REAL ESTATE

PRINCIPLES AND PRACTICES

FOURTH EDITION

RALPH A. PALMER

Revision Authors:
Joyce Thayer-Sword
Randall S. van Reken

GSP
GORSUCH SCARISBRICK, PUBLISHERS
Scottsdale, Arizona

The publisher makes every reasonable best effort to ensure the accuracy and completeness of the information and answers contained in this book. Due to the ever-changing nature of applicable laws and practices, the reader is cautioned and advised to always consult with the instructor when questions arise. Test answers have been checked for correct correlation with the question answered. If the reader encounters a questionable answer, the reader should always consult the text or the instructor for a more complete answer and analysis of the answer. Should the reader believe that an alternative interpretation of the information contained in this book is possible, he or she is encouraged to consult with the instructor.

Publisher:	Gay L. Pauley
Editor:	Shari Jo Hehr
Developmental Editor:	Katie E. Bradford
Production Manager:	Mary B. Cullen
Cover Design:	Kevin Kall
Typesetting:	Ash Street Typecrafters, Inc.

Gorsuch Scarisbrick, Publishers
8233 Via Paseo del Norte, Suite F-400
Scottsdale, AZ 85258

10 9 8 7 6 5 4 3 2 1

ISBN 0-89787-949-X

Printed in the United States of America.

Brief Contents

For the complete Contents, see p. iv.

Contents

CHAPTER 7 REAL ESTATE FINANCE PRINCIPLES 136

CHAPTER 8 Real Estate Finance Practices 156

CHAPTER 14

PROPERTY MANAGEMENT AND INSURANCE 282

CHAPTER 15

FEDERAL INCOME TAXATION AND BASIC PRINCIPLES OF REAL ESTATE INVESTMENT 296

Illustrations

Preface

This book provides beginning students with the principles and practices fundamental to a career in real estate. The subject matter and study materials are presented with the assumption that readers have no previous background in this subject. The overall goal of this book is to prepare each student with the appropriate material, guidance, and practice to enable him or her to pass the state licensing examination on the first attempt and in turn to become a successful practitioner.

This new edition includes the following learning tools to help make the material as accessible as possible:

- New to this edition: The *How Would You Respond?* chapter-end feature allows students to place themselves in practical, real-life scenarios and find legal, ethical solutions. Possible responses to these questions are also included.
- New to this edition: *Case Studies* summarize actual court cases and encourage understanding of how laws affect everyday real estate practice.
- *Putting It to Work* boxes throughout the text lend practical application to topics particularly relevant to today's practitioners.
- Chapters conclude with *Important Points* that summarize the chapters' key ideas in a succinct list format, facilitating student review.
- Chapters also include chapter-end *Review Questions* to allow students to self-test and apply what they have learned.
- Finally, two complete 100-question *Practice Exams* give students ample opportunity to prepare successfully for the licensing examination.

The book's clear, concise writing style and practical study features will aid students in understanding and retaining relevant information. More important, the text will help prepare them for a successful career in real estate.

Acknowledgments

This book is a joint effort of many talented writers, editors, reviewers, and educators. We extend our appreciation to Nancy Keck of North Carolina's Houser Associates for her ongoing contributions to the text. Our sincere thanks, also, to the following individuals, who reviewed all or portions of this text and offered suggestions as to how it might be improved: Larry Rickard, Realty School of Kansas; Richard Linkemer, American School of Real Estate; Elsie Keene, East Dale Realty; Yvonne Schluter, Academy of Real Estate; Robert W. Corl, Metropolitan Real Estate School; Donald White; Marcia Spada, Albany Center for Real Estate Education; Charles Stewart; and Charles Green of Casey Properties.

Learning Tools: The Complete Program

The Text

This easy-to-read text offers you all of the information you need to prepare for your licensing exam and a successful career in real estate. **Including two 100-question *Practice Exams!***

The Interactive Software Tutorial

Preparing for the Real Estate Salesperson Examination
625 questions cross-referenced specifically to your text by chapter and page number; you'll know exactly where to check to restudy an incorrect answer. Includes explanations of both correct and incorrect responses for each question. Take chapter quizzes and practice for your licensing text with a timed, comprehensive exam.

New! Audio Tapes

Important Point Review for Real Estate Principles and Practices
Make the most of your study time with this 2½ hour review of the most important points in each chapter. Great for use on the road!

For more information about the software tutorial and audio tapes, see your instructor. If these items are unavailable to you through your school, call (602) 991-7881.

CHAPTER 1

IMPORTANT TERMINOLOGY

allodial
code of ethics
feudal
highest and best use
immobility
indestructibility
investment
land use controls
listing contract
National Association of REALTORS® (NAR)
nonhomogeneity
personal property
real estate
real property
REALTOR®
realty
scarcity
situs
standards of practice
supply and demand

Basic Real Estate Concepts

IN THIS CHAPTER This chapter presents a brief introduction to real estate and the real estate business. It provides definitions of real property, personal property, and related terms and discusses the factors affecting real estate and the real estate business. Many of the topics introduced here are discussed in more detail in subsequent chapters.

GENERAL CHARACTERISTICS OF REAL ESTATE

Terminology and Classes of Property

Real estate or **realty** consists of *land and everything that is permanently attached to the land.* **Real property** *is real estate or realty plus all legal rights, powers, and privileges inherent in ownership of real estate.* Ownership of land encompasses not only the surface of the earth but also the area below the surface and the area above the surface, theoretically into outer space. These three components of land ownership are separable. The owner of the land may retain ownership of the surface but may sell the air space above and the mineral rights below.

All structures on the lands including improvements such as fences, swimming pools, flagpoles, as well as things growing in the soil naturally without cultivation, are included in the definition of real estate. When conveying the title to their property, property owners convey all aspects of real estate unless a prior agreement excludes some portion of the real estate from the conveyance.

The only category of property other than real property, as defined in law, is personal property. Therefore, by the definition of real property, we are able to classify **personal property** as *everything that is not real property*. Tangible personal property is everything that is readily movable. Personal property is entirely different from real property and does not have the special characteristics of real property.

Real property has specific characteristics that set it apart from other marketable and valuable commodities. These characteristics are both physical and economic. The physical characteristics of real property are:

1. Immobility
2. Indestructibility (permanence)
3. Nonhomogeneity (uniqueness)

The economic characteristics of real property are:

1. Scarcity/limited availability

2. Permanence of investment
3. Location (situs)
4. Modification by improvement

The physical characteristics define and pertain to the land itself. The economic characteristics define and pertain to value and change in value of the land. As a result of the interplay of all these characteristics, physical and economic, real estate is an exciting and challenging commodity to market.

Physical Characteristics Affecting Land Use

Immobility

A physical characteristic of major importance in real estate is the **immobility** of land. This is the primary difference between land and tangible personal property, which is highly mobile. Land *cannot be relocated.*

Immobility of land is a major factor affecting land value. Those who have specific knowledge of a local real estate market are better able to serve the buyers and sellers in that community.

Indestructibility

Land is a permanent commodity. Land cannot be destroyed. It may be altered substantially in its topography or other aspects of its appearance, but it remains. The **indestructibility,** or *permanence,* of land makes it attractive as a long-term investment. This is substantially different from most personal property, which often devalues, resulting in little or no salvage value. Land values, however, can change as a result of changing conditions in the area surrounding the land. Land values may suffer economic obsolescence, which results from changes in surrounding areas that adversely affect its value. For example, the construction of an interstate highway can radically affect land values of property located several miles away on a minor highway that loses traffic volume.

Nonhomogeneity (Uniqueness)

Nonhomogeneity means that *no two parcels of land are identical.* In agricultural land, fertility varies from location to location. In urban real estate, accessibility and zoning differ. Each parcel of real estate has its own topography, soil type, zoning, size, shape, and so on. These differences, whether minor or major, bestow on each parcel of realty its own unique functionality and appeal.

Basically, no two parcels of land occupy the same space on the earth's surface. This uniqueness of each parcel of land, even if there are no other differences, gives rise to the legal concept of *specific performance*, a legal remedy provided by the U. S. court system for breach of contract. If a seller contracts to sell her real property, the law does not consider money to be a substitute for her duty to convey that title. Therefore, if the seller intends to breach her contract and pay financial damages instead, the buyer may refuse to accept the money and insist on taking title to the agreed-upon land as the only acceptable contract performance.

FIGURE 1.1 The physical characteristics of real estate.

1. Immobility
2. Indestructibility (permanence)
3. Heterogeneity (uniqueness)

Economic Characteristics Affecting Land Use

Scarcity/Limited Availability

An important economic characteristic of real property is its **scarcity**, *its availability or lack of availability*. It follows the principle of **supply and demand**, which states that *the greater the supply of any commodity in comparison to demand, the lower the value will be*. Land is a commodity that is in *fixed supply*; no additional supply of land is being produced to keep pace with the ever-increasing population. Moreover, not all land is suitable for human use. The problems created by an ever-increasing demand for the limited supply of desirable land, however, have been eased substantially by the increase in economic supply of land.

An increase in economic supply comes from the increased utilization of land. For example, in agricultural land, fewer and fewer acres are needed to produce the world's supply of food. As a result of advances in technology, people are able to create high-rise office buildings, apartments, and multilevel shopping centers. Consequently, one acre of land now may serve many more people than could have utilized that land in the past.

Another factor that has increased the economic supply of land is the improvement and expansion of our public air, water, sewer, and land transportation systems through construction of highways, bridges, water reservoirs, purification plants, and public utilities. Accomplishments in construction and transportation have converted land that was previously useless into land that now can be utilized.

PUTTING IT TO WORK

Television real estate "gurus" often say, "Buy land because they ain't makin' no more of it," implying that any land purchase is wise. The concept of scarcity, however, is inseparable from the concepts of quality, desirability, and utility. The statement should be, "Buy good land, because everybody wants it and there's only so much of it."

Permanence of Investment

The permanence of land makes it an attractive investment. Because land is indestructible and immobile, owners of land are willing to invest large sums of money to improve the land itself or to place improvements on the land. Examples of this are found in the building of homes, office buildings, apartment buildings, golf courses, and so on. The permanence of land means that ownership of land is economically desirable.

Location (Situs)

Of all the characteristics of land, location has the greatest effect on property value. Land's immobility, a basic physical characteristic, dictates that the **situs**, or *location of a parcel of land*, is both unique and permanent. Therefore, if the land is located in an area where available land has a high demand, the land has a substantially higher value. Conversely, if the land is inaccessible from a practical standpoint or is located in an area with little or no demand, the economic value is depressed.

In addition, the value of the location can change as people's preferences change. During the 1950s people took flight from urban centers to the suburbs, which resulted in substantial property value reductions in many urban areas. Recently this trend has begun to reverse itself. People are rediscovering inner cities and rehabilitating older properties, restoring lost value.

Modification by Improvement

Improvements to the land or on the land can greatly affect the land's value. As a parcel of real estate is transformed from a plot of vacant land to a completed dwelling, the appeal of the land increases, resulting in increased value. Improvements to or on the land are not limited to buildings. They include, as examples, landscaping, grading, clearing, connection of public utilities, improved road access, better drainage, and even the building of golf greens and fairways for a new golf course. In addition, changes in surrounding areas can increase the value of neighboring real estate.

PUTTING IT TO WORK

Real estate is a huge factor in national and local economies; the value of real estate is greater than that of virtually all other "ownable" assets. The improvability of real estate provides jobs and even more value, and the permanence of real estate makes it desirable to own for the future. Think about which asset will hold its value or appreciate most to a buyer ten years after purchase: a $20,000 vacant lot, a $20,000 car, or $20,000 of clothing and furniture.

GENERAL CONCEPTS OF LAND USE AND INVESTMENT

Physical Factors Affecting Land Use

Physical factors affecting land utilization can be either natural or artificial. Natural factors include location, topography, soil conditions, size, shape, likelihood of flooding, action of the sun, and the presence or absence of minerals. Artificial factors include streets, highways, adjacent land use patterns, and availability of public utilities. Natural and artificial physical factors always must be considered in analyzing the utility of land.

Economic Factors Affecting Land Use

Local property tax assessments, tax rates, wage and employment levels, availability of financing, interest rates, growth in the community, zoning, fire regulations, building codes, and extent of community planning are all examples of economic factors that affect land use. All of these economic factors have a definite effect on the uses to which real estate can or should be put.

Highest and Best Use

The concept of **highest and best use** is of extreme importance in real estate. It is the *use of land that will preserve the land's utility, provide the greatest income, and result*

FIGURE 1.2 The economic characteristics of real estate.

1. Scarcity/limited availability
2. Permanence of investment
3. Situs (location)
4. Modification by improvement

in the greatest present value of the land. To achieve highest and best use, land is improved by the use of capital and labor to make the land productive.

All of the physical and economic factors set out above are taken into consideration to determine the highest and best use of land. A given parcel of land has only one highest and best use at any particular time. Loss of income to the land resulting from failure to use the land to its highest and best use will cause the value of the property to be less than fully realized.

PUTTING IT TO WORK

The highest and best use for most improved land is its current use, assuming that the use conforms to the expectations of the local marketplace. Highest and best use analysis and decisions become highly relevant in developing unimproved land and considering urban renewal and renovations in changing and blighted areas.

Land Use Restrictions

An owner's use of land is affected by government and private **land use controls**, or *limitations on land use*. In the past, under a **feudal** type of ownership, *land was owned or controlled by the king*. *Individual, private ownership of land*, called **allodial** ownership, did not come about in the United States until 1785. Even with the advent of private ownership of land, the general public had a vested interest in the use of all land, because of the effect on surrounding land. The use of land requires some regulations for the benefit of all. This is especially true in areas of high population density, where land uses are more intense and affect a greater number of people.

Government or public land use controls exist in the form of city planning and zoning, state and regional planning, building codes, suitability-for-occupancy requirements, and environmental control. In addition, direct public ownership exerts substantial public control of land uses. Direct public ownership exists in the ownership of public buildings, parks, watersheds, streets, and highways. Private restrictions on land use exist in the form of restrictive covenants established by developers, restrictions in individual deeds requiring the continuation of a specified land use or prohibiting a specified land use, and use restrictions imposed on tenants in lease contracts.

In both public and private land use regulation, the restriction must be reasonable, necessary, and legal. Certain types of zoning can be discriminatory and thus illegal. Certain private restrictions, especially those pertaining to race or gender, are illegal.

Investment Objectives

Investment is the *outlay of money expecting income or profit*. Therefore, the objective of a person who purchases a parcel of land for investment is to make an income or a profit. Different land owners may achieve this objective in various ways. Some owners desire to generate income from the land. Other owners are satisfied if the ownership of land indirectly provides income through tax savings. Some owners may be willing to wait many years for income or profit—buying vacant land, for example, in anticipation of extensive growth in 10 years, with the profit to be realized only upon final sale of the land.

The investment objective may be varied. Some common objectives are:

- To own land as a hedge against an inflationary economic trend.
- To own land for the tax savings generated by passive losses or depreciation deductions on improvements to the land.

- To own land as a means of providing regular income.
- To own land to build a strong portfolio of properties for resale at retirement or for other future needs.

In analyzing a property for investment purposes, in addition to their personal investment objectives, investors must consider the physical and economic characteristics of land, the highest and best use of the land, and any public or private restrictions that may affect the investment goal.

THE REAL ESTATE BUSINESS

The business of real estate is *big business*—big in the number of people it touches and big in the money it generates. For most people, buying and selling real estate represent the most significant monetary transactions of their lives. The business of bringing buyers and sellers together and assisting in negotiations and transactions concerning the sale of real estate is known as *real estate brokerage*. Real estate organizations at local, state, and national levels promote and police the real estate business. They also promote professionalism and specialization in the real estate business.

In addition to real estate sales, many other types of businesses are based on real estate. These include appraising, abstracting, lending, property management, development, construction, insuring, renovating, and remodeling. Various professional organizations at local, state, and national levels exist to regulate and promote professional conduct and standards.

National Association of REALTORS®

The largest professional association is the **National Association of REALTORS® (NAR)**, first organized in 1908. To be a full member of this association, a person must be licensed in an individual state to sell real estate and must join the local board of the NAR. In most areas this board is called the Board or Association of REALTORS®. To be an affiliate member of the NAR, a person must be closely affiliated with the real estate business, such as an attorney, a lender, or an abstractor. Only members of the NAR are REALTORS®. The term REALTOR® is a registered trademark owned and controlled by the NAR, indicated by the symbol "®" accompanying every use of the term.

A **REALTOR®** is a professional in real estate who subscribes to a strict code of ethics known as the **Code of Ethics and Standards of Practice**, a copy of which is available through the NAR.

The NAR at the local level promotes local real estate business. The local board or association may sponsor seminars on home ownership, civil rights, recycling, or other issues of public concern. The local board is also instrumental in policing the local real estate business. The goal of local NAR boards is to promote the highest ethical standards in the brokerage business. Also, cooperative agreements between brokers to share information, such as the Multiple Listing Service (MLS), usually are established at the local level. At the state and national levels, the NAR lobbies in the state legislatures and Congress on matters specific to the real estate business.

The NAR has developed special institutes that provide designations and certifications in specialized areas of real estate. This function of the NAR has added to the professional image of the real estate business. Some of the institutes and designations are listed in Figure 1.3.

FIGURE 1.3
Some of the many real estate institutes, societies, and councils, together with their related designations.

NATIONAL ASSOCIATION OF REALTORS®

REALTOR® Institute
- —Graduate, REALTOR® Institute (GRI)
- —Certified International Property Specialist (CIPS)

American Society of Real Estate Counselors (ASREC)
- —Counselor of Real Estate (CRE®)

Commercial-Investment Real Estate Institute (CIREI)
- —Certified Commercial-Investment Member (CCIM)

Institute of Real Estate Management (IREM)
- —Accredited Management Organization® (AMO®)
- —Accredited Residential Manager® (ARM®)
- —Certified Property Manager® (CPM®)

REALTORS® Land Institute (RLI)
- —Accredited Land Consultant (ALC®)

REALTORS® NATIONAL MARKETING INSTITUTE (RNMI®)
- —Real Estate Brokerage Council: Certified Real Estate Brokerage Manager (CRB®)
- —Residential Sales Council: Certified Residential Specialist (CRS®)

Society of Industrial and Office REALTORS® (SIOR®)
- —Professional Real Estate Executive (P.R.E.)

Women's Council of REALTORS® (WCR)
- —Leadership Training Graduate (LTG)

Pennsylvania Association of REALTORS®

NATIONAL ASSOCIATION OF RESIDENTIAL PROPERTY MANAGERS

Residential Property Managers (RPM)
Master Property Managers (MPM)
Certified Residential Management Company (CRMC)

APPRAISAL INSTITUTE

MAI —Appraisers experienced in commercial and industrial properties
SRA —Appraisers experienced in residential income properties
RM —Appraisers experienced in single-family dwellings and two-, three-, and four-unit residential properties
SREA —Appraisers experienced in real estate valuation and analysis
SRPA —Appraisers experienced in valuation of commercial, industrial, residential, and other property

PUTTING IT TO WORK

Holding a real estate license does not make one a REALTOR®. A licensee must apply to and join the Board of REALTORS® to become a member and be allowed to use the designation and logo. This involves membership fees, orientation classes, and induction into the Board.

Association of Real Estate License Law Officials

Another organization that has an impact on the real estate business is the Association of Real Estate License Law Officials (ARELLO). This organization was established in 1929 by license law officials on state commissions to assist each other in creating, administering, and enforcing license laws. The first licensing laws were passed in 1917 in California. Through the efforts of ARELLO, each state now has licensing laws. Also through the effort of ARELLO, uniform legislation has been developed and put into effect to protect the consuming public against misrepresentation and fraud in the real estate business. Such legislation relates, for example, to timesharing, real estate scams, and consumer fraud.

Real Estate Licensees

An individual licensed and engaged in the real estate business is not limited to selling residential real estate. A person licensed to sell real estate may specialize in one or more of many fields, such as farmland, multi-family dwellings, commercial, retail, or industrial sales. Some other areas in real estate aside from sales are appraising, building and development, property management, financing, and real estate consulting.

Effective real estate salespeople and brokers must have a clear picture of their role in the real estate transaction. Successful real estate licensees do not use "hard sell" techniques. Rather, they are advisors working diligently to assist buyers, sellers, and renters of real estate.

The real estate licensee's ability to serve the parties in a real estate transaction will determine his or her success. A career in real estate can provide a real estate licensee with satisfaction from serving the needs of others, as well as with financial rewards. Success in the real estate business is built upon knowledge, ethical conduct in all dealings, and, above all, service to others.

The Fundamentals of a Real Estate Transaction

The basic stages of a real estate transaction are the listing, the contract for sale, financing, and settlement. These aspects are highlighted briefly below, and each is discussed in more detail in later chapters.

Listing Contract

A **listing contract** is *a contract wherein a property owner employs a real estate firm to market a property for a prescribed period of time at a prescribed price and terms.* Under this contract the real estate firm becomes the agent of the seller. Listings represent the inventory of a real estate brokerage and are the lifeblood of the business. Without listings, a real estate firm is severely handicapped and is limited to marketing the listings of other real estate offices.

As agent for the seller, the real estate broker and his or her associates are empowered to market the listed property. The listing contract does not authorize the licensee to bind the seller in a contract to sell the property. The licensee's purpose is to find a ready, willing, and able buyer; "able" means a financially qualified buyer. The seller has the right to accept, reject, or counteroffer all offers to purchase.

Contract for Sale (Offer to Purchase)

A binding contract to buy and sell real property results from the written acceptance of a written offer to purchase or counteroffer. In presenting the offer, the real estate licensee must always remember for whom he or she works. The listing agent works for the seller and must always give the seller the benefit of all information regarding the buyer's qualifications and the quality of the offer.

In many instances, however, a real estate licensee establishes a contract for services with the buyer. This is called *buyer brokerage*. Under buyer brokerage, the real estate agent must represent the best interests of the buyer rather than the seller.

Finally, in some instances the licensee acts as limited agent to both buyer and seller. This form of contract for services requires explicit and specific disclosures to both buyer and seller. Under this form of service contract, the licensee is a *dual* agent and must be careful to treat both parties fairly.

Financing

Most buyers do not have cash funds available to purchase property; therefore, most real estate transactions cannot be completed without financing. If the property cannot be financed, it usually cannot be sold.

Because financing is so important, the real estate licensee needs a day-to-day working knowledge of the various loan programs available through local lending institutions. The real estate licensee must continually keep in touch with and establish a cordial working relationship with lenders. The lender is interested in placing the loan to make the sales transaction possible, but the licensee has to know the lender's guidelines to qualify the buyer and the property. A new salesperson should personally call on local lenders to establish a mutually supportive relationship.

When institutional financing is difficult to obtain at favorable interest rates, the real estate agent may need to look to the seller as the primary source of financing. This is typically for all or a portion of the purchase price in the form of a contract for deed or purchase money mortgage. Real estate licensees must be familiar with any existing mortgages that might restrict any type of seller financing.

Final Settlement

Completion of the real estate transaction occurs at closing or final settlement. At this time the buyer receives the deed, the seller receives compensation from the sale of the property, and the real estate broker receives the commission. Prior to closing, the real estate salesperson often coordinates various activities including inspections, appraisals, and so on.

In some states the real estate agent, along with an attorney, loan officer, buyer, and seller, attends the closing. In other states the final settlement is handled by an escrow agent who, pursuant to written instructions, processes all closing documents and distributes the sale proceeds.

The Real Estate Market

In the real estate market, properties are given substantial exposure, particularly at the local level. Properties are available for inspection by prospective buyers, and these buyers have the opportunity to inspect several properties before making a final selection. This is an example of a free market providing ample time for buyer and seller to effect a mutually beneficial purchase and sale without undue pressure or urgency.

The physical characteristics of land create special conditions in the real estate market that do not exist in other markets. The immobility of real estate causes the market to be local in nature, requiring local specialists who are familiar with local market conditions, property values, and availability.

The real estate industry traditionally has been subject to cyclical periods of recession and prosperity. It is often the first industry to feel the adverse effects of depressed conditions in the national and local economies. When supply substantially exceeds demand, existing properties cannot be withdrawn from the local market and relocated to an area with higher demand. Conversely, when the demand exceeds supply, new supplies of housing and business properties cannot be constructed quickly. Thus, the real estate industry takes longer than the economy as a whole to climb out of a recession, because of the inability to react quickly to radical changes in supply and demand. It is said to be relatively inelastic.

Changes in the real estate market are continuous. The goal of an effective real estate salesperson is to read the market and act. Effective real estate salespeople are aware of new industries coming to their community. They keep abreast of new legislation and local ordinances affecting real estate. They recognize trends in interest rates and closing costs. Effective real estate salespeople must learn to adapt to the ever-changing real estate market.

Supply and demand in the real estate market is affected by many factors: money supply, interest rates, population migrations, zoning, planning and environmental concerns, and local and federal tax laws. Informed real estate licensees strive to stay abreast of these factors.

Important Points

1. Real property includes the surface of the land, improvements attached to the land, minerals beneath the surface, and air space above the land.
2. Everything that is not real property is personal property. Tangible personal property is readily movable.
3. Real property has physical characteristics of immobility, indestructibility, and uniqueness.
4. Real property has economic characteristics of scarcity, permanence of investment, location, and improvements.
5. Land use controls are found both in private deed restrictions and in public laws.
6. The real estate business involves many specialties besides residential sales and requires knowledge of such fields as financing, housing codes, and other related matters.
7. The real estate industry is organized at local, state, and national levels primarily through the National Association of REALTORS®.
8. A real estate market is local in nature and is a good example of the free-market concept and the interplay of various market forces.
9. Real estate licensees act as advisors for the benefit of their clients and customers. Because a home's sale and purchase often involves the seller's most important financial asset and creates long-term financial obligations for the buyer, licensees have to be thoroughly knowledgeable and competent in their duties.

REVIEW QUESTIONS

Answers to these questions are found in the *Answer Key* section at the back of the book.

1. All of the following are separable ownership in land EXCEPT:
   a. surface of the land
   b. area below the surface
   c. nonhomogeneity
   d. air space above the land

2. The characteristic of land that causes the real estate market to be essentially a local market is the physical characteristic of:
   a. indestructibility
   b. immobility
   c. availability
   d. natural features

3. The basis for the legal remedy of specific performance when dealing with land is the:
   a. nonhomogeneity of land
   b. immobility of land
   c. indestructibility of land
   d. availability of land

4. All of the following have contributed to the increase in economic supply of land EXCEPT:
   a. increased utilization of the physical supply of land
   b. improvements to the land
   c. construction of condominiums
   d. lack of demand for land

5. The quality of the location of land, and consequently the value of the land, can be changed by:
   a. the principle of nonhomogeneity
   b. relocation of the land
   c. changes in the local trend of real estate business
   d. improvements to the land resulting in accessibility

6. The concept of highest and best use does NOT:
   a. include consideration of the physical and economic factors affecting land use
   b. result in the greatest present value of the land
   c. result in use in violation of present zoning
   d. include consideration for the improvements or modifications to the land

7. Public land use controls exist in the form of:
   a. restrictive covenants
   b. zoning laws
   c. deed restrictions
   d. conditions in a platted subdivision

8. Specializations within the real estate business include:
   a. transportation
   b. farming
   c. accounting
   d. property management

9. The type of land ownership that existed in colonial times was feudal. The private ownership of land is called:
   a. alliance
   b. allodial
   c. conservation
   d. fundamental

10. The real estate market may be described by all of the following EXCEPT:
    a. free market
    b. local market
    c. movable market
    d. slow to react to changes in supply and demand

11. The function of a real estate licensee in dealings with buyers and sellers in the real estate market may best be described as:
    a. financier
    b. advisor
    c. contractor
    d. adversary

12. The typical real estate licensee must have specialized knowledge in a variety of subjects that include all of the following EXCEPT:
    a. financing
    b. contracts
    c. excavation
    d. valuation

13. All of the following are real property EXCEPT:
    a. surface of the earth
    b. area below the surface
    c. readily movable items
    d. air space above the earth

14. Which of the following is a contract whereby a property owner employs a real estate broker to market the property?
    a. assumption
    b. contract for sale
    c. consummation
    d. listing

15. The Code of Ethics and Standards of Practice of real estate was established by:
    a. NAR
    b. ARELLO
    c. National Association of Real Estate Brokers
    d. MAI

CHAPTER 2

IMPORTANT TERMINOLOGY

alienation
bill of sale
bundle of rights
chattel
community property
condominium
convey
cooperative
co-ownership
corporeal rights
curtesy
declaration
deed
defeasible estate
dower
emblements
estate at sufferance
estate at will
estate for years
estate from year-to-year
estate in real property
estovers
fee simple absolute
fixture
freehold estates
fruits of industry
fruits of nature
hereditaments
incorporeal rights
intestate succession
joint tenancy
joint venture
land
leasehold estate
life estate
life tenant
master deed
nonfreehold estate
partnership
periodic estate
periodic tenancy
pur autre vie
remainder
reversion
right of first refusal
right of inheritance
right of survivorship
separate property
severalty
sole proprietorship
tenancy in common
tenants by the entirety
tenements
timesharing
trade fixture
trust
unities

Property Ownership and Interests

IN THIS CHAPTER The real estate business has a language all its own. So, mastering real estate terminology is like learning a new language—the more you use it, the easier it gets. As you read through the text, look for connections or associations—that is, things that are related. The more you *relate* or *link* one term with another, the more you will understand, comprehend, and retain. This chapter will begin the discussion of ownership of real property.

THE CONCEPT OF PROPERTY

The term *real estate* refers to the land and all improvements made both "on" and "to" the land. The term *real property* is broader in meaning. It is real estate plus all legal rights, powers, and privileges inherent in ownership of real estate. These legal rights, powers, and privileges are many in number and varied in nature. They have value, are usually salable, and affect the value of the underlying real estate. Real property encompasses things such as easements, options, water rights, and so on.

Real Estate Ownership as a Bundle of Rights

In days gone by it was the custom to exchange a handful of dirt or a bundle of sticks in a symbolic transfer of the rights to real property. This ritual evolved into the **bundle of rights** concept (see Figure 2.1), which is the idea that *various rights of ownership are transferred along with real property when it is transferred from one owner to another*. Each of these rights, powers, and privileges affects the value and marketability of a parcel of real estate; a parcel with less than the full bundle of rights may therefore have a reduced value.

Real estate licensees sell more than land and buildings. They also can sell *any rights to, interests in, and title to real property that affect the value of the real property*. Every bundle of sticks (piece of real property) can be divided in many ways. The division referred to here is not that of acres or lots. Instead, it refers to the various rights that can be held in real property, which will be discussed later in this chapter.

Real Property

We have learned that real property consists of land and everything permanently attached to the land, as well as legal rights to the land. Ownership of land includes not

FIGURE 2.1 Real estate ownership as a "bundle of rights."

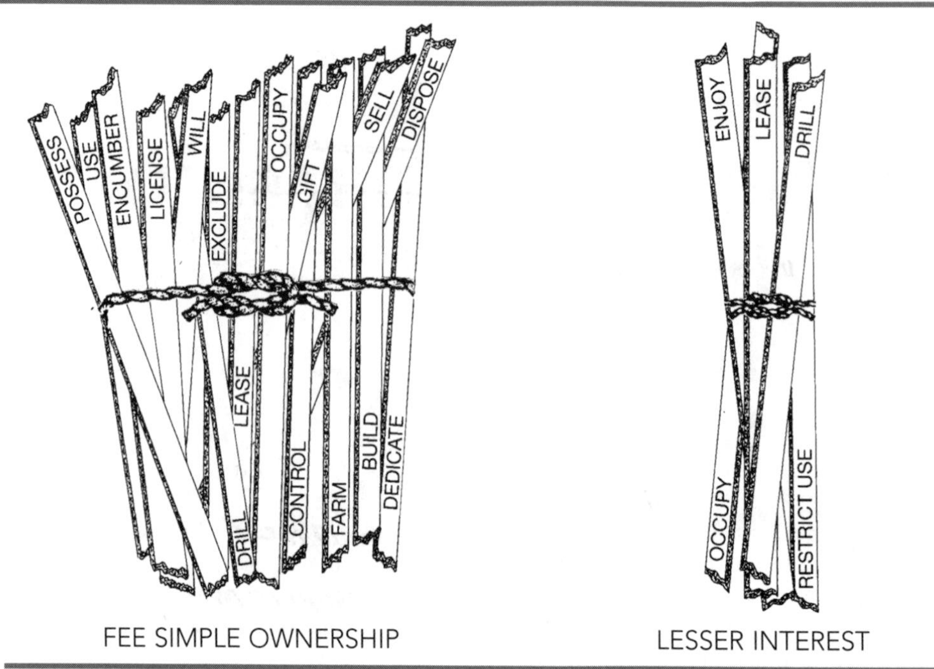

only the face of the earth but also the area below the surface to the center of the earth and the area above the surface theoretically to infinity. Real property also includes everything that is permanently attached to the land. Therefore, the land owner owns all structures on the land as well as other improvements to the land. Improvements *on* the land include things such as buildings, swimming pools, flagpoles, fences, and other structures. Improvements *to* the land refer to clearing the land, building roads, placing utilities, and the like.

Ownership of real property is transferred and evidenced by a document called a **deed**. A deed *conveys real property only and cannot convey personal property.*

Personal Property

Other than real property, the only category of property defined in law is personal property. Everything that is not real property is personal property. Tangible personal property is everything that is readily movable. Personal property is "your stuff," consisting of household furniture, cars, tractors, mobile homes, jewelry, and so on. Personal property also includes crops that are planted and cultivated annually. Another name for personal property is **chattel**. *Ownership of personal property is transferred and evidenced by a document called a* **bill of sale**.

Land, Minerals, and Fruits of the Soil

Land is defined as the earth's surface extending downward to the center of the earth and upward to infinity, including things permanently attached by nature. Land includes the dirt and soil, as well as boulders and growing things such as trees and bushes. Land also includes minerals located below the surface, such as oil, gold, silver, bauxite, and so on. The right to mine minerals in land is evidenced by ownership of subsurface rights.

Growing things that do not require regular planting or cultivation but continue to grow naturally (perennials) are called *fructus naturales*, **fruits of nature**, and are

FIGURE 2.2
Land, real estate, and real property.

LAND

REAL ESTATE
Land plus permanent improvements

REAL PROPERTY
Real estate and bundle of legal rights

Right to possession | Right to enjoyment | Right to farm | Right to development | Etc.

PUTTING IT TO WORK

Many states, particularly in the West, treat mineral rights under a body of law completely different from real estate. In these states a "non-owner" of land may have the legal right to take minerals without ever negotiating with the owner. Check your local regulations and practices for further information.

designated by law as real estate. These include forest trees, native shrubs, and wild berries. Fruits of nature pass to a buyer of real estate by execution and delivery of the deed from the seller unless specifically reserved by the grantor.

Growing things that require planting each season and cultivation are called *fructus industriales*, **fruits of industry**, and are designated by law as personal property. Examples include crops such as corn, wheat, melons, and soybeans. These *fruits of industry* are called **emblements**. Emblements are *the personal property of the tenant who cultivated them, and such a tenant has the common law right to reenter the property to harvest the crops even though the land has been sold or the lease terminated.* Fruits of industry or emblements do not pass to a buyer of real estate by deed; instead, they *pass via a bill of sale because they are personal property.*

Fixtures

An object that once was personal property but has been annexed to and become part of the real estate is a **fixture**. Lumber to build a structure is personal property or chattel when it is delivered to the building site. By attachment and intent of the builder, however, the lumber becomes a building on the land and thus real estate. The same is said for light fixtures, showers, bathtubs, toilets, windows, bricks, clotheslines, woodstoves, window shades, and so on.

Determining what is a fixture can be a problem during real estate transactions because the buyer and seller may have different perceptions. For example, an owner may have installed track lighting in the dining room and then want to remove it upon sale of the home, contending that it is his personal property. If the buyer wishes to establish that the lighting is a fixture and should remain with the home, the courts may apply several tests to resolve this issue. The typical tests ask:

1. How permanent is the attachment?
2. What was the intent of the person installing the item?
3. If it is removed, can the item be used elsewhere?

Because different people may view determination of fixture status differently, the real estate salesperson is responsible for ensuring that all parties to the contracts clearly understand who owns the fixtures. This can be achieved through a carefully written, explicit listing contract between real estate agent and seller and the purchase contract between buyer and seller. However, the purchase contract is the "final" contract between buyer and seller; the buyer is not bound by the listing because she is not a party to it. The purchase contract dictates ownership of the fixture. It should list any items that could cause confusion among the parties as included or excluded from the contract.

Trade Fixtures

The law of real estate recognizes an exception to the fixture rule. Items of personal property that a business operator installs in rented building space are presumed to remain the tenant's personal property. These are called **trade fixtures**. An example would be built-in shelves for displaying merchandise. Although they are attached to the property, these fixtures remain the personal property of the rental tenant and may be removed at the end of the lease period. Of course, the lease contract should be clear on the point of trade fixtures. The rental agreement may allow the landlord to retain these items. If the rental agreement does not have this provision, trade fixtures remain the property of the installing tenant.

Upon removal of a trade fixture, the tenant does have the responsibility to restore the property to its original condition. This may involve capping plumbing, repairing walls, filling holes, and so on.

Physically similar to trade fixtures, but legally different, are *leasehold improvements*. Even though a leasehold improvement may be physically identical to a trade fixture, the difference lies in who installed the item. If the landlord installed it, it remains with the building and is a leasehold improvement. If the tenant installed it, it is a trade fixture and removable.

Uniform Commercial Code (UCC)

A special situation occurs when a property owner has financed the purchase of a piece of personal property. The Uniform Commercial Code (UCC), adopted in most states, provides for the lender to retain a security interest in the personal property or chattel until the lender is paid in full. The security interest is available to the lender even though the chattel is installed in real property. The security interest is created by an instrument called a *security agreement*. An example of this type of financing and security agreement is a farmer financing the building of grain storage bins. The lender does not take a mortgage on the land on which the bins are built but instead takes a security interest in the bins themselves.

This type of agreement is evidenced on the public record by filing a notice, called a *financing statement*, in the office of the Register of Deeds or County Recorder. This filing provides constructive notice to all the world that a security interest exists in the personal property that is the subject of the security agreement. As a result, the attached item does not become a fixture or a part of the real estate. Consequently, if the buyer/borrower defaults in payment, the lender can remove the article of personal property even though it has been attached to real property.

Land, Tenements, and Hereditaments

Real property consists of land, tenements, and hereditaments. Land was described earlier as the earth's surface extending downward to the center of the earth and upward theoretically to outer space, including things permanently attached by nature. Land includes the dirt and soil, plus boulders and growing things such as trees and bushes. Land also includes minerals located below the surface.

Tenements include *land as well as the inherent rights of ownership that arise from owning land. Tenements may be corporeal or incorporeal.* **Corporeal rights** are *rights to things that are tangible*, such as the title and its transfer, the right of possession and control and also things that can be touched and seen such as buildings, trees, and fences. **Incorporeal rights** are *rights to things that are intangible*, that cannot be touched or seen, including easement rights, licenses, riparian rights, and so on.

Hereditaments are *property or property rights that are capable of being inherited. Hereditaments may be corporeal or incorporeal, personal or real.*

Thus real property can include the dirt (land); the inherent rights (tenements) that arise from owning the dirt such as transfer of the dirt, use of the dirt, use and control of the buildings on the dirt, and use of water that borders the dirt; and the right to pass the dirt and inherent rights at death by inheritance (hereditaments).

Estates in Real Property

Definition of Estate

An **estate in real property** is *an interest in the property sufficient to give the holder of the estate the right to possession of the property*. (This does not necessarily imply ownership of the property, only possession.) Here we must further distinguish between the right of possession and right of use. Referring to the earlier analogy of rights in real estate as being like a bundle of sticks, the owner of an estate in land has the right of possession, a bigger stick than a mere right to use or have access to the land, as in the case of an easement or a license.

The Latin root for the word "estate" is *status*, indicating the relationship in which the estate owner stands with reference to rights in the property. It establishes the degree, quantity, nature, and extent of interest a person has in real property.

The word "estate" is generally interchangeable with the word "tenancy." Both of these words imply a right to possession.

Under the feudal system of land ownership common in English law almost a thousand years ago, only the king could hold title to real property. The king granted feuds to loyal subjects. These feuds did not provide ownership in land but simply a right to use and possess the land as long as the holder of the feud provided certain services to the king. The feuds approximated the modern concept of leasing. Under the feudal system, outright ownership would never be obtained.

The feudal system of ownership was transplanted to America when people from England settled and founded the colonies. The King of England or his ambassadors owned and controlled all the land.

One of the basic reasons for the American Revolution was the colonists' insistence on outright and absolute ownership of land, called allodial ownership. Allodial, or private ownership of land, did not begin until 1785. The conveyance of lands from the government to individuals allowed after passage of the Ordinance of 1785 was by patent or land grant. With the transfer of land came the need for an accurate method of measurement or survey. The Ordinance of 1785 also provided the first official survey system, called *governmental* or *rectangular survey*. As a result, the present system of land ownership in the United States is the allodial system, not the feudal system. Individuals can hold title to real property outright.

Groups of Estates in Land

Estates in land are divided into two groups: (a) estates of freehold, and (b) nonfreehold estates. **Freehold estate** is *ownership for an undetermined length of time*. A nonfreehold, or leasehold, estate signifies possession with a determinable end. Each of these two major divisions has various groupings or subheadings, which will be discussed next. Figure 2.3 provides an outline of the estates in land.

Freehold Estates

Freehold estates are (a) the various fee simple estates, and (b) life estates. Fee simple estates are inheritable; life estates are not.

FIGURE 2.3 Estates and rights in real property.

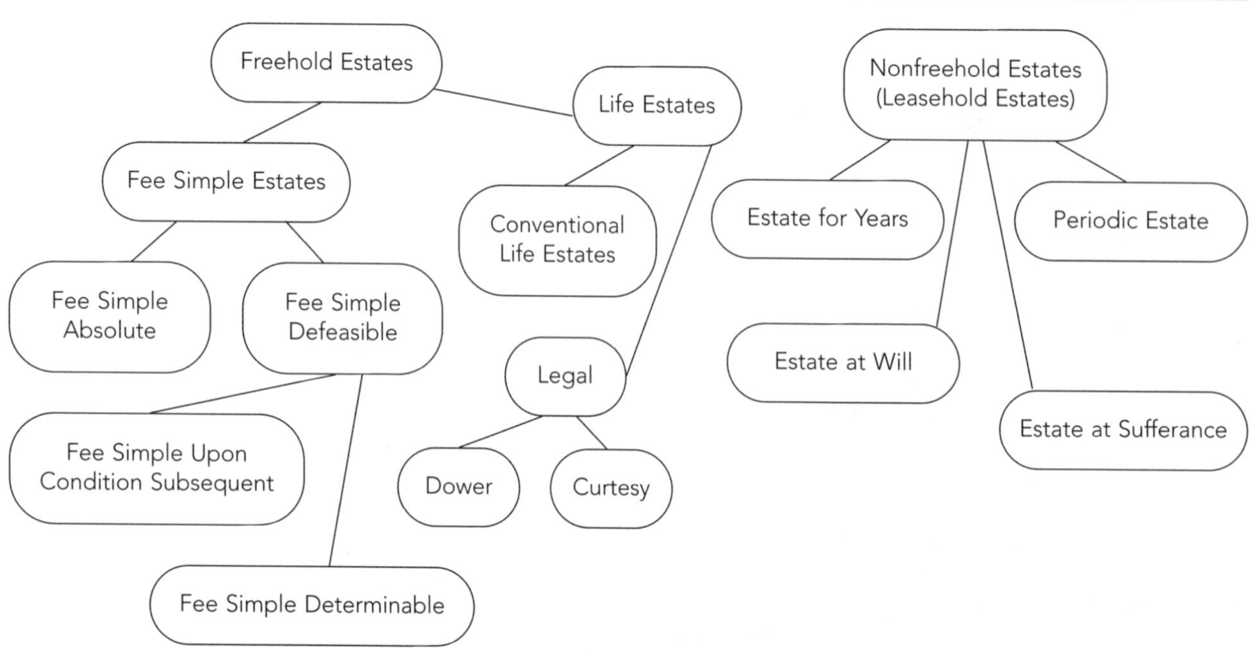

Fee Simple Estates

Fee Simple Absolute

The estate of **fee simple absolute** provides the most complete form of ownership and bundle of rights available in real property. This estate is also called fee simple or ownership in fee. Ownership in fee simple absolute *provides certain legal rights usually described as a bundle of legal rights*. This bundle includes the right to possession of the property; the right of quiet enjoyment of the property; the right to dispose of the property by gift, sale by deed, or by will; the right of exclusion; and the right to control use of the property within limits of the law. This is the typical estate owned by individual homeowners.

The owner in fee simple absolute may **convey**, or *pass to another*, a life estate in reversion or in remainder (defined and discussed later in this chapter); pledge the property as security for a mortgage debt; convey a leasehold estate to another; grant an easement in the land to another; or give to another a license to conduct some activity on the property. Certain of these rights may be removed from the bundle while leaving the other rights intact. For example, if the owner pledges the title as security for a mortgage debt, the balance remaining is a fee simple title subject to the mortgage debt. Also, if the owner conveys an estate for years or conveys an easement in the property to another, the remaining rights are fee simple subject to a lease or subject to the existence of an easement.

Most real estate transfers convey a fee simple absolute. No special words are required on a deed to create this freehold estate. It is the assumed estate.

Fee Simple Defeasible

A **defeasible estate** is *ownership with a condition or limitation attached. Defeasible* means destructible or defeatable. A frequent use of defeasible freeholds occurs when someone wishes to donate land to a church, school, or community for a specific purpose. The two types of defeasible fees are (a) fee simple subject to a condition subsequent, and (b) fee simple determinable.

Fee simple subject to a condition subsequent. The fee simple subject to a condition subsequent can continue for a potentially infinite time, as is the case with the fee simple absolute. The fee simple subject to a condition subsequent, however, can be defeated and is, therefore, a defeasible title. A fee simple subject to a condition is easily recognized by words such as "but if," "on condition that," "provided that," etc., in the transfer. For example, grantor conveys 40 acres to his son, but if alcoholic beverages are ever sold on the premises, his son's ownership terminates.

Fee simple subject to a condition subsequent is created by the grantor (the one conveying title) specifying in the conveyance of title a use of the property that is prohibited or required. The deed must specifically state the condition. In the example above, the grantor conveyed property to his son with the condition that it can never be used for the sale of alcoholic beverages. As long as the property is not used for this purpose, the title will continue indefinitely with the initial grantee, his son, or any subsequent grantee. If the property is used for the sale of alcoholic beverages at any time in the future, however, the original grantor or his heirs may reenter the property and take possession or go to court and sue to regain possession. By doing this, the titleholder's estate is terminated. Breach of the condition causes the termination.

Fee simple determinable. Fee simple determinable is another inheritable freehold estate in the form of a fee simple estate. It is also a defeasible fee, however, and therefore can come to an end. This type of estate is easily recognized by use of words such as "until" or "as long as" in the deed of transfer. For example, grantor transfers 10 acres to her daughter, as long as the property is used for educational purposes. Title received by her daughter can be for an infinite time. If the property is not used for the purpose specified in the conveyance, however, the title will terminate automatically and revert to the original grantor or her heirs.

In the case of a fee simple determinable, the estate in the grantee terminates automatically in the event the designated use of the property is not continued. This is called the *possibility of reverter*. It is contrasted with the fee simple subject to a condition subsequent, in which the termination is not automatic. In the fee subject to the condition subsequent, the grantor or heirs must either reenter the property or go to court to obtain possession of the property and to terminate the estate in the grantee. This is called *the right of reentry*. A major difference between reverter and reentry is where the burden of proof lies. With reverter, the burden of proof rests with the party trying to keep ownership. In reentry, the burden rests with the party trying to reclaim ownership.

In the case of very old conditions, the grantor or heirs may no longer remember the condition. Therefore, a condition may be broken with no consequences. If no one seeks termination of the defeasible fees, the title will not terminate. Also, some old conditions are no longer enforceable because they violate present laws. For instance, conditions that the property not transfer to other than white males are now discriminatory and unenforceable.

Putting It to Work

Defeasible fee estates are relatively rare. Most ownership positions are fee simple absolute. This latter form of ownership does not imply that all of these properties are free and clear of liens or other encumbrances but only that there are no involuntary conditions of ownership.

Life Estates

The **life estate** is a freehold estate that defines itself. It is *ownership, possession, and control of a parcel of real estate for the life of someone*. Ownership, possession, and control are contingent upon living; therefore, the ownership, possession, and control are lost at death. If ownership terminates as soon as a person stops breathing, the heirs of the deceased owner will inherit nothing. Under a life estate, ownership lies only with the living.

The life estate is a freehold estate that is *not* inheritable. It may be created for the life of the named life tenant or for the life of some other named person. A life estate created for the duration of the life tenant's own life is called an *estate for life* or *ordinary life estate*. For example: A conveys 40 acres to B for B's life. When the life estate is for the life of a person other than the life tenant, it is called an estate **pur autre vie**, meaning *for the life of another*. For example: C conveys 40 acres to D until the death of E.

Two outcomes are possible upon death: (a) an estate in remainder, or (b) an estate in reversion. If the *conveyance is from grantor to F for life and then to a named person or persons upon the death of F*, it is an estate in **remainder**. The *person or persons receiving the title upon the death of F*, the **life tenant**, are called *remaindermen*, and the conveyance is a *conveyance in remainder*. The remaindermen receive a fee simple title. The life tenant has only an estate or ownership for his or her life. Immediately upon his or her death or upon the death of some other person named in the conveyance, the title automatically vests in the remaindermen.

If the *conveyance does not specify a person or persons to receive the title upon the death of the life tenant or other specified person*, a life estate in **reversion** is created. Upon the death of life tenant, the title will revert to the grantor or the grantor's heirs. The grantor has a reversionary interest in the estate.

Let's use the following example:

Grantor A conveys title by deed to his son for life.

Grantor B conveys title by deed to his son for life, and after the death of his son to the Red Cross Association.

Each grantor has intentionally created a life estate in his son. Each has given his son a few sticks from the bundle of rights. As long as his son is alive, the son has control, title, and possession. In both examples, the son can sell his ownership interest, but he can sell only what he owns. His ownership ends at his death. Therefore, anyone who buys from the son will lose ownership when the son dies. This outcome makes the sale or mortgage of a life estate unlikely, although not impossible.

The real difference in the two examples exists in what occurs at the death of the son. Because Grantor A has not designated who or what gets the bundle of sticks at his son's death, the bundle reverts to Grantor A or his heirs if he is deceased. While his son lives, Grantor A has a *reversionary interest.* Grantor B designated that the Red Cross Association is to receive the bundle of sticks at his son's death. What the Red Cross Association has is called a *remainder interest.* The Red Cross Association is a remainderman.

Each example portrays a conventional life estate. A conventional life estate is one created voluntarily by the parties. This may be accomplished during one's life with a deed, or upon death in one's will. Someone or some entity is going to become the owner at some time in the future at the death of the life tenant. Figures 2.4 and 2.5 illustrate the difference between life estate in reversion and life estate in remainder.

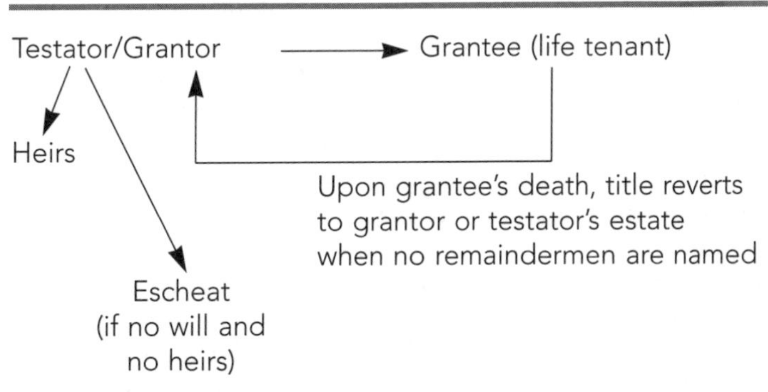

FIGURE 2.4 Life estate in reversion for Grantor A.

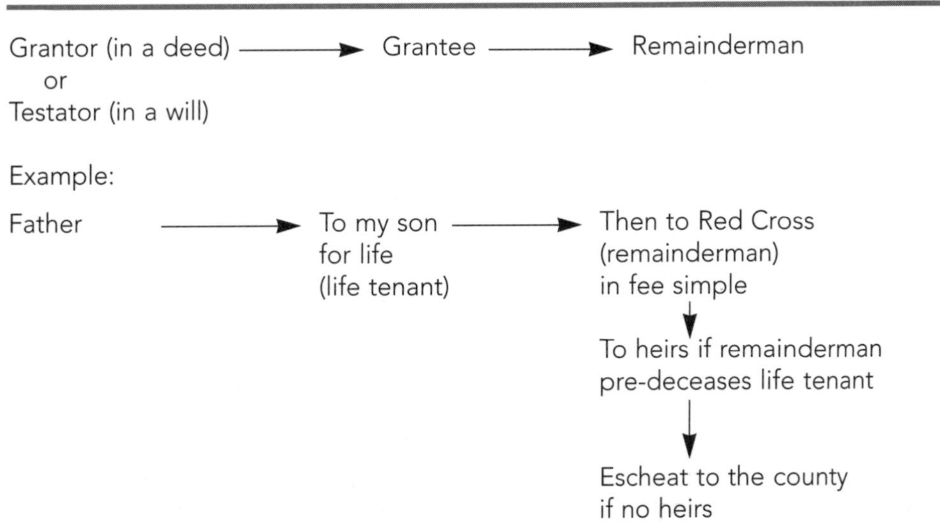

FIGURE 2.5 Life estate in remainder for Grantor B.

Life estates are by no means worthless. Any ownership right that gives title, possession, and control has value. Nevertheless, life estates are clearly temporary.

PUTTING IT TO WORK

Creation of life estates has become a common estate planning tool. The owners of real estate convey to themselves a life estate in the real estate and the remainder interest to their children. The ownership of the life estate allows use and control by parents until death, and then automatic transfer to children outside of probate.

In addition to being created by an intentional conveyance (conventional), life estates can also be created by law. Unlike life estates created by act of the parties, either by deed or in a will (conventional life estates), *life estates created by operation of law* are called *legal life estates* or *statutory life estates.*

Prior to adoption of the Uniform Probate Code, the most common life estates created by law or statute were dower and curtesy. Both **dower** and **curtesy** refer to an *automatic life estate owned by a surviving spouse in inheritable property owned by the deceased spouse alone during the marriage.* If the owner of the land was the *husband*, the wife has a life estate called dower. If the owner of the land was the *wife*, the husband has a life estate called curtesy (except in Arkansas, District of Columbia, Kentucky, Massachusetts, Missouri, and Ohio, where the husband's right is also called dower). Therefore, if John owns a home in his name only, upon his death his wife has an automatic life estate as a result of dower law. Until John dies, this is an *inchoate* (future) right of the surviving spouse. If the surviving spouse had not joined in a conveyance of the property, he or she has a right to a life estate (usually limited to one-third the value) in the property owned while they were married. This cannot be enforced until the death of the conveying spouse. Dower and curtesy should not be confused with community property laws.

Some states recognize a homestead life estate for a surviving spouse. A homestead life estate is available only on the family home, not on all the inheritable property, as with dower and curtesy.

In states where dower and curtesy have been abolished, a substitute usually is provided by intestate succession as set out in the Uniform Probate Code. **Intestate succession** statutes set forth *the manner in which the property of an intestate* (one who has died without leaving a valid will) *is distributed to heirs.*

PUTTING IT TO WORK

Dower and curtesy laws seem to be falling by the wayside in favor of statutory laws of intestacy. These laws provide for direct, timely passage of a decedent's assets to heirs and relatives in the absence of a will. Fewer and fewer states are recognizing dower and curtesy.

Rights and Responsibilities of Life Tenants

The life tenant under any type of life estate has the right of **alienation**, whereby the life tenant *may transfer title to another person or pledge the title as security for debt, but no more than the title.* Of course, the individual cannot give title for a duration longer than the life of the person named in the creation of a life estate to establish its duration, usually himself or herself. The life tenant also has the right to the net income produced by the property, if any.

The life tenant also may legally mortgage the life estate. A lending institution would not likely accept a life estate as security for a mortgage, however, because the estate terminates on the death of the life tenant or some other named person. This is possible, though, if a life insurance policy is obtained to protect the lender against the life tenant's premature death.

A life tenant has certain responsibilities. Basically, the individual must preserve and protect the estate for the benefit of the remainderman or reversionary interest. The life tenant, however, has a legal right called the right to **estovers**. This right provides that the *life tenant may cut and use reasonable amounts of timber from the land to repair buildings or to use for fuel on the property, but not for profit*. A violation of the right of estovers is called an *act of waste*.

A life tenant has an obligation to pay the real property taxes on the property in which he or she has a life estate. The life tenant also has the duty to pay any assessments levied against the property by a county or a municipality for improvements to the property. Assessments are levied against land for improvements made to the land, such as paving streets and laying water lines and sewer lines.

The life tenant has a duty to make repairs to improvements on the land. He or she cannot permit the property to deteriorate because of lack of repairs and thus cause depreciation to existing improvements. This is called the duty of preservation.

If a life tenant violates these responsibilities, those persons having the remainder or reversionary interest may bring suit to protect the real estate subject to the life estate.

Nonfreehold Estates (Leasehold Estates)

A **nonfreehold estate**, also called a **leasehold estate**, is a *less than freehold estate* (less than a lifetime) and therefore is of *limited duration*. Leasehold, or *rental* estates are *created by a contract called a lease or rental agreement*, which provides contractual rights and duties to both parties. Leasehold estates *grant possession to the tenant, but not title*. Title stays with the owner. Leasehold estates create the relationship of lessor (landlord) and lessee (tenant) between the parties. These estates may be called estates, tenancies, or leaseholds.

The nonfreehold estates or leaseholds are (1) estate for years, (2) periodic estate, (3) estate at will, and (4) estate at sufferance. An **estate for years** leasehold *exists only for a fixed period of time*. A **periodic estate**, also known as **estate from year-to-year**, however, *automatically renews itself for another period unless one party gives notice of termination to the other*. An **estate at will** has *no determinable period length and may be terminated by either party at will by simply giving notice*. An **estate at sufferance** describes a *tenant who originally was in lawful possession of property but refuses to leave after his possession is terminated*.

The characteristics of each nonfreehold estate are more fully described and discussed in Chapter 13, which deals with landlord and tenant.

Putting It to Work

The fact that a tenant is still, and improperly, in possession does not allow landlords the right to take matters into their own hands. They must take proper legal steps (court proceedings) to repossess the property. If the landlord "locks out" the tenant or terminates utility services, the landlord is subject to various legal actions and liability for wrongful or constructive eviction (discussed in Chapter 13).

Ownership of Real Property

Ownership of real property may be by one person alone or by many persons, or even non-natural entities such as partnerships and corporations. Co-ownership of property may be used to control transfer of the property at death or to allow pooling monies to purchase an investment, which then will be owned by several people. Co-ownership can happen accidentally or may require intentional action and words.

When acquiring property, buyers have many options in how to acquire the property. The various choices are referred to as *vesting options*. The vesting is shown in a deed (or will) immediately following the names of the grantee(s) (or devisees).

Vesting options may range from a basic tenancy in common to a complicated tenancy in partnership or trust agreement. The various options create stronger or weaker responsibilities and rights between co-owners with respect to one another. A co-owner's conduct may be very different under different vesting with different rights.

Putting It to Work

The decision regarding vesting is vastly important to buyers, although they probably do not realize this. Real estate licensees should know the vesting alternatives and inform the buyer of the importance of the decision, as well as the various alternatives available, but they should be careful not to practice law or give legal advice. A statement such as "Joint tenancy is always best for a married couple" exposes the licensee to liability, and deservedly so.

Ownership in Severalty

When *title to real property is held in the name of only one person or entity*, it is called ownership in **severalty**, because the interest is "severed" from all others. The person or entity holding title is the sole or only owner. If *the titleholder is married*, the property is called separate property. The owning spouse holds title separately from the other spouse.

Concurrent Ownership

Simultaneous ownership of real property by two or more people is called **co-ownership**. That term is used rather than joint ownership because the word "joint" describes a specific type of ownership. There are various types of co-ownership. The rights of the owners depend upon the type of ownership they have. The types of co-ownership are: tenancy in common, joint tenancy, tenancy by the entirety, and community property. To adequately understand the distinctions among the co-ownerships, the difference between right of survivorship and right of inheritance must be understood. **Right of survivorship** means that *if one (or more) of the co-owners dies, the surviving co-owners automatically receive the interest of the deceased co-owner.* Right of survivorship defeats passing of title by will. The last survivor of all of the co-owners owns the entire property in severalty. **Right of inheritance**, by contrast, means that *a co-owner's share of the real estate will pass at his death to his heirs or in accordance with his last will and testament.*

Concurrent ownerships such as tenancy in common, joint tenancy, and tenancy by the entirety require certain unities of ownership. The four possible **unities** are: *time, title, interest, and possession* (see Figure 2.6). For the co-ownership to be recognized, the different concurrent ownerships require one or more of the unities between the co-owners (see Figure 2.7).

FIGURE 2.6
Unities of co-ownership.

TIME:	The co-owners must receive title to the real estate in one document called a deed.
TITLE:	The co-owners each have the same type of estate such as fee simple absolute, fee simple defeasible, or life estate.
INTEREST:	The co-owners have the same percentage of ownership.
POSSESSION:	The co-owners have equal rights to access, possess, or use any of the co-owned property. They have undivided interest.

FIGURE 2.7
Comparison of the forms of co-ownership.

JOINT TENANCY WITH RIGHT OF SURVIVORSHIP	TENANCY IN COMMON	TENANCY BY THE ENTIRETY
▪ Four unities: time, title, interest, and possession ▪ must be created intentionally ▪ right of survivorship ▪ equal responsibility for expenses ▪ equal division of profits	▪ One unity: possession ▪ may happen accidentally ▪ no right of survivorship; right of inheritance ▪ co-owners share expenses and profits based upon percentage of ownership	▪ Four unities: time, title, interest, and possession ▪ must be legally married ▪ right of survivorship ▪ husband or wife cannot individually sell his or her interest ▪ divorce converts to tenancy in common

Tenancy in Common

Tenancy in common is characterized by *two or more persons holding title to a property at the same time.* The only required unity is that of possession. The unity of possession exists if all co-owners have the right to possess or access any and all portions of the property owned without physical division. This type of possession is called *possession of an undivided interest.* Any two or more parties can hold title as tenants in common. Each tenant in common holds an undivided interest in the entire property, rather than any specific portion of it. There is no right of survivorship; upon the death of a tenant in common, the deceased's share will go to the person's heir or as designated in the last will and testament.

Tenancies in common may occur when property is inherited by more than one person. If the will does not designate the type of co-ownership, or in the event of no will, the inheriting parties receive title as tenants in common.

A tenancy in common also is created if two or more purchasers do not request a vesting choice when they acquire property via a deed. If nothing is stated, a tenancy in common is created.

A tenant in common may sell his or her share to anybody without destroying the tenancy relationship. Each tenant in common also may individually pledge only his or her share of the property as security for a loan that creates a lien or encumbrance against that share only, not the entire property. If the loan is not repaid and the lien of one co-owner is foreclosed, the property foreclosed upon is only that share belonging to the defaulting co-owner. Tenants in common do not have to have equal interest in the property. For example, one co-tenant may hold one-half interest and two other co-tenants may hold one-quarter each.

A tenant in common may bring legal action to have the property partitioned so each tenant may have a specific and divided portion of the property exclusively. If this can be done equitably with a piece of land, each would receive title to a separate tract according to his or her share of interest. If this cannot physically be done to the land, the court may order the sale of the property with appropriate shares of the proceeds distributed to the tenants in common.

Joint Tenancy

The **joint tenancy** form of co-ownership *requires all four unities of time, title, interest, and possession.* The unity of time exists when co-owners receive their title at the same time in the same document or conveyance. The unity of title exists if the co-owners have the same type of ownership, such as a life estate, fee simple, or conditional fee. The unity of interest exists if the co-owners all have the same percentage of ownership. Joint tenants must have the same interest in the property, must receive their title at the same time from the same source, must have the same percentage of ownership, and must have the right to undivided possession in the property. For example, if there are three joint tenants, each must own one-third interest in the property, they must all receive their title from the same conveying document (will or deed), each must own the same type of interest (fee simple, life estate, or conditional fee), and each must have the right to possession and use of any and all portions of the property.

A special characteristic of joint tenancy is the right of survivorship. When one joint tenant dies, his or her share goes automatically to other surviving joint tenants equally, instead of passing to the heirs of the deceased. A joint tenant therefore cannot convey ownership by will. By acquiring as a joint tenancy, each joint tenant gives up the right of inheritance (control over passage of the property).

If a joint tenant, prior to his death, sells his share of ownership, the person purchasing this share will not become a joint tenant with the others. The necessary four unities will not exist. The document that gives title to the new purchaser is not at the same time as the document giving title to the original joint tenants. The unity of time has been destroyed. The new co-owner thus will enter the relationship as a tenant in common. The remaining original joint tenants continue as joint tenants, with the right of survivorship among themselves. The new purchaser, as a tenant in common with the original joint tenants, will be able to pass his share at his death to his heirs or by will.

PUTTING IT TO WORK

Many investment "partners" will acquire title as joint tenants thinking that the stronger link between co-owners will create a more desirable, stronger "partnership." This usually is not what unrelated investors really need. The partners will not likely want to waive their rights of inheritance and thereby "shut out" their heirs. What they probably want is a tenancy in common or a more formal tenancy in partnership outlining their rights and duties to each other. As indicated earlier, however, the real estate licensee should not offer advice on these matters but, instead, refer buyers to legal counsel.

The right of survivorship is not favored in all states today except in joint ownership by husband and wife as tenants by the entirety. In some states, a court will not recognize a joint tenancy unless the deed of conveyance makes it absolutely clear that the parties intend the right of survivorship. In other states, the right of survivorship is granted automatically without any more words than "as joint tenants."

A joint tenancy, just as a tenancy in common, is also subject to partition through legal action.

Tenancy by Entirety

Ownership as **tenants by the entirety** is *limited to husband and wife*. To receive title as tenants by the entirety, husband and wife must have a legal marriage at the time they receive title to the property. In many states, the deed does not have to read "to husband and wife as tenants by the entirety" to create a tenancy by the entirety. The deed only has to convey the property to John A. Jones and his wife, Mary A. Jones, and a tenancy by the entirety is created automatically. Like a joint tenancy, tenancy by the entirety contains the right of survivorship. Upon the death of one spouse, the surviving spouse automatically receives title to the property by operation of law. Creation of a tenancy by the entirety requires marriage and the unities of time, title, interest, and possession.

A husband or wife owning land as tenants by the entirety may not legally convey or pledge property as security to a third party without the other spouse joining in the deed or pledge instrument. A spouse who is a tenant by the entirety may convey her interest to the other spouse with only the signature of the conveying spouse on the deed. There can be no action for partition of real estate held as tenants by the entirety.

Tenancy by the entirety exists only as long as the tenants hold title to the property and are legally married. Tenancy by the entirety is abolished automatically by decree of divorce. A mere legal separation is not sufficient. When a final decree of absolute divorce is obtained, the ownership is automatically changed to tenancy in common by operation of law, eliminating the right of survivorship.

If they elect to do so, married people may own property as tenants in common. They do not have to take title as tenants by the entirety. A husband or wife also may own separate property in severalty. In most states, however, the other spouse has to join in the deed if the title is to be conveyed, to be certain that no spousal claim remains after the conveyance.

Community Property

Nine states (Arizona, California, Idaho, Louisiana, Nevada, New Mexico, Texas, Washington, and Wisconsin) are **community property** states. By law, in these states, *husband and wife automatically acquire title to real estate as community property*. A husband and wife may hold title to both real and personal property as community property. They also may hold title separately in severalty, as explained in the following paragraphs.

The theory of community property is that husband and wife share equally in the ownership of property acquired by their joint efforts during the community of marriage. The title to this property will vest in husband and wife as community property whether the deed is made only to the husband, only to the wife, or to both husband and wife.

This general rule is in effect in community property states with the exception of California and New Mexico, where there is a rebuttable presumption that property deeded to a married woman in her name only is separate property. The presumption may be rebutted by proof that the property was purchased with community funds.

Contrary to widely held opinion, there is no right of survivorship in community property, and therefore the one-half interest of a deceased spouse will descend to heirs and will not automatically go to the surviving spouse. To pledge or convey title to community property during life, both husband and wife must sign the pledge or deed.

In community property states, **separate property** is *any property acquired by one spouse during marriage by gift or inheritance. Also, any property purchased with the separate funds of the husband or wife* becomes separate property of the purchasing spouse. Property acquired prior to marriage by either husband or wife is also separate property. Because community property states do not recognize dower or curtesy, a spouse may mortgage or convey title to separate property without participation of the other spouse. In these states, separate property is completely under the ownership and control of the spouse holding title in severalty. In most of the community property states, however, both husband and wife must execute deeds and mortgages involving the separate property of either spouse if the property is being used as their home.

PUTTING IT TO WORK

Community property laws are subject to wide variations in interpretation by judges, lenders, title insurance companies, and others. Real estate licensees should be well-informed on the specific documents, expectations, and ramifications in a given community property state.

COMBINATION FORMS OF OWNERSHIP

Condominiums

The term **condominium** comes from the Latin words meaning "together" and "to exercise dominion over." Thus, condominium developments are *jointly controlled.* Since condominium ownership was not recognized under common law, special statutes were required to create this form of ownership. The first condominium statute enacted in the United States was the California Horizontal Property Act, in 1961, and condominium ownership is now recognized in all states.

PUTTING IT TO WORK

Condominium statutes are called "horizontal property acts" because they authorize a three-dimensional property description, with a property line above and below the condominium. These horizontal property lines create a cube of air space or a volume that is the privately owned condominium. Air rights and area below the land surface are owned as tenants in common.

Though laws creating condominium ownership vary from state to state, the fundamental principles are reasonably uniform. Condominium statutes set forth the manner in which a condominium is to be created and managed. These include a declaration (master deed), articles of association, and bylaws. The declaration, articles of association, and bylaws must be recorded in the public record in the county where the property is located.

Condominium ownership is a way of life as well as a type of concurrent ownership. Condominiums come in all shapes and sizes. They may be one story or many stories. They may be residential, industrial, or commercial. They may be new construction or conversion of a present structure. Condominium ownership is a combination of ownerships—individual unit plus co-ownership of the common areas available to all owners in the condominium project. The individual unit may be held as a fee in severalty, fee in joint tenancy, fee in common, or fee as tenants by the entireties. Common areas, such as the yard, roof, hallways, elevators, pool, tennis courts, and parking lots, are owned as tenants in common.

The *legal description of the condominium facility* is found in the **declaration**, or **master deed**. This description contains the height, width, and length of each unit. The declaration also contains a plat of the property showing the location of buildings, plans and specifications for the buildings and the various units, a description of the common areas, and the degree of ownership in the common areas available to each individual unit owner. The declaration also sets forth the specific purpose of the condominium facility. It also may include a *right of first refusal* clause, giving the association the first opportunity to purchase an individual owner's unit if the owner wishes to sell, though this is fairly rare.

Title to the individual unit may be transferred by deed or by leaving it to an heir by will. Title to the individual unit may be encumbered by a mortgage or a mechanic's lien (discussed in Chapter 3).

Title to the individual unit is assessed real property taxes. Marketable title to the individual unit is evidenced by an abstract of title or title insurance policy. In the real estate world the individual unit basically is treated like any other single-family dwelling. Condominium units may be purchased with cash or financed.

Since 1961, condominiums can be financed via an FHA mortgage. The Veterans Administration also will guarantee mortgage loans for the purchase of condominiums. (These concepts are discussed in Chapter 8.) Units also can be sold on contract for deed. If the individual unit's taxes or mortgage is not paid, only the individual unit will be placed in a tax sale or a foreclosure action. The other units in the condominium facility will not be affected.

Title to the common areas is held as tenancy in common with all other unit owners. The common areas are the responsibility of all unit owners. The *articles of association* establish an association to provide for maintenance and management of the common areas. The articles of association also establish the method and procedure for assessing the individual unit owners for each unit's share of the common maintenance items such as mowing, painting, and landscaping. If an individual unit owner fails or refuses to pay this assessment, the association may bring legal action against the unit owner to collect the unpaid assessment. If the individual unit owner files bankruptcy and thus cannot be forced to pay the assessment, the other unit owners will be required to pay an additional prorated assessment for the defaulting unit owner.

The *bylaws* are the operative rules for the condominium facility and individual unit owners. The bylaws set forth the officers of the association, who are usually owners of the individual units in the facility. They are elected by the individual unit owners and serve for the benefit of the whole. The bylaws also set out the method and procedure for amending the bylaws, declaration, and articles of association.

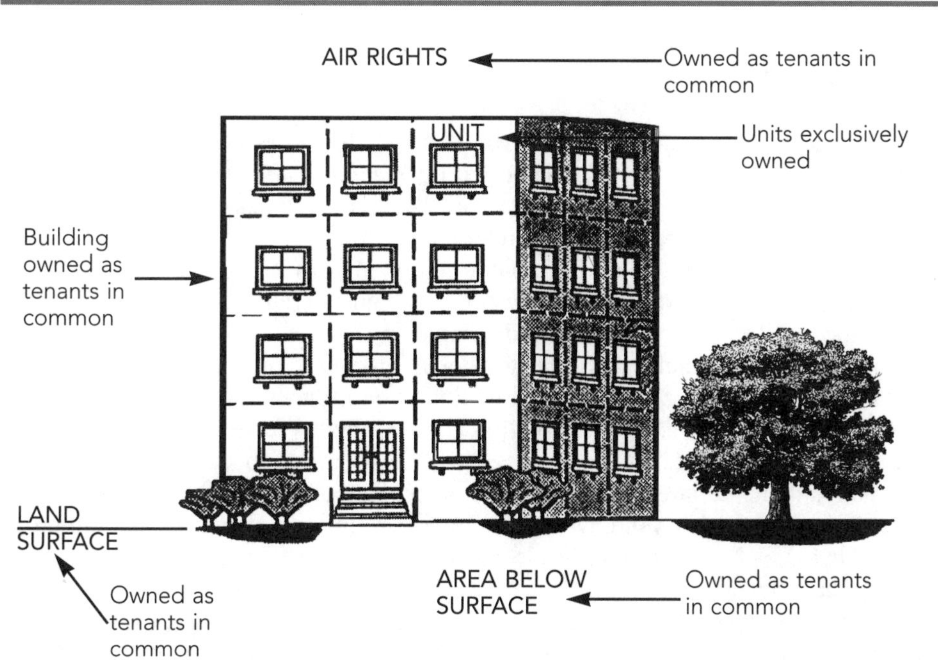

FIGURE 2.8 Condominium ownership.

Cooperatives

The same types of structures that house condominiums can also house cooperative ownership. Cooperatives can be new construction or conversion of a present structure. They can be residential or commercial. Cooperatives can be single story or multistory. The type and form of ownership in a cooperative, however, are vastly different from ownership in a condominium facility.

In a **cooperative**, the *buildings, land, all real property rights, and interests are owned by a corporation in severalty*. The title to the property, as shown on the deed, is in the name of the corporation. The shareholders of the corporation are tenants in the building. The tenants have the right of occupancy as evidenced by a *proprietary lease*, which is usually an estate for years and for a long period of time. Thus, ownership in a cooperative is really ownership of shares of stock in a corporation plus a long-term lease for the apartments. There is no tenancy in common ownership in the common areas, even though all tenants can use the common areas. The common areas, as all of the building, are owned in fee by the corporation.

A purchaser in a cooperative does not receive a deed, an abstract of title, or title insurance. An owner in a cooperative does not own real estate in the typical sense, although the Internal Revenue Service considers this as ownership by recognizing the traditional benefits of home ownership such as mortgage interest and property tax deductions (on a pro rata basis). The only property interest the shareholders hold is a leasehold estate providing the right to possession of an apartment and use of the common areas. As lessees, the shareholders pay no rent but do pay an assessment to cover the cost of maintaining and operating the building, real property taxes, and debt service if the corporation has placed a mortgage against the real estate. The shareholder's rights and obligations are specified in the lease and the corporation's bylaws.

A **right of first refusal** often exists in favor of the corporation. It *requires a selling shareholder to first offer the share of stock to the corporation before sale to an outside buyer is allowed*. If a right of first refusal does not exist, there is usually a right of approval before cooperative stock may be sold. Either of these features has a tendency to restrict or inhibit the resale potential for cooperatives. In addition, if there is high vacancy or some people do not pay assessments, the corporation may be forced to increase assessments among remaining owners to keep the bills paid.

Timesharing

Timesharing, another relatively new form of ownership, stretches the common law meaning of real estate ownership. Timesharing *combines the ownership of a condominium (or other separate unit) in fee with the sharing of use of the unit by many owners*. This co-ownership, based upon intervals of time, is called interval ownership. Several different people purchase the condominium unit in fee and then divide the use of the unit by weeks or months. Each owner of the unit purchases the exclusive right to use of the unit for the specified period of time.

Timesharing is especially attractive to people wishing to purchase a condominium for vacationing purposes. Many people vacation two to four weeks a year. Purchasing a timeshare allows them to enjoy a vacation home without year-round expense. Maintenance and repair costs, taxes, insurance, and general care of the timeshared property are prorated among the interval owners. The percentage of the expense equals the percentage of the year purchased. Owners of a timeshare interest also hope that the property timeshared will increase in value, building up equity and at the same time providing them housing while they vacation.

Timeshare ownership has become so popular that exchange programs for exchanging timeshare units are now available. The exchange programs allow the owner of specified time at a property to trade that time with the owner of a specified time at a totally different property. For example, the owner of a timeshare in Florida property could trade for a timeshare of equal time in Maine property.

Real Property Ownership by Business Organizations

Business organizations can take several different forms including sole proprietorship, partnership, corporation, syndicate, joint venture, and real estate investment trust. All of these business organizations can receive, hold, and convey title in the same ways individuals do.

Sole Proprietorship

A **sole proprietorship** is simply *a business owned by one individual.* An individual may use his or her own name as the name of the business or may assume a name for business purposes. Under the assumed name, the owner is sometimes referred to as DBA (doing business as) or AKA (also known as) or a fictitious name. The sole proprietor can receive, hold, and convey title to real estate either in his or her name or in the assumed name of the business.

The owner of a sole proprietorship is fully liable for all business debts. If business debts exceed business assets, the owner's personal assets may be attached by creditors to satisfy defaulted debts. Filing bankruptcy by the business alone will not alleviate possible attachment of the owner's personal assets to satisfy business debts. In a sole proprietorship, the business and the owner are one and the same.

Partnerships

A **partnership** is *a form of business organization in which the business is owned by two or more persons, called partners*. A partnership is created by contract between the partners. This contract or agreement should establish the partners' ownership and management rights and obligations. The partners do not have to have the same degree of interest in the partnership or the same extent of management authority or be the same type of partners, limited or general (see below). The contract or agreement also should contain the method and procedure for dividing ownership interest upon the withdrawal, death, or removal of a partner. The purpose of this portion of the agreement, usually called the buy-sell agreement, is to control the change in partners without significantly disrupting business operations.

The partners may be of two categories: general or limited. In *general partnerships*, the partners are personally liable for partnership debts exceeding partnership assets. Partners are jointly (together) and severally (separately) liable for these debts. Joint and several liability means that the creditors can attach the assets of all of the partners or any one of the partners to satisfy the debt. If one of the partners files bankruptcy, this does not relieve the other partners of the debt.

A *limited partnership* consists of one or more general partners who are jointly and severally liable, and one or more special, silent, or limited partners who contribute money or other assets of value to the extent of their ownership interest. Limited partners are not liable for the debts of the partnership beyond the amount of money they have contributed or have agreed to contribute to the partnership. To retain the protected status from partnership debts, a limited partner may not participate in managing the partnership. If limited partners exert any management authority, they lose the protection beyond limited liability. Limited partners thus may become general partners merely by their actions.

Corporation

A corporation is an artificial being, invisible, intangible, and existing only pursuant to law. A corporation is a taxable legal entity recognized by law with tax rates separate from individual income tax rates. Corporations did not exist at common law. A corporation is created by a charter granted by the state of incorporation. Evidence of incorporation is called a Certificate of Incorporation.

The corporation's activities are essentially limited to the state within which it is incorporated, and it may not "do business" in another state without permission. Thus, a corporation is initially geographically bound. Permission to conduct business in another state is granted by the Secretary of State in the state where business is desired to be conducted. A corporation is called a *domestic corporation* within the state in which it is incorporated. A corporation doing business in another state is called a *foreign corporation* in that state.

Corporations are divided into two basic classes according to their objectives and purposes. *Public corporations* are the various governmental corporations such as cities, towns, counties, school districts, and special bodies for public improvements. *Private corporations* are organized to perform nongovernmental functions. Private corporations can be further divided into "for profit" and "not for profit" corporations.

"Not for profit" corporations are churches, fraternal organizations, foundations, charitable organizations, and other groups that perform services for the public other than in a governmental capacity. "For profit" corporations are all other private corporations. "Not for profit" corporations may be exempt from the real property tax assessments and income tax assessments imposed upon "for profit" corporations.

Because a corporation exists only upon compliance with the laws of the state of incorporation, if the corporation ever fails to comply with the law, the corporation vanishes. The term for vanishing a corporation is *dissolution*. Dissolution of a corporation is by operation of law (automatic) if compliance with the law ceases. Dissolution of a corporation also may occur upon the vote of shareholders in the corporation.

A corporation has the power to receive, hold, mortgage, and convey title to real property for all purposes for which the corporation was created. The proper method for conveying property is set out in the corporation's bylaws. The bylaws expressly state what officers, directors, or other persons must sign conveying documents and whether a special corporate resolution or meeting is required to authorize the conveyance.

Syndications

Syndication denotes *multiple joint participation in a real estate investment*. The syndication may involve joining of assets and talents of individuals, general partnerships, limited partnerships, or corporations in some combination. Although the people and entities invest in real estate, some investors are hoping to make money based solely on the efforts of another without liability, so the organization may be considered to be dealing in securities. An investment is a security, as defined by the Federal Securities Act of 1933, if:

- It is an investment of money.
- The investment is a common or joint enterprise.
- The investment is undertaken for the purpose of making a profit.
- The investment is one in which profit will be derived solely or substantially from the management efforts of others.

Because most syndications intend to make a profit for many from the efforts of a few, they must comply with the rules and regulations of the Securities and Exchange Commission. Syndications typically are used in cases of multiple, continuing projects that require the investment of substantial amounts of money from many different sources.

Joint Venture

A **joint venture** is *an organization formed by two or more parties for the purpose of investing in real estate or any other type of investment.* The joint venture may be in the form of a corporation or a partnership, or the parties may hold title as joint tenants or as tenants in common. Joint ventures usually are devised for only one project.

Limited Liability Company

A limited liability company is a recent addition to forms of business organization. It is an artificial being existing only pursuant to law. In addition to filing statutory documents, a limited liability company must have an agreement signed by its members for operation of the business. A limited liability company may be managed jointly by all members of the company (called member managed) or it may be managed by one or more members in accordance with a management agreement (called manager managed). A limited liability company is similar to a partnership in many ways. It is taxed in the same manner as a partnership and it may distribute assets to individual members with minimal tax consequences as a partnership. In addition, a limited liability company is similar to a corporation in that it provides protection from liability to the members.

Trust

A **trust** is *an arrangement in which the trustor (owner of property) places property in the hands of a trustee for the benefit of a beneficiary.* A fiduciary relationship exists between the trustee and the beneficiary of the trust. In a fiduciary relationship, the trustee must be loyal to and protect the interest of the trust beneficiary. Anyone can create a trust, naming anyone, including oneself, as beneficiary or trustee, or both. A land trust is created by transferring the title of the land to a trustee, who holds the title for the benefit of the beneficiaries. The trustee's power and duties are expressly set out in the document establishing the trust.

Real Estate Investment Trust (REIT)

Real estate investment trusts (REITs) were created in 1967, stemming from changes in the Internal Revenue Code that became effective in September of 1967. As a result, the beneficiaries were not taxed doubly on trust income. The trust can now earn income from real estate investments without paying trust income tax. To avoid the trust income tax, however, the trust must distribute 95% of the ordinarily taxable income to the trust beneficiaries. The beneficiaries then report the income for tax purposes.

The two major investment choices for REITs are (a) to lend, or (b) to buy, rent, or sell property. If the REIT primarily lends money for the interest return, it is called a *mortgage REIT*. If the REIT primarily owns, manages, rents, and sells property, it is called an *equity REIT*.

IMPORTANT POINTS

1. Real property consists of land and everything attached to the land, including things that grow naturally without requiring planting and cultivation.
2. Annual crops that require planting and cultivation are personal property and are called emblements.
3. Ownership in land includes the surface of the earth and the area above and below the surface.
4. A fixture is formerly personal property that has become attached to real property and thus is now regarded as real property.
5. Trade fixtures are items of personal property used in business that even if attached do not become real estate.
6. The allodial system of real property ownership used in the United States provides for private ownership of real estate.
7. Estates in land are divided into two groups: freehold estates and estates of less than freehold (nonfreeholds or leaseholds).
8. Freehold estates include fee simple estates, which are inheritable, and life estates, which are not inheritable.
9. The most complete form of ownership in real property is fee simple absolute.
10. Life estates may be in reversion or in remainder.
11. The duration of a life estate may be measured by the life of the life tenant or by the life of another (pur autre vie).
12. Conventional life estates are those created by someone's intentional act. Legal or statutory life estates are created by operation of law.
13. A life tenant has the right of alienation, the right of encumbrance, the right of possession and enjoyment of the property, and the right to derive certain income from it.
14. A life tenant is obligated to preserve and maintain the property for the benefit of the future owners.
15. The less than freehold estates (also called leasehold estates or nonfreeholds) are estates of limited duration, providing possession and control but not title as in the case of freehold estates.
16. Leasehold estates are estate for years, periodic tenancy (estate from year-to-year), estate at will, and estate at sufferance.
17. Title held in the name of one person only is called ownership in severalty, and is also considered separate property if the owner is married.
18. When two or more persons or organizations hold title concurrently, it is called co-ownership or concurrent ownership. The forms of co-ownership are tenancy in common, joint tenancy, tenancy by the entirety, community property, and certain aspects of condominiums, cooperatives, and timeshares.
19. Joint tenancy and tenancy by the entirety include the right of survivorship and require the unities of time, title, interest, and possession. Tenancy by the entirety is restricted to husband and wife and adds the fifth unity: marriage (unity of person).
20. The owner of a condominium unit holds title to the unit either in severalty or as co-owner with another, as well as title to the common areas as tenants in common with the other unit owners.
21. Creating a condominium requires recording a declaration (also called master deed), articles of association, and bylaws.
22. A cooperative requires stock ownership in a corporation that owns a building containing cooperative apartments. Stockholders occupy apartments under a proprietary lease.

23. Interval ownership of land is called timesharing.
24. Business organizations may receive, hold, and convey title to real property.
25. Two or more people investing in a business or investment together without setting up a separate legal owner in the form of a corporation creates a partnership.
26. General partnerships have one class of partner only; all partners are fully liable.
27. Limited partnerships have two classes of partner; limited partners are liable only to their extent of investment, while general partners are fully liable.
28. A corporation is a separate legal entity created by investors.
29. Other business or investment structures include syndications, joint ventures, sole proprietorships, and real estate investment trusts (REITs).

How Would You Respond?

Betty inherited a life estate in 80 acres from her father. The remainder interest is owned by her two brothers. The farm is presently leased to Mr. Brown, who has planted corn.

1. Can the farm be listed for sale with only Betty's signature? Why or why not?
2. If the farm is sold, does the new owner receive any or all of the corn? Why or why not?

Review Questions

Answers to these questions are found in the *Answer Key* section at the back of the book.

1. Personal property attached to real property is prevented from becoming real property by which of the following?
   a. ownership in severalty
   b. ownership as tenants in common
   c. security interest and financing statement (UCC)
   d. right of survivorship

2. An estate in fee simple determinable is an example of a:
   a. freehold estate
   b. nondefeasible fee
   c. nonfreehold estate
   d. leasehold estate

3. If a widow inherits an estate by will, and the will grants her the right of use and possession of a parcel of land for the rest of her life with the provision that the estate will go to her children in fee simple upon her death, she has received:
   a. an inheritable freehold estate
   b. a life estate in remainder
   c. a life estate in reversion
   d. a fee simple absolute

4. The highest and best form of estate in real property is which of the following?
   a. leasehold for years
   b. defeasible fee
   c. life estate in reversion
   d. fee simple absolute

5. A life estate created by the exercise of the right of dower is a(n):
   a. conventional life estate
   b. estate pur autre vie
   c. legal life estate
   d. community property

6. All of the following are rights or responsibilities of a life tenant EXCEPT:
   a. estovers
   b. inchoate dower
   c. alienation
   d. preservation

7. A life estate for the life of another is a(n):
   a. dower
   b. estate pur autre vie
   c. curtesy
   d. statutory remainder

8. Title to real property held in the name of one person only is owned:
   a. in severalty
   b. as tenancy in common
   c. as tenancy by entirety
   d. as joint tenancy

9. Which type of ownership requires unity of interest, title, time, and possession?
   a. cooperative
   b. tenancy in common
   c. joint tenancy
   d. community property

10. If a person dies without a will, his property will pass in accordance with the laws of:
    a. testate succession
    b. testamentary authority
    c. intestate succession
    d. dower and curtesy laws

11. The purchaser of a condominium unit receives title to the land and common areas whereon the condominium is situated as a:
    a. tenant by entirety
    b. tenant in common
    c. joint tenant
    d. tenant in severalty

12. All of the following are true of the purchaser of a condominium timeshare EXCEPT:
    a. she receives a title for the same time period(s) each calendar year
    b. she may convey this title to anyone else
    c. she owns a share of stock in the land and a proprietary lease in the unit
    d. she will pay a prorated share of the maintenance

13. In the cooperative form of ownership:
    a. ownership is evidenced by shares of stock in a corporation holding title to the building
    b. each owner owns a fee simple interest in the land on which the building is located
    c. all owners pay real property taxes on their individual units
    d. each owner holds a freehold interest in the land

14. In most states a joint tenant may do all of the following with her interest EXCEPT:
    a. sell her interest in the property
    b. pledge her interest as security for a mortgaged loan
    c. pass her interest by will
    d. gift her interest prior to death

15. Ownership as tenants by the entirety includes which of the following?
    a. the right of one owner to convey title to his or her share of ownership without the participation of the other owner
    b. the right of survivorship
    c. ownership of an unequal interest in the property with another
    d. conversion to ownership as joint tenants if the owners are divorced

16. All of the following are tests to determine if an item is a fixture EXCEPT:
    a. manner of annexation
    b. intent of person who installed item
    c. utility of item at different location
    d. length of time at the premises

17. Bob transferred property to the Methodist Church as long as the property is used only for religious purposes. The estate created is:
    a. fee simple subject to condition subsequent
    b. fee simple determinable
    c. fee simple absolute
    d. fee tail

18. Ownership of property by two or more persons which passes by inheritance at the death of any co-owner is:
    a. ownership in severalty

    b. tenancy by entirety
    c. tenancy in common
    d. joint tenancy

19. In contrasting condominium ownership with co-operative ownership, which of the following is true?
    a. condominium ownership is limited to residential property while cooperative ownership is not limited
    b. the owner of a cooperative has a share of stock for his unit and a deed for the common areas while in a condominium the owner has a deed for his unit and a share of stock in the common areas
    c. the cooperative owner has a deed to real estate while a condominium owner has a share of stock and a lease
    d. the condominium owner has a deed to real estate while a cooperative owner has a share of stock and a lease

20. All of the following are considered part of real estate EXCEPT:
    a. trees
    b. fences
    c. growing crops
    d. garage

POSSIBLE RESPONSES TO "HOW WOULD YOU RESPOND?"

1. If only Betty signs the listing, only the life estate is being sold. Thus any buyer will purchase only Betty's right to use, control, and possession during Betty's life. The sale of just the life estate is legally possible but highly improbable.

2. The new owner would not receive any of the corn. The corn is an emblement and thus is personal property belonging to Mr. Brown who has leased the farm.

CHAPTER 3

Important Terminology

accretion
air rights
alluvion
appurtenances
assessment
avulsion
condemnation
dedication
dominant tenement
easement
easement appurtenant
easement by condemnation
easement by grant
easement by implication
easement by necessity
easement by prescription
easement in gross
eminent domain
encroachment
encumbrance
escheat
execution of judgment
general lien
intestate
judgment
judgment lien
license
lien
lis pendens
littoral rights
materialman's lien
mechanic's lien
merger
police power
priority liens
profit
profit à prendre
restrictive covenants
riparian water rights
running-with-the-land
servient tenement
special assessment
specific lien
subsurface rights
testate
trespasser
vendee
vendor
writ of attachment

Encumbrances, Government Restrictions, and Appurtenances

IN THIS CHAPTER An **encumbrance** is *anything that lessens the bundle of rights in real property*. It is a stick that has been given away, and thus the remaining bundle is of less value. Most encumbrances are interests in the property that create debt or give use or control, or both, to another. In this chapter we discuss easements, liens, restrictive covenants, and encroachments. We also discuss the inherent or automatic rights that arise from the ownership of real property. Chapter 11 focuses on other land use controls, private and governmental.

EASEMENTS

An **easement** is *a nonpossessory interest in land owned by another*. Someone who owns an easement right does not own or possess the land where the easement lies. The easement owner merely owns the right to use or have access to the land. The right of ingress and egress (entry and exit) to and from real estate is one primary use for easements. Other typical needs for easements are for a common wall in a duplex or condominium, the right to take water from the land of another, and the rights to receive light and air. The common terminology for easement is *right-of-way*. The two types of easements are easements in gross and easements appurtenant. Easements can be created by humans, by law, or by use.

Easements in Gross

Easements in gross are sometimes commercial easements in gross. This *category of easements is usually owned by the government, an agency of the government, or a public utility*. Examples are the water lines and electric lines that run underground in most lots in subdivisions. The owner of the easement (the utility company) does not own any land adjacent to the easement, merely the right to use the land of another. This right allows placement of the utility lines and extends to the easement owner the right to go onto the land to maintain and repair the utilities. Commercial easements in gross are assignable by the owner of the easement. The governmental agency or utility that owns the easement right can allow other utilities to use the same easement. The owner of the commercial easement in gross also can sell or assign the right to use the easement to others. An example is the sale by a telephone company to a cable television company of the right to place cable TV lines in the telephone easement.

The easement in gross is the most common form of easement, as virtually all urban and suburban property is subject to several government easements for things such as utilities, roadway widening, and alleyways. Easements in gross also may be held by the private sector. Examples are the right of access allowed to a Planned Unit Development association onto the land of private owners to repair walls or fences or gain access to other common areas.

Much controversy has arisen concerning abandoned railroad easements throughout the United States. The question is: Who owns the land where the railroad tracks used to lie? The answer depends on what kind of "stick" the railroad received when the tracks were laid. If the railroad received a deed for the land, the railroad holds ownership in fee. If, however, the railroad received only an easement in gross, the adjoining land owners own the land, subject to the easement rights of the railroad or the successors in interest of the railroad. The question of railroad rights-of-way has generated so much controversy and litigation that some states have passed laws designating ownership of the railroad easements by statute.

Easements Appurtenant

The **easement appurtenant** category includes *all easements that are not easements in gross*. For an easement appurtenant to exist, two separately owned parcels must be involved; one must receive a benefit and the other must accept a burden. The *land that benefits from an easement appurtenant* is called the **dominant tenement** or estate. The *land that must suffer and allow the use* is called the **servient tenement** or estate.

An example of an easement appurtenant is shown in Figure 3.1. In the illustration, if land owner B sells her property to X, the easement appurtenant follows the transfer of title to the land now owned by X. When *an easement appurtenant follows the transfer of title to land from one owner to another and attaches to the land*, this is called **running-with-the-land**. For an easement to run with the land, the owner of the easement must own land to which the easement attaches (dominant tenement). Just as the dominant nature of the easement appurtenant runs with the land, so does the servient nature run with the land. If A should sell his land to Z, Z must allow B use of the easement.

Putting It to Work

The typical purpose of an easement appurtenant is to allow access to some desirable feature, such as water, an access road, or perhaps other land owned by the dominant owner on the other side of the servient owner.

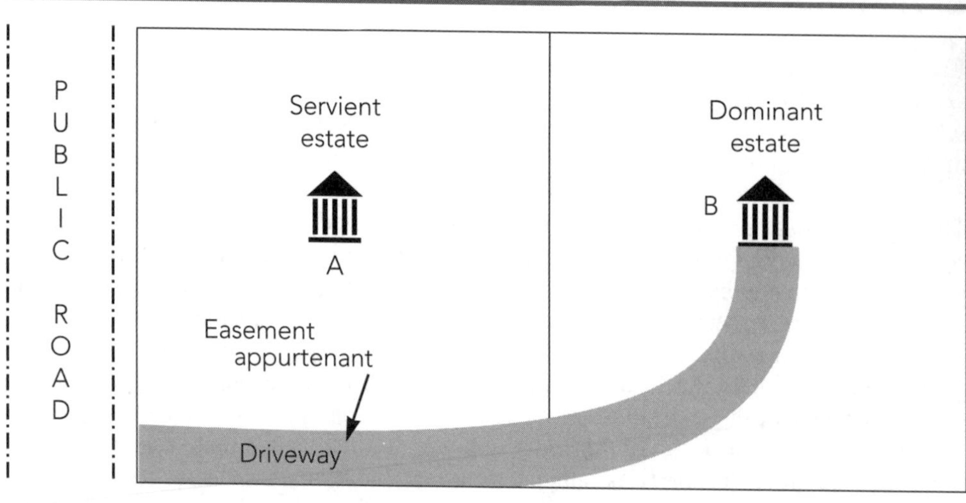

FIGURE 3.1 An example of an easement appurtenant.

PUTTING IT TO WORK

Many states and courts have determined that an owner of land has a natural "right" to sunlight, which cannot be violated without consent. By contrast, an owner generally does not have a natural "right" to a view.

Creation of Easements Appurtenant

Easements appurtenant are created:

1. By deed (grant or reservation)
2. By necessity and intent
3. By prescription
4. By implication
5. By condemnation

Easements created **by grant** or reservation are those *created by the express written agreement of the land owners*, usually in a deed. The written agreement sets out the location and extent of the easement. An owner may convey land and retain for himself an easement. This is the retention of an easement (retaining a stick in the bundle) on land conveyed to another. A common example of an easement by grant or deed is found when a developer, in the plat, *sets aside a portion of the land for common area, parks, sidewalks, and so on*. This practice is also called **dedication** of the land.

Easements created **by necessity** *exist when a land owner has no access to roads and is landlocked*. Access, also known as ingress and egress (entry and exit) is required by law. The servient tenement may be entitled to some compensation for the interest taken. Land owner B is landlocked. For land owner B to have access (ingress and egress) to the public road, land owner B must cross the property of land owner A. Land owner B receives the benefit of the easement. Land owner A must suffer and allow the use of access by land owner B.

Easements by prescription are *obtained by use of the land of another for the legally prescribed length of time*. The use must be open and well-known to others, without permission from the owners of the land, continued and uninterrupted for the period of time required by the laws of the state. The user must prove in court action that he or she has satisfied all the requirements for the intended use. (The easement by prescription gives only the right of continued use, not ownership of the land.) A common example of an easement by prescription is the driveway established by owner B at or near her boundary line without the benefit of a survey. After many years of using the driveway, a survey shows the driveway to be partially or completely on the land of owner C. Owner B will have an easement by prescription to use the driveway. Land owner B is the dominant tenement, and C is the servient tenement.

PUTTING IT TO WORK

Easements and boundary disputes often can be discovered only by a survey. If boundary problems are suspected, or if nearby construction is anticipated, real estate salespersons should suggest a survey.

Easements by implication *arise by implication from the conduct of the parties*. For example, when land owner X sells mineral rights to Company Y, Company Y has an easement by implication to go on the property of X to mine the minerals. Use of the easement by Company Y must be reasonable and only for the purpose of obtaining minerals.

Easements by condemnation are *created by the exercise of the government's right of eminent domain* (this government power is discussed later in this chapter). Through eminent domain the *government can take title to land and take the right to use land for some purpose in the future*. Most road widening, sidewalk, alley, and utility easements are created through eminent domain.

Termination of Easements Appurtenant

Easements may be terminated:

1. By the easement owner's release of the easement.
2. By *combining the dominant and servient lands into one tract*, called **merger**.
3. By the easement owner's abandonment of the easement.
4. When the purpose for the easement ceases to exist. An example is when land is no longer landlocked because a new road has been built.
5. By expiration of a specified time period for which the easement was created.
6. By condemnation or adverse possession.
7. By overburdening (use for an unapproved purpose).

LIENS

A **lien** is a *claim or charge against the property of another*. This stick in the bundle of sticks is usually security for a debt. In most cases, if the claim or lien is not satisfied in the prescribed time, the lienholder may execute on the lien—force payment of the claim or charge by forcing a sale of the property. In real estate terminology this is known as the process of foreclosure. Proceeds of the foreclosure sale are applied to the claims, charges, or liens in the order of priority.

Priority of Liens

At the execution and foreclosure of the liens, priority for payment is based upon the time (day and hour) they were recorded in the proper public office. Certain liens, however, have special priority or *receive preferential treatment*. Examples of special **priority liens** are mechanics' liens, or materialmen's liens in some states. The theory behind giving the priority treatment lies in the nature of the services and materials provided that increased the value of the real estate. Other lienholders benefit from the work and materials of the contractors and suppliers. Thus, the contractors and suppliers should be paid first. As explained below, in most states the highest priority of all liens is given to liens for real property taxes and special assessments.

Liens fall into two groups:

1. **Specific liens:** *claims against a specific and readily identifiable property, such as a mortgage.*
2. **General liens:** *claims against a person and all of his or her property, such as the disposition of a lawsuit.*

A chart of the various liens is shown in Figure 3.2.

FIGURE 3.2
Classification of liens.

1. *Specific liens:* claims against a particular property
   a. Mortgage
   b. Real property tax
   c. Mechanic's
   d. Materialman's
   e. Bail bond
   f. Vendor's and vendee's
   g. Lis pendens
2. *General liens:* claims against all assets of a person
   a. Judgment
   b. Writ of attachment
   c. Income tax
   d. Estate and inheritance tax

Specific Liens

Mortgage Lien

Mortgages are discussed in great detail in Chapters 7 and 8. The discussion here is limited to the type of lien created by a mortgage. A mortgage is a document pledging a specific property as collateral for payment of a debt. In most cases, the debt was incurred to purchase the property specified in the mortgage. The property is placed as security. If the borrower does not pay the debt as promised, the lender can foreclose the mortgage by having the property sold at public auction. Proceeds from the sale are utilized to satisfy the liens in order of priority.

Real Property Tax Liens

Taxes levied by a local government constitute a specific lien against the real estate. State laws provide that real property tax liens have priority over all other liens. If the assessed real estate property taxes are not paid when due, the local official responsible for collecting the tax can bring legal action to collect the taxes. The typical action for collection is the forced sale of the property at a tax sale. (Actual calculation of property taxes is detailed in Chapter 17.)

Ad valorem tax. Property is taxed on an ad valorem basis—that is, according to value. Some states use fair market value as the assessed value; other jurisdictions use a value substantially lower than market value. The assessed value is multiplied by the tax rate for the jurisdiction. The tax rate stated in dollars or mills (1/1000th of a dollar) is applied to the assessed value to determine the amount of tax. The rate must be sufficient to provide the amount of revenue required to accomplish the budgetary requirements of the local governmental unit. Real property taxes are by far the biggest source of revenue for local governments.

PUTTING IT TO WORK

Different localities state tax rates in a variety of ways—for example, dollars per hundred or thousand, mills, or percentages. Check to see what is the standard in your area.

Assessment of property for tax purposes involves establishing the value of each parcel of land to be taxed within the taxing unit, such as a city, town, or county. An official with the title of tax assessor is responsible for the *valuation of property for tax purposes*. Reassessment of property for tax purposes occurs on a regular basis established by statutes and when improvements are made to the real estate.

Special assessments. At times, taxing units levy special assessments in addition to real property taxes, to collect payment for a share of the cost of improvements made to areas near or adjoining the property. These assessments can be levied against property only if the property is benefitted by the improvement. Examples are assessments for streets, sidewalks, sewers, rural drainage ditches, and other public improvements. The **special assessment** becomes a *specific lien against the property until paid*. If the lien is not paid, the taxing unit may execute on the lien, forcing a sale of the property for payment of the assessments. These assessments may be calculated on an ad valorem basis or some alternative method, such as length of road frontage or percentage of cost.

Mechanics' and Materialmen's Liens

In real estate terminology, the term "mechanic" refers to a person, such as a carpenter or plumber, who provides labor to a specific property. A materialman is a supplier, such as a lumber company providing the wood materials that go into construction of a home. Therefore, a **mechanic's lien** is a *specific lien filed by a person who provides labor to a property*; a **materialman's lien** is a *specific lien filed by a supplier of products required in construction or improvement of a building*. In some states these two terms are used interchangeably or one or the other is used.

Most states do not recognize these liens at common law. Therefore, the "mechanic" or "materialman" must be careful to comply with state law to obtain a valid lien. State law typically requires that these liens must be filed in the public records within a specified number of days after furnishing the labor or materials. This requirement allows title companies and buyers of property time to assure that no unrecorded liens are lurking in the shadows upon purchasing a newly constructed or remodeled home.

Putting It to Work

A unique feature of mechanics' liens is that, although they must not be recorded until after the work or material has been supplied, when they are recorded, the effective date of the lien (and thus its priority for claims) is established based on the first day of delivery of the labor or material.

Mechanic's and materialman's lien laws typically attach only to the interest of the person ordering the work and materials. In most cases this person is the owner. In some cases, however, a tenant under a lease orders work done to a leased house. If the landlord did not give the authority for the tenant's actions, the lien attaches only to the leasehold interest of the tenant. If the tenant is evicted or the lease terminates naturally, the lien is null and void.

Bail Bond Liens

A bail bond is executed by or on behalf of a defendant under criminal charges to obtain temporary release from custody. The release is conditioned upon a later appearance in court to answer to the criminal charges. If real property is pledged as security for the bail bond, the bond creates a specific lien against the property pledged. If the defendant does not appear in court as scheduled, the bond is forfeited (lost) and the lien is executed. The result is a lien foreclosure sale of the property, with the proceeds applied to satisfy the financial obligations the bond created.

Vendors' and Vendees' Liens

A **vendor** is a *seller*. A **vendee** is a *buyer*. Vendors' liens come into existence upon the sale of real property and conveyance of title to the buyer without full payment of the purchase price. The vendor is given a specific lien against the property for the amount of the balance of the purchase price. If the buyer does not satisfy the lien, the vendor can foreclose to obtain the money to satisfy the lien.

Vendees' liens are created in the case of a sale of real estate when the vendor fails to deliver a deed. In this case, the vendee has a lien against the property in the amount of any money the vendee has paid toward the purchase price or put toward repairs or improvements. A vendee's lien also can be enforced by foreclosure.

Lis Pendens

The term **lis pendens** comes from the Latin words for *pending litigation*. This lien is *a notice to the world that a lawsuit has been filed and is awaiting trial concerning a specific property*. The notice is filed in the office of the county or local official responsible for the record keeping of pending litigation. The notice is a warning to a prospective purchaser of the property that the lawsuit could result in a judgment that in turn would create a lien against the property of the defendant in the suit. A lien resulting from the lawsuit will attach to the property even though the title was transferred to someone else prior to the final judgment in the suit, if the transfer occurred after the notice was placed on the public record in the county in which the property is located.

General Liens

Judgment Liens

A **judgment** is a *court decree resulting from a lawsuit*. The court decree establishes that one person is indebted to another, and the amount owed. The person who owes the judgment is called the judgment debtor. The person who is owed the judgment is called the judgment creditor. A **judgment lien** is *against all of the real and personal property the judgment debtor owns in the county* in which the judgment is recorded. A judgment lien does not apply to real property owned by husband and wife who hold as tenants by the entireties if the judgment is against only the husband or only the wife. For the judgment lien to attach to property of a husband and wife, the judgment obtained must be against both husband and wife on a debt they both incurred. A judgment creditor may record the judgment in any other county in the state (and possibly in other states), and it will become a general lien against all the property of the judgment debtor in that county. This is called *notice of lien*.

The lien takes effect at the time the judgment is entered in the court records. The lien attaches to all of the property of the judgment debtor at the time of the judgment. It also attaches as a lien to any property the judgment debtor acquires after the judgment and prior to satisfaction of the judgment. The judgment lien is enforced by an **execution of judgment**, *an order signed by the judge or clerk of the court instructing the sheriff to attach and seize the property of the judgment debtor*. The sheriff then is to sell the property, real and personal, of the judgment debtor. Proceeds from the sale are applied to satisfy the judgment.

A judgment lien remains in effect for a time specified by state statute unless the judgment is paid or discharged by filing a petition in bankruptcy. A judgment may be renewed and kept in force for additional periods if the judgment creditor brings another action on the original judgment. State law also may provide for interest on the judgment.

Judgment liens have a priority relationship based upon the time of recording in the court records. (The judgment creditor who obtains a judgment in the court records before another creditor will have the priority claim.) The judgment debtor's obligations to the creditors are paid in order of highest to lowest priority.

Writ of Attachment

Though similar to a lis pendens, a **writ of attachment** is stronger. It is an actual *court order preventing any transfer of the attached property during the litigation*. Violation of the order can result in a contempt of court citation.

Income Tax Liens

The Internal Revenue Service (IRS) of the United States and a State Department of Revenue may create a general lien against all of the taxpayer's property for taxes due and unpaid. The lien may be for a variety of types of taxes owed. The taxes due might be personal income tax, employee withholding tax, federal unemployment tax, FICA for employees, self-employment taxes, sales tax, use tax, or any other tax relating to income. The period of time for validity of these liens varies with the type of tax due and unpaid.

This lien is created by filing a certificate of lien against the land owner in the county in which the taxpayer's land is located. Liens held by the Internal Revenue Service or the individual states do not automatically receive priority status or preferential treatment for payment purposes. Priority of the tax lien is determined by the date the lien was placed on the real estate or against the individual, just as with a judgment lien.

Estate and Inheritance Tax Liens

Federal estate and state inheritance taxes are calculated and incurred at the time of death of an individual owning property. A general lien on the property in the estate passes through the estate to assure payment of the taxes due at death.

Most states impose some type of tax upon the inheritance of real and personal property. Called state inheritance tax, this tax is a lien on all property the heirs are to inherit. To satisfy the tax bill, the estate is allowed to sell sufficient property.

The federal government imposes a tax on the estates of deceased persons. Called the federal estate tax, this tax creates a lien that attaches to all of the property in the estate. However, the federal tax laws and most state tax laws allow property to pass to surviving spouses without taxation or with favorable tax treatment.

Restrictive Covenants

Restrictions placed on a private owner's use of land by a nongovernmental entity or individual are **restrictive covenants**. These are not to be confused with the restrictions on use of land by the government or the government's agencies (discussed in Chapter 11). The purpose of covenants by private owners is to preserve and protect the quality of land in subdivisions and to maximize land values by requiring the homogeneous use of land by purchasers of land in the subdivision. Covenants are promises by purchasers to limit their use of the property by complying with requirements of the restrictive covenants.

Typically, restrictive covenants are found in residential subdivisions. These may include minimum square feet in the homes to be constructed, prohibition against detached garages, prohibitions on exterior antennas, or other concerns of the owner/developer. Because these are private restrictions, they are enforced not by local zoning officials and building departments but, rather, by some agent of the subdivision or owner/developer.

If a land owner subject to a restrictive covenant violates the covenant, any other land owner in the subdivision can bring an action to end the violation. An injunction, a cease-and-desist order, or a restraining order is sought from a local court to enforce the restrictive covenant.

Encroachments

An **encroachment**, a *trespass on the land of another*, is created by the intrusion of some structure or object across a boundary line. Typical encroachments in real estate include tree limbs, bushes, fences, antennas, roof lines, driveways, and overhangs.

The encroaching owner is a **trespasser**. In most encroachment situations the encroachment is accidental and unintentional. The only method to accurately determine the existence of an encroachment is by a survey of the boundary line.

Almost every subdivision in the United States has classic examples of encroachments. At the time a new home is built, small trees and shrubs are planted on or near boundary lines to commemorate the boundaries. As the bushes and trees grow, the branches extend beyond the boundaries. The small apple tree planted many years ago is now dropping rotten apples in the neighbor's back yard. The lilac bush planted at the corner of the house has now grown to such a breadth that the branches rub the side of the neighboring house. The garage that was built within 6 inches of the boundary line has a roof line and eaves extending over the boundary line and draining on the neighbor's yard. These are all examples of accidental and unintentional encroachments.

Although accidental and unintentional, they are still an encumbrance on the real property. In most states a trespass or encroachment that continues for a prescribed time may become an easement by prescription or even ownership in fee. Until that time, the land owner being encroached upon has the right to bring legal action for removal of the encroachment or a suit for damages (judgment by that court requiring the encroacher to compensate the land owner for the encroachment).

An order to remove the encroachment of a branch over the boundary line does not mean that the tree will be cut down. The only part of the tree that must be removed is the portion encroaching.

Government Restrictions on Real Property

Since the Ordinance of 1785, land ownership by private individuals has been allowed in the United States. Even the allodial system of property ownership, however, is subject to four important powers of federal and local governments: (a) the power of eminent domain, (b) police power, (c) power of taxation, and (d) the power of escheat.

Power of Eminent Domain

The right or power of **eminent domain** is the *power of the government or its agencies to take private property for public use*. Governments exercise this power themselves and also delegate it to public utility companies. Actual *taking of property under the power of eminent domain* is called **condemnation**.

The power of eminent domain has two limitations. The right of eminent domain can be used only if (a) the property condemned is for the use and benefit of the general public, and (b) the property owner must be paid the fair market value of the property lost through condemnation. Property owners have the right to appeal to the courts if they are not satisfied with the compensation the condemning authority offers.

The bundle of rights concept as it relates to eminent domain prompts the question of who receives the money from the condemnation action. The answer is that the money is divided among any parties having an interest in the property, based upon the value of the interest owned by those individuals. For example, A rents a building to B for office space. The highway running in front of the building is widened, requiring the rented building to be demolished. Both A and B will receive compensation for the taking of the land and building under eminent domain because both have an estate or right in the real property.

Police Power

Police power *enables government to fulfill its responsibility to provide for public health, safety, and welfare*. The government may exercise this power even if it restricts some of the fundamental freedoms of the people. Exercise of the power, however, always must be in the best interest of the public.

Examples of the exercise of police power affecting property use are zoning ordinances, subdivision ordinances, building codes, and environmental protection laws. (Detailed discussion of the specifics of zoning, subdivision control, and the like are found in Chapter 11.) Property owners affected by the exercise of police power are not compensated for the restrictions and loss of use of their property resulting from the exercise of this power. Its underlying premise is that any restrictions imposed must reasonably provide for the health, safety, and welfare of the public.

Power of Taxation

Real property taxation was discussed earlier as a specific lien on real property. Exercise of the *power of taxation* is *one of the inherent burdens on private ownership of land*. Land owned by government, governmental agencies, or nonprofit organizations is exempt from real property taxation.

Power of Escheat

If a property owner dies **testate**—*leaves a valid will*—the individual's property is distributed to persons as specified in the will. If an owner dies **intestate**—*dies without having a valid will*—the decedent's property is distributed to heirs in accordance with state statutory provisions. These statutes, usually called "statutes of intestate succession," specify how property will be distributed based on the relationship of the deceased's heirs who come forth (or can be located).

If no one is qualified to receive title to property the deceased leaves, the state or other government entity uses its power of **escheat** and the property goes to the state or other government entity. *If someone dies with no valid will and no located heirs, all of the deceased's property goes to the state or other government entity.*

APPURTENANCES

The word appurtenance comes from a Latin word meaning "on to" or "attached to." **Appurtenances** in real property are the *inherent or automatic ownership rights that* *are a natural consequence of owning property.* The most common appurtenant rights are: profit, license, air rights, subsurface rights, and water rights. The right of accession, discussed below, also may bear on these ownership rights.

Profits

The word **profit**, also known as **profit à prendre**, is the legal term describing *the right to take products of the soil from the land of another.* This includes the right to take soil, minerals, or timber from another person's land. Profits are created in the same manner that easements are: by grant or deed, by necessity, and by prescription. In some areas of the nation, the term mineral lease or mineral rights lease is used to designate a profit.

A profit is salable, inheritable, and transferable. A profit in land easily could be more valuable than owning the land. For example, if land in Texas has oil fields, the right to take and sell the oil could be more valuable than use of the land for any other purpose.

License

A **license** is defined as *permission to do a particular act or series of acts on land of another without possessing any estate or interest in the land.* A license is a personal privilege that the licensor may revoke at any time unless the licensee has paid for the license. An example of a license that has been paid for is a right to fish or hunt in a specified lake or forest. The licensee has the right to be at the lake or forest for the purpose of fishing or hunting. The licensor may not revoke the license unless the licensee has gone outside the authority of the license. A license is not assignable and is not inheritable. A license is a *temporary privilege.*

Air and Subsurface Rights

Ownership of real property inherently includes ownership of the rights to the area above and below the earth's surface. *Rights to the area above the earth* are called **air rights**. The right of ownership of air space enables the land owner to use that space to construct improvements and to lease or sell the air space to others. Sale or lease of air space is becoming more common in high-density urban areas. In purchasing air rights, the purchaser must obtain an easement appurtenant over the ground if someone else controls the ground. For example, if owner A has a two-story building and sells the air rights above the two stories to owner B, A must include in the purchase and transfer an appurtenant easement allowing access over the first and second stories to the property above.

The right of ownership and control of air space, however, is limited by zoning ordinances and federal laws providing for use of the air space by aircraft. Zoning ordinances also can restrict the height of improvements constructed on the land so as not to overburden municipal support systems such as police, water, sewer, traffic, and so on.

Rights to the area below the earth's surface are called **subsurface rights**, often referred to as **mineral rights**. These rights also are subject to restriction by local, state, and federal laws. The owner of mineral rights may conduct mining operations or drilling operations personally or may sell or lease these rights to others on a royalty basis. A mineral lease permits use of the land for mineral exploration and mining operations. The lease may be for a definite period of time or for as long as the land is productive.

Water Rights

Water rights in real property include percolating water rights, riparian water rights, and surface water rights. Percolating water is the water underground, which can be drawn by wells. Land owners have the inherent right in that land to draw out the percolating water for their own reasonable use. Local health codes may restrict that use.

The right of natural drainage is at the heart of surface water rights. No land owner can substantially change the natural drainage of surface water (runoff) in such a manner as to damage neighboring land. The issue of surface water and drainage is an important consideration in building commercial developments with extensive paving, which reduces the absorption of water by the soil and intensifies runoff, possibly causing flooding.

Riparian water rights *belong to the owner of property bordering a flowing body of water*. **Littoral rights** *apply to property bordering a body of water that is nonflowing*, such as a lake or a sea. Generally, property adjacent to a river or a watercourse affords the land owner the right of access to and use of the water. Actual ownership of the water in a flowing watercourse, however, is complex and depends on numerous factors. Many states make a distinction between a navigable watercourse and a non-navigable watercourse. With a navigable watercourse, adjacent owners are limited to banks of the watercourse, and the state or the public owns the actual body of water. With a non-navigable watercourse, ownership lines extend to the center of the watercourse (see Figure 3.3). With littoral bodies of water, the boundary is at the average high-water mark.

Accession Rights

Owners of real property have the *right to all that their land produces or all that is added to the land, either intentionally or by mistake*—the ownership right of *accession*. This right becomes an issue when a watercourse changes gradually or rapidly. The *gradual building up of land in a watercourse over time by deposits of silt, sand, and gravel* is called **accretion**. The *land mass added to property over time* by accretion, called **alluvion**, is owned by the owner of the land to which it has been added. **Avulsion** is the *loss of land when a sudden or violent change in a watercourse results in its washing away*. Avulsion does not change boundaries or ownership as does the slow, gradual change of accretion.

FIGURE 3.3
Riparian rights.

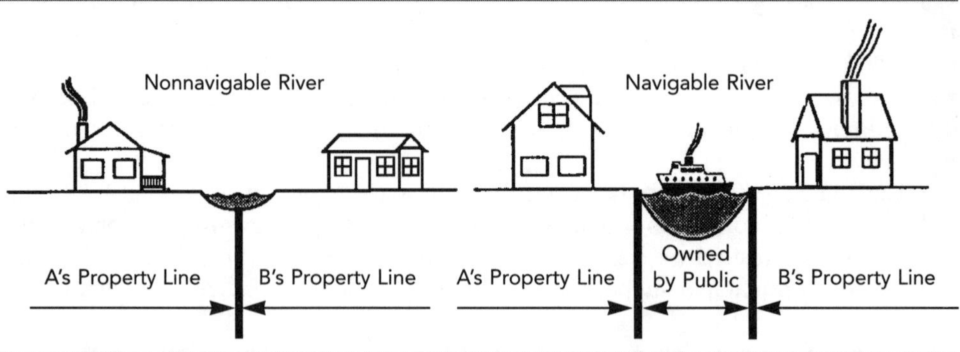

IMPORTANT POINTS

1. An encumbrance is a claim, lien, charge, or liability attached to and binding upon real property. Examples are encroachments, easements, liens, assessments, and restrictive covenants.
2. Easements are nonpossessory interests in land owned by another. Easements can be in gross or appurtenant in nature. Easements are created by grant, necessity, prescription, implication, reservation, and condemnation.
3. Easements appurtenant can be negative or affirmative.
4. Easements are terminated by grant, merger, abandonment, end of necessity, expiration of the prescribed time period, condemnation, adverse possession, or overburdening.
5. Specific liens are claims against a specific and readily identifiable property, such as a mortgage, a mechanic's lien, or a real property tax lien.
6. General liens are claims against a person and all of his or her property, such as a judgment resulting from a lawsuit.
7. The lien for real property taxes is a specific lien and in most states is given the highest priority for payment.
8. Real property taxation is on an ad valorem basis.
9. Mechanics' liens and materialmen's liens are specific liens that may receive preferential treatment for priority of liens.
10. The property of a judgment debtor is subject to execution and forced sale to satisfy an unpaid judgment.
11. Lis pendens notice provides constructive notice to the public that a lawsuit concerning certain real estate is pending.
12. Restrictive covenants are used to preserve the quality of land and maximize land values.
13. An encroachment is a trespass on land, an intrusion or breaking over the boundary of land.
14. Proof of the existence or lack of existence of an encroachment is evidenced by a survey of the boundary.
15. Private ownership of property is subject to the four powers of government: eminent domain, police power (such as zoning, health codes, and building codes), taxation, and escheat.
16. A profit in real property is transferable and inheritable. A license in real property is not transferable or inheritable.
17. Inherent ownership rights include air rights, subsurface rights, riparian water rights, and littoral rights.

HOW WOULD YOU RESPOND?

1. You are working as agent for buyer A who is looking for vacant land or a lot on which to place a manufactured home. What are some of the preliminary questions you and A should ask before A makes an offer on a piece of land or a lot?
2. B wishes to list for sale 20 acres of farmland through which an electric utility easement runs. Smith has farmed the entire area for over 10 years since the easement was granted. Prior to listing and advertising the property as suitable for a subdivision, what research should you do concerning the electric utility easement?

Review Questions

Answers to these questions are found in the *Answer Key* section at the back of the book.

1. The loss of land due to a sudden or violent change in an intercourse is called:
   a. avulsion
   b. accretion
   c. accession
   d. alluvion

2. All of the following statements about easements are true EXCEPT:
   a. an easement provides a nonpossessory interest in land
   b. a servient tenement is the land burdened by an easement
   c. a dominant tenement is the land benefitted by an easement
   d. an easement appurtenant is terminated by transfer of the benefitted tenement

3. One property owner held an enforceable right to prevent a second property owner from erecting a structure that would interfere with the passage of light and air to the property of the owner holding the enforceable right. This right is in the form of:
   a. implied easement
   b. easement by necessity
   c. easement by prescription
   d. negative easement

4. Easements may be created in all of the following ways EXCEPT:
   a. condemnation
   b. dedication
   c. prescription
   d. assessment

5. An easement may be terminated by all of the following EXCEPT:
   a. merger
   b. death
   c. grant or deed of release
   d. abandonment

6. A property owner gives another person permission to fish in a lake on the property. The permission is a temporary privilege and exists in the form of which of the following?
   a. license
   b. easement
   c. lease
   d. appurtenance

7. The creation of an easement by condemnation results from the exercise of which of the following?
   a. prescription
   b. eminent domain
   c. dedication
   d. implication

8. Liens, easements, encroachments, and restrictive covenants are all examples of:
   a. emblements
   b. estovers
   c. estates
   d. encumbrances

9. All of the following are examples of specific liens EXCEPT:
   a. mortgage
   b. mechanic's lien
   c. income tax lien
   d. vendor's lien

10. Creditor A, whose lien is secured by Owner's property, obtained a judgment against Owner on July 10; Banker B lent money to Owner and took back a mortgage on August 1; Creditor C obtained a judgment for failure to pay child support on August 20. Which of the above-listed liens will be paid first at foreclosure?
    a. creditor A
    b. banker B
    c. creditor C
    d. they will all be paid on a pro rata basis

11. If a property has liens for inheritance tax, income tax, estate tax, and property tax, which will receive priority in payment at foreclosure?
    a. inheritance tax
    b. income tax
    c. estate tax
    d. property tax

12. To enforce restrictive covenants in a subdivision, a land owner will bring legal action for:
    a. trespass
    b. nuisance
    c. injunction
    d. eviction

13. The doctrine of merger in easements means:
    a. the dominant tenement is larger and more valuable than the servient tenement
    b. the servient tenement must allow the dominant tenement complete access
    c. the easement will be terminated when the dominant tenement and the servient tenement are owned by the same person
    d. the easement is an easement in gross and is utilized by all of the government agencies in the jurisdiction for delivering utility services

14. The right to take sand, soil, and gravel from the land of another is called:
    a. license
    b. profit
    c. easement
    d. lien

15. All of the following are true about a profit EXCEPT:
    a. it is assignable prior to death
    b. it is inheritable
    c. it is transferable prior to death
    d. it is terminated at death

16. Permission to go onto the land of another for a specific purpose is called a(n):
    a. lien
    b. license
    c. profit
    d. easement

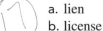

17. All of the following are inherent ownership rights in real estate EXCEPT:
    a. air rights
    b. mineral rights
    c. percolating water rights
    d. right of eminent domain

18. An act of taking land by the government is called:
    a. condemnation
    b. eminent domain
    c. escheat
    d. taxation

19. Escheat occurs when:
    a. a person dies testate with no living heirs
    b. a person dies intestate with no living heirs
    c. a person dies in an accident and has no living heirs
    d. a person dies intestate and has never been married

20. The government's right to protect the health and welfare of the public is called:
    a. public policy
    b. police power
    c. public domain
    d. police justice

21. When zoning laws create problems for a land owner:
    a. the land owner will receive just compensation with the passage of the laws
    b. payment will be made to the land owner under the rule of eminent domain
    c. no compensation is dictated by law
    d. a variance will be granted in lieu of compensation

22. A entered into a contract to purchase property from B. The property was located in two different counties. B breached the purchase contract. A filed suit for specific performance against B. Prior to the entry of judgment in the suit, what other action should A take to protect her equitable title in the real estate owned by B:
    a. record a certified copy of the filed court complaint in the recorder's office of each county
    b. file notice in the lis pendens file in the clerk's office of each county in which the real estate is located
    c. have the county sheriff serve the complaint on B
    d. petition the court to require B to post a surety bond in an amount equal to the appraised value of the real estate

23. A local court has awarded a judgment in favor of C and against D in the amount of $10,000 for personal injuries suffered in a car accident. Which of the following is true?
    a. the judgment is a specific lien, with priority over all other specific liens but not over general liens
    b. the judgment is a general lien, with priority over all other general liens but not over the specific liens
    c. the judgment is a general lien with priority over only those liens attaching after entry of the judgment
    d. the judgment is a vendor's lien with priority over all other liens, general or specific

24. The tenant on the second floor of a building hired ABC Contractors to install a new heating and air conditioning system for the second floor only. The tenant failed to pay for the materials and labor billed. The tenant also failed to pay his monthly rent and was evicted. Which of the following will be true of ABC Contractor's rights to a mechanic's lien?
   a. the mechanic's lien attaches only to the tenant's interest in the building; thus upon eviction, any mechanic's lien is void, but ABC Contractors' will have a right to sue the tenant for payment
   b. the mechanic's lien attaches to the tenant's interest in the building as a specific lien and to the owner's building as a general lien; thus, upon eviction, the mechanic's lien is void but ABC Contractors have a general lien against the building and a right to sue tenant for payment
   c. the mechanic's lien attaches to the tenant's interest in the building as a general lien and to the building as a specific lien; thus, upon eviction, the mechanic's lien against both the tenant and the building owner is void, but ABC Contractors can sue either the tenant or the owner of the building or both for payment
   d. no mechanic's lien can attach against the tenant's interest in the building either before or after eviction because the tenant did not own the building

25. E and F own adjacent properties and have a shared driveway created by written agreement. When E defaulted on his mortgage, the lender sued for foreclosure. G purchased the property at the sheriff's sale of the foreclosed property. Which of the following is true?
   a. the easement in gross that existed between E and F prior to foreclosure survives the foreclosure and exists between G and F
   b. the easement appurtenant that existed between E and F prior to foreclosure is extinguished. F receives the driveway for himself and G must put in a new driveway
   c. the easement appurtenant that existed between E and F prior to foreclosure has become an easement by implication. G will be able to use the driveway exclusively and may prohibit F's future use
   d. the easement appurtenant that existed between E and F survives the foreclosure without change. The new owner, G, will have the right to use the shared driveway, as will F

POSSIBLE RESPONSES TO "HOW WOULD YOU RESPOND?"

1. Does the land or lot have road access or an easement for ingress and egress?

   If the access is by easement, was the easement created by written agreement, necessity, or prescription?

   If the easement was created by prescription, will the prior use justify the new use as ingress and egress for a home?

   Is the land or lot subject to restrictive covenants prohibiting manufactured homes?

   Is the land or lot subject to any zoning or planning restrictions affecting the placement of a manufactured home?

2. You should obtain a copy of the electric utility easement and determine by mapping and/or survey the exact location. It is possible that no building can be done where the easement runs. If the easement is a general easement for the entire 20 acres, you will need to meet with representatives of the electric utility to better define where the easement lies.

CHAPTER 4

IMPORTANT TERMINOLOGY

agent
brokerage
buyer brokerage
client
customer
disclosure of information
dual agency
duty of disclosure
estoppel
express agency
fiduciary
general agent
implied agency
misrepresentation
multiple listing service (MLS)
principal
Property Disclosure Form
special agent
subagent
third party
unintentional misrepresentation
universal agent

Brokerage and Agency

IN THIS CHAPTER When one person enters into an agreement to act on behalf of another person, an agency relationship is created. The *person who is to act on another's behalf* is the **agent.** The *person who selects the agent to act on his or her behalf* is the **principal.** *Another name for principal* is **client.** Upon creation of the relationship, the agent is placed in a position of trust and loyalty to the principal (client). *The principal may authorize the agent to use other people to assist in accomplishing the purpose of the agency. These people are* **subagents**. (In some states, the concept of subagency is no longer in force, as will be discussed later in this chapter.)

Agency relationships do not exist in all business dealings. Services provided to people in the ordinary course of business create a *customer* relationship. A **customer** is *someone who is not a client but who must be treated ethically and honestly.* A customer is not a principal. In real estate brokerage, *another name for customer* is **third party.** Since no agency relationship exists with a customer, no special loyalty need be shown and no position of trust is created beyond honest dealing.

Payment of money by one party to another party does not create an agency relationship. The creation and existence of an agency relationship between parties is normally determined by the contract terms agreed to between the parties. However, as will be discussed later, an agency relationship can also be created unintentionally by certain words and actions.

A vast body of law controls the rights and duties in an agency relationship. This chapter covers the creation of agency, types of agencies, and obligations of a person under the law of agency, as well as the misconceptions and challenges that revolve around the subject of agency today.

AGENCY IN PRACTICE

Many of the concepts discussed briefly in this section will be treated in more detail later in the chapter.

The topic of agency has grown in significance in the past decade, not so much because of changing laws, although law changes have occurred, but because of changes in what's expected by home buyers. The traditional real estate scenario left most buyers of real estate unrepresented: in the old arrangement, the listing broker was the agent of the seller. In addition, brokers and salespersons who showed the home based on the listing offered in the multiple listing service (MLS) were subagents of the listing broker and therefore subagents of the seller. This subagency relationship occurred because until fairly recently the MLS was considered a "blanket offer of subagency," and in deciding to show a listing the practitioner was in effect agreeing to act as subagent to the seller.

Unfortunately, buyers often mistakenly believed that the broker working *with* them was in fact working *for* them. In other words, they assumed that the broker showing them homes was their agent and did not understand that, like the listing broker, he worked for the seller. This confusion of agency roles resulted in many problems.

For example, it placed the buyer in a disadvantaged position since she may have revealed information to the broker that she didn't want conveyed to the seller. In addition, it placed the broker in a legally and ethically perilous position since (1) if he kept the buyer information confidential he was in fact neglecting his fiduciary duties to his true client, the seller, and (2) by allowing the buyer to believe that he was acting in her behalf, the broker became party to an "implied" agency, thus making him an undisclosed dual agent (both implied agency and dual agency will be discussed later in this chapter).

Over the last decade, laws and practices have evolved to address this confusion regarding agency loyalties and relationships. Laws in almost every state now require "disclosure of agency relationships" by brokers early in a transaction. In addition, buyers today are more informed than ever and often request "buyer representation" from their brokers. Today, many transactions involve both a seller broker and a buyer broker and both parties thus enjoy representation.

Importance of the Fiduciary Duty

In its most basic terms, an agency relationship is a contract relationship to provide services. The person engaged to act on behalf of another is the agent. The person who seeks out the person to act on his behalf is the principal or client. As a result of the agency agreement, a fiduciary relationship exists between the agent and the principal. The term **fiduciary** means a *position of trust.* Because of the fiduciary relationship, the principal has faith, trust, and confidence in the agent hired.

The fiduciary relationship is basic to any agency contract. For this reason, an agent always must keep in focus who is the principal and what are the best interests of that principal. The agent must, however, maintain a course of honest and ethical dealings with all third parties as well. Specific duties and responsibilities of agents are discussed later in this chapter.

Classification of Agency Relationships

Most states recognize three classifications of agents: universal, general, and special. The differences among the types of agency revolve around the authority given to the agent by the principal and the services to be provided.

Universal

A **universal agent** is *someone authorized to handle all affairs of the principal.* An example is someone who has been given unlimited power of attorney over another's affairs. This person is called an attorney-in-fact.

General

A **general agent** is *someone authorized to handle all affairs of the principal concerning a certain matter or property,* usually with some limited power to enter into contracts. An example is a person who has been appointed property manager of an apartment complex by the owner of the complex. The property manager may collect rent, evict, enter into leases, repair the premises, advertise for tenants, and perform a range of activities on behalf of the principal concerning the specified property.

Special

A **special agent** has *narrow authorization to act on behalf of the principal.* An example is a real estate broker who has a listing on real estate. The broker can market the property for sale but cannot make decisions as to things such as price, repairs, or financing. A special agent cannot bind a principal to a contract. The range of authority is specialized and limited, and the services provided are specialized.

CREATION OF AGENCY

An *agency relationship created by an oral or written agreement between the principal and agent* is called an **express agency.** Typical examples are (1) the written listing agreement between seller and broker and (2) the buyer brokerage contract between buyer and broker.

An agency also may *be created by the actions of the principal and agent* indicating that they have an agreement. This is called an **implied agency** or ostensible agency. When a person claims to be an agent but has no express agreement, the principal can establish the agency by ratifying the actions the agent takes. For example, if a broker places an ad to sell a house without first having the seller's written consent, the seller, by approving and accepting the actions of the broker, creates an agency relationship. (The student should be aware that all license laws require a written agreement prior to placing an ad.)

An agency relationship also can be created by **estoppel.** This occurs *if an individual claims incorrectly that a person is his or her agent and a third party relies on the incorrect representation.* In these cases, the person making the incorrect statement is estoppel and prohibited from later claiming that the agency relationship does not exist. For example, Broker A states to Mr. and Mrs. R that B is a sales agent in the office of A when he knows this is not true. If Mr. and Mrs. R rely on this incorrect statement, Broker A cannot later claim that B is not an agent, and Broker A is liable for B's actions.

TERMINATION OF AGENCY

An agency relationship ends in accordance with the terms of the agency contract. An example is the expiration of a listing contract for the sale of real estate. When the contract terminates, so does any authority of the agent to act on behalf of the principal. Another means of terminating an agency relationship is by completing the terms of the agency, usually by completing the sale of listed real estate and the seller's paying commission.

In some cases, agency relationship may be terminated by operation of law. For instance, a listing terminates automatically at the death of either principal or agent. Another example is the termination of a listing contract held by a broker whose license is revoked.

Employment and Authority of Real Estate Agents

Brokerage Contracts

Brokerage is *the business of bringing buyers and sellers together and assisting in negotiations for the terms of sale of real estate.* In the real estate field a broker is defined as an individual licensed to assist a person who is trying to sell, buy, exchange, rent, lease, or option real property for a fee. Many states add collection of rents to this list.

A brokerage contract is created when the principal engages a broker (agent) to perform services relating to the real estate. Under the listing agreement, the seller engages a broker to assist in selling or renting real estate the principal owns. A brokerage contract also can be created between a prospective buyer and the broker. Under that agency agreement, the buyer is the principal. Under buyer brokerage the services typically involve finding a suitable property for the buyer to purchase, *as well as assisting the buyer* through all phases of the transaction and closing. Whether it is between broker and seller or broker and buyer, the typical brokerage contract is a *special agency with narrow authority.*

Extent of Authority

Every agency relationship is a contractual relationship. Thus, the authority given to the agent must be expressed in the brokerage contract. The principal controls the extent of authority delegated to the agent through the language in the brokerage contract.

If the type of agency created is a universal agency, such as an unlimited power of attorney, the agent has complete authority over the principal's property. The agent has the same authority as the principal. The agent has authority to bind the principal in any contract, including buying, selling, leasing, exchanging, or encumbering.

Under a general agency, the agent's authority is narrower than under a universal agency. Under a general agency, the agent has authority to bind the principal only on contract matters that directly relate to the authority given to the agent in the contract, such as accepting an offer at a specified price or executing leases on behalf of the principal under a property management agreement.

Under a special agency, as in the case of most real estate transactions, the agent has limited authority. A listing agreement represents a typical special agency, giving the agent authority only to market the property. The agent has no authority to bind the principal to a contract of any type.

Types of Commission Arrangements

The amount or rate of commission to be charged by or paid to a real estate broker is strictly negotiable between the broker and the seller or buyer. Federal law is violated if any person or organization even recommends a commission schedule to a broker or group of brokers. It is also illegal for two or more brokers to agree to charge certain rates of commission to listing sellers. This is regarded as price fixing and is an act in restraint of trade violating the Sherman Antitrust Act. The local real estate commission or Board of REALTORS® cannot establish by rule or regulation the amount of commission practitioners receive. Nor can these agencies or any other reprimand or punish a member who charges a lower rate of commission than other REALTORS® in the community.

In most real estate sales, the commission is paid at closing from the seller's proceeds.

Percentage of Final Sales Price

The most usual type of commission arrangement in listing contracts is for a specified percentage of the final sales price of the property. For example, the contract may call for the broker to be paid 6 percent of the home's sale price.

Net Listing

Another type of commission arrangement is the net listing, in which the seller specifies a net amount of money that he or she must receive upon sale of the property. All money above the net amount is designated as the broker's commission.

This type of commission arrangement is not recommended and is even illegal in some states. It can lead to a great deal of dissatisfaction by the seller if the property sells for substantially more than the listed price, as one of the broker's responsibilities is to establish a fair market price for the property. Thus, recommending a fair market price, including a reasonable rate of commission established as a percentage of the final sales price, is much more professional.

Flat Fee

Under the flat-fee listing arrangement, the broker and seller agree on a specified payment at the time of the listing. This may even be paid as an "up-front" fee. The broker is entitled to retain this fee for efforts in attempting to market the property. Compensation under this listing does not depend on the sale of the property, and thus the flat fee typically is substantially less than a percentage of sales price. Under this arrangement, the broker typically advertises the property but is not involved in showing the property or negotiating terms of the sale between seller and buyer.

PUTTING IT TO WORK

Under a flat-fee arrangement, if a seller wants a broker to open the listing to other brokers, the commission usually becomes a combination of flat fee (to the listing broker) and a specified percentage of the sales price (to cooperating brokers).

Commission of Sales Associates

Commission splits paid to sales associates in a real estate brokerage firm are established by the owner of the firm and the sales associates. Under the usual commission split agreement, the entire company commission is paid directly to the broker, who then pays a portion to the sales associate who listed the property and a portion to the sales associate who sold the property. If a sales associate sells a property that she has listed, she will receive both the listing and the selling portions.

For example, sales associate A of Lake Realty listed a property. She later found a buyer for the property. The total commission received by Lake Realty was $4,720. A's share was 30 percent for the listing ($1,416) and 25 percent for selling ($1,180). Her principal broker, Lake Realty, retained the balance of $2,124.

Commissions Paid to Cooperating Brokers

Upon sale of real estate through the cooperating efforts of two real estate firms, the commission to be paid pursuant to the listing agreement is paid to the listing broker by the property owner. This commission is then shared by the listing broker and the selling broker on a prearranged basis. In most cases, this sharing occurs even if the selling broker is employed as the buyer broker.

Referral Fees

Brokerage firms often pay a referral fee to licensees from other localities when the licensee refers prospective buyers or sellers. States differ in their requirements for payment and collection of referral fees. Before paying a referral fee, those involved should have complete knowledge of state laws and rules.

Agency and Subagency Relationships

Multiple Listing Service

A **multiple listing service (MLS)** is a *system that pools the listings of all member companies.* Members of the MLS are authorized to show any of the properties in the pool, an arrangement that greatly expands the offerings they may show to prospective buyers, as well as extending the marketing of their own listings. The pooling of listings is an offer of *cooperation and compensation* to all MLS members whether acting as subagents of the listing broker or buyer agents. The pooling is not a blanket offer of subagency.

When a cooperating broker accepts the offer of subagency associated with a listing, he or she works through the listing broker and is therefore the principal's subagent, just as are the sales associates in the listing agency's office. The cooperating broker has the same responsibility to work for the best interest of the owner who is paying the commission for both brokers.

The advantages of an MLS are obvious: Cooperating brokers and sales associates have more offerings, and the seller has more licensees working on his or her behalf.

Placing a property in the MLS permits subagency but does not automatically create it or require it. A broker might decide to work as a buyer's broker instead of working with the listing broker. In this situation, licensees acting as buyer's brokers must make their agency status clear to the listing broker before showing the property.

Brokerage Firm as Agent

A brokerage firm, or company, may be owned by a single licensed broker (a sole proprietor), or by more than one person, as in a partnership or a corporation. A brokerage firm is thought of as an independent broker if it is not associated with a national or local real estate franchise organization. Association with a real estate franchise organization licenses the brokerage firm to use the franchise's trade names, operating procedures, reputation, and referral services. The franchisee still owns and operates the brokerage firm.

Brokerage firms usually employ or have other licensed salespersons or brokers working with the firm. The sales associates affiliated with the brokerage firm are agents of the broker and subagents of the brokerage firm's principals (clients). The fiduciary duty of sales associates thus extends both to their employing brokerage firm and also to the firm's principals. The broker is in two separate agency positions: The broker is the agent for the principal (the seller in the case of a listing contract or the buyer in the case of a buyer brokerage agreement). The broker is also the principal of the sales associates under a subagency agreement in the brokerage firm. Therefore, the broker is responsible for the actions of the sales associates. As subagents of the broker in reference to the listing agreements, the sales associates are required to comply with the terms of the listing and all rules of the brokerage firm.

SINGLE AGENCY

In single agency, the broker represents either the buyer or the seller in a given transaction, but not both. In such transactions, the agent is required to impart fair dealing to both parties. Figure 4.1 summarizes the duties licensees owe to both customers and clients.

Seller Agency

In seller agency, an agency relationship is established between the owner of real estate and the broker by means of a listing contract. This is called a seller agency. In seller agency, the seller is the principal, and the principal is owed the fiduciary duties implicit to the agency relationship. Listing contracts are between the sellers and the brokerage firm; the brokerage firm owns the listing contracts.

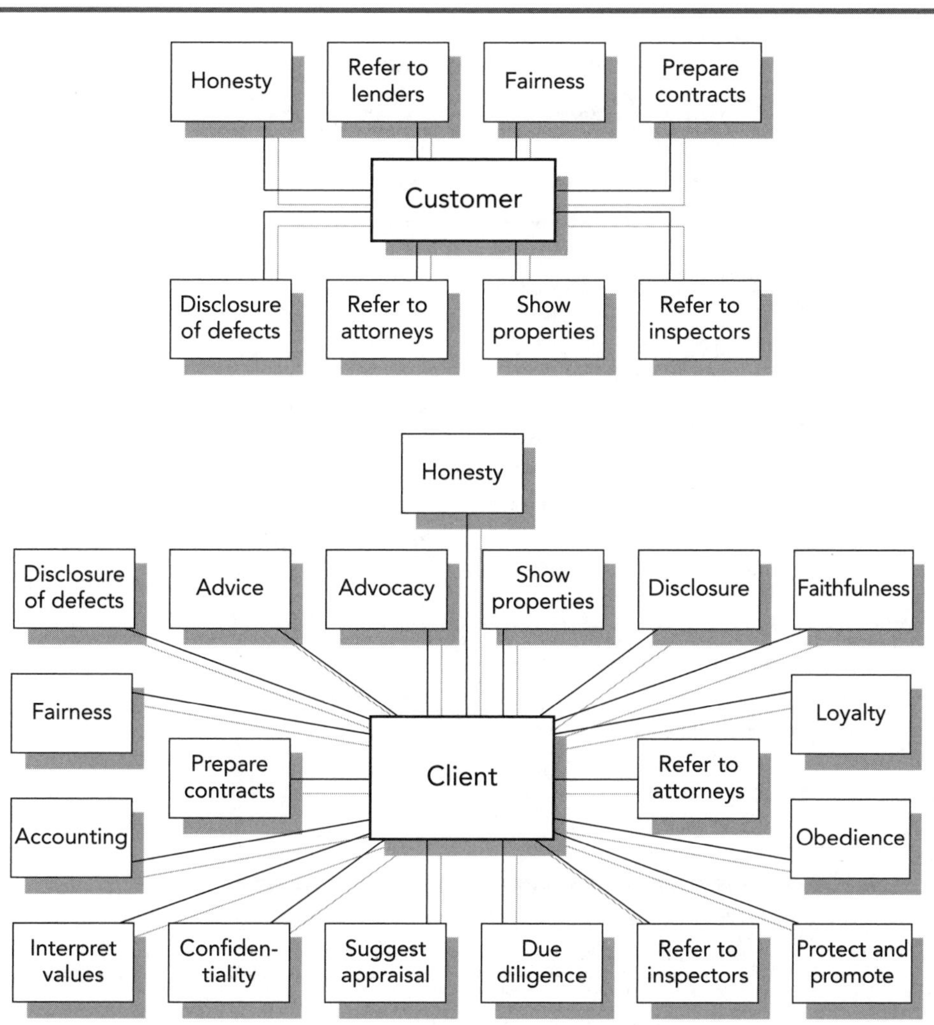

Source: Copyright © 1994 by Erle Rawlins III, (214) 363-7400. Used with permission.

FIGURE 4.1 Licensee duties to customers and clients.

Seller brokerages work *for* the seller, their client, and work *with* the buyer. In most states, agents and subagents of the seller must disclose their agency status to prospective buyers (see Figure 4.2).

Buyer Agency

Buyers of real estate are more frequently hiring real estate brokers to represent them. This relationship is referred to as **buyer brokerage** or buyer representation. In such cases the *agency relationship exists between the buyer and the broker:* The buyer is the principal/client, and the broker is the agent. In some cases, the buyer may agree to compensate the broker upon the purchase of property by the buyer. More frequently, however, the seller of the property is offering a commission upon sale, a portion of which is paid to the buyer's broker.

Buyers moving into a new area recognize the value of broker representation in locating a house for purchase. The advantages to the buyer in establishing this type of a relationship include gaining the technical expertise to negotiate a better price and the fiduciary confidentiality and trust of the broker. As might be expected, buyers want assurance that they are paying a reasonable and fair price for a property. A buyer's broker may perform a market analysis and advise the buyer on his or her offer. A buyer broker also may be able to suggest creative financing that is in the buyer's interest.

FIGURE 4.2 An example of an agency disclosure form.

NOTICE TO PROSPECTIVE REAL ESTATE PURCHASERS/TENANTS

In Ohio, real estate licensees are required to disclose which party they represent in a real estate transaction. Under Ohio law, a real estate licensee is considered to be an agent of the owner of real estate unless there is an agreement to the contrary and that agreement is disclosed to all parties.

Some of the duties of the licensee, as the agent of the owner, are to:

- Treat all parties to a transaction honestly
- Offer the property without regard to race, color, religion, sex, ancestry, national origin or handicap
- Promote the best interest of the owner
- Obtain the best price for the owner
- Fully disclose to the owner all facts which might affect or influence a decision
- Present all offers to the owner

As a buyer, if you choose to have a real estate broker represent you as your agent, you should enter into a written contract that clearly establishes the obligations of both you and your agent and specifies how your agent will be compensated.

Under Ohio law, the disclosure statement below must be submitted to the prospective purchaser/tenant in each transaction. This form has been approved by the Ohio Real Estate Commission for use by Ohio real estate licensees. Please sign below.

AGENCY DISCLOSURE STATEMENT

The listing broker and all agents associated with the listing broker represent the owner. The ____________ and ____________ represent (please check
(Selling Broker) *(Selling Agent)*
one): the purchaser/tenant ___; the owner ___.

If a broker/agent is representing both the purchaser/tenant and the owner as a dual agent, he/she must attach a copy of the agreement signed by the purchaser/tenant and owner acknowledging their agreement to this arrangement.

By signing below, the parties confirm that they have received, read and understood the information in this Agency Disclosure Form and that this form was provided to them before signing a contract to purchase/lease real estate.

Purchaser/Tenant	*Date*	*Owner*	*Date*
Purchaser/Tenant	*Date*	*Owner*	*Date*

Any questions regarding the role or responsibilities of real estate brokers or agents in Ohio can be directed to an attorney or to:

State of Ohio
Department of Commerce
Division of Real Estate
Telephone: 614/466-4100

PUTTING IT TO WORK

Services a Seller Broker Can Provide to a Buyer/Customer

A broker representing the seller can

1. provide the buyer with information on available properties and sources of financing
2. show the buyer available properties and describe their attributes and amenities
3. assist the buyer in submitting an offer to purchase/lease

Both the listing broker and the cooperating broker (acting as subagent) and their sales agents are obligated by law to treat the buyer honestly and fairly. They must

1. present all offers to the seller promptly
2. respond honestly and accurately to questions concerning the property
3. disclose any latent or hidden defects the broker knows about the property
4. disclose all facts known by the broker that materially affect the value of the property and are not known by or readily observable to the buyer

A buyer's broker relationship is common in commercial real estate, in which a buyer employs a broker to locate a certain type of property for purchase. Today this approach is becoming more common in residential real estate as well.

With the establishment of buyer agency, the direction of agency responsibility is reversed from the traditional sales situation. When a buyer engages a broker, the broker owes all duties of loyalty and disclosure to the buyer and not to the seller. The seller is the third party. A written buyer broker agreement signed by both buyer and broker is essential to prevent any disputes. Typically, a disclosure of this relationship is required to be made in writing to the seller or his agent prior to any showing of the property.

Subagency

As indicated earlier, the principal may authorize the agent to use other people to assist in accomplishing the purpose of the agency. These people are subagents and owe the same fiduciary loyalties to the principal as are owed by the agent. In the case of seller agency, those practitioners accepting subagency status agree to represent the best interests of the seller; in working with buyers, these subagents of the seller must offer customer-level service only.

The concept of subagency was once tied closely to use of the MLS. Until recently, the MLS required that cooperating brokers accept subagency status, but this policy is no longer in effect. The MLS permits subagency but does not require it.

In an attempt to further reduce confusion regarding agency relationships, individual states continue to enact legislation aimed at protecting both consumers of real estate services and practitioners themselves. Some states are moving away from the concept of subagency and toward such concepts as "designated agency," under which a broker names a licensee to act as legal agent of the client.

DUAL AGENCY

A **dual agency** exists when *a real estate firm attempts to represent both the buyer and seller in the same transaction.* Dual agency may be intended or unintended. Dual agency must be disclosed to both buyer and seller, and both must agree to that dual relationship in writing. Undisclosed dual agency is a breach of a broker's fiduciary duty, and usually a violation of state licensing law.

An intended dual agency can arise when a listing broker acts as a buyer's broker and shows an in-house listing with the seller's full knowledge and agreement. The real estate firm then represents both the buyer and the seller in a dual agency capacity and cannot give either of them exclusive loyalty and confidentiality. In this situation it is important to convey to both buyer and seller that neither can receive full representation. The dual agent takes on the role of *facilitator*, giving assistance to both sides in an effort to close the transaction.

PUTTING IT TO WORK

Salespeople who work for the listing broker and wish to sell the firm's listings are now considered in many states to be acting as dual agents. These salespeople must take special steps to avoid *undisclosed* dual agency, in which the buyer mistakenly assumes that the practitioner is working for them. In such instances, disclosure of dual agency status to both seller and buyer is usually required.

As might be expected, maintaining this balance of neutrality is difficult because the responsibilities to both buyer and seller are difficult to define. Brokers who choose to engage in dual agency may find that when the transaction has ended, either client may think the other received more effective representation and may challenge the broker's actions in court. Because of the difficulties of achieving successful dual agency, this agency relationship is discouraged and usually prohibited without full disclosure and consent of both buyer and seller. Figure 4.3 is an example of a dual agency disclosure agreement.

DUTIES AND LIABILITIES OF AGENTS

Agent's Responsibility to Principals

Every agency creates a fiduciary relationship between principal and agent. It is a position of trust. The agent has certain obligations to the principal, as required of every agent by law. The agent's duties and responsibilities include loyalty, obedience, skill, care, diligence, disclosure of information, and accounting.

Loyalty

An agent must be loyal to the principal and must work diligently to serve the best interests of the principal under the terms of the employment contract creating the agency. The agent may not work for personal interest or interest of others adverse to the principal's interest. The agent cannot legally represent any other person who directly affects the principal without disclosing the fact of that representation to the principal and obtaining the principal's consent. An agent cannot enter into a dual agency and attempt to represent both buyer and seller in the same transaction whether or not receiving a commission from both without the knowledge and consent of both buyer and seller.

Obedience

The agent must obey reasonable and legal instructions from the principal. For example, the seller, as principal, may specify that the property be shown only

FIGURE 4.3
Informed written consent of dual agency shall be presumed to have been given by any client who signs such a document.

CONSENT FOR DUAL AGENCY REPRESENTATION

The undersigned, [insert name(s)], agree that [licensee] may undertake a dual representation (represent both the seller or landlord and the buyer or tenant) for the sale or lease of the property located at [insert address]. The undersigned acknowledge they were informed of the possibility of this type of representation.

BEFORE SIGNING THIS DOCUMENT PLEASE READ THE FOLLOWING:

Representing more than one party to a transaction presents a conflict of interest since both clients may rely upon Licensee's advice and the clients' respective interests may be adverse to each other. Licensee will undertake this representation only with the written consent of ALL clients in the transaction.

Any agreement between the clients as to a final contract price and other terms is a result of negotiations between the clients acting in their own best interests and on their own behalf. Clients acknowledge that Licensee has explained the implications of dual representation, including the risks involved, and understand that they have been advised to seek independent advice from their advisors or attorneys before signing any documents in this transaction.

WHAT A LICENSEE CAN DO FOR CLIENTS WHEN ACTING AS A DUAL AGENT

1. Treat all clients honestly.
2. Provide information about the property to the buyer or tenant.
3. Disclose all latent material defects in the property known to Licensee.
4. Disclose financial qualifications of the buyer or tenant to the seller or landlord.
5. Explain real estate terms.
6. Help the buyer or tenant arrange for property inspections.
7. Explain closing costs and procedures.
8. Provide information about comparable properties that have sold so both clients may make educated decisions on what price to accept or offer.

WHAT A LICENSEE CANNOT DO FOR CLIENTS WHEN ACTING AS A DUAL AGENT

1. Disclose confidential information that Licensee may know about either client without that client's permission.
2. Disclose the price the seller or landlord will take, other than the listing price, without permission of the seller or landlord.
3. Disclose the price the buyer or tenant is willing to pay, without permission of the buyer or tenant.
4. Recommend or suggest a price the buyer or tenant should offer.
5. Recommend or suggest a price the seller or landlord should counter with or accept.

If either client is uncomfortable with this disclosure and dual representation, please let Licensee know. Clients are not required to sign this document unless clients want to allow Licensee to proceed as Dual Agent in this transaction.

By signing below, clients acknowledge that they have read and understand this form and voluntarily consent to Licensee acting as Dual Agent (that is, to represent BOTH the seller or landlord AND the buyer or tenant) should that become necessary.

Date:____________________________

____________________________ ____________________________

____________________________ ____________________________

during certain times of the day, or not on certain days of religious observance. The buyer being represented might instruct the broker not to disclose the buyer's identity to the parties without buyer's consent. Of course, the principal cannot require the agent to do any illegal acts, such as violating the Fair Housing Laws. If the principal does insist on an illegal act, the broker cannot disobey; he must withdraw from the relationship.

Skill, Care, and Diligence

In offering services to the principal, agents assert that they possess the necessary skill and training to perform the services. In performing their duties, agents must exercise the skill, care, and diligence the public is entitled to expect of the them in that field. If an agent's principal incurs a financial loss as a result of the agent's negligence and failure to meet the standards of skill, diligence, and reasonable care, the agent is liable for any loss the principal incurs. Further, the principal is not required to pay any compensation to the agent as agreed in the employment contract.

Disclosure of Information

Agents are required to keep the principal fully aware of all important matters through **disclosure of information.** They must *promptly and totally communicate to the principal any information that is material to the transaction for which the agency is created.* As an example, the requirement for disclosure of information requires that a broker present every offer to the seller. The seller has the prerogative to decide whether to reject or to accept any offer for purchase of the property. In presenting the offer, the broker should provide the seller with any knowledge of all circumstances surrounding the offer. If a buyer broker, the broker should indicate to the buyer what market value the property has and use all negotiating techniques possible to obtain the most favorable terms for the buyer. The requirement to disclose all information material to the transaction is modified under a dual agency. Disclosure must be with consent of both seller and buyer. However, material facts about the subject property must always be disclosed to all parties of the transaction.

Accounting

An agent must account for and promptly remit as required all money or property entrusted to the agent for the benefit of others. The agent is required to keep adequate and accurate records of all receipts and expenditures of other people's money to be able to provide a complete accounting. For example, a real estate broker must maintain a special account for depositing other people's money. This account should be labeled either "trust account" or "escrow account" and be maintained in an insured bank or insured savings and loan association. It is a violation of the law of agency for real estate brokers to commingle funds or property they are holding in trust for others with personal money or property, or with the operating account of the business.

Putting It to Work

Handling other people's money is one of the most serious fiduciary responsibilities of licensees. Check with your state department of licensing for information on the proper handling of deposits and disbursements.

Agent's Responsibility to Third Persons

Even though one of the agent's obligations to the principal consists of the requirement not to disclose certain confidential information to third parties that would be injurious to the principal, the agent may not engage in misrepresentation of fact in any way to a third party. A **misrepresentation** by a seller broker occurs when he or she *conceals a defect in the property from the buyer or makes a misrepresentation to the buyer regarding the existence of a defect.* Agents *must disclose any material facts of which they have knowledge or should have had knowledge* regarding the condition of any service or item provided. This disclosure is in addition to the seller's disclosure form discussed later in this chapter. For example, a seller broker must disclose to prospective buyers any condition of the property that may be defective, such as the septic system, wet basement, boundary disputes, and so on. Liability may be imposed upon the agent for concealing defects in the property or for failing to disclose the existence of defects, or even failing to make reasonable attempts to discover the defects.

The basis for imposing liability in the case of misrepresentation consists of (a) a false representation of a material fact; (b) the fact that the person making the false representation knew or should have known it to be false; (c) the fact that the misrepresentation was made with an intent to induce the party to act or refrain from acting in reliance upon the misrepresentation; (d) the fact that the party relied upon the misrepresentation in acting or failing to act; (e) the fact that there was damage to the party who relied upon the misrepresentation in acting or not acting.

A misrepresentation also occurs by omission of facts about the property even if the buyer does not ask. For example, when A listed a property owned by B, B disclosed a faulty septic system. This defect was not revealed in any advertisements or a property disclosure. When showing the property, A revealed the defect only when specifically asked by a prospective buyer. A will be liable to any purchaser who is not aware of the defect for damages based upon his failure to disclose.

An **unintentional misrepresentation** occurs when the seller broker *makes a false statement to the buyer about the property and the broker does not know whether the statement is true or untrue.* In either of these situations, the broker is liable to a customer who suffers a loss as a result of acting or failing to act in reliance upon the misrepresentation. The broker is not excused from liability for making a misrepresentation based upon statements the principal makes to the broker. The broker is required to make a personal, diligent investigation before passing on information of any type. For example, C listed a property owned by D. D thought the property was zoned for small industry. C advertised the property as zoned for small industry without verifying the zoning. After closing on the property, the buyers were unable to use the property for small industry. C and D will be liable for damages suffered by the buyers for the unintentional misrepresentation.

Basically, brokers are liable for (a) what they know from disclosure by the principal; (b) what they should know because of their skill and training; and (c) what they should know by an inspection of the property.

Even though the maxim of caveat emptor, or "buyer beware," still applies, the buyer does not have to beware of a seller broker lying or hiding defects. The seller broker must disclose, and if he or she does not, legal recourse by the buyer may be available.

PUTTING IT TO WORK

The term "stigmatized" is applied to properties that are considered in some way undesirable as a result of a crime or other tragedy that occurred there. Some states now require disclosure regarding stigmatized properties, and in these and all states practitioners should be aware of such issues and should seek advice and legal counsel when necessary.

Duties and Liabilities of Principals

Duties to Agents

Under an agency agreement, the principal is obligated to the agent for cooperation, compensation, and indemnification. The agency agreement should clearly set out the amount of compensation to be paid and the conditions that must be met to earn the compensation. Because an agency agreement is for providing services to the principal by the agent, the principal must not hinder the agent's efforts in providing services. For example, the seller of listed property must not refuse to allow the broker to show the property to prospective buyers in accordance with terms of the listing.

For compensation, the seller typically agrees to pay the broker a set percentage of the accepted sales price of the property when a ready, willing, and able buyer (discussed in Chapter 5) is produced. If the broker brings a buyer with an offer completely in accordance with the listing agreement and no conditions (full cash offer), the broker is entitled to commission whether the seller does or does not accept the offer or is later unable to close the transaction.

Finally, the agent is entitled to be free from liability if the principal has withheld information that causes the agent to make incorrect representations to third parties. If the agent is found liable to the third parties for the principal's misrepresentation, the agent is entitled to repayment from the principal for all monies paid. The repayment from the principal is indemnification to the agent and makes the agent financially whole. For instance, if the seller of listed property knows of a latent defect (such as hidden termite or water damage) and fails to disclose the defect to the broker, any legal action brought by an innocent buyer against the broker shall be indemnified to the broker by the seller.

Property Disclosure by Seller

The principal of an agency agreement has no express contract with anyone except the agent. The principal, however, does have a common law **duty of disclosure** and fairness to any third parties. This duty complements the duty the principal has to the agent for *revealing all information that affects the agency agreement.* This duty requires that the principal disclose, completely, any and all information that has a bearing on the subject of the agency agreement. The seller's duty to disclose to the broker any and all hidden defects known by the seller also runs to any buyer brokers, prospective buyers, and subagents of the listing broker.

In many states, the seller must complete and provide to any prospective buyer a detailed **Property Disclosure Form** listing the condition of the property being sold. This form, to be completed by the seller, *is a comprehensive checklist pertaining to the condition of the property including its structure and any environmental hazards in and around the property.*

In states requiring such a form, failure to provide it may invalidate any offer to purchase made by a prospective buyer. Incomplete disclosure or intentional falsification of information on the disclosure form may subject the seller to liability for misrepresentation, fraud, and damages incurred by the buyer as a result of the misinformation. If sellers fail to correctly disclose, they will be liable for the statutory penalties.

Important Points

1. Agency is usually created with an agreement but also can be created by the agent's conduct. A fiduciary relationship exists between principal and agent in an agency relationship.
2. The types of agents are universal, general, and special.
3. The type of agency depends on the scope and duration of authority given by the principal.
4. The types of real estate agency relationships are: seller agency, buyer agency, and dual agency.
5. Compensation does not determine agency because either client or customer may pay commission.
6. A multiple listing service (MLS) offers cooperation and compensation to participating members. It permits subagency but does not automatically create or require it.
7. Responsibilities of agent to client include loyalty, obedience, skill, care, diligence, disclosure, and accounting.
8. The agent has the responsibility to deal fairly and honestly with all customers.
9. The principal has a common law duty of disclosure and fairness to all parties.

How Would You Respond?

1. You have sold property listed by H. H now wishes you to assist him in the purchase of another property. He has asked to look at a property listed with your principal broker. What are the areas of concern in this situation? How should this situation be handled?
2. J is a newly licensed salesperson. He has some property he wishes to sell. Can J advertise the property "for sale by owner" without mentioning his principal broker or his status as a licensee? What should J do to sell his property and comply with the law of agency?

Case Studies

SELLER'S AGENT NOT LIABLE FOR LOSS SUFFERED BY BUYER

Parnell listed property with Edwards REALTORS®. Taylor, agent of Edwards REALTORS® consummated the sale to McAdams.

The sale was on contract with over 50 percent of the purchase price paid down by McAdams. Parnell had an outstanding mortgage on the property. Although information concerning the mortgage was not specifically discussed with McAdams, it was not hidden from McAdams. The contract signed by McAdams specifically allowed Parnell to have a mortgage on the property.

Closing was held with Taylor acting as closing agent. The down payment from McAdams was distributed to pay commissions, satisfy a second mortgage, attorney fees, and recording fees. The balance went to Parnell.

Parnell left town and defaulted on the mortgage. McAdams was named in the foreclosure suit and was forced to buy the property at the foreclosure sale.

McAdams sued Taylor, stating that he should have warned them of the possible risk involved with the underlying mortgage. They also claimed that since he acted as closing agent, he should have distributed the funds at closing to the first mortgage holder and given none to Parnell.

The Court, although sympathetic to McAdam's predicament, stated that Taylor as Parnell's agent had no duty to McAdams other than to treat McAdams openly and honestly. Taylor withheld no information from McAdams. McAdams was not prevented by words or actions from seeking independent legal advise prior to closing.

Taylor was not held liable for McAdam's loss.

McAdams v. Edward REALTOR®s, 1992, 604 N.E. 2d 607.

CULVER v. JAOUDI

In a 1991 California Court Appeal decision in *Culver v. Jaoudi* (1 Cal. Rptr. 2d 680), a judge decided against the award of a commission to a broker who had failed to tell the seller that he was representing the buyer.

The broker had a buyer/client who was looking for a parcel of land to develop. The broker contacted an owner who had a parcel for sale. The broker asked for a one-time listing from the seller, who agreed to pay a 3 percent commission if a buyer could be found. The broker presented the seller with his buyer/client's offer, and after negotiation, the buyer and seller agreed upon a sales price. At closing, the sale was consummated but the seller refused to pay the $52,500 commission to the broker for failure to disclose that he was representing the buyer in the transaction. The broker sued. The judge ruled against the broker, saying, "The agent has a fiduciary duty to his principal to disclose all information in the agent's possession relevant to the subject matter of the agency." The broker was representing both the buyer and the seller, and in this case, the dual agency must be clearly disclosed to both parties. Since the broker failed to tell the seller that he was representing the buyer, the penalty for failure to disclose the dual representation is loss of the sales commission.

REVIEW QUESTIONS

Answers to these questions are found in the *Answer Key* section at the back of the book.

1. An agent's duties to the principal include all of the following EXCEPT:
   a. loyalty
   b. accounting
   c. obedience
   d. legal advice

2. All of the following represent an agency relationship EXCEPT:
   a. the relationship between an owner of rental property and the tenant
   b. the relationship between an owner of rental property and the property manager
   c. the relationship between a listing agent and a cooperating agent participating in marketing the listed property
   d. the relationship between the seller of property and the broker under a listing

3. A real estate salesperson presents an offer to the property owner during the listing term for the listed price payable in cash with no contingencies and the specified earnest money deposit. In this situation, which of the following statements is correct?
   a. the property owner is required to accept the offer
   b. the listing brokerage company is legally entitled to the commission agreed upon in the listing contract
   c. the sales agent will get the earnest money deposit if the offer is refused
   d. the property owner will forfeit the earnest money deposit if she refuses to accept the offer

4. A real estate broker advises a buyer that a property is zoned for commercial use of the type for which the buyer intends the property. Relying upon the broker's advice, the buyer contracts to purchase the property. In making the statement regarding the zoning, the broker did not know what zoning applied to the property. The buyer subsequently learns that the zoning will not allow use of the property as he intended. Which of the following is (are) correct?
   a. the broker committed an act of misrepresentation and is liable to the buyer for any loss the buyer suffered as a consequence
   b. because the broker did not know the true facts regarding the zoning, no misrepresentation of the property to the buyer took place, and therefore the broker is not liable
   c. caveat emptor applies, and thus the broker is not liable
   d. the broker is not liable because the property was for commercial use instead of residential

5. When a licensed real estate salesperson desires to buy property listed with her broker's office, she may:
   a. buy the property at any time and on any terms
   b. not buy the property because of the subagency relationship with the seller through her office
   c. buy the property provided her interest is made known to all parties
   d. buy the property if she informs her broker but doesn't notify the principal

6. All of the following terminate an agency agreement EXCEPT:
   a. expiration of time period set out in the agreement
   b. death of the principal
   c. bankruptcy of the salesperson
   d. completion of sale of property subject to the agency agreement

7. A licensee can accept compensation from both buyer and seller:
   a. only if there is a written listing from both buyer and seller
   b. only if the total amount is equal to the total commission
   c. under no circumstances
   d. only after full disclosure and agreement of both buyer and seller

8. When a cooperating broker accepts an MLS offer of subagency, the broker becomes the fiduciary of the:
   a. listing agency
   b. seller
   c. buyer
   d. both the listing agency and the seller

9. The listing broker can discuss with the buyer all of the following EXCEPT the:
   a. agency relationship that exists
   b. property disclosure sheet
   c. bankruptcy the seller is facing
   d. problem with inadequate septic system

10. Someone who has an unlimited power of attorney is typically a:
    a. special agent
    b. general agent
    c. universal agent
    d. trust agent

11. MLS is best defined as:
    a. listings of multiple-unit properties in one area
    b. listings of properties that have multiple owners
    c. a means of sharing listings between member brokers and their agents, allowing for cooperation and shared compensation
    d. sharing lists of buyers with builders in an effort to multiply the magnitude and construction of home sales

12. A property manager is typically a:
    a. special agent
    b. general agent
    c. universal agent
    d. trust agent

13. A principal is one who:
    a. empowers another to act for her
    b. buys direct from the owner, without a broker's representation
    c. expects care, obedience, accounting, and loyalty from the buyer of her property
    d. the owner of a brokerage firm

14. When taking a listing, the agent is told by the property owner that the septic system has not been working properly. This fact is disclosed on the listing sheet and on the MLS sheet. At a showing of the property, which of the following is true?
    a. the agent does not have to disclose this information unless the prospective buyer asks about the septic system
    b. the agent does not have to disclose this information because it was disclosed on the listing sheet and MLS sheet
    c. the agent does have to disclose this information whether asked or not, because the agent must be fair, open, and honest in all dealings
    d. the agent does not have to disclose this information unless in a dual agency situation, in which case the agent represents both buyer and seller

15. The difference between client and customer is:

    a. a client is someone who is the principal in an agency relationship whereas a customer is someone who is merely provided services in the ordinary course of business
    b. a customer is someone who is the principal in an agency relationship whereas a client is someone who is merely provided services in the ordinary course of business
    c. a client is always the seller, whereas the customer is always the buyer
    d. a customer is always the seller, whereas the client is always the buyer

16. Double Duty Realty has a written listing of B's property. Which of the following is true?
    a. the written listing creates an express agency agreement with Double Duty Realty as agent and B as principal
    b. the written listing creates an implied agency agreement with Double Duty Realty as agent and B as principal
    c. the written listing creates an agency relationship by estoppel with Double Duty Realty as agent and B as principal
    d. the written listing creates a universal agency agreement with B as agent and Double Duty Realty as principal

17. C, a licensed broker, is best friends with D. D has asked C to sell his house but no written listing agreement has been signed. C advertises and shows the property to prospective buyers. D knows of the ads and the showings. However, D and C failed to disclose to the prospective buyers that the basement floods during a rain. Which of the following is true?
    a. an express agency exists between C and D and both are liable to any buyers as a result of innocent representation
    b. an agency by estoppel exists between C and D and both are liable to any buyers as a result of positive misrepresentation
    c. an express agency exists between C and D and both are liable to any buyers as a result of positive misrepresentation
    d. No agency relationship exists between C and D, thus only D is liable for the innocent representation

18. E has listed three parcels of real estate with a total listing price of $950,000 and commission of 7 percent. E sells all three parcels to buyers she has found. What is the total commission E receives if she receives 30 percent of the total commission for listing and 30 percent of the total commission for selling?
    a. $37,200
    b. $39,900
    c. $42,750
    d. $66,500

19. F has listed property owned by G. After showing the property to several prospective buyers, F decides to offer to purchase the property for himself. Which of the following is true?
    a. F is not allowed to purchase the property since he is the special agent of G
    b. F is not allowed to purchase the property unless he discloses to G that he is the purchaser
    c. F is allowed to purchase the property but only if his principal broker terminates him as a sales associate
    d. F is not allowed to purchase the property unless an appraisal is done, and he offers more than the appraised value

20. Sellers of property state that the property is not to be shown or sold to any Catholic. Which of the following is true?
    a. the listing agent must obey the seller's instructions under the law of agency
    b. the listing agent can write the listing as sellers indicate and then show and sell the property to anyone including Catholics
    c. listing agent cannot disobey seller's instructions, but neither can he obey and violate the law. He must withdraw from the agency agreement
    d. listing agent must notify the local Civil Rights Commission of the seller's request

POSSIBLE RESPONSES TO "HOW WOULD YOU RESPOND?"

1. Since you have just acted as H's agent in the sale of his property, he may assume that you are his agent in all real estate transactions. However, when H becomes a buyer, H may be a customer or a client. To be a client, H will need to enter into an express agreement with you. This agreement would create a buyer broker agency.

   If H wishes to see a property that is already listed by your principal broker, then you cannot work solely for H. You must disclose to H prior to the showing of the listed property that you represent the seller. You can offer to represent both H and the seller under a dual agency, but only if the seller and H both agree to this arrangement. If both H and the seller agree to this arrangement, then a written agreement authorizing the dual agency must be signed by H and the seller.

2. In most states, any advertisement placed by a licensee associated with a principal broker must include the name of the principal broker. Also in most states, a licensee, whether or not associated with a principal broker, must disclose that he is licensed in the purchase or sale of any real estate.

   Thus in the situation above, J would be required to "list" his property with his principal broker prior to sale. Thus any advertisement would include the name of the principal broker. This does not mean that J would have to pay a commission to his principal broker upon the sale of the property. J's principal broker has the right to waive any commission or to accept a lower commission. If J is not associated with a principal broker, he must disclose in the advertisement that he is licensed.

   The specific disclosures by J would vary from state to state. Check the law in your particular state.

CHAPTER 5

Important Terminology

acceptance
accord and satisfaction
assignee
assignment
assignor
bilateral contract
breach of contract
carryover clause
compensatory damages
competence
complete performance
conditional sales contract
consideration
contract
contract for deed
counteroffer
duress
earnest money
equitable title
exclusive agency listing
exclusive right-to-sell listing
executed contract
executory contract
express contract
fraud
implied contract
installment land contract
land contract
liquidated damages
listing contract
misrepresentation
mutual assent
mutual mistake
novation
offer and acceptance
open listing
operation of law
option
parol evidence rule
punitive damages
ready, willing, and able
reality of consent
rescission
right of first refusal
specific performance
Statute of Frauds
undue influence
unenforceable contract
unilateral contract
valid contract
voidable contract
void contract
with reserve

Real Estate Contracts

In This Chapter Contracts are involved in every aspect of real estate. Some of the most common real estate contracts are listings, purchase agreements, leases, options, mortgages, and land contracts (contracts for deed). Before learning the specifics of the various contracts normally encountered in the real estate business, we must understand the basics of contract law, which apply to real estate contracts as well as all other contracts. Nearly every controversy or question arising in the real estate business involves the contracts between parties and can be answered by applying basic contract law.

Basic Contract Law

Terms and Classifications

A **contract** is *an agreement between legally competent parties to do some legal act or to refrain from doing some legal act in exchange for lawful consideration.* A contract establishes both the rights and the duties or responsibilities of the parties to the contract. Because the rights and responsibilities can differ from contract to contract, various classifications or types of contracts have evolved. Contracts can be classified as:

1. Express versus implied
2. Unilateral versus bilateral
3. Executory versus executed
4. Valid, enforceable or unenforceable, void or voidable

Express Contracts

Under an **express contract**, *the parties to the contract have definitely agreed on all the terms and conditions in the contract.* An express contract can be written or spoken (oral). Among real estate contracts, which include listings, offers to purchase, mortgages, land contracts, options, and leases, the majority are in writing and thus are express contracts. In some cases, parties have oral leases. Oral contracts are also express contracts.

PUTTING IT TO WORK

People often question the validity of an oral contract because of the difficulty in proving it when parties dispute the contract terms. Though proof may be a problem, this does not affect the validity of oral contracts when there is proof.

Implied Contracts

An **implied contract** (or ostensible contract) is one *inferred from the conduct and actions of another without express agreement.* Implied contracts arise when the conduct of the parties clearly illustrates the intention to contract. A court implies the existence of a contract if one party has received the benefit at the expense of the other party. The court requires the recipient of the benefit to pay a reasonable compensation to the party rendering the benefit. An exception is if the benefit received is truly a gift. An implied contract is created, for example, if C hires D to cut his hair without stipulating the price to be paid for the haircut. An implied contract to pay the reasonable value of the service delivered is created by C's allowing the haircut.

The law does not favor implied contracts because of the uncertainty of terms of the agreement of the parties and because the parties are placed in a contract relationship without actual express consent to contract. Implied contracts should be avoided in real estate. They arise most often when a licensee is showing property to a customer (buyer). Under the listing, the seller and the real estate agent have an express contract setting out the agreement and terms of the parties. Because the seller's agent also may spend much time with the prospective buyer, the buyer may infer that a contract for services exists between the buyer and the seller agent. This may occur when the seller agent is involved in negotiating the terms of the offer to purchase between the seller and the buyer. Each party believes the real estate broker is working in his or her own best interest. This is a classic example of an implied contract in real estate that may result in an unintended dual agency.

Bilateral Contracts

"Bi" means two. In its meaning here, "two" does not refer to two parties to a contract, as every contract has at least two parties; instead, "bi" refers to the number of parties to the contract *who are making promises or performing acts.* A **bilateral contract** is one in which *two parties have made promises of some kind to each other.* The promise could be for the payment of money or for the performance of some act such as painting a house. Because both parties make promises, both are bound or obligated under the contract from the onset of the contract.

The offer to purchase a home is bilateral because it is based on the exchange of promises whereby the seller will sell and the buyer will buy. Other examples of bilateral contracts in real estate are mortgages, many exclusive listings, leases, and land contracts (contracts for deed).

Unilateral Contracts

The "uni" in unilateral means "one." Again, this does not refer to the number of parties to a contract but, instead, to the number of parties making promises in the contract. In a **unilateral contract**, *one party makes a promise in order to induce a second party to do something.* The party making the promise is bound and obligated under the contract. The other party, however, has made no promise and thus is not bound or obligated in any way to perform or act.

An example of a unilateral contract outside of real estate is an offer for a reward for the return of a pet. No one is obligated to look for and return the pet. If someone does return the pet, however, the one who promised the reward is obligated to pay.

The typical unilateral contract in the real estate business is an option contract. Under an **option**, the *owner of the property (optionor) promises to sell his or her land to another (optionee) at a certain price for a certain time period.* The optionee is not obligated to purchase the land; however, if the optionee does desire to purchase the land, the optionor is obligated to sell on the terms promised. The optionor cannot legally sell the land to any other person during the term of the option.

Executed Contracts

A *contract that has been fully performed* is an **executed contract**. An example in the real estate business is an offer to purchase in which all contingencies and conditions have been met and closing takes place. After the closing, nothing more is to be performed under the offer to purchase.

Executory Contracts

A *contract that is not fully performed or completed* is called an **executory contract**. In real estate, most contracts begin as executory. A mortgage is a contract whereby the borrower pays money over a term of years to the lender. The action yet to be done—the monthly payments—will go on for years. A lease is a contract whereby the tenant will pay rent on an ongoing basis or face eviction. A listing contract sets a definite time period during which the real estate broker tries to sell the property, and activity continues during the term of the listing. The best example may be the contract of sale itself, prior to closing.

PUTTING IT TO WORK

Although a real estate sales contract becomes executed upon closing, it often gives rise to many other ongoing contracts. Closing may present a new mortgage, an insurance contract, and a homeowner's warranty, all of which are executory.

Valid Contracts

A **valid contract** is one that is *binding and enforceable on all parties to it.* It contains all the essential elements of a contract (discussed later in this chapter). The parties to a valid contract are legally obligated to abide by the terms and conditions of the contract. If a party to a valid contract defaults in performing an obligation under the contract, that individual is subject to legal action by the nondefaulting party in a court of law. In drawing up contracts, every effort should be made to create a valid contract.

Unenforceable Contracts

An **unenforceable contract** is one that *appears to meet the requirements for validity but would not be enforceable in court.* A contract will be unenforceable if it does not satisfy the **Statute of Frauds**. The Statute of Frauds states that *contracts for the sale or exchange of real estate must be in writing to be enforceable.* Thus an oral contract to sell real estate between A and B may be valid, but if A refuses to complete the contract, B is unable to obtain the court's assistance in enforcing the terms of the oral contract. Even though the contract would not be enforceable in court, unenforceable contracts may still be completed by the parties. This is discussed more fully later in this chapter.

Void Contracts

A **void contract** has *absolutely no legal force or effect even though all of the essential elements for a contract exist.* The phrase "null and void" is often used to mean "does not exist in the eyes of the law." Two circumstances cause a contract to be void:

1. The purpose of the contract is illegal; or
2. The contract is impossible to complete because of an act of God or operation of law.

A contract between two people to murder a third person for money is void. The purpose of the contract is illegal. Neither party is obligated by the terms to which they have agreed. No contract exists.

Impossibility to complete a contract is more common in real estate. Parties to an offer to purchase real estate may agree on the price and terms of purchase, yet if the State condemns the property for a highway, neither party can sue the other for failing to complete the contract. The contract is impossible to complete under the operation of law. The same impossibility to complete can occur if the object of the contract is destroyed by fire, flood, tornado, or other natural causes. If the contract is impossible to complete, it is void; it does not exist.

Voidable Contracts

A **voidable contract** may or may not be enforceable between the parties. It *results from the failure of the contracting parties to meet some legal requirement in negotiating the agreement.* Usually in the voidable contract situation, one party to the contract is the victim of wrongdoing by the other party. For example, Mr. Smith contracts to buy property owned by Mrs. Brown; Mrs. Brown states that the property has no defects when she knows the septic system does not function properly; Mr. Smith relies on Mrs. Brown's statement and buys the property. Mrs. Brown has committed fraud (intentional lying); thus, Mr. Smith can choose to complete the contract or choose to nullify the contract.

The parties to a voidable contract are not required to set aside or void the contract. The parties may fulfill their obligations under the contract and receive their benefits. A voidable contract can be voluntarily performed by the parties. At any time prior to complete performance of the contract, however, the party that is wronged can elect to discontinue. Other examples of conditions that result in voidable contracts appear in the subsequent discussion of requirements for contracts.

Essential Elements of Contracts

The first step in understanding contract law is to recognize when a contract exists and, conversely, when it does not exist. The essential elements required for the existence of a contract are:

1. Offer and acceptance (meeting of the minds)
2. Consideration
3. Legal capacity of the parties

4. Reality of consent
5. Legality of object
6. Possibility of completion

In analyzing any controversy concerning real estate, the first step taken by a lawyer should be to run down the checklist of contract elements to assure that in fact a contract exists.

Offer and Acceptance

For a contract to exist, an offer and an unconditional acceptance of the offer must be present. Another name for **offer and acceptance** is *meeting of the minds*. Meeting of the minds is evident when the *parties to the contract reach agreement on the terms of the contract. Agreement of the parties* is also called **mutual assent**. The party making the offer is the *offeror* and the party to whom the offer is made is the *offeree*.

In the typical real estate purchase agreement, the buyer begins as the offeror. An offer that has not been accepted can be withdrawn at any time prior to acceptance and the notification of that acceptance. Once the offeror (or his or her agent) has knowledge of the acceptance, the offer may not then be withdrawn.

The offer must be *definite and specific* in its terms. If the offer is vague and indefinite and, therefore, subject to various interpretations, its acceptance will not result in a valid contract. For example, if an offer is made to Seller A to purchase a home in the Executive Heights Subdivision without setting forth a specific legal description and Seller A owns three houses in that subdivision, the offer is vague and an acceptance will not result in the creation of a valid contract.

PUTTING IT TO WORK

In real estate, the agreement should be complete in every detail. An offer to buy will include price, terms, financing, performance, dates, closing costs, warranties, and many other details.

FIGURE 5.1 Comparison of void, voidable, and unenforceable contracts.

VOID CONTRACT

- caused by illegal purpose or impossibility of completion
- if void, no contract obligation exists for either party

VOIDABLE CONTRACT

- caused by lack of consideration, lack of reality of consent, lack of legal capacity, lack of meeting of minds
- if voidable, contract exists, but one of the parties may choose to invalidate it due to lack of an essential contract requirement. The party who was "victim" of any wrongdoing can invalidate the contract.

UNENFORCEABLE CONTRACT

- caused by failure to comply with Statute of Frauds or by failure to enforce before time expires limiting enforcement (Statute of Limitations)
- if unenforceable, neither party can obtain court assistance in enforcing the terms of the contract

The offer *must not be illusory* in nature. An offer that is so indefinite and totally in the control of the offeror is illusory. For example, an offer to buy a home in Security Estates, when and if the offeror decides to move, is too indefinite and totally within the offeror's control. The offer is not binding upon the offeror and thus is illusory. Acceptance of an illusory offer will not result in the creation of a valid contract.

If the offer is clear and definite, the offeree has the right to accept unconditionally, reject, or counteroffer. The contract comes into existence only at the time unconditional acceptance of the offer is communicated to the offeror or his or her agent.

An acceptance that varies in any way from the offer as presented will not qualify as an acceptance. An *acceptance that varies from the offer* is a **counteroffer**. If the seller makes a counteroffer, no contract exists regarding the first offer. The making of a counteroffer terminates and destroys the original offer much like rejection of the offer. The seller has now become the offeror, and the buyer is the offeree. In the typical real estate transaction where many offers and counteroffers can be made before consummating the deal, the parties switch "hats" of offeror and offeree often.

A unilateral offer may be accepted only by performance of the action specified in the offer—for example, a promise to pay money upon the delivery of goods. Acceptance of this unilateral offer is made by delivery of the goods. A bilateral offer is accepted by an agreement to do the things requested in the offer. Acceptance of a bilateral offer must be communicated to the offeror for a contract to be created. The acceptance must be absolutely unconditional in the case of either the unilateral or bilateral offer.

Sometimes an offer specifies the manner in which acceptance of the offer must be communicated to the offeror by the offeree. In the absence of any specific provision in this regard, the offeree should communicate acceptance in the same manner as the offer. If the offer is made in writing, the acceptance should be made in writing. If acceptance is by mail, the communication is effective and a contract is created at the time the offeree deposits the acceptance in the mail.

Offers may be terminated in the following ways:

1. By the expiration of a time limit specified by the offeror prior to acceptance.
2. By the death or insanity of either the offeror or the offeree prior to acceptance.
3. By revocation of the offer by the offeror prior to acceptance and notification of that acceptance.
4. By the expiration of a "reasonable" period of time after the offer is made without an acceptance.
5. By failure of the offeree to comply with the terms of the offer as to the specific manner in which the acceptance must be communicated.
6. By rejection of the offer.
7. By acceptance of the offer; the offer now becomes a contract.

When the offer is accepted, a contract is created and the buyer acquires an interest in the land known as equitable title. The seller retains legal title until transfer by deed to the buyer. **Equitable title** is *an interest in real estate of sufficient worth for court protection of that interest,* although this interest may be less than full ownership.

Consideration

Consideration is the *giving of something of value*. For a contract to be valid, consideration must be present. Consideration is anything of value, including money, property, and even a promise of performance. One of the most common errors real estate licensees make is stating that for an offer to purchase to be valid, the buyer must pay "earnest money." Buyers almost always give earnest money in an offer to purchase, but earnest money is not required. The buyer's promise in the offer to buy the property is sufficient consideration for a valid contract.

In the case of a unilateral contract, a promise is made in exchange for the performance of a specified act. A bilateral contract entails mutual promises for future performance. Each party must promise simultaneously. If one party promises to make a gift to another party, a valid contract does not exist because the other party has made no promise in return. There must be consideration from both sides. This is called *mutuality of contract. Each party to a contract must do something or promise to do something*.

Legal Capacity of the Parties

For a contract to be valid, the parties to the contract must have the capacity to enter into a contract. Age is one consideration in the legal capacity of a party. Minors—those who have not reached the age of majority as established by the statute in each state—do not have the legal capacity to contract. An exception for minors is made in some jurisdictions for minors who are married or who are contracting for essential services such as housing or medical care.

Legal capacity of a party also is determined by the **competence** of the party, *the mental and/or emotional capacity to enter into contracts*. An adjudicated insane person does not have legal capacity to contract.

The legal capacity of a person to contract also can be affected by alcohol and drugs. An individual who is intoxicated or under the influence of drugs to the extent that he or she does not understand what is happening is temporarily incompetent to contract. Any contract signed under these conditions is not enforceable against the person who was temporarily incompetent.

Contracts entered into by parties lacking legal capacity are voidable by the party lacking capacity. In the case of minors, the contract is voidable at the option of the minor. The minor may hold an adult to a contract, but the adult cannot legally hold the minor to the contract. The contract is not legally enforceable against the minor. If a minor fulfills the terms of the contract and does not take steps to terminate the contract prior to reaching the age of majority or soon after, the individual is said to have ratified the contract as an adult and thus is bound.

The legal capacity of entities other than individuals also must be considered. Entities that may enter into contracts include corporations, partnerships, churches, schools, towns, cities, and other governmental agencies. The legal capacity of these "things" does not involve age, insanity, or drunkenness. The legal capacity of entities created by the statutes of a state is determined by the documents and instruments that create the entities. For example, in a corporation, the bylaws of the corporation determine what actions must be taken and what officers or directors must sign contracts for the agreements to be valid.

Reality of Consent

For a valid contract to be created, the parties must enter into it voluntarily. They must mutually agree to the terms and conditions in the contract. If a person enters into a written contract, as evidenced by his or her signature on the contract, the individual is presumed to have assented to the terms and conditions of the contract.

The consent of the parties to enter into a contractual agreement must be a real consent. **Reality of consent** is *based on the parties having an accurate knowledge of the facts concerning the terms and conditions of the contract*. If one or both parties does not have full knowledge or accurate knowledge, the contract will fail to be valid because of the lack of mutual assent. Typical factors causing the lack of mutual consent are fraud, misrepresentation, mutual mistake, undue influence, and duress. Any of these factors can defeat the voluntary assent of the parties and, therefore, invalidate the contract and make it voidable.

Fraud

Fraud is *intentional deceit or lying*, a misstatement of material facts to induce someone to rely on the facts and enter into a contract. A false statement is deemed to be fraudulent when (a) the party making the statement knows it to be false; or (b) the party making the statement does not know in fact whether the statement is true or false but proceeds without determining its truth or falsehood.

As an example of a fraudulent statement, a prospective buyer asks the listing agent for the owner of a property if the house has termites. Actually knowing that the house has termites, either by his own personal inspection or by a report from an independent inspector, the agent tells the prospective buyer that there are no termites. The agent has committed fraud. Based upon this misstatement of facts, the prospective buyer may rescind any contract entered into. The listing agent also could be held personally liable to the buyer for any damages arising from the falsehood or face disciplinary action.

Misrepresentation

Misrepresentation is *the intentional or unintentional misstatement of facts*. Misrepresentation can be the result of a misunderstanding of the facts by the person making the misrepresentation. A party to a contract who has relied on the misrepresented facts is legally entitled to rescind the contract. It is voidable.

For example, a prospective buyer asks a listing agent for a property how much land the seller owns. Upon checking the local records, the agent finds that the owner owns 50 acres. The owner, however, is selling only 10 acres. The buyer makes an offer assuming that the sale will be of 50 acres and not 10 acres. The real estate agent has unintentionally misled the buyer. The confusion is innocent. The buyer will be able to invalidate or void the contract.

Both fraud and misrepresentation involve the material representation of facts that may turn out to be false or misleading.

Mutual Mistake

A **mutual mistake**, *a mistake of material fact by both parties*, may nullify a contract. An example is in using an incorrect street address. In this case, the contract is voidable.

Mutual mistake does not cover a misunderstanding of the law by one party or the other, only a mistake of fact. Mistake of law will not invalidate an otherwise valid contract. An example of mistake of law may occur in an offer to purchase. The prospective buyer has in mind to open a beauty shop at a given address. The buyer does not state in the offer that the purchase is conditional upon proper zoning. After the offer is accepted, the buyer finds that local zoning will not allow a beauty shop. The buyer does not have the right to invalidate the contract.

Undue Influence

Undue influence is *any improper or wrongful control or influence by one person over another*. As a result, the will of one person is overpowered so that he or she is induced to act or prevented from acting of his or her own free will. Undue influence occurs when one person takes advantage of another person's lack of knowledge or takes advantage of a special relationship between the parties. Such a relationship may exist between a legal advisor and a client or between employer and employee. If a person is induced to enter into a contract as a result of undue influence, the contract is voidable by the disadvantaged party.

Duress

Duress is the *threat of violence or placing a person in fear for his or her safety.* The essential element of duress is physical fear or threat. The presence of duress in contract negotiations renders the contract voidable by the victim. It defeats the requirement of a voluntary meeting of the minds.

Legality of Object

Legality of object means that *the contract must be for a legal purpose.* A contract for an illegal purpose is void. Examples of illegal contracts include contracts in restraint of trade, contracts to stifle or promote litigation, and contracts in restraint of marriage.

Possibility of Completion

The parties must be able to complete the contract without interference from operation of law or acts of God. A contract that is impossible to complete is void. Examples of contracts that are impossible to complete arise in times of national emergency. A steel company may have contracted to deliver steel to a manufacturer of household appliances but because of a declaration of war, the steel company is ordered by the government to send all steel to battleship manufacturers. Examples of contracts that are impossible to complete in times of natural disaster are those affected by tornadoes, hurricanes, fires, and floods. A contract to paint a house on a certain day is impossible to complete if the house is destroyed by hurricane or other act of God.

STATUTE OF FRAUDS

Nowhere in the list of essential elements for a valid contract is a requirement for writing. In most cases an oral contract is just as valid as a written contract. Both oral and written contracts are express contracts. The difficulty with oral contracts lies in the chance for misunderstanding as to the parties' rights and obligations. Terms of an oral contract may be extremely difficult to prove in a court proceeding should that become necessary.

Because of the potential for misunderstandings in oral contracts, all states have adopted the **Statute of Frauds**. This law states that *contracts involving the creation of an interest in real property or the conveyance of an interest in real property must be written to be enforceable.* "Enforceable" means that a party to the contract may ask the court to order that the terms of the contract be carried out.

The Statute of Frauds requires that real estate contracts be written and contain all of the essential elements for a valid contract. Oral testimony (parol evidence) is not sufficient to create a contract involving the transfer of title to real property. A primary purpose of the Statute of Frauds is to prevent presentation of fraudulent proof of an oral contract. This issue is also addressed by a concept known as the **parol evidence rule**, which essentially states that *oral explanations can support the written words of a contract but cannot contradict them.* (Oral contracts entered into after a written contract, however, can be considered a "new" contract or modifications to the prior written contract.)

The statute does not require any particular form of writing. To satisfy the requirements of the statute, the writing may be a short memorandum, a telegram, a receipt, and so forth. The contract need not necessarily be contained in one document. It can be a series of letters or invoices. The best format, however, is to have the entire contract in one writing and signed by all parties.

All real estate contracts fall under the Statute of Frauds, including contracts to buy and sell real estate, options, contracts for deeds, and contracts for the exchange of real estate. Lease contracts also fall under the Statute of Frauds, but an exception exists for leases of short duration. A lease whose term exceeds a statutory time period in that particular state (usually one year) falls under the Statute of Frauds. Leases with shorter terms are enforceable even if not written.

Discharge of Contracts

Contracts can be discharged or terminated by: (a) agreement of the parties, (b) full performance, (c) impossibility of performance, or (d) operation of law.

Agreement of the Parties

Just as contracts are created by agreement of the parties, any executory contract can be terminated by agreement of the parties. This is typically called a *release of contract*. The release is itself a contract and thus must have consideration to be valid. The consideration is found in the relief from the obligations under the original contract. The release also must be voluntarily given and with full knowledge of all material facts.

In some instances a contract is terminated not by agreed release but by **accord and satisfaction**, *a new agreement between the parties*, often the result of a negotiated compromise. An example of accord and satisfaction is when one party to the contract wishes to be released but the other party desires money for the attempted default. The parties enter into a new contract for the payment of money as a substitution for performance of the contract. In real estate, the typical example of accord and satisfaction occurs when the buyer of property wishes to be relieved from the contract to buy and the seller agrees to take the earnest money in place of selling the property.

Another form of agreement that discharges or terminates contracts is **novation**, *the substitution of a new contract for a prior contract or the substitution of a new party for an old party*. It typically involves the substitution of parties in the contract. A new party to the contract agrees to satisfy the former contracting party's obligation. Upon reaching the agreement to substitute parties, the novation or new contract is created, terminating the original contract and the original party's liability.

Full Performance

The usual and most desirable manner of terminating contracts is by **complete performance** of all terms of the contract. The contract is said to be executed when *all parties fully perform all terms*.

Impossibility of Performance

The general rule is that even if a party to a contract is unable to perform obligations under the contract, the party is still liable. The reasoning is that the one who cannot perform should have provided against this possibility by including a provision in the contract for relief in the event of impossibility.

There are exceptions to the general rule. One is in the case of personal service contracts. If a person contracts to render services such as representing one in court, but is unable to complete the services as a result of death or incapacity, the obligated person is relieved of liability. This is one of the few instances in which death or incapacity affects contractual obligations. In most other contract cases, death does not affect the contract obligation or rights.

Another exception to the general rule is when the performance of an obligation under a contract becomes illegal as a result of a change in law after the contract was created, such as contracting for the drainage of farmland that has been recently designated as wetlands. The prohibition against drainage of wetlands renders the contract between the parties impossible to complete through no fault of either party, and the obligated parties are relieved of responsibility.

Operation of Law

The term **operation of law** describes *the manner in which the rights and liabilities of parties may be changed by the application of law without cooperation or agreement of the parties affected.* Contracts can be terminated or discharged by operation of law. Examples of discharge of contracts by operation of law are:

1. *Statute of limitations.* If a party to a contract fails to bring a lawsuit against a defaulting party within a time period set by statute, the injured party loses the right of remedy because of operation of law. The mere passage of time and expiration of the statutory time period affect the injured party's right to recover. Every state limits by statute the time to bring legal action against a party.

2. *Bankruptcy.* The filing of a petition in bankruptcy under federal law has the effect of terminating contracts in existence as of the date of filing the bankruptcy petition. The purpose of bankruptcy law is to relieve the bankrupt from liability of outstanding contracts and to provide a fresh start.

3. *Alteration of contract.* The intentional cancellation or alteration of a written agreement has the effect of discharging the agreement. The alteration must be material and intentional. This frequently involves negotiable instruments such as checks, stocks, and bonds in which the date of payment, amount of payment, or changes in interest rates are altered.

Assignment of Contract Rights

Contract rights are considered a personal property right. The contract itself may concern real estate, and thus the ownership of contract rights is ownership of a stick in the bundle of sticks of that real estate. Either party to a contract may transfer or sell the contract rights unless the contract specifically prohibits such a sale or transfer. The *transfer or sale of contract rights* is called **assignment**. *The party assigning or transferring his or her rights* is the **assignor**. *The party receiving the rights* is the **assignee**.

Any assignment of contract rights pertains to rights only and does not eliminate the contract obligations. For the contract obligations to be eliminated, a release or novation must occur.

A typical assignment in real estate happens when a landlord sells rental property to a new owner. Sale of the property does not terminate the lease; thus, the new owner not only owns the real estate but also has been assigned the old owner's rights under the lease to rent. Another assignment in real estate transactions is more commonly called "mortgage assumption." For example, Mr. Adams owns a house with a mortgage owed to a local bank. Mr. Adams sells to Mr. and Mrs. Brown, who assume the mortgage of Mr. Adams. The contract rights belonging to Mr. Adams concerning monthly payments and interest rate are transferred to Mr. and Mrs. Brown. Mr. Adams, however, is still obligated under the mortgage contract in the event Mr. and Mrs. Brown do not make the monthly payments.

Interpretation of Contracts

A contract that is clear, concise, and unambiguous will rarely become the center of a dispute requiring interpretation by a court. However, when a contract is unclear, ambiguous, or confusing, a dispute between the parties may arise requiring court interpretation. The court has established rules for contract interpretation. These rules do not allow the court to amend or change a contract between parties. If the essential elements of a contract cannot be proved, the court will hold that no contract exists.

If a contract exists, the court will enforce the contract in accordance with what is typical and customary, giving it a practical interpretation, if possible, and considering the circumstances leading to the contract. The court will look to the intent of the parties making the contract. The court will look to the entire contract as a whole but will stay within the "four corners" of the document. The court cannot add terms to the contract.

If a printed contract form, such as a listing or offer to purchase, is used, with blanks filled in by the parties, the handwritten words supersede the printed words if a contradiction exists. The same is true of typewritten words in a preprinted contract.

Any ambiguity in a contract is construed *against* the party preparing the contract. This has been established as good public policy so one providing the confusing contract cannot benefit from the ambiguity. As a consequence, real estate licensees must use extra care in preparing offers to purchase. Any ambiguity in the contract will work against the party the licensee represents.

Contract Remedies

In some cases, a party to a contract *fails to complete the contract or fails to perform for no legal cause*. This is **breach of contract**. Breach of contract is also called *default*. The effect of breach of contract by a party is to terminate that party's contract rights. The breach, however, does not terminate the contract obligations of the breaching party. The nondefaulting party has the following legal remedies against the defaulting party. The remedies are obtained by filing suit in a court of law.

1. Specific performance
2. Rescission
3. Compensatory damages
4. Liquidated damages

Specific Performance

Every piece of real estate is unique. All are in different locations; no piece can be substituted for another and have an exact match. As a result, a party contracting to buy a parcel of real estate does not have to accept a similar, or even almost identical, parcel. Because of the unique nature of real estate, the remedy of specific performance is available to nondefaulting parties. An order from the court requiring **specific performance** means that *the contract must be completed as originally agreed.*

For example, Buyer B has contracted to buy 123 Hickory Lane from Seller H. Seller H attempts to convey 456 Hickory Lane, which is an exact mirror image of 123 Hickory Lane. Buyer B does not have to accept the substitute and files suit for specific performance. The court orders Seller H to deed 123 Hickory Lane to Buyer B.

Rescission

This court remedy is the opposite of a suit for specific performance. **Rescission** means *to take back, remove, annul, or abrogate*. A marriage of short duration is rescinded or annulled. This contract remedy is applied when a contract has not been performed by either party and when it has been breached by a party. Upon suit for rescission, the court orders the parties placed back in their original positions as if the contract had never existed.

For example, Vendor Smith enters into a contract for deed (land contract) with Vendee Black, possession to be immediate. Within two months, Vendee Black loses his job, tells Vendor Smith that he will not move out or pay the agreed payments, and refuses to sign a release of contract. Vendor Smith files suit for rescission of the contract. The court order places Vendor Smith in possession and control and shows that Vendee Black has no interest in the real estate, just as before the contract. If Vendee Black had paid a down payment, the down payment would be ordered returned to Vendee Black, minus a fair amount for rental during the period Vendee Black had possession of the premises.

Compensatory Damages

When a contract is breached, one party usually suffers monetary loss as a result of the contract breach. The *amount of money actually lost* limits the amount of **compensatory damages** the court will award.

The amount of compensatory damages should be an amount sufficient to put the nondefaulting party in the same economic position that he or she would be in if the contract had not been breached. The amount ordered paid should total what the injured party lost from the contract breach. The amount must be able to be calculated with some certainty. For example, Landlord T must evict Tenant G for failure to pay rent in the amount of $500. Upon inspection of the premises, damage to windows, walls, and appliances has been done in the amount of $850. In addition, Landlord T must move and store Tenant G's belongings at a cost of $235. The compensatory damage award should be the total of $500, $850, $235, plus any court costs to file suit.

The items usually included are lost rent, unpaid taxes, repair cost to the premises, title search fees, lost interest, commissions, and lost profits. Traditionally, attorney fees incurred to litigate the contract breach are not included in calculating compensatory damages. Some states, however, have passed laws that allow attorney fees to be recoverable as part of compensatory damages for contract breach. Each state's statutes must be consulted on this issue.

Punitive damages or exemplary damages are not typically allowed in breach of contract cases. Punitive or exemplary damages are *awarded for extremely bad behavior by a party*. They are to punish and send a message to society that the bad behavior will not be tolerated. An award of punitive damages is made most often in cases in which one party has taken fraudulent advantage of another.

Liquidated Damages

Instead of compensatory damages or in addition to compensatory damages, the parties to the contract can stipulate in the contract an amount of money to be paid upon certain breaches of the contract. *Damages agreed to be paid in the contract* are called **liquidated damages**. Liquidated damages usually consist of forfeiture of some money or late fees held by one party in the event of breach.

Courts do not favor forfeiture. Thus, for liquidated damages to be collectible and enforced by the court, the amount must be reasonable as compared to the damage caused by the breach. To be enforceable, the amount must not appear to be a penalty.

Examples of liquidated damage clauses exist in many real estate contracts. The most typical one is the forfeiture of earnest money by the buyer to the seller in the event the offer to purchase is not completed for legal cause. Another example is found in the typical offer to purchase. The buyer and the seller agree on a date of possession; they also agree what amount of money the seller will pay the buyer if possession is not given as agreed. A further example is the late fee agreed to be paid in leases and mortgages in the event of late payments.

Auction Sales

The sale of real estate by auction is becoming more and more common. Sellers who wish a quick sale with the greatest potential for interested buyers are turning to the services of an auctioneer.

Even at an auction sale, the issue of contract existence and terms of the contract are present. In most types of auctions, the seller places the property for sale with reserve unless specifically stated otherwise. **With reserve** means *the seller does not have to accept any bids*. In this type of auction, the bidder is the offeror. The auctioneer, as agent for the seller, may accept the bid and thus form the contract. After bidding begins and before acceptance, however, the seller or the auctioneer may remove the property from the sale. If the property is removed, no contract exists. Likewise, prior to accepting a bid at auction, the bidder may withdraw his or her offer. Thus, no contract will exist.

If the sale is without reserve or an absolute auction, the seller is the offeror. Any bid will result in acceptance of the offer and thus form a contract. Once the bidding has begun, no property may be removed from a sale without reserve or absolute auction.

Under an auction sale, the seller and the auctioneer, as agent for the seller, can disclaim all warranties as to the property except:

1. The seller and the auctioneer warrant that what is claimed to be sold is in fact being sold.
2. The seller and the auctioneer have the legal right to sell the property and transfer title.

Listing Contracts and Practices

Definition and Purpose

The first contract we encounter in the real estate business is usually the listing contract. A **listing contract** is one whereby the owner of property engages a real estate broker to find a buyer for his or her property. This contract *creates an agency relationship in which the seller is the principal and the broker is the seller's special agent for this purpose*. If a buyer hires a broker to obtain property that he or she may purchase, the broker is the agent of the buyer, who is his or her principal. The latter is a fast growing area of representation in the real estate business, and many brokers are becoming solely buyer specialists. The more common situation, however, is that the broker is employed by the seller and is, therefore, the seller's agent.

Under this contract, no transfer of interest in real property is going to occur. No title will pass between seller and broker. Most states following the Statute of Frauds require the listing contract to be in writing because listing contracts relate to the sale of real property. Listing contracts must be in writing for the broker to be eligible to receive a commission (although some states allow open listings to be oral and still valid and enforceable for receipt of a commission).

Thus, in most states, the broker must prove the existence of an employment contract. A written contract clearly spells out that the broker actually has been hired by the seller, and it sets forth all the terms and conditions of employment. The requirement for the listing contract to be in writing substantially reduces lawsuits between brokers and property owners concerning matters of the broker's employment. In addition, listing contracts should include a definite time period. In some states a definite expiration date is required for a valid listing.

Commission Entitlement

The broker's entitlement to commission is determined by two tests:

1. **Ready, willing, and able**. If the broker brings to the seller a *buyer who is ready to buy, is willing to buy, and is able (financially) to buy under the terms and conditions of the listing contract*, the broker is legally entitled to the commission. The broker has done the job he or she was hired to do in the listing contract—find a buyer who will pay the listed price in cash or other specified, accepted terms. When the broker does this, the commission has been earned under the ready, willing, and able test. Whether the owner actually agrees to sell the property to the prospective buyer does not matter. The seller may reject any offer, but rejection of an offer that conforms to the terms of the listing contract does not remove the duty to pay the commission.
2. **Acceptance**. If the *broker brings a buyer the seller accepts*, the broker is legally entitled to the commission, as he or she has been instrumental in procuring a buyer for the property. Acceptance is based on some price or terms other than the listed price in cash. For example, the listing contract may specify $80,000 to be payable in cash. A broker may bring an offer to the seller of $78,500. This offer may not be for payment in cash but instead may be subject to the buyer's assuming the seller's existing mortgage. If the seller accepts this offer, the broker is legally entitled to the commission on the basis of acceptance. The broker has brought the seller a buyer who is acceptable to the seller.

These tests are not both required. This is an either/or situation. The broker earns a commission either on the basis of having brought a ready, willing, and able buyer or on the basis of having brought an offer that the seller accepts. However, some listing contracts stipulate that no commission is due unless settlement takes place.

PUTTING IT TO WORK

In reality, most listings do not attract offers at full list price and terms (a mirror offer). Usually an offer is somewhat less than the asking price or on slightly different terms. Thus, of the two tests discussed above, the second is met more often.

Types of Listings

The three types of listing contracts in general use are the open listing, the exclusive agency listing, and the exclusive right-to-sell listing. Each of these contracts gives different rights to the broker and the seller.

Open Listing

Under an **open listing**, the *seller lists a property with the assistance of one or more brokers*. The broker effecting the sale is entitled to the commission. If the owner sells the property (to a prospect not generated by any broker), however, the owner owes no commission.

This type of listing is usually not beneficial to the owner or to the broker. Usually a broker cannot afford to spend advertising dollars and sales staff on such an uncertain type of listing. The broker is competing rather than cooperating with the owner and every other broker who has an open listing on the property. This type of listing also can lead to disputes over commissions between brokers and can present legal problems for the owner. The lack of protection for the broker provides little incentive for aggressive marketing.

Exclusive Agency Listing

In an **exclusive agency listing**, the *property is listed with one broker as the only agent.* If the broker effects sale of the property, he or she is legally entitled to the commission agreed upon, but if the owner sells the property, the broker earns no commission.

This type of listing is somewhat better than the open listing in that only one broker is involved, but the broker is still competing with the owner. The broker's advertising programs, including "for sale" sign on the property, may generate prospects for the owner. Here, as with open listings, litigation may arise as to who was the "procuring cause" of the sale.

PUTTING IT TO WORK

If the owner already has commenced negotiations with a prospect, he or she may still grant an exclusive agency listing. The owner does not have to pay a commission if that prospect purchases the home. An alternative solution would be to list with an exclusive right-to-sell with a clause excluding by name only those persons with whom the owner is currently negotiating.

Exclusive Right-to-Sell Listing

An **exclusive right-to-sell listing** contract is recommended by the National Association of REALTORS®. Under this listing contract, the *property is listed with only one broker.* If anyone else sells the property during the term of the listing contract, the broker is legally entitled to the commission. The seller is legally obligated to pay the broker's commission if the broker or the seller or some third party effects a sale of the property during the term of the listing contract.

The exclusive right-to-sell listing contract benefits the owner because the broker is secure enough in the opportunity to earn a commission that he or she can afford to spend time and advertising dollars to effect a quick and satisfactory sale of the listed property. Also, with the seller's agreement, the broker may place the listing in a multiple listing service and thereby provide significantly increased market exposure for the property.

Listing Contract Provisions

A sample listing contract is shown in Figure 5.2. The sample is an express bilateral contract. Under most listings, the seller agrees to cooperate with the broker and to pay a commission if the listed property is sold, and the broker agrees to make his or her best efforts to procure a sale of the listed property. Specific provisions must be included to make the terms of the contract between the seller and the broker clear and unambiguous. Examples of the specific provisions are found in Figure 5.2.

FIGURE 5.2
A sample listing contract.

LISTING CONTRACT

This is a legally binding contract. If not understood, seek competent legal advice.

Date:____________________

In consideration of your listing for sale and undertaking to find a
purchaser for the real estate below described, the undersigned, hereinafter
called Owner, gives and grants to you, hereinafter called REALTOR®, the sole and
exclusive right, for a period of______________from this date expiring 12
1 midnight of__________________to sell the property described as deeded to
____________________________located at____________________________
for the sum of____________________________in cash or upon any other price,
terms or exchange to which the Owner may hereafter consent.

As a condition of this listing the property herein described ☐shall
2 ☐shall not be placed with others members of the__________Board of REALTORS®
through their Multiple Listing Service.

If said real estate is sold or exchanged during the term of this agreement,
or within 6 (six) months after the expiration thereof, to any person or firm with
whom, during the exclusive period of this listing, the REALTOR®, Owner, or other
person may have negotiations, for said price, and upon said terms, or for a price
3 and upon such terms as are acceptable to Owner, Owner agrees to pay REALTOR® a
commission equal to ______% of the gross sales or exchange price thereof. The
above extension clause shall be null and void, if said real estate is relisted
with another REALTOR® or licensed broker.

Said real estate shall be conveyed in the same condition as it now is, ordinary wear and tear excepted, to purchaser by general warranty deed: and in support of title purchaser shall be furnished at Owner's expense, either an Owner's policy of title insurance in the amount of the purchase price or a complete and merchantable abstract of title continued to date. Said policy or abstract to show respectively an insurable or merchantable title to said real estate in the name of the Owner, subject only to easements and restrictions of record, if any, and free and clear of all other liens and encumbrances, except as therein stated.

REALTOR® is hereby authorized to place a "For Sale" sign and a lock box on the real estate, to remove any other signs and to show the property at any reasonable time.

Owner represents that all improvements on the real estate are structurally
4 sound and that all heating, air conditioning, plumbing, electrical systems and
all appliances that are to be included in the sale of this real estate are now
in good or satisfactory operating condition and will be upon date of possession
by the Buyer, except:____

It is understood that REALTOR® is relying on all information pertaining to this Listing Contract provided by Owner. Owner hereby agrees that REALTOR® may disclose all information pertaining to this Listing Contract to any and all parties connected with this transaction. Owner hereby authorizes the lending institution to divulge any mortgage information required by the REALTOR®.

This property is offered for sale without regard to race, creed, color, sex or national origin, in accordance with all State and Federal laws.

Owner hereby states that he has read the property description herein, this listing contract and that the information given is true and accurate to the best of his knowledge and belief. Owner acknowledges receipt of a copy of this Listing Contract, and agrees that this contract is binding also upon his or their heirs, administrators, executors or assigns.

______________is hereby authorized to send referral information to a cooperating broker at the seller's destination location.

Listed by Sales Agent ____________________________

Accepted:

5 Owner (Signature)____________________ (Print)____________________

Owner (Signature)____________________ (Print)____________________

Res. Phone____________________ Off. Phone____________________

Owner's Address____

By (Authorized Broker)____

Section 1 of the sample sets forth the beginning date and expiration date of the listing contract. This section also gives an informal description and location of the listed property. Also found in this section are the listed price for sale and any specific terms upon which the seller will sell, such as contract for deed, assumption of existing mortgage, or cash only.

Section 2 of the sample describes the procedure for handling any earnest money deposits. It also contains an agreement to place the listing information in the multiple listing service. Finally this section gives a specific statement of the broker's responsibility to use "best efforts" to procure sale of the property, including advertising requirements.

Section 3 in the sample specifies the rate of commission that will be paid upon completion of the listing contract. This section also provides a **carryover clause**, or protection clause, stating that *the broker will be entitled to a commission if sale of the listed property occurs after expiration of the listing when sold to a buyer generated by the broker's efforts*.

Section 4 of the sample sets forth language requiring the broker and the seller to offer the listed property for sale in total compliance with all state and federal laws dealing with civil rights and illegal discrimination. A blank space is included for any miscellaneous provisions specific to this listing contract.

Section 5 of the sample has the signature lines for the owners of the listed property and the broker who has listed the property. If the property is owned by a married couple, both husband and wife must sign the listing. Even if the property is owned in severalty by a married person, both the husband and the wife should sign to avoid any dower, curtesy, or community property claims in states where these rights exist.

Data Sheet

As a part of the listing contract, the broker attaches a data sheet with detailed information on the specific property listed. A sample data sheet is found in Figure 5.3. The information contained on the data sheet is to be gathered from personal inspection and measurement by the broker, contacts with government offices to verify taxes, zoning, assessed value, age, lot size, type of ownership, and deed restrictions, as well as contacts with the seller's mortgage company to verify the existing loan terms. Information on the data sheet usually is included in all multiple listing information and, thus, all member brokers rely upon it. This is added reason for the reported information to be accurate.

In some states the listing broker also must complete a state disclosure form, provided to all prospective buyers. This form is to be signed by the seller, the broker, and the prospective buyer. The purpose of this form is to solicit disclosure from the seller of any possible defects on the property prior to sale.

FIGURE 5.3 A sample data sheet.

ADDRESS MLS # PRICE				Instructions to Show: Lockbox in use ☐
LOC. AREA SQ. FT. RM BR BA				House vacant ☐ Occupied ☐
L/O PH 372-2200		CO-OP BROKER		
AGNT PH		COMM.		
CONST	HEAT	SIZE	LVL	Smoke Detector Installed Yes ☐ No ☐
AGE/COND	COST	LR		Pest Control:
BSMT F ☐ U ☐	A/C C ☐ W ☐	DR		Attic Insulation: Attic Storage:
SLAB ☐ CRAWL ☐	WATER HEATER	KIT		Wood Stove ☐ Attic Fan ☐
POSS	WALLS	BRF		Washer ☐ H.U. ☐
LOT SZ	ROOF	FAM		Dryer ☐ H.U. ☐
MTG BAL	TV ANT. ☐ CABLE ☐	UTIL		Microwave ☐ Refrigerator ☐ 220 V Elec. ☐
INT RT	FIREPLACE	BA		All Window Coverings ☐
MTGEE	CITY WATER ☐ WELL ☐	BR		Curbs Sidewalks
SEMI-TAX	SEWER ☐ SEPTIC ☐	BR		Owner Financing:
ASSESS	PAVED ST ☐ DRIVE ☐	BR		
ZONING	GARAGE __ DR OPNR ☐	BR		
SCHOOL	PATIO ☐ PORCH ☐	CRPT WINCVR		
FLOOD HAZ	OVEN RNGE ☐ DISP ☐	SD ☐ SW ☐ T ☐		INFORMATION HEREIN IS CONSIDERED ACCURATE BUT IS NOT WARRANTED.
FENCE	KIT VENT ☐ DISHW ☐	WTR SOFTENER R ☐ O ☐		ALL MEASUREMENTS, TAXES, AND AGE ARE APPROXIMATE.

REMARKS ______________________________

Termination

Listing contracts terminate after expiration of the time period agreed to by the seller and the broker in the listing or sale of the property. They also terminate upon the death or incapacity of the seller, destruction of the listed property, condemnation of the listed property, bankruptcy of the seller, revocation of the broker's license, mutual agreement of the seller and the broker, or breach of the listing terms by either the seller or the broker.

PUTTING IT TO WORK

Termination should be handled on a case-by-case basis in situations of material change in the property, such as damage to the property, a zoning change, or discovery of minerals. The change may or may not terminate a listing. Obviously, some renegotiation or pricing changes should be considered.

Competitive Market Analysis

Part of the listing process involves recommending to the owner a market price that will be the listed price. This price should be determined by comparison of the listed property with other similar properties that have sold recently. No two properties are exactly alike; however, many are comparable or similar in quality, location, and utility. In comparing the listed property and the selected comparables, allowances are made for differences in things such as lot size, age, number of rooms, square footage, and so on.

A minimum of three comparables is desirable. Comparables should be as similar as possible in all respects to the listed property. Comparables are found in office real estate files, in county assessor files, in MLS closed sales data, and from appraisers. The more recent the date of sale of the comparable, the more valuable the comparable is to the analysis. Also of great importance is the extent of similarity of physical characteristics of the comparable and location of the comparable in relation to the listed property. A sample of a competitive market analysis is found in Figure 5.4.

PUTTING IT TO WORK

In addition to knowing what has sold recently, the seller should be shown what is currently available. Knowing the competition may influence pricing and marketing strategies.

SALES CONTRACTS AND PRACTICES

Offer to Purchase

The parties to an accepted offer to purchase are the buyer and the seller, also called offeror and offeree, respectively. Other names for the accepted offer to purchase are *purchase agreement, sales contract*, and *contingent proposition*. This contract is the road map for the real estate transaction. The contract relationship between the parties

FIGURE 5.4 Competitive market analysis of a subject property and three comparables.

COMPETITIVE MARKET ANALYSIS

Prepared Especially for:
John and Susan Mitchell

Prepared by:
Grace Sanford,
Levittown Real Estate

Date:
January 9, 1996

Medium Range Adj ADDRESS PROXIMITY	SUBJECT 2735 Hawthorne Carriage Estates	COMPARABLE 1 of 3 2815 Hemingway Carriage Estates		COMPARABLE 2 of 3 3270 Melville Heath Heights		COMPARABLE 3 of 3 4520 Thoreau Ct. Foxpointe	
Style	Ranch/Rambler	Ranch/Rambler		Ranch/Rambler		Ranch/Rambler	
Construction	Fr Stucco	Ced Stone	0	Brick	0	Brick	0
Date Sold		June 1996	238	Apr 1996	856	Apr 1996	907
Effective Age	12	12	0	14	1,000	11	(500)
Sq Ft Total	1,544	1,442		1,654		1,608	
Sq Ft Main	1,544	1,442	2,040	1,654	(2,200)	1,608	(1,280)
Sq Ft Up	0	0	0	0	0	0	0
Sq Ft Down	0	0	0	0	0	0	0
Pct Down Finished	0	0		0		0	
Acreage/Lot Size	120 x 80	120 x 85		125 x 80		115 x 97	
Value of Lot	$4,500	$4,500	0	$4,500	0	$4,500	0
Price/Sq Ft Inc Lot	$60 (Adj Avg)	$66		$56		$57	
Price/Sq Ft Exc Lot	$57 (Adj Avg)	$62		$54		$54	
Bedrooms Total	3	3	0	3	0	3	0
Bedrooms Main	3	3		3		3	
Bedrooms Up	0	0		0		0	
Bedrooms Down	0	0		0		0	
Bathrooms Total	2.0	2.0	0	2.5	(1,000)	2.0	0
Baths Main	2.0	2.0		2.5		2.0	
Baths Up	0.0	0.0		0.0		0.0	
Baths Down	0.0	0.0		0.0		0.0	
Fireplaces	1	1	0	1	0	1	0
Air Conditioning	Central	Central	0	Central	0	Central	0
Garage	2.0	2.0	0	2.0	0	2.0	0
Swimming Pool	0	0	0	0	0	0	0
Semiannual Tax	$852.16	$697.12	0	$691.04	0	$820.51	0
Assessment	22360	21400	0	22060	0	25530	0
Fenced Yard	Privacy		0	Privacy	0	Privacy	0
Double Storage Bldg			0		0		0
Fruit Trees			0		0		0
Listed Price		$94,500	Adjustment	$96,000	Adjustment	$93,500	Adjustment
Sales Price		$94,500	$2,278	$93,000	($1,344)	$92,000	($873)
ADJ SALES PRICE		$96,778		$91,656		$91,127	

Comp 1: 35% × $96,778 = $33,872
Comp 2: 25% × $91,656 = $22,914
Comp 3: 40% × $91,127 = $36,451

Reconciled Price: $33,872 + $22,914 + $36,451 = $93,237

is described as "arms length." The parties are not in an agency relationship. The parties are assumed to have equal bargaining power and equal ability from opposing viewpoints.

The purchase contract is a bilateral express contract. The buyer promises to buy the property if certain terms and conditions are met; the seller promises to convey marketable title to the property as prescribed by the offer to purchase. The consideration given consists of the promises made by the parties. Although most offers to purchase are accompanied by earnest money, earnest money is not legally required for a valid offer to purchase. **Earnest money** *is given (a) to show sincerity of the buyer; (b) to demonstrate his or her financial capability to raise the money called for in the agreement; and (c) to serve as possible liquidated damages to the seller in the event of default by the buyer.*

All terms and conditions of sale of the property are contained in this sales contract. They include sales price, type of financing, interest rate if a mortgage is to be obtained or if seller financing is to be used, inspections required, proration of taxes and insurance, listing of personal property to be included in the purchase, designated party with risk of loss from fire, flood, and other causes, time periods for possession and transfer of title, type of deed to be used, type of title acceptable to buyer, amount of earnest money, liquidated damages upon breach, and period of time for acceptance or rejection.

PUTTING IT TO WORK

Many brokerages use prepared addenda to cover supplemental issues of the agreement. Some examples are personal property lists, homeowner's warranties, presale or postsale rental agreements, and contingency clauses.

If the offer to purchase is written clearly and concisely, the parties should be able to close the deal without controversy. Conversely, if the offer to purchase is unclear or ambiguous, the road to closing will be difficult.

In accordance with the Statute of Frauds, the offer to purchase is required to be in writing. It is not a contract until the seller unconditionally accepts it. Unlike the listing contract, an accepted offer-to-purchase contract does obligate the seller to sell his or her property or face litigation for specific performance. The accepted offer to purchase is binding on the heirs and estates of the buyer and the seller. Upon the seller's acceptance of the offer to purchase, the buyer has equitable title in the real estate, which is an interest such that a court will take notice and protect the rights of the owner of the equitable title.

Because most purchase contracts contain specific deadlines to be met, parties to the contract or agents of the parties must keep close track of the calendar. If it appears a deadline is not going to be met, to keep the contract in force, all parties to the contract must agree to any extension and initial the extension as written on the purchase contract. Failure to meet all of the conditions in the purchase contract excuses the buyer and the seller from the obligations of the contract. If failure to meet all of the conditions in the purchase contract was outside the seller's control and not caused by the seller, the seller will be excused from payment of a commission per the listing contract.

Discharge or termination of offer to purchase occurs when all terms and conditions are met and the seller conveys title to the buyer. Discharge or termination also occurs when all of the terms and conditions are not met or when the deadlines set out in the offer to purchase expire with no extension acknowledged by the parties. Termination occurs, too, when the property is condemned under right of eminent domain; when the property is destroyed by fire, flood, or other natural disaster; or when insanity or incapacity of either party occurs.

A sample offer to purchase is found in Figure 5.5. The specific provisions are outlined below.

Section 1 gives the names of the real estate brokers, the address and legal description of the property, the offered purchase price, and amount of earnest money.

Section 2 specifies the terms for financing that must be met to complete the offer to purchase, such as cash sale, assumption of present mortgage, contract sale, or new mortgage.

Section 3 designates the possession date and liquidated damages to be paid by seller for failure to give possession.

Section 4 states how any rents and security deposits will be handled and when purchaser is to begin paying real property taxes.

Section 5 provides for title evidence requirements; closing date; and that seller is liable for risk of loss to the property due to fire, flood, etc., until date of closing.

Section 6 lists the personal property, if any, included in the offer.

Section 7 sets forth disclaimer language relieving the broker from the guarantees of an inspector. This section also states what inspections will be required prior to closing.

Section 8 provides the agreement on disbursement of earnest money in the event of default by either buyer or seller. This section also contains language stating clearly that both brokers work for the seller. This language should be stricken if the selling broker has signed a contract with the buyer to represent the buyer solely or is acting as a dual agent.

Section 9 gives any miscellaneous provisions of the agreement specific to this contract.

Section 10 provides for the signature(s) of the buyer(s) and the time given seller(s) to accept the offer.

Section 11 provides for the signature(s) of the seller(s) evidencing acceptance of the offer, counteroffer, or rejection of the offer.

Land Contract/Contract for Deed

A **land contract** is also called a **contract for deed**, an **installment land contract**, an agreement of sale, or a **conditional sales contract**. The essence of this contract is that the *buyer is contracting to obtain legal title to the property by paying the purchase price in installments, and the seller is agreeing to transfer the legal title to the buyer by the delivering of a deed upon buyer's full payment of the purchase price*. The seller, rather than a mortgage company, is "loaning" the purchase price to the buyer. Under the land contract, the seller will usually receive an agreed-upon down payment and monthly payments from the buyer. The seller is deferring receipt of full payment of the purchase price from the buyer over the term of the contract. Figure 5.6 is a sample contract for deed.

The parties to a contract for deed are the vendor and the vendee. Under this contract the vendor is the seller and the vendee is the buyer. A contract for deed is an express bilateral executory contract. The vendor promises to give possession to the vendee during the contract, accept payments toward the purchase price, and convey marketable title to the vendee upon payment of the full purchase price. The vendee promises to make the agreed-upon payments, pay taxes, obtain insurance on the property, and maintain the property in good condition during the term of the contract. The vendor's security for payment of the purchase price is retention of legal title until all payments are made. Upon execution of the contract for deed, the vendee has equitable title in the real estate.

In accordance with the Statute of Frauds, a contract for deed must be in writing to be enforceable. The contract for deed also must include the legal description of the property sold. A contract for deed is recorded in the locality where the real estate is

FIGURE 5.5 A sample offer to purchase, also called a purchase agreement.

This is a legally binding contract. If not understood, seek competent legal advice.

PURCHASE AGREEMENT

Selling Broker ______________________ By ______________________

Listing Broker ______________________ By ______________________

Any and all written offers to purchase or authorization to purchase shall be communicated to the Seller for his formal acceptance or rejection immediately upon receipt of such offer. (Per Indiana Real Estate Commission Rule #24)

The undersigned, hereinafter called "Purchaser", hereby agrees to purchase from the owner, hereinafter called the "Seller", through you as Realtor, the real estate known as ______________________ St., in the City (or Town) of ____________, County of ____________, State of Indiana, the legal description of which is: ______________________

and to pay as the purchase price therefor the sum of ______________________ Dollars ($ ____________) payable as follows: ______________________ Dollars ($ ____________) as earnest money deposited with the broker herewith, which shall be applied on the purchase price at the closing of this transaction, and the balance of the purchase price shall be payable in accordance with Paragraph ________ as hereinafter set forth:

PARAGRAPH 1 (SALE BY DEED) The balance of the purchase price shall be paid in cash upon delivery of warranty deed.

PARAGRAPH 2 (SALE BY DEED ASSUMPTION OF MORTGAGE) A down payment of ______________________ Dollars ($ ____________), of which the earnest money is a part, subject to a mortgage now of record in the unpaid amount as of ____________, 19____ of ______________________ Dollars ($ ____________), interest at ______% ☐ fixed ☐ variable monthly payments of $ ____________, including principal and interest ____________, which the Purchaser agrees to assume and pay. Purchaser agrees to pay any points or fees charged by Mortgagee in connection with the assumption of mortgage.

PARAGRAPH 3 (CONTRACT SALE) ______________________ Dollars ($ ____________), down upon the delivery of a properly executed form of real estate contract embodying the terms contained herein; and the balance of the purchase price at the rate of $ ____________ per month including interest at the rate of ______% per annum, computed monthly on balances remaining unpaid. The contract is to be for ______ years and amortized over ______ years. The first of said monthly payments shall be made within 30 days following the closing of this transaction and succeeding payments shall be made on the same day of each month thereafter. Taxes and insurance are to be paid by Purchaser separately when due. The contract shall include a ______ day default clause and provide for Seller's attorneys fees. 1

FINANCING —This Offer is subject to the Purchaser(s) obtaining a $ ____________ financing commitment within ______ days from date of acceptance hereof, at a ______% ☐ fixed ☐ variable interest rate and ______ points for a ______ year term. Purchaser shall use due diligence in applying for such commitment. 2

POSSESSION — Purchaser shall have (complete) (landlord) possession on or before ____________. Failure of Seller to deliver possession within this time limit shall not make Seller a tenant of Purchaser, but in such event Seller shall pay Purchaser $ ____________ per day as liquidated damages for breach of contract and not as rent. This provision shall not prevent Purchaser from pursuing any other legal or equitable remedy available under the law. 3

INTEREST– RENTS – DUES – SECURITY AND/OR DAMAGE DEPOSITS – Interest on encumbrances assumed by the Purchaser shall be prorated to date of closing the transaction. Rents, if any, shall be prorated to date of closing the transaction. Security and/or damage deposits, if any, shall be transferred to Purchaser at time of closing the transaction. Any mandatory lot owner assessments shall be prorated to day of closing. 4

FLOOD INSURANCE – If it is determined that this real estate is located in a flood hazard area, and if flood insurance is required by the lender, then Purchaser hereby agrees to provide such required insurance.

TAXES – Purchaser will assume and agree to pay all installments of taxes on said real estate beginning with the installment due and payable in ____________, 19______, and all installments subsequent thereto. Seller shall pay all prior taxes and penalties.

Seller shall be charged with and shall pay all assessments or charges upon or applying to the real estate for public or municipal improvements or services which on the date of acceptance of this Offer are constructed or installed on or about the real estate or are serving the real estate.

TITLE EVIDENCE – Purchaser shall be furnished at Seller's expense, ☐ a complete abstract of title **OR** ☐ an owners' title insurance continued to date as quickly as the same can be prepared, said abstract or title insurance to show a merchantable title to said real estate in the name of the Seller who will execute and deliver a general warranty deed (or contract of sale if so specified herein) conveying said real estate (or in case of a contract of sale, agreeing to convey) in the same condition as it now is, ordinary wear and tear excepted, free and clear of all liens and encumbrances except as stated herein and subject to easements or restrictions of record, if any. Should additional time be required for making or continuing such abstract, or for correcting defects of title, reasonable extension of time shall be given. 5

CLOSING DATE –This transaction is to be closed on or before ____________ after said abstract showing merchantable title or binder for owners' title insurance is delivered to Purchaser or the Purchaser's lending institution.

LOSS OR DAMAGE – All risk of loss or damage to improvements on said real estate shall be borne by Seller until delivery of deed or execution of Real Estate Contract. If all or a substantial portion of said buildings are destroyed or damaged prior to the delivery of deed or execution of Real Estate Contract, this Purchase Agreement, at the option of the Purchaser may be terminated, and in such event the earnest money deposit shall be returned to Purchaser without delay. Current insurance may be cancelled by Seller upon date of closing. If required Purchaser(s) shall show proof of insurance.

(continued)

FIGURE 5.5 Continued.

6 **IMPROVEMENTS AND FIXTURES**—The above sales price includes all improvements permanently installed and affixed, such as, but not limited to, electrical and/or gas fixtures, heating equipment and all attachments thereto, central air conditioning, built-in kitchen equipment, hot water heaters, water softener (if not leased), gas grills, incinerators, window shades, curtain rods, drapery poles, and fixtures, storm doors, storm windows, screens, awnings, TV antennas & rotor, permanently installed carpeting, all landscaping, mailbox, garage door opener(s) with control(s) and the following: ______________________________

____

____

which belong to the above property and are now in the premises. All said items will be fully paid for by Sellers at time of closing the transaction.

7 **CONDITION OF PROPERTY**—Purchaser and Seller acknowledge that they have been advised that the Realtor(s) is not a professional building inspector and that the Realtor(s) has not made any warranties or guarantees (implied or otherwise) as to the condition or functioning of the real estate or its improvements. Purchaser and Seller further acknowledge that they have been advised by the Realtor(s) to seek professional, independent inspection(s) of the condition of the real estate and its improvements and that the findings of such inspections are not warranted or guaranteed by the Realtor(s). If inspections are requested, such inspections are to be completed within _____ working days after ☐ this offer is accepted OR ☐ after the date of loan approval. Purchaser shall report results of inspection to Seller or Seller's agent in writing within 5 days after inspection, but no later than 5 days prior to closing. This offer is further subject to the following inspection at Purchaser's expense: ______________________________

____

____

If above said inspections reveal that repairs are necessary, Seller agrees to pay for repairs exceeding ____________ cumulative, but not greater than ____________.

Yes ☐ **No** ☐ This offer is subject to an inspection for wood destroying insects at the Purchaser's expense. If found, treatment is to be by a licensed pest control operator at Seller's expense. If structural damage is found, the Purchaser shall have the option to void this contract.

Yes ☐ **No** ☐ This offer is subject to an inspection of well water and septic system by a member of the Health Department at the Purchaser's expense. If a satisfactory test does not result, it is to be corrected to the satisfaction of the Health Department at the Seller's expense. If repairs are not made by Seller, then Purchaser may terminate this purchase agreement and recover his earnest money.

8 The said earnest money deposit above mentioned shall be returned in full to Purchaser promptly in event this proposition is not accepted. In the event this proposition is accepted, and Purchaser shall, without legal cause, fail or refuse to complete the purchase of said real estate in accordance with the terms and conditions hereof, said earnest money deposit shall be forfeited by Purchaser as liquidated damages and shall be retained one-half (½) by the Seller, one-fourth (¼) by the Listing Broker, and one-fourth (¼) by the Selling Broker. Seller may pursue any other legal remedy available to Seller under the law.

It is expressly agreed that all terms and conditions of this contract are included herein, and no verbal agreements of any kind shall be binding upon the parties, and this contract shall be binding upon the parties hereto, their heirs, administrators, executors, successors and assigns.

AGENCY DISCLOSURE— Seller and Buyer hereby acknowledge that, unless otherwise agreed in writing hereon, the selling broker, including a listing broker selling his/her own listing; is exclusively the agent of the seller, and not the agent of the buyer; however, the selling broker is under a duty to treat all parties in the transaction fairly.

9 **FURTHER CONDITIONS**— ______________________________

____

____

____

____

SEE ATTACHED ADDENDUM(S) Yes ☐ No ☐

The Realtor hereby acknowledges receipt of earnest money in the amount of $ ____________ cash ☐ or check ☐

10

REAL ESTATE OFFICE	PURCHASER (Signature)	DATE
	PURCHASER (Print)	S.S.# ____________
REALTOR	PURCHASER (Signature)	DATE
Time ________ Date ________	PURCHASER (Print)	S.S.# ____________

EXPIRATION AND APPROVAL—This Offer to Purchase is void if not accepted in writing on or before ____________ o'clock (A.M.) (P.M.) (Noon) (Midnight) of the ____________ day of ____________, 19 _____.

11 **ACCEPTANCE BY SELLER**—As the Owner and Seller of the property described herein ____________ hereby accept the foregoing Offer to Purchase this ____________ day of ____________, 19 _____, and agree to sell in accordance therewith and to pay to ____________ Company (licensed broker) the sum of ____________ Dollars ($ ____________) commission for services rendered in this transaction.

SEE COUNTER OFFER ADDENDUM(S) Yes ☐ No ☐ **ACCEPTED PER ATTACHED ADDENDUM(S)** Yes ☐ No ☐

SELLER	SELLER
S.S.# ____________	S.S.# ____________
	Time ________ Date ________

REJECTION CLAUSE—As the Owner and Seller of the property described herein ____________ hereby reject the foregoing Offer to Purchase this ____________ day of ____________, 19 _____.

SELLER	SELLER
	Time ________ Date ________

FIGURE 5.6 A sample contract for deed, also called a land contract.

CONTRACT FOR DEED

This agreement by and between_______________________________, of_______________County, Indiana herein called the Sellers and_______________________________ _______________of_______________County, Indiana, herein called the buyers.

WITNESSETH THAT:

The Sellers agree to sell and the Buyers agree to buy for a price and upon terms and conditions herein set out the real estate in_______________County, Indiana, described as follows:

Lot Numbered Sixty-four (64) in Wehmeier's First Addition to the Town of Bethel Village, in the Northwest Quarter of Section Twelve (12), Township Eight (8) North of Range Five (5) East, as recorded in Plat Book "E," page 5 in the Office of the Recorder of Bartholomew County, State of Indiana. Situated in Wayne Township.

1. PURCHASE PRICE. The Buyers agree to pay to the Sellers as the purchase price therefore the sum of_______________________and_________/100 dollars ($______) payable as follows:

a. ____________________/100 dollars ($_______) as down payment receipt of which is acknowledged by execution herein.

b. _______________(____) monthly payments of _______________dollars ($_____) with the first payment due ______________________.

c. The unpaid balance shall accrue interest of _______% per annum.

d. Any payment that is made after the ____ of any month shall accrue a late penalty of $______.

e. Buyers shall have the right at any time to prepay this contract without penalty or discount.

2. CONVEYANCE. Upon payment of the purchase price in full as herein set out Sellers agree to convey the real estate to the Buyers by proper general warranty deed free of all liens except taxes as herein set out. Any abstract update or title insurance shall be the Sellers' expense. Deed preparation costs shall also be paid by Sellers. Title insurance, if used, shall be in an amount not less than the full purchase price.

3. TAXES AND INSURANCE. The sale is subject to fall taxes on the real estate for the year 19__, due and payable in __________, 19__ and all subsequent taxes and assessments, which taxes and assessments the Buyers assume. The Buyers agree to keep the improvements, if any, on the real estate insured against loss by fire and extended coverage in the amount not less than the unpaid balance under this contract for the benefits of the Sellers and Buyers as their interest may appear. Said insurance shall begin from the execution of this contract. Buyers to provide proof of insurance upon closing and thereafter upon reasonable request from Sellers. It is acknowledged that the insurance provided by Buyers shall show the Sellers as the insureds but that any insurance proceeds paid under the policy shall be for payment of the contract balance therein. In the event the insurance proceeds exceed the unpaid balance of the contract, all excess shall belong to Buyers.

4. POSSESSION. The Buyers shall be entitled to possession of the real estate during the terms of this contract but they shall not commit waste or damage thereto. It is understood by Buyers and Sellers that the Buyers shall hold Sellers harmless from any and all liabilities of damages occasioned by Buyers' use, occupancy, and possession of tract. It is further understood that the real estate and improvements, if any, are being purchased "as is."

5. IMPROVEMENTS. The Sellers shall have the right upon reasonable notice to enter upon and in said tract for the purpose of inspecting the same, and shall have a representative of the Buyers with them. The Buyers may make improvements only with the written consent of the Sellers. This provision shall apply both to present improvements and improvements that may be placed thereon by Buyers. In the process of making any changes to real estate the Buyers shall do no act that will allow the taking or claiming of a mechanic's lien against the real estate. However, should notice of the taking or claiming of the mechanic's lien be filed against the real estate the Buyers agree to promptly discharge same.

6. DEFAULT. Upon failure by the Buyers to pay any installments of purchase price or interest when due or upon failure to pay taxes as agreed or to keep the premises insured or any other breach of this contract and such default continues for a period of _______ (____) days the Sellers may, upon giving the ten (10) day written notice to the Buyers, treat this agreement as void and be entitled to immediate possession of the real estate. In such event Sellers shall have all rights entitled under Indiana Law. In addition Buyers shall be liable for Sellers' reasonable attorney fees.

The failure or forbearance on the part of said Sellers for any length of time to declare this contract forfeited upon any of the contingencies or conditions herein provided for shall not be deemed a waiver by said Sellers to terminate said contract as herein provided for or to bring suit for foreclosure or quiet title. If the default is failure to pay the monthly payments, taxes or insurance premium, Sellers have the right to pay any sum in default and add the amount paid to the unpaid balance under this contract. Any sum so paid shall draw the same interest as the unpaid balance.

7. ASSIGNMENT OF CONTRACT; RENT. Buyers will have no right to sell premises on contract or to assign their rights in this contract in the premises without consent of the Sellers. Buyers shall have the right to lease or rent the premises without consent of Sellers.

8. MORTGAGE. It is acknowledged by the parties that Sellers have an outstanding mortgage at ____________________________ dated __________ in the original amount of $________. If the financial institution declines to waive in writing the due on sale clause contained in the mortgage and a foreclosure ensues, the parties agree to renegotiate the terms of this sale. The parties agree to proceed with this contract knowing these facts. Sellers agree to provide Buyers copies of any notice received from the date of execution which affects Buyers' ownership interest.

10. NOTICES. Any written notices that need to be given to the Buyers or Sellers may be given at the following addresses:

SELLERS: _________________________ _________________________

BUYERS: _________________________ _________________________

This contract and the rights and obligations established herein are binding and inure to the benefit to the assigneds, heirs, executors and successors in interest to the parties hereto. In the event either party files suit for enforcement of this contract, the party found to be in default shall pay full court costs and reasonable attorney fees of the prevailing party.

Witness the signatures and seals of the parties this _____ day of_______________, 19__.

SELLERS: _________________________ _________________________

BUYERS: _________________________ _________________________

STATE OF INDIANA)
COUNTY OF ___________)

Before me, a Notary Public in and for said county and State, personally appeared ___ _______________________________________ who acknowledged the execution of the foregoing Contract for Sale of Real Estate and who, having been duly sworn, stated that any representations herein contained are true.

Witness my hand and Notarial Seal this _____ day of _____________, 19___.

My Commission Expires_______________

Signature ______________________________
Printed: ______________________________
Resident of ______________________________
County ______________________________

THIS INSTRUMENT PREPARED BY ______________________
ATTORNEY AT LAW.

situated. This provides constructive notice to the world of the vendee's equitable title and vendor's legal title and right to payment from vendee.

A contract for deed is binding on the heirs and estates of the parties. It is discharged by payment in full by the vendee with conveyance of the title by deed from the vendor. It also may be discharged by suit for breach of contract by the parties or mutually agreed release of the contract.

This type of contract originally was used to purchase relatively inexpensive pieces of land, but it can be used for any type of property. It has major advantages to the buyer, particularly in times of tight credit (high interest rates) markets or when the buyer does not qualify for conventional loans. In these cases, the seller may be willing to provide the financing, especially because this form of contract puts the seller in a strong position.

Most mortgage documents today contain a "due on sale" clause, specifying that the entire principal balance due on the mortgage must be paid in full if a sale of the property is to take place. A contract for deed must never be used to circumvent these loan assumption clauses. The lending institution holding the mortgage may declare the execution of a contract for deed to be a sale of the property and thereby require the seller to pay off the mortgage.

Consultation with legal counsel prior to creating the contract for deed is advised for the protection of all parties.

Options

An **option** is *a contract wherein an optionor (owner) sells a right to purchase the property to a prospective buyer, called an optionee, at a particular price and terms for a specified time period.* An option is an express unilateral contract. Only one party to the option contract makes a promise. The optionor promises to allow the optionee the sole right to purchase the real estate during the specified time. The optionee pays for this right but makes no promise to purchase the real estate. The optionee is merely "buying time" to decide or arrange financing. The money the optionee pays to the optionor for the option right may or may not apply to the purchase price of the property. The parties to the option will negotiate this matter.

Putting It to Work

Many times an option to purchase is a viable alternative when a buyer is serious but does not have the required down payment or cannot qualify for a loan. After renting for a certain amount of time, the buyer will have accumulated the down payment, or the financing situation may have changed, or both, allowing the transaction to be completed to the satisfaction of buyer and seller.

In accordance with the Statute of Frauds, options to purchase must be in writing to be enforceable. Options to purchase are binding on the heirs and estates of the parties. All owners of the real estate must sign the option.

If the optionee desires to complete the purchase, he or she exercises the option right. At this point, the option becomes a purchase agreement as in any other real estate transaction. Because an option can become a purchase agreement between the parties, the original option should be specific as to type of title to be conveyed, terms of financing if other than cash, and any other provisions typically contained in an offer to purchase. These issues should not be left to be addressed at the time of exercise.

Options to purchase are discharged by expiration of the time period agreed upon in the option or by exercise of the option by the optionee.

A sample option is found in Figure 5.7. The various sections of this document are outlined here.

Section 1 gives the names of the optionor and the optionee and the price paid for the option.

Section 2 sets forth the legal description of the property that is the subject of the option.

Section 3 states the length of the option, the price to be paid for the property upon exercise of the option, and the method of payment of the purchase price at exercise of the option.

Section 4 sets forth the procedure to exercise the option.

Section 5 specifies the settlement date, type of title to be conveyed upon exercise of the option, and the date for transfer of title and possession.

Section 6 provides for the signature(s) of the optionor(s).

Section 7 sets forth the language to exercise an option.

PUTTING IT TO WORK

An option is often tied to a lease. If this is the case, additional issues must be addressed. For example, does any of the rent apply toward the purchase price? Who bears the expense of repairs? If the tenant breaches the lease, how does that affect the option?

RIGHT OF FIRST REFUSAL

A **right of first refusal** is another type of unilateral contract whereby the *property owner agrees to give an individual the first right to refuse the property if and when it is offered.* This contract (see Figure 5.8) is very different from the option to purchase, in that the owner does not promise to sell the property to the individual, nor is a price established for sale. The owner merely promises to give the individual first chance to purchase the property at whatever price and terms anyone else offers for the property, if it is sold.

This is an express unilateral contract. To be enforceable under the Statute of Frauds, it must be in writing. It will be binding on the heirs and estate of the owner of the real estate. The right of first refusal is discharged upon sale of the property to the named individual or upon the named individual's refusal to purchase the property when offered for sale.

This type of contract is often found in real estate transactions when a family member has gifted property or sold property to another family member. In an effort to control ownership of the property, the right of first purchase is given to the original owner.

FIGURE 5.7 A sample option to purchase.

OPTION TO PURCHASE

This option to purchase is granted this ________________ day
of ________________, 19cy, by ______________________________
1 ____________, hereinafter called Optionor to ______________
________________, hereinafter called Optionee. Optionor for
consideration of ______________________________ paid by Optionee
grants to Optionee the exclusive right to purchase the real property
described as follows:

Northwest 1/4, of Northwest 1/4, of Section 10, Township 2
2 North, Range 3 East of the Michigan Meridian, Home County,
State of Homestate.

This option shall be binding upon the Optionor from the date
until noon ________________, 19cy. The option purchase price of
3 the above described property shall be ____________________, paid
as follows:

____

____

This option shall be exercised by written notice to the
4 Optionor and signed by the Optionee within the time limit set forth
above. Should the Optionee not exercise this option within the time
limit, the consideration for the option in the amount of _________
_______________ will be retained by Optionor.

Should Optionee exercise this option as provided, final
settlement is to be made on or before ____________________, 19cy.
Optionor to convey a marketable title free from encumbrances except
5 restrictive covenants, recorded easements, zoning regulation, and ad
valorem taxes which are to be prorated as of the date of closing.
Possession of the property to be given Optionor on date of final
settlement.

Additional conditions: ______________________________________

____

6 This contract contains the entire agreement between the
parties.

OPTIONOR: ______________________ ______________________

OPTIONEE: ______________________ ______________________

Exercise of Option to Purchase

To: ____

This is to notify you that pursuant to the option executed by
us on the _________ day of ___________, 19cy, we hereby elect to
7 exercise said option to purchase the real property described therein
in accordance with the terms and conditions agreed upon.

OPTIONEE:

____

____

I, ______________________________
______________, owner of real estate described as

hereby grant to ______________________________ the first right to purchase the above described property at the price offered by any other buyer. ______________ ______________ shall have ________ hours to match the price offered by any other buyer with no contingencies or conditions.

This right of first refusal will terminate ______ ______________.

Date:

Owner ______________ Owner ______________

Figure 5.8 A sample right of first refusal.

Important Points

1. A contract is an agreement between competent parties, upon legal consideration, to do or abstain from doing some legal act.
2. An express contract is spoken or written. An implied contract is one inferred from the actions of the parties.
3. Bilateral contracts are based on mutual promises. Unilateral contracts are based on a promise by one party and an act by another party.
4. An executed contract has been fully performed. An executory contract has provisions yet to be performed.
5. A contract is created by the unconditional acceptance of a valid offer. Acceptance of bilateral offers must be communicated. Communication of the acceptance of unilateral offers results from the performance of an act by the promisee.
6. Contracts that have an illegal purpose or are missing an element are void.
7. A voidable contract is one that may not be enforceable at the option of one of the parties to the contract.
8. The requirements for contract validity are (a) competent parties, (b) reality of consent, (c) offer and acceptance, (d) consideration, (e) legality of object, and (f) possibility to complete.
9. An offer must not be indefinite or illusory.
10. An offeror may revoke an offer at any time prior to knowledge of acceptance.
11. Consideration is anything of value, including a promise.
12. Reality of consent is defeated and a contract made voidable by (a) misrepresentation, (b) fraud, (c) undue influence, (d) duress, or (e) mutual mistake.
13. Contracts are assignable in the absence of a specific prohibition against assignment in the contract.
14. The remedies for breach of contract are (a) compensatory damages, (b) liquidated damages, (c) specific performance, and (d) rescission.
15. If a contracting party defaults in the performance of contractual obligations, the injured party may sue for damages in a suit for breach of contract. If the contract is for the purchase and sale of real property, an alternative remedy in the form of a lawsuit for specific performance is available to the injured party.
16. A listing contract is one in which a property owner employs a broker to find a buyer for his or her property. The contract creates an agency relationship wherein the seller is the principal and the broker is the special agent of the seller.

17. A contract for deed is also called an installment land contract, a conditional sales contract, or a land contract. It is a contract of sale and a method of financing by the seller for the buyer. Legal title does not pass until the buyer pays all or some specified part of the purchase price. The contract buyer holds equitable title until transfer of legal title.
18. An option provides a right to purchase property under specified terms and conditions. During the option term, the contract is binding on the optionor but not the optionee (and thus is unilateral). When an option is exercised, it becomes a contract of sale and is, therefore, binding on both parties (bilateral).

How Would You Respond?

1. Real estate to be listed for sale is owned by Fast Express, Inc. Who must sign that listing? Explain your answer.
2. Green made an offer on property owned by Smith. Green gave Smith 72 hours to consider the offer. Within three hours of making the offer, Green found another property he likes better than the Smith property. Can Green revoke his offer? Why or why not?

   If Green does revoke the offer, can Smith sue Green for revoking it? Why or why not?

Review Questions

Answers to these questions are found in the *Answer Key* section at the back of the book.

1. A contract in which mutual promises are exchanged at the time of signing (execution) is termed:
   a. multilateral
   b. unilateral
   c. bilateral
   d. promissory
2. Termination of contract by mutual agreement of the parties is called:
   a. partition
   b. patent
   c. rescission
   d. reintermediation

3. For contracts in general, all are essential elements EXCEPT:
   a. competent parties
   b. offer and acceptance
   c. legality of object
   d. writing
4. All of the following statements about contracts are true EXCEPT:
   a. a contract may be an agreement to do a certain thing
   b. contracts may arise out of implication
   c. a contract may be an agreement not to do a certain thing
   d. all contracts must be based upon an express agreement
5. Brown listed his home for sale with Ace Realty for six months. During the listing period, several people viewed the home and made offers of less than the listing price. Brown rejected all offers. Two days before the listing was to expire, another offer was made for 95 percent of the listing price. An agent for Ace Realty bluntly told Brown that if the offer was not accepted, Ace Realty would sue for their commission. Brown, fearing suit, accepted the offer. Brown was a victim of:
   a. duress
   b. mistake
   c. misrepresentation
   d. illusory tactics

6. An otherwise valid contract that cannot be enforced by legal action because of lack of compliance with the Statute of Frauds is:
   a. voidable by either party
   b. void on its face
   c. voidable by the offeree
   d. unenforceable

7. A contract to sell real property may be terminated by all of the following EXCEPT:
   a. complete performance
   b. death
   c. mutual assent
   d. breach of contract

8. Which of the following has the effect of terminating contracts?
   a. consideration
   b. bankruptcy
   c. exercise
   d. assignment

9. Upon the receipt of a buyer's offer, the seller accepts all of the terms of the offer except the amount of earnest money; the seller then agrees to accept an amount 50% higher than the buyer had offered. This fact is promptly communicated to the offeree by the real estate agent. Which of the following most accurately describes these events?
   a. the communication created a bilateral contract
   b. the seller accepted the buyer's offer
   c. the seller conditionally rejected the buyer's offer
   d. the seller rejected the buyer's offer and made a counteroffer to the buyer

10. Brown has listed his house for sale for $90,000. Cox makes a written offer of $86,500, which Brown accepts. Under the terms of this agreement:
    a. Brown was the offeror
    b. Cox was the offeree
    c. there was a meeting of the minds
    d. a unilateral contract was created

11. A contract between an adult and a minor is usually:
    a. voidable by either party
    b. voidable by the minor
    c. voidable by the adult
    d. void on its face

12. An owner employs a broker to market the owner's property and agrees to pay the broker a percentage of the sales price if the property is sold by anyone during the specified time period of the broker's employment. This agreement is which of the following?
    a. exclusive right-to-sell listing
    b. net listing
    c. exclusive agency listing
    d. open listing

13. Deliberate misrepresentation of a material fact, made with the intent that the other party act upon it to his or her detriment, is:
    a. misrepresentation
    b. undue influence
    c. fraud
    d. duress

14. The clause in the listing contract that protects the broker's commission entitlement beyond the listing period in the event of a sale by the owner to a prospect who was in fact introduced to the property by the broker or another agent of her listing firm is called:
    a. forfeiture clause
    b. carryover clause
    c. settlement clause
    d. exclusive right clause

15. All of the following should always be present in offers and contracts of sale EXCEPT:
    a. date of final settlement
    b. date possession will be given purchaser
    c. date of commission payment
    d. date of contract inception

16. Which of the following most accurately describes an agreement wherein a property owner agrees to convey title to the property when another party satisfies all obligations agreed to in the contract?
    a. lease contract
    b. listing contract
    c. level contract
    d. land contract

17. When a purchaser and seller have a valid contract for the sale of real property, the purchaser has:
    a. legal title
    b. no title
    c. equitable title
    d. constructive title

18. When a party purchases an option, the optionee is purchasing which of the following?
    a. contract liability
    b. time
    c. land
    d. exercise

19. Owner Appleton has given Miller an option for 30 days to purchase Appleton's farm at a specified price. Under the terms of an option, which of the following statements would NOT be correct?
    a. Appleton is the optionor
    b. Miller is the optionee
    c. Miller can require Appleton to sell at any time during the 30 days
    d. Appleton can require miller to purchase within 30 days

20. All of the following are requirements of options EXCEPT:
    a. an option must be in writing to be enforceable
    b. an option must contain a description of the property
    c. an option must be exercised
    d. an option must contain a recital of consideration

POSSIBLE RESPONSES TO "HOW WOULD YOU RESPOND?"

1. To be valid, a listing must be signed by the owners of the real estate. The owner of the real estate is a corporation, thus the listing must be signed by the parties authorized to enter into contracts for the corporation. To determine who are the proper parties authorized to enter into contracts, the documents creating the corporation must be reviewed. These documents include the Articles of Incorporation, minutes of corporate meetings, and the bylaws of the corporation.

   The designated parties could be the corporate officers, the board of directors, the secretary of the corporation, or any other party set out in the corporate documents.

2. Any offer can be revoked prior to acceptance. An offer is not yet a contract. It is merely an attempt to enter into a contract.

   Green can revoke his offer to Smith at any time up to acceptance of the offer. Thus if Smith has not accepted Green's offer, Green can revoke his offer. The revocation of the offer by Green should be in writing just like the original offer. If Smith has already accepted Green's offer prior to revocation by Green, revocation is not allowed.

   If Green can and does revoke his offer, Smith cannot sue Green even if the 72-hour period has not expired. Green and Smith do not have a contract until the offer is accepted. Thus Smith has no legal standing or right upon which to sue Green. Green cannot breach a contract that does not exist.

CHAPTER 6

Important Terminology

abstract of title
acknowledgment
administrator/administratrix
adverse possession
alienation
baseline
beneficiary
bequest
bona fide purchaser (BFP)
certificate of title opinion
chain of title
constructive notice
contract buyer's policy
covenant
deed of bargain and sale
deed of confirmation
deed of gift
deed of release
deed of surrender
delivery and acceptance
descent
description by reference
devise
devisee
executor/executrix
general warranty deed
grant deed
grantee/grantor
granting clause
habendum clause
intestate
involuntary alienation
judicial deeds
leasehold policy
legacy
lien foreclosure sale
marketable (merchantable) title
metes and bounds
mortgagee's policy
owner's policy
plat
principal meridian
probate
property description
quarter-section
quitclaim deed
ranges
recordation
rectangular survey system
section
special warranty deed
subrogation of rights
testator/testatrix
title examination
title insurance
title transfer taxes
torrens system
township
voluntary alienation

Transfer of Title to Real Property

IN THIS CHAPTER The transfer of real property between buyer and seller is the goal of the typical real estate transaction. Assuring the transfer of good title involves the recording system, legal descriptions, abstracts of title, title insurance, surveys, deeds, and the requirements to be a bona fide purchaser. *Transfer of title to real property* is described in law as **alienation**. In a transfer, the property owner is alienated or separated from the title. Alienation may be voluntary or involuntary. Transfer may be during an owner's life or upon the owner's death.

METHODS OF TRANSFERRING TITLE

Descent

When a person dies and leaves no valid will, the laws of **descent** *determine the order of distribution of property to heirs*. The typical order of descent is to spouses, children, parents, brothers, and sisters and then more remote lineal and lateral descendants. State statutes are enacted for this purpose and are called intestate succession statutes because *a person dying without leaving a valid will* has died **intestate**. Escheat occurs when no one is eligible to receive the property of the decedent as provided by statute. If a diligent search fails to reveal qualified heirs as specified by the statute, the property escheats to the State or other government entity. This means that in the absence of heirs, the State or other government entity takes title to the deceased's property. Because *the deceased has no control over the transfer of title* to the State or other government entity, this results in an **involuntary alienation** after death. This is the only form of involuntary alienation after death.

The *person appointed by a court to distribute the property of a person dying intestate*, in accordance with provisions of the statute, is called an **administrator** (man) or **administratrix** (woman).

Will

When death is accompanied by *a valid will* or, in the absence of a valid will, *with qualified heirs located* to receive title to the property, the applicable term is **voluntary alienation**. If a person dies and leaves a valid will, he or she is said to have died testate. The deceased is called a **testator** if a man and a **testatrix** if a woman. A *person appointed in a will to carry out provisions of the will* is called an **executor** (man) or an **executrix** (woman). **Probate** is the *judicial determination of the validity of a will* by a court of competent jurisdiction *and subsequent supervision* over distribution of the estate. *A gift of real property by will* is a **devise**, and *the recipient of the gift of real property by will* is the **devisee**. A *gift of personal property by will* is a **bequest** or **legacy**, and the *recipient of the gift of personal property* is the **beneficiary**.

PUTTING IT TO WORK

Although wills are relatively simple documents, certain absolute requirements must be met or the will may be declared invalid. Wills are best drafted by an attorney specializing in estate planning. After all, when it is discovered that a will has been inadequately drawn, it is too late to change it.

Voluntary Alienation

Voluntary transfer is the type of alienation that is of primary importance to the real estate business. Voluntary alienation, or transfer of title during life, is accomplished by the delivery of a valid deed by the grantor to the grantee during the life of both of them. The contract for sale of real property is consummated when the grantor delivers to the grantee a valid deed as required in the contract.

Involuntary Alienation

During the life of an owner, title to real property may be transferred by involuntary alienation as a result of a lien foreclosure sale, adverse possession, filing a petition in bankruptcy, or condemnation under the power of eminent domain.

Lien Foreclosure Sale

In Chapter 3 we discussed the concept that real property may be sold at public auction to satisfy a specific or general lien against the property. The **lien foreclosure sale** is *without consent of the property owner who incurred the debt resulting in a lien*. Foreclosure sales are ordered by a court or authorized by state law, and title is conveyed to a purchaser at the sale by judicial deed (discussed under types of deed, later in the chapter). A judicial deed is executed by the official whom the court or state authorizes to conduct the sale and transfer the title. In these cases, titles typically are conveyed by a sheriff's deed, a trustee's deed, a commissioner's deed, or similar document, usually without the participation of the property owner who is losing the title as the result of foreclosure.

Adverse Possession

A *person other than the owner can claim title to real property* under **adverse possession** if the other person makes use of the land under the following conditions:

1. The possession or occupation must be open and well-known to others (notorious).
2. The possession must be hostile; that is, without the permission of the true owner and must be exclusive (not shared with the true owner). Thus, co-owners cannot adversely possess against each other.
3. The possession must be continuous and uninterrupted for a period specified by statute in the state where the property is located. The states provide by statute a shorter period of time if possession is under "color of title" than when possession is under a *claim of title*. In a claim of title, *possession is based on some type of claim against the land rather than on some written document*, as in the case of

color of title. Statutory requirements vary from state to state, but the period may be as short as 5 to 7 years under color of title and as long as 21 years without color of title.

4. The possession must be actual.
5. In most states, possession of the property must be under color of title or claim of title; that is, the occupant of the property must have some reasonable basis to believe that he or she is entitled to possession of the property. This basis typically is in the form of a defective deed or a quitclaim deed (discussed later).

The adverse possessor does not automatically acquire title to the property by merely meeting the five requirements just listed. To perfect the claim and obtain a title to the property, the claimant must satisfy the court that he or she has fulfilled the requirements of the adverse possession statute of that state in an action to "quiet title." If the court is satisfied that the statutory requirements have been met, the court will award the title to the claimant under adverse possession.

Filing of Bankruptcy

If the owner of real estate files a bankruptcy petition under Chapter 7 of the United States Code, title to the real estate is transferred by operation of bankruptcy law to the bankruptcy trustee. Any further conveyance requires the approval and execution of documents by the bankruptcy trustee.

Condemnation Under Eminent Domain

The federal government, states and their agencies, counties, cities, towns, and boroughs have the power of eminent domain. This power confers the right to condemn, or take private property for public use. The condemned property must be for the use and benefit of the general public. The property owner must be compensated for the fair market value of the property lost through condemnation. The condemning authority must adhere to due process of law (that is, adequately notify the property owner of the condemnation), and the property owner must have the right to appeal the value of the property as established by the condemning authority through the court system. The property owner, however, cannot prevent the condemnation and, therefore, the loss of title is involuntary.

DEEDS

Essential Elements of a Valid Deed

The requirements necessary for creation of a valid deed and conveyance of title vary from state to state in some of the terms, so the following is a generalized discussion to be adapted to your own specific state.

Writing

The deed must be in writing. As required by the Statute of Frauds, every deed must be written. An oral conveyance is ineffective. The written form of the deed must meet any legal requirements of the state in which the property is located.

Grantor

The **grantor**, *the one conveying the title*, must be legally competent; the individual must have the capacity to contract. This is the same requirement that exists for all parties to a valid contract. The grantor must have reached the age of majority and must be mentally competent at the time of deed execution. Also, the grantor must be named with certainty; it must be possible to positively identify the grantor.

A corporation may receive, hold, and convey title to real property in the corporate name. Therefore, a corporation may be a grantor. If the conveyance of title by the corporation is in the corporation's ordinary course of business, the deed may be executed on behalf of the corporation by the corporate president or vice president and countersigned by the secretary or assistant secretary. If the transfer of title is not in the ordinary course of the corporation's business, the board of directors of the corporation authorizing the transfer of title must make a resolution authorizing the conveyance. When the resolution has been made, the signatures of the individuals named above are sufficient. A partnership may receive, hold, and convey title to real property in the partnership name, in the name of an individual general partner, or in the name of a trustee acting for the partnership for this purpose.

Title to real property may be held in an assumed name, and it can be transferred under that name. Examples are titles in the name of a corporation or partnership. Although title may be held or transferred under an assumed name, the person or organization must actually exist.

Grantee

A **grantee**, the person receiving title, does not have to have legal capacity; a minor or a mentally incompetent person can receive and hold title to real property. These people, however, cannot convey title on their own, because they are not qualified to be grantors. To effect a conveyance of title held in the name of an incompetent, a guardian's deed must be executed by the incompetent's guardian as grantor. The conveyance by the guardian may be accomplished only with court authority.

Grantees must be named with certainty. It must be possible to identify the grantee. The grantee must actually exist and be either a natural person or an artificial person such as a corporation or partnership. The grantee must be alive at the time of delivery of the deed. A deceased person cannot be a grantee.

Property Description

The deed must contain an adequate formal legal description of the property. The three methods of providing this description are discussed later in this chapter.

Consideration

The deed must provide evidence that consideration (something of value such as money) is given. In some states the deed does not have to recite the actual amount of consideration (money) involved; thus, a phrase such as "ten dollars, and other consideration" is sufficient to accomplish this purpose. This is called *nominal* consideration. A recital of consideration is shown in Figure 6.1 in conjunction with words showing conveyance.

Good consideration is often present in gift or charitable conveyances. State laws vary in whether "for love and affection" or "for the continued use of the [charity]" are acceptable in a deed or if a statement indicating valuable consideration is required.

Words of Conveyance

The deed must contain *words of conveyance* demonstrating that it is the *grantor's intention to transfer the title to the named grantee*. These *words of conveyance* are contained in the **granting clause**. In the case of warranty deeds, typical wording is "as given, granted, bargained, sold and conveyed."

PUTTING IT TO WORK

The words of the granting clause indicate the type of deed. "Conveys and warrants to" indicates a warranty deed. "Quits any and all claims to" indicates a quitclaim deed.

In addition to the granting clause, the deed sometimes contains a **habendum clause**, which *describes the estate granted and should be in agreement with the granting clause*. This clause begins with the words "to have and to hold." A typical habendum clause in a deed conveying a fee simple title reads "to have and to hold the above described premises with all the appurtenances thereunto belonging, or in anywise appertaining, unto the grantee, his heirs, and/or successors and assigns forever." By contrast, the typical habendum clause in a deed conveying a life estate reads, "to have and to hold the premises herein granted unto the grantee for and during the term of the remainder of the natural life of the herein named grantee." An example of a habendum clause is shown in Figure 6.1.

If the property is being sold subject to specific encumbrances of record, such as an easement or a mortgage lien, the habendum clause recites these encumbrances. Two points in regard to encumbrances are:

1. Transfer of fee simple absolute title does not mean an absence of encumbrances.
2. The warranty against encumbrances in a deed, discussed below, is only a warranty against encumbrances that have not been disclosed (those not on record).

Execution

Proper execution of the deed means that it *must be signed by each grantor conveying an interest in the property*. Only the grantors execute the deed. In most cases the grantee does not sign (the exceptions to this rule are deeds involving a corporation, a minor, or a court-ordered transfer). In a minority of states, proper execution includes execution under seal. In these states the word "seal" in parentheses must appear at the end of the signature line provided for each grantor. Sometimes the letters LS (locus sigilli), rather than the word "seal," follow the grantor's signature. Locus sigilli means "the place of the seal." The deed will not convey the title unless it is properly executed by the grantors.

Witnessing

For the deed to be valid, a few states require witnessing. One person or more must be present when the grantor signs the deed. Witnessing is called "attestation."

Acknowledgment

For a deed to be eligible for recording, it must have an **acknowledgment**. The *grantor must appear before a public officer* such as a notary public who is eligible to take an acknowledgment, *and state that signing of the deed was done as a voluntary act*. A deed is perfectly valid between grantor and grantee without an acknowledgment. Without the acknowledgment, however, the grantee cannot record the deed and thereby have protection of title against subsequent creditors or purchasers of the same property from the same grantor who record their deed. The grantee should insist upon receiving a deed that has been acknowledged.

Delivery and Acceptance

To effect a transfer of title by deed, there must be **delivery and acceptance**. The *grantor must deliver a valid deed to the grantee, and the grantee must accept the deed.* Delivery may be directly to the grantee or to an agent of the grantee. The agent for this purpose is typically the grantee's attorney, his or her real estate broker, or the lending institution providing the mortgage loan to finance purchase of the property. In

FIGURE 6.1 A sample general warranty deed.

WARRANTY DEED

THE STATE OF
COUNTY OF
That

of the County of State of for and in consideration of the sum or Ten and no/100 Dollars, and other good and valuable consideration, to the undersigned cash in hand paid by the grantee(s) herein named, the receipt of which is hereby acknowledged,

have GRANTED, SOLD AND CONVEYED, and by these presents do GRANT, SELL AND CONVEY unto

of the County of State of , all of the following described real property in County, State, to-wit:

TO HAVE AND TO HOLD the above described premises, together with all and singular the rights and appurtenances thereto in anywise belonging unto the said grantee(s) heirs and assigns forever; and do hereby bind heirs, executors and administrators to WARRANT AND FOREVER DEFEND all and singular the said premises unto the said grantee(s) heirs and assigns, against every person whomsoever lawfully claiming or to claim the same or any part thereof.

EXECUTED this day of , A.D. 19

____________________ ____________________

THE STATE OF
COUNTY OF

Before me, the undersigned authority, on this day personally appeared known to me to be the person(s) whose name subscribed to the foregoing instrument, and acknowledged to me that he executed the same for the purpose and consideration therein expressed.

Given under my hand and seal of office on this the day of , A.D. 19

PREPARED IN THE LAW OFFICE OF:

Notary Public in and for County, State
RETURN TO:

almost every case there is a presumption of acceptance by the grantee. This presumption is especially strong if the deed has been recorded and the conveyance is beneficial to the grantee.

Types of Deeds

Deeds may be classified both by the form of warranty of title contained in the deed and by the special purpose for which the deed is drawn. The various types of deeds are discussed next, both by type of warranty and by special purpose.

General Warranty Deed

The **general warranty deed** *contains the strongest and broadest form of guarantee of title of any type of deed* and therefore provides the greatest protection to the grantee. The general warranty deed usually contains six **covenants**, or *binding agreements*, as discussed below. Exact wording of these covenants may vary.

1. **Covenant of Seisin.** Typical wording of this covenant is, "Grantor covenants that he is seised of said premises in fee." This covenant, like the others in the general warranty deed, is a specific covenant and provides *an assurance to the grantee that the grantor holds the title that he or she specified in the deed* that he or she is conveying to the grantee. In the example cited, the grantor promises the grantee that he or she has fee simple title to the property.

2. **Covenant of Right to Convey.** This covenant, which usually follows the covenant of seisin in the general warranty deed, typically reads, "and has the right to convey the same in fee simple." By this covenant the grantor provides *an assurance to the grantee that the grantor has legal capacity to convey the title and also has the title to convey.*

3. **Covenant Against Encumbrances.** This covenant typically states that, "said premises are free from encumbrances (with the exceptions above stated, if any)." The grantor assures the grantee that there are *no encumbrances against the title except those set forth in the deed itself.* Typical encumbrances that are acceptable to grantees are a lien of a mortgage when grantee is assuming grantor's existing mortgage, recorded easements, and restrictive covenants.

4. **Covenant of Quiet Enjoyment.** This covenant typically reads, "the grantee, his or her heirs and assigns, shall quietly and peaceably have, hold, use, possess, and enjoy the premises." This covenant is an assurance by the grantor to the *grantee that the grantee shall have quiet possession and enjoyment of the property being conveyed* and will not be disturbed in the use and enjoyment of the property because of a defect in the title being conveyed by the grantor. In warranty deeds not containing a specific covenant of quiet enjoyment, the covenant of warranty itself assures the grantee of quiet enjoyment of the property.

5. **Covenant for Further Assurances.** This covenant typically reads, "that he or she (grantor) will execute such further assurances as may be reasonable or necessary to perfect the title in the grantee." Under this covenant, *the grantor must perform any acts necessary to correct any defect in the title being conveyed and any errors or deficiencies in the deed itself.*

6. **Covenant of Warranty.** The warranty of title in the general warranty deed provides that the grantor "will warrant and defend the title to the grantee against the lawful claims of all persons whomsoever." This is the *best form of warranty for protecting the grantee* and contains no limitations as to possible claimants protected against, because the grantor specifies that he or she will defend the title against "the lawful claims of all persons whomsoever." The covenant of warranty is the most important of all the covenants.

PUTTING IT TO WORK

In many states, the form of warranty deed may not specifically outline in words what is warranted. These promises, or warranties, are merely implied with the word "warrants" in the granting clause, but still would be recognized in the event of a dispute over title.

If the covenant of seisin or the covenant of warranty is broken, a grantee may recover from the seller any financial loss up to the price paid for the property. If the covenant against encumbrances is broken, the grantee may recover from the grantor any expenses incurred to pay off the encumbrance. The amount the grantee may recover in this case also is limited to the price paid for the property.

The covenant of quiet enjoyment is not considered to be broken unless the grantee is actually dispossessed of the property. The mere threat or assertion of a claim by another party to some right in the property does not constitute a breach of the covenant of quiet enjoyment. In the case of dispossession, the grantee may recover from the grantor an amount up to the price paid for the property.

The covenant for further assurances is not broken until the grantee has to execute some instrument to perfect the grantee's title. Neither the covenant of quiet enjoyment nor the covenant of warranty is broken until the grantee actually is evicted from the property by someone holding a superior title.

Special Warranty Deed

In the **special warranty deed**, the warranty is *limited to claims against the title arising out of the period of ownership of the grantor.* This warranty goes back in time only to the date when the grantor acquired the title, as contrasted with the general warranty deed, in which the warranty is against defects in the title going back for an unlimited time.

PUTTING IT TO WORK

The special warranty deed usually is used by a non-owner acting on behalf of the true owner. Examples include the executor or administrator of an estate, guardian, custodian, trustee, receiver, or anyone acting in a fiduciary capacity.

Quitclaim Deed

The **quitclaim deed** contains no warranties whatsoever. It is simply a *deed of release.* It will release or convey to the grantee any interest, including title, that the grantor may have. The grantor, however, does not state in the deed that he or she has any title or interest in the property and certainly makes no warranties as to the quality of title. Execution of the quitclaim deed by the grantor prevents the grantor from asserting any claim against the title at any time in the future.

Quitclaim deeds may be used to clear a "cloud on a title." This terminology describes the situation when someone has a possible claim against a title. As long as this possibility exists, the title is clouded and therefore not a good and marketable title. To remove this cloud and create a good and marketable title, the possible claimant executes a quitclaim deed as grantor to the true titleholder as grantee.

PUTTING IT TO WORK

Common clouds include lingering spousal claims (particularly after a divorce), liens that appear to have been paid but not released (mortgages and mechanics' liens), and claims of relatives after estate probate.

Quitclaim deeds also are used in community property states to enable a married individual to own property purchased during the marriage in severalty.

The granting clause in the quitclaim deed shown in Figure 6.2 contains the words "quitclaims, remises and releases" instead of "grant, sell and convey," as used in the warranty deed shown in Figure 6.1.

Grant Deed

The **grant deed** is a special form of statutory deed used in western states where warranty deeds are rarely used. Rather than being expressly set forth in the deed, *the warranties are implied from state statute*. These implied warranties include a warranty against encumbrances created by the grantor or anyone claiming title under his or her deed and a warranty that the grantor has not previously conveyed the same title to anyone else. The form of an individual grant deed is the simplest of all the various types of deed.

FIGURE 6.2
A sample quitclaim deed.

QUITCLAIM DEED

THIS INDENTURE WITNESSETH, that ____________ (Grantor) of ____________ County in the State of ____________ QUITCLAIMS, REMISES AND RELEASES to ____________ of ____________ County in the State of ____________ for the sum of One Dollar ($1.00) and other valuable consideration, a receipt of which is hereby acknowledged, her interest in the following described real estate in ____________ County, ____________:

Lots Numbered One Hundred Three (103) and One Hundred Four (104) in Robbins and Scott Addition to the Town of Anywhere as recorded in Plat Book "A", page 22, in the Office of the Recorder of ____________ County, State of ____________.

IN WITNESS WHEREOF, the Grantor has executed this deed, this ____________ day of ____________, 19________.

____
Grantor:

STATE OF ____________

COUNTY OF ____________

Before me, a Notary Public in and for said County and State, personally appeared ____________, who acknowledged the execution of the foregoing Quitclaim Deed, and who, having been duly sworn, stated that any representations therein contained are true.

Witness my hand and Notarial Seal this ____________ day of ____________, 19________.

My commission expires:____________

Signature:____________ Printed:____________
Residing in Bartholomew, County

THIS INSTRUMENT PREPARED BY ____________
ATTORNEY AT LAW.

Return deed to: ____________

Send tax bill to: ____________

Deed of Confirmation

The **deed of confirmation**, also called a deed of correction, is *used when a deed contains an error that requires correction*. Examples of the types of errors corrected by this type of deed are errors in names of the parties, errors in the property description, and mistakes made in execution of the deed.

Deed of Release

The **deed of release** is *used primarily to release a title from the lien of a mortgage when the debt secured by the mortgage has been paid in full* or, in the case of a blanket mortgage, to release individual parcels of land from the lien of the blanket mortgage. A deed of release also is used to release a dower right in property.

Deed of Surrender

A life tenant may use the **deed of surrender** *to convey his or her estate to the reversioner or to the remainderman*, depending on the form of the life estate. This same result may be accomplished through a quitclaim deed.

Deed of Bargain and Sale

Deed of bargain and sale may be with or without covenants of warranty. In either case, there is an *implied covenant on the part of the grantor that he or she has a substantial title and possession of the property*. Grantees in these deeds, for their protection, should require that the deed contain specific warranties such as the warranty against encumbrances.

Deed of Gift

A **deed of gift** of *real property may be conveyed by either general warranty deed or by quitclaim deed*. If using the warranty deed, the grantee cannot enforce the warranties against the grantor; the grantor received no consideration for conveying the title to the grantee, as the conveyance was a gift. Either a warranty deed or a quitclaim deed conveys the property provided the grantor has title to convey.

Judicial Deed

Execution of **judicial deeds** *results from a court order to the official executing the deed*. The various types of judicial deeds receive their names from the title of the official executing the deed. They include sheriff's deed (in some states, referee's deed in foreclosures), tax deed, guardian's deed, commissioner's deed (in some states, referee's deed in partition), executor's deed, and administrator's deed. Judicial deeds contain no warranties.

Title Transfer Taxes (Revenue Stamps)

At the time of this writing, most states impose *a tax on the conveyance of title to real property*. We use the term **title transfer taxes**, though the name of the tax varies from state to state. Examples are: revenue stamps, real estate excise tax, documentary stamps, real estate transfer tax, deed tax stamps. State statutes usually require the seller to pay this tax. The amount of tax is based on the consideration the seller receives in selling the property.

The amount of tax charged on the purchase price varies by state. Some subtract the amount of any mortgage being assumed, which is called "old money," and therefore charge the tax only on the "new money" brought into the transaction above the amount of the assumed loan. In those states, an examination of tax stamps provides only an indication of the new money, which is below the sales price if a mortgage is assumed. The real estate licensee needs to learn the rate and application of this tax, as well as the collection procedures, in his or her own state. Some states require a sworn statement of consideration paid, called a *declaration of value*.

TITLE ASSURANCE

Title Examination

Before the title can be transferred, the seller must provide evidence of **marketable or merchantable title**, one that is *readily salable in a locality*. Marketable title is not perfect title. It is not necessarily title free of all liens. In the case of a sale with mortgage assumption, the buyer has bargained for and will accept seller's title with the present mortgage as a lien on the title.

Evidence of marketable title through **title examination** can be provided by a commercially hired search or by a personal *search of the records that may affect real estate titles*. The records searched include public records of deeds, mortgages, long-term leases, options, contracts for deed, easements, platted subdivisions, judgments entered, deaths, marriages, bankruptcy filings, mechanics' liens, zoning ordinances, real and personal property taxes, miscellaneous assessments for improvements, mortgage releases, and lis pendens notices.

PUTTING IT TO WORK

Given the extent and complexity of records to be searched, as well as future legal implications, use of a skilled service, such as a title insurance company or an abstractor, is recommended for title examination.

The search of the records on a given piece of real estate will establish a **chain of title**, which must be unbroken for the title to be good and, therefore, marketable. It involves *tracing the successive conveyances of title* starting with the current deed and going back an appropriate time (typically 40 to 60 years), quite often researching back to original title (the last instance of government ownership).

The two most often-used forms of commercial title evidence are abstract of title with attorney opinion and policy of title insurance.

PUTTING IT TO WORK

Any missing links in the chain of title create uncertainty as to the path of ownership and proof thereof. These missing links could be the result of oversight (failing to record a deed), fraud, or a dispute between parties. Any of these uncertainties is of sufficient concern to a buyer to threaten the marketability of title. If these missing links can be bridged by obtaining proper title-clearing documents, the transaction may safely occur. If not, the sale should not close.

Abstract of Title with Attorney Opinion

An **abstract of title** is a *condensed history of the title*, setting forth a summary of all links in the chain of title plus any other matters of public record affecting the title. The abstract contains a legal description of the property and summarizes every related instrument in chronological order. An abstract continuation is an update of an abstract of title that sets forth memoranda of new transfers of title. The preparer of the abstract certifies that all recorded matters relating to the real estate in question are included in the abstract. When the abstract is completed, an attorney must examine it to assure that the chain of title is unbroken and clear. The attorney then gives a written **certificate of title opinion** as to *what person or entity owns the real estate and the quality of title*.

The abstractor certifies that the public records have been searched. The attorney certifies that the abstract has been examined and states the quality of title and exceptions, if any, to clear title.

Policy of Title Insurance

A **title insurance** policy is a contract of insurance that *insures the policy owner against financial loss if title to real estate is not good*. Title insurance policies are issued by the same companies that prepare abstracts of title. The company issuing the insurance policy checks the same public records as abstractors do, to determine if it will risk insuring the title.

The typical title insurance policy requires the title insurance company to compensate the insured for financial loss up to the face amount of the policy resulting from a title defect (plus cost of litigation or challenge). The policy protects the insured only against title defects existing at the time of transfer of title. If a claim is filed and the title insurance company pays the claim, it may have the right to bring legal action against the grantor for breach of warranties in the deed. The title insurance company has obtained from the insured grantee this right to file suit by payment of the claim. The *substitution of the title insurance company in the place of the insured for filing a legal action* is called **subrogation of rights**.

Like any other insurance policy, a title insurance policy has a list of risk items that are included and excluded. A typical title insurance policy does not cover financial loss from adverse possession, adverse parties in possession, easements by prescription, or any unrecorded documents. A title insurance policy does insure against financial loss by forgery of any document affecting real estate. A title insurance policy also may include special endorsements that increase the areas of coverage. Typical endorsements in commercial real estate, particularly, are to insure ingress and egress and proper zoning.

The title insurance policy is issued only upon an acceptable abstract or title opinion. A title that is acceptable to the title insurance company is called *insurable title*. The premium for a title insurance policy is a one-time premium paid at the time the policy is placed in effect. The four forms of title insurance policies are: owner's policy, mortgagee's policy, leasehold policy, and contract buyer's policy.

Owner's Policy

The **owner's policy**, *for the protection of the new owner*, is written for the amount the new owner paid for the property. The amount of coverage remains the same for the life of the policy. The policy remains in effect for the duration of the insured's ownership of the property and continues in effect after the death of the owner to benefit heirs receiving an interest in the property.

Mortgagee's Policy

A **mortgagee's policy** *protects only the mortgagee (lender)*. Under the terms of the policy, the mortgagee is insured against defects in the title to property pledged as security in the mortgage. The mortgagee's insurable interest is only to the extent of the outstanding loan balance at any given time. Therefore, the mortgagee's policy decreases in face amount as the loan principal decreases but always provides coverage equivalent to the amount of the loan balance.

Leasehold Policy

The **leasehold policy** *protects the lessee (tenant) and/or a mortgagee against defect in the lessor's title*. This policy is issued to a mortgagee when the mortgagor has pledged a leasehold interest instead of a fee simple title as security for the mortgage debt.

Contract Buyer's Policy

A **contract buyer's policy** *protects the contract buyer against defects in the contract seller's title* prior to the contract. This policy is issued when a contract for deed (land contract) is executed between vendor and vendee.

Recordation

Title insurers, abstractors, and attorneys all rely on recorded documents concerning real estate. Some documents are not required to be recorded. **Recordation** of a deed provides *protection for the owner's title against subsequent claimants*. This protection is provided by the theory of **constructive notice**: *All of the world is bound by knowledge of the existence of the conveyance of title if evidence of the conveyance is recorded.*

Documents do not have to be acknowledged or notarized to be valid, but they must be acknowledged or notarized to be recorded. Recording an invalid document does not make it valid.

Constructive notice is contrasted with actual notice. Constructive notice is binding on everyone, even though they have not actually read the deed, because recording it gives notice to the world. Actual notice requires that the person in fact knows about and sees the document. Constructive notice, provided by recording, protects the title for the grantee. This protection is against everyone with a later claim, including other purchasers of the same property from the same grantor.

A buyer of property who relies on the records and is unaware of an unrecorded prior document is called a **bona fide purchaser** (BFP). A bona fide purchaser's real estate title is protected because of recording.

Figure 6.3 illustrates the possible effects of a grantee's failure to record a deed and the protection provided to a grantee who does record a deed. In the figure, title is transferred effectively from Grantor to Grantee #1, but the title is defeated by her failure to record the deed. The Grantor conveys the same title to Grantee #2, who records

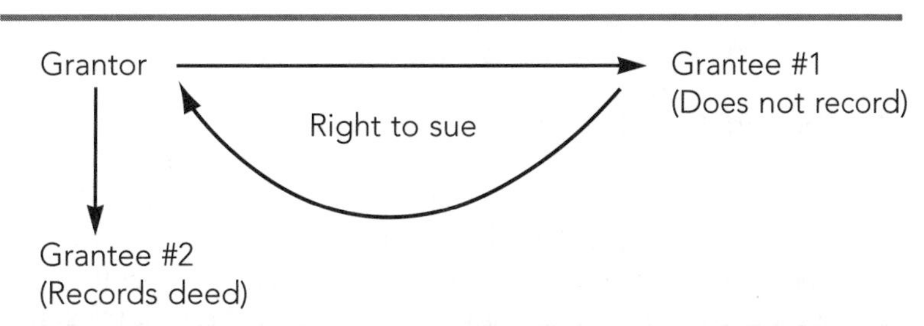

FIGURE 6.3 The possible effects of failure of grantee to record a deed.

the deed. Grantee #2 now holds the title, and Grantee #1 has the right to sue Grantor to recover her money. This right may be worth pursuing provided that Grantor can be found and has money or property. In doing this, Grantee #2 must be a bona fide purchaser for value. He must be completely unaware of the prior conveyance to Grantee #1 and must have paid fair market value for the property.

In summary, Figure 6.3 illustrates that a valid conveyance of title can take place between grantor and grantee without the deed being recorded. Nevertheless, the deed must be recorded to protect grantee's title from third parties, such as purchasers, from the grantor, subsequent creditors, or other lienholders of the grantor.

Title Registration/Torrens System

In addition to the regular method of recording titles, a special form of recording called the **torrens system** of title recordation is available in some states. Under the torrens system the *titleholder applies to the court to have property registered.* The court orders the title to be examined by official title examiners, who report the examination results to the court. If results of the examinations are satisfactory, the court issues instructions to the Register of Titles to record the title, and issues certificates of registration of title after giving adequate public notice so anyone contesting the title has ample opportunity to appear.

The certificate of registration of title contains the type of title the applicant has and sets forth any encumbrances against the title. One certificate is issued to the Register of Titles and the other to the titleholder who applied for registration of the title. The certificate of registration provides conclusive evidence of the validity of the title, and it cannot be contested except for fraud. Title to properties recorded under the torrens system cannot be obtained by adverse possession.

Property Descriptions

For effective and accurate title transfers, title insurers, abstractors, and attorneys also rely on an *accurate legal description of the land.* The type of legal description for title transfer must be a formal description. Informal descriptions, such as street addresses or assessor/tax numbers, are acceptable on listings but not on documents for transferring or encumbering title.

Property descriptions are of three acceptable types: metes and bounds, description by reference, and government or rectangular survey system.

Putting It to Work

If a legal description and informal reference do not identify the same property, the legal description is recognized and the informal reference is ignored. Because most people readily recognize street addresses and do not recognize legal descriptions, it is essential to verify that both describe the same property.

Metes and Bounds

The property description used in the states comprising the original thirteen colonies is the metes and bounds description. It also is used in states in which the primary description is the government or rectangular survey system; in those states, the metes and bounds type of description is used to describe small, irregular land areas.

In the **metes and bounds** description, the metes are *the distances from point to point in the description* and the bounds *are the directions from one point to another.* An example of a metes and bounds description is given in Figure 6.4.

A metes and bounds description is made from a survey performed by a licensed, registered land surveyor. One of the most important aspects of the metes and bounds description is the selection of the point of beginning. This point should be one that is reasonably easy to locate and well established. After starting at the point of beginning, the surveyor sights the direction to the next point or monument. A "monument" may be a tree, a rock, or an artificial boundary such as a road or a concrete marker. The directions in the metes and bounds description might read "north 45 degrees east." Refinement of the direction might include degrees (symbolized by °), divided into minutes (1 degree = 60 minutes; minutes are symbolized by the symbol '), and each minute divided into seconds (symbolized by "). A description, then, might read "north 45°, 30'10" east." These bearings are illustrated in Figure 6.4. A metes and bounds description always must end at the point of beginning.

FIGURE 6.4 Metes and bounds description in conjunction with a description by reference.

An example of a typical metes and bounds description and the plat resulting from that description follow.

*Being all of Lot No. 20 of the subdivision of a portion of the property of Mortgage Heights Land Company, Inc., Centre County, as shown by plat thereof prepared by Worley and Gray, Consulting Engineers, dated October 1, 1995, and recorded in Book 5, page 40, Records of Plats for Centre County, and more particularly bounded and described as follows:

**BEGINNING on a stake in the northeast margin of Amortization Drive, south corner of Lot No. 20 of the subdivision or a portion of the property of Mortgage Heights Land Company, Inc., and running thence North 6° 18' East 215.2 feet to a stake; thence North 8° 49' West 241.0 feet to a stake, common corner of Lot Nos. 20 and 19 of said subdivision; thence with the dividing line between said Lot Nos. 19 and 20, South 87° 50' West 138.5 feet to a stake in the east margin of a cul-de-sac; thence with the east margin of said cul-de-sac in a southwesterly direction along a curve with the radius of 50.0 feet, 61.2 feet to a stake in said margin; thence with the east margin of a drive leading to Amortization Drive, South 5° 19' West 132.8 feet to a stake in the point of intersection of said margin of said drive with Amortization Drive; thence with the northeast margin of said Amortization Drive, South 51° 17' East 84.7 feet to a stake in said margin; thence still with said margin of said drive, South 42° 27' East 47.2 feet to a stake in said margin; thence still said margin of said drive, South 29° 36' East 199.9 feet to the BEGINNING.

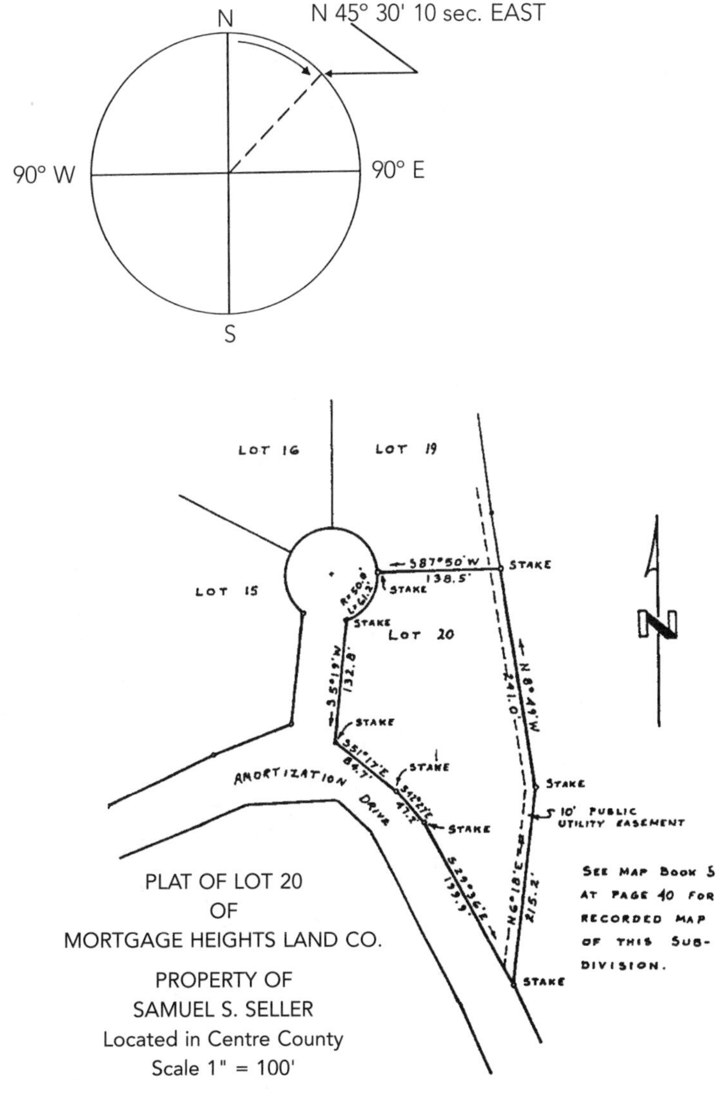

*Description by reference
**Description by metes and bounds

Description by Reference, Plat, or Lot and Block

A description by reference, plat, or lot and block, also shown in Figure 6.4, is another valid legal description. Sometimes an attorney incorporates into the deed a description by reference in addition to a metes and bounds description. At other times the description by reference is the only description in the deed. A **description by reference** *may refer to a* **plat** *(map) and lot number that has been recorded or to a previous deed conveying the same property*. The former description states the plat book number and page number in which the plat or map is recorded so interested parties can look it up and determine the exact location and dimensions of the property. Two examples of subdivision plats are shown in Figures 6.5 and 6.6.

When a property is described by reference to a previous deed that conveyed the same property, the reference incorporates the description in the previous deed by reference into the deed being prepared. If the description in the previous deed is accurate, all is well and good. If the description in the previous deed is faulty, the subsequent deed is still bound by that description.

Often a description also contains a statement as to the number of acres or quantity of land being conveyed. If this quantity is inconsistent with the description by metes and bounds, the quantity of land is established by the metes and bounds description.

Government or Rectangular Survey System

The government or **rectangular survey system** is used for the *transfer of regularly shaped tracts of real estate*, such as rectangles and squares. In this system, the country is divided by *36 north-south lines* called **principal meridians**, and by *east-west lines* called **baselines**. Imaginary lines, called range lines, are located every 6 miles

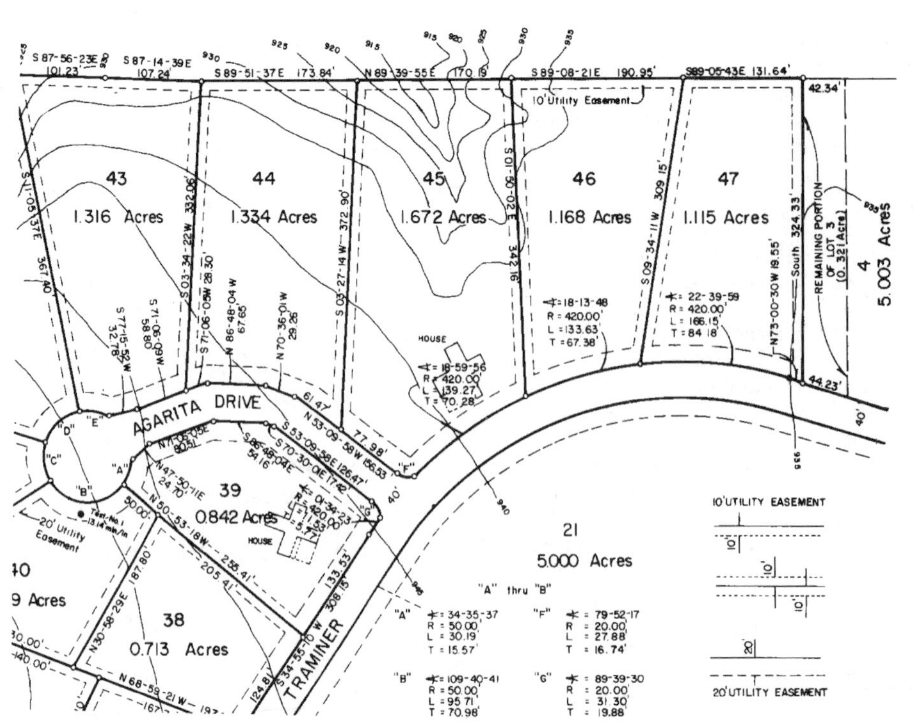

FIGURE 6.5
A sample plat map.

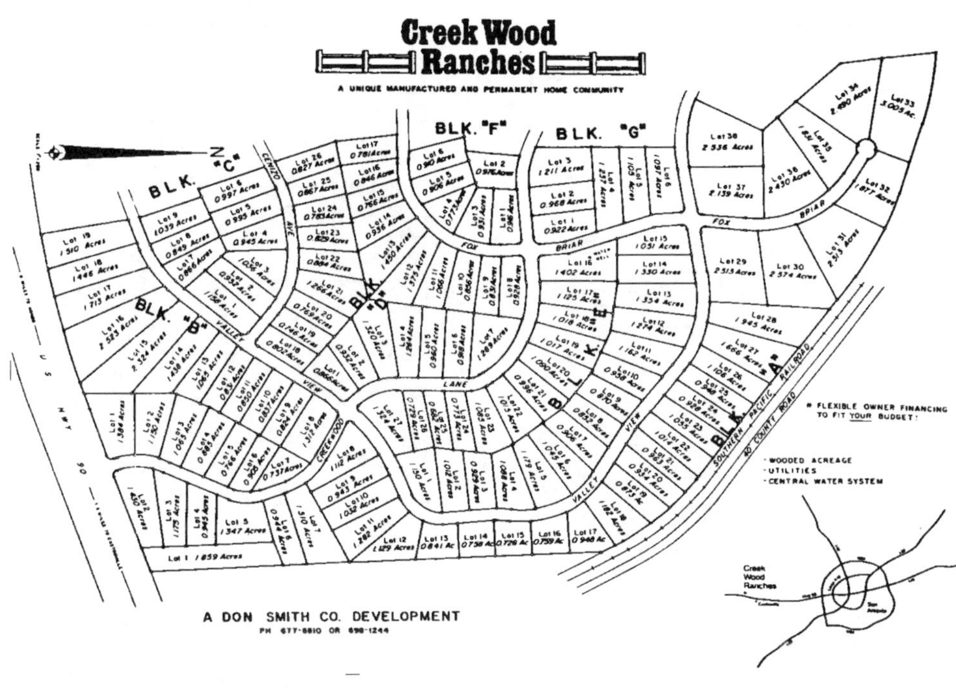

FIGURE 6.6
A sample subdivision plat.

east and west of a principal meridian. The *6-mile "strips" of land between lines*, called **ranges**, are numbered east and west of a principal meridian as Range 1 East (R1E), Range 2 East (R2E), Range 5 West (R5W), and so on.

Township lines are located every 6 miles north and south of baselines. These "rows" of land, called tiers, are numbered every mile north and south of a baseline as Township 1 South (T1S), Township 2 South (T2S), and so on. Each **township** is *a square, 6 miles by 6 miles in area, divided into 36 sections, each one mile in length and width.* Figure 6.7 illustrates a township. The sections are numbered beginning in the northeast section and counting backward 6 miles, forward 6 miles, forward again, and so on through the township.

Each *one-mile square* **section** may be divided into **quarter-sections** and may then be subdivided into areas less than a quarter-section. Each section contains 640 acres and, therefore, a quarter-section is 160 acres. A legal description of the partial section shown in Figure 6.8 would read as follows: "The northwest quarter of the northwest quarter of Section 25 (range 1 east, township 1 north, Huntsville meridian and baseline)."

Examination of these sections as a measurement of land area can provide an introduction to the simple arithmetic of real estate. You can calculate the number of acres in a section by recalling one familiar number of 5,280 feet per mile and learning the new number of 43,560 square feet per acre. The number of acres in any rectangular parcel therefore is figured by calculating the total square feet and dividing by the number of square feet per acre:

$$\text{Acres in a section (square mile)} = \frac{5{,}280 \times 5{,}280}{43{,}560} = 640$$

Further, you can divide a section into quarter-sections by dividing by 4 (160 acres per quarter-section) and further if necessary.

Due to the curvature of the earth, all townships are not six miles square. Because range lines extending northward grow closer together and would finally meet at the North Pole, the north line of a township is automatically shorter than the south line. To

FIGURE 6.7
A township divided into sections.

|←——— 6 miles ———→|

6	5	4	3	2	1
7	8	9	10	11	12
18	17	16	15	14	13
19	20	21	22	23	24
30	29	28	27	26	25
31	32	33	34	35	36

6 miles

FIGURE 6.8
One section subdivided.

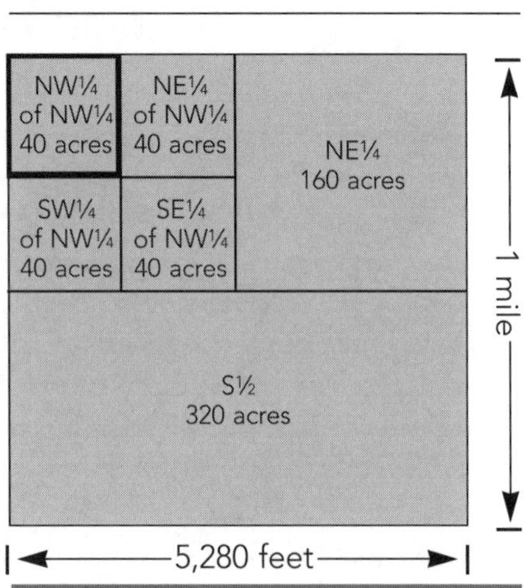

correct for this shortage, every fourth township line north and south of the baseline is specified as a *correction line*. On each correction line, the distance between range lines is measured to a full six miles. Guide meridians are designated every 24 miles east and west of a principal meridian. The distance between the guide meridians and the correction lines is approximately 24 miles square and is referred to as a *check*.

Because each township does not contain 36 square miles, surveyors follow established rules to adjust for the variation. Any overage or shortage in a township is adjusted in designated sections of that township. The sections adjusted are called *fractional sections*. All non-adjusted sections are called *standard sections*.

IMPORTANT POINTS

1. Transfer of title is termed alienation. Involuntary alienation occurs during life as a result of adverse possession, lien foreclosure sale, or condemnation under the power of eminent domain. Involuntary alienation after death is escheat. Voluntary alienation after death is by will or descent. Voluntary alienation during life can occur only by delivery of valid deed.
2. The requirements for deed validity are: (1) deed in writing, (2) competent grantor, (3) competent or incompetent grantee, (4) grantor and grantee named with certainty, (5) adequate property description, (6) recital of consideration, (7) words of conveyance, (8) habendum clause, (9) proper execution by grantor, (10) witnessing (in some states), and (11) delivery and acceptance to convey title.
3. To be eligible for recording on the public record, a deed must be acknowledged. Recording protects the grantee's title against creditors of the grantor and subsequent conveyances by the grantor.
4. A general warranty deed is the strongest and broadest form of title guarantee. The general warranty deed typically contains six covenants: seisin, right to convey, against encumbrances, quiet enjoyment, for further assurances, and warranty.
5. A quitclaim deed is a deed of release and contains no warranties. It will convey any interest the grantor may have. The quitclaim deed is used mainly to remove a cloud from a title.

6. The purpose of a title examination is to determine the quality of a title. Lenders require that the examination be made by an attorney or a title company. Only an attorney can legally give an opinion as to the quality of a title.
7. A title insurance policy protects the insured against financial loss caused by a title defect. The four types of policies are: owner's, mortgagee's, leasehold, and contract buyer's.
8. The three methods of property description in use in the United States are metes and bounds, reference, and rectangular survey.

How Would You Respond?

1. Black sold his property to Big Red Grocery Store. The owner's title insurance policy shows the title vested in Ralph Scott Black. The deed signed at closing was signed as R. Scott Black. Does this create any title problem? Why or why not? If yes, what steps should be taken to correct the title problem?
2. Your client wishes to purchase real property being sold by an estate. The estate will not provide title insurance. Should your client have a title search prepared or a title insurance binder issued before purchasing the real property? Why or why not?

Review Questions

Answers to these questions are found in the *Answer Key* section at the back of the book.

1. Voluntary alienation may occur by which of the following?
   a. condemnation
   b. will
   c. escheat
   d. adverse possession

2. If the owner of real property dies testate, title to the real property will transfer by:
   a. executor's deed to the devisee
   b. trustee's deed to the legatee
   c. warranty deed to the owner's descendants
   d. quitclaim deed to the testator

3. Essential elements of a valid deed include all of the following EXCEPT:
   a. acknowledgment
   b. writing
   c. competent grantor
   d. execution by grantor

4. The purpose of a deed being acknowledged is to:
   a. make the deed valid
   b. make the deed eligible for delivery
   c. make the deed eligible for recording
   d. identify the grantee

5. The type of notice provided by recording is which of the following?
   a. actual
   b. reasonable
   c. protective
   d. constructive

6. Of the following types of deeds, which provides the grantee with the greatest assurance of title?
   a. special warranty
   b. deed of confirmation
   c. sheriff's deed
   d. general warranty

7. Which of the following covenants assures the grantee that the grantor has the legal capacity to transfer title?
   a. covenant of quiet employment
   b. covenant of right to convey
   c. covenant of seisin
   d. covenant for further assurances

8. A deed in which the wording in the granting clause is "remise and release" is which of the following?
   a. quitclaim deed
   b. special warranty
   c. grant deed
   d. bargain and sale deed

9. Either a general warranty deed or a quit claim deed is equally suitable for which of the following?
   a. judicial deed
   b. trustee's deed
   c. official deed
   d. deed of gift

10. A grantor left a deed for the grantee to find after the grantor's death. The result was to:
    a. convey the title during the grantor's life
    b. convey the title after the grantor's death
    c. convey no title as the deed was not delivered
    d. convey no title as the deed was not recorded

11. The type of deed used to remove a mortgage lien when the debt is satisfied is:
    a. deed of surrender
    b. grant deed
    c. deed of release
    d. special warranty deed

12. At the time of his death, Brown owned a house on a lot. He has a debt of $40,000 on the house and land. Which of the following is true concerning the debt on the house and lot passed through his estate?
    a. the debt remains on the property
    b. the debt was terminated by Brown's death
    c. the debt was released from the real estate but is still owed by Brown's estate
    d. the debt escheats to the State

13. A claim of title by adverse possession may be defeated by the property owner by which of the following?
    a. permission
    b. confirmation
    c. will
    d. condemnation

14. The type of deed that guarantees the title against defects that were created only during the grantor's ownership is which of the following?
    a. bargain and sale
    b. special warranty
    c. surrender
    d. release

15. A mortgagee's title insurance policy protects:
    a. owner
    b. lending institution
    c. seller
    d. grantee

16. The successive conveyances of a title are called:
    a. releases
    b. remises
    c. links in the chain of title
    d. abstracts of title

17. Which of the following is a system of title registration?
    a. abstract continuation
    b. records of liens
    c. record of acknowledgment
    d. torrens

18. A title insurance policy may be written to protect all of the following EXCEPT:
    a. owner
    b. licensee
    c. lessee
    d. mortgagee

19. A title insurance policy protects the insured against loss caused by:
    a. defects in the title existing at the time the insured acquired title
    b. defects in the title created during the insured's ownership
    c. defects in title created in the past 40 years
    d. defects in title created by the assumed mortgage

20. A description as follows describes how many acres? "The NE 1/4 of the NE 1/4 of Section 12":
    a. 40 acres
    b. 160 acres
    c. 320 acres
    d. 640 acres

POSSIBLE RESPONSES TO "HOW WOULD YOU RESPOND?"

1. The signing of the deed as R. Scott Black does create a title problem. This deed creates a gap in the chain of title. Transfer of property by Grantor must be in exactly the same name as received as Grantee. The slightest deviation creates a title problem.

   To correct the problem, a corrective quitclaim deed signed properly can be recorded. Another remedy is to record an affidavit stating that R. Scott Black is one and the same as Ralph Scott Black.

   Correction of the problem requires that a new document be recorded.

2. Title to property in an estate is no better than the title held by the deceased owner. Mortgages, judgments, liens, etc., owed by the deceased owner pass through to the estate and are owed by the estate. In addition, property purchased from an estate is transferred by judicial deed. Judicial deeds have no warranties or guarantees as to title.

   Thus if your client wants assurance that title to the real property is marketable, a title search or title insurance binder is needed.

CHAPTER 7

IMPORTANT TERMINOLOGY

acceleration clause
alienation clause
amortization
arrears
conditional sales contract
conforming loans
contract for deed
deed in lieu of foreclosure (friendly foreclosure)
deed of trust
defeasance clause
deficiency judgment
disintermediation
"due on sale" clause
equity of redemption
Fannie Mae (FNMA)
FNMA pass-through certificate
foreclosure
foreclosure under the power of sale
Freddie Mac (FHLMC)
Ginnie Mae (GNMA)
hypothecate
installment land contract
interest
intermediate theory
judicial foreclosure
junior mortgage
land contract
lien (or mortgage) theory
liquidity
mortgage
mortgage assumption
mortgage bankers
mortgage broker
mortgagee
mortgage principal
mortgagor
nonjudicial foreclosure
nonrecourse note
novation
prepayment penalty
promissory note
release of liability
right of assignment
savings and loan associations (S&Ls)
secondary mortgage market
statutory redemption
strict foreclosure
title theory
trustee
trustor

Real Estate Finance Principles

IN THIS CHAPTER Most people do not have enough cash to buy property outright. Many existing loans are not assumable by the buyer, and many sellers are not willing to carry back any part of the price for future payment. For these reasons, most buyers must borrow some part, often a very substantial part, of the purchase price. Described in a single word, financing is *borrowing*. This chapter discusses financing instruments, such as mortgages and deeds of trust, and the various sources of real estate funds. Because cash sales are unusual, knowledge or lack of knowledge of the ways to finance a sale makes the difference between a successful or unsuccessful career in real estate. Federal government regulations of lending institutions that make mortgage loans and the secondary mortgage market are also covered.

NOTES

When a person borrows money the lender requires the borrower to sign a **promissory note**, also called a bond in some states. *The note, which must be in writing, provides evidence that a valid debt exists.* The note contains a promise that the borrower will be personally liable for paying the amount of money set forth in the note and specifies the manner in which the debt is to be paid. Payment is typically in monthly installments of a stated amount, commencing on a certain date. The note also states the annual rate of interest to be charged on the outstanding principal balance.

PRINCIPAL, INTEREST, AND PAYMENT PLANS

Understanding the terms *interest* and *principal* is essential to understanding notes, mortgages, deeds of trust, and all real estate financing methods. **Interest** is the *money paid for using someone else's money for a period of time*. The **mortgage principal** is the *amount of money that has been borrowed*. In the case of an interest-bearing note, principal is the amount of money the lender has lent the borrower and on which the borrower will pay interest to the lender.

The note can be an interest-only note on which interest is paid periodically until the note matures and the entire principal balance is paid at maturity. Construction notes are often of this type. Or the note can be a single-payment loan that requires no payments on either principal or interest until the note matures, and the entire principal and interest is paid at maturity. This is seen more frequently in short-term notes. The note also can be an amortizing note in which periodic payments are made on both principal and interest until such time as the principal is completely paid. Most mortgage loans are of this type.

The original principal is the total amount of the note. This amount remains the same in an interest-only or a one-payment loan until the entire principal is paid in one lump sum.

In an **amortizing** loan, *periodic payments are applied first toward the interest accrued since the last payment and then toward the principal.* As the principal portions of these payments are applied, the amount of principal gradually decreases. As each successive payment is made, the interest is applied to the declining principal balance; therefore, with each successive payment, the interest portion of the payment decreases and the principal portion increases but the combined principal and interest payment remains the same. The first payment is mostly interest, and the last payment is mostly principal. The payments can be set at a fixed rate for the life of the loan, or they can fluctuate based on a specified index, or they can change at set intervals according to a set formula. This subject is covered in more detail under types of mortgages in Chapter 8.

Simple interest is usually used for mortgage loan interest. This means that the interest is recalculated each time a payment is made and only charged on the decreasing outstanding balance. The annual rate of interest is used to calculate payments even though payments normally are made monthly. Payments sometimes are set up to be paid quarterly or annually. Recently, a payment plan in which payments are made every two weeks (biweekly) has become popular because it reduces the term of the loan and saves a significant amount of interest over the life of the loan. An existing loan can sometimes be switched to this payment plan.

Mortgage loan interest almost always is calculated in arrears, although it sometimes is calculated in advance. If interest is calculated in **arrears**, *a monthly payment due on the first of the month includes interest for using the money during the previous month.* If interest is calculated in advance, a monthly payment due on the first of the month includes interest for the month in which the payment is due. When paying off or assuming a loan, one must know if the interest is paid in advance or in arrears to determine the amount of interest owed or to be prorated at closing. Interest must be paid in arrears on all loans sold in the secondary mortgage market.

PUTTING IT TO WORK

Unlike rent, which is usually paid in advance of the month the rental property is used, interest is paid in arrears on most loans. When a borrower makes the September 1 payment, the interest out of that payment was for the past month, August, not the upcoming month.

MORTGAGE AND DEED OF TRUST

Typically, the borrower's personal promise to pay the debt is not enough security for the large amount of money involved in a mortgage loan. The lender therefore requires the additional security of the property itself as collateral for the loan. *Pledging property as security for the loan* **(hypothecating)** is accomplished through the mortgage or deed of trust instrument. Therefore, every mortgage loan has two instruments: (a) the note (a personal IOU), and (b) the mortgage or **deed of trust** (*a pledge of real property*). Pledging the property does not require the borrower to give up possession except in case of default. Then the property may be claimed by the lender.

The two main lending practices, or theories of financing, are:

1. **Lien (or mortgage) theory**, in which the *loan constitutes a lien against the real property*. The mortgage is a two-party instrument between the lender and borrower.
2. **Title theory** (granting theory), in which the lender or a third party actually holds legal title to the property as security for the loan. This may be either a mortgage (if held by the lender) or a deed of trust.

Some states have a modified plan of either the title or lien theory referred to as the intermediate theory. The **intermediate theory** *functions much like a mortgage or lien theory, but the lender does not have to wait until the foreclosure to obtain possession of the property*. In all states the mortgage or deed of trust creates a lien against the property pledged to secure payment of the note. Some states have, in addition to the lien, an actual conveyance of title within the mortgage or deed of trust for the purpose of securing the debt pending payoff.

A **mortgage** is a *two-party instrument in which the borrower gives a piece of paper (mortgage) to the lender in return for the borrowed funds*. The *borrower who gives the mortgage* is called the **mortgagor**. The *lender who receives the mortgage* is known as the **mortgagee**. The borrower (mortgagor) retains title to the property, but this title is encumbered by the lien created by the mortgage in favor of the lender (mortgagee). If the lender is not paid according to the terms of the mortgage and note, the lender can execute the lien, or foreclose.

In contrast, the title theory of finance requires the **trustor** *(borrower)* to convey title to the property to a **trustee**, a type of third-party referee, through a deed of trust. When the trustor completes paying off the debt, the trustee is required to return title to the trustor, by executing a deed of release. If the borrower defaults in his or her obligation to pay back the funds, the lender (beneficiary) may instruct the trustee to sell the title to recover the lender's funds. Because the lender therefore benefits from the title placed in trust, he or she is also known as the beneficiary.

Putting It to Work

The concepts of note and mortgage might become clearer by giving them "plain English" titles. The note's title would be "I promise to pay you back." The mortgage or deed of trust would be titled "and if I break any rules of our agreement, this is what you can do to me."

Requirements for Validity of a Mortgage or Deed of Trust

1. The mortgage or deed of trust must be in *writing*, as required by the Statute of Frauds, because the mortgage or deed of trust pledges or conveys title to real property to secure payment of the note.

2. The borrower (mortgagor) in a mortgage or the trustor in the deed of trust must have *contractual capacity*. This is the same requirement of competency necessary for creation of a valid contract as discussed in Chapter 5.

3. The mortgagee or trust beneficiary in a deed of trust and the trustee must have contractual capacity.

4. There must be a *valid debt* to be secured by the mortgage or deed of trust. The existence of the valid debt is evidenced by the note.

5. To secure the debt in the mortgage or deed of trust, the mortgagor or trustor must have a *valid interest* in the property pledged or conveyed.

6. A legally acceptable *description of the property* must be included.

7. The mortgage or deed of trust must contain a *mortgaging clause*. In lien theory states that use a mortgage form, the mortgaging clause is a statement demonstrating the mortgagor's intention to mortgage the property to the mortgagee. In title theory states, this clause takes the form of a deed of conveyance. The mortgaging clause in this case reads like the granting clause in a deed. This is not an absolute conveyance of title by the borrower but, rather, is a conditional conveyance made only to secure payment of the note.

8. The mortgage or deed of trust has to contain a *defeasance clause* that defeats the lien and conveyance of title when the mortgage debt is fully satisfied.

9. The *borrower must properly execute* the mortgage or deed of trust. Only the borrower signs the mortgage or deed of trust. The lender does not sign.

10. The mortgage or deed of trust must be *delivered* to and *accepted* by the mortgagee or trust beneficiary (lender).

Figure 7.1 shows the relationships in a deed of trust transaction.

Mortgage Clauses and Covenants

The following are examples of the various clauses and covenants that may be included in a mortgage or deed of trust.

1. The mortgage is dated and contains the names of mortgagor and mortgagee. If the deed of trust form is used, the borrower's name appears, identified as trustor, grantor, or mortgagor. The name of the trustee or grantee and the name of the lender, who is both the trust beneficiary and the noteholder, also appear.

2. The note executed by the borrower is reproduced in the mortgage or deed of trust. The note includes an **acceleration clause** *enabling the lender to declare the entire balance remaining immediately due and payable if the borrower is in default for any reason.*

Putting It to Work

Although failure to make payment is certainly the most common reason for default of a loan, there are also many other reasons. For example, the borrower may have failed to pay taxes; failed to keep the property insured (or to name the lender, if any, as an additional insured party to the policy); caused disrepair to the property (causing waste); used the property without zoning compliance; sold the property with a due-on-sale clause (discussed below); or other possibilities detailed in the mortgage document.

3. The note may provide that the borrower is permitted to pay off the loan any time prior to expiration of the full mortgage term without incurring a financial penalty for the early payoff, or it may provide for *a penalty to be imposed on the borrower* **(prepayment penalty)** *if the debt is satisfied prior to expiration of the full term.* FHA, VA, and conforming loans (discussed in Chapter 8) cannot have a prepayment penalty.

4. The mortgage requires the borrower to pay all real property taxes and assessments on a timely basis, keep the buildings in a proper state of repair and preservation,

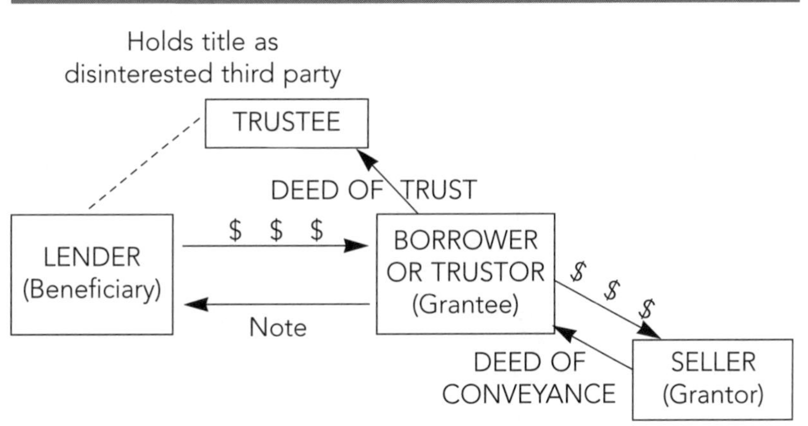

FIGURE 7.1 Relationships in a deed of trust transaction.

and protect the buildings against loss by fire or other casualty by an insurance policy written in an amount at least 80% of the value of the structures. Many lenders require insurance for 100% of the loan value.

5. The mortgage contains a **defeasance clause** *giving the borrower the right to defeat and remove the lien by paying the indebtedness in full.*

6. The mortgage provides the right of foreclosure to the lender if the borrower fails to make payments as scheduled or fails to fulfill other obligations as set forth in the mortgage.

7. In the deed of trust form, a clause gives the lender irrevocable power to appoint a substitute trustee or trustees, without notice and without specifying any reason, by recording an instrument of appointment on the public record where the deed of trust is recorded.

8. In both the mortgage form and the deed of trust form, a covenant always specifies that the mortgagor has a good and marketable title to the property pledged to secure payment of the note.

9. The mortgage or deed of trust may contain an **alienation** or **due on sale clause** entitling *the lender to declare the principal balance immediately due and payable if the borrower sells the property during the mortgage term; this makes the mortgage unassumable* without the lender's permission. The alienation clause may provide for the release of the original borrower from liability if an assumption is permitted. This release is sometimes referred to as a *novation* or *release of liability.*

10. Permission to assume the mortgage at an interest rate prevailing at the time of assumption can be given at the discretion of the lender. This is called an *escalation.*

11. The mortgage or deed of trust always provides for execution by the borrower. In some states witnesses also may be required.

12. The mortgage or deed of trust provides for acknowledgment by the borrower to make the document eligible for recording on the public record for the lender's protection.

Rights of Borrower

1. The borrower has the right to possession of the property during the mortgage term as long as the borrower is not in default.

2. The defeasance clause gives the borrower the right to redeem the title and have the mortgage lien released at any time prior to default by paying the debt in full.

3. The borrower has the right of **equity of redemption**. After default, the *borrower can redeem the title pledged or conveyed to secure a mortgage debt up to the*

time of a foreclosure sale by paying the debt, interest, and costs (discussed later in the chapter).

Rights of Lender

1. The lender has the right to take possession of the property (after foreclosure) if the borrower defaults in mortgage payments.

2. The lender has the right to foreclose on the property if the borrower defaults in the payments. The property may be sold at a foreclosure sale, and the proceeds of the sale, after certain other items are paid, are applied to satisfy the mortgage debt.

3. The lender has the right to assign the mortgage or deed of trust. This enables the lender to sell the mortgage, if he or she so desires, and thereby free up the money invested. The **right of assignment** provides liquidity to mortgages because *the lender can sell the mortgage at any time and obtain the money invested rather than wait for payment* of the loan over an extended time. Because of the right of assignment notes and mortgages are negotiable (transferable) instruments.

4. In title theory states the lender has the right to collect rents on a mortgaged property between default and foreclosure sale.

Foreclosure

If the borrower (mortgagor) does not make the payments as required, he or she is in default on the loan. The lender's ultimate power is to foreclose. **Foreclosure** is the *liquidation of title to the real property pledged, to recover funds to pay off the mortgage debt.* The two types of foreclosure are judicial and nonjudicial.

Judicial Foreclosure

In **judicial foreclosure**, *the lender brings a lawsuit against the borrower and obtains a judgment in the amount of the borrower's debt.* When the judgment is obtained, the lender requests the court to issue an execution instructing the sheriff to take possession of the mortgaged property and sell it for cash at public auction to the highest bidder. Many states require the public auction to be advertised for several weeks prior to the auction. Title is conveyed to the purchaser by a sheriff's deed or a trustee's deed.

Nonjudicial Foreclosure

Nonjudicial foreclosure, or **foreclosure under the power of sale**, *requires the mortgagee or trustee to advertise sale of the property* by posting notice at the courthouse in the county where the property is located for a period required by state law. The mortgagee or trustee also must advertise the sale in a newspaper published in the county in which the property is located, at least once a week for a minimum of three to five consecutive weeks (depending upon state requirements). In both the courthouse and newspaper notices the advertisement must describe the property and appoint a day and hour for the sale to be held. The sale is conducted by the trustee or sheriff, who conveys the title to the purchaser by a trustee's deed or a sheriff's deed.

PUTTING IT TO WORK

The major difference between judicial and nonjudicial foreclosure is the requirement of court action in judicial foreclosures. In other aspects, the events are much the same: default, advertisement, and auction.

PUTTING IT TO WORK

Who is purchasing all of these properties at the foreclosure sales? While technically these auctions are open for bidding by any interested party, the buyers are usually the foreclosing lienholder (lender). This lender-forced sale and usual purchase by the same lender is how the lender "wrestles" title away from a defaulting borrower.

Equity of Redemption

After default, and up to the time a foreclosure sale is held, the borrower has an equitable right to redeem his or her property by paying the remaining principal amount of the debt, accrued interest, and lender's costs incurred in initiating the foreclosure. The borrower's equity of redemption cannot be defeated by a mortgage clause. This right is terminated by the foreclosure sale. Some states, however, have passed statutes that allow redemption after foreclosure.

Statutory Redemption

Some states provide a benefit to the borrower by statute by allowing the borrower *the right to pay the debt plus accrued interest and costs in full after the foreclosure sale, and thereby recover the property*. This is called **statutory redemption**. The period of time during which the borrower may recover the property in this way varies from state to state, but it is usually 90 days to two years after the date of the foreclosure sale. Some statutes provide for possession of the property by the borrower during this period and the appointment of a receiver to collect rent from the borrower and see that the property is adequately maintained.

Strict Foreclosure

Under **strict foreclosure**, the *lender may file a foreclosure petition with a court after the mortgagor is in default*. The court then issues a decree requiring the mortgagor to satisfy the mortgage debt within a stated period of time or lose his or her equitable right to redeem the title. Once this right is lost, the mortgagor cannot assert any rights in the title or any remaining equity, which passes to the mortgagee. This type of foreclosure is not in favor in the United States.

Deed in Lieu of Foreclosure

In a measure sometimes called a **friendly foreclosure** but more formally a **deed in lieu of foreclosure**, a *borrower in default simply conveys the title to the property to* *the lender*, to avoid record of foreclosure. The disadvantage is that it does not eliminate other liens against the property. Furthermore, the lender may lose the right to any claim against mortgage insurance or guarantee programs such as FHA or VA.

Distribution of Sale Proceeds

Proceeds of the mortgage foreclosure sale are distributed in the following order of priority:

1. All expenses of the sale are paid. These include court costs, trustee's fee, advertising fees, legal fees, accounting fees, and the like.
2. If there are no other lienholders with liens having priority over the lien of the mortgage or deed of trust, the lender is paid including accrued interest.
3. Any other creditors holding liens against the property are paid; however, unsecured creditors are not paid with sale proceeds of the foreclosed property.
4. Any remaining monies (equity) after items 1 through 4 have been satisfied are paid to the borrower.

Whether or not real property tax liens and special assessments must be paid at the foreclosure sale is a matter of state law. Some states require these liens also to be included at the foreclosure sale; other states do not include them and the purchaser of the property will be responsible for those liens at a later time.

Deficiency Judgment

The borrower in a mortgage loan is personally liable for payment of the note. Therefore, if the proceeds of a foreclosure sale are not sufficient to satisfy the balance due the lender, the lender can sue for a **deficiency judgment** on the note. A deficiency judgment is *a court order stating that the borrower still owes the lender money.* Even though the collateral has been seized, there is still a valid debt evidenced by the note. Deficiency judgments are often sought by junior lienholders.

PUTTING IT TO WORK

Some states do not allow deficiency judgments under any circumstances. Others allow deficiencies only in auction sales in which the lender did not participate in the bidding. In essence, if lenders bid, they must bid the mortgage balance due to them. Thus, no deficiency is possible in these cases. Some other states prohibit deficiency judgments under specific conditions, such as those on properties financed by the seller.

Nonrecourse Note

One situation in which deficiency judgments are not available to the lender is in the case of a **nonrecourse note**. This type of note typically is used in mortgage loans secured by commercial property. Nonrecourse means the *borrower assumes no personal liability for paying the note*; therefore, the lender may look only to the property pledged in the mortgage to obtain the money owed in the case of default by the borrower. There are a few states that treat all mortgage notes as nonrecourse.

Other Aspects of Mortgages

Recordation

Recordation gives order to the system of land ownership and transfer. Recorded documents affecting real estate can be found in public records in the county in which the property is located.

Mortgages and deeds of trust should always be recorded. This protects those with any present or future interest in the property by providing constructive notice to the general public of claims against the property. Real estate documents do not have to be recorded to be valid between the parties involved. If they are not recorded, however, someone obtaining and recording a future interest in the property may have an interest superior to that of the person who gained an interest earlier but did not record the document before the future interest holder.

Priority and Subordination

Priority usually is established by the time (date and hour) the lien is recorded. The priority of certain liens, such as property tax liens, special assessment liens, and mechanics' liens, is not based on the time of recording but on other factors, as discussed in Chapter 3. In the event of a foreclosure sale, the holder of the first lien has the first claim against the sale proceeds, and that debt must be fully satisfied, including accrued interest, before the holder of the second lien is fully satisfied, and so on down the line of priorities. In some instances, the priority can be modified by a subordination agreement, whereby an earlier lender may be willing to subordinate (take a position of lower priority) to a later lender. Typically a lender will only subordinate his mortgage to another mortgage if he is certain the property value is sufficient to pay off both mortgages should foreclosure become necessary. An example of subordination occurs when the lien holder on a building lot subordinates his mortgage lien to the later construction mortgage lien.

Junior Mortgage

Junior mortgage describes *any mortgage that is subordinate (lower in priority) to another mortgage*. A junior mortgage may be a second mortgage, a third mortgage, or a fourth mortgage. Each of these is subordinate to any prior mortgage secured by the same property. The second mortgage is subordinate to a first mortgage, the third mortgage is subordinate to the second, and so on. Junior mortgages are usually for a shorter term and at a higher interest rate because they pose a greater risk to the lender than a first mortgage.

Releases

Recording a release of a mortgage, note, claim, or deed of trust is just as important as recording the original document. Failure to do so may continue to cloud the title to the property by showing a lien that no longer exists.

Types of Sales Transactions

Cash Sales

Although cash sales are the exception in real estate, they are perhaps the simplest real estate transaction to process. They can be as simple as the seller providing a deed and the buyer providing the cash. Unfortunately, the simplicity of these cash transactions may cause an inexperienced real estate salesperson to make costly mistakes. No mortgage company is involved in the transaction demanding an appraisal, a survey, a wood-destroying insect inspection, a structural inspection, deed recordation, payment of taxes or transfer fee, title search, and so on. Nonetheless, real estate practitioners have an obligation to make a reasonable effort to know and disclose to the buyer anything materially affecting the value of the property. Whether the deal is closed by a broker, an attorney, or an escrow, abstract, or title company, brokers are responsible for safeguarding the interests of their clients and for fairness to the other party.

New Financing

Most real estate transactions require new financing. The relatively recent savings and loan problems and skyrocketing mortgage foreclosures in many areas of the country have prompted mortgage lenders, FHA, VA, and private mortgage insurance companies to tighten requirements for new financing. To help buyers choose the most advantageous method of new financing, today's real estate practitioner needs a thorough knowledge of real estate finance. Knowledge of down payments, closing cost regulations, amounts of allowable seller or third-party contributions to closing costs, and methods of structuring the best possible payment plan are essential to a successful real estate transaction involving new financing. These aspects of finance and closing are discussed more fully in Chapters 8 and 9.

Mortgage Assumption

Although most conventional fixed-rate real estate loans are not assumable, some are, along with some older FHA-insured and VA-guaranteed loans. When a purchaser assumes the seller's existing mortgage, the purchaser assumes liability for the mortgage as well as personal liability for payment of the note. Therefore, such purchasers who default in mortgage payments are subject to the loss of their property as a result of a foreclosure sale and also are subject to a possible deficiency judgment obtained by the lender. Just like the original borrower, the wording of the contract is often "assumes and *agrees to pay.*"

In a **mortgage assumption**, the *seller whose mortgage was assumed remains liable for the mortgage and payment of the note* unless specifically released from liability by the lender. If the purchaser defaults and the proceeds of a foreclosure sale are insufficient to pay off the mortgage, the seller whose mortgage was assumed may be subject to a possible deficiency judgment by the lender. The lender can foreclose against the current titleholder and possibly sue the original borrower, or anyone who has assumed the mortgage, for a deficiency judgment if the proceeds of the foreclosure sale do not satisfy the mortgage debt. The seller's agent has a responsibility to inform the seller of a property sold under a loan assumption of any liability and recommend that the seller obtain a release of liability from the lender at the time of sale if possible. This **release of liability** *based upon substituting the buyer for the seller on the mortgage and note*, is sometimes called a **novation**.

Taking "Subject to" a Mortgage

If property is sold and title conveyed subject to the lien of an existing mortgage (but that lien is not actually "assumed"), the lender can still foreclose against the property in the event of a default in mortgage payments. In taking title subject to a mortgage, the purchaser does not become personally liable for payment of the note. Therefore, the lender cannot sue the purchaser for a deficiency judgment but may only obtain a deficiency judgment against the seller, who remains personally liable for paying the debt as evidenced by the note.

Land Contract/Contract for Deed

A **land contract** is also called a **contract for deed**, an **installment contract**, an agreement of sale, or a **conditional sales contract**. The essence of this contract is that the *buyer (vendee) is contracting to obtain legal title to the property by paying the purchase price in installments, and the seller (vendor) is agreeing to transfer the legal title to the buyer by the delivery of a deed* upon the buyer's full payment of the price.

Primary Sources of Real Estate Finance

Savings and Loan Associations

Savings and loan associations (S&Ls) lend money to construct housing, to purchase existing housing, and to effect improvements in existing housing. Traditionally, these organizations supplied more money for financing the purchase and construction of single-family dwellings than any other type of lending institution. During the late 1980s, however, S&Ls encountered a great deal of difficulty, losing billions of dollars. Hundreds of S&Ls have merged or closed, and the government has taken over hundreds more. Costs to taxpayers will be measured in the billions of dollars, and the effects on the economy will be felt for years to come. Nevertheless, these institutions continue to invest a larger portion of their assets in residential real estate than any other type of institution. Commercial banks, however, recently have surpassed S&Ls in actual number of mortgage loans originated and the amount of money invested in mortgage loans. Savings institutions, including S&Ls and savings banks, continue to provide more funds for one- to four-family housing than commercial banks provide; however, the gap has been steadily narrowing since 1988.

Savings and loan associations may be state-chartered or federally chartered; however, the practical difference has been blurred by passage of the Financial Institutions Reform, Recovery, and Enforcement Act (FIRREA) in 1989. This act, passed to curb the abuses and problems that led to the S&Ls' problems, affects all federally insured depository institutions. This legislation substituted (a) the Office of Thrift Supervision for the Federal Home Loan Bank Board, and (b) the Savings Association Insurance Fund for the Federal Savings and Loan Insurance Corporation. The Federal Deposit Insurance Corporation (FDIC) now regulates both banks and savings and loan associations; however, the insuring funds are maintained separately.

Some S&Ls have changed their names to "savings banks" to avoid the negative connotations now associated with S&Ls. Although some of these S&Ls changed their structure and function, others changed only their names. These savings banks differ from mutual savings banks (discussed below), some of which also have changed their names to savings banks.

The primary purposes for which savings and loan associations exist are (a) to encourage thrift (hence the term "thrifts"), and (b) to provide financing for residential properties. Although there are far fewer thrifts in existence today than in the early 1980s, in general they are enjoying profit and continue to play a major role in residential real estate financing.

Mutual Savings Banks

Mutual savings banks are similar to savings and loan associations in that their main objectives are to encourage thrift and to provide financing for housing. These organizations exist primarily in the northeast portion of the United States and are chartered and regulated by the state in which they are located. Mutual savings banks play a prominent role in financing housing in those states.

During the late 1970s and the 1980s, regulatory changes allowed these institutions to branch out into other types of loans and to become more like commercial banks. They now are more commonly called "savings banks." These depositor-owned institutions currently differ from other depository institutions primarily in form of ownership: they are still depositor-owned.

Commercial Banks

Commercial banks can be either federally chartered or state-chartered. In both cases, commercial banks are sources of mortgage money for construction, purchase of existing housing, and home improvements. Their loan policies usually are more conservative than those of other types of lending institutions. Commercial banks have steadily increased their mortgage holdings in recent years.

Mortgage Bankers

Mortgage bankers, also called mortgage companies, *make mortgage loans for the construction of housing and purchase of existing housing*. They often specialize in FHA-insured loans and VA-guaranteed loans, although most also make conventional loans.

Mortgage banking and mortgage brokering are quite different. Mortgage banking involves making and servicing mortgage loans. **Mortgage brokering** *brings together a lender and a borrower for a fee paid by the lending institution*, just as a real estate broker brings together a buyer and seller of real property for a fee. Mortgage brokers generally work with and represent many lending institutions. Often a mortgage company will perform both functions.

Life Insurance Companies

At one time a number of life insurance companies were active in making loans directly to individual mortgage borrowers. Today, they provide funds to lending institutions to lend to individual borrowers and to provide funds for the purchase or construction of large real estate projects such as apartment complexes, office buildings, and shopping malls.

PUTTING IT TO WORK

Currently, some life insurance companies are experimenting with the concept of mortgage divisions geared to residential borrowers. This is likely to be an area of expansion for insurance companies in the future.

Credit Unions

Credit unions may be an excellent source of mortgage money for their members. Usually, credit unions offer mortgage loans to their membership at an interest rate below the commercial rate at any given time. To be financially able to make long-term mortgage loans, the credit union must be of substantial size. The Federal Employees Credit Union, a state employees credit union, and the credit union of a major industry are examples of large credit unions.

Real Estate Investment Trusts (REITs)

Real Estate Investment Trusts (REITs) make loans secured by real property. REITs are owned by stockholders and enjoy certain federal income tax advantages. They provide financing for large commercial projects, such as second-home developments, apartment complexes, shopping malls, and office buildings. REITs may invest in properties as owners and managers, known as equity REITs, or they may choose to lend money on projects owned by others, known as mortgage REITs.

Individual Investors

Individuals in every area invest in mortgages. These investors usually are an excellent source for second mortgage loans. The seller of real property is definitely not to be overlooked as an individual investor. These sellers may finance the sale of their properties by taking a regular second mortgage, taking a second mortgage in the form of a wraparound, taking a purchase money first mortgage, or financing by means of a contract for deed. (These concepts are discussed in Chapter 8.) In times of extremely high interest rates, a sale often cannot be made unless the seller provides a substantial part of the financing for the buyer.

Secondary Mortgage Market

The primary mortgage market consists of lending institutions that make loans directly to borrowers. In contrast, the **secondary mortgage market** *buys and sells mortgages created in the primary mortgage market.* One of the requirements for mortgage liquidity is that it be assignable. This assignability feature allows the lender holding the mortgage to assign or sell the rights in the mortgage to another; thus, the money invested in the mortgage is freed without waiting for the borrower to repay the debt over the long mortgage term.

Sale of the mortgage by the lender does not in any way affect the borrower's rights or obligations. The original mortgagor may not even be aware that the mortgage has been sold, because the original lending institution often continues to service the loan for the purchaser of the mortgage and the mortgagor continues to make the necessary mortgage payments to the same lending institution that made the mortgage loan. If the purchaser of the mortgage prefers to service the mortgage itself, the original lender simply notifies the mortgagor to make payments to a different lender at a different address.

The secondary mortgage market benefits lending institutions and, in turn, the borrowing public, by providing **liquidity** to mortgages. The mortgage is a liquid asset because it *can be readily converted to cash* by the lending institution selling the mortgage in the secondary market. Sale of the mortgage by the lender is especially beneficial in low-yield mortgages—those mortgages for which the lender receives a lesser return on his or her investment in terms of both discount and interest rate, expressed as an annual percentage rate. The lender may get at least some money out of these mortgages to reinvest in new mortgage loans at current higher yields. This provides stability in the supply of money for making mortgage loans. Therefore, the secondary mortgage market benefits the borrowing public by enabling lending institutions to make money available for loans to qualified applicants.

Mortgage liquidity available in the secondary market reduces the impact of disintermediation on lending institutions. **Disintermediation** is the *loss of funds available to lending institutions for making mortgage loans, caused by the withdrawal of funds by depositors for investment in higher-yield securities in times of higher interest rates.* Without the secondary mortgage market, disintermediation can result in funds available to lenders "drying up" to the extent that these loans would be practically unavailable.

Secondary Market Activities

Some lending institutions limit their mortgage loans to their own assets rather than participate in the secondary mortgage market. For lenders that do participate in the secondary market, two types of markets are available: (a) the purchase and sale of mortgages among lending institutions, and (b) the sale of mortgages by lending institutions to three organizations that provide a market for this purpose (FNMA, GNMA, and FHLMC, discussed on the following pages).

Activities Between Lending Institutions

A major activity of the secondary mortgage market is the purchase and sale of mortgages by and among lending institutions. In this way, the market facilitates movement of capital from institutions that have available funds to invest to lenders that do not have enough money for this purpose.

For example, at any given time the demand for mortgage loans may be low in a given locality. Institutions with funds available for making loans in those areas are unable to invest these funds in the local market by making primary mortgage loans. Their funds should be invested in mortgages where they could earn interest instead of lying idle. At this same time, another part of the country may have a high demand for mortgage loans. A lender in that area may have a short supply of available funds to lend to qualified loan applicants. The problems of both of these lending institutions can be solved if the institution whose funds are in short supply sells its existing mortgages on hand to a lender in another area having a surplus of available funds and a low demand for mortgage loans. As a result, the lender with otherwise idle funds has them invested in mortgages earning interest as they should be, and the lender in short supply of money frees up capital invested in mortgages to meet the high demand for new mortgage loans in that area.

The direct sale of loans from investor to investor is legal and occurs relatively frequently, especially among small investors who sell to larger investors to make "pools." Much more likely are sales to organizations that buy and sell mortgages, as discussed in the following paragraphs.

Sale to Organizations

Three organizations that actively participate in purchasing mortgages from financial institutions are the Federal National Mortgage Association (FNMA), the Government National Mortgage Association (GNMA), and the Federal Home Loan Mortgage Corporation (FHLMC).

Federal National Mortgage Association (FNMA). The **FNMA** usually is referred to by its nickname **Fannie Mae**. It is the *oldest secondary mortgage institution and the single largest holder of home mortgages.* Fannie Mae was created in 1938 as a corporation completely owned by the federal government to provide a secondary market for residential mortgages. By 1968, it had evolved into a privately owned corporation. It is a profit-making organization, and its stock is listed on the New York Stock Exchange.

As a government-owned corporation, Fannie Mae was limited to purchasing FHA-insured mortgages and VA-guaranteed mortgages. As a privately owned corporation, it now may also purchase conventional mortgages, which currently are a major portion of its business.

Fannie Mae buys mortgages regularly. Mortgage bankers are major sellers of mortgages to Fannie Mae. Savings and loan associations, mutual savings banks, commercial banks, and life insurance companies also sell mortgages to Fannie Mae. Fannie Mae *sells interest-bearing securities (bonds, notes, and debentures) to investors.* These securities are backed by specific pools of mortgages purchased and held by Fannie Mae. These are sometimes called **pass-through certificates**.

Government National Mortgage Association (GNMA). The popular name for **GNMA** is **Ginnie Mae**. It was established in 1968, when Fannie Mae was fully converted to a private corporation. Ginnie Mae, *an agency of the Department of Housing and Urban Development* (HUD), *purchases mortgages to make capital available to lending institutions.* As a government agency, Ginnie Mae is *limited to the purchase of VA and FHA mortgages.*

Ginnie Mae guarantees the "Ginnie Mae Pass-Through," a mortgage-backed security providing participation in a pool of FHA-insured or VA-guaranteed mortgages. The pass-throughs are originated by lending institutions, primarily mortgage bankers. Ginnie Mae guarantees these securities and thereby makes them highly secure investments for purchasers. The yield on each pass-through issue is guaranteed by the full faith and credit of the U.S. government; the pass-throughs are secured by the FHA-insured and VA-guaranteed loans; and the lending institution originating the pass-through provides a guarantee as well. The government does not guarantee that investors in Ginnie Mae securities will make or not lose money on their investments. It only guarantees the loans backing the securities. If the interest rates change dramatically, the investor can either make or lose money as a result of these fluctuations.

Federal Home Loan Mortgage Corporation (FHLMC). Like the other organizations, **FHLMC** has a nickname, **Freddie Mac**, and likewise *exists to increase the availability of mortgage credit and provide greater liquidity for savings associations.* It achieves these objectives by purchasing mortgages.

Freddie Mac was created by Congress in 1970 *primarily to establish a reliable market for the sale of conventional mortgages.* At that time, Fannie Mae purchased only a small number of conventional mortgages, although this number has now increased; Ginnie Mae does not purchase conventional mortgages. Therefore, prior to Freddie Mac, lending institutions holding conventional mortgages were fairly well limited to the purchase and sale of these mortgages among themselves.

Freddie Mac sells mortgage-participation certificates (PCs) and guaranteed-mortgage certificates (GMCs). These are securities that represent an undivided interest in specific pools of mortgages. Freddie Mac guarantees payment of principal and interest to purchasers of PCs and GMCs.

Freddie Mac was part of, and was wholly owned by, the Federal Home Loan Bank (FHLB) System. When Freddie Mac began, approximately 3,000 savings and loan associations held its stock. In 1988, these associations released the stock for sale, which provided another source of funds for Freddie Mac's operations. Any member of the system and any other financial institution whose deposits or accounts are insured by an agency of the federal government is eligible to sell mortgages to Freddie Mac. Although Freddie Mac purchases residential conventional mortgages primarily from savings and loan associations, it also purchases residential conventional mortgages from mutual savings banks and commercial banks.

Other Aspects of the Market

Primary lenders wishing to sell mortgages to Fannie Mae or Freddie Mac must use uniform loan documents that meet criteria established by FNMA and FHLMC. Loans *processed on uniform loan forms and according to FNMA/FHLMC guidelines* are called **conforming loans**. For example, these organizations will not purchase any mortgage containing a **prepayment penalty**, an *extra charge for paying off a mortgage sooner than specified in its terms*. This requirement is particularly advantageous to individual borrowers when they are required to pay off their mortgage as a condition of a contract of sale. In some cases, prepayment penalties on nonconforming loans are extremely high and, therefore, pose a real hardship to sellers.

In late 1980, Fannie Mae announced a new program that is highly beneficial to home sellers who are willing to finance the sale for a buyer by taking a purchase money first mortgage (discussed in Chapter 8). Under the Fannie Mae program, the seller can have the mortgage prepared by a lending institution qualified to sell mortgages to Fannie Mae using uniform FNMA and FHLMC documents. The lending institution will close the transaction between seller and buyer and continue to service the loan for the seller for a fee. The institution collects the payments of principal and interest from the buyer and forwards them to the seller. In this way, sellers have an onsite expert to protect their interests and rights in the mortgage.

An important aspect of this Fannie Mae program is Fannie Mae's guarantee to purchase the mortgage if the sellers/mortgagees desire to sell and get their money out without waiting to complete a series of payments over the mortgage terms. Prior to this, sellers holding purchase money first mortgages had no reliable market for these mortgages if they wished to sell. This Fannie Mae program should provide additional incentive to home sellers to take purchase money first mortgages.

Important Points

1. The purpose of a mortgage or deed of trust (trust deed) is to secure the payment of a promissory note.
2. The two legal theories regarding a mortgage or deed of trust are the lien theory and the title theory.
3. A mortgage is a two-party instrument. A deed of trust is a three-party instrument.
4. The requirements for mortgage or deed of trust validity are: (1) writing, (2) competent parties, (3) valid debt, (4) valid interest, (5) property description, (6) mortgaging clause, (7) defeasance clause, (8) execution by borrower, (9) delivery to and acceptance by lender.
5. The borrower's rights are: (1) possession of the property prior to default, (2) defeat of lien by paying debt in full prior to default, and (3) equity of redemption.
6. The lender's rights are: (1) possession of the property upon default, (2) foreclosure, and (3) right to assign the mortgage.
7. The two categories of foreclosure are judicial and nonjudicial. Foreclosure sale proceeds are distributed in a special order of priority. If the sale proceeds available to the lender are insufficient to satisfy the debt, the lender may sue for a deficiency judgment if the laws of his or her state allow for deficiency judgments under the specific circumstances.
8. A buyer assuming a seller's mortgage assumes liability on both the mortgage and the note. The seller, however, remains liable on the note unless specifically released by a mortgage clause or by the lender. A buyer taking title "subject to" an existing mortgage has no liability on the note.
9. A fully amortizing mortgage requires payments of principal and interest that will satisfy the debt completely over the mortgage term.
10. The major sources of residential financing are savings and loan associations, mutual savings banks, commercial banks, and mortgage bankers. Of these, savings and loan associations have traditionally provided more funds for one- to four-

family housing than any other single source, though the gap between savings institutions and commercial banks narrowed significantly after the S&L shake-up in the 1980s. When all types of mortgages (residential, commercial, and farm) are considered, commercial banks hold more mortgage loans than do savings institutions.

11. In the primary mortgage market, lending institutions make loans directly to individual borrowers. In the secondary market, lending institutions purchase and sell mortgages among themselves and sell mortgages to Fannie Mae (FNMA), Ginnie Mae (GNMA), and Freddie Mac (FHLMC). The market provides liquidity to mortgages, thereby reducing the effect of disintermediation for the benefit of lending institutions and borrowers as well.

How Would You Respond?

You have just taken a listing on a property for six months. The sellers cannot remember whether it is a conventional or FHA loan and the mortgage company has changed at least four times in the last two years. They do remember the agent telling them something about "assumable" when they bought it seven or eight years ago, but not whether anything was said about qualifying. The sellers are also about six weeks behind on their mortgage payments as the husband has been out of work for two months. What are some of the issues facing you and the sellers in marketing this property?

1. What information do you need to know regarding the origination date of the loan?
2. How is this information important if the existing loan is FHA? VA? Conventional?
3. What is the difference between "freely assumable" and "assumable with qualifying"?
4. How does the sellers' current delinquency on the loan affect things?
5. What does the sellers' current delinquency do to your marketing strategy?

Review Questions

Answers to these questions are found in the *Answer Key* section at the back of the book.

1. All of the following statements are applicable to promissory notes EXCEPT:
   a. they must be written
   b. the borrower is personally liable for payment
   c. they provide evidence of a valid debt
   d. they are executed by the lender

2. Which of the following statements concerning a mortgage is (are) correct?
   a. the purpose of a mortgage is to secure the payment of a promissory note
   b. a mortgage is a lien on real property
   c. a mortgage is a two-party instrument
   d all of the above

3. Which of the following is NOT a right given to lenders by a deed of trust?
   a. assignment
   b. possession after default
   c. foreclosure
   d. equity of redemption

4. The clause that makes a mortgage unassumable is which of the following?
   a. defeasance
   b. alienation
   c. mortgaging
   d. prepayment

5. Which of the following gives the borrower the right to pay the debt in full and remove the mortgage lien at any time prior to default?
   a. defeasance
   b. acceleration
   c. equity of redemption
   d. foreclosure

6. The borrower's right to recover the title after the foreclosure sale is which of the following?
   a. strict
   b. statutory
   c. equitable
   d. judicial

7. A deed in lieu of foreclosure conveys a title to which of the following?
   a. lender
   b. borrower
   c. trustee
   d. mortgagor

8. Which of the following is paid first from the proceeds of a foreclosure sale?
   a. mortgage debt
   b. real property taxes
   c. mortgagee's equity
   d. sale expenses

9. A deficiency judgment may be available to:
   a. mortgagee
   b. mortgagor
   c. trustee
   d. trustor

10. A buyer assumed the seller's mortgage without providing release of liability and subsequently defaulted. Which of the following is (are) correct?
    a. only the buyer is personally liable for payment of the note
    b. only the seller is personally liable for payment of the note
    c. both the buyer and the seller may be personally liable for payment of the note
    d. neither the buyer nor the seller is personally liable for payment of the note

11. When one refers to a second mortgage, the word *second* addresses the issue of:
    a. where the loan was obtained
    b. priority
    c. a co-borrower
    d. assignment

12. The activity of lending institutions making mortgage loans directly to individual borrowers occurs in the:
    a. secondary mortgage market
    b. money market
    c. institutional market
    d. primary mortgage market

13. Which of the following is a government-owned corporation that purchases FHA and VA mortgages?
    a. Fannie Mae
    b. Ginnie Mae
    c. Freddie Mac
    d. Maggie Mae

14. The major benefit of the secondary mortgage market is to provide lenders which of the following?
    a. amortization
    b. liquidity
    c. disintermediation
    d. expensive settlement charges

15. Which of the following organizations would NOT originate a mortgage loan for a borrower?
    a. bank
    b. mortgage banker
    c. FNMA
    d. savings and loan

POSSIBLE RESPONSES TO "HOW WOULD YOU RESPOND?"

1. The origination date will have bearing on whether the loan is assumable with or without qualifying if it is FHA or VA.

2. FHA's cutoff date on this issue is a conditional commitment on 12-15-89. VA's cutoff date is origination on 3-1-88. A conventional loan is likely to be assumable only with qualifying if it is assumable at all.

3. "Freely assumable" is without significant fees or qualifying. Qualifying requires approval of the lender according to certain guidelines or possibly arbitrary guidelines of the lender.

4. The sellers' delinquency may cause the lender to be less likely to cooperate on an assumption if they have discretionary guidelines.

5. The fact that your listing is for six months may be irrelevant if the sellers are two payments behind. The lender may commence foreclosure proceedings long before the listing expires. There will be a greater sense of urgency which may or may not need to be disclosed to assist in the marketing.

CHAPTER 8

IMPORTANT TERMINOLOGY

adjustable rate mortgage (ARM)
annual percentage rate (APR)
appraisal
balloon payment
blanket mortgage
certificate of reasonable value (CRV)
construction mortgage
conventional mortgage loan
cooling-off period
disclosure statement
discount points
down payment
Equal Credit Opportunity Act (ECOA)
escrow account
Federal Housing Administration (FHA)
FHA-insured loans
good faith estimate
graduated payment adjustable mortgage
graduated payment mortgage (GPM)
growing equity mortgage (GEM)
impound account
junior mortgage
leasehold mortgage
loan-to-value ratio
margin
mortgage insurance premium (MIP)
negative amortization
open-end mortgage
package mortgage
participation mortgage
prepaid items
prepayment penalty
private mortgage insurance (PMI)
purchase money mortgage
qualifying
Real Estate Settlement Procedures Act (RESPA)
Regulation Z
release clause
release of liability
settlement
shared appreciation mortgage (SAM)
substitution of entitlement
take-out loan
term mortgage
Truth-in-Lending Simplification and Reform Act (TILSRA)
underwriting
VA-guaranteed loan
wraparound mortgage

Real Estate Finance Practices

IN THIS CHAPTER In this chapter, we discuss the various loans the buyer may use to finance the purchase of real property with a lending institution. The types of mortgage loans that may be obtained from lending institutions can be divided into two groups:

1. Conventional loans, those that are not backed by an agency of the federal government.
2. FHA or VA mortgage loans, those in which the federal government participates either by insuring the loan to protect the lender (FHA-insured loans) or by guaranteeing that the loan will be repaid (VA-guaranteed mortgage loans).

DOWN PAYMENTS, LOANS, AND QUALIFYING

A person buying a home rarely pays all cash. The *portion of the price that is paid in cash* is called the **down payment**. The balance of the price involves some form of loan. The seller may accept part of the price with future payments or allow an existing loan to be assumed. Most often, however, the buyer will have to get a new loan from some type of a financial institution—a bank, savings and loan, or mortgage broker.

Analysis of a buyer's ability to borrow money for a purchase is referred to as **qualifying**. This ability to obtain new financing depends upon many things: value of collateral, size of down payment, buyer's credit, buyer's income and debts, and financial market conditions (interest rates). A problem in any one of these areas can affect the interaction of all of them, possibly causing a loan to be rejected by the lender. See Figure. 8.1 for an example of a qualifying worksheet for a conventional loan.

LOAN-TO-VALUE RATIO

Relying solely on the borrower's income, creditworthiness, and the property as collateral, the lender will set a limit as to how much an applicant can borrow. Sometimes this limit is set by law or the type of loan or is simply left up to the lender's discretion. The **loan-to-value** ratio is the *loan amount divided by the value of the property expressed as a percentage*. If the lender allows a $60,000 loan against a property valued at $80,000, this would be $60,000 ÷ $80,000 = .75 or a 75 percent loan-to-value ratio. The balance of the price must be paid as a cash down payment. Without additional guarantees or assurances, most lenders will not lend more than 80 percent of the value on owner-occupied residential property. The amount loaned gets lower as lenders feel that a loan carries more risk. On an investor's rental property, the limit may be only 70 percent, on land 50 percent or even less. Different types of loan programs have different loan-to-value ratios, and while lenders have similar standards, there are many individual differences.

CONVENTIONAL LOANS

A **conventional mortgage loan**, one that has *no participation by an agency of the federal government*, can be either uninsured or insured. In an uninsured conventional loan, the borrower's equity in the property provides sufficient security for the lender

FIGURE 8.1
Qualifying income worksheet for a conventional loan.

Before approving a conventional mortgage loan, the lender must determine if the borrower will be able to meet the financial obligation of monthly house payments. Most often, the lender requires that the monthly home payments not exceed 28% of the borrower's gross monthly income and that the total of all long-term obligations not exceed 36% of this income; this is referred to as the 28/36 rule.

For example, assume a sales price of $125,000, a loan amount of $100,000,* and an annual interest rate of 8.5% with a 30-year loan term. (Please use the amortization chart on p. 161 if you don't have a financial calculator.) Tax and insurance escrow numbers are given. In this case, the formula would be applied as follows:

1. The lender will first calculate the total monthly payments:

$769.00	(P & I)
116.80	for tax escrow (T)
54.00	for insurance escrow (I)
$939.80	P.I.T.I. (total monthly payment)

2. Next the borrower's gross monthly income will be calculated by dividing the annual household salary by 12:

   $55,000 ÷ 12 = $4,583.33

3. The ratio of home payments to gross monthly income is then determined by dividing the payment by monthly income:

   $939.80 ÷ $4,583.33 = 20.5%

   The first part of the 28/36 rule has been satisfied since this ratio is under 28%.

4. All other long-term expense payments are then added to determine the borrower's other long-term debt:

$340.00	car payments
75.00	credit card payments
100.00	personal loan
$515.00	total monthly payment for long-term debt

5. Add this total to the house payment:

   $ 515.00
   939.80
   $1,454.80

6. Divide this total by monthly income to determine the ratio of long-term debt:

   $1,454.80 ÷ $4,583.33 = 31.7%

   The borrower will qualify for the loan since this ratio is under 36%.

*This is an 80% loan-to-value ratio; therefore, it requires no private mortgage insurance (PMI). A higher loan-to-value ratio requires PMI to be included in payments. Also, a higher loan-to-value ratio often will use a 25/33 rule instead of the 28/36 rule.

to make the loan; therefore, any further insurance to protect the lender in case of the borrower's default is not required. In most cases, the borrower obtains a loan that does not exceed 75 to 80 percent of the property value and has a remaining equity of 20 or 25 percent. An insured conventional loan typically is one in which the borrower has a down payment of only 5 or 10 percent and therefore borrows 90 to 95 percent of the property value. In these cases, insuring repayment of the top portion of the loan to the lender is necessary in the event the borrower defaults. The insurance is called **private mortgage insurance (PMI)**, and private insurance companies, not government agencies, issue the policies. Today, private mortgage insurance companies insure more mortgage loans than the FHA does. The premiums and features of private mortgage insurance have grown more varied and complex in recent years. The examples that follow are just that—examples.

Premiums and program features vary greatly. Some premiums are one-time fees; others are paid up front and include a yearly premium (factored into the monthly payment). Some plans are refundable, which means that if the loan is paid off early, part of the PMI is returned. Sometimes the PMI may be financed; other times part or all may be required in cash. Occasionally the PMI can be dropped if the loan-to-value ratio drops to 80 percent or less due to amortization of the loan or appreciation in the value of the property. And, in all cases, the lower the down payment, the more expensive PMI premiums become due to the higher risk. The cost is usually blocked out into loan-to-value ratio segments of 80–85 percent, 85.01–90 percent, or 90.01–95 percent to determine the premiums.

Aspects of Conventional Mortgages

Conventional mortgages can take many shapes with varied terms. In the early 1980s, more innovations appeared in the types of mortgages than in the preceding 50 years because of inflation and the accompanying increases in interest rates. Often these increases were radical and on very short notice. As a result and for their protection, lending institutions tried to shift the burden resulting from rapid increases in interest rates from themselves to the borrowing public by making substantial modifications to mortgage loan programs. We discuss here various types of mortgages, including those of long-standing duration and those that have come into existence more recently. If more than one mortgage exists on the same property or properties, one of them is the first mortgage and all others are junior mortgages.

Junior Mortgage

Junior mortgage describes *any mortgage that is subordinate to (lower in priority than) another mortgage.* Second mortgages, the most common form of junior mortgage, frequently are used to finance part of the difference between the purchase price of a property and the loan balance being assumed in a purchase involving assumption of the seller's existing mortgage. The seller often offers a short-term (5-, 7-, or 10-year) purchase money second mortgage to the buyer for part of the difference when the buyer does not have the funds to pay the full assumption amount. Second mortgages also are available from other sources, such as finance companies, credit unions, and others when the borrower has sufficient equity in the property.

Term Mortgage

In a **term mortgage**, *the borrower pays only interest for the term of the loan, and at the end of the term the borrower is required to pay the entire principal.* This was the type of mortgage generally in use before and during the depression of the 1930s.

Many borrowers were unable to pay the principal when it came due, and lenders were unable to refinance the principal for the borrower as they had done in more prosperous times. As a result, many homeowners lost their property through foreclosure.

PUTTING IT TO WORK

In today's markets a seller often provides financing for three to five years with interest-only payments and the full balance to be paid at the end of this period. This is a common term mortgage.

Amortizing Mortgage

The **Federal Housing Administration (FHA)** was created by the National Housing Act of 1934 for the purpose of *insuring mortgage loans to protect lending institutions in case of borrower default*. FHA will insure only amortizing mortgages (mortgages that retire the debt). As a result of this and of the potential hardship for borrowers under the term mortgage, the typical home mortgage loan today is the amortizing mortgage whether the loan is FHA, VA, or conventional.

As explained in Chapter 7, amortization provides for paying a debt by installment payments. A portion of each payment is applied first to the payment of interest and the remainder to reduction of principal. The interest is computed only on the outstanding principal balance due at the time of an installment payment, not on the original balance. This is also called simple interest.

The rate of interest is an annual percentage rate as specified by the note and mortgage. The interest rate is calculated by multiplying the annual percentage rate by the unpaid principal balance and dividing the result by 12 (months) to determine the amount of interest due and payable for any monthly installment.

After deducting the interest, the remainder of the payment goes to reduce the principal balance. Therefore, the amount of interest paid with each installment declines because the interest rate is applied against a smaller and smaller amount of principal. In this way, the loan is amortized so the final payment in a fully amortizing mortgage will pay any remaining interest and principal.

The payment may be a fixed amount and remain the same over the life of the loan, or it may be a graduated payment. Possibly the payment may change as a result of a varying interest rate specified in the note and mortgage.

Figure 8.2 shows an abbreviated version of an amortization chart, used to determine monthly payments on an amortized loan.

Fifteen-Year Mortgage

The 15-year mortgage has gained popularity in recent years. In reality, this is a regular fully amortized mortgage with a 15-year term. By cutting the loan term from 30 years to 15 years, the borrower greatly reduces the interest paid, and therefore the cost of funds, for a moderate increase in monthly payment. The shorter term also provides for faster equity accumulation in the property.

Balloon Mortgage

The balloon mortgage provides for installment payments that are not enough to pay off the principal and interest over the term of the mortgage, so *the final payment*

AMORTIZATION CHART (Monthly payments per $1,000)				
Annual interest rate	Years to fully amortize loan			
	15	20	25	30
6.50	8.71	7.46	6.75	6.32
6.75	8.85	7.60	6.91	6.49
7.00	8.99	7.75	7.07	6.65
7.25	9.13	7.90	7.23	6.82
7.50	9.27	8.06	7.39	6.99
7.75	9.41	8.21	7.55	7.16
8.00	9.56	8.36	7.72	7.34
8.25	9.70	8.52	7.88	7.51
8.50	9.85	8.68	8.05	7.69
8.75	9.99	8.84	8.22	7.87
9.00	10.14	9.00	8.39	8.05
9.25	10.29	9.16	8.56	8.23
9.50	10.44	9.32	8.74	8.41
9.75	10.59	9.49	8.91	8.59
10.00	10.75	9.65	9.09	8.78

Note: This is an abbreviated amortization chart intended for example and learning purposes. Most real estate salespersons find it easier to use a calculator to compute and compare payments and to quickly solve other real estate math problems.

FIGURE 8.2 An abbreviated amortization chart.

(called a **balloon payment***) is substantially larger than any previous payment, to satisfy the remaining principal and interest.* If this balloon payment is to be a substantial amount, the note may provide for refinancing by the lender to provide the funds to the borrower if he or she cannot otherwise make the final payment.

Open-End Mortgage

An **open-end mortgage** *allows additional borrowing without rewriting the mortgage* or incurring additional closing costs. The original mortgage provides the security for additional funds to be advanced to the borrower up to a specified amount and sometimes functions as a line of credit. This is not the typical residential first mortgage, but home equity loans that became instantly popular in 1987 with the new tax law may be considered in this category. These loans are currently a popular form of junior financing.

Graduated Payment Mortgage (GPM)

In the **graduated payment mortgage (GPM)**, *monthly payments are lower in the early years of the mortgage term and increase at specified intervals* until the payment amount is sufficient to amortize the loan over the remaining term. The monthly payments are kept down in the early years by not requiring the borrower to pay all the

PUTTING IT TO WORK

Although GPM loans do make qualifying for a loan easier, the greater financial burden of the "peak" payments actually may make default more likely. In addition, adding unpaid accrued interest to the balance may cause owners to find themselves "upside down" in the property, meaning that they owe more than the property may be worth.

interest, which is added to the principal balance. This increase in the balance is called negative amortization.

The purpose of this type of mortgage is to enable individuals to buy homes by offering lower initial monthly payments. An outstanding example of this type of mortgage loan is the FHA 245 graduated payment mortgage, discussed later in this chapter.

Adjustable Rate Mortgage (ARM)

To say that the 1980s and 1990s have been turbulent decades for real estate finance would be an understatement. In the late 1970s, no sage would have predicted that interest rates would soar from 9 percent to 18 percent or higher. Who would have predicted in 1982 the 7.5 percent rates seen in mid-1986 and again in the early and mid-1990s? Given these circumstances, the motivation of lending institutions to shift the burden of unpredictability from themselves to the mortgagor is easier to understand. We therefore can appreciate the adjustable rate mortgage from the lender's standpoint. Suppose you had $50,000 to commit to a 30-year, fixed-rate loan. What interest rate would you accept?

The **adjustable rate mortgage (ARM)** (or *variable rate mortgage*) evolved as one solution to the uncertainty of future financial rates. With the ARM, the *parties agree to float mortgage rates based on the fluctuations of a standard index.* Common indices include the cost of funds for savings and loan institutions, the national average mortgage rate, and the one-year rate for the government's sale of Treasury Bills.

An ARM designates an index and then adds a **margin** *(measure of profit)* above this index. For example, if the Treasury Bill (T-Bill) index were 7 and the lender's margin were 2.50, the ARM would call for an interest rate of 9.5.

The ARM has definite advantages for some buyers, especially for the short-term owner who expects to sell the home in the near future, perhaps because of an employment transfer. Long-term owners may fear the possibility of an ever-increasing mortgage rate, but apprehension should be moderated by the understanding that economic cycles rise and fall and, in the case of inflation, the value of the property likely will rise as well. The potential long-term buyer may choose an ARM with a conversion feature allowing him or her to convert to a fixed-rate mortgage when interest rates are more favorable.

A significant concern in an ARM is the possibility of **negative amortization**. When the index rises, and if the payment is fixed, it may cause the payments to fall below the amount necessary to pay the interest required by the index. This *shortfall is added back into the principal, causing the principal to grow larger after the payment.*

Modern ARMs are structured with caps (ceilings) that limit both the annual adjustment and the total adjustment during the lifetime of the loan. For example, annual increases could be limited to perhaps 1 or 2 percent interest, and the lifetime loan ceiling might be no higher than perhaps 5 or 6 percent above the original rate. There may similarly be a floor. Many ARMs also prohibit negative amortization. Conventional lenders and FHA have authorized adjustable rate mortgages for several years.

Renegotiated Rate Mortgage

Similar to an ARM is a renegotiable rate mortgage. The major difference is the duration of each interval before a rate change is allowed. On ARMs this can be as short as one month to as long as two years. With renegotiable rate mortgages the interval is typically every three to five years. Renegotiable rate mortgages are often capped but are rarely indexed.

FIGURE 8.3
Understanding loan payments.

(a)
Using the amortization chart.

Example: Assume a home purchase price of $87,500 with a conventional mortgage of 80% of the sales price at an annual interest rate of 8.5% for 30 years.

1. Calculate the amount of the loan:
   $87,500 × 80% = $70,000
2. Figure 8.2 lists a factor for each $1,000 of a loan. Divide $70,000 (our loan amount) by $1,000 (as per Figure 8.2) to determine the number of units of $1,000, which is 70. Jot down this figure before completing step 3.
3. Go to the 8.5% row (our annual interest rate) on Figure 8.2. Read across to the 30-year column (our loan term). The factor listed is 7.69. This is the payment per month per $1,000 of the loan.
4. Multiply the 70 from step 2 by the 7.69 figure from step 3 to arrive at $538.30. This is the monthly payment of principal and interest (P & I) needed to amortize (pay off) a loan of $70,000 at 8.5% for 30 years.

(b)
Calculating interest paid per month.

Use the data from (a) to calculate how much of the payment (P & I) went toward interest (I).

1. Interest (I) equals the principal (P) times the rate (R) times the period of time (T) you have had the money, or:
   I = P × R × T
2. In our example,
   I = $70,000 × 8.5% × 1⁄12 of one year, or
   I = $70,000 × 0.085 = $5,950.00 ÷ 12 = $495.83
3. Therefore, of the total payment of $538.30 in the first month, $495.83 went to interest.

(c)
Calculating principal reduction per payment.

How much did this monthly payment of $538.30 reduce the loan principal? Subtract the amount that went toward interest from the total payment amount; the remainder went to principal:

	$538.30	(P & I)
–	495.83	(I)
	$ 42.47	(P)

(d)
Calculating principal balance after one payment.

1. Calculate the amount that went to principal: $42.47
2. Subtract this amount from the previous balance:
   $70,000.00
   – 42.47
3. The remainder is the new principal balance: $69,957.53

(e)
Calculating total interest paid over the life of this loan.

1. Calculate the monthly payment: $538.30
2. Calculate the total number of months to be paid; in this case:
   30 (years) × 12 (months per year) = 360 payments
3. Multiply the monthly payment times the total number of months to be paid to calculate the total of the payments:
   $538.30 × 360 payments = $193,788 total payback
4. Subtract the amount of the loan borrowed from the total payback to calculate the amount that went toward interest:
   $193,788.00
   – 70,000.00
   $123,788.00 total interest paid

FIGURE 8.4 Comparing monthly payments and interest paid between a 15-year and a 30-year loan.

As we determined in Figure 8.3, the monthly payment needed to amortize an 8.5% interest loan of $70,000 in 30 years (360 payments) is $538.30.

Using the same formula, we can determine that the monthly payment to amortize an 8.5% interest loan of $70,000 in 15 years (180 payments) is $689.50. With these two figures, we can now make the following comparisons:

30-year loan		15-year loan
$ 538.30	*Monthly payment*	$ 689.50
× 360	*Number of payments*	× 180
$193,788.00	*Total $ paid over life of loan*	$124,110.00
– 70,000.00	*Minus amount of original loan*	– 70,000.00
$123,788.00	TOTAL INTEREST PAID	$ 54,110.00

Thus, with the 30-year loan, the borrower paid $69,678 more interest.

Note: While this is a substantial savings in actual dollars, the benefit may be reduced by several factors:

1. The borrower will have less of a tax deduction for interest paid.
2. The dollars paid in extra principal each month could possibly earn more money if invested elsewhere.
3. Due to inflation, dollars paid toward the mortgage in later years are actually worth less than those paid in early years.

The effect of these factors varies depending upon an individual's tax bracket, his or her expertise at investing money, and the rate of inflation.

New variations in recent years are the very popular 5/25 and 7/23 loans. Interest rates are locked in for the first five or seven years respectively with only one rate adjustment possible at the end of that term. Then the rate will remain the same for the remaining 25 or 23 years of the loan. Many of these have provisions that if interest rates get too high at the interval point, the loan must be paid off or refinanced.

Graduated Payment Adjustable Mortgage

The **graduated payment adjustable mortgage** is a *combination of the graduated payment mortgage and the variable rate mortgage*. Its purpose is to make more borrowers eligible for mortgage loans by keeping the payments down in the early years as a result of the graduated payment and the variable rate features.

Federal regulation of lending institutions has been liberalized in an effort to protect financial institutions making long-term loan commitments from extreme fluctuations in short-term interest rates. These institutions borrow funds at the short-term rate but lend money on a long-term basis. As a result, they sometimes are caught in a situation in which the price they must pay in the form of interest for use of money is more than the interest they earn on a long-term basis from making mortgage loans. The addition of ARMs, GPMs, and combinations of the two has shifted some of the burden of fluctuating interest rates from lending institutions to mortgage loan borrowers.

Shared Appreciation Mortgage (SAM)

The **shared appreciation mortgage (SAM)** *allows the lender to benefit from the appreciation of property value in exchange for a lower rate of interest to the borrower*. Typically, for a one-third share in appreciation, the lender makes the loan at a rate one-third less than the going rate for a fixed-term conventional loan at the time the loan is created.

The increase in value that the lender shares is evidenced by the price for which the borrower sells the property, as compared to the price paid for the property. Federal regulations require that if the property is not sold within 10 years, the property must be appraised and the lending institution must receive its one-third share of the value increase as shown by the appraisal. This could result in a substantial hardship for the borrower who does not sell within the 10-year term. This borrower may have to refinance to obtain the money to pay the lender the one-third share of value increase.

Growing Equity Mortgage (GEM)

The **growing equity mortgage** is *a loan in which the monthly payments increase annually, with the increased amount applied directly to the loan's principal*, thus allowing the loan to be paid off more quickly.

Bi-Weekly Mortgage

A long-term mortgage will have total interest paid over the life of the loan that is substantial, or, to many borrowers, staggering. In an effort to pay off loans more quickly, many borrowers have opted for biweekly mortgage payments plans. These may be arranged directly with some lenders or through a third party collection account.

By paying half of a monthly payment every two weeks, the borrower will make 26 "half payments" or the equivalent of 13 full payments in one year. The extra payment is applied entirely to the principal balance, which speeds up the payoff. In many cases this shortens the payoff by several years and saves thousands of dollars in interest charges. A borrower can achieve the same basic result by paying an extra portion each month to the principal. Most lenders allow this partial prepayment without penalty and even invite it in a section on the payment coupon for "additional prepayment."

Participation Mortgage

Participation mortgage describes two different types of mortgages.

1. *A mortgage in which two or more lenders participate in making the loan.*

2. *A mortgage in which the lender participates in the profits generated by a commercial property used to secure payment of the debt in the mortgage loan.* The borrower agrees to the lender's participation in the net income as an inducement for the lender to make the loan. This allows the lender to receive interest as well as a share of the profits. This is similar to the shared appreciation mortgage except that the lender receives part of the annual income instead of a one-time capital gain.

Wraparound Mortgage

A **wraparound mortgage** is *a second mortgage for an amount larger than the existing balance owed on a first mortgage against the same property.* This mortgage "wraps around" the existing first mortgage, which stays in place. The seller of the property makes a wraparound loan to the buyer, who takes title to the property subject to the existing first mortgage. The seller continues to make the payments on the first mortgage, and the buyer makes the payments to the seller on the wraparound.

The wraparound mortgage can be beneficial to both seller and buyer. The seller makes payments on the existing first mortgage at an old and often lower interest rate and on a smaller loan amount. The seller receives the buyer's payments on a substantially larger loan amount at a higher rate of interest than the seller is paying on the existing first mortgage. In this way, the seller receives principal payments on the second mortgage and earns interest income on the amount by which the interest received on the wraparound exceeds the interest being paid on the existing first mortgage. In addition, the wraparound may enable the seller to effect a sale that otherwise may not have been accomplished in times of high interest rates and tight money. The benefits to the buyer in this situation include purchasing the property with a small down payment and obtaining seller financing at a rate usually several percentage points below the prevailing market rate for new financing at that time. Additionally, the closing costs on a wraparound are substantially lower than with institutional financing.

Wraparounds work only when the existing first mortgage is assumable. If the existing first mortgage contains a due-on-sale or alienation clause, a wraparound mortgage cannot be used. The alienation clause provides that the existing first mortgage must be paid in full if the title to the property is transferred by the first mortgage borrower without the lender's authorization. Lenders will often give their approval provided the interest rate on the existing mortgage is increased to the current rate charged by the lender.

Package Mortgage

In a **package mortgage**, *personal property in addition to real property is pledged to secure payment of the mortgage loan.* Typical examples of these items are washer and dryer, range and oven, dishwasher, and refrigerator. The package mortgage is used frequently in sales of furnished condominium apartments and includes all furnishings in the units. This is also common in commercial real estate lending where the business assets are also offered as collateral.

Blanket Mortgage

In a **blanket mortgage**, *two or more parcels of real estate are pledged as security for payment of the mortgage debt.* The blanket mortgage usually contains a **release clause** that *allows certain parcels of property to be removed from the mortgage lien if the loan balance is reduced a specified amount.* The mortgage always should provide that sufficient property value remains subject to the mortgage lien to secure the remaining principal balance at any given time.

Real estate developers typically use blanket mortgages with release clauses. In this way, the mortgagor can obtain the release of certain parcels from the lien of the mortgage and convey clear title to purchasers to generate a profit and provide the funds to make future mortgage payments.

Construction Mortgage

The **construction mortgage** is a form of *interim, or temporary, short-term financing for creating improvements on land.* The applicant for a construction loan submits, for the lender's appraisal, the plans and specifications for the structure to be built and the property on which the construction is to take place. The lender makes the construction loan based on the value resulting from an appraisal of the property and the construction plans and specifications. The loan contract specifies that disbursements will be made as specified stages of the construction are completed; for example, after the foundation is laid or upon framing. Interest is not charged until the money has actually been disbursed. Upon completion, the lender makes a final inspection and closes out the construction loan, which is then converted to permanent, long-term financing or replaced by financing obtained by a buyer of the property.

Often the lender requires the builder to be bonded for completion of the property. The bond is made payable to the lender in the event the builder goes bankrupt and is unable to complete the structure. In this way, the lender can obtain the funds to complete the construction and have a valuable asset to sell and recover the monies extended under the construction loan.

If the mortgage commitment is strictly a short-term construction loan, permanent financing (e.g., 30 years) will have to be established. *Permanent financing on a short-term construction loan* is known as a **take-out loan**. This commitment is necessary to assure long-term financing within the mortgagor's means.

Purchase Money Mortgage

The **purchase money mortgage** is a *mortgage given by a buyer to the seller to cover part of the purchase price*. Here, the seller becomes the mortgagee and the buyer the mortgagor. The seller conveys title to the buyer, who immediately reconveys or pledges it as security for the balance of the purchase price. The seller is financing the sale of his or her property for the buyer in the amount of the purchase money mortgage. The purchase money mortgage may be a first mortgage, a typical junior mortgage, or a junior mortgage in the form of a wraparound.

Contract for Deed

As discussed in Chapter 5, the contract for deed (or installment land contract) is both a contract of sale and a financing instrument. The seller provides a method of purchasing the property, and the buyer makes installment payments.

The distinction between the contract for deed and the purchase money mortgage method of financing between buyer and seller is that in the purchase money mortgage, the seller conveys title to the buyer, who pledges it as security for payment of the mortgage debt. In the contract for deed, no title passes until the buyer completes the required installment payments totaling the purchase price, unless the contract for deed stipulates that the title pass at some other specified time.

Leasehold Mortgage

The **leasehold mortgage** *pledges a leasehold estate rather than a freehold estate to secure payment of a note*. The leasehold acceptable to the lender is a long-term estate for years. The usual case is a lease for vacant land whereon the lessee is to construct an improvement such as a shopping mall, a hotel, or an office building as an investment.

Begin

FHA-Insured Loans

Part of the mission of the Federal Housing Administration (FHA), created during the Depression of the 1930s, was to make home ownership available to more people, to improve housing construction standards, and to provide a more effective and stable method of financing homes. It succeeded in this mission and provided the leadership to standardize procedures for qualifying buyers, appraising property, and evaluating construction. FHA has been an agency of the U.S. Department of Housing and Urban Development (HUD) since 1968.

FHA does not make mortgage loans. Instead, **FHA-insured loans** *protect lenders against financial loss*. The buyer pays for this insurance protection by paying an upfront mortgage insurance premium at closing and an annual mortgage insurance premium prorated monthly and paid with the monthly mortgage payment (discussed later in this section). This insurance enables lenders to provide financing when the **loan-to-value ratio** is high. Loan-to-value ratio *compares the loan amount to the property value*. With a high ratio, the borrower has to make only a small down payment. The amount of insurance protection to the lender is always sufficient to protect the lender from financial loss in the event of a foreclosure sale because these loans are insured for the entire loan amount.

Many of the FHA programs available in the past are no longer available or are no longer widely used. The most popular program still in existence is the FHA 203(b) loan, which allows an owner-occupant to purchase a one- to four-family dwelling with an FHA-insured loan. The FHA 245 graduated payment mortgage, the FHA 203(b)(2) FHA-VA mortgage, and the FHA 234(c) condominium loan also are available when circumstances warrant.

FHA 203(b) Loan Program

The FHA 203(b) regular loan program is the original and still the basic FHA program. It provides for insuring loans for the purchase or construction of one- to four-family dwellings. FHA does not set a maximum sales price, only a maximum loan amount. A buyer may purchase a home for more than the FHA maximum loan amount, but he or she will have to pay anything above the maximum loan amount in cash. As of this writing, maximum loan amounts range from $77,197 to $152,362 for the purchase or construction of a single-family dwelling, and from $148,300 to $292,800 for the purchase or construction of a four-family dwelling, depending upon approved limits for a specific area. The maximum loan amount is based on acquisition cost, which is the combination of FHA-appraised price or sales price, whichever is lower, plus those buyer's closing costs that FHA will allow to be financed. With the 203(b) loan the principal and interest payment and interest rate are both fixed for the term of the loan. The most common terms of FHA 203(b) loans are 15 or 30 years.

Other FHA Loan Programs

FHA has a variety of other loan programs available to borrowers. In periods of higher interest rates (over 12 percent) the FHA 245 loan is popular. This is a graduated payment loan with the monthly payment lower in the early years, usually not enough to pay the interest; consequently, the balance rises. The payments increase yearly over the first five or 10 years of the loan to reverse this negative amortization.

The FHA 203(b)(2) loan, sometimes called FHA-Vet or FHA-VA, is not related to the regular VA loan program, and does not affect a veteran's entitlement. The benefit is that there is no down payment on the first $25,000 of value. This reduces the down payment by $750 (.03 x $25,000).

The FHA 234(c) is the condominium version of a "standard" FHA loan. The condominium project must meet certain FHA conditions regarding construction, owner occupancy, and homeowner association structure.

FHA Mortgage Insurance Premium (MIP)

In 1990, the U.S. Congress revised FHA **mortgage insurance premium (MIP)** calculations again. In July 1991, the 3.8 percent MIP, which was calculated on the base loan amount and paid at closing or added to the loan amount, was renamed an upfront mortgage insurance premium (UFMIP). The amount of this UFMIP decreased to 3.0 percent in October 1992 (the beginning of fiscal year 1993) and again in April

1994 to 2.25 percent. An additional annual MIP is charged at the rate of 0.5 percent, applied to the average unpaid principal balance. This amount is divided by 12 to arrive at the premium to be paid monthly. The length of time this annual MIP must be paid depends upon the loan-to-value ratio and the fiscal year in which the loan is made.

FHA Loan Qualification

FHA loan qualification procedures changed dramatically on December 1, 1989, when FHA changed from a net income to a gross income approach. This change simplified qualifying a buyer for an FHA loan. Under these guidelines, the monthly housing expenses composed of principal, interest, taxes, homeowner's insurance, MIP paid monthly, and homeowners' association dues or assessments, if any, cannot exceed 29 percent of gross income. This total mortgage payment, plus any recurring monthly debts which will either extend for six months or more or have payments of more than $100 per month, cannot exceed 41 percent of effective gross income.

FHA Maximum Loan Amount

Several changes in legislation and regulations from 1990 until late 1992 have affected FHA maximum loan amount calculations. The net effect of the changes is that the determination of maximum loan amount is now a two-step process. In the first step, the loan amount calculation is based on acquisition cost (or mortgage basis), which consists of the FHA appraised value or sales price, whichever is lower, plus 100 percent of the buyer's allowable closing cost. These loan amounts are 97 percent of the first $25,000 of acquisition cost, 95 percent of the acquisition cost between $25,001 and $125,000, and 90 percent of acquisition cost above $125,000. A special case exists if the adjusted sales price or appraised value is $50,000 or under. The 97 percent loan-to-value ratio is applied to the whole acquisition cost, even that amount between $25,000 and $50,000. The loan amounts discussed in this paragraph cannot exceed the area's FHA loan limit, which equals 95 percent of the area's median home price or 75 percent of the loan amount allowed by Fannie Mae and Freddie Mac, whichever is lower.

The second step in the maximum loan amount calculations applies a 97.75 percent maximum loan-to-value ratio to the appraised value, excluding closing costs, if the value is over $50,000 and 98.75 percent if the value is $50,000 or less. The lesser amount derived from step 1 and step 2 is the maximum loan amount. This calculation of maximum loan amounts is current as of early 1995; however, real estate practitioners are advised to keep abreast of changes in this area.

Maximum loan amounts are available for dwellings that are more than one year old or, if less than one year old, were built to FHA specifications and under FHA supervision or with an acceptable 10-year homeowner warranty. If the dwelling is less than one year old and not built to specifications and under supervision or with an acceptable 10-year homeowner warranty, the loan amount is 90 percent of the total acquisition cost. These guidelines require that the borrower occupy the property.

FHA Loan Assumption Policies

In 1986, FHA began changing its policies on assumptions of FHA-insured loans. FHA mortgages originated before December 1, 1986, are freely assumable without qualification by owner-occupants and investors alike. The Housing and Urban Development Reform Act of 1989 effectively stopped new investor loans and nonqualifying loan assumptions. A creditworthiness review is required for the assumption of all FHA loans originated after December 15, 1989. This requirement remains in effect throughout the life of the loan.

FHA Changes

Significant changes have taken place in the FHA home loan program since its inception, but especially since 1983, and will most certainly change many times in the future. Salespeople must understand these changes because they will likely be selling properties purchased with FHA loans that originated under rules different from those currently in effect. When such a property is listed, the salesperson should obtain copies of the documents relating to the original sale to determine what rules apply to the sale in the case of either a loan assumption or a loan payoff. Rules for loan assumption qualification, release of liability, notification and time of payoffs, and possible partial refunds of mortgage insurance premiums are important, and these differ according to when the loan was underwritten.

PUTTING IT TO WORK

Comprehensive changes pertaining to FHA loans have occurred in the past decade and changes are ongoing. Salespeople can remain current regarding FHA guidelines by looking to their broker-in-charge, the firm's training or loan processing department, a trade publication, or a mortgage lender.

DEPARTMENT OF VETERAN AFFAIRS GUARANTEED LOAN PROGRAM

Whereas the FHA programs insure loans, the Department of Veteran Affairs offers a guaranteed loan program. Under a **VA-guaranteed loan** the VA *guarantees repayment of the top portion of the loan to the lender in the event the borrower defaults*. Unlike the FHA, the VA does not set maximum loan amounts.

The VA-guaranteed loan is a 100 percent loan requiring no down payment. The loan amount may be 100 percent of the VA appraisal of the property set forth in the Veterans Administration **certificate of reasonable value (CRV)** or 100 percent of the sales price, whichever is less. The VA provides this certificate, sometimes informally called the VA appraisal, to the lending institution as a basis for making the loan. VA-guaranteed loans are available for the purchase or construction of one- to four-family dwellings. The VA does not have a program for loans in which the veteran borrower will not occupy the property being purchased or constructed. When obtaining the loan, the veteran must certify in writing that he or she will occupy the property being purchased with the loan proceeds. (If veteran is on active duty, spouse must occupy.) If the property is a multi-family dwelling (maximum of four units), the veteran must occupy one of the apartments.

Eligibility

For the borrower to be eligible for a VA-guaranteed loan, he or she must qualify as a veteran under requirements of the Department of Veteran Affairs. Three groups of qualifying periods are as follows:

Group I

Qualification in this group consists of at least 90 days of active duty during any one of four wartime periods:

- World War II: September 16, 1940, to July 25, 1947

- Korean War: June 27, 1950, to January 31, 1955
- Vietnam: August 5, 1964, to May 7, 1975
- Persian Gulf War: August 2, 1990, to present

The veteran must have been discharged or released from duty under conditions other than dishonorable or may still be on active duty.

Group II

The three periods in Group II fall between the wars and from the conclusion of U.S. involvement in Vietnam to September 8, 1980. To qualify in any of these groups, the veteran must have served at least 181 days of active duty and must have been discharged or released under conditions other than dishonorable or still be on active duty. (The period between September 8, 1980, and August 2, 1990, is covered under Group III even though it is technically between the Vietnam War and the Persian Gulf Conflict.)

- Post-World War II: July 26, 1947, to June 26, 1950
- Post-Korean: February 1, 1955, to August 4, 1964
- Post-Vietnam: May 8, 1975, to September 8, 1980

Group III

From September 8, 1980 (enlisted), and October 17, 1981 (officers), to August 2, 1990, 24 months on active duty are required if the veteran is no longer on active duty. During this time, the veteran could get a VA loan after 181 days on active duty as long as he or she was still on active duty at the time of the loan or was discharged for a service-connected disability, the convenience of the government, or hardship.

The spouse of a deceased veteran who had qualified under one of the three groups and died as a result of a service-connected disability or in the line of duty is qualified as the veteran would have been. Eligibility is not allowed for children, spouses who remarry, or spouses in cases in which the deceased veteran did not die as a result of service.

In October, 1992, President Bush signed HR 939 into law. This legislation provides for VA entitlement to certain members of the National Guard and the military reserves with over six years of service. These individuals will have to pay a higher VA funding fee, and their entitlement will end after seven years.

If a contract of sale subject to the buyer's obtaining a VA-guaranteed loan is created prior to an appraisal and commitment by the VA, the contract must contain the following statement, as required by the Department of Veteran Affairs:

> It is expressly agreed that, notwithstanding any other provisions of this contract, the purchaser shall not incur any penalty by forfeiture of earnest money or otherwise be obligated to complete the purchase of the property described herein, if the contract purchase price or cost exceeds the reasonable value of the property established by the Department of Veteran Affairs. The purchaser shall, however, have the privilege and option of proceeding with the consummation of this contract without regard to the amount of the reasonable value established by the Department of Veteran Affairs.

Qualifying for VA Loans

Since 1986, VA standards require the borrower to qualify under both a net family support standard and a gross monthly income ratio.

VA Loan Analysis Form 26-6393 is used to organize information on estimated home payments, long-term debts (six months or longer), and family dependents, and to evaluate the reliability of monthly income. Net take-home pay is determined by taking the gross monthly income minus federal taxes, state taxes, social security tax, and other pension plans or deductions. This net income is then reduced by the amount of the estimated home payments and long-term debts to determine a residual balance available for family support. This residual balance must meet regional standards established by the VA. A family of four must have a monthly residual balance of $986 in the Northeast, $964 in the Midwest, $964 in the South, and $1,074 in the West.

The next step in the qualification is to compare the total of home payments, special assessments, homeowners' association dues, and debts that either will extend for six months or more or will have payments of more than $100 per month to the gross monthly income. This ratio is limited to 41 percent. A VA loan analysis form is used to organize information on income and long-term debts to determine if the 41 percent ratio will be met.

PUTTING IT TO WORK

Qualifying a veteran for a VA loan is not difficult; however, it requires consulting several tables to determine various taxes, maintenance costs, residual requirements, and child care expenses. Military pay tables for active duty veterans also are helpful. VA qualification can be time consuming. Even though all practitioners should understand this qualification process, using a computer program to perform the qualification is highly recommended. Many inexpensive, easy-to-use programs incorporating these tables are available.

Anyone can assume a VA loan. The person assuming the loan does not have to be a veteran. He or she can either be an owner-occupant or an investor and can provide release of liability in both situations. Only an assuming owner-occupant veteran can substitute entitlement to restore the selling veteran's entitlement. All VA loans closed after March 1, 1988, require qualification and release of liability for assumption.

Restoration of Eligibility

When a veteran is discharged from the service, he or she receives a "certificate of eligibility." This certificate states the maximum guarantee in effect at the time the veteran is discharged. Today, the certificate provides an eligibility of $36,000 for loans $144,000 or less and up to $50,750 for loans of more than $144,000. If a veteran has used either full or partial eligibility in obtaining a VA loan, he or she may have that eligibility fully restored in one of the two following ways:

1. The loan is paid in full and the veteran has disposed of the property.
2. A veteran purchaser with as much remaining eligibility as the original veteran used to obtain the loan and who also satisfies the VA requirements for income, credit, and occupancy assumes the VA loan from the original veteran borrower. The assuming veteran must meet the same requirements as an original VA loan applicant and agree to substitute his or her entitlement for that of the original veteran purchaser.

A mere **release of liability** by the lender and the VA does not in itself restore eligibility. Anyone can assume a VA loan; however, only a qualified veteran can give a **substitution of entitlement**. As pointed out in item 1 above, simply *paying the loan in full is not sufficient to restore the entitlement; the veteran must no longer own the property.*

PUTTING IT TO WORK

There is a widespread misunderstanding that VA financing is a "once-in-a-lifetime" loan. This is not true. The VA entitlement may be fully restored (see above) or any remaining partial guarantee may be used (see below).

Unused Eligibility

If a veteran has used part of his or her eligibility and sold the property to a nonqualifying veteran or nonveteran who assumed the loan, the veteran may still have some eligibility remaining. For example, if the veteran obtained the loan between May of 1968 and December of 1974, the maximum guarantee in effect was the lesser of $12,500 or 60 percent of the loan amount. Even if the veteran used all eligibility at that time by obtaining a loan for $50,000 (all of the entitlement would have been used at that time for any loan of $20,833.33 or above), the remaining eligibility is at least $23,500 (up to a $144,000 loan) to $38,250 (up to a $203,000 loan), depending on the loan amount. These numbers are derived by subtracting the maximum eligibility of $12,500 existing at the time the loan was made from the current two-tiered maximums of $36,000 or $50,750.

History of Loan Guarantees

The loan guarantee the Department of Veteran Affairs gives to lenders making VA loans has steadily increased over the years from the lesser of $2,000 or 50 percent of the loan amount, when the program was first initiated in 1944, to the present multi-layered system outlined in Table 8.1. In all, there have been eight increases since the initial program.

On December 18, 1989, the VA changed its guarantee to the lender to the present structure (Table 8.1). These guarantees are the same as the guarantees put into effect February 1, 1988, except for the addition of a $50,750 guarantee for loans of more than $144,000. This change complicates the calculation of remaining entitlement when a veteran has used part of his or her entitlement. Because the loan amount determines whether the remaining entitlement is based on $36,000 or $50,750, the loan amount must be determined before it is known whether all or any of the extra $14,750 can be used.

OTHER ASPECTS OF FHA AND VA LOANS

Down Payment

If the VA Certificate of Reasonable Value is less than the price the veteran is willing to pay for a home, the veteran still may obtain the VA loan and make a down payment

TABLE 8.1 VA loan guarantees.

LOAN AMOUNT	PERCENT OR AMOUNT OF GUARANTEE
$45,000	50% of loan amount
$45,001 to $144,000	40% of loan amount or $36,000, whichever is less
$144,001 to $203,000	25% of loan amount or $50,750, whichever is less

for the difference between the loan amount and the purchase price. In this case, as well as with the down payment required under an FHA-insured loan program, the borrower may not finance the down payment unless it is secured by other collateral. The borrower must have these funds on hand and certify in writing that he or she has not borrowed this money, and is under no obligation to repay the money if the money is a gift.

Miscellaneous

The maximum term of either an FHA or a VA loan is 30 years. Both of these types of loan are assumable, although with qualification after certain origination dates, and at the same interest rate at which the loan was originally created. The presence or absence of qualification requirements and the dates they became effective are given under each loan type. Mortgages securing these loans may not contain a due-on-sale (alienation) clause as long as the purchaser meets the qualification requirements in effect at the time the loan was made and the loan is transferred in accordance with applicable regulations. In either an FHA or a VA assumption, the difference between the loan amount assumed and the purchase price can be financed, although the loan payment on the amount financed must be considered in the qualification process on loan assumptions requiring release of liability. FHA and VA mortgages never require a **prepayment penalty**, a *charge for paying off the loan before the end of the mortgage term.*

As of October 1, 1992, all FHA loans require that the borrower sign a lead-based paint notice if the property was built before 1978. This notice must be signed on or before date of contract of sale.

Closing or Settlement Costs

At the time of **settlement** or *closing of a real estate transaction*, both the buyer and the seller must satisfy the various expenses and obligations incurred in the transaction. If this is a new first mortgage from a lending institution, the buyer's cost typically is at least 3 percent of the loan amount plus discount points. The seller's closing cost varies widely depending on the obligations that must be satisfied at the closing. One substantial obligation that the seller may have is the requirement to satisfy (pay off) an existing first mortgage against the property.

Putting It to Work

At various points in the process, the salesperson provides the buyer or the seller, or both, with an estimate of closing costs. This typically occurs during the prequalification process and again as needed when offers or counteroffers are presented. At the time of listing the property, and again when offers are presented, the salesperson usually gives the seller an estimate of net proceeds.

The various closing or settlement costs buyers and sellers incur in real estate transactions are discussed in detail in Chapter 9.

Residential Lending Practices and Procedures

Loan Origination

Once a borrower has contracted to purchase a home, the process of arranging for mortgage financing commences. The main document in the loan origination process is the loan application. Customarily, the borrower and the lender's representative meet, and the borrower completes the loan application at this initial meeting.

At the time of loan application, the borrower is required to sign the following authorization forms, so the lender can verify the data the borrower gives on the loan application:

1. Verification of employment. If the borrower is self-employed, the most recent two years' tax returns (personal and business) are required in place of this verification.
2. Verification of rent or mortgage.
3. Verification of bank account balance.
4. Verification of outstanding loans.
5. Verification of sales contract deposit.
6. Verification of pension (if applicable).
7. Authorization to release information.
8. Consent to credit check and verification.

Sometimes substitute documentation may be used in place of verifications. For example, pay stubs or employee year-end W-2 statements may be used in place of employment verification; bank account statements for two months prior to loan application may substitute for bank account verification. In addition to the documents listed, most lenders require a copy of the borrower's driver's license and social security card for identification purposes. The loan origination documentation, along with the purchase contract, the borrower's check to cover the cost of the credit report and the property appraisal, and an application fee, is delivered to the lender's loan processing department for action.

Putting It to Work

Many lending institutions have implemented a "one-button" loan application process whereby most loans can be approved or declined by confidential computer analysis, without upfront human processing. Check to see if lenders in your area offer this service.

Loan Processing

For general information, the following steps, among others, are involved in loan processing.

Appraisal

An **appraisal**, *an evaluation of the subject property by a qualified professional,* normally is ordered from an appraiser who has obtained recognized training and experience through membership in a professional appraisal organization. For most lending that requires appraisals, the appraiser now must be licensed or certified according to state regulations. A Uniform Residential Appraisal Report form has been created to standardize appraisals nationally (see Chapter 10, Figure 10.1).

Credit Report

In ordering a credit report, the reporting agency will contact at least two national repositories of accumulated credit records covering each residence of the borrower over the prior two-year period. Several national credit organizations meet the repository definition: Trans Union, TRW, Credit Bureau, Chilton Corporation, Associated Credit Services, and Associated Credit Bureau Service. All information on the credit report must be verified from sources other than the borrower; otherwise, the credit agency must report that they are unable to verify or that the credit source refused to verify. The borrower may be required to provide other explanations or documentation concerning these accounts.

Application Review

The purpose of loan processing is to verify all data the borrower presents in the loan application. This is done by comparing the verified information with the application data. The borrower must explain items that do not match and must obtain additional verification or data. For example, employment income, bank deposit, and outstanding debts must be the same on the credit report and the loan application.

Although the loan processor is not the loan underwriter, the processor sometimes may decline the loan before submitting to underwriting if the borrower clearly will not qualify because of excessive debts or insufficient income, or if the property fails to meet the lender's standards as to condition or value.

Loan Underwriting

Once all information has been verified and the loan documentation assembled, the loan processor submits the loan to **underwriting**. The underwriter is responsible *for reviewing the loan documentation and evaluating the borrower's ability and willingness to repay the loan and the sufficiency of the collateral value of the property*. The underwriter may be someone on the lender's staff or, in the case of a loan designated for sale, someone on the investor's staff. In the case of FHA and VA loans, these agencies have delegated underwriting responsibility to the lender. For conventional loans over 80 percent loan-to-value and requiring mortgage insurance, an underwriting submission also must be made to the private mortgage insurance company.

Many factors govern loan underwriting. The following are only representative of the basic factors that must be considered in the loan approval process. Loan underwriting can be divided into three categories: buyer ability to pay, buyer willingness to pay, and property evaluation.

Buyer Ability to Pay

The buyer's ability to pay consists of the following considerations:

1. *Employment.* Borrower employment for the past two years is verified as evidence of ability to pay. Also, the underwriter must determine the probable stability and continuance of that employment.

2. *Income.* Even if employment is stable, income may not be. Borrowers who are self-employed, work on commission, or are employed by a close relative must submit signed federal income tax returns for the most recent two years.

3. *Closing funds.* The borrower has to show sufficient funds on hand to close the mortgage transaction. The verified borrower's deposit on the sales contract plus

verified bank balances must equal the down payment plus closing costs and prepaid items. The underwriter must look for the possibility of last-minute unsecured borrowed funds being used for all or part of the required closing costs (evidenced by large, unexplained recent bank deposits).

Gift funds from a family member are acceptable to meet cash requirements for closing FHA or VA loans if they are actually transferred to the borrower and verified.

Stocks and bonds also are acceptable as closing funds if the market value can be verified and a 5 percent borrower cash down payment is made.

4. *Debt ratio.* The underwriter must calculate the borrower's two debt ratios: (a) monthly housing expense to income, and (b) total payment obligations to income. These ratios determine the borrower's ability to meet home ownership responsibilities. The ratios most lenders in the secondary market recognize are:

	Monthly Housing Expense	*Total Obligations*
Conventional Loans		
Fixed-rate	28%	36%
Adjustable-rate	28%	36%
FHA loans	29%	41%
VA loans	None	41%

Monthly housing expense includes: fixed mortgage payment plus deposits for hazard insurance premium; real estate taxes and mortgage insurance premium; owners' or condominium association charges, less the utility charge portion; any ground rents or special assessments; and payments under any secondary financing on the subject property.

These ratios do not constitute absolute requirements. For example, compensating factors allow for approval of a borrower with higher housing expense and total obligation ratios than set forth here. Some factors or conditions allowing for higher ratios are:

a. For mortgage loans with 20 percent or larger down payment:
   - Borrower's demonstrated ability to delegate a higher percentage of income to mortgage payments.
   - Borrower's demonstrated ability to accumulate savings.
   - Borrower's property qualifying as an energy-efficient dwelling.
   - Borrower's potential for higher long-term earnings.

b. For mortgage loans with less than 20 percent down payment, the lender has risks in addition to the above ratios; therefore, the underwriter must determine that:
   - Borrower will have adequate cash reserves after closing, usually the equivalent of two months' mortgage payments.
   - Borrower has the ability to make mortgage payments in excess of his or her previous housing expense.
   - Borrower has demonstrated an ability to accumulate savings and to properly manage debt.
   - Borrower has maintained an excellent credit history.
   - Borrower has a capability for future increased earnings and savings.

c. For adjustable rate mortgages with less than 20 percent down payment, the debt ratio usually is calculated based on the fully indexed adjustable rate (loan margin plus index), not the initial rate, which in many instances can be up to 2 percent lower. Thus, when mortgage rates are at 10 percent, the borrower may have to qualify on the basis of 10 percent.

d. For adjustable rate mortgages with greater than 20 percent down payment, the borrower under an ARM may qualify on the basis of the lower first-year rate.

Thus, under the same interest rate conditions, a buyer might qualify on the basis of 8 percent if he or she has the larger down payment.

Buyer Willingness to Pay

The buyer's willingness to pay is reflected by credit history. This can be demonstrated by the borrower's mortgage payment record, number and amount of outstanding credit obligations, and payment history on other credit obligations.

In determining the acceptability of borrower credit, the underwriter examines the total credit history, the borrower's written explanations of any problems, and offsetting factors.

Bankruptcy and prior poor credit history are not disqualifying factors (a) if they are caused by extraordinary circumstances, such as health problems, or (b) if in the two-year period prior to loan application, the borrower has reestablished credit and demonstrated an ability to now manage his or her financial affairs.

Property Evaluation

The property appraisal is an estimate of value that the underwriter must evaluate. Some of the major considerations the underwriter must include in this evaluation process are: neighborhood, site analysis, improvements, economic life, and valuation. Property evaluation and each of these factors are discussed in detail in Chapter 10.

Based on the gathered data, the appraiser makes a final reconciliation of value. This is the appraised value, and the underwriter, after totally reviewing and evaluating the appraisal, makes his or her own conclusion as to value.

Escrow or Impound Account

These loans require that the borrower maintain an **escrow account** (also called an **impound account**) with the lending institution. The *borrower must pay into this account an impound each month to accumulate money to pay the annual real property tax bill and the annual homeowner's insurance policy premium.* In addition, if the loan is used to purchase a condominium apartment, escrow deposits may include an amount to pay the property owner's assessment.

At closing, the borrower must put money into the account to get it started and provide a head start for accumulating the necessary funds. This includes two months' payments toward the next hazard insurance premium, several months toward payment of the real property tax bill, and, if the loan is insured by the FHA, the equivalent of one month's FHA mortgage insurance premium. The number of months of property tax placed in escrow usually is determined by the lender, depending upon the length of time since the last payment of taxes. These *insurance and tax monies deposited at the time of closing* are called **prepaid items** and are not a part of the borrower's actual closing costs; they are in addition to the closing costs.

The FHA requires the borrower to pay these prepaid items but allows the seller to pay buyer closing costs within the limits specified and stated above under FHA loans, provided that these closing costs are taken into consideration in determining maximum loan amount. Under the VA program, sellers are permitted, if they agree, to pay the closing costs and prepaid items for the buyer.

Discount Points

In making mortgage loans, lending institutions may charge **discount points**. The purpose is to increase the yield to the lender by raising the effective interest rate in an amount exceeding a maximum rate that may be charged under certain conditions.

Each point that the lender charges costs someone (either the buyer or the seller, depending upon the situation) *1 percent of the loan amount*, paid at the time of loan closing.

Lenders may charge discount points in making conventional loans. These situations have no prohibition against the borrower paying the points, and the borrower usually is the one who pays. In times of high interest rates and short supply of money for making mortgage loans, lenders often charge one or two points in making 90 percent and 95 percent conventional loans. Also, in states having usury laws that fix a maximum allowable interest rate lower than the average national rate prevailing at any given time, lenders require payment of sufficient points to increase their yield above the statutory maximum to the equivalent of the national average rate. Borrowers sometimes volunteer to pay discount points to "buy down" a mortgage interest rate at the time the loan is made.

Sellers traditionally have had to pay discount points in order for a veteran buyer to purchase their home using a VA loan when the maximum VA rate was below the current market rate. In late 1992, Congress abolished the ceiling on VA interest rates and made both interest rates and discount points negotiable between buyer and seller and between buyer and lender. A three-year trial period during which buyers are allowed to pay discount points will likely be extended to on-going practice.

FINANCING LEGISLATION

Truth-in-Lending Simplification and Reform Act (TILSRA)

The Truth-in-Lending law is part of the Federal Consumer Credit Protection Act, which became effective July 1, 1969. It subsequently was amended and became known as the **Truth-in-Lending Simplification and Reform Act (TILSRA)** of 1980. The Truth-in-Lending Act empowered the Federal Reserve Board to implement regulations in the Act. TILSRA now *requires four chief disclosures: annual percentage rate, finance charge, amount financed, and total of payments*. The Federal Reserve Board implemented these regulations by establishing Regulation Z. This law is enforced by the Federal Trade Commission.

Regulation Z does not regulate interest rates but instead *provides specific consumer protections in mortgage loans for residential real estate*. It covers all real estate loans for personal, family, household, or agricultural purposes. The regulation does not apply to commercial loans. Regulation Z also standardizes the procedures involved in residential loan transactions and requires that the borrower be fully informed of all aspects of the loan transaction. In addition, the regulation addresses any advertisement of credit terms available for residential real estate.

Disclosure

At time of application or within three days thereafter, the lender must provide the borrower with a **disclosure statement**. The disclosure *must set forth the true, or effective, annual interest rate on a loan*, called the **annual percentage rate (APR)**. This rate may be higher than the interest as expressed in the mortgage. For example, when certain fees and discount points charged by the lender are subtracted from the loan amount, the result is an increase in the true rate of interest. As a result of the subtraction, the borrower receives a smaller loan amount and pays interest on a larger amount. Therefore, the effect is to increase the interest rate being received by the lender.

In addition to stating the true or effective annual interest rate on the loan, the disclosure statement must specify the finance charges, which include loan fees, interest, and discount points. The finance charges do not have to include things such as title examination, title insurance, escrow payments, document preparation fees, notary fees, or appraisal fees.

PUTTING IT TO WORK

The APR provides a method for consumers to compare costs when lenders charge quite differently. For example, a loan for which a lender charges 8½ percent interest with a 2 percent origination fee and 4 discount points may be more costly than a 9 percent loan with only a 1 percent origination fee and no points. The APR allows the true loan cost to be accurately compared.

Cooling-off Period

If the borrower is refinancing an existing mortgage loan or obtaining a new mortgage loan and is pledging a principal residence already owned as security for the loan, the disclosure statement must provide for a **cooling-off period**, or *three-day right of rescission for the loan transaction.* The borrower must exercise the right to rescind, or cancel, the loan prior to midnight of the third business day after the date the transaction was closed. The three-day right of rescission *does not* apply if the loan is to finance the purchase of a new home, or to finance the construction of a dwelling to be used as a principal residence, or to refinance an investment property. It therefore usually applies only on junior liens and refinancing.

Advertising

Regulation Z also applies to advertising the credit terms available in purchasing a home. The only specific thing that may be stated in the advertisement without making a full disclosure is the annual percentage rate, spelled out in full, not abbreviated as APR. If any other credit terms are included in the advertisement, it must provide a full disclosure. For example, an advertisement mentioning a down payment triggers the requirement to make a complete disclosure of all of the following credit terms: cash price of the property, annual percentage rate, amount of down payment, amount of each payment, date when each payment is due, and total number of payments over the mortgage term. If the annual percentage rate is not a fixed rate but is instead a variable rate, the ad must specify the rate to be a variable or adjustable rate.

Statements of a general nature regarding the financing may be made without a full disclosure. Statements such as "good financing available," "FHA financing available," and "loan assumption available" are satisfactory. Real estate agents must take special care not to violate advertising requirements of Regulation Z.

Penalties

Violators of Regulation Z are subject to criminal liability and punishment by fine of up to $5,000, imprisonment for up to a year, or both. If the borrower suffers a financial loss as the result of the violation, he or she may sue the violator under civil law in federal court for damages.

Real Estate Settlement Procedures Act (RESPA)

Congress enacted the **Real Estate Settlement Procedures Act (RESPA)** in 1974. It *regulates lending activities of lending institutions in making mortgage loans for housing*. RESPA has the following purposes:

1. To effect specific changes in the settlement process resulting in more effective advance disclosure of settlement costs to home buyers and sellers.
2. To protect borrowers from unnecessarily expensive settlement charges resulting from abusive practices.
3. To ensure that borrowers are provided with more information, on a more timely basis, on the nature and cost of the settlement process.
4. To eliminate referral fees or kickbacks that increase the cost of settlement services, lenders are permitted to charge only for services actually provided to home buyers and sellers, and in an amount that the service actually costs the lender.

Enforcement of RESPA is by the Department of Housing and Urban Development (HUD).

RESPA Requirements

The Act requires:

1. *Good faith estimate.* Within three working days of receiving a completed loan application, the lender is required to provide the borrower with a **good faith estimate** of the *costs likely to be incurred at settlement.* A sample form is shown in Figure 8.5.

2. *Buyer's guide to settlement costs.* At the time of loan application, the lender must provide the borrower with a booklet entitled *Homebuyer's Guide to Settlement Costs,* which contains the following information:

   a. Clear and concise language describing and explaining the nature and purpose of each settlement cost.
   b. An explanation and sample of the standard real estate settlement forms required by the Act.
   c. A description and explanation of the nature and purpose of escrow/impound accounts.
   d. An explanation of choices available to borrowers in selecting persons or organizations to provide necessary settlement charges.
   e. Examples and explanations of unfair practices and unreasonable or unnecessary settlement charges to be avoided.

3. *HUD Form No. 1.* In making residential mortgage loans, lenders are required to use a standard settlement form designed to clearly itemize all charges to be paid by borrower and by seller as part of the final settlement. The form (see Figure 8.6), which has become known as HUD Form No. 1, or the HUD 1, must be made available for the borrower's inspection at or before final settlement. This form is not required for assumptions and nonresidential loans.

A recent federal rule affecting portions of RESPA now allows brokers to assist home buyers in selecting and prequalifying for a mortgage and to charge a reasonable fee for these services. Any fees must be disclosed and agreed to in writing by the buyer. Brokers can even begin the loan application process. In providing these services brokers typically use computerized loan origination (CLO) systems that list the various loan programs for lending institutions.

Equal Credit Opportunity Act (ECOA)

The **Equal Credit Opportunity Act (ECOA)** was enacted by Congress in 1975 *to prevent lending institutions from discriminating in the loan process.* The Act requires

FIGURE 8.5 A lender's good faith estimate of settlement costs.

Applicant(s): ______________________ Sale Price: ______________

Property Address: ______________________ Loan Amount: ______________

______________________ LTV: ______________

Loan Type: __________ Term: __________ Interest Rate: ______________

Occupancy Status: ______________________ Purchase ☐ Refinance ☐

THIS IS NOT A COMMITMENT TO LEND

I. Estimated Closing Costs:	**Buyer**	**Seller**
Loan Origination (_____ %)	______	______
Loan Discount (_____ %)	______	______
Appraisal Fee	______	______
Credit Report	______	______
Doc Stamps - Deed	______	______
Doc Stamps - Mortgage	______	______
Intangible Tax - Mortgage	______	______
Title Insurance - Owners	______	______
Title Insurance - Mortgage	______	______
Title Search	______	______
Recording Deed	______	______
Recording Mortgage	______	______
Recording Satisfaction	______	______
VA Funding Fee	______	______
FHA - MIP	______	______
Mortgage Insurance 1st Yr.	______	______
Tax Service Fee	______	______
Underwriting Fee	______	______
Doc Prep Fee	______	______
Inspection Fee	______	______
Survey	______	______
Termite/Pest Inspection	______	______
Roof Inspection	______	______
Courier Fee	______	______
Packaging Fee	______	______
Other __________	______	______
TOTAL CLOSING COSTS	______	______
	Buyer	**Seller**

II. Estimated Prepaids & Escrows	
Prepaid Interest - 30 days (Per Diem ____)	______
Prepaid Hazard & Flood Ins. - 1 yr.	______
Escrow Hazard & Flood Ins. - 2 mo.	______
Escrow RE Taxes - 4 mo.	______
Escrow Mortgage Ins. - 2 mo.	______
TOTAL	$ ______

III. Purchase Details	
a. Purchase Price	______
b. Buyer & Seller Closing Costs	______
c. Prepaids & Escrows	______
d. Total a + b + c	______
e. Less Mortgage	(______)
f. Less Deposit	(______)
g. Less Seller's Costs	(______)
h. Less Application Fees	(______)
i. Less __________	(______)
Buyer's Cash Required	$ ______

IV. Payment Details	______
Principal + Interest	______
Real Estate Taxes	______
Insurance - Hazard	______
Insurance - Flood	______
Mortgage Ins. - PMI	______
Homeowners Dues	______
TOTAL	$ ______

THIS IS ONLY A GOOD FAITH ESTIMATE OF THE ITEMS STATED. THE ACTUAL CHARGES MAY BE MORE OR LESS. CERTAIN OF THE ABOVE ESTIMATES ARE BASED ON THE AMOUNT OF THE LOAN AND RATE APPLIED FOR; IF THESE CHANGE, THE CHARGES WILL CHANGE. THIS FORM MAY NOT COVER ALL ITEMS YOU WILL BE REQUIRED TO PAY IN CASH AT CLOSING. YOU MAY BE REQUIRED TO PAY OTHER ADDITIONAL AMOUNTS AT SETTLEMENT.

FIGURE 8.6
HUD Form No. 1, required by RESPA for settlement cost calculations.

U.S. DEPARTMENT OF HOUSING AND URBAN DEVELOPMENT — OMB No.2502-0265

A. SETTLEMENT STATEMENT

B. TYPE OF LOAN

1. ☐ FHA 2. ☐ FMHA 3. ☐ CONV. UNINS. 4. ☐ VA 5. ☐ CONV. INS.	6. File Number	7. Loan Number	8. Mortgage Insurance Case Number

C. NOTE: This form is furnished to give you statement of actual settlement costs. Amounts paid to and by the settlement agent are shown. Items marked "(p.o.c.)" were paid outside the closing; they are shown here for informational purposes and are not included in the totals.

D. NAME AND ADDRESS OF BORROWER	E. NAME AND ADDRESS OF SELLER	F. NAME AND ADDRESS OF LENDER

G. PROPERTY LOCATION	H. SETTLEMENT AGENT	
	PLACE OF SETTLEMENT	I. SETTLEMENT DATE rec: cls:

J. SUMMARY OF BORROWER'S TRANSACTION		K. SUMMARY OF SELLER'S TRANSACTION	
100. GROSS AMOUNT DUE FROM BORROWER		400. GROSS AMOUNT DUE TO SELLER	
101. Contract sales price		401. Contract sales price	
102. Personal Property		402. Personal Property	
103. Settlement charges to borrower (line 1400)		403.	
104.		404.	
105.		405.	
ADJUSTMENTS FOR ITEMS PAID BY SELLER IN ADVANCE		ADJUSTMENTS FOR ITEMS PAID BY SELLER IN ADVANCE	
106. City/Town taxes to		406. City/Town taxes to	
107. County taxes to		407. County taxes to	
108. Assessments to		408. Assessments to	
109.		409.	
110.		410.	
111.		411.	
112.		412.	
120. GROSS AMOUNT DUE FROM BORROWER		420. GROSS AMOUNT DUE TO SELLER	
200. AMOUNTS PAID BY OR IN BEHALF OF BORROWER		500. REDUCTIONS IN AMOUNT DUE TO SELLER	
201. Deposit or earnest money		501. Excess Deposit (see instructions)	
202. Principal amount of new loan(s)		502. Settlement charges to seller (line 1400)	
203. Existing loan(s) taken subject to		503. Existing loan(s) taken subject to	
204. Application deposit		504. Payoff of first mortgage loan	
205. Second lien mortgage		505. Payoff of second mortgage loan	
206.		506.	
207.		507.	
208.		508.	
209.		509.	
ADJUSTMENTS FOR ITEMS UNPAID BY SELLER		ADJUSTMENTS FOR ITEMS UNPAID BY SELLER	
210. City/Town taxes to		510. City/Town taxes to	
211. County taxes to		511. County taxes to	
212. Assessments to		512. Assessments to	
213.		513.	
214.		514.	
215.		515.	
216.		516.	
217.		517.	
218.		518.	
219.		519.	
220. TOTAL PAID BY/FOR BORROWER		520. TOTAL REDUCTION AMOUNT DUE SELLER	
300. CASH AT SETTLEMENT FROM OR TO BORROWER		600. CASH AT SETTLEMENT TO OR FROM SELLER	
301. Gross amount due from borrower (line 120)		601. Gross amount due to seller (line 420)	
302. Less amounts paid by/for borrower (line 220)	( )	602. Less reduction amount due seller (line 520)	( )
303. CASH ☐ FROM ☐ TO BORROWER		603. CASH ☐ TO ☐ FROM SELLER	

Buyer ____ Date ____ Seller ____ Date ____

Buyer ____ Date ____ Seller ____ Date ____

Settlement Agent ____ Date ____

Previous Edition Is Obsolete
F1061.LMG (7/94)

HUD-1 (07-87) RESPA, HB 4305.2

(continued)

FIGURE 8.6
Continued.

U.S. DEPARTMENT OF HOUSING AND URBAN DEVELOPMENT
SETTLEMENT STATEMENT
Page 2

L. SETTLEMENT CHARGES	PAID FROM BORROWER'S FUNDS AT SETTLEMENT	PAID FROM SELLER'S FUNDS AT SETTLEMENT
700. TOTAL SALES/BROKER'S COMMISSION(based on price)		
Division of commission (line 700) as follows: $ @ %= $		
701. $ to		
702. $ to		
703. Commission paid at Settlement		
704.		
800. ITEMS PAYABLE IN CONNECTION WITH LOAN		
801. Loan Origination Fee %		
802. Loan Discount %		
803. Appraisal Fee to		
804. Credit Report to		
805. Lender's Inspection Fee		
806. VA Funding Fee to		
807. Assumption Fee		
808. to		
809. Underwriting Fee		
810. Tax Service Fee		
811		
900. ITEMS REQUIRED BY LENDER TO BE PAID IN ADVANCE		
901. Interest from to @ $ /day		
902. Mortgage Insurance Premium for mos. to		
903. Hazard Insurance Premium for yrs. to		
904. yrs. to		
905		
1000. RESERVES DEPOSITED WITH LENDER FOR		
1001. Hazard Insurance mos. @ $ /mo.		
1002. Mortgage Insurance mos. @ $ /mo.		
1003. City Property Taxes mos. @ $ /mo.		
1004. County Property Taxes mos. @ $ /mo.		
1005. Annual Assessments mos. @ $ /mo.		
1006. mos. @ $ /mo.		
1007. mos. @ $ /mo.		
1008. mos. @ $ /mo.		
1100. TITLE CHARGES		
1101. Settlement or Closing Fee to		
1102. Abstract or Title Search to		
1103. Title Examination to		
1104. Title Insurance Binder to		
1105. Document Preparation to		
1106. Notary Fees to		
1107. Attorney's Fees to		
(includes above items No.:)		
1108. Title Insurance to		
(includes above items No.:)		
1109. Lender's Coverage $		
1110. Owner's Coverage $		
1111.		
1112.		
1113		
1200. GOVERNMENT RECORDING AND TRANSFER CHARGES		
1201. Recording Fees: Deed $; Mortgage $; Release $		
1202. City/County tax/stamps: Deed $; Mortgage $		
1203. State tax/stamps: Deed $; Mortgage $		
1204.		
1205		
1300. ADDITIONAL SETTLEMENT CHARGES		
1301. Survey to		
1302. Pest Inspection to		
1303.		
1304.		
1305		
1400. TOTAL SETTLEMENT CHARGES (enter on line 103, Section J and line 502, Section K)		

Items marked "(p.o.c.)" were paid outside the closing; they are shown here for information purposes and are not included in the totals.

The Undersigned Acknowledges Receipt of This Settlement Statement and Agrees to the Correctness Thereof.

Buyer ____________ Seller ____________

SS# ____________ SS# ____________

Buyer ____________ Seller ____________

SS# ____________ SS# ____________

Buyer ____________ Date ____________

SS# ____________

Buyer ____________

SS# ____________

HUD-1B Settlement Statement
F1006.LMG (7/94)

financial institutions that make loans to do so on an equal basis to all creditworthy customers without regard to discriminatory factors. The Equal Credit Opportunity Act is implemented by Regulation B of the Federal Reserve Board.

The ECOA makes it unlawful for any creditor to discriminate against any loan applicant in any aspect of a credit transaction:

1. On the basis of race, color, religion, gender, national origin, marital status, or age (unless the applicant is a minor and, therefore, does not have the capacity to contract).
2. Because part of the applicant's income is derived from a public assistance program, alimony, or child support.
3. Because the applicant has in good faith exercised any right under the Federal Consumer Credit Protection Act of which the Truth-in-Lending Law (Regulation Z) is a part.

Compliance with the Equal Credit Opportunity Act is enforced by different agencies depending on which agency has regulatory authority over the type of financial institution.

IMPORTANT POINTS

1. Methods of financing include insured and uninsured conventional mortgage loans, FHA-insured loans, VA-guaranteed loans, and the various types of seller financing.
2. Lenders usually do not require a conventional loan to be insured if the loan amount does not exceed 80 percent of the property value. Most conventional insured loans are 90 and 95 percent loans. The insurance is called private mortgage insurance (PMI). The premium is paid by the borrower and insures the lender against loss due to borrower's default.
3. Various types of mortgages include junior, term, amortizing, balloon, open-end, graduated payment, adjustable or variable rate, shared appreciation (SAM), growing equity (GEM), participation, wraparound, package, blanket, construction, purchase money, and leasehold mortgages.
4. FHA and VA loans are made by specifically qualified lending institutions, not by FHA and VA.
5. The FHA-insured programs include 203(b), 245, 203(b)(2), and 234(c). FHA insurance, called mortgage insurance premium (MIP), protects the lender from financial loss in the event of foreclosure. The borrower pays the premium. FHA establishes a maximum loan amount.
6. VA loans are guaranteed loans. The current guarantee is a multitiered system. VA loans may be made for up to 100 percent of the sales price or of the property value established by a VA appraisal and stated in the Certificate of Reasonable Value (CRV), issued by the VA, whichever is less.
7. FHA and VA loans require escrow accounts and are for 30-year terms or shorter. Both are assumable with certain restrictions and do not impose a prepayment penalty. The down payment can be borrowed if it is secured by collateral.
8. Prior to October 28, 1992, the VA fixed the maximum interest rate a lending institution could charge in making these loans. The allowable rate was usually below the market rate for conventional loans at any given time. Therefore, lenders charged discount points to increase the yield to an approximate equivalent of the conventional loan rate. Borrowers could not pay these points on a VA loan unless they were refinancing a home they already owned, but the seller could pay them, and usually agreed to do so in the sales contract. Borrowers could and still may

pay points in an FHA or a conventional loan when required or to buy down the rate.

9. On October 28, 1992, Congress established a three-year trial period in which there is no maximum VA interest rate and the borrower is now allowed to pay discount points. During this three-year period, veteran buyers can negotiate interest rates and discount points in the same way as FHA and conventional buyers do.
10. Federal laws that regulate lending institutions in making consumer loans include Regulation Z, RESPA, and ECOA.

HOW WOULD YOU RESPOND?

Most buyers do not pay cash; fewer and fewer loans can be found that are assumable. Those that are assumable are becoming more difficult to qualify for. Therefore, most buyers need new loans. If they cannot get a loan, there will be no sale and no commission. The buyers will have to live with their decision on financing every month for many years to come. The buyer has a few questions for you: "What's best, 15 years or 30 years? A fixed-rate loan or ARM? Or a 5–25 or 7–23 or 30-year fixed? FHA, VA, or Conventional? What's PMI and MIP? Can I use my VA eligibility again on this home? Where do I go for my loan?" Examine each of these issues and explore some of the pros and cons concerning various options for the borrower. Remember, strive to convey information regarding options, avoid offering advice or recommendations.

REVIEW QUESTIONS

Answers to these questions are found in the *Answer Key* section at the back of the book.

1. Insurance for the protection of lending institutions making conventional loans is called:
   a. mutual mortgage insurance
   b. conventional mortgage insurance
   c. institutional insurance
   d. private mortgage insurance
2. The FHA programs are for which of the following purposes?
   a. making housing loans
   b. guaranteeing housing loans
   c. purchasing housing loans
   d. insuring housing loans
3. Which federal law deals with closing costs of a real estate transaction?
   a. RESPA
   b. ECOA
   c. Regulation Z
   d. FHA
4. Which federal law deals with costs of credit for a consumer?
   a. RESPA
   b. ECOA
   c. Regulation Z
   d. FHA
5. Which of the following statements about VA loans is correct?
   a. repayment of 100 percent of VA loans in the event of borrower default is guaranteed to the lender
   b. VA loans may be for 100 percent of the property value established by the VA
   c. a veteran can use his or her VA entitlement to purchase a single-family home for use as a rental property
   d. once a veteran has purchased one home using a VA loan, he can never get another VA loan

6. All of the following statements about FHA and VA loans are correct EXCEPT:
   a. they are assumable with qualifying
   b. they require a prepayment penalty
   c. the maximum term is 30 years
   d. they require an escrow (impound) account

7. Which of the following statements about discount points is (are) correct?
   a. points increase the lender's yield on the loan
   b. each point charged by the lender costs 1 percent of the loan amount
   c. buyers can pay points on VA, FHA, and conventional loans
   d. all of the above

8. All of the following statements about Regulation Z are correct EXCEPT:
   a. it applies to commercial mortgage loans
   b. it requires lenders to furnish a disclosure statement to the borrower
   c. it provides for a three-day right of recession if a residence already owned is pledged
   d. it regulates the advertising of credit terms of property offered for sale

9. RESPA requires the lender to furnish the borrower all of the following EXCEPT:
   a. buyer's guide to the settlement costs
   b. good faith estimate
   c. standard settlement form
   d. three-day right of recession

10. ECOA requires lenders to make consumer loans without regard to all of the following EXCEPT:
    a. age
    b. occupation
    c. gender
    d. marital status

11. The type of mortgage requiring the borrower to pay only interest during the mortgage term is:
    a. balloon
    b. open
    c. term
    d. closed

12. The amount of interest paid in an amortizing mortgage for a month in which the principal balance is $73,000 and the rate is 12 percent is:
    a. $876
    b. $730
    c. $600
    d. $1,369

13. A mortgage that is not on a fully amortizing basis and, therefore, requires a larger final payment is called:
    a. graduated mortgage
    b. balloon mortgage
    c. open mortgage
    d. flexible mortgage

14. The type of mortgage in which the lender reduces the interest rate in exchange for a part of the profit realized when the property is sold is a:
    a. participation mortgage
    b. price-level adjusted mortgage
    c. wraparound mortgage
    d. shared appreciation mortgage

15. A mortgage in which two or more parcels of land are pledged is called:
    a. blanket
    b. package
    c. all-inclusive
    d. wraparound

16. PMI is generally NOT required if the loan-to-value ratio is:
    a. 80%
    b. 85%
    c. 90%
    d. 95%

17. A mortgage given by buyer to seller to secure payment of part of the purchase price is a(n):
    a. purchase money mortgage
    b. earnest money mortgage
    c. participation mortgage
    d. graduated payment mortgage

18. Which of the following statements regarding wraparound mortgages is true?
    a. the wraparound is a junior mortgage in an amount larger than the existing first mortgage
    b. it is not necessary that the existing first mortgage is assumable
    c. both a and b are true
    d. neither a nor b is true

19. A biweekly mortgage's major advantage is:
    a. a lower interest rate
    b. lower payments
    c. faster payoff of the loan
    d. easier qualifying

20. An index is relevant for:
    a. an ARM
    b. a GPM
    c. a blanket mortgage
    d. a wraparound mortgage

POSSIBLE RESPONSES TO "HOW WOULD YOU RESPOND?"

15 or 30 years?

Total interest paid will be less over 15 years, but the 15-year loan will also involve a higher payment and more difficult qualifying. The 30-year loan will be easier to qualify for, but the total interest paid will be higher. The 30-year loan probably can be paid off sooner with optional larger payments. The interest rates for the two loans will likely be different.

A fixed-rate loan or ARM?

The fixed-rate loan gives security of knowing the rate, but usually begins at a higher rate than an ARM. Depending on the expected duration of ownership, the ARM may be cheaper.

A 5–25 or 7–23 or 30-year fixed?

This mostly depends on the expected duration of ownership. The 5–25 and 7–23 will likely offer lower rates, but must be renegotiated at the fifth or seventh year or be paid off at that time. These loans are appealing to buyers who expect to own their home for a limited time.

FHA, VA, or conventional?

VA is available only to vets and their spouses. FHA and VA have much tighter rules for qualifying and other issues than conventional. Conventional lenders tend to be more flexible. Qualifying standards are quite different among these programs.

What's PMI and MIP?

PMI is private mortgage insurance on conventional financing. MIP is the mortgage insurance on FHA. There is greater opportunity to avoid the expense of PMI than MIP, which cannot be avoided.

Can I use a VA eligibility again on this home?

Only if the former use of the entitlement has been fully restored. There may be a partial entitlement if the veteran did not use the total current entitlement on the former home.

Where do I go for my loan?

This is one of the most important questions about which you can offer information for the buyer. Banks, saving and loans, mortgage bankers and brokers, hard money lenders, etc., all offer different benefits that you can explore with your buyer.

CHAPTER 9

IMPORTANT TERMINOLOGY

accrued expenses
closing statement
credits
debits
escrow instructions
impound accounts
perc test
prepaid expenses
proration
reconciliation
vendor's affidavit

Closing Real Estate Transactions

In This Chapter Closing is the consummation of the sales effort that began when the broker or salesperson obtained a listing or found a prospective buyer. This event has different names in different parts of the country. These include settlement, passing of papers, and coming out of escrow. At the closing, the buyer receives a deed and the seller receives payment for the property. Some states use escrow companies or abstract and title companies for all the preparatory work necessary to close the transaction and actually do the final closing. In many states an attorney, a real estate broker, and (when a new loan is involved) a lending institution perform the functions necessary for closing a real estate transaction.

This chapter covers the various methods of closing, items required at closing, and proration calculations. Four examples and four closing problems allow practice in preparing for closing.

Methods of Closing

The two common types of closing methods are the face-to-face closing and the escrow closing.

Face-to-Face Closing

At the *face-to-face closing, the parties and other interested persons meet to review the closing documents, execute the closing documents, pay money, receive money, and receive title to real estate*. The face-to-face closing typically is held at the office of the lender, attorney for one of the parties, or the title company. Those present at this type of closing are buyers, sellers, real estate brokers, and lender representatives. Before executing the closing documents and disbursing the closing funds, the parties should assure themselves that the conditions and contingencies of the purchase agreement have all been met. In a face-to-face closing, the title to the real estate is transferred upon execution and delivery of the deed.

Escrow Closing

In an *escrow closing a disinterested party is authorized to act as the closing or escrow agent, in charge of all closing documents, monies, and activities.* The escrow agent may be any of the following (depending on state laws):

1. Attorney
2. Title company
3. Escrow company
4. Escrow department of a lending institution
5. Trust company

Prior to selecting the escrow agent, the buyer and seller often execute **escrow instructions** in a detailed offer to purchase, *outlining the escrow agent's authority and what must occur prior to and at closing.*

Putting It to Work

The escrow instructions should exactly parallel the offer and acceptance. Reference should be made in the escrow instructions to include the terms, conditions, contingencies, and addenda of the sales contract.

After the escrow agent is chosen, the earnest money, escrow instructions, and all pertinent documents are delivered to the escrow agent for completion of the transaction. The documents provided to the escrow agent by buyer and seller are all executed by the providing party prior to or upon delivery. This means that the seller executes the deed and delivers it to escrow, where it is held by the escrow agent until all contingencies and conditions of the offer to purchase have been met. Title to the real estate technically transfers when the deed is deposited with the escrow agent. Thus, death of either the buyer or the seller prior to completing the conditions of the offer to purchase will not invalidate the deal.

The escrow agent has the authority and obligation to examine the title evidence to assure marketable title. When marketable title is shown and all other contingencies of the escrow instructions are met, the escrow agent disburses the purchase price to the seller minus all charges and expenses attributable to the seller. The escrow agent also records the deed, mortgage, deed of trust, and any other documents set out in the escrow instructions.

If the seller cannot give marketable title or if any contingencies of the offer are not able to be met and the buyer will not accept title or waive the contingency, the escrow instructions provide that the closing will not be completed. Title remains with the seller, and all monies are returned to the buyer or handled in accordance with the sales contract and escrow instructions.

The Role of Title and Escrow Companies

Title and escrow companies selected as the escrow or closing agents schedule the closing, assure that the escrow instructions are completed accurately, prepare all documents needed to close the transaction, deposit and disburse monies, and record all documents to transfer title and secure any debt. Title or escrow companies usually are paid for their work and expertise based upon a percentage of the monies handled at closing. The escrow agent is liable for any damages resulting from an improperly handled closing, either in disbursement of funds or inaccurate documents. The closing agent is also responsible for preparing the 1099-S form to report the sale of real estate to the Internal Revenue Service.

PRELIMINARIES TO CLOSING

Before closing, the closing agent must assure that all conditions and contingencies of the offer to purchase are met. Some typical items or documents of concern for the closing agent are described next.

PUTTING IT TO WORK

The obligation for paying various costs is determined by local custom, state law, and the type of financing incurred, if any. Local closing officers should be consulted to determine who bears responsibility for each item. Many closing costs are negotiable and should be disclosed as such with clients in the negotiations.

Parties

The legal names and marital status of the parties must be identified prior to closing. This is to assure accurate completion of the closing documents to transfer title and secure debt.

Survey

In some real estate transfers, the buyer or the buyer's lender requires either a full staked survey or a mortgage survey to assure that no encroachments exist. The cost of the survey is typically the buyer's responsibility.

Pest Inspection

Often the buyer or the buyer's lender requires proof that no wood-destroying pest, infestation, or damage is present. The cost of this inspection is typically the seller's. If infestation is found, the seller has to pay for treating and repairing any damage.

Title Examination, Insurance, and Defects

The seller must provide evidence of marketable title for transfer. This proof can be provided by the update of an abstract of title or by issuance of a title insurance binder. The seller often bears the cost of either, but this varies from region to region.

If an updated abstract of title is provided, the buyer must hire an attorney to prepare an opinion as to the quality of title shown in the abstract. If title defects are found, the seller is responsible for the cost of curing or removing the defects. Until marketable title is available, closing will not likely be completed.

If the buyer is borrowing money from an institutional lender, a mortgagee's title insurance policy also is needed. The buyer bears the cost of this title insurance policy.

Because abstract updates and title insurance binders typically are issued several days or weeks before closing, an update of the abstract or title binder should be obtained prior to closing with an effective coverage date to the date of closing. In addition, the seller may be required to sign a **vendor's affidavit**, a *document stating that the seller has done nothing since the original title evidence to adversely affect title.*

Property Inspection

Usually the buyer wants to inspect the premises prior to closing. The inspection most often is performed by a professional inspection company. This is called a "whole house inspection." The inspection report indicates any mechanical, electrical, plumbing, design, or construction defects. The buyer bears the cost of this inspection.

In addition to the professional inspection, the buyer usually arranges for a final "walk through" the day of closing or immediately prior to closing. This is to ensure that no damage has been done since the offer to purchase and that no fixtures have been removed.

Insurance

Prior to closing, the buyer usually provides homeowner's fire and hazard insurance on the real estate being purchased. If the buyer is borrowing money for the purchase, the lender/mortgagee is listed on the policy as an additional insured. The cost of this insurance is the buyer's, and it must be purchased to cover the lender.

Perc and Soil Tests

If the property is not connected to a public sewer, the seller is required to provide the results of what is commonly called a **perc test**, an *inspection on percolation of the septic system to assure proper functioning and drainage and to show compliance with local and state health codes.* In addition, if the property is for commercial use, the seller is responsible for a soil test to assure the absence of hazardous waste or EPA problems.

Additional Documents

Depending on the state and the transaction, any of the following documents also may be involved in closing the real estate transaction. Accurate preparation of all relevant documents must be completed before closing.

- Bill of sale of personal property
- Certificate of occupancy
- Closing or settlement statement (HUD Form No. 1)
- Contract for deed
- Deed
- Deed of trust or mortgage
- Note
- Disclosure statement
- Estoppel certificate
- Homeowner's policy or hazard insurance policy
- Lease
- Lien waivers
- Mortgage guarantee insurance policy

- Option and exercise of option
- Sales contract
- Flood insurance policy

Not all of the above are applicable at each closing, but each is possible at typical real estate closings.

PRORATIONS AT CLOSING

Items Prorated

A closing sometimes involves the *division of expense between buyer and seller* for items such as rent, taxes, insurance, interest, and homeowner's association dues. This division, called **proration**, is necessary to ensure fair apportioning of expenses between buyer and seller. Prorated items are either accrued or prepaid. **Accrued expenses** are *costs the seller owes at the day of closing but that the buyer will eventually pay*. The seller therefore gives the buyer a credit for these items at closing. Typical accrued items to be prorated are:

1. Unpaid real estate taxes.
2. Rent collected by seller from tenant.
3. Interest on seller's mortgage assumed by the buyer.
4. Unpaid association fees.

Prepaid expenses are *costs the seller pays* in advance and are not fully used up. At closing, these items are shown as a credit to the seller and a debit to the buyer. Typical prepaid items to be prorated are:

1. Prepaid taxes and insurance premiums.
2. Rent paid by the seller under lease assigned to the buyer.
3. Utilities billed and paid in advance.
4. Association fees paid in advance.

Proration Rules and Methods

Methods for prorating expenses and the calculations involved follow.

1. Either the buyer or the seller may pay the costs of the day of closing. For purposes of the calculations in this book, the seller will pay the costs of the day of closing.
2. Mortgage interest, taxes, insurance, and like expenses usually are prorated using 360 days per year and 30 days for each month. Mortgage interest generally is paid in arrears, so the parties must understand that the mortgage payment for August will include interest not for August but instead for the month of July. In many areas, taxes are paid in advance. This means the seller will receive reimbursement at closing for the remaining days of the tax year following closing.
3. Accrued real estate taxes that are assessed but not yet due are typically prorated to the day of closing, with the seller having a debit and the buyer a credit for the amount owed as of the day of closing.
4. In prorating rent, the seller typically receives the rent for the day of closing.
5. Personal property taxes may be prorated between buyer and seller, or they may be paid entirely by the seller. In the calculations here, personal property taxes are not prorated.

6. Every year is considered to have 360 days; every month, 30 days.

The arithmetic for proration is discussed completely in Chapter 17. Basically, the computation involves determining a yearly, monthly, or daily charge for the item being prorated. This charge then is multiplied by the number of months or days of the year for which reimbursement or payment is to be made. A synopsis of the method is set out in Figure 9.1.

FIGURE 9.1 Exercises for determining prorated costs.

EXERCISE 1

Accrued Items: The closing of a property is to be held on October 14, 1996. The real estate taxes of $895 for the year have not been paid and are due at the end of the year. What entry will appear on the seller's and buyer's closing statements?

January 1 — October 14 / — December 30

	YEAR	MONTH	DAY
Closing Date	1995 ~~1996~~	21 ~~9~~ ~~10~~	44 ~~14~~
– Paid to Date (previous year)	– 1995	12	30
= Proration Time	0	9	14

Accrued period for taxes owed by seller at closing

$895 ÷ 12 = $74.58 taxes per month

$74.58 ÷ 30 = $2.49 taxes per day

$ 74.58	plus	$ 2.49		
× 9 full months		× 14 days		
$671.22	plus	$34.86	=	$706.08

Thus, the accrued taxes owed by seller at closing are $706.08. This will be a seller debit and a buyer credit at closing.

EXERCISE 2

Prepaid Items: The closing of a sale of a rental is to be held March 10, 1997. The seller has received the rent for March in the amount of $500. What entry will appear on the seller's and buyer's closing statements?

March 1 — March 10 / — March 30

Prepaid period not earned by seller prior to closing and assigned to buyer at closing

	YEAR	MONTH	DAY
Paid to Date	1997	3	30
– Closing Date	– 1997	3	10
= Proration Time	0	0	20

$500 ÷ 30 = $16.67 rent per day

$ 16.67
× 20 days not used
$333.40 unused rent

Thus, the prepaid rent credited to the buyer at closing is $333.40. This will be a seller debit and a buyer credit at closing.

Preparation of Closing Statements

The **closing statement** is prepared before the closing, but it records what must happen at closing. The statement *sets forth the distribution of monies involved in the transaction*—who is to pay a specific amount for each expense and who is to receive that amount. The closing statement is to be prepared by the person in charge of disbursing monies at closing. This could be an escrow agent, an attorney, a broker, a lender, or a title company.

Format and Entries

The first step in preparing statements is to list all items in the transaction. Some of these items involve both the buyer and the seller, other items are of concern only to the buyer, and still others are of concern only to the seller. Entries that involve both parties will appear on the settlement statement of both parties. Items that involve only the buyer will appear only on the buyer's section of the settlement statement. Those that involve only the seller will appear only on the seller's section of the settlement statement.

Items included on the settlement statement fall into one of two categories: debits or credits. *Items that are owed* are **debits**. Those to be paid by the buyer are called buyer debits, and those owed and to be paid by the seller are seller debits. *Monies received* are **credits**. Items representing money to be received by the buyer are called buyer credits. Items representing money to be received by the seller are called seller credits.

In the RESPA settlement statement form shown in Chapter 8 (Figure 8.6), the areas for debits and credits have been marked. Although real estate agents typically do not have to complete that form, they should be sufficiently familiar with the format to explain the entries to buyer and seller. For purposes of the examples and practice problems at the end of this chapter, a simplified, basic buyer and seller statement is used. The typical debits and credits of buyer and seller are set out below.

Buyer Debits

Purchase price
Hazard or homeowner's insurance
Document preparation fee (mortgage and note)
Survey
Mortgagee's title insurance
Credit report
Loan origination fee
Mortgage assumption fee
Prepaid mortgage interest
Mortgage insurance
Discount points
Real estate property taxes paid in advance by seller
Recording of deed
Recording of mortgage documents

Buyer Credits

Earnest money deposit
New mortgage money proceeds
Purchase money mortgage
Assumed mortgage and seller's accrued interest on mortgage
Contract for deed balance
Unpaid real property taxes prorated
Balance due from buyer at closing (this is a balancing entry only, as buyer owes this money)

Seller Debits

Unpaid real property taxes prorated
Existing mortgage and seller's accrued interest
Deed preparation fee
Contract for deed balance
Purchase money mortgage taken back from buyer

Seller Credits

Purchase price
Overpaid real property taxes
Overpaid insurance premium
Sale of personal property
Escrow balance on assumed loan

Termite inspection and treatment
Soil test (perc test)
Unpaid utility bills
Mortgage interest on assumed loan
Transfer tax on transfer of real estate
Broker's fee
Balance due to seller at closing
(this is a balancing entry only, as seller gets this money)

Handling Closing Funds

At the closing, the monies the buyer owes are to be received by the closing agent. The monies owed to the seller are to be disbursed by the closing agent. All other expenses of the sale are to be paid from the closing proceeds and disbursed by the closing agent. The closing agent basically begins with an empty account, receives money, disburses money, and ends with an empty account.

The money available for disbursement must equal the amount to be disbursed. The closing agent should perform a **reconciliation**, *a check of the money available and money owed prior to closing.*

RECONCILIATION

A good check to perform on statements for both buyer and seller is to verify that the money available for disbursement equals the expenses and money to be disbursed. The closing agent is to begin with a zero balance and, after disbursements at closing, end with a zero balance. To recap the reconciliation for the purchase money mortgage sample for the buyer and seller immediately preceding:

Money Available	
Earnest money	$ 2,000.00
Balance due from buyer	$12,737.47
Total available	$14,737.47
Money to Disburse	
Preparation of note and mortgage	$ 45.00
Deed recording	3.50
Mortgage recording	4.50
Title insurance binder	300.00
Seller's existing mortgage	5,000.00
Preparation of deed	40.00
Broker's commission	3,600.00
Proceeds due seller	5,744.47
Total to disburse	$14,737.47

The money available and the money to be disbursed to pay expenses and the seller are equal. The closing statement figures have been reconciled, and the closing agent can be assured that at the closing the exact funds needed will be available.

CASH SALE STATEMENT

Our first illustration and analysis is the cash sale statement. This statement is usually the least complex of the four types because it has fewer items. The items involved in the transaction are listed below, developed from the offer to purchase between buyer and seller, expenses incurred prior to closing, and expenses owed at closing.

The statement prepared from this list and shown in Figure 9.2 is a typical example of a cash sale statement. The subsequent analysis, when related to each entry in the figure, should clarify the cash sale statement.

Closing date: February 15, 1996
Sales price: $45,000
Earnest money deposit: $3,000
Annual insurance premium paid by buyer: $235
Annual real property taxes, unpaid: $720
Deed preparation: $25
Recording fee: $3.50
Owner's title insurance policy: $315
Transfer taxes charged on transfer of real estate: $45
Broker's commission due (7%): $3,150

Analysis of the Cash Sale Statement

Settlement Date

The settlement date shown for this transaction is February 15, 1996. This is the date on which the closing took place, and this date becomes the calendar basis for all prorations involved in the closing statement. In making prorations, the day of closing or settlement date is charged to the seller. Expenses for this date in a prorated item are to be paid by the seller. For purposes of this book and most licensing examinations, all prorations are performed on the basis of a 360-day year.

FIGURE 9.2 Cash sale closing statement.

Settlement Date: February 15, 1996	Summary of Buyer's Transaction		Summary of Seller's Transaction	
	Debit	Credit	Debit	Credit
Purchase Price	$45,000.00	$	$	$45,000.00
Earnest Money		3,000.00		
Insurance Premium	235.00			
Prorated Real Property Taxes		90.00	90.00	
Deed Preparation			25.00	
Deed Recording	3.50			
Title Insurance			315.00	
Transfer Taxes			45.00	
Commission Due to Broker			3,150.00	
Balance Due from Buyer		42,148.50		
Proceeds Due to Seller			41,375.00	
Totals	$45,238.50	$45,238.50	$45,000.00	$45,000.00

Purchase Price

Both buyer and seller are involved with the purchase price. The buyer is paying, and the seller is receiving. Because the buyer is paying, this is a debit on the buyer's statement. The seller is receiving, and thus it appears as a credit on the seller's statement. This appears in both seller's and buyer's statements.

Earnest Money

When the buyer entered into the contract for purchase with the seller, he made a deposit of $3,000 in the form of earnest money, escrow money, or binder, as it is variously called. The buyer receives credit in his statement for having paid this amount. This money usually is held in the broker's trust or escrow account until closing. The broker brings a check for the $3,000 to closing for the benefit of the buyer. This money is available at the closing, to be applied to the buyer's debits. This affects only the buyer.

Hazard Insurance Premium

Buyers want to be protected against financial loss resulting from total or partial destruction of their property. Therefore, the buyer has in force at closing a hazard or homeowner's insurance policy. This policy is for the buyer's benefit and thus is a debit to the buyer. This affects only the buyer.

Real Property Taxes

The annual real property taxes in the cash sale example are $720, and these taxes are not paid. This is an accrued item. At the end of the year, when the tax bill is due, the property will belong to the buyer, and thus the buyer will have to pay the taxes. The unpaid taxes constitute a specific lien on the real estate. To make an equitable division of these taxes at closing, the seller should pay the taxes from January 1 through February 15. The seller owes the prorated tax bill, and thus it is a seller debit. The money is owed to the buyer for use at the end of the year and thus is a buyer credit. The seller's share for the 45 days (30 days of January and 15 days of February) is $2 per day, or a total of $90 for entry on the settlement statement. This affects both parties.

Title Insurance and Deed Preparation

In the offer to purchase, the seller agreed to convey a marketable title to the buyer. To accomplish this conveyance, the seller must provide a title insurance policy or updated abstract. In this example, the seller provided title insurance at a cost of $315. Most often this is an expense solely of the seller, to be paid to the title company at closing; thus, it is usually a seller debit. In some geographic areas, however, this is treated as a buyer expense.

Once marketable title is provided, the seller must complete the conveyance by execution of a deed. Because the deed is necessary to complete the seller's promise in the offer to purchase, the seller is responsible for the cost of deed preparation. This is a seller debit only.

Deed Recording

The purpose of recording a deed is to provide notice of title for the buyer. Therefore, the buyer usually pays the recording fee although this does vary locally. This is a buyer debit only.

Transfer Taxes

Most states impose a tax on the conveyance of real estate, based on the consideration that the seller receives in the transaction. The usual statutory requirement is that the seller pay these taxes; therefore, this item usually appears as a seller debit on the settlement statement. The name of this tax varies from state to state. It may be known as deed stamps, real estate excise tax, or real estate conveyance tax.

Broker's Fee (Commission Due)

In the listing contract, the seller has hired the broker to market the property. In the listing, the seller has agreed to pay the broker a fee or commission of 7 percent of the final sales price of the property. Therefore, an entry of $3,150 is made as seller debit. This affects only the seller.

Balance Due from Buyer

The balance due from the buyer is the amount the buyer must bring to closing to fulfill his obligations in the transaction. The combination of the $3,000 earnest money and the $42,148.50 balance due from the buyer will fulfill the financial responsibility. The balance due from the buyer is determined by totaling the buyer debits and subtracting the buyer credits. The total debits are $45,238.50. The total credits are $3,090.00. The difference is $42,148.50. The buyer has $42,148.50 more debits than credits; thus, the buyer must pay this amount at closing to satisfy his obligations. This amount is entered in the buyer credit column because he must bring this amount and pay it at closing.

Balance Due Seller

In this illustration, the seller has only one credit, the purchase price. We subtract the seller's debits from this credit to arrive at the balance due the seller at closing. The difference is $41,375. The seller has $41,375 more in credits than debits. Therefore, to satisfy the obligations due him at closing, seller must receive a check in the amount of $41,375. Because he received this check at closing, it is entered as a debit. With the entry of the amount due the seller, the seller debit and credit columns are equal.

Other Comments

Notice that the totals of the buyer's statement and seller's statement in the illustration are different. This is because the two statements are not completely interrelated. The buyer has certain expenses and credits that the seller does not, and the seller has certain expenses that the buyer does not. For this reason, the two statements are not the same.

A typical entry on a seller's statement that did not appear in this example is the payoff of an existing mortgage. In the example, if the seller had a mortgage on the property, the seller would have to pay off the mortgage balance to convey clear title to the buyer. The cost of paying off the mortgage would be a debit to the seller only.

Purchase Money Mortgage Statement

This type of closing statement involves the use of a mortgage given by the buyer to the seller for part of the purchase price. The seller is financing the sale of her property to the extent of the amount of the purchase money mortgage taken back from the buyer. In the discussion of this type of statement and in the next two statements, various terms are used to identify mortgage. These are: mortgage, deed of trust, and trust deed. For purposes of the closing statement, these terms are interchangeable.

Typical items for a settlement statement involving a purchase money mortgage are listed below. Figure 9.3 shows closing statements for buyer and seller that would result from the listed information.

Settlement date: September 27, 1996
Sales price: $60,000
Earnest money: $2,000
Insurance policy: On Jan. 31, the seller paid $240 for a full year in advance. At closing, the buyer is purchasing the remaining portion of the policy from the seller.
Annual real property tax: $536 unpaid
Seller's existing mortgage: $5,000
Purchase money mortgage: $45,000
Deed preparation: $40
Mortgage and note preparation: $45
Deed recording: $3.50
Mortgage recording: $4.50
Owner's title insurance policy: $300
Broker's commission: 6% of the sales price

FIGURE 9.3 Purchase money mortgage closing statement.

Settlement Date: September 27, 1996	Summary of Buyer's Transaction		Summary of Seller's Transaction	
	Debit	Credit	Debit	Credit
Purchase Price	$60,000.00	$	$	$60,000.00
Earnest Money		2,000.00		
Insurance Prorated	82.00			82.00
Real Property Taxes		397.53	397.53	
Seller's Existing Mortgage			5,000.00	
Purchase Money Mortgage		45,000.00	45,000.00	
Deed Preparation			40.00	
Mortgage and Note Preparation	45.00			
Deed Recording	3.50			
Mortgage Recording	4.50			
Title Insurance			300.00	
Commission Due to Broker			3,600.00	
Balance Due from Buyer		12,737.47		
Proceeds Due to Seller			5,744.47	
Totals	$60,135.00	$60,135.00	$60,082.00	$60,082.00

Analysis of Purchase Money Mortgage Statement

In the following analysis of the purchase money mortgage statement, only the entries that were not in the cash sale statement are discussed.

Prorated Insurance Premium

In the example, the seller has paid for a full year's premium in advance, and the buyer is purchasing the unused portion of the policy. This is a prepaid item requiring proration.

On January 31, the seller paid $240 for one year, but used only a portion of the year. She used the full months of February through August, which is $7 \times 30 = 210$ days, plus 27 days of September, for a total of 237 days used by the seller. The total of unused days is $360 - 237 = 123$. Thus, the buyer owes the seller for 123 days. This is a seller credit and a buyer debit on the settlement statement. It is an entry in the amount of $123 \times \$.6666 = \$81.99$.

Purchase Money Mortgage

The buyer is given credit for having given the seller a purchase money mortgage at closing. A purchase money mortgage simply means the seller lends the buyer the money to purchase the property by agreeing to wait for the actual cash to be paid over a period of time. The seller is not going to get the cash at closing. This is treated just as if the buyer had given the seller $45,000 in cash toward the purchase price of $60,000 and thus is placed as a buyer credit. The fact that the seller received this mortgage results in an offsetting entry in the seller's debit column. This affects both parties.

Seller's Existing Mortgage

To have clear title to convey to the buyer, the seller must satisfy the existing mortgage. Because this is a seller expense, the payoff amount appears as a seller debit.

Cost of Preparing Mortgage

The buyer must have the purchase money mortgage to deliver to the seller; therefore, the buyer will pay for the preparation of the mortgage and note. This is a buyer debit.

Other Comments

All other entries appearing in Figure 9.3 are similar to those in Figure 9.2 for the cash sale statement. If you are unclear as to the other entries, refer to Figure 9.2 and the discussion of Figure 9.2.

Mortgage Assumption Statement

In the next example (see Figure 9.4), the buyer is assuming the seller's existing mortgage. The buyer is paying part of the purchase price by the assumption of this mortgage. In assuming the seller's existing mortgage, the buyer is agreeing to make the payments of the principal and interest as well as assuming the responsibility for the other conditions set out in the mortgage contract between the seller and seller's lender. In the illustration, $49,000 of the $65,000 purchase price is paid by the buyer's assumption.

Closing date: November 13, 1997
Sales price: $65,000
Earnest money deposit: $1,500
Annual premium for new homeowner's insurance: $280
Annual real property taxes: $300 prepaid
Mortgage assumption to be assumed by buyer: $49,000
Interest rate on mortgage to be assumed: 9%
Mortgage balance fee: $135
Deed preparation: $50
Recording fee: $3.50
Broker's commission: 6.5%

Analysis of Mortgage Assumption Statement

Prorated Real Property Taxes

The closing date in this sample is November 13, 1997. The seller is responsible only for the real property taxes through the date of closing. Because the seller has paid the taxes for the entire year, the seller will be reimbursed for 30 + 17 days of taxes. The amount represented by 47 days is $39.17 ($300 ÷ 360 days = $.8333 per day). This will appear as a credit to the seller and a debit to the buyer.

FIGURE 9.4 Mortgage assumption closing statement.

Settlement Date: November 13, 1997	Summary of Buyer's Transaction		Summary of Seller's Transaction	
	Debit	Credit	Debit	Credit
Purchase Price	$65,000.00	$	$	$65,000.00
Earnest Money		1,500.00		
Insurance Premium	280.00			
Prorated Real Property Taxes	39.17			39.17
Assumed Mortgage Balance		49,000.00	49,000.00	
Mortgage Interest Nov. 1–13		159.25	159.25	
Mortgage Assumption Fee	135.00			
Cost of Preparing the Deed			50.00	
Deed Recording	3.50			
Commission Due to Broker			4,225.00	
Balance Due from Buyer		14,798.42		
Proceeds Due to Seller			11,604.92	
Totals	$65,457.67	$65,457.67	$65,039.17	$65,039.17

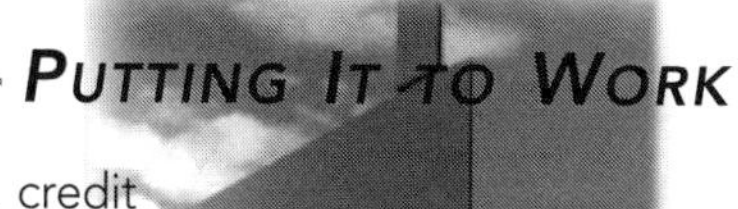

Examples of items commonly paid outside closing (POC) include appraisal, credit report, loan application fee, and hazard insurance premium.

Mortgage Interest Through November 13

In transactions involving the buyer's assumption of the seller's existing mortgage, the interest rate is important in calculating the monthly interest. Monthly interest must be prorated to the date of closing for an equitable division between buyer and seller for the interest owed. Most mortgage loans are set up for the interest to be paid in arrears rather than in advance. In this illustration, the seller's interest was paid in arrears. The mortgage payment to be paid by the buyer on December 1 will include interest for the month of November. The seller is responsible for the first 13 days of the interest in November. Therefore, the buyer will be credited with 13 days of interest. A corresponding debit will appear in the seller's statement. The accrued interest will be an entry to both parties. The calculation is:

\$49,000 (mortgage assumed) × .09 (interest rate) =	\$4,410.00	annual interest
\$4,410.00 ÷ 12 =	\$367.50	monthly interest
\$367.50 ÷ 30 =	\$12.25	daily interest
\$12.25 × 13 =	\$159.25	owed by seller

Mortgage Assumption Fee

Lending institutions typically charge a fee to transfer the mortgage record from the seller to the buyer. The buyer who is assuming the mortgage pays the fee. Therefore, it appears as a single-entry buyer debit on the closing statement.

Other Comments

If the seller has a mortgage escrow or impound account with the lender for the purpose of accumulating funds to pay the annual tax and insurance bills when they come due, the escrow account balance must be considered at the closing and shown on the closing statement. One way to handle this on the closing statement is to have the buyer purchase the account from the seller on a dollar-for-dollar basis. The buyer would have a debit, and the seller would have a credit for the amount of the escrow account.

An alternative method would be for the buyer to establish *a new escrow account with the lender*. These accounts are also called **impound**, budget, or reserve **accounts**. The buyer then would make her own contributions to the account. This would require an entry as a buyer debit for the amount to be contributed to the new account at closing. The old escrow account could be refunded to the seller at closing or after the closing. If the refund is at the closing, the seller will have a credit for the amount of the account. If the refund is to be after the closing, no entry will appear.

(See Practice Problem 1: Mortgage Assumption on page 208 for an opportunity to apply the information studied in this section.)

NEW FIRST MORTGAGE STATEMENT

A new first mortgage statement represents a transaction in which the buyer is obtaining a new loan from a lending institution. The security for this loan is a first mortgage given by the buyer to the lending institution.

Closing date: August 20, 1997
Sales price: $94,000
Earnest money deposit: $2,500
Annual premium for new insurance: $382
New first mortgage: 80% of the sales price
Annual real property taxes: $1,128 unpaid
Seller's existing mortgage: $46,000
Deed preparation: $60
Mortgage preparation: $55
Lender's title insurance: $2.50 per $1,000 of loan amount
Credit report: $35
Survey: $175
Termite inspection: $50
Loan origination fee: $752
Deed recording: $7
Mortgage recording: $10.50
Broker's commission: 7% of sales price

Analysis of New First Mortgage Statement

The new first mortgage is shown as an entry only on the buyer's statement (see Figure 9.5). It is shown as a credit because this money is available to the buyer to be applied to the satisfaction of his obligations in the transaction. In this illustration, three sources of funds contribute to payment of the buyer's cost: earnest money, new first mortgage, and balance of money due from the buyer at closing. Several new expenses are reflected as buyer debits; these are additional expenses associated with the new first mortgage. The other entries have been covered in prior analysis.

(See Practice Problem 2: New First Mortgage on page 209 for an opportunity to apply the information studied in this section.)

FIGURE 9.5 New first mortgage closing statement.

Settlement Date: August 20, 1997	Summary of Buyer's Transaction		Summary of Seller's Transaction	
	Debit	Credit	Debit	Credit
Purchase Price	$94,000.00	$	$	$94,000.00
Earnest Money		2,500.00		
Insurance Premium	382.00			
First Mortgage		75,200.00		
Prorated Real Property Taxes		720.67	720.67	
Existing Mortgage			46,000.00	
Deed Preparation			60.00	
Mortgage Preparation	55.00			
Title Insurance	188.00			
Credit Report	35.00			
Survey	175.00			
Termite Inspection			50.00	
Loan Origination	752.00			
Deed Recording	7.00			
Mortgage Recording	10.50			
Commission Due to Broker			6,580.00	
Balance Due from Buyer		17,183.83		
Proceeds Due to Seller			40,589.33	
Totals	$95,604.50	$95,604.50	$94,000.00	$94,000.00

PRACTICE PROBLEM 1: MORTGAGE ASSUMPTION STATEMENT

Use the following information to prepare statements on the provided worksheet. The solution to this practice problem is found at the end of the chapter.

Settlement date: July 10, 1997
Purchase price: $69,500
Earnest money deposit: $4,500
New insurance policy premium: $278
Annual real property taxes: $900 unpaid
Assumed mortgage balance: $42,000
Mortgage interest rate for July: 9% paid in arrears
Mortgage assumption fee: $50
Purchase money second mortgage from buyer to seller: $9,000
Seller's escrow account for taxes and insurance (to be purchased by buyer at closing): $735
Deed preparation: $25
Second mortgage preparation: $30
Recording of deed and second mortgage: $8
Title insurance binder: $320
Lighting allowance given to buyer by seller for fixtures being removed by seller: $180
Broker's commission: 7½%
Transfer taxes: 2% total, paid by seller

PRACTICE PROBLEM 1 Worksheet.

Settlement Date: Items:	Summary of Buyer's Transaction		Summary of Seller's Transaction	
	Debit	Credit	Debit	Credit
Totals				

PRACTICE PROBLEM 2: NEW FIRST MORTGAGE STATEMENT

Use the following information to prepare statements on the provided worksheet. The solution to this practice problem is found at the end of the chapter.

Settlement date: July 18, 1998
Purchase price: $140,000
Earnest money deposit: $10,000
New insurance premium: $497
New mortgage: 90% of the purchase price; 4 points to be paid by buyer
Annual real property taxes: $1,700 unpaid
Additional property assessment: $1,540 unpaid to be prorated
Prepaid interest at 9.5%
Seller's existing mortgage: $83,760 at 7%
Private mortgage insurance: 1% of the loan
Deed preparation: $60
Deed of trust preparation: $50
Credit report: $50
Survey: $225
Termite clearance: $650
Loan origination charge: 1% of the loan
Mortgagee's title insurance: $385
Recording fees: $12
Broker's commission: 6% of the sales price
Owner's title insurance: $785
Transfer taxes: 2% of the sales price to be split

PRACTICE PROBLEM 2 Worksheet.

Settlement Date: Items:	Summary of Buyer's Transaction		Summary of Seller's Transaction	
	Debit	Credit	Debit	Credit
Totals				

SOLUTION TO PRACTICE PROBLEM 1: MORTGAGE ASSUMPTION STATEMENT

Settlement Date: July 10, 1997	Summary of Buyer's Transaction		Summary of Seller's Transaction	
	Debit	Credit	Debit	Credit
Purchase Price	$69,500.00	$	$	$69,500.00
Earnest Money Deposit		4,500.00		
Insurance Premium	278.00			
Prorated Real Property Taxes		475.00	475.00	
Assumed Mortgage		42,000.00	42,000.00	
Mortgage Interest		105.00	105.00	
Mortgage Assumption Fee	50.00			
Purchase Money Second Mortgage		9,000.00	9,000.00	
Seller's Escrow Account	735.00			735.00
Cost of Preparing the Deed			25.00	
Cost of Preparing Second Mortgage	30.00			
Cost of Recordings	8.00			
Cost of Title Abstract			320.00	
Light Fixture Allowance		180.00	180.00	
Commission Due to Broker			5,212.50	
Transfer Taxes			1,390.00	
Balance Due from Buyer		14,341.00		
Proceeds Due to Seller			11,527.50	
Totals	$70,601.00	$70,601.00	$70,235.00	$70,235.00

SOLUTION TO PRACTICE PROBLEM 2: NEW FIRST MORTGAGE STATEMENT

Settlement Date: July 18, 1998	Summary of Buyer's Transaction		Summary of Seller's Transaction	
	Debit	Credit	Debit	Credit
Purchase Price	$140,000.00	$	$	$140,000.00
Earnest Money		10,000.00		
Insurance Premium	497.00			
First Mortgage		126,000.00		
Discount Points	5,040.00			
Real Property Taxes		935.00	935.00	
Assessment		847.00	847.00	
Prepaid Interest	399.00			
Existing Mortgage			83,760.00	
Accrued Interest			293.16	
P.M.I.	1,260.00			
Deed Preparation			60.00	
Deed of Trust	50.00			
Credit Report	50.00			
Survey	225.00			
Termite Clearance			650.00	
Loan Origination	1,260.00			
Mortgagee's Title Insurance	385.00			
Recording Fees	12.00			
Commission Due to Broker			8,400.00	
Owner's Title Insurance			785.00	
Transfer Taxes	1,400.00		1,400.00	
Balance Due from Buyer		12,796.00		
Proceeds Due to Seller			42,869.84	
Totals	$150,578.00	$150,578.00	$140,000.00	$140,000.00

How Would You Respond?

It is the day before closing and you are reviewing the proposed closing statement with your sellers before they sign the final documents tomorrow. Several items confuse them and you explain these to their reluctant satisfaction. Several items show up that they do not recall in the original offer and acceptance. In reviewing the O & A, it seems that they are right; but, in reviewing the escrow instructions, the items were listed as the sellers' expenses. These total $925. The sellers complain that they never agreed to these in the sales contract and should not have to pay them. They did not review the escrow instructions in detail since you assured them it was just like the O & A. They are refusing to close the sale.

1. Can the sellers legitimately refuse to close the sale?
2. Who is at fault?
3. Who should have to pay these items?

Review Questions

Answers to these questions are found in the *Answer Key* section at the back of the book.

1. The amount of an assumed mortgage appears on the buyer's statement as a:
   a. credit
   b. debit
   c. reconciliation
   d. format

2. The amount of the earnest money deposit appears as a:
   a. seller's debit
   b. seller's credit
   c. buyer's debit
   d. buyer's credit

3. If property was listed for sale at $30,000 and sold for $28,500, the 6% broker's fee would appear in the seller's statement as a:
   a. debit of $1,800
   b. credit of $1,800
   c. debit of $1,710
   d. credit of $1,710

4. The cost of preparing a deed appears as a:
   a. seller's debit
   b. seller's credit
   c. buyer's debit
   d. buyer's credit

5. If the closing date is June 30 and seller's real property taxes of $664 for the calendar year are unpaid, the appropriate entry on the buyer's statement would be a:
   a. credit of $332
   b. debit of $664
   c. debit of $332
   d. credit of $664

6. The proper entry on the closing statements for a transaction closed on April 15, in which the buyer is purchasing the seller's insurance policy for which the seller paid an annual premium of $156 on November 30, would be:
   a. credit to seller of $97.50
   b. debit to buyer of $58.50
   c. debit to seller of $97.50
   d. credit to buyer of $58.50

7. A buyer purchased a rental property and closed the transaction on July 20. The tenant had paid rent for the month of July in the amount of $540 on July 1. The rent should be shown as a:
   a. debit to seller of $180
   b. debit to buyer of $180
   c. debit to seller of $360
   d. credit to buyer of $360

8. A purchase money mortgage appears as a:
   a. credit to seller
   b. debit to seller
   c. debit to buyer
   d. prepaid by seller

9. The responsibility for certain closing costs to be paid by the buyer or seller is determined by:
   a. negotiations
   b. the type of new loan
   c. local custom
   d. all of the above

10. Which of the following is true regarding closing statements items?
    a. all items appear on both statements
    b. a new insurance policy appears only on the buyer's statement
    c. earnest money affects only the seller
    d. a mortgage payoff affects both the buyer and seller

POSSIBLE RESPONSES TO "HOW WOULD YOU RESPOND?"

1. The sellers may have a right to refuse the sale based on your misrepresentation of the terms of the escrow instructions. This would be determined with certainty only by a court.

2. The sellers bear some responsibility for their failure to read the escrow instructions. As a licensee, you have some liability for the misrepresentation based on your negligence or failure to do due diligence. The escrow agent should have paralleled the O & A in the escrow instructions, but is not technically a party to that contract.

3. On a contract basis between the buyer and seller, the seller will likely have to bear the responsibility. In practice, the agent often will pay various expenses for these types of oversights and inconsistencies. The agent probably bears the greatest responsibility.

CHAPTER 10

IMPORTANT TERMINOLOGY

anticipation
appraisal
appraisal report
assessed value
book value
capitalization formula
capitalization rate (cap rate)
change
chronological age
comparables
comparison approach
competition
condemnation value
conformity
contract rent
contribution
cost approach
cubic-foot method
depreciation
economic obsolescence
effective age
effective demand
evaluation
fixed expenses
functional obsolescence
gross effective income
GIM (gross income multiplier)
GRM (gross rent multiplier)
income approach
insurance value
liquidity
market data method
market value
mortgage loan value
narrative report
net operating income
operating expenses
operating statement
overimprovement
paired sales analysis
rate of return
reconciliation
replacement cost
replacement reserve
reproduction cost
risk factor
scarcity
square-foot method
substitution
supply and demand
transferability
underimprovement
utility
vacancy rate
valuation
weighted average

Property Valuation

IN THIS CHAPTER Appraising is not an exact science. Uniformity in appraising, however, has developed by applying proven appraisal techniques developed by appraisal organizations such as the Society of Real Estate Appraisers and the Institute of Real Estate Appraisers, now merged to form the Appraisal Institute. These organizations offer continuing education programs for members to assure high quality standards of appraisers and the appraisals they produce. Specialized designations and certifications have been available to members for many years. In 1989 federal laws and regulations mandated licensing or certification of persons acting as appraisers.

The new regulations pertaining to residential appraisers and appraisals are the first mandatory federal regulations in the field. The federal regulations apply to mortgage loans packaged for sale to the regulated secondary mortgage market. As of July 1, 1991, lenders who wish to sell mortgages to the secondary mortgage market must use only appraisers certified by the state in which the appraised property is located, and all appraisals so used must meet the new federal criteria. Similar regulations have been implemented for commercial appraisals pertaining to federally related transactions. Professional fee appraisers concentrate their time, knowledge, and skill in appraising real estate. Even though real estate brokers and salespersons are not required to be professional appraisers, they need to have a working knowledge of the approaches to determining value of property to be listed and sold.

PUTTING IT TO WORK

Most states allow a person to hold both a real estate license and an appraisal license/certificate. Because of the obvious conflict, these people should never act as appraiser in transactions in which they, their friends, or others employed by their broker are also an agent or a principal.

This chapter covers the various types of value that can be established by appraisals, factors and forces affecting appraisals, and the three approaches used in arriving at the appraised value.

BASIC APPRAISAL CONCEPTS

Definition

An **appraisal** is *an estimate of value, based on factual data, on a particular property, at a particular time, for a particular purpose.* It is an opinion as to the worth of a given property. The opinion must be supported in writing with collected data and logical reasoning. The reasoning must follow one or more of the three appraisal approaches discussed later in the chapter. As the definition implies, date of the appraisal affects the opinion of value. Also affecting the opinion is the reason or purpose for the appraisal, also called the "problem."

Valuation Versus Evaluation

Valuation of a property *establishes an opinion of value utilizing a totally objective approach.* The person assigned to perform the valuation must base his or her opinion wholly upon facts relating to the property, such as age, square footage, location, cost to replace, and so on. A valuation is done to determine the market value of the property. **Market value** is defined by the Appraisal Institute as:

> *The highest price in terms of money which a property will bring in a competitive and open market under all conditions requisite to a fair sale, the buyer and seller, each acting prudently, knowledgeably, and assuming the price is not affected by undue stimulus.*

Market value is the most probable price a property will bring if:

1. Buyer and seller are equally motivated.
2. Both parties are well-informed or well-advised, and each is acting in what the individual considers his or her own best interest.
3. A reasonable time is allowed for exposure in the open market.
4. Payment is made in cash or its equivalent.
5. Financing, if any, is on terms generally available in the community at the specified date and typical for the property type in its locale.
6. The price represents a normal consideration for the property sold, unaffected by special financing amounts or terms, services, fees, costs, or credits incurred in the transaction.

Market value implies nonrelated buyer and seller in an "arms-length" transaction in which the buyer and seller are motivated by their own interests. Related-party sales or sales in which one party is in a "distress" situation obviously are not indicative of "fair" market value.

Evaluation, on the other hand, is *a study of the usefulness or utility of a property without reference to the specific estimate of value*. Evaluation studies take the form of land utilization studies, highest- and best-use studies, marketability studies, and supply and demand studies. Evaluation of a property does not result in an estimate of value of the property.

Types of Value

The usual purpose of an appraisal is to estimate the market value of a particular property. Market value is defined above. In addition to market value, the following values are often the subject or purpose of an appraisal:

Assessed value
Insurance value
Mortgage loan value
Condemnation value
Book value (historic value for accounting purposes)

Assessed Value

The **assessed value** of real property is determined by a local or state official. It is *the value to which a local tax rate is applied to establish the amount of tax imposed on the property*. The assessed value, as set by statute or local ordinance, is normally a percentage of market value. This percentage is called an assessment rate or ratio and may be up to 100 percent. Therefore, a combination of the rate of assessment and the tax rate applied to the property is what determines the annual tax bill. Assessed value is calculated by using the formula: market value × assessment rate = assessed value.

Insurance Value

In estimating the value of property as a basis for determining the amount of insurance coverage necessary to adequately protect the structure against loss by fire or other casualty, the insurance company is concerned with the cost of replacing or reproducing structures in the event of a total loss caused by an insured hazard. **Insurance value** is *the cost of replacing or reproducing the structure in the event of a total loss*. This cost is calculated by multiplying a square-foot replacement cost by the number of square feet in the structure, or it may involve more detailed analysis of component costs. Land value is not included in calculating insurance value.

Mortgage Loan Value

In making a mortgage loan, the lender is interested in the value of the property pledged as security for the debt. In the event of a foreclosure, the lender must recover the debt from sale of the property. Consequently, the **mortgage loan value** is *whatever the lender believes the property will bring at a foreclosure sale or subsequent resale*. Some lenders make a conservative value estimate; others are more liberal. Therefore, the mortgage value may be more or less than the market value.

Condemnation Value

When real property is taken under the power of eminent domain, the property owner is entitled to receive the fair market value of the property to compensate for the loss. This is what the owners would have received had they chosen to sell rather than being forced to sell. **Condemnation value** in the case of condemnation of the entire property is not difficult to estimate. In the case of a partial condemnation, however, it becomes more complex. In this case, the property owner is entitled to be compensated for the difference in the market value of the property before and after condemnation. This amount is typically an amount greater than the value of the portion of property condemned as a percentage of the entire property value.

Book Value or Historic Value

Book value is *an artificial value used for accounting or tax purposes, in connection with establishing a depreciation schedule* for a property based on the property's useful life. Often, this value has nothing to do with the actual useful life of the property but is used for tax or other financial accounting purposes. In 1980 the tax schedule assumed a property had a useful life of 40 years; in 1981 this became 15 years, later 18 years, then 19 years, and now the useful life is 27.5 or 39 years depending on its use as residential or commercial.

Assuming a property currently may be assigned a tax life of 27.5 years, this provides a straight line depreciation of 3.636% per year. If the property is 8 years old, the depreciation claimed is 3.636% × 8, or 29.09%; thus 70.91% (100% − 29.09%) has not depreciated. If the original cost of the property is $100,000, the present book value is $70,910.

Original cost	$100,000
8 years' depreciation	− 29,090
Present book value	$70,910

Appraisal Versus Competitive Market Analysis

An appraisal is an estimate of property value applying collected data in three appraisal approaches: market data approach, cost approach, and income approach. Each of these three approaches may yield a different value. The appraiser then reconciles the differing values, applying accepted appraisal principles and methods. In some cases, one or more of the approaches may not be utilized in the reconciliation (such as ignoring cost approach on older properties or the income approach in appraising single-family residential property with little likelihood of rental).

As discussed in Chapter 5, a competitive market analysis (CMA) is an analysis of the competition in the marketplace that a property will face upon sale attempts. This procedure is not an appraisal although many of the same principles apply. A CMA takes into consideration other properties currently on the market, as well as properties that have recently sold. An appraisal is only concerned with actual sales, not listings. A CMA is similar to the market data approach of a true appraisal, which is only one of the three approaches to the value applied in each appraisal. A CMA is a comparison of properties and is prepared in a similar fashion as the market data approach described later in this chapter.

Basic Real Estate Appraisal Concepts

Characteristics of Value for Real Property

An appraisal is an opinion of value. For property to have value, it must have certain legal and economic characteristics. These characteristics basic to all real property are:

1. Utility
2. Scarcity
3. Transferability
4. Effective demand

Utility

For the property to have value, it must have **utility**, *the ability to satisfy a need or desire.* A property must be useful. It must be possible to use or adapt the property for some legal purpose. If a property cannot be put to some beneficial use to fill a need, it will not have value; nobody will want it. This is also simply referred to as demand.

Scarcity

The characteristic of **scarcity** is *based on the supply of the property in relation to the effective demand for the property*. The more abundant the supply of property in comparison to the effective demand for property, the lower the value. Conversely, the fewer properties available on the market in comparison to the effective demand or bidding for these properties, the greater the value of the properties. The relationship of scarcity and utility is the classic economic principle of supply and demand.

Transferability

Transferability is a legal concept that must be present for a property to have value. The owner must *be able to shift the ownership interest to a prospective buyer*. This ownership interest includes all of those factors previously discussed in the bundle of rights theory.

PUTTING IT TO WORK

Examples of property that may not have transferability include property in probate proceedings, property held in trust, property with options against it or with defeasible conditions, and co-owned properties.

Effective Demand

Effective demand is a *desire or need for property coupled with the financial ability to satisfy the need*. In times of excessively high interest rates, many people with a strong desire and substantial need for housing are priced out of the mortgage market; therefore, the demand for the property is *not* effective. The people who wish to buy do not have the ability to satisfy the demand. In creating housing or other types of properties, such as office buildings, shopping malls, and hotels, a developer must take into consideration not only the need for these types of property but also the financial ability of prospective tenants or purchasers to satisfy their needs.

Factors Affecting Value

Once a property is shown to be of value because it has utility, scarcity, transferability, and effective demand, many factors affect the value of the property in a negative or a positive way. Collectively these factors are referred to as a neighborhood analysis. Specifically these factors are divided into four categories:

1. Physical
2. Economic
3. Social
4. Governmental

Physical Factors

The forces in this category are both natural and manmade. Natural physical factors that affect value are things such as land topography, soil conditions, mineral resources, size, shape, climate, and location. Manmade physical factors include public utilities, streets, highways, available public transportation, and access to streets and highways.

Economic Factors

Economic factors are typically separate from the real property being appraised. They include employment levels, median family income, interest rates, inflation, recession, and availability of credit.

Social Factors

Social factors include rates of marriage, births, divorces, and deaths; the rate of population growth or decline; and public attitudes toward things such as education, cultural activities, and recreation.

PUTTING IT TO WORK

In compliance with Fair Housing regulations, questions or comments regarding race and ethnicity are not appropriate in either the appraisal or marketing of property.

Governmental Factors

Governmental factors affecting value include regulations such as zoning laws, building codes, subdivision control ordinances, fire regulations, taxation, and city or county planning.

BASIC ECONOMIC VALUATION PRINCIPLES

Many economic principles may affect the value of real property. In establishing an estimate of value, an appraiser considers the following principles.

Highest and Best Use

The appraiser must consider four aspects of "use": possible use, permissible use, feasible use, and highest and best use.

1. *Possible use* considers the physical characteristics of the property.
2. *Permissible use* is the use legally available for the land under existing zoning, planning, deed restrictions, and so on.
3. *Feasible use* refers to the physical characteristics of the property and legal controls that make land appropriate for the market, neighborhood, and economic conditions.
4. *Highest and best use*, as defined in Chapter 1, is the feasible use that will produce the highest present value. The highest and best use in the context of market value is the most probable use. It may or may not be the present use of the property. Highest and best use can change over time as market forces change.

Highest and best use always takes into consideration present improvements on the property. The present use of an improved property is presumed to be the highest and best use unless change is imminent in market demand or in legal controls. To determine the highest and best use, knowledge of the subject property, community, market forces, and principles of land utilization is required.

PUTTING IT TO WORK

A common example of changing conditions dictating change to a higher and better use is an older home in a downtown area being converted to professional office space.

To accomplish the highest income and the highest present value of land, care must be taken not to create an overimprovement or an underimprovement. An **overimprovement** represents *an added investment in property that does not yield a return to the owner*. For example, creating too many apartment units with a high cost of maintenance may not yield sufficient income after paying capital and labor costs. Investment in the improvement exceeds the ability of the improvement to provide sufficient net income to cover the priority demands and still leave a residual income that will result in the highest land value. The same result occurs from **underimprovement**—*insufficient investment in improving property*. For example, if an insufficient number of apartment units are constructed, the improvement will not produce the greatest potential income to create maximum value.

Either an underimprovement or an overimprovement will result in loss of property value (or failure to realize the property's full potential). Therefore, in adhering to the principle of highest and best use, the owner not only must establish a feasible use but also a use capable of supporting the improvements constructed plus a return of investment return to the owner. Owners want both return on and return of their investment.

The *income allocated to the land as residual income under the principle of highest and best use* is defined as *economic rent*. This is the rent that land is capable of producing if it is put to its most efficient use. *Rent agreed upon in a contract between landlord and tenant* is called **contract rent**.

The principle of highest and best use also can be applied to the construction of a single-family residence. For example, if a house costs $125,000 to construct in a neighborhood of $75,000 houses, the result is an overimprovement. Conversely, a $50,000 house constructed in an area of homes valued at $125,000 and higher is an underimprovement. The principle of conformity, discussed later, also applies to this example.

Substitution

Under the principle of **substitution**, the *highest value of a property has a tendency to be established by the cost of purchasing or constructing another property of equal utility and desirability*, if the substitution can be made without unusual delay. Therefore, if two properties are on the market, each having the same degree of desirability and utility, one priced at $95,000 and the other at $100,000, a buyer would substitute the $95,000 property instead of purchasing the $100,000 property. The buyer will select the property that gives him or her the same amenities at the lesser price. Both the cost approach and the market data approach are heavily based upon the principle of substitution.

Supply and Demand

The economic principle of **supply and demand** is applicable to the real estate industry just as it is to other economic activities in the free enterprise system. This principle states that *the greater the supply of any commodity in comparison to the demand for that commodity, the lower the value will be*. Conversely, the smaller the supply and the greater the demand, the higher the value will be. Therefore, factors influencing the demand and supply of real estate affect property values either positively or negatively.

Conformity

Conformity means *"like kind" or compatible uses of land within a given area*. Adhering to the principle of conformity results in maximum property values. Failure to adhere to the principle results in inharmonious and incompatible uses of land within the area, with the consequence of depreciating property values. In residential subdivisions, conformity is achieved through restrictive covenants. In other areas, conformity is accomplished through zoning laws and subdivision ordinances. An example of a noncompatible use might be a "dome" home or "submerged home" in a subdivision of ranch-style houses.

If a property fails to conform to an area, either regression or progression may be the result. *Regression* occurs when the worth of a better property is diminished by the presence of a lesser quality property. An example is a large, elegant home in a neighborhood of modest ranch-style homes. *Progression* signifies an increase in the worth of a lesser property because of its location near higher quality properties. An example is an older, smaller home in an area of new construction of larger homes.

The greatest value will be shown in giving the market what the market expects to see. Buyers will not overpay because a property has been overimproved.

Anticipation

Under the principle of **anticipation**, *property value is based on the expectation of future benefits of ownership*. The future, not the past, is what is important in estimating property value. Changes in the expected demand for property can stem from various improvements such as schools, shopping centers, freeways, or other developments deemed beneficial to the area. Therefore, real estate licensees and appraisers have to be aware of plans for future development in their local market area. Other changes adversely affect the expected demand for property. Changes in surrounding land use patterns, such as re-routing of traffic via a by-pass, have an adverse effect on future demand. Changes producing an increase in demand increase property value; changes leading to a reduction in demand cause a loss in value.

Contribution

The principle of **contribution** states that *various elements of a property add value to the entire property*. For example, if a typical buyer is willing to pay $5,500 more for a property with a garage than for the same property without the garage, we infer that the element (garage) adds a value of $5,500 by itself.

The market data approach to valuing property utilizes this principle. To establish value, adjustments are made for differences between the comparable properties and the property that is being appraised. For example, the appraisal property has a fireplace—the element of contribution—whereas a comparable does not. The appraiser must estimate the value the fireplace contributes to the property as a whole and compare it to the value the property has in the absence of the fireplace. The appraiser extracts the contributed value from comparisons of properties in the market with and without the element. The values extracted will vary from area to area.

This can occasionally be determined by a **paired sales analysis**. This occurs when an appraiser has *two extremely comparable sales with only one significant difference in features*. If the only difference in the two sales is a two-car garage versus a three-car garage, the entire difference in price can be attributed to the extra space in the garage.

PUTTING IT TO WORK

An element's contribution may not be related to its cost. For example, a fireplace upgrade in a new home may cost $1,200, but when the home is resold, the buying market may be willing to pay only an additional $500 for the improvement. The contribution of the fireplace is thus $500.

Increasing Returns/Diminishing Returns

Under the principle of increasing or diminishing returns, an improvement to a structure is not valued as a separate element. The cost of the improvement is compared to the increase in value to the property after the improvement is completed. Under *diminishing returns, the increase in value is less than the cost of the improvement.* Under *increasing returns, the increase in value is more than the cost of the improvement.*

This principle becomes important when a property owner is considering placing property for sale. Any fix-up expenses the owner incurs prior to sale should have an increasing return effect. If the fix-up cost is greater than the potential increase in sales price, the owner may not want to do the fix-up.

This concept is basically a cost–benefit type of analysis. For example, if a feature such as a covered patio would cost $4,000 and the typical buyer is only willing to pay $2,500 extra for a home with a covered patio, this would not be a cost-effective addition. By contrast, if paying $400 additionally for thicker carpet pads extends the life of the carpeting for several years, this extended life is most certainly worth the extra cost.

Competition

The principle of **competition** states that *when the net profit a property generates is great (excessive), others will be drawn to produce similar properties.* Excessive profits are generated when demand exceeds supply. For example, if a growth area contains only one or two properties of a certain type, such as apartment complexes, these properties will produce excess profits because of the high demand. Competitors who build apartment complexes will come to the area eager to share in the market and profits. Competition will work to reduce excess profits, and the supply of competing services will increase until excess profits are finally eliminated.

Change

The principle of **change** states that *constantly differing conditions affect land use and therefore continually impact the value.* Every property and every area are constantly undergoing change. Nothing remains the same. The only constant is that change will occur. Change may cause a value to go up (appreciate) or go down (depreciate). Change may come from a physical or an economic condition relating to the property or surrounding property.

Appraisal Methodology

An appraisal is an estimate of property value based on factual data. In estimating property value, an organized and systematic program must be followed. The following steps provide an orderly progression of the appraisal process.

1. Define the appraisal problem or purpose. This includes determining the purpose of the appraisal and the type of value to be estimated. The purpose of the appraisal may prescribe the approaches to be implemented. If the appraisal is for repairs from fire damage, the cost approach may be more relevant. For a lender's appraisal, the market data approach makes more sense.
2. Obtain a complete and accurate description of the property that is to be appraised. The appraisal report must contain a legal description of the property to precisely locate and identify the property. The identification must specifically define the limits of the area included in the appraisal.

3. Inspect the surrounding area and the property to be appraised. Determine which properties in the area will be used in comparison.
4. Collect the specific data required as the basis for the value estimate. This information will be gathered from several sources including government offices, recent real estate sales records, zoning changes, and so on.
5. Analyze the data and consider the three approaches of market, cost, and income. Arrive at a value estimate by each of these three appraisal methods if each can be applied.
6. Correlate and reconcile the results obtained by each of the three methods. The reconciliation will determine the estimate of value.
7. Prepare the appraisal report. A sample Uniform Residential Appraisal Report form is shown in Figure 10.1.

Approaches to Value: Market, Cost, Income

Market Data or Comparison Approach

The **comparison approach**, or **market data method**, is the primary appraisal approach for estimating the value of single-family, owner-occupied dwellings and vacant land. It involves *comparing the property that is the subject of the appraisal (subject property) with other properties offering similar utility that have sold recently.* These are called **comparables**, or comps. No two properties are exactly alike; however, many are similar in desirability and utility. Adjustments are made for the differences by following the principle of contribution, or what a typical buyer may be willing to pay for extras. Figure 10.2 outlines the three approaches to determining value.

A minimum of three comparables is absolutely necessary. If available, as many as six comparables are appropriate. Comparables should be as similar as possible to the subject property in all respects. Comparables may be found in real estate office files of closed sales, in the closed sales data of a multiple listing service, in the county clerk or recorder's office, the assessor's office, and from other appraisers. The more recent the date of sale of the comparable, the more relevant the comparable is to the appraisal process. Also of great importance is the degree of similarity of physical characteristics of the comparables and the location of the comparables.

In selecting the comparables, certain property characteristics and nonproperty characteristics of each comparable must be specifically identified. Property characteristics include things such as size, type of construction, age, design, special features, and location. Nonproperty characteristics include the date of sale, verified sales price, method of financing, length of time on the market, and the seller's motivation in the sale. The fewer adjustments that need to be made, the better that comparable indicates the subject property's value.

Data values assigned as adjustments are the result of careful analysis of appraiser records. The numbers are not pulled arbitrarily from the air but, rather, derive from comparable sales analysis data from the appraiser's files. The appraiser should verify all comparable data provided by a party involved in the sales transaction. The amount used in the adjustments is not the cost to build the element being compared. *Cost* is defined as *the dollars needed to construct the element*; market value is defined as what the market will pay for the element. This is an application of the principle of contribution. Cost is not the same as market value. To arrive at the value of an element, the agent must constantly determine from the marketplace what the average buyer will pay for the element being compared. This value is based upon facts determined to exist in the area of the subject property and the comparables.

FIGURE 10.1
A uniform residential appraisal report.

Property Description UNIFORM RESIDENTIAL APPRAISAL REPORT **File No.**

Property Address | City | State | Zip Code
Legal Description | County
Assessor's Parcel No. | Tax Year | R.E. Taxes $ | Special Assessments $
Borrower | Current Owner | Occupant: ☐ Owner ☐ Tenant ☐ Vacant
Property rights appraised ☐ Fee Simple ☐ Leasehold | Project Type ☐ PUD ☐ Condominium (HUD/VA only) | HOA$ /Mo.
Neighborhood/Project Name | Map Reference | Census Tract
Sale Price $ | Date of Sale | Loan charges/concessions to be paid by seller $
Lender/Client | Address
Appraiser | Address

Location	☐ Urban	☐ Suburban	☐ Rural	**Predominant occupancy**	**Single family housing** PRICE $ (000) AGE (yrs)	**Present land use %**	**Land use change**
Built up	☐ Over 75%	☐ 25-75%	☐ Under 25%			One Family	☐ Not Likely ☐ Likely
Growth Rate	☐ Rapid	☐ Stable	☐ Slow	☐ Owner	Low	2-4 family	☐ In process
Property values	☐ Increasing	☐ Stable	☐ Declining	☐ Tenant	High	Multi-family	To:
Demand/supply	☐ Shortage	☐ In balance	☐ Over supply	☐ Vacant (0-5%)	Predominant	Commercial	
Marketing time	☐ Under 3 mos.	☐ 3-6 mos.	☐ Over 6 mos.	☐ Vacant (over 5%)			

Note: Race and the racial composition of the neighborhood are not considered reliable appraisal factors.

Neighborhood boundaries and characteristics:

Factors that affect the marketability of the properties in the neighborhood (proximity to employment and amenities, employment stability, appeal to market, etc):

Market conditions in the subject neighborhood (including support for the above conclusions related to the trend of property values, demand/supply, and marketing time -- such as data on competitive properties for sale in the neighborhood, description of the prevalence of sales and financing concessions, etc.):

Project Information for PUDs (If applicable) -- Is the developer/builder in control of the Home Owners' Association (HOA)? ☐ Yes ☐ No
Approximate total number of units in the subject project . Approximate total number of units for sale in the subject project
Describe common elements and recreational facilities:

Dimensions | Topography
Site area | Corner Lot ☐ Yes ☐ No | Size
Specific zoning classification and description | Shape
Zoning compliance ☐ Legal ☐ Legal nonconforming (Grandfathered use) ☐ Illegal ☐ No zoning | Drainage
Highest & best use as improved: ☐ Present use ☐ Other use (explain) | View

Utilities	Public	Other	**Off-site Improvements**	Type	Public	Private	
							Landscaping
Electricity	☐		Street		☐	☐	Driveway Surface
Gas	☐		Curb/Gutter		☐	☐	Apparent easements
Water	☐		Sidewalk		☐	☐	FEMA Special Flood Hazard Area ☐ Yes ☐ No
Sanitary sewer	☐		Street lights		☐	☐	FEMA Zone Map Date
Storm sewer	☐		Alley		☐	☐	FEMA Map no.

Comments (apparent adverse easements, encroachments, special assessments, slide areas, illegal or legal nonconforming zoning, use, etc.):

GENERAL DESCRIPTION	EXTERIOR DESCRIPTION	FOUNDATION	BASEMENT	INSULATION
No. of Units	Foundation	Slab	Area Sq. Ft.	Roof ☐
No. of Stories	Exterior Walls	Crawl Space	% Finished	Ceiling ☐
Type (Det./Att.)	Roof Surface	Basement	Ceiling	Walls ☐
Design (Style)	Gutters & Dwnspts.	Sump Pump	Walls	Floor ☐
Existing/Proposed	Window Type	Dampness	Floor	None ☐
Age (Yrs.)	Storm/Screens	Settlement	Outside Entry	Unknown ☐
Effective Age (Yrs.)	Manufactured House	Infestation		Adequacy ☐

ROOMS	Foyer	Living	Dining	Kitchen	Den	Family Rm.	Rec. Rm.	Bedrooms	# Baths	Laundry	Other	Area Sq. Ft.
Basement												
Level1												
Level 2												

Finished area **above** grade contains: Rooms; Bedroom(s); Bath(s); Square Feet of Gross Living Area

SURFACES Materials/Condition	HEATING	KITCHEN EQUIP.	ATTIC	AMENITIES	CAR STORAGE:
Floors	Type	Refrigerator ☐	None ☐	Fireplace(s) # ☐	None ☐
Walls	Fuel	Range/Oven ☐	Stairs ☐	Patio ☐	Garage # of cars
Trim/Finish	Condition	Disposal ☐	Drop Stair ☐	Deck ☐	Attached
Bath Floor	COOLING	Dishwasher ☐	Scuttle ☐	Porch ☐	Detached
Bath Wainscot	Central	Fan/Hood ☐	Floor ☐	Fence ☐	Built-In
Doors	Other	Microwave ☐	Heated ☐	Pool ☐	Carport
	Condition	Washer/Dryer ☐	Finished ☐		Driveway

Additional features (special energy efficient items, etc.):

Condition of the improvements, depreciation (physical, functional, and external), repairs needed, quality of construction, etc.:

Adverse environmental conditions (such as, but not limited to, hazardous wastes, toxic substances, etc.) present in the improvements, on the site, or in the immediate vicinity of the subject property.:

Freddie Mac Form 70 6-93 12 CH. PAGE 1 OF 2 Fannie Mae Form 1004B 6-93

(continued)

FIGURE 10.1 Continued.

Valuation Section

UNIFORM RESIDENTIAL APPRAISAL REPORT

File No.

COST APPROACH

ESTIMATED SITE VALUE .... = $ ______

ESTIMATED REPRODUCTION COST-NEW-OF IMPROVEMENTS

Dwelling ______ Sq. Ft @ $ ______ = $ ______

______ Sq. Ft @ $ ______ = ______

______ = ______

Garage/Carport ______ Sq. Ft @ $ ______ = ______

Total Estimated Cost New .... = $ ______

Less | Physical | Functional | External

Depreciation ______ = $ ______

Depreciated Value of Improvements .... = $ ______

"As-is" Value of Site Improvements .... = $ ______

INDICATED VALUE BY COST APPROACH = $ ______

Comments on Cost Approach (such as, source of cost estimate, site value, square foot calculation, and for HUD, VA and FmHA, the estimated remaining economic life of the property): ______

SALES COMPARISON ANALYSIS

ITEM	SUBJECT	COMPARABLE NO. 1		COMPARABLE NO. 2		COMPARABLE NO.3	
Address							
Proximity to Subject							
Sales Price	$		$		$		$
Price/Gross Liv. Area	$ ⌀	$ ⌀		$ ⌀		$ ⌀	
Data and/or Verification Sources							
VALUE ADJUSTMENTS	DESCRIPTION	DESCRIPTION	+(-) $ Adjustment	DESCRIPTION	+(-) $ Adjustment	DESCRIPTION	+(-) $ Adjustment
Sales or Financing Concessions							
Date of Sale/Time							
Location							
Leasehold/Fee Simple							
Site							
View							
Design and Appeal							
Quality of Construction							
Age							
Condition							
Above Grade Room Count	Total Bdrms Baths	Total Bdrms Baths		Total Bdrms Baths		Total Bdrms Baths	
Gross Living Area	Sq. Ft.	Sq. Ft.		Sq. Ft.		Sq. Ft.	
Basement & Finished Rooms Below Grade							
Functional Utility							
Heating/Cooling							
Energy Efficient Items							
Garage/Carport							
Porch, Patio, Deck Fireplaces, etc.							
Fence, Pool, etc.							
Net Adj. (total)		+ -	$	+ -	$	+ -	$
Adjusted Sales Price of Comparable		Gross % Net %	$	Gross % Net %	$	Gross % Net %	$

Comments on Sales Comparison (including the subject property's compatibility to the neighborhood, etc.): ______

ITEM	SUBJECT	COMPARABLE NO. 1	COMPARABLE NO. 2	COMPARABLE NO.3
Date, Price and Data Source for prior sales within year of appraisal				

Analysis of any current agreement of sale, option, or listing of the subject property and analysis of any prior sales of subject and comparables within one year of the date of appraisal:

INDICATED VALUE BY SALES COMPARISON APPROACH .... $ ______

INDICATED VALUE BY INCOME APPROACH (If Applicable) Estimated Market Rent $ ______ /Mo. x Gross Rent Multiplier ______ = $ ______

RECONCILIATION

This appraisal is made ☐ "as is" ☐ subject to the repairs, alterations, inspections or conditions listed below ☐ subject to completion per plans and specifications.

Conditions of Appraisal: ______

Final Reconciliation: ______

The purpose of this appraisal is to estimate the market value of the real property that is the subject of this report, based on the above conditions and the certification, contingent and limiting conditions, and market value definition that are stated in the attached Freddie Mac Form 439/Fannie Mae Form 1004B (Revised ______).

I (WE) ESTIMATE THE MARKET VALUE, AS DEFINED, OF THE REAL PROPERTY THAT IS THE SUBJECT OF THIS REPORT, AS OF ______ (WHICH IS THE DATE OF INSPECTION AND THE EFFECTIVE DATE OF THIS REPORT) TO BE $ ______.

APPRAISER:		SUPERVISORY APPRAISER (ONLY IF REQUIRED):	
Signature		Signature	☐ Did ☐ Did Not Inspect Property
Name		Name	
Date Report Signed		Date Report Signed	
State Certification #	State	State Certification #	State
Or State License #	State	Or State License #	State

Freddie Mac Form 70 6-93 12 CH. PAGE 2 OF 2 Fannie Mae Form 1004B 6-93

The Market Data Method	Compares subject to similar properties and makes appropriate adjustments.
The Income Method	Applies capitalization formula to forecast income or income produced (rent).
The Cost Approach	Theoretically rebuilds the structure new and then adjusts to its present condition.

FIGURE 10.2 Approaches to determining value (appraisal methods).

PUTTING IT TO WORK

Many people are frustrated by the adjustments appraisers make for differences in features; they often think the adjustments are too low or too high. No book or single resource says, "Bathroom: $1,500" or "Garage: $2,500." Instead, the appraiser's files, experience, and expertise justify the adjustment figures.

Data used in making adjustments between the comparable properties and the subject property is summarized, by appraisers, on page 2 of the URAR. The comparison sets forth all the property and nonproperty characteristics utilized in this specific value estimate.

Plus and minus adjustments are made to the comparable properties to reconcile the differences and arrive at a value estimate for the subject property on the basis of the prices for which the comparables sold (see Figures 10.3 and 10.4). A plus adjustment to a comparable is made when the comparable is deficient in some respect when compared to the subject property. A minus adjustment is made to a comparable when it contains an additional feature that the subject property does not, rendering the comparable superior to the subject property. For example, in Figure 10.3 an adjustment of minus $1,000 is made to Comparable #2 because it has 2.5 bathrooms instead of the 2.0 in the subject property. In other words, if Comparable #2 had only 2 bathrooms, theoretically it would have sold for $1,000 less.

After making all adjustments, the net adjustment amount for each comparable is calculated and the result is applied to the price for which the comparable sold, to arrive at an adjusted price. The adjusted price is an estimate of the price for which the comparable would have sold if all features and factors had been the same as the subject property. The three adjusted prices are correlated or reconciled to arrive at an indicated market value for the subject property. This reconciliation is reached by calculating a **weighted average**, in which *comparables with a high degree of similarity are given more weight than comparables with less similarity*. In Figure 10.3, comparable #3 is given the greatest weight because it requires the fewest adjustments; 40 percent of the weighting has been given to comparable #3. Next in order of similarity is Comparable #1, which is located in the same subdivision as the subject property (35 percent of the weighting). Comparable #2 is given the least weight because it is located in a different subdivision (25 percent of the weighting).

Income Approach

The **income approach**, also called appraisal by capitalization, is the primary method used to estimate the present value of properties that produce income. Properties included in this category are apartment complexes, single-family rental houses, mobile home parks, office buildings, shopping malls, parking lots, leased industrial plants, and any individual properties occupied by commercial tenants. The *value of the property is estimated by converting net annual income into an indication of present value by application of a capitalization rate.* The capitalization rate can be described as a

FIGURE 10.3 The market data approach.

Date:
July 9, 1996

Prepared Especially for:
John and Susan Mitchell

Medium Range Adj ADDRESS PROXIMITY	SUBJECT 2735 Hawthorne Carriage Estates	COMPARABLE 1 of 3 2815 Hemingway Carriage Estates		COMPARABLE 2 of 3 3270 Melville Heath Heights		COMPARABLE 3 of 3 4520 Thoreau Ct. Foxpointe	
Style	Ranch/Rambler	Ranch/Rambler		Ranch/Rambler		Ranch/Rambler	
Construction	Fr Stucco	Ced Stone	0	Brick	0	Brick	0
Date Sold		June 1996	238	Apr 1996	856	Apr 1996	907
Effective Age	12	12	0	14	1,000	11	(500)
Sq Ft Total	1,544	1,442		1,654		1,608	
Sq Ft Main	1,544	1,442	2,040	1,654	(2,200)	1,608	(1,280)
Sq Ft Up	0	0	0	0	0	0	0
Sq Ft Down	0	0	0	0	0	0	0
Pct Down Finished	0	0		0		0	
Acreage/Lot Size	120 x 80	120 x 85		125 x 80		115 x 97	
Value of Lot	$4,500	$4,500	0	$4,500	0	$4,500	0
Price/Sq Ft Inc Lot	$60 (Adj Ave)	$66		$56		$57	
Price/Sq Ft Exc Lot	$57 (Adj Ave)	$62		$54		$54	
Bedrooms Total	3	3	0	3	0	3	0
Bedrooms Main	3	3		3		3	
Bedrooms Up	0	0		0		0	
Bedrooms Down	0	0		0		0	
Bathrooms Total	2.0	2.0	0	2.5	(1,000)	2.0	0
Baths Main	2.0	2.0		2.5		2.0	
Baths Up	0.0	0.0		0.0		0.0	
Baths Down	0.0	0.0		0.0		0.0	
Fireplaces	1	1	0	1	0	1	0
Air Conditioning	Central	Central	0	Central	0	Central	0
Garage	2.0	2.0	0	2.0	0	2.0	0
Swimming Pool	0	0	0	0	0	0	0
Semi Annual Tax	$852.16	$697.12	0	$691.04	0	$820.51	0
Assessment	22360	21400	0	22060	0	25530	0
Fenced Yard	Privacy		0	Privacy	0	Privacy	0
Double Storage Blg			0		0		0
Fruit Trees			0		0		0
Listed Price		$94,500	Adjustment	$96,000	Adjustment	$93,500	Adjustment
Sales Price		$94,500	$2,278	$93,000	($1,344)	$92,000	($873)
ADJ. SALES PRICE		$96,778		$91,656		$91,127	

Comp 1: 35% × $96,778 = $33,872
Comp 2: 25% × $91,656 = $22,914
Comp 3: 40% × $91,127 = $36,451

Reconciled price: $33,872 + $22,914 + $36,451 = $93,237

In this example, the inferior property has no garage, the subject property has a one-car garage, and the superior property has a two-car garage. The appraiser must adjust for these discrepancies.

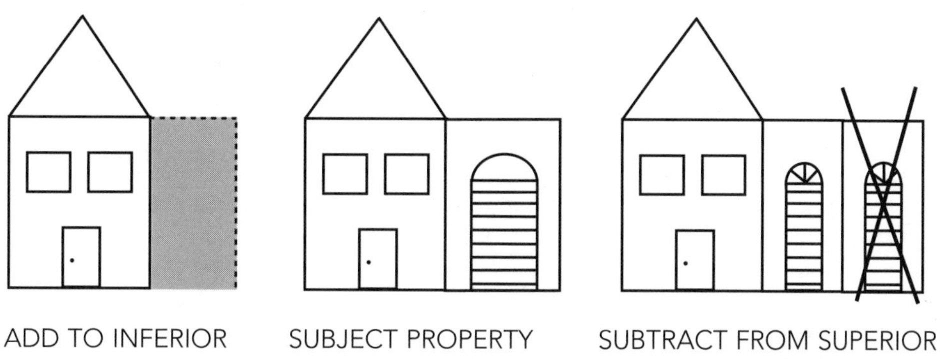

FIGURE 10.4 When adjusting comparables to subject property, an appraiser must add to inferior and subtract from superior comparables to arrive at an adjusted comparison.

desired rate of return by the marketplace for a type of investment. This procedure is illustrated in Figure 10.5 and the accompanying analysis. It shows an **operating statement** *stating income, vacancy rate, and expenses*. The information provided is used in the analysis, which applies the **capitalization formula**:

Annual net income ÷ capitalization rate = value

Analysis of Operating Statement

The apartment complex has a potential gross income of $1,350,000. This is the income that would be produced if every apartment were rented 100 percent of the time at $450 per month for a 12-month period. To expect any rental property to be occupied 100 percent of the time on a continuing basis is unrealistic. Therefore, the potential gross income must be reduced by the **vacancy rate** and credit loss. This example estimates the vacancy rate at 6 percent. The credit loss may include uncollected rent from defaulting tenants. In the example, the vacancy and credit losses are expected to reduce the gross potential income by $81,000 (6% × $1,350,000).

This apartment complex has other income generated by vending machines and laundry facilities that the tenants use. This income is projected to be $25,000 per year. *Any income added to the rental income yields the* **gross effective income**. The gross effective income in our example is $1,294,000. This is the amount of money the complex may realistically be expected to generate in a 12-month period.

To arrive at the net income, which is the number used in the capitalization formula, various expenses must be subtracted from the gross effective income. These expenses are categorized into fixed expenses, operating expenses, and replacement reserve.

Fixed expenses are *costs that do not fluctuate with the operating level of the complex*. They will remain the same whether the occupancy rate is 95 percent or 50 percent. These include real property taxes, insurance, licenses, and permits. The fixed expenses in the illustration total $121,000.

Operating expenses in general *fluctuate with the operating level* or occupancy of the property. As in the example, maintenance is the major operating expense, totaling $106,000. This expense varies with level of operation and is related to the age and condition of the property. Older properties naturally have more expenditures for maintenance than newer properties do. The property manager's fee also is an operating expense. Property managers typically are paid on a percentage of gross income. This fee increases with high occupancy and decreases with lower occupancy. Total operating expenses of the sample complex are $402,400. Of the three types of expenses, operating expenses typically represent the largest dollar amount.

FIGURE 10.5 An operating statement.

OPERATING STATEMENT

250-unit apartment complex with rent schedule of $450 per month per unit

Potential Gross Income: 250 × $450 × 12		$1,350,000
Less Vacancy and Credit Losses (6%)		(81,000)
Plus Other Income		25,000
Gross Effective Income		$1,294,000
Less Expenses		
Fixed Expenses:		
Property Insurance	$24,500	
Property Taxes	95,300	
Licenses & Permits	1,200	($121,000)
Operating Expenses:		
Maintenance	$106,000	
Utilities	103,200	
Supplies	16,000	
Advertising	7,500	
Legal & Accounting	15,000	
Wages & Salaries	90,000	
Property Management	64,700	($402,400)
Replacement Reserve:		($ 25,000)
Total Expenses		$548,400
Net Operating Income		$745,600

A **replacement reserve** represents *an amount of money set aside to replace equipment* and make improvements. Replaced equipment may be hot water heaters, ranges, ovens, dishwashers, and disposals, for example. Typical improvements are pavement and roofs. Setting aside an amount of money for this purpose each year enables the project to avoid the impact of substantial expenditures in any given year when a number of the items must be replaced. In the illustration, the replacement reserve is $25,000.

The total of the three types of expenses equals $548,400. For appraisal purposes, debt service (mortgage principal and interest payments) is not included in the list of expenses. Debt service is considered to be a personal obligation of the property owner. The building would have the same income whether it is free and clear or financed with a 14 percent loan. Thus, the appraisal process puts all comparable properties on the same basis by eliminating items that vary substantially from one property to another and one owner to another.

Also not included is any tax or accounting depreciation on the building. These items do not reflect expenditures that will adjust the cash flow. **Net operating income** is determined by *subtracting the expenses from the gross effective income*. The annual net operating income in the illustration is $745,600.

The final step in estimating the value of the property by the income approach is to apply the capitalization formula given earlier. This involves dividing the annual net income by the capitalization rate. The difficulty lies in arriving at the proper capitalization rate. A number of complex methods are used to establish this rate. They are beyond the scope of this discussion and typically are not covered in pre-licensing courses. In essence, the **capitalization**, or **cap rate**, is *the rate that other investors are achieving on like investments in the same area*. The **rate of return**, or *percentage of income per money invested that the investor gets back on an investment*, includes a consideration for a **risk factor**. The *greater the risk of loss, the greater potential rate of return* the investor is entitled to expect. Another major factor is the **liquidity** of the investment or *the ability to quickly convert the investment to cash without significant loss or costs*.

In the illustration of the apartment complex, we will use the capitalization rate of 12 percent. Dividing the annual net operating income by .12 yields a value estimate of $6,213,333. If an investor paid $6,213,333 for the complex and continues to realize a net operating income of $745,600, the investor will have a return of 12 percent before deductions for debt service and income tax. The numbers used in our example are estimates, based on projection and speculation that the property and economy will continue to perform as in the past. These figures and assumptions are not guaranteed. Further, the computations do not account for the investor's income tax or financing efforts.

The importance of selecting a proper capitalization rate cannot be overemphasized. Even a slight variation in this rate will result in a substantial change in the estimate of value. For example, if a 13 percent rate had been used in the foregoing example, the value estimate would be $5,735,385, which represents a reduction in estimated value of 7.69 percent. The higher the capitalization rate, the lower the estimated value; the lower the capitalization rate, the higher the estimated value. Other examples applying the capitalization rate are found in Chapter 17, on real estate mathematics.

Gross Rent Multiplier

A simplified variation from the capitalization appraisal is found in the **gross rent multiplier (GRM)** also called gross income multiplier (GIM). This approach is not truly a part of the income approach but may be used to estimate income-producing properties by sales comparison. GRM is *a factor calculated from comparing sales prices of properties with their gross rental income* (see Figure 10.6). Monthly GRM is usually used for one- to four-unit residential properties while annual GRM is used for larger residential and commercial and industrial properties.

This method has a degree of unreliability because calculations are based on the gross income rather than the net income. If the property is managed efficiently, the gross income provides a reliable basis for calculating an estimate of value. If expenses are extraordinary, however, gross income does not accurately reflect the property value.

Gross rent multipliers are calculated by dividing the price for which a property sold by the monthly rental income. A gross income multiplier uses the gross annual income in calculations on larger residential (more than one to four family), commercial, and industrial properties.

In estimating the value on an income-producing property, gross rental incomes may be obtained for comparable income-producing properties that have sold recently. A weighted average of the gross rent multipliers obtained can be used as a multiplier for the monthly gross (or annual gross) income produced by a property that is being valued. Figure 10.7 illustrates sales prices and annual gross income of several income-producing properties.

A. $\dfrac{\text{Comparable's Sales Price}}{\text{Rent}} = \text{GRM}$

B. Subject's Rent × GRM = Estimate of Subject's Value

FIGURE 10.6 Computation and application of gross rent multiplier.

FIGURE 10.7
Calculating gross rent multipliers.

COMPARABLE	PRICE	ANNUAL GROSS	GRM/ YEAR
No. 1	$6,213,000	1,294,000	4.8
No. 2	5,865,000	1,212,000	4.8
No. 3	5,125,000	1,080,000	4.7
No. 4	6,060,000	1,236,000	4.9
No. 5	7,250,000	1,500,000	4.8
No. 6	6,588,000	1,332,000	4.9
Average GRM			4.8

Cost Approach or Approach by Summation

The **cost approach** in appraisal is the *main method for estimating the value of properties that have few, if any, comparables and that are not income-producing.* Examples of the types of structures appraised by this method are schools, owner-occupied factories, fire stations, hospitals, government office buildings, and libraries. Virtually any new construction can be appraised by the cost approach also.

The first step in the cost approach is to estimate the value of the site as if it were vacant. The site value is estimated by the market data approach, which uses comparable parcels of land to arrive at the value estimate. As a basis for the land value, the site is compared to comparable parcels of land that have sold recently.

The second step in the cost approach is to estimate the cost of reproducing or replacing the structure. Replacement cost and reproduction cost are different. **Reproduction cost** is the *price to construct an exact duplicate of the property when it was new.* **Replacement cost** is *based on constructing a building of comparable utility using modern building techniques and materials.* If the subject property was constructed many years ago, estimating the cost of reproducing that property today may be impossible. The materials and craftsmanship may not be available. Therefore, the basis of the cost approach for older structures is replacement cost new. Reproduction cost new may be used for properties that have been constructed recently or have special historical interest.

Methods of estimating reproduction or replacement costs include the quantity survey method, the unit-in-place method, the square-foot method, and the cubic-foot method. Of these, the quantity survey method is the most accurate but is also the most complex and time-consuming.

1. Most builders use the *quantity survey method* in calculating a cost estimate for a construction job. It involves the *detailed determination of the exact quantity of each type of material to be used in the construction and the necessary material and labor costs* applicable to each unit. The final estimate includes a profit to the builder.
2. In the *unit-in-place* method, the *cost of each major component or section of the structure is calculated, including material, labor, and overhead costs plus a profit to the builder.*
3. In the **square-foot method**, cost is *calculated by multiplying the number of square feet in the structure being appraised by the current cost per square foot to construct the building.*
4. The **cubic-foot method** is mathematically similar to the square-foot method, except the *measurement is of the volume of the structure.* This method is most applicable to warehouse or storage space. The measure of cubic footage is also relevant for measuring the capacity of air conditioning and heating units. The formula for cubic feet is:

   length × width × height = cubic feet

The estimated cost figures employed in any of these methods are available through construction cost services that publish construction cost estimates for various types of structures and structural components.

The third step in the value estimate by the cost approach is to deduct from the estimated cost of replacing or reproducing the property with new construction any observed depreciation existing and resulting from any of the three forms of depreciation. Deduction of the dollar amount of depreciation provides the depreciated value of the structure as it presently exists.

Fourth, the depreciated value of any other site improvements is added to the value of the structure to provide an estimate of the total depreciated value of all improvements.

The estimate of the land value by the market data approach is added to the estimate of the total depreciated value of the improvements to provide a value estimate for the total property by the cost approach.

The various steps and calculations employed in the cost approach are illustrated by the example of the cost approach calculations in Figure 10.8.

Depreciation

Depreciation is defined as *a loss in value from any cause*. The loss in value is estimated by the difference in the present market value and the cost to build new. Depreciation results from the following: physical deterioration, functional obsolescence, and economic obsolescence. Each of these three types of depreciation is caused by forces having an adverse effect on the land and structure.

Physical Deterioration

Physical deterioration, or erosion in the condition of property, is caused by:

- Unrepaired damage to the structure caused by fire, explosion, vandalism, windstorm, or other action of the elements, and damage caused by termites or other woodburning insects.
- Wear and tear resulting from normal use of the property and lack of adequate maintenance measures to keep the property in good condition.

Replacement or Reproduction Cost:		
21,000 square feet @ $52.50 sq ft		$1,102,500
Less structure depreciation:		
Physical deterioration	$33,075	
Functional obsolescence	44,100	
Economic obsolescence	-0-	77,175
Depreciated value of structure		1,025,325
Plus depreciated value of other improvements:		
Retaining walls	10,000	
Paved drive and parking	15,000	
Exterior lighting	2,000	
Fencing	1,500	28,500
Depreciated value of all improvements		1,053,825
Land value by market data approach		253,000
Total Property Value		$1,306,825
Rounded down		$1,306,800

FIGURE 10.8 Cost approach calculations.

Functional Obsolescence

Functional obsolescence refers to *flawed or faulty property, rendered inferior because of advances and change*, such as:

- Inadequacy or superadequacy of things such as wiring and plumbing, heating and cooling systems, and insufficient or oversufficient number of bathrooms, closets, and other facilities.
- Equipment that is out of date and not in keeping with current style and utility.
- Exposed wiring or plumbing; lack of automatic controls for things such as furnaces and hot water heaters; inadequate insulation.
- Faulty design resulting in inefficient use of floor space, poor location of various types of rooms in relation to other types, such as bathrooms in relation to bedrooms; too-low ceilings.

Economic Obsolescence (External, Environmental, or Locational Obsolescence)

Economic obsolescence refers to *property that is out of date for external, environmental, or locational reasons*, such as:

- Changes in surrounding land-use patterns resulting in increased vehicular traffic, air pollution, noise pollution, inharmonious land uses, and other hazards and nuisances adversely affecting the quality of the area.
- Failure to adhere to the principle of highest and best use, thereby creating an overimprovement or underimprovement on the property.
- Changes in zoning and building regulations that adversely affect property use.
- Reduction in demand for property in the area caused by local economic factors, changes in growth patterns, population shifts, and other economic factors adversely affecting property value.

Curable and Incurable Depreciation

Depreciation in the form of physical deterioration and functional obsolescence results from forces at work within the property. These two forms of depreciation may be curable or incurable. If it is physically possible and economically practical to correct the causes of physical deterioration and functional obsolescence, the depreciation is considered *curable*. If the necessary corrections are not possible or economically feasible, depreciation is considered *incurable*. In the case of incurable depreciation, the structure typically is torn down and replaced with a new structure or the owner simply endures the flaw.

Economic obsolescence is caused by forces outside the property. Economic obsolescence is never curable by the property owner. The owner has no control over properties others own and therefore is not able to take necessary corrective measures.

Age

Every structure may have two different ages: chronological and effective. The **chronological age** of a structure is measured by *the number of years the structure has existed.* This is similar to the age of a person. The **effective age** refers to *the age that the structure appears to be, based on its condition.* If a property is well-maintained, it may seem to be younger than it actually is chronologically. Conversely, the effective age may be greater than the chronological age if adequate maintenance and modernization measures have not been taken.

Reconciliation

In making an appraisal, a professional appraiser uses as the primary appraisal method the most relevant approach to the value estimate. The most relevant method depends on the type of property that is the subject of the appraisal and the purpose for the appraisal. For example, in estimating the value of an existing single-family, owner-occupied dwelling, the most relevant method is the market data approach. In addition, the qualified appraiser also estimates the property value by each of the other two methods. In the case of the single-family dwelling, the appraiser treats the property as if it were rental property and estimates the value using the income approach. Last, the appraiser arrives at a value estimate by the cost approach. As a practical matter, the results obtained by these three methods will not be identical. To provide the most reliable estimate of value, there must be a correlation or reconciliation of the three different results.

In the **reconciliation** process, three factors are taken into consideration:

1. The *relevancy of each of the three methods to the subject property and the client's use for the appraisal.*
2. The *reliability of the data on which each estimate is based.*
3. The *strong points and weak points of each method.*

After considering these factors, the greatest weight should be given to the estimate resulting from using the most appropriate or relevant method for the type of property that is the subject of the appraisal.

If the property is an office building, the most relevant approach, and the one to receive the greatest weight, is the income approach. Even though the results obtained by the different approaches will not be exactly the same, they should be reasonably close. Therefore, each approach provides a check on the other two. If the result by one method varies considerably from the others, it indicates a calculation error, an error in the data used as a basis, or inappropriateness of that method.

Putting It to Work

The purpose for which the appraisal will be used helps determine the most appropriate approach in reconciliation. For example, if the appraisal is to estimate fire damage to a home, the best approach would be cost. If the appraisal is to estimate loan value for a lender, the best approach would be market data. If the appraisal is to determine value of an older home in a declining area dominated by rental properties, the income approach would be the best.

The final step in the appraisal process is to prepare the **appraisal report**. The report contains *the appraiser's opinion of value based on observation of the results obtained by the three methods and the appraiser's reasons for adopting the final estimate of value*. The appraisal report may be in narrative form or may be a form report. The **narrative appraisal report** provides *all the factual data about the property and the elements of judgment the appraiser used in arriving at the estimate of value.* When a standard form is used to report the various property data and the appraisal method employed, it is called a form report. A form report does not contain narrative information as does the narrative report but simply sets forth various facts and figures used in the appraisal process and correlation of the final estimate of market value.

PUTTING IT TO WORK

The most common appraisal form in use today is the URAR, or Uniform Residential Appraisal Report. This form gives a brief recap of the property and the site, a neighborhood analysis, and a fairly detailed analysis of the mathematics of all three approaches. On the URAR form, the most attention and emphasis is given to the market data, or sales comparison, approach.

IMPORTANT POINTS

1. An appraisal is an estimate (not a determination) of value based on factual data at a particular time for a particular purpose on a particular property.
2. Market value is the amount of money a typical buyer will give in exchange for a property.
3. The various types of value include market value, assessed value, insurance value, mortgage loan value, condemnation value, and book value.
4. Property value is dependent on utility, scarcity, transferability, and effective demand.
5. The basic valuation principles are: highest and best use, substitution, supply and demand, conformity, anticipation, contribution, increasing or diminishing returns, competition, change, depreciation, and age.
6. Depreciation is the loss in value from any cause. In structures, the causes of depreciation are: (a) physical deterioration, (b) functional obsolescence, and (c) economic obsolescence.
7. The market data or comparison approach to value estimate is the most relevant appraisal method for estimating the value of single-family, owner-occupied dwellings, and vacant land.
8. The income approach, or appraisal by capitalization, is the most appropriate appraisal method for estimating the value of property that produces rental income.
9. A gross rent multiplier may be appropriate for estimating the value of rental property.
10. The cost approach is the main appraisal method for estimating the value of property that does not fall into the other categories. These properties, known as special-use properties, include museums, hospitals, schools, and churches, as well as new construction.
11. An appraisal report provides a value estimate based on a reconciliation of the estimates obtained by all three approaches.

HOW WOULD YOU RESPOND?

You have an appointment with some prospective clients to prepare a CMA on their home. You know the neighborhood well and similar homes have sold for $125,000 to $132,000 in the last few months. As you pull up to the home you see that it has excellent landscaping and tremendous curb appeal. This home will show very well. As you get inside you find some outstanding improvements. Marble floors, ceiling fans in every room, intercom, three fireplaces, an indoor spa, totally remodeled bathrooms and a kitchen with very expensive European cabinets. They proudly state that they have over $60,000 in these upgrades and their house is the best in the neighborhood by far.

1. What reaction do you think you will get when you suggest a list price of $139,000?
2. How will you handle their reactions?
3. What can you tell your clients about the effect these factors will have on an appraisal?

REVIEW QUESTIONS

Answers to these questions are found in the *Answer Key* section at the back of the book.

1. Reconciliation between the three appraisal approaches would be best achieved by:
   a. taking the highest number of the three approaches
   b. calculating a simple average
   c. taking the middle number of the three approaches
   d. calculating a weighted average

2. All of the following characteristics must be present for a property to have value EXCEPT:
   a. utility
   b. obsolescence
   c. transferability
   d. effective demand

3. The amount of money a property will bring in the marketplace for sale in an area is called:
   a. extrinsic value
   b. intrinsic value
   c. market value
   d. GRM factor

4. If the contribution of a feature or improvement outweighs its cost, this shows:
   a. conformity
   b. increasing returns
   c. the highest and best use
   d. anticipation

5. Which of the following is described as the cost of constructing a building of comparable utility using modern techniques and materials?
   a. reproduction cost
   b. operating cost
   c. unit cost
   d. replacement cost

6. Physical deterioration is caused by all of the following EXCEPT:
   a. unrepaired damage
   b. lack of adequate maintenance
   c. inefficient floor plan
   d. inadequate exterior maintenance

7. Functional obsolescence results from:
   a. faulty design and inefficient use of space
   b. changes in surrounding land use patterns
   c. inadequate exterior maintenance
   d. extensive and poorly planned urban redevelopment

8. Which of the following causes of depreciation is not curable by the property owner?
   a. economic obsolescence
   b. functional obsolescence
   c. competitive obsolescence
   d. physical deterioration

9. The principle followed in making adjustments to comparables in an appraisal by the market data approach is:
   a. competition
   b. change
   c. contribution
   d. conformity

10. An appraisal is which of the following?
    a. estimate of value
    b. appropriation of value
    c. correlation of value
    d. determination of value

11. All of the following are approaches to value EXCEPT:
    a. cost approach
    b. contribution approach
    c. income approach
    d. comparison approach

12. The primary appraisal method for estimating the value of vacant land is which of the following?
    a. cost approach
    b. market data approach
    c. income approach
    d. appraisal by capitalization

13. All of the following are important data in selecting comparables EXCEPT:
    a. size of the lot
    b. income of the owners
    c. location of the properties
    d. condition of the properties

14. Using the capitalization formula, the income used as a basis for estimating value is:
    a. monthly net
    b. annual gross effective
    c. monthly gross effective
    d. annual net

15. If the income used in the appraisal by capitalization is $480,000 and the capitalization rate is 11%, which of the following will be the estimate of property value?
    a. $2,290,000
    b. $2,990,000
    c. $4,363,636
    d. $5,280,000

16. For appraisal purposes, all of the following are deductible from gross effective income to arrive at net operating income EXCEPT:
    a. maintenance
    b. legal fees
    c. replacement reserve
    d. debt service

17. In the income approach, which of the following is deducted from gross potential income to calculate gross effective income?
    a. fixed expenses
    b. vacancy loss
    c. other income
    d. replacement service

18. If a property produces a gross income of $103,000 and the GIM is 7.5, which of the following is the indication of value?
    a. $137,333
    b. $772,500
    c. $927,000
    d. $1,373,333

19. Which of the following would use the cost approach as the primary method of appraisal if comparable sales are not available?
    a. shopping mall
    b. courthouse
    c. parking garage
    d. condominium apartment

20. All of the following are methods used for estimating replacement cost EXCEPT:
    a. quantity survey
    b. square foot
    c. unit in place
    d. quality survey

POSSIBLE RESPONSES TO "HOW WOULD YOU RESPOND?"

1. Sellers often have an inflated view of their property value. While sellers typically want and expect dollar-for-dollar value for their original cost of improvements, in reality these improvements have relatively little resale value. They will likely be surprised and perhaps displeased with your suggested list price.

2. Indicate to them the reality of the buying market not being willing to pay for overimprovements. Relate similar stories from your experience and ask them how much extra they would pay for something like "built-in aquariums." Also point out that while they may not get full value back on these improvements, the improved curb appeal and presentation of the property will likely speed up the sale and overcome any price objections.

3. Let them know that the appraiser will try to represent the critical perception of a typical buyer. The appraisal will likely be somewhere near the $139,000 price rather that the seller's actual cost (somewhere around $185,000).

CHAPTER 11

IMPORTANT TERMINOLOGY

- building codes
- certificate of occupancy
- cluster zoning
- conditional use permit
- conditions
- covenant
- cumulative zoning
- declaration of restrictions
- deed restrictions
- enabling acts
- Environmental Policy Act
- Environmental Protection Agency (EPA)
- general plan
- Interstate Land Sales Full Disclosure Act
- nonconforming use
- planned unit development (PUD)
- property report (Full Disclosure Act)
- restrictive covenants
- setback
- spot zoning
- subdivision regulation
- variance
- zoning map
- zoning ordinance

Land Use Controls

IN THIS CHAPTER Understanding land use controls is important to real estate salespeople. Almost every property is subject to some form of control, whether it is the result of city zoning ordinances, general subdivision restrictions, deed restrictions unique to one parcel of land, or federal legislation. Any of these forms of land control may have a major impact on the owner's rights.

Real estate practitioners are obligated to be knowledgeable regarding existing public and private land use controls within their market area and must keep abreast of changes in requirements as they happen. Lack of knowledge in these areas may subject them to civil liability and even possible criminal liability under certain federal laws.

HISTORICAL DEVELOPMENT OF LAND CONTROL

Private control of land use was the forerunner of public controls. In 1848, U.S. courts first recognized and enforced restrictive covenants regulating land use in residential subdivisions. In 1926, the U.S. Supreme Court upheld the validity of zoning ordinances. Before these two important legal events, a developer or governmental unit had no way to regulate land use, even though the need for controls was readily apparent.

The need for land use controls has increased along with the increasing population density. Abuse by even one property owner in the use of land can have a substantial adverse effect on the rights of other property owners and cause severe depreciation of their properties.

PUBLIC LAND USE CONTROLS

Private land use controls, discussed later in this chapter, are limited in scope. Only a specific area can be subject to private use controls. For example, property owners in a subdivision with private controls have absolutely no control over land uses outside that subdivision. Therefore, a subdivision may be affected adversely by uncontrolled use of an adjoining property outside the subdivision. As people became aware of the need for planning and land use controls for larger areas of land, zoning ordinances came into being, the first of which was enacted in 1916.

Urban and Regional Planning

The purpose of planning is to provide for the orderly growth of a community that will result in the greatest social and economic benefits to the people in the community. Over the years, state legislatures have passed **enabling acts** that *provide the legal basis for cities and counties to develop long-range plans for growth.* Planning and zoning are based on the police power of government to enable it to protect the health, safety, and welfare of the people.

In urban planning, the first step is typically to conduct a survey to determine the city's present physical composition. This is done through a survey of the community's physical and economic assets. This information serves as a basis for developing a master plan for orderly growth. The resulting plan designates the various uses to which property may be put in specific areas.

Regional planning has its origins in the grassroots of a community. This planning may occur in communities located in unzoned county areas where property owners see the need to plan for orderly community growth; thus, they adopt and enforce a plan through zoning ordinances. In the absence of this planning, haphazard development often ensues. A plan *created and based on a strong consensus of property owners in the community* is the result of *community-based planning*. Along with the plan, the community agrees on certain proposed zoning requirements. The proposal is presented by referendum to all of the property owners in the community. If a substantial majority of the community endorses the plan and zoning, the county government adopts the plan and enacts the necessary zoning ordinances to enforce the plan as conceived by the property owners.

Zoning

Zoning begins with city or county planning, and zoning laws implement and enforce the plan. Violations of zoning laws can be enforced by fines, corrected by a court injunction requiring the violation to be discontinued, or corrected by extreme measures such as demolishing an unlawful structure.

Zoning ordinances consist of two parts: (a) the **zoning map**, which *divides the community into various designated districts*, and (b) text of the **zoning ordinance**, which *sets forth the type of use permitted under each zoning classification and specific requirements for compliance*. The extent of authority for zoning ordinances is prescribed by the enabling acts passed by state legislatures. These acts specify the types of uses subject to regulation. They also limit the area subject to the ordinances to the geographic boundaries of the government unit enacting the zoning laws. For example, city zoning ordinances may not extend beyond city limits into the county. A county government, however, sometimes authorizes the extension of city zoning for some specified distance into the county, and in some cases the State empowers cities to specifically extend zoning beyond the city limits.

Several types of zones may be established by local ordinances:

1. Residential, which can be subdivided into single-family homes and various levels of multi-family dwellings.
2. Commercial.
3. Light manufacturing.
4. Heavy industrial.
5. *Multiple use* or **cluster zoning**.

The last category provides for **planned unit developments (PUD)**, which create a *neighborhood of cluster housing and supporting business establishments*.

Zoning ordinances may provide for either exclusive-use zoning or cumulative-use zoning. In *exclusive-use zoning, property may be used only in the ways specified for that specific zone*. For example, if the zone is commercial, residential uses will not be permitted. In contrast, **cumulative zoning** *may permit uses that are not designated in the zone*. For instance, if an area is zoned commercial, a residential use could still be made of the property. In cumulative zoning, however, uses are placed in an order of priority: residential, commercial, industrial, where residential represents the highest priority. A use of higher priority may be made in an area where the zoned use has a lower priority.

Zoning laws also define certain standards and requirements that must be met for each permitted type of use. These requirements include things such as minimum **setbacks**, or *distances from the front property line to the building line, as well as from the interior property lines*; minimum lot size on which a structure may be placed; height restrictions to prevent interference with the passage of sunlight and air to other properties; regulations against building in flood plains; and requirements for off-street parking.

Nonconforming Use

When zoning is first imposed on an area or when property is rezoned, the zoning authority generally cannot require the property owners to discontinue a current use that does not now conform to the new zoning ordinance. A **nonconforming use** occurs when a *preexisting use of property in a zoned area is different from that specified by the zoning code for that area*. The nonconforming use must be permitted because requiring the property owners to terminate the nonconforming use would be unconstitutional. In these cases, the property owner is permitted to lawfully continue a nonconforming use. This is called a *preexisting nonconforming use* or a use "grandfathered" in.

Although nonconforming use is permitted under these circumstances, the nonconforming user is subject to certain requirements designed to gradually eliminate the nonconforming use. Examples are:

1. If the property owner, over time, abandons the nonconforming use, the owner cannot resume that type of use at a later date but may use the property only in a manner that conforms to the zoning ordinance.
2. The property owner may not make structural changes to the property to expand the nonconforming use. The owner is permitted to make only normally necessary repairs to the structure.
3. The nonconforming use cannot be changed from one type of nonconforming use to another type of nonconforming use.
4. If a nonconforming structure is destroyed in fire or other casualty, it cannot be replaced by another nonconforming structure without specific approval.
5. Some ordinances provide for a long-term amortization period, during which the nonconforming owner is permitted to continue the nonconforming use. At the end of this period, the owner must change the property use to conform with the zoning ordinance, rebuilding the structure if necessary. This long-range "notice" to the owner should allow sufficient time to relocate or modify the use without causing an economic shock to the owner.
6. Nonconforming uses may or may not be transferable to another owner. This may depend on who the acquiring owner is (for example, a relative) or on local ordinances.

Variance

A **variance** is a *permitted deviation from specific requirements of the zoning ordinance*. For example, if an owner's lot is slightly smaller than the minimum lot size restrictions set by zoning ordinances, the owner may be granted a variance by petitioning the appropriate authorities.

Variances are permitted where the deviation is not substantial, where variance will not severely impact neighboring owners, and where strict enforcement would impose an undue hardship on the property owner. The hardship must be applicable to one property only and must be a peculiar or special hardship for that property under the zoning law. The special hardship does not exist where all of the property owners in the zoned area have the same difficulty.

A *variance with additional restrictions upon the owner's use* is called a **conditional use permit**.

Spot Zoning

With **spot zoning**, a *specific property within a zoned area is rezoned to permit a use different from the zoning requirements for that zoned area.* If the rezoning of a property is solely for the benefit of the property owner and has the effect of increasing the land value, the spot zoning is illegal and invalid; however, when spot zoning is used for the benefit of the community and not for the benefit of a certain property owner (or owners), the spot zoning is not illegal and is valid even though the owner may benefit. An example of legal spot zoning occurs in residential urban areas when lots are rezoned to allow retail shops for the benefit of the community.

Subdivision Regulations

States may empower local government, cities, and counties, through **subdivision regulations**, *to protect purchasers of property within the subdivisions and taxpayers in the city or county from an undue tax burden* resulting from the demands for services that a new subdivision generates and which might otherwise not be provided. Subdivision ordinances typically address the following requirements:

1. Streets may have to be of a specified width, be curbed, have storm drains, and not exceed certain maximum grade specifications.
2. Lots may not be smaller than a specified minimum size.
3. Dwellings in specified areas must be for single-family occupancy only. Specific areas may be set aside for multi-family dwellings.
4. Utilities, including water, sewer, electric, and telephone, must be available to each lot; or plans must include easements to later provide utilities.
5. All houses must be placed on lots to meet specified minimum standards for setbacks from the front property line, as well as from interior property lines.
6. Drainage must be adequate for runoff of rainfall to avoid damage to any properties.

Developers must obtain approval from the appropriate officials before subdividing and selling lots. Compliance with most subdivision ordinances requires the platting of land into lots. Then the subdivision plat is recorded on the public record and development can begin.

PUTTING IT TO WORK

Until the subdivision plat is approved and recorded, a subdivision reference may not be used in a legal description. Once approved, this lot, block, and subdivision type of description is legally acceptable.

Building Codes

Building codes provide another form of land use control to protect the public. These codes *regulate things such as materials used in construction, electrical wiring, fire and safety standards, and sanitary equipment facilities.* Building codes require a permit from the appropriate local government authority before constructing or renovating a commercial building or residential property. While construction is in progress, local government inspectors perform frequent inspections to make certain that code requirements are being met.

After a satisfactory final inspection, a **certificate of occupancy** is issued, *permitting occupation of the structure by tenants or the owner.* Many cities today require a certificate of occupancy, based upon satisfactory inspection of the property, prior to occupancy by a new owner or tenant of any structure even though it is not a new construction or has not been renovated. Inspection is required to reveal any deficiencies in the structure requiring correction before the city will issue a certificate of occupancy to protect the new purchaser or tenant.

Federal Regulation

Interstate Land Sales Full Disclosure Act

The federal **Interstate Land Sales Full Disclosure Act** *regulates interstate* (across state lines) *sale of unimproved lots.* It became effective in 1969 and was made more restrictive by a 1980 amendment. The Act is administered by the Secretary of Housing and Urban Development (HUD) through the office of Interstate Land Sales registration. Its purpose is to prevent fraudulent marketing schemes that may transpire when land is sold sight unseen. The Act requires that a developer file a statement of record with HUD before offering unimproved lots in interstate commerce by telephone or through the mails. The *statement of record requires disclosure of information about the property as specified by HUD.*

Developers of these properties also are required to provide each purchaser or lessee of property with a printed **property report,** which *discloses specific information about the land* before the purchaser or lessee signs a purchase contract or lease. Information required on these property reports includes things such as the type of title a buyer will receive, number of homes currently occupied, availability of recreation facilities, distance to nearby communities, utility services and charges, and soil or other foundation problems in construction. If the purchaser or lessee does not receive a copy of the property report prior to signing a purchase contract or lease, the purchaser likely will have grounds to void the contract.

The Act provides for several exemptions, the most important of which are:

1. Subdivisions in which the lots are of five acres or more.
2. Subdivisions consisting of fewer than 25 lots.
3. Lots offered for sale exclusively to building contractors.
4. Lots on which a building exists or where a contract obligates the lot seller to construct a building within two years.

If a developer offers only part of the total tract owned and thereby limits the subdivision to fewer than 25 lots to acquire an exemption, the developer may not then sell additional lots within the tract. HUD considers these additional lots to be a part of a "common plan" for development and marketing, thereby eliminating the opportunity for several exemptions for the developer as a result of piecemeal development of a large tract in sections of fewer than 25 lots at a time.

The Act provides severe penalties for violation by a developer or a real estate licensee who participates in marketing the property. The developer or the real estate licensee, or both, may be sued by a purchaser or a lessee for damages and are potentially subject to a criminal penalty by fine of up to $5,000 or imprisonment for up to five years or both. Therefore, prior to acting as an agent for the developer in marketing the property, real estate salespersons must be certain to ascertain that a developer has complied with or is exempt from the law.

PUTTING IT TO WORK

Because this law addresses sales across state lines only, many states have adopted similar laws to address intrastate (within the state) land sales. In some cases, these state laws are much more restrictive than the federal law.

ENVIRONMENTAL PROTECTION LEGISLATION

The National **Environmental Policy Act** of 1969 *requires filing an environmental impact statement with the* **Environmental Protection Agency (EPA)** *prior to changing or initiating a land use or development,* to ensure that the use will not adversely affect the environment. Typical subject areas regulated by the Act include air, noise, and water pollution, as well as chemical and solid waste disposal.

Since 1969, several amendments and companion legislation have been passed to more clearly define the EPA's role in land use. The Resource Conservation and Recovery Act (RCRA), passed in 1976, defined hazardous substances. Then, in 1980, Congress passed the Comprehensive Environmental Response, Compensation and Liability Act (CERCLA) to provide solutions to the environmental problems created over the years by uncontrolled disposal of wastes. Under CERCLA, a program was created to identify sites containing hazardous substances, ensure that those sites were cleaned up by the parties responsible or by the government, and establish a procedure to seek reimbursement for clean-up from the party responsible for placing the hazardous substance.

In 1986, CERCLA was amended by the Superfund Amendments and Reauthorization Act (SARA). The amendments imposed stringent clean-up standards and expanded the definition of persons liable for the costs of clean-up. Under CERCLA and SARA, every land owner is potentially affected.

In addition to federal legislation, some states now require full disclosure, prior to title transfer by deed, if real estate is listed by a federal or state agency as contaminated by hazardous substances.

More recent environmental issues include protection of habitats for wildlife, wetlands, shorelines, and endangered species, as well as issues such as lead-based paint, radon, formaldehyde, and asbestos. These topics are discussed in Appendix B.

PRIVATELY IMPOSED LAND USE CONTROLS

Individual owners have the right to place private controls on their own real estate. These restrictions take the form of individual deed restrictions or subdivision restrictive covenants affecting the entire subdivision.

Individual **deed restrictions** are *in the form of covenants or in the form of conditions.* A **covenant** may be included in a deed *to benefit property that is sold or to benefit a property that is retained when an adjoining property is sold.* For example, an owner who retains one property and sells an adjoining property may provide in the deed that a structure may not be erected in a certain area of the property being sold, to protect the view from the retained property or to prevent loss of passage of light and air to the retained property. These restrictions are covenants that run with the land (move with the title in any subsequent conveyance). Covenants may be enforced by a suit for damages or by injunction. *Restrictions that provide for a reversion of title if they are violated* are called **conditions**. If a condition is violated, ownership reverts to the grantor. These conditions thus create a defeasible fee estate.

Restrictive covenants are *limitations placed on the use of land by the developer of a residential subdivision*. The purpose of these covenants is to preserve and protect the quality of land in subdivisions and to maximize land values by requiring the homogeneous use of the land by purchasers. The covenants are promises by those who purchase property in the subdivision to limit the use of their property to comply with requirements of the covenants; therefore, they are restrictive in the nature of the owner's use. The deed conveying title to property in the subdivision contains a reference to a recorded plat of the subdivision and a reference to recording of the restrictive covenants; or the restrictions may be recited in each deed of conveyance. Restrictions must be reasonable, and they must benefit all property owners alike.

PUTTING IT TO WORK

Subdivision restrictions typically address issues related to maintaining quality and consistency of the subdivision. These may be concerns of a relatively minor nature, such as exterior lighting and clean-up of rubbish, or things such as speed limits, landscaping, and even construction and architectural review and approval.

If the subdivision is in a zoned area, restrictive covenants have priority over the zoning ordinance to the extent that the covenants are more restrictive than the zoning requirements. For example, if the zoning permits multi-family dwellings and the restrictive covenants do not, the restrictive covenants can be enforced. If restrictive covenants are contrary to public law and public policy, they cannot be enforced. For example, a restrictive covenant requiring discrimination on the basis of race, religion, gender, or national origin is invalid. Also, restrictive covenants are not valid unless they are recorded on the public record in the county in which the land is located.

Typical Private Restrictions

Restrictive covenants provide a **general plan** *setting forth development of a subdivision*. Prior to beginning development, the developer establishes a list of *rules each lot purchaser will be required to adhere to in use of the property*, as recorded in an instrument called **declaration of restrictions**. The declaration is recorded simultaneously with the plat and includes a reference to the plat. Examples of typical restrictive covenants are:

- Only single-family dwellings may be constructed in the subdivision.
- Dwellings must contain a specified minimum number of square feet of living area.
- Only one single-family dwelling may be constructed on a lot.
- No lot may be subdivided.
- Dwellings must be of a harmonious architectural style. To ensure this, a site plan and plans and specifications for the structure must be submitted to and approved by a committee prior to start of construction.
- Structures must be set back a specified distance from the front property line and a specified distance from interior property lines.
- Temporary structures may not be placed on any lot.

- Covenants may be enforced by any one property owner or several property owners of land within the subdivision by taking appropriate court action.
- The covenants will remain in effect for a specified time period. (Restrictive covenants, in some cases, are subject to automatic renewal periods, during which time they may be changed by a vote of the property owners.)

PUTTING IT TO WORK

Real estate licensees must be aware of restrictive covenants in subdivisions in which they are selling property. The salesperson should provide prospective buyers with a copy of the covenants, which may be obtained from the developer, if still selling on the site, or from the office of title registration in the county in which the property is located. In preparing offers to purchase in the subdivision, the real estate licensee should include a provision that the prospective buyer acknowledges receipt of a copy of the restrictive covenants.

Termination of Covenants

Restrictive covenants may be terminated in the following ways:

1. Expiration of the time period for which the covenants were created.
2. Unanimous vote of the property owners to end the restrictions, unless the restrictions provide for termination by vote of a smaller number of land owners.
3. Changes in the character of the subdivision that render it unsatisfactory to continue the type of use specified by the restrictions. For example, if property owners in a subdivision fail to restrict it to single-family residential use, the area might gradually change to commercial use; consequently, the subdivision is no longer suitable for limitation to residential use.
4. Abandonment, which occurs when the property owners have violated their restrictions and in many instances have participated in the violations. As a result, a court may rule that the property owners have abandoned the original general plan and therefore the court will not enforce the restrictions.
5. Failure to enforce restrictions on a timely basis. Owners cannot sit by idly and watch someone complete a structure in a subdivision in violation of the restrictive covenants and then attempt to enforce the restrictions by court action. If property owners do not act to enforce restrictive covenants on a timely basis, the court will not apply the restriction against the violator and it will be terminated. Termination of a covenant in this manner is an application of the Doctrine of Laches, which states that if a land owner delays in protecting her rights, she may lose them.

Enforcement of Covenants

Private land use controls are enforced through the courts. This is accomplished by an action of a court known as an injunction. An injunction prevents a use contrary to the restrictions of record, or orders the removal of any such uses that have been implemented. In a practical sense, the individuals who bear primary responsibility for making sure the restrictions are enforced are the other owners of property in the affected area. Their failing to enforce the restrictions on a timely basis might lead to the eventual loss of the right to enforce the restrictions at all.

Enforcement of covenants is not limited to the original purchasers of property in the subdivision. Subsequent purchasers must abide by and may enforce the restrictive covenants until such time as the covenants may be terminated, as previously discussed. In this sense, the restrictions run with the land.

Important Points

1. Public plans for development are enforced by zoning ordinances. Planning and zoning are exercises of police power.
2. Types of zones include residential, commercial, planned unit developments (PUDs), industrial, and agricultural.
3. Zoning may be either exclusive-use or cumulative-use.
4. In addition to specifying permitted uses, zoning ordinances define standards and requirements that must be met for each type of use.
5. A nonconforming use is one that differs from the type of use permitted in a certain zone. It is allowed to continue since the use was in effect prior to the law.
6. A variance is a permitted deviation from specific requirements of a zoning ordinance because the property owner would be subject to a special hardship imposed by the strict enforcement.
7. Spot zoning occurs when a certain property within a zoned area is rezoned to permit a use that is different from the zoning requirements for that area. Spot zoning may be valid or invalid.
8. The purpose of planning is to provide for the orderly growth of a community that will result in the greatest social and economic benefits to the people.
9. Subdivision ordinances regulate the development of residential subdivisions to protect property purchasers as well as taxpayers in the area from increased tax burdens to provide essential services to those subdivisions.
10. Building codes require certain standards of construction. The codes are concerned primarily with electrical systems, fire and safety standards, and sanitary systems and equipment.
11. The Interstate Land Sales Full Disclosure Act regulates sale of unimproved lots in interstate commerce to hinder fraudulent schemes involving the sale of land sight unseen.
12. Environmental protection legislation is a form of land use control to protect the public against abuses of the environment in the development of real estate.
13. Private land use controls are in the form of deed restrictions and restrictive covenants.
14. Restrictive covenants must be reasonable and must be equally beneficial to all property owners.
15. Restrictive covenants are recorded on the public record in an instrument called a declaration of restrictions. These covenants must be recorded to be legally effective and enforceable.
16. Restrictive covenants are enforced by court injunction upon petition by the property owners on a timely basis.

How Would You Respond?

A prospective buyer is considering buying a vacant commercial lot to build a store on a major street. There are several other stores and businesses all with parking in front of the buildings; your buyer wants the store at the sidewalk with parking in the rear. She also wants to have a sign on the roof of the building rather than a fascia sign. There are other businesses with similar signs on the street. Her business will also require deliveries by very large trucks several times daily. What are the various sources of information you should verify to determine whether she can locate this business?

Review Questions

Answers to these questions are found in the *Answer Key* section at the back of the book.

1. All of the following statements about land use controls are correct EXCEPT:
   a. deed restrictions are a form of private land use control
   b. public land use controls are an exercise of police power
   c. enforcement of private restrictions is by injunction
   d. public land use controls are limited to state laws

2. Most legislation regarding environmental issues originates at which level of government?
   a. county
   b. local
   c. state
   d. federal

3. All of the following statements about restrictive covenants are correct EXCEPT:
   a. they must be reasonable
   b. they are enforceable even though not recorded
   c. they are not enforceable if contrary to law
   d. they provide for a general plan for development

4. The instrument used for recording restrictive covenants is called:
   a. plat
   b. master deed
   c. covenant
   d. declaration of restrictions

5. Restrictive covenants may be terminated in all of the following ways EXCEPT:
   a. expiration
   b. transfer of title
   c. failure to enforce on a timely basis
   d. abandonment

6. Restrictive covenants are enforced by:
   a. zoning
   b. injunction
   c. police power
   d. condemnation

7. The type of zoning that permits a higher priority use in a lower priority zone is called:
   a. exclusive use
   b. nonconforming use
   c. amortizing use
   d. cumulative use

8. Rezoning of an area caused the use by one property owner to be in noncompliance with the new zoning ordinance. If the owner continues this use, it is called:
   a. variance
   b. nonconforming use
   c. spot zoning
   d. exclusionary zoning

9. A permitted deviation from the standards of a zoning ordinance is called:
   a. variance
   b. nonconforming use
   c. spot zoning
   d. unlawful nonconforming use

10. Rezoning of a specific property for the owner's benefit is called:
    a. variance
    b. nonconforming use
    c. spot zoning
    d. unlawful nonconforming use

11. Which of the following is a purpose of subdivision ordinances?
    a. to protect taxpayers from increased taxes caused by increased demand for services to those subdivisions
    b. to protect developers during the development period from excessive costs and thereby encourage residential development
    c. to protect homeowners in existing subdivisions from an oversupply of residential property
    d. to protect developers from excessive building code requirements

12. When the initiative for zoning and planning ordinances comes from property owners, it is called:
    a. owner planning
    b. community-based planning
    c. general planning
    d. exclusive-use planning

13. Building codes require which of the following?
    a. property report
    b. PUDs
    c. certificate of occupancy
    d. statement of record

14. Which of the following statements concerning the Interstate Land Sales Full Disclosure Act is NOT correct?
    a. it regulates sales of unimproved lots across state lines
    b. it is administered by HUD
    c. the developer is required to record a property report in the local recorder's office
    d. subdivisions of fewer than 25 lots are not subject to the law

15. Exemptions to the Interstate Land Sales Full Disclosure Act include all of the following EXCEPT:
    a. subdivisions of fewer than 25 lots
    b. lots offered only to building contractors
    c. lots on which there is a building
    d. subdivisions in which the lots are 2 acres or more

16. Cluster zoning applies in the establishment of:
    a. variances
    b. planned-unit developments
    c. nonconforming uses
    d. enabling acts

17. Which of these issues would NOT be part of building code regulations?
    a. setbacks
    b. permits
    c. inspections
    d. safety standards

18. The regulations of subdivision development would address which issue?
    a. building codes and health codes
    b. street widths and utility access
    c. spot zoning and variances
    d. buffer zones

19. While deed conditions and deed restrictions may address the same use of property, they differ regarding:
    a. their enforcement at the federal or local level
    b. their enforcement by government officials or private parties
    c. loss of title as opposed to forced compliance through litigation without loss of title
    d. the extent of fines for violations

20. A neighbor is building an addition to his home that comes right to the property line along your eastern boundary. Your concern is that he is violating which of the following?
    a. the buffer zone
    b. your right of lateral support
    c. the setback
    d. your right to quiet enjoyment

POSSIBLE RESPONSES TO "HOW WOULD YOU RESPOND?"

1. Check with zoning on the setbacks, roof sign, parking, trucks on the street, delivery driveways and whether there is a variance required for any of these issues.
2. Check title records to see if there are any private deed restrictions or conditions, covenants, or restrictions that will affect the setbacks, roof sign, parking, and deliveries.
3. Check with the landlord and other tenant leases to verify that these are acceptable to the landlord and do not violate other tenants' rights, signage, parking, etc.

CHAPTER 12

IMPORTANT TERMINOLOGY

administrative law judge
Americans with Disabilities Act
blockbusting
Civil Rights Act of 1866
Civil Rights Act of 1968
disability
discriminatory advertising
Fair Housing Act of 1968
Fair Housing Amendments Act of 1988
familial status
handicap
redlining
steering

Fair Housing

IN THIS CHAPTER Two federal laws prohibit discrimination in housing: (a) the Fair Housing Act of 1968, together with its important 1974 and 1988 amendments, and (b) the Civil Rights Act of 1866. The Fair Housing Act of 1968 and its subsequent amendments apply specifically to residential property. The 1866 law prohibits all discrimination based on race in both real and personal property.

CIVIL RIGHTS ACT OF 1866

The first significant statute affecting equal housing opportunity is the federal **Civil Rights Act of 1866**. Far from being obsolete, this statute has had a major impact on fair housing concepts through a landmark case in 1968, the year the federal Fair Housing Act became law. Although the 1968 statute, discussed later, provides for a number of exemptions, the 1866 law has no exemptions and contains the blanket statement that *all citizens have the same rights to inherit, buy, sell, or lease all real and personal property*. This statute is interpreted to prohibit all racial discrimination in property transactions.

In the case of *Jones* v. *Alfred H. Mayer Company*, the U.S. Supreme Court applied the Civil Rights Act of 1866 to prohibit any racially based discrimination in housing. The ruling provides an interesting interplay between the 1866 act and the 1968 amendments to the federal Fair Housing Act, because the exemptions provided for in the 1968 law cannot be used to enforce any racial discrimination.

Enforcement

Based on the 1866 law, if discrimination on the basis of race occurs, the aggrieved party can file an action in federal district court for an injunction and damages.

FEDERAL FAIR HOUSING ACT OF 1968

Originally enacted by Congress as *Title VIII* of the **Civil Rights Act of 1968**, the **Fair Housing Act** *prohibits discrimination in housing on the basis of race, color, religion, or national origin*. An amendment in the Housing and Community Development Act of 1974 added the prohibition against discrimination on the basis of sex. The **Fair Housing Amendments Act of 1988** added *provisions to prevent discrimination based on mental or physical handicap or familial status* (see Figure 12.1).

FIGURE 12.1 Listing of protected classes by law.

YEAR	LAW	PROTECTED CLASS
1866	Civil Rights Act	Race
1968	Federal Fair Housing Act	Race, religion national origin, color
1974	Amendment to Housing and Community Development Act	Sex
1988	Fair Housing Amendments Act	Familial status, handicap

1988 Amendments to Fair Housing Act

Although the Fair Housing Act of 1968 was clear in its intent to provide fair housing for the nation, it essentially lacked means for enforcement. Until 1988, the role of the U. S. Department of Housing and Urban Development (HUD) was limited to that of negotiator, trying to effect a voluntary conciliation between the affected parties through the force of persuasion. Although aggrieved parties could always take their complaints to a federal court and seek civil damages, this often was not a reality because the victim of discrimination was often unable to afford the legal expense.

In addition, Congress found that although racial complaints were becoming less frequent, a major problem was discrimination against families with young children, as well as the special needs of people with handicaps. To address these concerns, Congress passed sweeping amendments to the Act, which became effective March 12, 1989. Here is a synopsis of those amendments.

1. Protected classes now include individuals with a **handicap**, a *mental or physical disability that impairs any of their life functions*. Landlords must allow people with handicaps to make reasonable modifications to an apartment, at the tenant's expense, to accommodate their special needs. Tenants, for example, must be allowed to install a ramp or widen doors to accommodate a wheelchair, or install grab bars in a bathroom. At the end of their tenancy, they must return the premises to their original condition, also at their own expense.

   Since 1990, new multi-family construction provides certain accommodations for people with handicaps—for example, switches and thermostats at a level that can be operated from a wheelchair, reinforced walls to install grab bars, and kitchen space that will permit maneuverability in a wheelchair.

2. Another added protected class is **familial status**. Familial status is granted to *an adult with children under 18, a person who is pregnant, and one who has legal custody of a child or who is in the process of obtaining such custody*. Thus, landlords are prohibited from advertising "Adults Only" in most circumstances. The amendments, however, provided for elderly housing if (a) all units are occupied by individuals age 62 or older, or (b) 80 percent of the units have persons age 55 or older and the facility has accommodations to meet the physical and social needs of the elderly.

3. The 1988 amendments added major enforcement provisions. Previously, HUD could use only persuasion, but now HUD can file a formal charge and refer the complaint to an **administrative law judge (ALJ)** unless the aggrieved party or the charged party elects for a jury trial in a civil court. The ALJ, who *hears complaints regarding violations of the 1988 amendments*, can impose substantial fines from $10,000 to $50,000 for subsequent offenses.

4. Enforcement is further strengthened by an expanding role of the U. S. Attorney General to initiate action in the public interest that could result in fines of as much as $50,000 on the first offense. This will occur only upon the finding of a "pattern of discrimination." The Attorney General will take the role of the aggrieved party, freeing the actual aggrieved party from the legal expense of pursuing the case.

Real estate brokers should be aware of an amendment to the 1968 law that requires all offices to prominently display the Fair Housing Poster shown in Figure 12.2. Upon investigation of a discrimination complaint, failure to display the poster could be conclusive proof of failure to comply with the federal law.

As the law presently exists, discrimination on the basis of race, color, religion, sex, national origin, handicap, or familial status is illegal in the sale or rental of housing or residential lots, advertising the sale or rental of housing, financing housing, and providing real estate brokerage services. The Act also makes blockbusting and racial steering illegal. (These terms are defined on page 256.)

Prohibited Acts

A few special exemptions are available to owners in renting or selling their own property (examined later in the chapter). In the absence of an exemption, the following specific acts are prohibited:

1. Refusing to sell or rent housing, or to negotiate the sale or rental of residential lots on the basis of discrimination because of race, color, religion, sex, national origin, handicap, or familial status. This includes representing to any person on discriminatory grounds "that any dwelling is not available for inspection, sale, or rental when in fact such dwelling is available." It is also illegal "to refuse to sell or rent after the making of a bona fide offer, or to refuse to negotiate for the sale or rental of, or otherwise make unavailable or deny a dwelling to a person" because of race, color, religion, sex, national origin, handicap, or familial status. Examples of violations of these prohibited acts are:
   - Advising a prospective buyer that a house has been sold, because of the prospect's national origin, when it has not.

U.S. Department of Housing and Urban Development

We Do Business in Accordance With the Federal Fair Housing Law

(The Fair Housing Amendments Act of 1988)

It Is Illegal to Discriminate Against Any Person Because of Race, Color, Religion, Sex, Handicap, Familial Status, or National Origin

- In the sale or rental of housing or residential lots
- In advertising the sale or rental of housing
- In the financing of housing
- In the provision of real estate brokerage services
- In the appraisal of housing
- Blockbusting is also illegal

Anyone who feels he or she has been discriminated against may file a complaint of housing discrimination with the:

U.S. Department of Housing and Urban Development
Assistant Secretary for Fair Housing and Equal Opportunity
Washington, D.C. 20410

Previous editions are obsolete — form HUD-928.1 (3-89)

FIGURE 12.2 Poster for equal housing opportunity.

- Refusing to accept an offer to purchase because the offeror is a member of a certain religion.
- Telling a rental applicant that an apartment is not available for inspection because the applicant is a female (or male) when the apartment is actually vacant and available for inspection.
- Refusing to rent to a person confined to a wheelchair or make reasonable modifications (at the tenant's expense) to an apartment to accommodate the wheelchair.
- Refusing to rent to a family with children.

2. The Act makes it illegal "to discriminate against any person in the terms, conditions, or privileges of sale or rental of a dwelling, or in the provision of services or facilities in connection therewith, because of race, color, religion, sex, national origin, handicap, or familial status." Examples of prohibited acts in this category are:
   - The manager of an apartment complex routinely requires tenants to have a security deposit in an amount equal to one month's rent except when the rental applicant is Hispanic, in which case the required deposit is increased to two months' rent.
   - The manager of an apartment complex restricts use of the complex swimming pool to white tenants only.
   - The owner of a condominium includes in the purchase of a condo apartment a share of stock and membership in a nearby country club provided the purchaser is not Jewish.
   - A landlord charges a larger deposit to a couple with young children.
   - A landlord charges a higher rent to a person in a wheelchair.

Blockbusting

The Act specifically makes **blockbusting** illegal. This practice is defined as: *"for profit, to induce or attempt to induce any person to sell or rent any dwelling by representations regarding the entry or prospective entry into the neighborhood of a person or persons of a particular race, color, religion, sex, national origin, handicap or familial status."* Blockbusting occurs when real estate salespersons induce owners to list property for sale or rent by telling them that persons of a particular race, color, national origin, sex, religion, handicap, or familial status are moving into the area.

Steering

In **steering**, real estate licensees *direct prospective purchasers, especially minority purchasers, toward or away from specific neighborhoods to avoid changing the ethnic and/or racial makeup of neighborhoods*. The prohibition against steering falls under the general prohibition of refusing to sell, rent, or negotiate the sale or rental of housing or residential lots. Examples of steering are:

- Showing a white prospect properties only in areas populated only by white people.
- Showing African-American prospects properties only in integrated areas or areas populated only by African-Americans.
- Showing Polish prospects properties only in areas populated by Poles.
- Placing tenants with handicaps in a separate building.

Discriminatory Advertising

Discriminatory advertising that *shows preference based on race, color, religion, sex, national origin, handicap, or familial status* is illegal. The Act specifies that it is illegal to make, print, or publish, or cause to be made, printed, or published any notice, statement, or advertisement, concerning the sale or rental of a dwelling, that indicates any preference, limitation, or discrimination based on race, color, religion, sex, national origin, handicap, or familial status. Examples of violations are:

- An advertisement for the sale of condominium units or rental apartments containing pictures that show owners or tenants on the property of only one race.
- An advertisement stating that the owner prefers tenants who are male college students.
- A "For Sale" sign specifying "No Puerto Ricans."
- A statement to prospective white tenants by a real estate salesperson that black tenants are not permitted.
- An apartment advertisement stating "Adults Only."

PUTTING IT TO WORK

Most people can clearly recognize the negative discrimination in advertising that states "no children" or "no blacks." Equally illegal, however, are advertisements that show discriminatory practices such as "Catholics preferred" or "Bachelor apartment available." "Adult community" also is forbidden unless the community meets strict federal guidelines.

Financing of Housing

In the past, areas populated by minorities were redlined. Prior to enactment of the Fair Housing Act, some lending institutions circled certain local areas with a red line on the map, refusing to make loans within the circled areas based upon some characteristic of property owners in the area. The Act prohibits lending institutions from **redlining**, or *refusing to make loans to purchase, construct, or repair a dwelling by discriminating on the basis of race, color, religion, sex, national origin, handicap, or familial status.* The prohibition also extends to individuals who discriminate in fixing terms of the loan, including interest rates, duration of loan, or any other terms or conditions of the loan.

Real Estate Brokerage Services

The Act prohibits discrimination in providing brokerage services and states "It is unlawful to deny any person access to or membership or participation in any multiple listing service, real estate broker's organization, or other service relating to the business of selling or renting dwellings, or to discriminate against him in the terms or conditions of such access, membership or participation on account of race, color, religion, sex, national origin, handicap or familial status."

Exemptions

The Fair Housing Law provides exemptions to property owners under certain conditions. Exemptions from the 1968 Fair Housing Act as amended include:

1. An owner of no more than three single-family dwellings at any one time is exempt upon sale of one of the dwellings. However, the owner is limited to only one exemption in any 24-month period, unless he or she is living in or was the last occupant of the dwelling sold. An example of this exemption is a builder of single-family homes who builds only one or two a year. He may build a home,

move in until it sells, then build another home. In the sale of such a home, the builder/owner can legally discriminate against the protected classes, perhaps by excluding handicapped individuals because he doesn't wish ramps added to any of his construction.

2. An owner of an apartment building containing no more than four units, one of which is occupied by the owner, is exempt in renting the units. An example of this exemption is an owner of a duplex in a college town where the owner rents one side to college students and resides in the other side. If the owner is female, she may wish to exclude all male tenants. Under this exemption she can legally discriminate against most protected classes in the rental of the duplex.
3. Religious organizations are exempt as to properties owned and operated on a non-commercial basis for the benefit of their members only. This exemption is only available to them if membership in the organization is not restricted on account of race, color, national origin, sex, familial status, or handicap. An example of this exemption is a Baptist home for unwed mothers. Excluding non-Baptists will be allowable as long as the home is run as a non-profit venture and not as a commercial venture, and as long as it does not discriminate on the basis of race, color, national origin, gender, familial status, or handicap.
4. A private club, not open to the public, which provides housing to members as a benefit to them and not as a commercial venture, is exempt in the rental of such housing. An example of this exemption is an exclusive men's club that has overnight lodging for members. The club can refuse overnight lodging to a woman, even though doing so discriminates on the basis of sex, one of the protected classes.

None of these exemptions is available if either of the following has occurred:

1. Discriminatory advertising has been used.
2. The services of a real estate broker, associate, salesperson, or any person in the business of selling or renting dwellings are used.

A person is deemed to be in the business of selling or renting dwellings if:

- The individual has, within the preceding 12 months, participated as principal in three or more transactions involving the sale or rental of any dwelling or any interest therein.
- The person has, within the preceding 12 months, participated as agent (excluding the sale of personal residence) in providing sales or rental facilities or services in two or more transactions involving the sale or rental of any dwelling or any interest therein.
- The individual is the owner of any dwelling designed or intended for occupancy by five or more families.

Enforcement and Penalties

The Fair Housing Act may be enforced in three ways:

1. By administrative procedure through the Office of Equal Opportunity, Department of Housing and Urban Development (HUD). HUD may act on its own information and initiative. HUD must act in response to complaints. If a state or local law where the property is located is substantially equivalent, HUD must refer the complaint to the state or local authorities. Complaints must be in writing and state the facts upon which an alleged violation is based. If HUD or the state organization is unable to obtain voluntary conciliation, a charge will be filed and the case referred to an administrative law judge, unless either party elects to have the case tried in a civil court.

   The ALJ may impose a civil penalty of up to $10,000 for a first offense, $25,000 if another violation occurs within five years, and $50,000 if two or more violations occur in seven years. An individual can be fined $25,000 or $50,000 without limitation of time periods if he or she engages in multiple discriminatory practices.

2. The aggrieved party, with or without filing a complaint to HUD, may bring a civil suit in Federal District Court within one year of the alleged violation of the Act unless a complaint has been filed with HUD, in which case the period is two years. If the aggrieved party wins the case, the court may issue an injunction against the violator and award actual damages and punitive damages with no limitation by the statute.
3. The U.S. Attorney General may file a civil suit in any appropriate U. S. District Court where the Attorney General has reasonable cause to believe that any person or group is engaged in a pattern of violation of the Act and, as such, raises an issue of general public importance. The court may issue an injunction or restraining order against the person responsible and impose fines of up to $50,000 to "vindicate the public interest." A first-time fine of $50,000 may be imposed where a "pattern of practice" of discrimination is discovered.

State Fair Housing Acts

The individual states have the authority to pass their own civil rights acts. State laws may adopt the same protected classes as the federal laws, and they may add more protected classes, such as marital status. If the state has a law that is substantially the same as the federal law, complaints based upon the federal law must be referred to the state enforcement agency.

Exemptions

A state law cannot increase the exemptions found under the federal law. It may be more restrictive, however, and provide for *no* exemptions.

Enforcement and Penalties

Enforcement of state laws typically is through injunctive relief or damages, or both, after a hearing or negotiated settlement. The amount of damages is determined by a civil court. The State also may require a person found guilty of violating the state laws to take affirmative action. The affirmative action could be in the form of relevant community service, advertisements concerning fair housing, sponsorship of a seminar on fair housing, or the like.

Equal Housing Opportunity Today

Many people have the idea that the issue of fair housing has long been resolved through actions such as the civil rights movements of the 1960s. Despite the intention of both the 1866 and the 1968 civil rights acts to provide equal housing opportunity for all citizens, this goal has not been achieved in practice. Although the Fair Housing Act has been in effect for many years, recent HUD studies find that minorities are still confronted with discrimination in purchasing homes and in leasing rental units.

Many proposals have been developed to correct this situation. One means of enforcing the law is through an organized program of testing by civil rights groups. In 1968 the administration supported a Fair Housing Initiative Program (FHIP) to provide funding for testers. The National Association of REALTORS® negotiated an agreement with HUD to ensure that the funded testing will be objective, reliable, and controlled, and then it endorsed the program.

To address attitudes against discrimination, NAR developed a Voluntary Affirmative Marketing Program. The Association encourages its affiliates and members to adopt the program by signing an affirmative marketing agreement. Provisions of the agreement pledge signatories to adopt affirmative advertising, recruitment, and educational programs. As each April is celebrated with observances of passage of the Fair Housing Act of 1968, it is hoped that the spirit and intention of the law will be fulfilled.

PUTTING IT TO WORK

Salespersons should be well-informed on the laws of their state as they apply to discrimination issues. Not only is discrimination socially offensive, but it also can jeopardize a transaction or one's license and expose one to legal liability.

AMERICANS WITH DISABILITIES ACT

The **Americans with Disabilities Act**, which took effect on January 26, 1992, specifically *protects the rights of individuals with disabilities by requiring that they have access to public transportation, commercial buildings, and public buildings.* **Disability** is defined in USC 42, Sec. 12101, as a *physical or mental impairment that substantially limits one or more of the major life activities of a person.*

Under this law, individuals with disabilities cannot be denied access to public transportation, any commercial facility, or public accommodation. This Act applies to all owners and operators of public accommodations and commercial facilities, regardless of the size or number of employees. It also applies to all local and state governments.

Public accommodations are defined as private businesses that affect commerce and trade, such as inns, hotels, restaurants, theaters, convention centers, bakeries, laundromats, banks, barber shops, attorneys' offices, museums, zoos, places of education, day care centers, and health clubs. Commercial facilities are those intended for nonresidential use and affect commerce, such as factories.

Under ADA requirements, public, retail commercial establishments must have parking, bathrooms, seating, and work areas that are usable by persons with disabilities. ADA also prohibits discrimination in hiring practices of public, retail, and commercial establishments.

To comply with this law, public accommodations and commercial facilities are to be designed, constructed, and altered to meet the accessibility standards of the new law if readily achievable. "Readily achievable" means easily accomplishable and able to be carried out without much difficulty or expense. Considerations in determining if the commercial facility or public accommodation can be made accessible are:

1. Nature and cost of the needed alteration.
2. Overall financial resources of the facility involved and number of persons employed.
3. Type of operation of the entity.

Public accommodations must remove structural, architectural, and communication barriers in existing facilities if the removal is readily achievable. Examples of barriers to be removed or alterations to be made include placing ramps, lowering telephones, making curb cuts in sidewalks and entrances, widening doors, installing grab bars in toilet stalls, and adding raised letters on elevator controls. Commercial facilities are not required to remove the barriers in existing facilities.

In the construction of new public accommodations and commercial facilities, all areas must be readily accessible and usable by individuals with disabilities. The Americans with Disabilities Act is enforced by the U. S. Attorney General. Punishment for violating this law includes injunctions against operation of a business, a fine up to $50,000 for the first offense, and a fine of $100,000 for subsequent offenses.

Be aware that individuals with AIDS, alcoholism, or mental illness are included in the category of people with a mental or physical disability that impairs any of their life functions.

Although ADA does not deal with housing, its provisions will impact licensees who wish to open an office or manage commercial property. Because of the requirements set out in ADA, some office buildings, and commercial and retail properties will not be usable. If property is not usable, it is not as valuable. Thus, properties that do not meet ADA requirements may have lower appraised values.

Important Points

1. The Civil Rights Act of 1968, as amended, prohibits discrimination in housing because of race, color, religion, sex, national origin, age, handicap, or familial status.
2. Discrimination is prohibited in (a) sale or rental of housing, (b) advertising the sale or rental of housing, (c) financing of housing, and (d) provision of real estate brokerage services. The Act also makes blockbusting illegal.
3. Four exemptions are provided to owners in selling or renting housing: (a) owners who do not own more than three houses, (b) owners of apartment buildings with not more than four apartments and owner occupies one of the apartments, (c) religious organizations, as to properties used for the benefit of members only, and (d) private clubs, as to lodging used for the benefit of members only. The owners' exemptions are not available if the owner used discriminatory advertising or the services of a real estate broker.
4. Enforcement of Title VIII of the 1968 Civil Rights Act was amended significantly in 1988. Enforcement procedures now include: (a) administrative procedure through the Office of Equal Opportunity of HUD, which first attempts voluntary conciliation and then can refer the case to an administrative law judge, who can impose financial penalties of $10,000 to $50,000; (b) civil suit in federal court; and (c) action by the U. S. Attorney General, who may file a suit in federal court and impose penalties of up to $50,000 on the first offense in a "pattern of discrimination."
5. The Civil Rights Act of 1866 prohibits discrimination only on the basis of race. The prohibition is not limited to housing but includes all real estate and personal property transactions. The Act may be enforced only by civil suit in federal court. This law has no exemptions.
6. The individual states may pass their own civil rights acts that are mirror images of the federal law or add protected classes. If the state law is substantially equivalent to the federal law, complaints filed with HUD will be referred to the state agency for investigation and enforcement.
7. The Americans with Disabilities Act provides that individuals with disabilities cannot be denied access to public transportation, any commercial facility, or public accommodation. Barriers in existing buildings must be removed if readily achievable. New buildings must be readily accessible and usable by individuals with disabilities. It does not address residential properties.

How Would You Respond?

1. As office manager for a property management firm, you notice discrimination by office staff in response to maintenance requests. The discrimination appears to be based upon the national origin of the tenants. What steps would you take to correct the situation?
2. Brown has listed his real estate with you. He states that he will not accept an offer from an individual that is from a foreign country. What should you do?

Case Studies

REAL ESTATE AGENTS GUILTY OF STEERING

In 1987, the Open Housing Center of New York (OHC), investigated AM Realty. Once a month for five months, OHC sent a white "tester" to see apartments managed by AM Realty in certain New York neighborhoods. On the same days, OHC sent an African-American or Latino "tester" to see the same apartments in the same neighborhoods. The testers all had similar income and family size.

Each time the white tester was taken to white neighborhoods; the African-American or Latino testers were told to check other ethnic neighborhoods or that no apartments were available.

In addition to investigating AM Realty, OHC also investigated the landlords who used AM Realty. The investigation showed that the landlords knew of the steering and in some cases encouraged it.

Both AM Realty and the landlords who used AM Realty were found guilty of violating the Fair Housing Law.

Catrera v. Jakabovitz, 24 F.3d 372, (New York) 1994.

LANDLORD FOUND GUILTY OF DISCRIMINATORY ADVERTISING

Jancik, who owns a large housing complex, advertised an apartment for lease; the ad stated that a mature person was preferred. Two testers were sent to pose as potential tenants; one was white, the other African-American. When Jancik spoke with the white tester on the telephone he asked her race and the number of children she had. When Jancik spoke with the African-American tester by telephone he asked her race, stating he needed that information to screen applicants. When the testers arrived to see the apartment, they were told it had been rented.

The administrative law judge found Jancik guilty of discriminatory advertising that showed a preference against families. The term "mature person" suggests an unlawful preference to an ordinary reader and is set out in the Fair Housing regulations as being among the most often used term to convey discriminatory preferences or limitations.

The ALJ also found Jancik guilty of discrimination based upon race in his questions to testers, and he admitted that he used race to screen applicants.

Jancik v. Dept. of HUD, decided 1/6/95, Case #93-3792

REVIEW QUESTIONS

Answers to these questions are found in the *Answer Key* section at the back of the book.

1. Sam Seller refuses to accept an offer to purchase his home from Juan Pedro from Spain because Sam considers the $50 of earnest money insufficient. As to Sam's refusal, which of the following is correct?
   a. Sam is in violation of the Fair Housing Act of 1968 because he has discriminated on the ground of national origin
   b. Sam refused the offer because of the small of earnest money, so he is not in violation of the 1968 Act
   c. Sam is in violation of the Civil Rights Act of 1866 because he discriminated on the basis of race
   d. Sam is guilty of redlining

2. Which of the following is NOT a basis of discrimination prohibited by the original 1968 Act?
   a. race
   b. national origin
   c. sex
   d. religion

3. Larry Landlord refuses to rent one of five apartments in his building to Barbara Barrister, an attorney. Which of the following statements about Larry's refusal is correct?
   a. if Larry's refusal to rent to Barbara is because she is an attorney, he is not in violation of the 1968 Act
   b. if Larry's refusal to rent to Barbara is because she is female, Larry is not in violation of the 1968 Act
   c. if Larry's refusal to rent to Barbara is because she is a female, he is guilty of redlining
   d. it doesn't matter what Larry's reason is because he can claim an exemption

4. The Our Town Multiple Listing Service refused to accept a listing because the home's owner is Russian. Which of the following is correct?
   a. a multiple listing service does not come under the 1968 Act because it is a private non-profit organization
   b. the 1968 Act does not prohibit discrimination against Russians
   c. the listing broker's membership in the MLS may be terminated for taking the listing
   d. the MLS is in violation of the 1968 Act for denying access to the service because of the owner's national origin

5. A property manager refuses to rent an office because the rental applicant is an African-American. The applicant has legal recourse under the:
   a. Civil Rights Act of 1968
   b. Civil Rights Act of 1866
   c. Civil Rights Act of 1988
   d. Civil Rights Act of 1974

6. In an advertisement offering her only house for sale, the owner states that she will give preference to cash buyers who are female and members of the Catholic religion. The owner subsequently refuses a cash offer because the offeror is a male Presbyterian. Which of the following is correct?
   a. because the seller only owns one house, she is exempt from the 1968 Act
   b. because the advertisement only stated a preference, it is not discriminatory
   c. because the seller's main purpose was to obtain cash, the refusal is not discriminatory
   d. because the advertisement was in fact discriminatory, the seller's exemption is lost and she has violated the 1968 Act in two ways

7. A real estate salesperson shows white prospects homes only in all-white areas. This discriminatory practice is called:
   a. redlining
   b. blockbusting
   c. steering
   d. directing

8. Which of the following is exempt from the provisions of the 1968 Act?
   a. an owner of four houses
   b. an owner occupying one of four apartments in his building
   c. a religious organization renting one of 16 apartments it owns and operates for commercial purposes
   d. an owner who has listed a residential lot for sale with a real estate broker

9. The Civil Rights Act of 1968 as amended in 1988 may be enforced by all of the following EXCEPT:
   a. a civil suit for damages in federal court
   b. administrative procedures through HUD
   c. action by the U. S. Attorney General
   d. arbitration with the National Labor Relations Board

10. A homeowner avails herself of the exemption provided by the 1968 Act and refuses to accept an offer because the offeror is a white person. The offeror may do which of the following?
    a. bring suit in federal district court under the Civil Rights Act of 1866
    b. bring suit in federal district court under the Civil Rights Act of 1968
    c. bring suit in federal district court under the Civil Rights Act of 1988
    d. ask for arbitration with HUD

11. The following ad appears in a local paper: "Home for rent; limited to mature persons; 2 bedrooms; 1 bath." Which of the following is correct?
    a. the ad is in compliance with the Fair Housing Act of 1968 as amended in 1988
    b. the ad violates the Civil Rights Act of 1866
    c. the ad is in compliance with the Civil Rights Act of 1974
    d. the ad violates the Fair Housing Amendments of 1988

12. A person confined to a wheelchair requests that an apartment be modified to meet her physical needs. Which of the following is correct?
    a. the owner must make appropriate modifications at the owner's expense
    b. at the end of the tenancy, the renter must pay for returning the premises to their original condition
    c. the owner may refuse to rent to the disabled tenant because of the needed modifications
    d. the owner may charge increased rent because of the disability and the needed modifications

13. Which of the following laws allows no exemptions from its provisions?
    a. Americans with Disabilities Act
    b. Civil Rights Act of 1866
    c. Federal Fair Housing Act of 1968
    d. Federal Fair Housing Act of 1988

14. Betty Jones has her only house for sale. She does not use a real estate agent. She places a simple sign in the yard that states: House for Sale. On the first day, two people stop to look at the house. One is black, the other is Asian-American. Betty Jones tells both parties that she will not sell to them because of their race. Which of the following is true?
    a. Betty Jones' actions fall under an exemption of the 1866 Civil Rights law
    b. Betty Jones' actions fall under an exemption of the 1968 law
    c. Betty Jones' actions fall under an exemption of the ADA law
    d. Betty Jones' actions are lawful under all of the Civil Rights laws and ADA

15. If a physically handicapped person is a tenant at an apartment complex with assigned parking, all of the following are true EXCEPT:
    a. the landlord is not required to provide preferential parking for the handicapped tenant
    b. the landlord is required to provide preferential parking for the handicapped tenant
    c. the tenant is allowed to make modifications to the rental unit at the tenant's expense
    d. the landlord can require any modifications made by the tenant to be similar in architectural style to the unit

POSSIBLE RESPONSES TO "HOW WOULD YOU RESPOND?"

1. The immediate response to the problem is to meet with all office staff and explain that discrimination is occurring. In some instances, the staff may not even be aware of what is happening. An immediate training session on the federal and state laws relating to discrimination should be held. It is sometimes possible to have the Director of the local Human Rights Commission present a training program. Tapes and materials are also available for NAR. If any staff member states that he or she will not adhere to the laws, then you must dismiss this staff member to avoid the penalties of the laws.

   To assure that future discrimination does not occur, establish standard office procedures for the handling of maintenance requests. These procedures should include the use of forms which set out the date and time of the request and the date and time of the response to the request. If the forms are used, you as office manager should be able quickly to determine and assure that maintenance requests are handled in order of time or receipt.

2. It is unlawful for Brown to discriminate in the sale of his real estate on the basis of national origin since he has listed his property with a licensee. It may be that Brown has a concern that is not based upon national origin but upon finances. Discuss with Brown his reason for his statement. If you find that Brown's concern is for a reason that is not unlawfully discriminatory, then you can continue the listing and address his concern in the sale documents with a prospective buyer.

   If however you find that Brown's concern is truly based upon the national origin of any prospective buyer, you should advise Brown that his position is a violation of the federal and possibly state law. You should advise him to seek legal counsel if he insists on the discrimination. You cannot agree to violate the law, thus you must terminate the listing agreement. Any termination should be in writing with the writing stating your specific reason for termination.

CHAPTER 13

IMPORTANT TERMINOLOGY

escalated lease
eviction
fixed lease
graduated lease
gross lease
ground lease
holdover clause
holdover tenant
index lease
lease
lessee
lessor
negligence
net lease
option to renew
percentage lease
periodic lease
privity of contract
quiet enjoyment
reappraisal lease
reversionary interest
sale and leaseback
security deposit
sublease

Leasehold Estates (Landlord and Tenant)

IN THIS CHAPTER Landlord–tenant law revolves around the lease contract. The basic law of contracts, discussed in Chapter 5, applies to the leases discussed in this chapter. The history of landlord–tenant law is vast. Most of the law prior to recent time was established by court decisions called common law. Today, many new statutes drastically change the relationship of landlord and tenant. This chapter defines and explains the parties in a lease agreement; the essential elements of a valid lease; duties, obligations, and rights of the parties to the lease agreement; and various legal leaseholds.

DEFINITIONS CONCERNING THE LANDLORD/TENANT RELATIONSHIP

A **lease** is a *contract between the owner of the property and the tenant to transfer possession temporarily to the tenant.* Under the lease agreement, the owner transfers to the tenant a property interest, possession, for a prescribed period of time. The *owner of the property* is called the *landlord* or **lessor**. The *tenant placed in possession* is called the **lessee**. The tenant is to have quiet enjoyment of the premises, and the landlord is to receive money plus a **reversionary interest** in the property; *possession of the property will go back to the owner at the end of the lease.*

Under a lease, the lessor and lessee agree to the terms of possession and the rent to be paid. The benefit of the lease runs both to the lessor and the lessee, so either the lessor or lessee can demand to receive the contracted benefit. The *right to demand and receive the specific benefit* is based upon **privity of contract** that exists only between lessor and lessee.

Individuals who are not a party to the lease contract cannot demand to receive any benefit from the lease contract. For example, a guest of the lessee has no right to bring legal action against the lessor for lessor's breach of the lease; the guest does not have privity of contract. A person who receives the rights of the lessee by assignment, however, has privity of contract to bring suit against the lessor. Assignment of contract rights transfers the privity of contract necessary for suit.

ESSENTIAL ELEMENTS OF A LEASE

In creating a lease, the requirements of offer, acceptance, legal capacity, legal purpose, consideration, and reality of assent apply, just as they do in any contract.

Property Description

A formal legal description of the property is not required. A street address or other informal reference that is sufficiently identifying to both parties is acceptable. If the lease is for a long term, a formal legal description is recommended to accommodate recordation of the contract.

Term

The term of the lease is the period of time for which the lease will exist between landlord and tenant. The term should be sufficiently clear so that all parties will know the date of expiration and the method to terminate. The term may be cut short prematurely by breach of the lease by one of the parties or by mutual agreement. The death of one party may or may not terminate the estate, depending on the type of leasehold estate.

Rent

Rent is the consideration the tenant pays to the landlord for possession of the premises. In addition to possession, the rent paid assures the tenant quiet enjoyment of the premises (explained later in the chapter).

Other Lease Provisions

Leases may contain additional provisions setting out specific agreements between the landlord and tenant. One common provision is an **option to renew** the lease. This *sets forth the method for renewal and the terms* by which the renewed lease will exist. The parties also may include in the lease an option to buy. This provision allows the tenant to purchase the leased premises for a certain price for a certain period of time. In commercial leases, a right of first refusal often is given to a tenant to allow an opportunity to expand into additional space before it is leased to another tenant. This option *may* be at a different rental rate than originally agreed upon.

In most written leases, provisions stating who has the responsibility for maintenance and repair are included. Also, the landlord usually includes a provision prohibiting assignment of lease rights or subleasing of the premises by the tenant (discussed later in the chapter) without the landlord's approval. Examples of these provisions are found in the sample lease in Figure 13.1.

Written or Oral Provisions

The Statute of Frauds in most states requires that, to be enforceable by the court, a lease of real estate must be in writing if the term is for more than one year. Oral leases under one year in length are generally enforceable by the courts. If a written lease is used, both landlord and tenant should sign. To be safe, regardless of the time period, any lease should be written.

Recordation

Most short-term leases are not recorded, but in the case of ground leases (discussed later), leases of more than one year in duration, and leases with an option to buy, it is in the best interest of the tenant to record the lease in the jurisdiction where the property lies. Recordation provides constructive notice of the tenant's rights in the event of sale or death of the landlord.

FIGURE 13.1
A sample lease.

RESIDENTIAL RENTAL APPLICATION, AGREEMENT AND RECEIPT FOR DEPOSIT

The printed portion of this agreement has been approved by the Arizona Association Of REALTORS®. This is intended to be a binding agreement. No representation is made as to the legal validity or adequacy of any provision or the tax consequences thereof. If you desire legal or tax advice, consult your attorney or tax advisor.

Agency Confirmation: Unless otherwise disclosed in writing, Landlord and Tenant acknowledge that Brokers represent the Landlord. Brokers agree to treat fairly all parties to the transaction.

RECEIPT

Earnest Money: Received From: ______________________________

Earnest money shall be held by Leasing Broker named in Line 13 until offer is accepted, subject to prior lease. Upon acceptance, Leasing Broker is instructed as follows:

a. Amount of Earnest Money	b. Form of Earnest Money:	c. Deposited With:
$ __________	☐ Personal Check ☐ Cashier Check ☐ Other: ________	☐ Leasing Broker's Trust Account ☐ Listing Broker's Trust Account ☐ Landlord ☐ Other: ________

If check is payable to either Broker, Broker may deposit in Broker's Trust Account or endorse the check without recourse to the Landlord. All earnest money is subject to collection.

In the event of Tenant's breach of this agreement all earnest money shall be deemed a security deposit.

Received by Leasing Broker:

______________ PRINT FIRM NAME ______________ PRINT AGENT'S NAME ______________ AGENT'S SIGNATURE ______________ MO/DA/YR

RENTAL OFFER

Property Description & Offer: Tenant offers to lease the real property and all fixtures and improvements thereon and appurtenances incident thereto, plus personal property described below (collectively the "Premises")

Property Address: ______________________________

City: ______________________________ AZ, Zip Code: ______________

Personal Property: ______________________________

____

Term: The lease shall begin on ______ (MO/DA/YR) and end on ______ (MO/DA/YR)

Rent: Tenant shall pay monthly installments of $ __________ plus any applicable sales taxes, which are currently $ __________, totaling $ __________ ("Rent"). Rent shall be payable in advance without deductions or offsets.

If the first month's Rent is for a period other than the full month, the Rent shall be $ __________ plus any applicable sales taxes, which are currently $ __________, totaling $ __________ for the period beginning ______ (MO/DA/YR) and ending ______ (MO/DA/YR).

Rent installments in the full amount shown on line 22 shall be due and payable no later than 5 p.m. on the __________ day of each month during the term of this Agreement. When the rental term is for part of a month, the rent shall be prorated.

A late charge of ______________________________ shall be added to all rent installments not received by the due date and shall be collectible as Rent.

Tenant shall pay Landlord a charge of $ __________ for all checks returned from the bank unpaid for any reason plus appropriate late charge from the due date until good funds are received. These additional charges shall be collectible as Rent. If a check has been returned from the bank unpaid for any reason, the Landlord reserves the right to demand that all sums due under this Rental Agreement be paid in the form of a cashier's check or money order and to return any personal or company check previously accepted by Landlord and demand a cashier's check or money order in its place.

The Rent shall automatically increase ______________________________ on all holdover periods. The new monthly rent amount shall be valid for the term of the holdover period.

Application Fee/Credit Report(s): $ __________ is non-refundable by separate payment. This Agreement is conditioned on satisfactory verification and approval by Landlord prior to possession of Tenant's employment, credit, banking references and past rental history. Tenant consents to an employment and credit check along with an investigation of prior rental history through Landlord or Broker. Tenant shall complete a separate rental and/or credit application containing the necessary information. Tenant warrants that the information is correct and complete and that Tenant has disclosed all pertinent information and has not withheld any information, including but not limited to poor credit, early terminations of leases, evictions or bankruptcy. The failure to accurately disclose all requested information relating to Tenant's employment history, credit history, and prior rental history shall be deemed to be a material and irreparable breach of this Agreement, entitling Landlord to immediately terminate this Agreement pursuant to A.R.S. 33-1368. If Landlord terminates this Agreement based on Tenant's failure to disclose the aforementioned information, Landlord may pursue any remedies available under applicable law, including but not limited to, a claim for rent for the remainder of the term of this Agreement. The credit history of Tenant with respect to this Agreement may be reported to any credit bureau or reporting agency.

Additional Terms: ______________________________

____

____

____

____

____

Deposits: Tenant shall pay by cashier's check or money order the amounts shown below on or before ______ (MO/DA/YR).

Deposits will be held: ☐ Broker's trust account: ______________ (FIRM NAME)
☐ By Landlord

Security deposit:	$ ______	Refundable		
Pet deposit:	$ ______	Refundable		
Other deposit:	$ ______	Refundable		
Cleaning deposit:	$ ______	☐ Refundable	$ ______	☐ Non-refundable
Redecorating deposit:	$ ______	☐ Refundable	$ ______	☐ Non-refundable
Total required deposits:			$ ______	
First month's rent:			$ ______	
Total required payment:			$ ______	
Less earnest money on line 8 (becomes deposit upon acceptance by all parties)			$ ______	
Balance due:			$ ______	

Note: Total payments and deposits shown above, including pet deposit but excluding any cleaning or redecorating deposit and first month's rent, may not exceed one and one-half month's rent. Any cleaning or redecorating deposit must be reasonable. The breakdown of the deposit amounts shown above is solely for the purpose of showing how such amounts were calculated and does not limit Landlord's right to use all deposit amounts as permitted by A.R.S. § 33-1321 and § 33-1341. Tenant shall not be entitled to use any portion of a deposit except any first or last month's rent as a credit for rent. Under A.R.S. § 33-1321(A) a tenant may voluntarily pay more than one and one-half month's rent in advance.

If deposits are held by Landlord, Tenant and Landlord agree to hold Broker and Property Manager harmless of all liability regarding said deposits.

This form is available for use by the entire real estate industry. The use of this form is not intended to identify the user as a REALTOR®. REALTOR® is a registered collective membership mark which may be used only by real estate licensees who are members of the NATIONAL ASSOCIATION OF REALTORS® and subscribe to its Code of Ethics.

PAGE 1

(continued)

FIGURE 13.1
Continued.

Refundable Deposits: If the premises are surrendered to Landlord at the termination or expiration of this Agreement in a clean and undamaged condition acceptable to Landlord, Landlord shall refund the Refundable Deposits to the Tenant. However, if the premises are delivered to Landlord in an unclean or damaged condition not acceptable to Landlord, Landlord may, at Landlord's option, retain all or a portion of the Deposits, and may hold the Tenant liable for any additional charges.

Pets: ☐ No pets allowed. Tenant agrees not to keep or permit any pets on the Premises without prior written consent of the Landlord.
☐ Landlord hereby grants Tenant permission to keep the following pets on the premises: ______________________________

____

Keys: Landlord agrees to deliver to Tenant _____ sets of keys to the premises and _____ garage door openers upon possession. Tenant shall be responsible for the security of the premises until all keys and garage door openers have been returned to Landlord or otherwise satisfactorily accounted for. Tenant is not authorized to change the locks or add a deadbolt lock. Tenant agrees to pay $ _______________ as cost of re-keying the property unless all keys are returned and $ _______________ for each garage door opener not returned.

Utilities. Tenant agrees to arrange and pay for, when due, all utilities except ______________________________

____

Miscellaneous Matters: The following shall be the responsibility of the party indicated:

A. Pool Maintenance: ☐ Landlord ☐ Tenant ☐ Association ☐ Not applicable
B. Pest Control: ☐ Landlord ☐ Tenant ☐ Association ☐ Not applicable
C. Yard Maintenance: ☐ Landlord ☐ Tenant ☐ Association ☐ Not applicable

Occupancy: The Premises shall be used only for residential purposes for the following named persons, including any children: ______________________________

______________________________.

Addenda: ☐ Property Disclosure ☐ Agency Disclosure ☐ Other: ______________________________

THE TENANT HAS READ THIS ENTIRE AGREEMENT. THE TENANT ACKNOWLEDGES THAT HE UNDERSTANDS THE TERMS AND CONDITIONS CONTAINED HEREIN. THE TENANT ACCEPTS AND AGREES TO THE TERMS AND CONDITIONS OF THIS RENTAL AGREEMENT AND AGREES TO BE BOUND BY THEM. THE TENANT HAS RECEIVED A COPY OF THIS AGREEMENT.

____
TENANT(S): PRINT NAME(S)

______________________________ (MO/DA/YR) ______________________________ (MO/DA/YR)
(TENANT SIGNATURE) (TENANT SIGNATURE)

______________________________ ______________________________
(TENANT ADDRESS) (TENANT ADDRESS)

Time for Acceptance: This offer must be accepted by Landlord on or before ______________________________
Written acceptance of this Offer given to the Broker named on Line 13 of this Contract shall be notice to Tenant.

ACCEPTANCE

COMMISSIONS PAYABLE FOR THE SALE, LEASING OR MANAGEMENT OF PROPERTY ARE NOT SET BY ANY BOARD OR ASSOCIATION OF REALTORS® OR MULTIPLE LISTING SERVICE OR IN ANY MANNER OTHER THAN BETWEEN THE BROKER AND CLIENT.

Landlord shall pay a commission of:

_______________ to ______________________________.
LISTING BROKER

_______________ to ______________________________.
LEASING BROKER

Property Manager shall be compensated as per written property management agreement.
The entire commission shall be due and payable upon payment of first month's rent and acceptance of this Agreement by both parties. If completion of the rental is prevented by default of Landlord, or with the consent of Landlord, the entire compensation shall be paid directly by Landlord. If the earnest money is forfeited for any other reason, Landlord shall pay a Broker's compensation equal to one-half of the earnest money deposit, provided such payment shall not exceed the full amount of the compensation.
Upon any extension or renewal of the rental of the premises. Landlord agrees to pay a commission of:

_______________ to ______________________________.

_______________ to ______________________________.

If the premises are sold to Tenant, Landlord agrees to pay a commission of:

_______________ to ______________________________.

_______________ to ______________________________.

Property Manager, if any, authorized to manage the Premises and act on behalf of Landlord under **separate written agreement.**

______________________________ (_______) ______________________________
NAME TELEPHONE

____
FIRM

____
ADDRESS CITY STATE ZIP

The Landlord or the person authorized to act on behalf of the Landlord for receiving service of process, notices, and demands is:

______________________________ (_______) ______________________________
NAME TELEPHONE

____
FIRM

____
ADDRESS CITY STATE ZIP

No refund of any commission will be made if this Agreement is terminated because of its breach by Landlord or Tenant or by mutual consent of Landlord and Tenant.

LANDLORD HAS READ THIS ENTIRE AGREEMENT. THE LANDLORD ACKNOWLEDGES THAT HE UNDERSTANDS THE TERMS AND CONDITIONS CONTAINED HEREIN. THE LANDLORD ACCEPTS AND AGREES TO THE TERMS AND CONDITIONS OF THIS RENTAL AGREEMENT AND AGREES TO BE BOUND BY THEM. THE LANDLORD HAS RECEIVED A SIGNED COPY OF THIS AGREEMENT AND DIRECTS THE BROKER TO DELIVER A SIGNED COPY TO THE TENANT, AND TO ANY OTHER BROKER INVOLVED IN THIS LEASE. LANDLORD AGREES TO PROVIDE TENANT A COPY OF THE COVENANTS, CONDITIONS AND RESTRICTIONS AND ANY APPLICABLE RULES AND REGULATIONS AS SOON AS PRACTICABLE.

Counter Offer is attached, which is incorporated herein by reference. If there is a conflict between this Agreement and the Counter Offer, the provisions of the Counter Offer shall be controlling. (Note: If this box is checked, Landlord should sign both Agreement and Counter Offer.)

Rent shall be payable to: ______________________________ at: ______________________________
(NAME) (ADDRESS)

____
CITY STATE ZIP CODE

____
LANDLORD(S): PRINT NAME(S)

______________________________ (MO/DA/YR) ______________________________ (MO/DA/YR)
(LANDLORD/PROPERTY MANAGER SIGNATURE) (LANDLORD/PROPERTY MANAGER SIGNATURE)

For Broker Use only: File No. _______________ Manager's Initials _________ Broker's Initials ____________ Date _______________

This form is available for use by the entire real estate industry. The use of this form is not intended to identify the user as a REALTOR®. REALTOR® is a registered collective membership mark which may be used only by real estate licensees who are members of the NATIONAL ASSOCIATION OF REALTORS® and subscribe to its Code of Ethics.

Obligations of Landlord and Tenant

The common law of leases, which is the law set by past court decisions, has established the obligations of landlord and tenant in many states. In recent years, however, with an increase in the number of residential tenants, some states have passed specific legislation setting out the obligations of landlord and tenant. The most widely used statute is called the Uniform Landlord and Tenant Act. As of 1991, Arizona, Hawaii, Alaska, Iowa, Kansas, Mississippi, Montana, Nebraska, New Mexico, Oklahoma, Oregon, South Carolina, and Tennessee have adopted this law totally or with modifications.

Whether under the common law or under specific statute, terms of the lease control the obligations and duties of landlord and tenant. Without a lease agreement to indicate which party is responsible for certain items, common law or the specific state law dictates the responsible party.

Mutual Obligations

Under contract law, the validity of a contract can be challenged if both parties are not bound or if both parties have not received consideration. Under a lease, the landlord's consideration is receipt of rent. The tenant's consideration is possession of the premises and the right of quiet enjoyment. The landlord's obligation to give possession of the premises to the tenant is directly tied to the tenant's payment of rent. If one party fails in his or her responsibility (consideration), the other party may be relieved of his or her duty. (Because of the interplay of many of the rights and duties—payment, maintenance, liquidated damages, and so on—one should never assume the relief of one's duties without court support of this position.)

PUTTING IT TO WORK

Landlord–tenant law varies dramatically from state to state and even from city to city. Many states are pro-tenant; others favor the landlord regarding maintenance, payment, eviction proceedings, and so on. Real estate salespeople involved in leasing or property management should be well aware of local laws and court policy.

Landlord's Duties

The landlord is required to put the tenant in possession of the premises. The tenant is entitled to **quiet enjoyment** of the premises, meaning that *no one will interrupt the tenancy or invade the premise without the tenant's consent.* This includes the landlord. The landlord does not have an automatic right to inspect the leased premises although the tenant may agree, in the lease, to the landlord's right to inspect. The landlord also has the right to enter the premises in an emergency, such as fire or burst water pipes, to protect the premises.

In the case of residential property, the landlord usually is obligated to have the premises in *habitable*, or *livable*, condition at the beginning of the lease and to maintain the premises in habitable shape during the term of the lease. The requirement for maintenance may be shifted to the tenant by agreement of the parties. The landlord also is required to warn the tenant of any dangers that are not obvious (latent dangers) such as electrical circuit problems, loose floor boards or steps, or holes in the floor hidden by carpet.

Unless the lease agreement specifically states to the contrary, the lease allows the tenant to assign his or her lease rights. Similarly, the landlord must allow the tenant to create a *lesser lease estate*, called a **sublease**, unless specifically prohibited in the lease. The lease of the original tenant becomes the *sandwich lease*.

Tenant's Duties

The tenant's basic obligation under any lease (apart from the payment of rent) is to maintain the premises in the same condition they are in at the beginning of the lease, with *ordinary wear and tear* excepted. This is the *usual deterioration caused by normal living circumstances*. The tenant will be held responsible for damage or waste. During occupancy, the tenant is expected to use the premises only for legal purposes and to conform to all local laws.

The tenant is obligated, of course, to pay the agreed-upon rent in a timely fashion. Under common law, rent is due at the end of the lease period unless the lease agreement states otherwise. Because this is typically unacceptable to the landlord, lease agreements usually require rent to be paid in advance on a month-to-month basis.

At the end of the lease, the tenant is obligated to vacate the premises without the need for legal eviction by the landlord.

If the tenant has guests (invitees) or customers (licensees), the tenant must warn them of any hidden dangers that might cause harm.

PUTTING IT TO WORK

Because of the many variables involved and the subjective nature of the words "reasonable" and "wear and tear," the lease should outline specifics such as "lawn maintained in present condition," "carpets cleaned by tenant annually," and so on.

Law of Negligence

Negligence is defined as a *failure to use that care that a reasonable person would use in like circumstances*. The term is relative and depends on the circumstances of each case. Under the law of negligence, a person is liable for damages that result to another person if a duty to that person is owed and the duty is not performed in a reasonable fashion.

Under landlord–tenant law, the landlord is responsible for damage that occurs to the tenant, tenant's guests or clients, or tenant's possession only if the landlord has a duty to that person and the landlord fails to perform his or her duty. An example of landlord negligence is if the landlord assures that all plumbing apparatus is properly maintained at the premises and the plumbing then ceases to function because of improper maintenance, and as a result of the faulty plumbing, the tenant's possessions are damaged. Negligence law does not apply where, through no lack of maintenance, the plumbing ceases to function or if the plumbing ceases to function as a result of the tenant's action and damage occurs to the tenant's possessions.

The duty of care imposed upon the landlord is the care that a reasonable and prudent person would exercise under like conditions. A landlord's liability also may be created by failure to comply with basic safety codes and laws. Examples of this might be failure to install a smoke alarm or porch railing. Any injury because of the absence of these features results in liability on the part of the landlord.

The law of negligence also applies to tenants. If tenants do not exercise reasonable care in their use of the premises and damage occurs to the landlord's property, the tenant is liable for the resulting damages.

Withholding Rent

Under the common law of landlord–tenant relationships, withholding rent was not allowed for any reason. Today, in jurisdictions that have adopted specific landlord–tenant legislation, withholding rent or a rent strike is sometimes allowed.

Rent strikes are seen in "slumlord" situations where the landlord refuses to maintain the property and basic needs such as heat, water, and electricity are deficient, or life-threatening conditions, such as rat infestation, exist. Tenants are allowed to withhold rent from the landlord but are required to pay the rent into the court for disbursement as the court may equitably decide.

In some cases, the tenant can claim *constructive eviction* and thus be relieved of the obligation to pay rent. In such cases, through the landlord's lack of care, the tenant has been evicted, for all practical purposes, because *enjoyment of the premises is not available*. This may happen when heat and water are not available to the tenant because of the landlord's lack of care or the landlord fails to perform certain repairs. To claim constructive eviction in most states, however, the tenant must actually vacate the premises while the conditions that make the premises uninhabitable still exist. The lease is terminated under the claim of constructive eviction. This is not an automatic right that the tenant can assume; it may have to be litigated.

Security Deposits

Most landlords require the tenant to deposit a certain *sum of money that will be refunded at the end of the lease* based upon the condition of the premises. This **security deposit** often is negotiated as one month's rent. The money is intended for repair of only that damage the tenant causes beyond ordinary wear and tear, and the landlord is not to use it for basic cleaning and repainting. However, the landlord is allowed to charge the tenant a separate sum for cleaning and repainting if both parties agree. The security deposit usually must be held separate from the landlord's personal funds in a trust account. In some states the landlord is to pay interest to the tenant on the monies held as deposits.

At the end of a lease, the landlord is to refund the security deposit or provide to the tenant an itemized list of the damages (and cost) repaired beyond ordinary wear and tear.

Because of landlords' abuses in using and not returning security deposits, some states passed legislation limiting the amount of deposit and setting a deadline for returning the deposit or mailing the itemized repair statement to the tenant. The tenant must provide the landlord with a forwarding mailing address in writing to enable the landlord to comply with the law. If the landlord does not comply with the law, the tenant typically can recover in court the total deposit, court costs, and attorney fees.

Termination and Eviction Remedies

A lease may terminate in a variety of ways. The simplest way is for the lease term to expire. At expiration of the lease, if proper notice to terminate the lease was given and no renewal agreement is reached, the duties and rights of the landlord and tenant terminate. The tenant vacates the premises, and possession reverts to the landlord.

The landlord and tenant also can mutually agree to cancel a lease prior to expiration of the term. Mutual cancellation also terminates the parties' duties and rights. Possession reverts to the landlord. Cancellation of the lease, sometimes by mutual agreement, occurs after a breach of the lease by either party.

The lease also can be terminated by the landlord's evicting the tenant. This can occur during the term of the lease if the tenant breaches the agreement—for example, by failing to pay rent. Eviction also can occur *after the lease agreement expires if the tenant fails or refuses to vacate the premises.* At this point, the tenant is called a **holdover tenant**, and the landlord requests ouster of the tenant and his or her belongings and return of possession of the premises. In some cases, the landlord requests a landlord's lien on the tenant's belongings as security for payment of rent owed. This type of lien on personal property falls under the Uniform Commercial Code (UCC); thus, reference to the local statute is necessary.

Eviction is a *legal action in the court system for removal of the tenant and his or her belongings and a return of possession of the premises to the landlord.* Eviction is different from self-help whereby the landlord physically removes the tenant and his or her belongings from the premises or takes action to prevent tenant access to the premises. This is a violation of the common law by the landlord. Self-help is not allowed.

The timetable for eviction proceedings and the evidentiary requirements to prove right to eviction are governed by local court rules. A landlord seeking eviction is well-advised to hire an attorney to handle an eviction proceeding or to obtain a copy of the court rules and forms to assure compliance.

PUTTING IT TO WORK

In some states, a property manager may handle an eviction proceeding for the owner; in other states, this is prohibited as it constitutes the unauthorized practice of law without a license. Interested property managers should check with state law as to whether they can represent the owner and file for the eviction.

A lease also can terminate if the tenant abandons the premises and the landlord reenters to accept return of possession of the premises. This is similar to cancellation of the lease. Upon the tenant's abandonment, the landlord does not have to accept return of the premises; instead, he or she can pursue the tenant for rent under the lease. If the landlord does accept return of the premises, he or she may still pursue the tenant for lost rent under the old lease. The landlord must use his or her best efforts to re-rent the premises and minimize the lost rent. This is called *mitigating damages*.

A lease agreement typically does not terminate upon the death of the landlord or the tenant. The type of leasehold existing between the landlord and tenant determines whether the lease survives at death of a party. These leaseholds are discussed next. The lease agreement does not terminate upon a landlord's selling the premises. The new owner is bound by the terms of the lease.

LEASEHOLD (NONFREEHOLD) ESTATES

Nonfreehold estates or leaseholds were discussed initially in Chapter 2, in conjunction with the bundle of rights in ownership of real estate. These estates are less than a lifetime. Leasehold (rental) estates are created by a contract providing contractual rights and duties to both parties, as discussed earlier in this chapter. Leasehold estates provide possession, but not title (ownership), to the tenant. The owner retains the title and the right of reversion of possession upon termination of the lease. The relationship of landlord and tenant exists between the parties. These estates may be called estates, tenancies, or leaseholds and are more fully described below as well as illustrated in Figure 13.2.

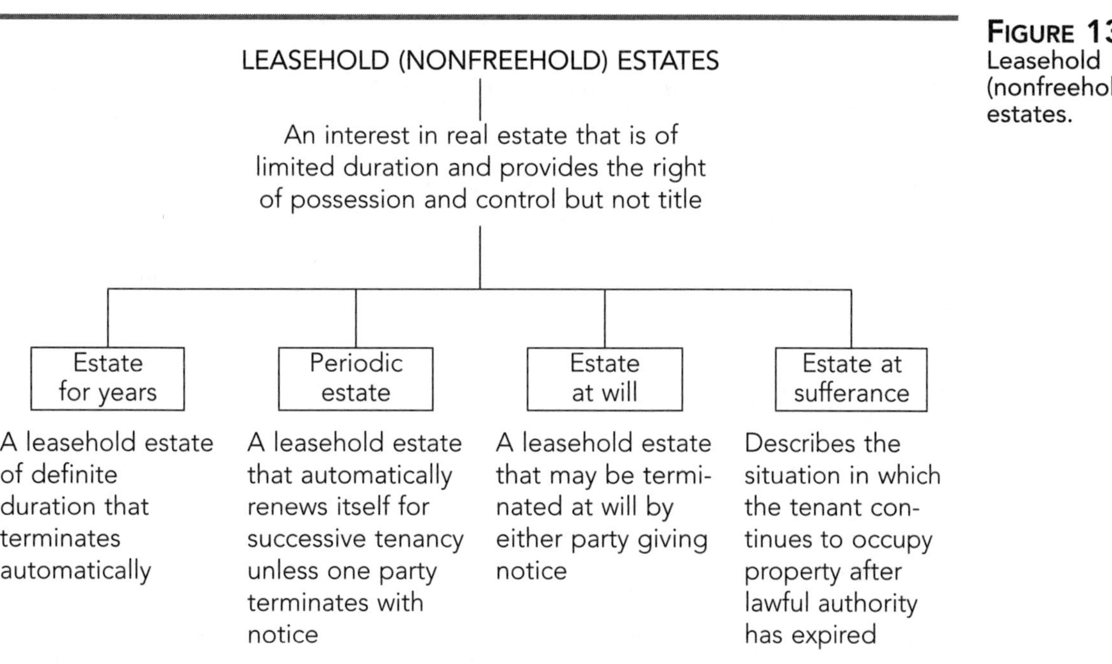

FIGURE 13.2 Leasehold (nonfreehold) estates.

Estate for Years

The key feature of the estate, tenancy, or leasehold for years is that it exists for only a fixed period of time. The term "years" is misleading in that the estate does not have to be in effect for a year or more but simply for a fixed period, which can be as short as a week or even one day. At the end of that stated time, the estate (rental agreement) terminates automatically without any need for either party to give notice to the other. If any uncertainty exists about the duration of the lease, it is not an estate for years.

The Statutes of Frauds of many states require that if this estate lasts more than one full year, the lease must be in writing to be valid. If a property is sold with a tenant in possession at the time of sale, the purchaser will have to honor the lease. At the death of either the landlord or the tenant, heirs of the deceased party are bound by the terms of the lease. The lease is considered to be inheritable because the obligations and rights of the lease pass to the estate or heirs of the decedent.

Periodic Estate (Estate from Year-to-Year)

The estate, tenancy, or leasehold from year-to-year is commonly known as a periodic tenancy. The term "year-to-year" is misleading in that the estate does not have to be in effect for one year or more. The period can be a week, a month, or any other negotiated time period. The key feature of a **periodic lease** is that it *automatically renews itself for another period at the end of each period unless one party gives notice to the other* at the prescribed time prior to the end of the lease. Notice is usually one period. For longer periodic leases (year-to-year), the notice would likely be 30 to 90 days. This notice period may be one to three months, depending upon the state in which the property is located. For example, if the required notice period is one month and the parties enter the last 30 days of the lease without notifying the other of any change, a new lease is created automatically for another period at the same terms. At the death of either the landlord or the tenant, heirs of the deceased party are bound by terms of the lease, including giving notice if the heirs wish to terminate.

Estate at Will

In the estate at will, duration of the term is completely unknown at the time the estate is created, because either party may terminate the lease simply by giving notice to the other party. The duration is open-ended. Statutes often require that notice of termination be given at least 30 days before the date upon which termination is to be effective. This type of leasehold is typical in a casual arrangement, such as a family setting in which a parent rents to an adult child. At the death of either the landlord or the tenant, this leasehold terminates. This differs from the estate for years and the periodic lease.

Estate at Sufferance

An estate at sufferance is not an estate that the parties voluntarily establish. This term is used simply to describe the rights of a tenant who was originally in lawful possession of another's property but refuses to leave after his right to possession terminates. This might be upon termination of any of the three previously discussed leases. The term "estate at sufferance" differentiates between the tenant at sufferance, who originally was in lawful possession of the property, and someone who has been on the property illegally from the beginning (trespasser). The estate at sufferance continues until the property owner brings a legal action to evict the person wrongfully holding over or until the one holding over vacates voluntarily. During this period, the occupier is called a tenant at sufferance. A tenant at sufferance is not a trespasser. The legal action to remove a tenant at sufferance is eviction (suit of possession), not an action in trespass.

Putting It to Work

Rights and duties of the parties regarding notice, termination, and inheritance are determined first by which one of the four leaseholds exists. The difference between the leaseholds is not in how long they last but, rather, in the agreement as to when and how termination is established. The termination may be at a fixed date (estate for years), at the end of a recurrent period (periodic estate), or open-ended (estate at will).

Holdover Clause

Many leases have a clause prediting and addressing the possibility of a tenant's failure to vacate upon the expiration of an estate for years. Such a clause is called a **holdover clause**. *This usually results in the extended tenancy being treated as a periodic estate.* In commercial leases, a holdover clause may have with it a severe penalty in the absence of renegotiation such as a doubling or tripling of the rent.

Types of Leases

Gross and Net Leases

The two primary classifications of leases, based on arrangement of payment of expenses of the rental property, are gross lease and net lease. A **gross lease** provides for *the owner (lessor) to pay all expenses*, such as real property taxes, owner's insurance, liability insurance, and maintenance. In a **net lease**, *the tenant (lessee) pays some or all of the expenses*. Sometimes the net lease is referred to as net, double net, or triple net, depending upon how many property expenses the tenant pays. Certain other expenses of the property, such as income taxes, depreciation, and mortgage payments, are not considered operating expenses. These are the owner's personal expenses, not expenses of the building.

Variations of the standard lease are discussed next. Any of these variations can be either gross or net. The arrangement for paying property expenses is the determining factor of gross or net leases.

Graduated (Step) Lease

A **graduated lease** is one in which the *rental amount changes from period to period* over the lease term. The lease contract specifies the change in rental amount, which usually is an increase in stair-step fashion. This type of lease could be utilized for a new business tenant whose income is expected to increase with time.

"Escalated" Lease

An **escalated lease**, usually a gross lease, *provides for rental changes at agreed-upon intervals, in proportion to changes in the lessor's cost of ownership and operation of the property*. As the lessor's obligations for the real property taxes and operating expenses change, the lease rent changes in specified proportions.

Index Lease

In an **index lease**, the *rental amount changes at agreed-upon intervals, in proportion to changes in the government cost of living index or some other index* agreed to by the parties.

Fixed Lease

A **fixed lease** is one in which the *rental amount remains constant during the term of the lease*. This is sometimes called a flat lease.

Reappraisal Lease

With a **reappraisal lease**, *changes in rental amount are based on changes in property value, as demonstrated by periodic reappraisals of the property*. These appraisals may occur at three- or five-year intervals in the case of a long-term lease. The rent changes a specified percentage of the previous year's rent as spelled out in the lease.

Percentage Lease

Many retail commercial leases are percentage leases. A **percentage lease** has *a base rent plus an additional monthly rent that is a percentage of the lessee's gross sales*. Most commercial leases in cases where the lessee is using the property to conduct a retail business are percentage leases. This is especially true of shopping malls. The percentage lease provides the lessor with a guaranteed monthly rental plus the opportunity to participate in the lessee's sales volume on a percentage basis.

Ground Lease

A **ground lease** is a *lease of unimproved land*, usually for construction purposes. The ground lease normally contains a provision that the lessee will construct a building on the land. Ownership of the land and improvements is separated. The ground lease is typically a long-term lease to allow the lessee sufficient time to recoup the cost of improvements. This type of lease also is typically a net lease in that the lessee is required to maintain the improvements, pay the property taxes, and pay the expenses of the property.

Oil and Gas Leases

In oil and gas leases, the land owner usually receives a one-time lease payment in exchange for giving the oil and gas company the right to drill for oil or gas for a long period of time. Sometimes the owner is compensated with a percentage of the revenues. If no drilling occurs but the oil and gas company wishes to continue the lease, it typically pays a small flat monthly or annual fee. If no drilling occurs and the company does not make any further payments, the lease expires and terminates.

Sale and Leaseback

A **sale and leaseback** is a *transaction wherein a property owner sells a property to an investor and the investor agrees to lease back the property to the seller immediately.* This type of transaction usually is used by an owner of business property who wishes to free up capital invested in the real estate and still retain possession and control of the property under a lease.

The motivation of a sale and leaseback transaction for the owner/tenant may also be based on income tax benefits. Depreciation, capital gains, deduction of rent, and operating expenses are all affected by the sale and leaseback decision.

IMPORTANT POINTS

1. A lease is created by contract between the owner of property and the tenant. The landlord or owner is the lessor; the tenant is the lessee.
2. The landlord and tenant are bound by contractual rights and obligations created by the lease agreement.
3. The transfer of the entire remaining term of a lease by the lessee is an assignment. A transfer of part of the lease term with a reversion to the lessee is a subletting.
4. In a lease of residential property, the landlord has the duty to provide habitable premises to the tenant.
5. The tenant has a duty to maintain and return the premises to the landlord, at expiration of the lease, in the same condition as at the beginning of the lease, ordinary wear and tear excepted.
6. The tenant can make a claim of constructive eviction when the premises become uninhabitable because of the landlord's lack of maintenance (failure to maintain habitability). A claim of constructive eviction will terminate the lease.
7. Leases are terminated by (a) expiration of lease term, (b) mutual agreement, (c) breach of condition, (d) actual (court-ordered) eviction, or (e) constructive eviction. The law does not favor actual eviction.
8. Leases are nonfreehold estates. The four leasehold estates are estate for years, periodic estate, estate at will, and estate at sufferance. A tenant at sufferance is not a trespasser.

9. The two main classifications of leases are gross lease and net lease. Under a gross lease, the landlord pays the real property taxes, insurance, and maintenance of the property. Under a net lease, the tenant pays some or all of these expenses.
10. Types of lease include the graduated lease, escalated lease, index lease, fixed lease, reappraisal lease, percentage lease, ground lease, and oil and gas leases.

How Would You Respond?

One of your residential clients has decided to open her own business and asks you to help her find some space and to help negotiate the lease. She knows her business well, but knows very little about leasing. You get some help from your commerical division manager in the office, who opens your eyes to a brand-new real estate vocabulary. Outline some of the differences for your client in some of these choices and features.

1. A gross lease versus a net lease?
2. Graduated lease versus fixed lease?
3. Estate for years versus month-to-month?
4. Holdover clause?
5. Percentage lease?
6. Security deposits?

Review Questions

Answers to these questions are found in the *Answer Key* section at the back of the book.

1. A transaction in which a lessee transfers the remainder of a lease term without reversion is a(n):
   a. assignment
   b. option to renew
   c. sandwich lease
   d. sublease

2. Which of the following leaseholds has the characteristic of a definite termination date agreed upon by the parties?
   a. periodic estate
   b. estate for years
   c. estate at will
   d. estate a sufferance

3. Under an indexed lease with first-year rent of $700 per month, inflation during the first year is 7%. The second year rental rate will be:
   a. $700 per month
   b. $707 per month
   c. $749 per month
   d. none of the above

4. When a lease terminates with no right to renew and the tenant fails to vacate, the tenant is holding a(n):
   a. estate for years
   b. estate at will
   c. estate at suffereance
   d. periodic estate

5. According to the Statute of Frauds, an oral lease for five years is:
   a. enforceable
   b. unenforceable
   c. assignable
   d. renewable

6. A lease with term from January 1 to July 1 of the same year is a(n):
   a. estate for years
   b. estate at will
   c. estate at sufferance
   d. periodic estate

7. The right of the lessee to uninterrupted use of the leased premises is called:
   a. conveyance
   b. quiet enjoyment
   c. quiet commencement
   d. letting the premises

8. If cost of maintenance is increasing and rents are increasing, a fixed lease arrangement for a long term is advantageous to:
   a. the tenant
   b. the landlord
   c. both landlord and tenant
   d. neither landlord nor tenant

9. Mr. A buys a building owned by Mrs. X. Mrs. X has leased the building to ABC Company for seven years. Mr. A must:
   a. renegotiate the lease with ABC
   b. evict ABC to get possession
   c. share the space with ABC
   d. honor the lease agreement

10. Which of the following lease arrangements is designed to allow the lessee to receive her capital investment from the leased property?
    a. percentage lease
    b. index lease
    c. step-up lease
    d. sale and leaseback

11. A lease from period to period will not be terminated by:
    a. mutual agreement of the lessor and lessee
    b. eviction by the court
    c. death of the lessor
    d. abandonment by lessee and acceptance by lessor

12. When a tenant, under a valid lease, gives up possession of the leased premises to the landlord prior to expiration of the lease, it is called:
    a. novation
    b. abatement
    c. abandonment
    d. renunciation

13. A lease that provides for an adjustment in rent to cover the lessor's operating expenses is called:
    a. escalated
    b. accelerated
    c. sufferance
    d. gross lease

14. Under a residential lease, if the lessor does not provide habitable premises, the lessee can claim:
    a. eviction
    b. constructive eviction
    c. habitability damages
    d. mitigation of damages

15. Annual sales of a retail business are $240,000. A percentage lease entitles the landlord to $825 per month base rent plus 4% of gross sales. The monthly rent will be:
    a. $825
    b. $858
    c. $1,625
    d. none of the above

16. A lease with a fixed low base rent plus an additional amount based upon gross receipts of the lessee is a(n):
    a. percentage lease
    b. gross lease
    c. net lease
    d. escalated lease

17. Who is the final tenant in the sale and leaseback?
    a. seller
    b. buyer
    c. lessor
    d. mortgagor

18. Under a lease, the reversionary interest is owned by the:
    a. lessor
    b. lessee
    c. tenant for years
    d. life tenant

19. At the death of the landlord under an estate for years, the lease is:
    a. terminated
    b. expired
    c. not affected
    d. cancelled

20. A tenant has vacated ten months prior to the expiration of his lease. The landlord has made no attempt to re-rent the space. The landlord has failed to:
    a. properly evict the tenant unde the law
    b. constructively evict the tenant
    c. mitigate damages
    d. establish quiet enjoyment

POSSIBLE RESPONSES TO "HOW WOULD YOU RESPOND?"

1. The issue here is who pays which of the operating expenses, the landlord or the tenant. How much is allocated to each?
2. Does the business need the "jump start" of the lower rent in a graduated lease's earlier years?
3. Is the business strong and established to take the risk of a fixed term in the estate for years? Or does the flexibility of the month-to-month lease afford more security for the new, insecure business?
4. If there is a fixed term, how does a holdover clause provide for any automatic renewal of any portion of the lease terms and at what rate? Or does the holdover clause financially penalize the tenant and therefore force renegotiation?
5. In the case of a retail center, does the landlord expect a percentage of the profits? If so, how should this be demonstrated?
6. Financially, security deposits can be very burdensome to a fledging business. Moreover, there is no deduction for this and usually no interest paid on the deposit.

CHAPTER 14

IMPORTANT TERMINOLOGY

anchor stores
capital reserve budget
coinsurance clause
corrective maintenance
endorsement
extended coverage
face amount
fire insurance policy
homeowner's policy
homeowner's warranty policy
insurable interest
management agreement
management proposal
operating budget
package policy
preventative maintenance
property management
property management report
property manager
resident manager
risk management
stabilized budget
standard fire policy
strip center

Property Management and Insurance

In This Chapter Property management is one of a number of specializations within the real estate industry. A **property manager** is *a person who manages properties for owners as their agent.* In acting as agent, the property manager is a fiduciary and therefore owes all the obligations imposed by the law of agency to each owner-principal. The discussion in this chapter centers on the functions and purpose of property managers. Property insurance and homeowner's warranty (HOW) policies also are explained.

The Basics of Property Management

By applying real estate knowledge and expertise, a property manager strives to produce the greatest net return possible for the owner. He or she is responsible for protecting the owner's investments. Because the property manager acts as the owner's agent in managing and, typically, renting, leasing, and perhaps selling the property, the property manager must have a real estate license. (A few states provide for limited exceptions to this requirement.) The property manager also must have comprehensive, specialized training to be able to satisfactorily perform the functions expected under the typical contract with the property owner. Some of this knowledge may be acquired through courses provided by the Institute of Real Estate Management, an affiliate of the National Association of REALTORS®. After completing this program, individuals receive the professional designation Certified Property Manager (CPM). Other associations for property managers include the National Apartment Association, the National Association of Residential Property Managers, the Building Owners and Managers Institute, and the Community Association Institute.

A **resident manager** is *a person living on the premises who is a salaried employee of the owner.* In some states, this person is not required to have a real estate license if he or she is employed directly by the owner rather than a managing broker.

Expert management is often needed for income property to be a profitable investment. Competent **property management** provides a *comprehensive, orderly program, on a continuing basis, analyzing all investment aspects of a property to ensure a financially successful project.* The need for property management has increased in recent years as a result of the trend toward absentee ownership by investors and larger and more complicated properties in need of management. As a result, many brokerage firms have separate staffs of property managers.

Types of Properties and Management

Many different types of properties can benefit from real estate management services, including (a) residential property management, which includes apartments, condominiums, single-family homes, and vacation property; (b) retail or commercial property management, which includes offices, small retail stores, office condominiums, and large shopping malls; (c) industrial property management, including industrial parks and industrial warehouses; (d) farm property management; and (e) management by homeowners' association, which provides physical property management.

Residential Property Management

Residential property includes apartments, single-family housing, multi-family housing, condominiums, vacation houses, and mobile home parks. The concerns of a property manager when selecting tenants for residential properties include credit history of tenants, past landlord references, and employment status. The manager also must be involved with maintenance and repair of the premises and eviction of tenants. The manager has to be in tune with the local housing market.

Putting It to Work

Although the manager's function is to represent the owner in most situations regarding the property (with tenants, repair people, city officials, and so on), the manager may not be able to represent the owner in court proceedings such as evictions. These actions may require an attorney. Consult your local law.

Retail Property Management

Most retail properties managed by a property manager are in strip centers, neighborhood shopping centers, and regional malls. A **strip center** consists of *more than four stores located conveniently and with easy access to a main roadway*. Neighborhood shopping centers usually are made up of several buildings grouped together with common parking and common access. Regional malls typically are under one roof and include *several nationally recognized stores* called **anchor stores**. A manager of these properties must select tenants suitable for this type of center. The manager also must be aware of the desires of retail tenants as to noncompetition from like tenants, group or common advertising, common area maintenance, and security.

Industrial Property Management

Based upon the desired economic growth of many cities and towns, industrial developments and industrial parks are common. These are often handled by a professional manager. Property managers must be aware of the transportation systems and utility services available in the area. In addition, they must be knowledgeable about tax rates, tax incentives, available labor force, commercial financing, and community services.

Farm Property Management

Farm property can consist of grain crops, animal production, dairy production, or a combination of these. Besides understanding accounting methods, the property manager must be familiar with crop production, commodity prices, soil types, environmental controls, and soil conservation. As more and more farms are owned by corporations, the property manager becomes indispensable.

Management by Homeowners' Associations

Although not always involved with leasing or renting, a manager for a condominium, townhome, or PUD association is tremendously involved in the physical management of property for owners and occupants. The responsibility begins with budgeting expenses and collecting assessments and progresses to coordinating common facility maintenance, landscaping, security, and enforcement of the association's regulations.

THE OWNER–MANAGER RELATIONSHIP

Authority

The owner–manager relationship is established and defined by a **management agreement**. This contract creates *an agency relationship wherein the owner is the principal and the property manager is the agent* for the purposes specified in the agreement. This relationship imposes the same serious fiduciary duty as demanded of agents toward their principals in the sale of a home.

Provisions of the typical property management agreement include:

1. Inception date and names of the parties.
2. Property location and description of the premises.
3. Duration of the agency.
4. Method of termination by either party.
5. Agent's fee (a base fee plus a percentage of the rent actually collected is common).
6. Agent's authority.
7. Agent's duties.
8. Owner's duties.
9. Handling of security deposits, rents, and expenses by agent.
10. Execution of the agreement by owner and agent.

The authority of the manager comes from and must be explicitly set out in the management agreement. The management agreement creates a general agency and should be in writing. This agreement creates the responsibility in the property manager to realize the highest return on the property while obeying the owner's instructions and the laws of agency and landlord/tenant relations.

Duties

One of the first duties of a prospective property manager is to submit a **management proposal** to the property owner, *setting forth the commitments of the manager* if employed by the owner.

A typical proposal includes:

1. A complete description of the land and all improvements.
2. A listing of all maintenance required and existing curable obsolescence.
3. Information regarding maintenance records and accounting procedures the manager will use.

4. Schedules of property inspections and owner conferences.
5. A thorough operating budget, capital improvement budget, and stabilized budget (all discussed later).
6. A document citing the management fee.

Fee

The property manager's fee is negotiated between the property owner and the manager. It commonly consists of a base fee and/or a percentage of the rents actually collected.

Principal Functions of Property Managers

Although renting space, collecting rents, and paying expenses are basic functions of property managers, their functions and responsibilities go far beyond these activities. In essence, the property manager's overall responsibilities are (a) to produce the highest possible net operating income from the property, and (b) to maintain and increase the value of the principal's investment. The property manager fulfills these responsibilities by performing the specific activities discussed next.

Rental Schedule

In setting the rental rates, the property manager must be aware of the owner's goals for return on investment, as well as the current market for rental rates. Consideration must be given to current rates in like properties. Supply and demand for rental properties and present vacancy rates also must be considered. Adjustments in rental rates should be made only after a careful survey and analysis of the factors affecting rental.

Putting It to Work

Many owners justify increasing rents by citing increased expense. In fact, this is often the only allowable increase for rent-controlled units. In a free rental market, however, rental rates are totally independent of expense level. An owner may want to raise rent 12 percent because expenses have increased by that percentage. Tenants, however, may not accept the increase if comparable lower-cost space is available elsewhere.

Budget

Before rental of a project can be organized and structured, an operating budget, capital reserve budget, and stabilized budget should be established. The budgets are always subject to adjustments, particularly in the first months of a project. The **operating budget** is *an annual budget and includes only the items of income and expense expected for week-to-week operation*. The **capital reserve budget** is *a projected budget over the economic life of the improvements of the property* for variable expenses such as repairs, decorating, remodeling, and capital improvements. The **stabilized**

budget is *a forecast of income and expenses as may be reasonably projected over an intermediate term*, typically five years.

PUTTING IT TO WORK

The budgeting practices described above are common, expected, and necessary on larger projects. With smaller buildings, however, budgets may be subject to extreme fluctuations as expenses are not always predictable. For example, if three of four air conditioners fail in a single year in a four-plex, this could easily exhaust the typical repair budget.

Marketing

The manager's strategy of marketing available rental space is shaped by the present demand for space, newness of the project, and the tenant selection process. In designing and implementing any marketing activity, managers must comply with all federal, state, and local fair housing laws.

Handling Funds

The property manager collects or attempts to collect all monies owed to the owner. Any monies collected are to be held in a trust account for the benefit of the owner. The only monies taken from the account are to be used for expenses in the property management budget. In handling security deposits, the property manager must comply with local laws with regard to collecting and retaining security deposits.

PUTTING IT TO WORK

State license laws typically have specific requirements regarding handling rents, deposits, and expenses. The broker must be scrupulous in maintaining records and must avoid any commingling or conversion.

Legal Actions

If the property manager is careful in selecting tenants, legal actions for eviction and collection of rents will be minimal. Effective property managers attempt to resolve any disputes before they institute a lawsuit. If a lawsuit is necessary, the property manager's file must show his or her compliance with all terms of any lease agreement with the tenant.

In filing a suit, the property manager must be familiar with local court rules and procedure. Some courts require that the property manager be represented by an attorney. If so, the property manager should consult with legal counsel prior to any court date to assure that any witnesses will attend and that all exhibits for the hearing are available.

Maintenance

One of the most important functions of a property manager is to supervise physical property maintenance. Efficient maintenance requires accurate analysis of the building's needs, coupled with consideration of the costs of any work done. Maintenance can include preventative maintenance, corrective maintenance, and construction.

Preventative maintenance requires a *periodic check of mechanical equipment* on the premises, to *minimize excessive wear and tear from improper operation*. An example of preventative maintenance is changing the air filters on air conditioners and furnaces.

Corrective maintenance is the *work performed to fix a nonfunctioning item* that a tenant has reported. An example of this type of maintenance is the repair of a leaking faucet.

Construction is done after money has been budgeted for remodeling, interior redecorating, or new capital improvements. Renovation often increases a property's desirability and thus can lead to increased income.

Records

The property manager should provide a *periodic* (usually monthly) *accounting of all funds received and disbursed.* This accounting is called a **property management report.** It contains detailed information of all receipts and expenditures for the period covered (plus the year-to-date) and relates each item to the operating budget for the period. In addition to the reports to the owner, the manager should maintain whatever records are necessary for compliance with local laws on fair housing, security deposits, trust accounts, and so on.

Americans with Disabilities Act

Property managers of commercial facilities and public accommodations will be required to comply with the Americans with Disabilities Act (ADA). Effective January 1993, the ADA states that all such facilities must have barrier-free design. The law does not apply to residential use property or to properties already built prior to 1993. However, new commercial construction and modified properties will have to be in compliance. For more information on ADA, see Chapter 12.

Basic Insurance Concepts and Terminology

The modern term **risk management** *embodies the concern for controlling and limiting risk in property ownership.* Ownership and use of real estate necessarily entails risk, but the questions are: How is the risk to be controlled? Can some risk be transferred by means of an insurance policy? The manager should find a competent insurance agent who is familiar with the type of property to be insured. Written specifications by the manager to competing agents will ensure comparable quotes for consideration. The insured property will be the property being managed. The person or entity insured will be the person or entity who owns the property.

Property Insurance

Most insurance policies in the United States are based on the New York **standard fire policy** form as revised in 1943. This **fire insurance policy** *indemnifies the insured against loss caused by fire.* If the insured wishes to have protection against losses from other hazards, he or she must obtain an extended coverage endorsement to the fire policy. This endorsement, in the form of a rider attached to the fire policy, requires an additional premium. The **extended coverage** endorsement *usually includes coverage for losses resulting from hail, explosion, wind storm, aircraft, civil commotion, vehicles, and smoke from friendly fires*. A fire confined to the place where it is intended to be, such as a fireplace or furnace, is a friendly fire; otherwise it is a hostile fire.

Liability Insurance

Public liability insurance covers the risks an owner assumes when the public enters the premises. Payments under this coverage are to pay claims for medical expenses incurred by the person injured on the property as a result of the landlord's negligence.

Flood Insurance

If improved property is located within a flood-prone zone, a federally insured or guaranteed loan program will not approve loans on such property without flood insurance being obtained. This insurance is available through selected insurance carriers in local areas or the National Flood Insurance Program. Most lenders have access to flood zone maps to determine whether a property falls within this definition.

Package Policy

A **package policy** is available to homeowners. This form of policy, called a **homeowner's policy**, provides *coverage for the structure and its contents* (casualty insurance). A homeowner's policy provides coverage against loss by fire, wind storm, hail, dust, surface waters, waves, frozen plumbing, vandalism, and industrial smoke damage, and provides personal financial liability coverage to the policyholder for personal injury and property damage caused by the policyholder.

Standardized Homeowner's Insurance Policies

Homeowner's policies are identified as *HO-1, HO-2, HO-3, HO-4, HO-5, and HO-6*. An HO-4 is a tenant's policy, and HO-6 is designed for condominiums and cooperatives. HO-1, HO-2, HO-3, and HO-5 cover owners of single-family dwellings.

Every hazard insurance policy must contain a description of the insured property. The street address usually is adequate, although some insurers require a full legal description. Specific provisions of the various homeowner's policies are:

HO-1 "Named perils." Perils covered are damage or loss from fire at the premises.

HO-2 "Broad form." Coverage extends to loss or damage as a result of fire, vandalism, malicious mischief, wind, hail, aircraft, riot, explosion, and smoke.

HO-3 A special "all risk" policy. It covers loss for damage resulting from anything not specifically excluded from coverage.

HO-4 "Tenant's broad form." Its coverage is like HO-2 except it applies only to the tenant's contents at the premises.

HO-5 A special "all risk" policy offering automatic replacement cost for contents and dwelling.

HO-6 Like a tenant's broad form but applies to condominium owners and cooperative owners and covers their contents. (The structure would be insured by the association.)

The HO-2, 3, 4, 5, and 6 are all package policies that include medical payments coverage and personal liability coverage for negligence.

Selected Legal Issues

Insurable Interest

To be eligible for insurance coverage of any type, the insured must have a *legitimate financial interest*, known as an **insurable interest**, in the property. In the absence of an insurable interest, the policy is void. Examples of people having an insurable interest are buyer and seller in a contract of sale or land contract, the owner, owner of a partial interest, trustee, receiver, life tenant, mortgagor, and mortgagee. A mortgagee is an individual, a group of individuals, or an insurable organization with interest in the property based upon lending money. The mortgagee usually requires, in the mortgage, that the borrower maintain adequate hazard insurance coverage on the property to satisfy the debt in the case of destruction. The policy is issued in the names of both the mortgagee and the mortgagor. The policy section that names the lender is called mortgagee clause or additional insured. The policy protects the mortgagee up to the amount of the principal balance owed on the loan if within the coverage limits the policy provides. In the event of partial loss, the insurance company pays mortgagors so they may make the appropriate repairs. In the event of total loss, the mortgagee is paid first up to the amount of the mortgage debt still outstanding and the mortgagor receives any surplus.

Coinsurance

Most homeowner's insurance policies contain a **coinsurance clause** *requiring the property owner to insure for a face amount that is at least 80 percent of the property value*. **Face amount**, typically set out on the first page of the policy, is the *maximum amount of coverage specified in the policy and sets the insurance company's maximum liability*. Some policies require 90 percent or 100 percent but 80 percent is the typical requirement in policies insuring an owner-occupied residence. If the coverage is for less than 80 percent of value, the policy will pay only part of the loss in proportion to the percentage of value insured by the policy owner.

For example: A structure is worth \$100,000, the coinsurance clause is 80 percent, and the insurance carried is only \$60,000. In the event of a partial loss of \$30,000, the insurance company's liability is only \$22,500. The amount of the insurance company's liability is calculated using the following formula:

$$\frac{\text{Insurance carried}}{\text{Insurance required}} \times \text{loss} = \text{Company's limit of liability}$$

$$\frac{\$60{,}000}{\$80{,}000} \times \$30{,}000 = \$22{,}500$$

If the loss had been \$80,000 or more, the insurance company's liability would be the amount of insurance carried. If the loss equals or exceeds the amount of insurance required by the coinsurance clause, the company pays the face amount of the policy. This is illustrated by the following example:

Value of structure	\$100,000
Insurance required (80%)	80,000

Insurance policy amount	60,000
Loss	90,000

$$\frac{\text{Insurance carried}}{\text{Insurance required}} \times \text{loss} = \text{Company's limit of liability}$$

$$\frac{\$60,000}{\$80,000} \times 90,000 = 67,500$$ but because the policy was for only $60,000, the company pays only $60,000

Because the loss equals or exceeds the amount of insurance required by the coinsurance clause, the insurance company pays the policy amount even though the requirement of the coinsurance clause is not met. In no event, however, will the policy pay an amount in excess of the amount of coverage specified in the policy.

Unoccupied Building Exclusion

Insurance coverage available on a property varies depending upon whether the premises are unoccupied or occupied. If occupied, the homeowner's coverages set out above apply. If unoccupied, the maximum coverage available is similar to the HO-1 "named perils." The premises are insured against loss from fire only at the premises.

PUTTING IT TO WORK

Many insurance policies cover vacant properties for a maximum of 30 days, after which time the coverage lapses. This should be brought to the attention of owners of a vacant house for sale.

Policy Assignment

Insurance policies generally are assignable with the written consent of the insurance company. Often a seller assigns his or her interest in a hazard insurance policy to a buyer of the property as of the date of closing, and the premium is prorated between buyer and seller. The assignment is not valid, however, without the *written consent of the insurer*. This consent typically is evidenced by the insurance company's **endorsement** to the policy, *changing the name of the insured*.

Homeowner's Warranty Policies

The **homeowner's warranty policy** *protects home buyers against certain defects in a house they purchase*. In the case of a new house, the builder may provide the policy. Typical policies extend a 1-year warranty against defective workmanship, a 10-year warranty against major structural defects, and a 2-year warranty against defects in mechanical and electrical systems. In the resale of an existing house, the seller may transfer the policy to the buyer if the warranty is still in effect. If the policy is no longer in force or if the house was never protected by a homeowner's warranty policy, policies are available through many insurance companies as well as many real estate brokerages. The premium usually is paid by the seller, who transfers the policy to the home buyer.

Several real estate franchise companies also provide warranties to purchasers. These buyer protection programs are attractive and effective marketing tools. The salesperson, seller, and buyer have to realize that these warranties are not coverage from "foundation to roof." Instead, the coverage has many exclusions of which the agent must be keenly aware in discussions with customers and clients. Overrepresenting the warranty's provisions can result in personal liability to the agent.

Putting It to Work

Generally, the builder's warranties regarding new homes are much more comprehensive than homeowner's warranties offered by third-party insurers on resale properties.

Important Points

1. Property managers are agents engaged in the management of property for others and, therefore, must have a real estate license (with exceptions in some states).
2. The management agreement is a contract in which a property owner employs a property manager to act as his or her agent.
3. The property manager's basic responsibilities are (a) to produce the best possible net operating income from the property, and (b) to maintain and increase the value of the principal's investment.
4. Properties that may require management are condominiums, cooperatives, apartments, single-family rental houses, mobile home parks, office buildings, shopping malls, industrial property, and farms.
5. Property managers fulfill their basic responsibilities by formulating a management plan, soliciting tenants, leasing space, collecting rent, hiring and training employees, maintaining good tenant relations, providing for adequate maintenance, protecting tenants, maintaining adequate insurance, keeping adequate records, and auditing and paying bills.
6. The property management report is a periodic accounting provided by a property manager to the property owner.
7. A fire insurance policy indemnifies the insured against loss by fire. Protection from losses by other hazards may be obtained by an extended coverage endorsement.
8. Package policies, called homeowner's policies, provide all the usual protections in one policy. These policies are available to both homeowners and renters.
9. To be eligible for insurance, the applicant must have an insurable interest in the property, such as buyer and seller in a contract, owner, part owner, trustee, receiver, tenant, mortgagor, and mortgagee.
10. Every hazard insurance policy contains a coinsurance clause requiring the property owner to insure the property for at least 80 percent of the property value to recover up to the face amount of the policy in the event of a partial loss. If the loss equals or exceeds the amount of coverage required by the coinsurance clause, however, the insurance company will pay the policy amount even though the requirement of the coinsurance clause is not met.
11. Insurance policies usually are assignable with the written consent of the insurance company. The consent is evidenced by an endorsement to the policy.
12. Homeowner's warranty policies are available to purchasers of newly constructed houses and of existing houses. These policies insure against many, but not all, structural and mechanical defects.

How Would You Respond?

A client of yours who has bought six rentals from you in the last three years has just been transferred to Denver. He has been managing his own rentals until now. He has asked you not only to find him a tenant for his own home when he moves but to manage all seven properties now that he will be out of the area. You agree to do the management. What are some of the responsibilities and questions that will apply in this new area of property management?

Review Questions

Answers to these questions are found in the *Answer Key* section at the back of the book.

1. All of the following statements about property management are correct EXCEPT:
   a. property management is a specialized field within the real estate industry
   b. a property manager acts as an agent of the property owner
   c. the terms *property manager* and *resident manager* always have the same meaning
   d. a property manager is a fiduciary

2. A budget based on forecast of income and expense anticipated over a period of years is called a(n):
   a. stabilized budget
   b. targeted budget
   c. anticipated budget
   d. operating budget

3. When building occupancy reaches 98 percent, this tends to indicate that:
   a. rents should be lowered
   b. rents should be raised
   c. management is ineffective
   d. the building needs remodeling

4. An HO-4 insurance policy offers coverage for:
   a. condominium's contents
   b. cooperative contents
   c. tenant's contents
   d. owner's contents

5. Which of the following statements about hazard insurance policies is NOT correct?
   a. they are not assignable
   b. they contain a coinsurance clause
   c. there must be an insurable interest
   d. they protect only the person or persons named in the policy

6. If a home valued at $200,000 and insured for $120,000 by a policy with an 80 percent coinsurance clause suffers a loss of $175,000 from an insured hazard, what amount will the insurance company pay?
   a. $96,000
   b. $120,000
   c. $160,000
   d. $175,000

7. Which of the following identifies a policy insuring against loss caused by structural defects?
   a. fire and extended coverage
   b. HOW
   c. HO-1
   d. HO-6

8. A condominium building would be insured by:
   a. an HO-6 policy
   b. an HO-5 policy
   c. an HOW policy
   d. the association funded by the association dues

POSSIBLE RESPONSES TO "HOW WOULD YOU RESPOND?"

1. The management agreement
2. Compensation structure
3. Your arrangement with your broker
4. Handling the rents and deposits
5. Handling money for repairs
6. Being available to the tenants in the event of emergency
7. A power of attorney
8. Arranging for repairs and maintenance
9. Tenant screening
10. Collections
11. Evictions
12. Advertising

CHAPTER 15

Important Terminology

accelerated depreciation
adjusted basis
age-55-and-over exclusion
boot
capital gain
deductible expenses
depreciation
economic depreciation
fix-up expenses
gross operating income
income shelter
inheritance basis
installment sale
investment syndicate
like-kind property
multiple exchange
net operating income
opportunity cost
rollover rule
Starker exchange/Starker trust
straight-line depreciation
tax basis
tax-deferred exchange
tax depreciation
time value of money
unlike-kind property

Federal Income Taxation and Basic Principles of Real Estate Investment

IN THIS CHAPTER Although all real estate licensees must have basic knowledge and understanding of the federal income tax laws affecting real property, they must not give tax advice to buyers and sellers. Because each taxpayer's situation is different, only competent professional tax consultants who are familiar with the taxpayer's position should give advice of this nature. Real estate licensees should recommend that buyers and sellers seek this specialized expertise when appropriate. It is appropriate for an agent to recommend a professional if the client does not already have one.

This chapter presents the fundamentals of tax implications in the ownership and sale of a principal residence and business and investment property. It illustrates and explains the special tax benefits provided to owners and sellers of real property to enable you to understand these advantages.

In addition, a working knowledge of basic real estate investment principles allows licensees to better understand the needs of their clients. Such an introduction is provided in this chapter.

TAX REFORM ACT OF 1986 AND REVENUE RECONCILIATION ACT OF 1993

The Tax Reform Act (TRA) of 1986 brought some sweeping changes to the tax laws, a number of them less generous to the real estate industry than previous regulations. Although the top individual income tax rate was reduced from 50 percent to 28 percent, eliminating other favorable aspects of the code meant that certain real estate investors actually saw their taxes increase significantly.

The Revenue Reconciliation Act (RRA) of 1993 brought with it several changes, some that benefit the real estate industry and some that do not. The RRA eased passive activity loss restrictions for real estate professionals, but it also increased the maximum tax bracket on income to 39.6 percent.

Capital Gain

For example, the older laws provided for long-term **capital gain** treatment that allowed investors to exclude a portion of their gain (profit) on real estate investments from taxation on a qualifying transaction. The new law reduced this beneficial capital gain treatment. Under the TRA of 1986, an investor now pays a maximum of 28 percent on the entire profit.

PUTTING IT TO WORK

The tax code, and particularly the aspects that address real estate, have been "political footballs" over the years. During the last two decades, capital gains alone have been reduced, expanded, repealed, brought back, extended, and shortened. The situation regarding capital gain may well change again in the near future. Licensees should keep abreast of current federal and state tax laws.

Depreciation

Depreciation is a *deductible allowance from net income of property when arriving at taxable income*. Under the generous Tax Act of 1981, the Accelerated Cost Recovery System (ACRS) was established as an alternative to straight-line depreciation. Under **straight-line depreciation** a *taxpayer deducts equal amounts of a depreciable assets cost each year*. **Accelerated** (or front-loaded) **depreciation** meant that *more depreciation could be taken in early years, and less in later years*. Also, depreciation initially was taken over 15 years, and later modified to 18, then to 19 years. Under ACRS, the first-year depreciation on a $100,000 depreciable asset could have been as high as $12,000. After 1986, however, depreciation on real property has been allowed only on a straight-line basis. Under the TRA of 1986, the schedule is set at 27.5 years for residential property ($3,636 in this example), and 31.5 years for non-residential property ($3,175 in this example). The RRA of 1993 has stretched this out to 39 years for non-residential property ($2,564).

A purchase made under pre-1987 law, however, still uses those pre-1987 depreciation schedules. A purchase after 1986 uses the newer schedules that were in effect on the date of the purchase. The same taxpayer may have several different depreciation schedules for several different investment properties on the same tax return.

Passive Income

Further, under the TRA of 1986, any tax losses from investment property are allowable only to offset income from passive activities, called passive income.

A passive activity involves conducting any trade or business in which the taxpayer does not materially participate. A taxpayer will be considered materially participating if during a tax year one of the following tests is satisfied:

1. Taxpayer participates more than 500 hours.
2. Taxpayer is the only participant in the activity.
3. Taxpayer participates 100 hours, and no other participant has more hours involved.
4. Taxpayer participates materially for any 5 years in a 10-year period.
5. The activity is a personal service activity, such as health fields, engineering, architecture, accounting, and actuarial service.

If the taxpayer materially participates, the income derived is not passive income.

Passive losses cannot be used to offset active income, which is income from wages, interest, dividends, and so on, but can offset other passive income. If excess passive losses exist in any tax year, they may be carried over to later years and deducted then against passive income, or claimed when the asset is sold.

A limited exception to this rule applies to taxpayers with adjusted gross income of less than $100,000 who actively manage their own rental property. These taxpayers may shelter up to $25,000 of other passive income or active income. This exception begins to phase out when the taxpayer's adjusted gross income reaches $100,000 and is completely phased out at $150,000.

Pursuant to the RRA of 1993 certain taxpayers involved in real property trades or businesses are not subject to the passive activity rules including the $25,000 limitation. This allows these taxpayers to use unlimited rental losses against non-passive income.

To be eligible for this treatment the taxpayer must:

1. Materially participate and perform more than 50 percent of his or her personal services in real property trades or businesses, and
2. Perform more than 750 hours of service in the real property trades or businesses in which the individual materially participates.

Real property trades or businesses include development, redevelopment, construction, reconstruction, acquisition, conversion, rental, operation, management, leasing, or brokerage. Material participation requires that the taxpayer be involved in the operations of the activity on a regular and continuous basis. Limited partners cannot be considered material participants.

Consumer Tax Issues in Real Estate

Certain deductions for real property, such as most mortgage interest and property taxes, are maintained. These deductions apply to both a principal residence and a second home. Previous residential energy tax credits that expired at the end of 1985 were not reinstated in the new laws. Many consumers were dismayed to lose, also, favorite deductions for consumer interest, such as that on credit cards and automobile loans, as well as the very popular deduction for individual retirement accounts (IRAs). Applications of the new tax laws are discussed in the following sections.

Putting It to Work

As a result of lost deductions for consumer interest on cars and credit cards, many taxpayers are borrowing against the equity in their houses (which may be fully deductible) to pay off nondeductible interest debts. The risk in this, however, is that the home may be lost if payments are not made per the loan agreement; this risk is not typically associated with failure to pay monthly credit card installments per a credit agreement.

Tax Implications of Home Ownership

Interest and Taxes

The tax-deductible expenses involved in home ownership are mortgage interest (not principal) and ad valorem real property taxes paid to local taxing authorities. In addition, taxpayers who can deduct mortgage interest usually find it advantageous to itemize and take advantage of other tax-deductible expenses not associated with home ownership. The combination of mortgage interest and other itemized expenses provides greater tax relief than is available by taking the more modest standard deduction.

Let's assume a home buyer purchases a residence for $100,000 with a $10,000 down payment and finances the balance for 30 years at 8 percent interest. The monthly payment of principal and interest necessary to fully amortize the remaining $90,000 over a 30-year period is $660.39. During the first 12 months of loan payments, the borrower will pay a total of $7,172.83 in mortgage interest. This interest is available as a tax deduction for the year in which it is paid. Negative amortization, which reflects unpaid but accrued interest added to the principal balance, is not deductible. Prepayment penalties charged on the early payoff of a loan are deductible as interest.

Rollover Rule or Deferred Reporting

The federal tax laws provide that *a gain realized from the sale of a principal residence is not taxed in the year of the sale provided the seller buys or constructs another residence, within 24 months before or after the sale, for a price equal to or greater than the adjusted sales price of the home sold.* If the transaction qualifies under the requirements set forth above, the **rollover rule** is mandatory. The taxpayer does not have a choice. He or she must indefinitely defer the tax on the gain.

A taxpayer may be involved in a number of qualifying transactions, and therefore many mandatory rollovers of tax, during his or her lifetime. Any gain in the sale of a residence that is not currently taxed under the rollover rule is used to reduce the **tax basis** of the new residence purchased (as discussed below). The tax basis is essentially *the original cost of the property plus any improvements that increase its value*. The tax basis of the new residence is reduced by the untaxed amount. This results in a lower tax basis for the new property in calculating the gain when that home is sold and therefore more profit at that time.

If the transaction does not qualify under the rollover rule, the gain realized in the sale of the residence is taxable for the tax year in which the sale transpires, not when the 24-month period has expired. The taxpayer will have to pay the tax due for the year of sale plus any statutory IRS interest, but there is no penalty.

To compute gain or loss in the sale of a principal residence, the first step is to establish the owner's tax basis in the property. Tax is owed only on the gain and not on the full sales price. Gain is determined by subtracting the tax basis of the property from the sales price of the property.

Sales price
– Tax basis
Gain

The tax basis consists of the price paid for the property, less any gain deferred from the sale of the previous residence under a prior rollover, plus expenses incurred in acquiring the property (other than those to arrange financing), plus the cost of any capital improvements (not repairs) made during ownership.

Certain costs of acquiring the property may be added to the basis. We can see that it is to the homeowner's advantage to have as large a basis as possible, to reduce the tax gain realized when the property is eventually sold. It is important that accurate records are kept by the taxpayer of any permanent improvement to the home. Alternatively, the gain is reduced by being able to deduct certain items from the sale price. Some of these are outlined in the next section. If the basis is higher than the adjusted sale price and results in a loss, the loss is *not* deductible. Personal residence losses are not deductible. Losses on the sale of investment property may be deductible. The sale of the home is reported to the IRS whether or not there is a profit, repurchase, or contemplated rollover. The taxpayer must report the sale of the home on the tax return in the year of sale. The reporting to the IRS is done with form 1099-S, which reports the sellers' names, social security numbers, date of the sale, identification of the property, and the gross sales price (not the net proceeds).

Effect of Purchase and Sale

In the purchase and sale of a personal residence, both the buyer and the seller have certain expenses. Examples of these expenses, and their application to buyer and seller in calculating taxable gain, are offered below.

1. The premium paid for a title insurance policy may be subtracted from the selling price if the seller pays it. If the buyer pays that premium, the amount paid is added to the buyer's basis.
2. Transfer taxes, ordinarily paid by the seller at the transfer of the real estate, are based upon the seller's equity or sales price. They may be deducted by the seller from the selling price. If the tax is paid by the buyer, however, the amount is added to the buyer's basis.
3. Attorney fees paid by the seller are deductible from the selling price. Attorney fees paid by the buyer are added to the buyer's basis. Attorney fees incurred by the buyer to obtain financing, however, may not be added to the buyer's basis.
4. If the seller pays the attorney's fee for preparation of a deed, the seller may deduct this fee from the selling price. If the buyer pays the fee for drawing the deed, it may be added to the buyer's basis.
5. Buyer's closing costs that are allocable to purchasing the property may be added to the buyer's basis. Expenses of borrowing the purchase price, however, may not be added to the buyer's basis. Expenses involved with obtaining the loan include things such as appraisal fees, mortgage insurance premiums, charges by the lender's attorney, and credit report cost.
6. The seller often pays discounts points and other financing expenses charged by lending institutions in making home loans to buyers. These may be deducted from the selling price if the seller pays them to enable the buyer to obtain a loan; therefore, this lowers the seller's profit. They may not be deducted by the seller as interest because the seller has not borrowed the money and has no obligation to repay. The discount points and loan origination fee may be deducted by the buyer as interest in the year in which they are paid if the loan is to purchase a principal residence. This is true even if the seller paid the points, but if the seller paid the points, the buyer must lower his or her cost basis in the home.

Putting It to Work

In 1986, the IRS ruled that discount points paid by the buyer to refinance an existing loan have to be spread out over the term of the loan. The essential difference is that if a buyer pays $2,000 in points for a new home, she can deduct all $2,000 in the year paid. If she refinances her present loan for 20 years, however, she can deduct only $100 per year. If a mortgage loan is not obtained to purchase or improve a principal residence, deduction of the discount points as interest must be spread out over the life of the loan. For example, if a borrower pays $2,000 in discount points to obtain a 20-year conventional loan to purchase an apartment building, the discount points are deductible at a rate of $100 per year for 20 years. Any remaining undeducted points may be deducted in the year the loan is paid off.

7. With the exception of discount points and loan origination fee, few other financing fees are deductible by the buyer. Any other buyer closing costs that are attributable to buying the property may be added to the cost basis of the property.

However, any costs of closing to borrow on the property may not be added to the cost. These are personal nondeductible expenses.

8. Other expense items, such as surveys, escrow fees, title abstracts, recording fees, and advertising costs, may be added to the buyer's basis if paid by the buyer, or subtracted from the selling price if paid by the seller.

9. The real estate commission a seller pays may be deducted, but only from the selling price. The commission paid is not deductible from the seller's ordinary income.

10. **Fix-up expenses** are *costs the seller incurs in preparing a residence for sale.* To qualify as adjustments from the amount realized to establish the adjusted sale price, these costs must have been incurred within 90 days prior to signing the contract of sale that results in the completed sale of the home and must be paid for within 30 days after the sale. Fix-up expenses, however, are not deductible unless the seller purchases or builds a new home within the limits specified by the rollover rule. Also, these expenses are deductions only to determine the amount of gain on which tax is to be postponed and may not be used as deductions in arriving at gain.

11. A financial penalty required by a lender for early payoff of a mortgage loan (a prepayment penalty) is deductible as interest by the borrower for the year in which the prepayment penalty is paid.

Moving Expenses

Moving expenses are deductible if the taxpayer itemizes and the expenses are incurred moving to a new job that would require 50 miles increased travel one way for the taxpayer without the move. A deduction is available for employees and for self-employed taxpayers.

Deductible moving expenses are used to calculate adjusted gross income. These expenses may include transportation of furniture and effects, and expenses of transportation and lodging when traveling from the former home to the new home. These amounts are fully deductible by any working taxpayer.

The tax-deductible costs of moving household goods and personal effects and the tax-deductible expenses incurred for travel to the new location are not limited in dollar amount. Pre-move house-hunting trips, temporary living quarters, and sale and purchase costs, which, under previous laws, were partially deductible under certain circumstances, are no longer deductions pursuant to the RRA of 1993.

The Age-55-and-over Exclusion

The **age-55-and-over exclusion** is available to sellers of a principal residence provided the seller is age 55 or over. The *seller may exempt from tax up to $125,000 of gain in the sale of a principal residence.* The seller must have used the property as his or her principal residence for at least three of the five years immediately preceding the date of the sale. The tax on any remaining gain in excess of the $125,000 exemption will be deferred under the rollover rule, if applicable.

This is a once-in-a-lifetime exemption. After it is used, it is gone. This is true even if the exclusion is taken on a gain of only $40,000. The seller does not have an additional $85,000 to exempt in another sale of property in the future.

An unmarried co-owner of property used as his or her principal residence qualifies for the exclusion. In this case, the qualifying owner may take the exemption even though the other does not qualify. If they both qualify, one may elect to take the exclusion for his or her portion of the gain, and the other may elect not to do so. Single owners in severalty also qualify for the $125,000 exclusion.

If the property is owned by a married couple, only one spouse has to be at least age 55 for the transaction to qualify for the exemption. If a married couple takes the exemption, even if only one spouse qualifies, it is binding upon both of them. If they are divorced after the sale in which the exemption is taken and both subsequently acquire a new spouse, the fact that each of them took the exclusion previously disqualifies the new spouse in each case as well, even if the new spouse would have qualified otherwise.

A taxpayer who has been in the house for less than three years does not normally qualify for the exclusion. In meeting the ownership and use tests, the taxpayer may add the time he or she owned and lived in a previous home destroyed by fire or other casualty or condemned under eminent domain to the time he or she owned and lived in the home for which he or she desires to exclude a gain under the age-55-and-over exclusion. The three years may be reduced to one year if the taxpayer moves into a qualified nursing facility.

Computation of Gain

Figures 15.1 and 15.2 illustrate the steps taken in computing taxable gain and arriving at the **adjusted basis** for a new residence. Figure 15.1 depicts the situation in which the homeowner purchases a new home for a price greater than the amount realized on the sale of his previous residence. The gain realized in the sale is calculated by subtracting the adjusted basis from the amount realized (the sale price minus expenses of the sale). The original cost (basis) of the old home has been increased by a portion of the closing costs to obtain it, as well as the costs of improvements to the property.

The rollover rule does not require that the seller use the same funds received in the sale of his or her old principal residence to buy or build a new home. The seller may invest a lesser amount of cash and obtain a larger mortgage loan with which to purchase another qualifying residence.

An example in Figure 15.1 is the $40,000 proceeds the seller received from his old home. If he is purchasing a new $110,000 home with a VA loan (no down payment), he does not have to actually invest any of the cash proceeds in the new purchase. Therefore, he has $40,000 cash, tax free, to use as he likes. He has not totally escaped the consequences of this profit, however, as the basis of the new home is reduced by the $40,000. If, in the future, he sells this new home for the same $110,000 amount and does not purchase another home, he will be subject to taxation on $40,000 of profit from the first home.

Selling price of old home	$85,000
Less: Selling expenses	– 7,000
Amount realized	= $78,000
Basis of old home	$35,000
Plus: Closing costs	+ 1,000
Improvements	+ 2,000
Adjusted basis of old home	= $38,000
Amount realized	$78,000
Minus: Adjusted basis	–38,000
Gain realized	= $40,000
Cost of new home	$110,000
Less: Gain postponed	–40,000
Basis of new home	= $70,000

FIGURE 15.1 The rollover rule applied to a more expensive new home.

FIGURE 15.2 The rollover rule applied to a less expensive new home.

Selling price of old home	$85,000
Less: Selling expenses	– 5,600
Amount realized on old home	= $79,400
Basis of old home	$52,400
Plus: Capital improvements	+ 1,200
Adjusted basis of old home	= $53,600
Amount realized on old home	$79,400
Less: Adjusted basis	–53,600
Gain on old home	= $25,800
Amount realized on old home	$79,400
Cost of new home	–76,000
***Gain taxed now**	= $ 3,400
Gain on old home	$25,800
Less: Gain taxed	– 3,400
Gain postponed	= $22,400
Cost of new home	$76,000
Less: Gain postponed	–22,400
Basis of new home	= $53,600

*Taxable for year of sale.

Figure 15.2 illustrates the situation in which the homeowner does not purchase a new home for a price greater than the amount realized on the sale of her previous residence. The taxable gain for the year of the sale is $3,400 and not the full gain of $25,800. The taxable gain in the year of sale is incurred because the price of the new residence was not equal to or greater than the adjusted basis of the old home. The tax on the gain postponed, $22,400, is deferred indefinitely under the mandatory rollover rule. The gain postponed, however, is used to reduce the tax basis of the new residence purchased and is the tax basis for the new residence when it is sold some time in the future. Therefore, the tax basis of the new residence to the purchaser will be $53,600 ($76,000 – $22,400). Had the taxpayer purchased a new residence costing $79,400 or more, all of the gain realized would have been postponed.

PUTTING IT TO WORK

Taxpayers and real estate licensees alike often misunderstand the fundamental provision of the tax code regarding rollovers. The issue is so important in selling (and repurchasing) decisions that the licensee should be clearly versed in the technical rules applied. They are not difficult, but they are important. While licensees should not give tax advice, they should point out to the parties that tax concerns are an important aspect of any real estate decision.

Inheritance Basis

The tax basis for all real property received by heirs is the *market value of the property on the date of the decedent's death*, not the price the decedent paid. As a result of this stepped-up **inheritance basis**, any tax on gains deferred under the rollover rule during the decedent's lifetime is eliminated. Therefore, gains deferred under the rollover rule are not taxed in the decedent's estate or final tax return. The only time these deferred taxes must be paid is in the event of sale of property, during the taxpayer's lifetime, that does not qualify for tax deferment under the rollover rule and also does not qualify for the $125,000 once-in-a-lifetime exclusion, discussed earlier.

Vacation Homes

Under the TRA of 1986, homeowners are allowed to deduct mortgage interest on both a principal residence and a second home, such as a vacation property. Special rules apply in classifying this second property. The vacation property is considered a second home if it is occupied for personal use more than 14 days per year or 10 percent of its useful rental period. In this case, the mortgage interest and property taxes on both the principal residence and the second home can be deducted to the extent the mortgages do not exceed the original purchase price of the properties plus improvements.

If, however, personal use of the second property is limited to less than 14 days or 10 percent of the useful rental period, the home is treated as a business property. In this case, it is eligible for the 27½-year depreciation schedule and repairs and maintenance deductions, as well as full deduction of the mortgage interest and property taxes, subject to the passive loss rules.

Installment Sales

The subject of installment sales is included at this point because tax law applications in installment sales apply both to a personal residence and to property held for investment or for use in a trade or business. An owner may sell his or her principal residence on an **installment sale** basis, in which *at least one payment is received by the taxpayer in a tax year after the sale*, and avoid the total impact of the tax in one year. The typical installment sale is by contract for deed or land contract with relatively fewer sales financed by a seller mortgage or deed of trust. If the seller does not plan to purchase a new residence within the time period required for the rollover rule and also does not qualify for the $125,000 maximum tax exemption, an installment sale can be used to provide tax relief.

Installment sales may be used to spread the impact of federal income taxes on gains over several years or to postpone taxes to a future year or years as the principal is received. This enables the taxpayer to avoid the impact of tax on gain in the sale of property in a single year. Installment sale rules apply to the sale of real property, businesses, securities, and personal property.

The TRA of 1986 makes the installment sale method much less attractive than under previous laws. Retroactive to March of 1986, for installment sales of business property it is assumed that the seller has received a minimum cash payment each year. This means the payment is recognized for tax purposes, regardless of whether any cash is actually received during that year.

Investment Property

As we have seen, ownership and sale of a principal residence have special tax benefits. Ownership and sale of real property held as an investment or for use in a trade or business also have special tax benefits including depreciation, deductible expenses, and tax-free exchanges of like-kind property.

Depreciation

The two types of depreciation are tax depreciation and economic depreciation. **Economic depreciation** *results from physical deterioration of property caused by normal use, damage caused by natural and other hazards, and failure to adequately maintain the property.* **Tax depreciation** is a provision of the tax law (called cost recovery in the Internal Revenue Code) applicable to certain types of assets, that permits a property owner to take an *ordinary business deduction for the amount of annual depreciation.* This permits the owner to recover the cost or other basis of an asset over the period of the asset's useful life. Tax depreciation is a deduction from net income in calculating taxable income.

PUTTING IT TO WORK

Tax depreciation is an accounting concept only. The property being "depreciated" actually may be appreciating in value. When the property is sold, tax may have to be paid on the "real" appreciation plus recapture of the "artificial" tax depreciation.

The Tax Reform Act of 1986 and Revenue Reconciliation Act of 1993 established two depreciation schedules for real property: 27½ years for residential property and 39 years for nonresidential property. All depreciation on new purchases must be taken on a straight-line basis. Under TRA 1986, the amount of claimed investment losses must equal an amount no more than the income received from similar passive activities. For example, if an investor loses $35,000 on her properties but the properties' income is only $21,000, the investor can claim only $21,000 in loss this tax year. The excess loss of $14,000 ($35,000 – $21,000) cannot be used in the year of the loss. The excess loss may be carried over to future tax years.

A limited exception to this rule applies to owners with adjusted gross income of less than $100,000 who actively manage their own property. It is phased out for taxpayers with adjusted gross income between $100,000 and $150,000. These owners may shelter up to $25,000 of other wages or active income in the same tax year. Passive investors who do not actively manage their own property cannot apply excess losses to other active income in the same tax year. In the above example, if the investor manages her own properties and has an adjusted gross income of $70,000, she can use the $14,000 excess loss to reduce the adjusted gross income to $56,000. This allowance is not limited to $25,000 for taxpayers who are engaged in real estate trades or businesses.

Depreciable property includes assets such as buildings, equipment, machinery, and other things that are used in business to produce income (other than inventories) or that are held as investments. Assets held for personal use, including a personal residence, are not depreciable assets. Also, land is not a depreciable asset. Therefore, the value of the land and the value of structures on the land must be separated to arrive at a basis for determining depreciation. This basis normally is the cost of acquiring the property reduced by the estimated salvage value of the property at the end of its useful life.

When a depreciable asset is sold, *the basis of the asset used to compute the taxable gain from the sale is the depreciated value.* For example, if a depreciable asset is purchased for $100,000 and the purchaser had taken $40,000 of tax depreciation at the time the property was sold for $130,000, the taxable gain is $70,000 ($130,000 sales price minus $60,000 depreciated value = $70,000 taxable gain). In essence, the basis of a depreciable asset is reduced by any depreciation deduction taken. The tax treatment of this gain can vary greatly as either capital gain or depreciation recapture. Careful tax analysis prior to the sale of a depreciated property is critical.

Deductible Expenses

Unlike the expenses of operating property held for personal use, such as a personal residence, the *costs of operating property held for use in business or as an investment* are **deductible expenses**. These operating costs may be deducted from gross income in arriving at net income. Before deducting operating expenses, *losses from vacancies and credit losses are deducted from gross scheduled rental income* to arrive at **gross operating income**. Operating expenses are deducted from gross operating expenses. Examples of operating expenses are:

accounting and legal fees	services
advertising	maintenance and repairs
property management fee	supplies
property insurance	property taxes
licenses and permits	utilities
wages and salaries	

The *result of deducting operating expenses* is **net operating income**. Mortgage interest and depreciation are deducted from net operating income to arrive at net taxable income. This otherwise taxable income may be completely or partially sheltered from tax liability as a result of the depreciation allowance. Consequently, the building may generate no taxable income but still have positive cash flow.

Income Shelter

Deductible allowances from net income of property to arrive at taxable income and tax losses allowed to offset passive and active income are **income shelters** for individual taxpayer owners. Examples of expenses and allowances deductible from gross income include depreciation, operating expenses, real estate taxes, and mortgage interest.

To see the benefit of this concept, let's reconsider the operating statement for an apartment building introduced in Chapter 10 (Figure 10.5) and further discussed in Chapter 14. We assumed the subject property was purchased for $6,200,000. Because land does not depreciate, we have to make an allocation between the land and the improvement (the building). If we assume that 15 percent of the price is allocated to the land, the depreciable property becomes 85 percent of $6,200,000, or $5,270,000. Because the property can be depreciated over a 27½-year period, one year's depreciation is 1/27.5th or $191,636, which may be used to offset (shelter) income from the property itself. Further interest on the debt service is deductible. The final figures are illustrated in Figure 15.3.

Viewed another way, we can see that if the property owner is in a 28 percent tax bracket, the exclusion (sheltering) of the depreciation allowance of $191,636 means that she saved 28 percent of this figure, or potentially $53,658 in federal income taxes, without having to "write a check" for the depreciation.

Tax-Deferred Exchanges

The Internal Revenue Code provides that, in cases of qualified exchange of property, some or all of the gain may not have to be recognized for tax purposes. The property

Net Operating Income	$745,600
Less: Interest	−463,836
Depreciation	−191,636
Net Taxable Income	$ 90,128

FIGURE 15.3
Determination of net taxable income.

exchanged must be investment property or business property. In a qualified **tax-deferred exchange**, *the tax on the gain is postponed and the deduction of a loss also must be postponed*. These requirements are not discretionary with the taxpayer or the government. If a transaction qualifies as an exchange, no gain or loss may be recognized in the year of the exchange. The basis of the property each exchanger received is treated as if it were the same basis as the property each owned prior to the exchange, plus any additional expenditures or debt incurred on the new property.

Like-Kind Property

To qualify as an exchange, the properties must be like-kind. **Like-kind property** is *property of the same nature and character,* such as real property for real property, depreciable personal property for depreciable personal property, and so on. Exchanges of like-kind real property may be an office building for a shopping mall, an apartment house for a tract of land, or an office building for an apartment building. Examples of personal property exchanges are a truck for a machine or an automobile for a truck. Personal residences and foreign property do not qualify for an exchange.

Business or Investment Property

The property exchanged must be held for use in business or as an investment. Property held for personal use does not qualify. An exchange of residences by homeowners does not qualify as a tax-free exchange but is treated as a sale and a purchase and thus may qualify for the rollover rule discussed earlier in this chapter.

Property Not Held for Sale

The property exchanged must not be held for sale to customers in the regular course of business, such as lots held for sale by a developer.

Boot

If an exchangor receives cash or some other type of nonqualifying property in addition to like-kind property, the transaction may partially qualify as a tax-deferred exchange. The *recipient of the cash in the exchange*, called the **boot**, or other nonqualifying property must pay the tax liability on the boot received or other unlike-kind property received in the calendar year of the exchange. **Unlike-kind property** is *property that is not similar in nature and character to the property exchanged*. Boot may be given or paid by the taxpayer, but not received tax-free.

Basis

The basis of the property an exchangor receives is the basis of the property given up in exchange plus new expenditures or debt incurred. Therefore, an exchangor does not change the basis of an asset as a result of the exchange. For example, Exchangor #1 trades a property with a market value of $100,000 and a basis of $20,000 for another property also worth $100,000. The property Exchangor #1 receives also is considered to have a basis of $20,000 plus any new debt assumed, or cash or boot paid, regardless of the other exchangor's basis.

Multiple Exchange

A **multiple exchange** is one in which *more than two properties are exchanged in one transaction*. Usually, multiple exchanges are three-way exchanges. For example, A, B, and C each own like-kind real property held for business purposes of investment. In the exchange, A acquires the property owned by C, B acquires the property owned by

A, and C acquires the property owned by B. Multiple exchanges qualify as tax-deferred exchanges in the same way two-way exchanges do. An exchangor does not have to receive property from the same person with whom he or she is exchanging property.

Starker Exchange (Starker Trust)

In the case for which the Starker exchange was named, Starker sold land to a corporation. The purchaser, however, withheld the purchase price until Starker subsequently found a suitable property to be purchased with proceeds from the sale. The U. S. Circuit Court of Appeals in 1979 held that the **Starker exchange** qualified for treatment as a tax-deferred exchange because the sale proceeds were held beyond the control of the taxpayer seeking the tax-deferred exchange. The court viewed the exchange as one continuous transaction.

Therefore, *if the proceeds of a sale of property are held beyond the seller's control until the seller can locate the like-kind property in which to invest the proceeds, the transaction may constitute a tax-free exchange. Proceeds from a Starker exchange* are held in a **Starker trust**. Some time limitations apply. The property for exchange must be identified in writing within 45 days of the time the Starker trust is established (first closing date), and the closing on the property must be within 180 days of establishment of the Starker trust, or April 15, whichever comes first.

PUTTING IT TO WORK

Exchanges are becoming more and more common. This is especially true in areas of strong appreciation. Taxpayers would rather exchange and defer taxation than sell and pay tax.

INVESTMENT SYNDICATES

As a result of the tax implications and advantages in owning real estate, many people want to invest in real estate. To achieve maximum purchasing power, some investors pool their resources in a real estate **investment syndicate**, *a joint venture typically controlled by one or two persons hoping for return to all investors*. Profit for investors is generated when the syndicate buys, sells, and develops real estate.

To protect investors from fraud by syndicate promoters, the federal and state governments have enacted securities laws and regulations. Because these laws are designed to protect investors from buying "blue sky" without substance, they are commonly referred to as *blue sky laws*.

The Security Act of 1933 was the first federal securities law. This law regulated companies' initial issuance of securities, outlined fraudulent practices, and required registration of securities prior to sale. Since that time, many additional laws have been passed requiring further disclosure, regulating insider trading, and requiring disclosure of any conflicts of interest.

The goals of the 1933 act and subsequent laws are to protect the investing public. The act requires full disclosure by companies wishing to issue and sell stock to the public. Companies also are required to file a registration statement with the Securities and Exchange Commission (SEC). In all sales, a pamphlet or prospectus must be provided to all potential investors. The SEC does not pass judgment on the quality of the investment. It merely requires all disclosures necessary for investors' full knowledge.

In certain situations, securities legislation provides for exemptions from the registration process. The most typical exemptions relate to minimum number of investors and minimum amount of money to be pooled by the investors. If a pool of investors (syndicate) does not comply with federal and state securities laws, the penalty is a fine up to $10,000 and imprisonment of up to five years.

Real Estate Investment

Many real estate professionals, in addition to their clients and customers, will be interested in investment in real estate. While some of these issues have been discussed elsewhere in this text, such as the income or capitalization approach to appraisal (Chapter 10), some additional comments may be helpful. Investors in real estate have different investment preferences motivated by capital appreciation, cash flow, tax advantages, tax deferral, or combinations of some or all of these.

Time Value of Money

A dollar received today is more important, and therefore more valuable, than a dollar received next year. The dollar received next year is better than a dollar received 10 years from now. This is due to inflation as well as the **opportunity cost** to the investor. This is the fact that the investor is *passing up many other investment alternatives by not having the money available to him or her now*. Computers and financial calculators have programs that will equate what a dollar received in 1 or 5 or 10 years is worth in today's dollars. Analyzing inflows and outflows over a series of years is called cash flow analysis. These types of computations are referred to as present value calculations or the time value of money. While most state pre-licensing examinations do not require candidates to compute these figures, the more sophisticated investment markets require an understanding of this concept.

Putting It to Work

The investor records the expected initial outlay to make the investment. He or she then determines the current income and expenses, including debt service and tax consequences. The investor makes certain assumptions about future expenses, income, capital improvement, capital appreciation, and tax law. Next, the investor makes certain predictions regarding the expected future income due to positive cash flow or additional contributions for negative cash flow or capital improvements. Next, the investor must decide approximately when the sale of the property will take place and what the net sales proceeds will be at that time. Each year's net cash flow will be recorded as to the amount as well as when it is expected to be received. The same is true for the year of sale. From this data we can determine what the investor's internal rate of return is on the property. This is the rate that the investment markets use when it is said that one makes a particular rate of return such as 12 percent or 14 percent. This is similar to a capitalization rate in appraisal but on a much more sophisticated scale.

The less sophisticated but common practice of "averaging" the total percent of gain by dividing by the number of years the investment is held is less accurate than the internal rate of return based on the time value of money.

Tax Aspects of Various Types of Real Estate Investments

The most basic component of real estate, land, is an investment many people prefer. In a growth area, land can appreciate very rapidly, often far outpacing inflation. Land rarely provides any cash flow, but ownership of land offers some deductible expenses, such as property taxes. Other expenses such as survey, insurance, and engineering costs must be added to the cost basis, which reduces profit upon sale. As the property goes up in value, the investor does not pay tax on the increase in value until the property is sold. Any net profit or appreciation of the property qualifies for preferential capital gain treatment under the tax code.

A taxpayer who holds appreciated property with a sizable equity may decide to borrow money and offer the property as collateral. This receipt of the money is not a taxable event and the loan proceeds are not taxable income. Tax is paid only upon the sale of the property, not upon borrowing.

Rental property is often the first real estate investment undertaken by investors. Previously discussed regulations regarding deductible expenses, depreciation, loss limitation, and passive activity losses all pertain to rental properties, whether residential or non-residential. While property may be depreciated for tax and accounting purposes, in reality it may be appreciating in value. This legal curiosity is corrected when the investor sells the property. Any depreciation claimed that was not actually realized must be deducted from basis upon sale. While some of this depreciation may be eligible for capital gain treatment, excess depreciation (over straight-line) must be recaptured in full in the year of sale. Any of the depreciation eligible for capital gain treatment as well as the "real profit" (appreciation) may be taxed as capital gain it the year of sale or recognized on the installment basis if the investor carries back some form of seller financing. The installment recognition of gain effectively defers the gain substantially by spreading it over a number of years. If the investor wishes to structure the "sale" as a tax-deferred exchange (discussed earlier in this chapter), any profit that is eligible for capital gain treatment is exchangeable.

Putting It to Work

Investment in rental real estate has many advantages. The property may actually show a positive cash flow with the depreciation allowed under the tax code sheltering this cash flow and possibly other income subject to the limitations discussed earlier. Thus, the investor may save tax dollars with an asset that provides him or her with current income that is actually increasing in value.

On the downside, a surprise many investors discover upon sale is that the depreciation they have been allowed to deduct over the years far exceeds the amortization of any loan balance. When this occurs, and the investor sells the property, the taxable profit may well be greater than the equity after paying the selling and closing expenses. Taxpayers are often confused by the fact that they pay tax on much more than the net proceeds check they received at closing. This is sometimes referred to as "phantom income." The explanation is the "phantom deduction" that they have been allowed in the form of depreciation they have claimed (without ever writing a check).

Losses that have been incurred on investment property are usually deductible. Losses on the sale of land are deductible as capital losses, which are limited to $3,000 per year against other ordinary income with the excess carried over to later years.

Rental real estate sold at a loss can be deducted in full in the year of sale under the Internal Revenue Code.

Important Points

1. Real estate licensees should be knowledgeable about tax legislation but should encourage clients to seek professional tax advice when necessary.
2. The Tax Reform Act of 1986 and Revenue Reconciliation Act of 1993 reduced capital gains benefits and lengthened depreciation schedules for investment property.
3. Depreciation is a deductible allowance from net income in arriving at taxable income. Therefore, it provides a tax shelter for the property owner.
4. A homeowner's real estate property taxes and mortgage interest, subject to certain limits, are deductible expenses in calculating federal taxable income.
5. Losses incurred in the sale of a personal residence are not tax-deductible.
6. The rollover rule is mandatory for purchasing a new personal residence, and it enables the owner to postpone taxation on the gain from the former personal residence if the purchase price of the new home is more than the amount realized from sale of the former home.
7. The amount of gain deferred under the rollover rule is used to reduce the tax basis of the new home purchased.
8. The age-55-and-over exclusion allows an exemption of up to $125,000 of gain in the sale of a principal residence occupied for at least three of the last five years immediately preceding the sale. The exclusion may be taken only once.
9. The installment sale recognition of gain applies to the principal residence as well as to business and investment properties.
10. Depreciation enables the owner of business or investment property to recover the cost or other basis of the asset.
11. Land is not depreciable. Only structures and improvements on the land are depreciable real property.
12. Depreciation for real property is now calculated at 27½ years for residential property and 39 years for other property.
13. When a depreciable asset is sold, the basis of the asset used to compute taxable gain is the depreciated value, not the price the seller pays for the property.
14. Expenses of operating a business or investment property are deductible expenses in arriving at taxable income.
15. To qualify as a tax-deferred exchange, like-kind property must be exchanged. An exchangor receiving cash (boot) or other unlike-kind property in addition to like-kind property is taxed on the value of the boot or other unlike-kind property received.
16. To qualify as a tax-deferred exchange, the property exchanged must have been held for use in business (other than inventory) or as an investment. Property held for personal use does not qualify.
17. Investors in real estate syndicates are protected from fraudulent promoters by "blue sky" laws and the Security Act of 1933.
18. Investment analysis requires careful attention to tax consequences as well as cash flow analysis.

How Would You Respond?

Many real estate practitioners avoid tax issues at all costs. While real estate licensees are not expected to be tax experts, they must understand certain basic issues in a conversational sense. Consider the following questions that Pauline has encountered in just the previous month:

1. A renter interested in buying a home asks Pauline how much can be deducted of the closing costs, mortgage interests, and taxes.
2. A seller of a home in escrow needs to extend the escrow, but the buyers would then miss their deadline for reinvesting their proceeds from the sale of their former home two years ago.
3. Another seller is considering two different offers on the sale of a rental home with a large profit. One offer is a cash sale, the other is a wraparound with a strong 25 percent down payment. He asks Pauline how this will impact his income taxes.
4. A buyer is relocating to the area from another state. He wants to know what moving expenses and closing costs will be deductible.
5. Pauline has a listing seller who expects to realize a $200,000 profit in the sale of his land. He wants to structure a sale or an exchange to minimize his tax liability.
6. Pauline's sellers realize a large profit form the sale of their home. The husband is 56 and the wife is 53. Do they qualify for the age-55-and-over exclusion?

Pauline feels that if she can't talk intelligently about these issues she might lose these clients.

Review Questions

Answers to these questions are found in the *Answer Key* section at the back of the book.

1. Which of the following is an expense deductible for tax purposes resulting from home ownership?
   a. operating expenses
   b. depreciation
   c. mortgage interest
   d. energy use

2. The rollover rule providing for deferment of an otherwise taxable gain in qualifying transactions is:
   a. optional
   b. mandatory
   c. conditional
   d. flexible

3. Discount points paid by a borrower or seller to obtain a conventional mortgage loan to purchase a principal residence:
   a. are not deductible by the borrower as interest
   b. are deductible by the borrower as interest
   c. increase the basis of the new residence
   d. decrease the basis of the new residence

4. With regard to a real estate commission paid by a seller, which of the following is (are) correct?
   a. the commission may be deducted from the selling price as a selling expense in calculating the amount realized in the sale of a principal residence
   b. the commission paid is deductible from ordinary income (wage income) by the seller when itemizing tax deductible expense
   c. the commission paid increases the basis of the residence sold
   d. the commission paid decreases the basis of the residence sold

5. A mortgage prepayment penalty paid by a borrower as a requirement for early loan payoff:
   a. may be deducted as interest in the year paid
   b. may be deducted as interest over a five-year period
   c. may only be deducted from selling price as a selling expense
   d. may not be taken as a deduction for any purpose

6. The amount of gain on which tax is postponed under the rollover rule is used to:
   a. increase the basis of the new residence
   b. reduce the basis of the new residence
   c. increase the allowable moving expenses
   d. reduce the inheritance basis of the new residence

7. The age-55-and-over exclusion provides all of the following EXCEPT:
   a. the choice of excluding from taxation up to $125,000 of gain resulting from the sale of a principal residence
   b. the exclusion may be taken only once in lifetime and, if taken by a married person, is binding on the other spouse even though the other spouse was below age 55
   c. the choice of excluding from taxation up to $125,000 of gain resulting from the sale of business property
   d. the exclusion is available only on sale of real estate that has been the principal residence three of the last five years

8. Which of the following is a benefit depreciation provides?
   a. tax credit
   b. tax deduction
   c. tax evasion
   d. tax deferral

9. Deductible expenses for a business property include all of the following EXCEPT:
   a. advertising
   b. utilities
   c. mortgage principal
   d. insurance

10. Raul Ramirez and Sarah Gildar trade office buildings. In the trade, Raul receives $20,000 in cash in addition to Sarah's office building. With regard to this transaction, which of the following is (are) correct?
    a. the transaction does not qualify as a tax-free exchange
    b. the cash Raul receives is called boot and is taxable for the year in which the exchange occurs
    c. the exchangors, Raul and Sarah, exchange basis in the traded properties
    d. the cash Raul receives is deductible for the year the exchange occurs

11. The basis of property received in a tax-free exchange is:
    a. the basis as it was to the prior owner at the time of the exchange
    b. the average of the difference in the basis of all properties exchanged
    c. the same basis as the basis of the property given up in the exchange plus any debt assumed and cash paid
    d. the value of the property received in the exchange

12. In 1996, Ed and Margaret take advantage of the low interest rates to refinance their existing 30-year, 13.5% mortgage with a 15-year, 9.5% mortgage on their present home. They pay $1,500 in discount points to refinance this loan. How will the cost of these points be treated in their income tax?
    a. the cost is added to the basis of their home
    b. since all discount points are fully deductible in the year paid, they may deduct the $1,500 from their 1996 income
    c. they may deduct only $100 per year
    d. there is no deduction benefit at all

13. Bill and Betty purchase a home for $40,000 and later add a new room to the home at a cost of $5,000. They subsequently sell this home for $60,000 minus a 6% real estate commission. What will be the minimum purchase price of their new home in order to postpone taxation from all of the gain on the old home?
    a. $40,000
    b. $45,000
    c. $56,400
    d. $60,000

14. Victor and Valerie own a vacation property at the beach, which they use only one week per year. The property is rented out at fair market value the rest of the year. Which items of this property can they deduct?
    a. mortgage principal only
    b. mortgage interest only
    c. mortgage interest, repairs, depreciation, maintenance, and property taxes
    d. mortgage interest and property taxes only

15. An investor says that her rate of return is 12.5% after selling a rental property. This means:
    a. the IRS allows 12.5% depreciation per year
    b. the IRS charges only 12.5% tax due to a capital gain deduction
    c. her original investment accrued 12.5% average per year
    d. the property has appreciated by 12.5% per year

POSSIBLE RESPONSES TO "HOW WOULD YOU RESPOND?"

1. Typically only the following closing costs are deductible: prorated taxes, interest, and points. Mortgage interest and taxes are deductible if the taxpayer itemizes deductions.
2. It takes both parties to agree to any modification or extension of an escrow. This delay could cost the buyer thousands of dollars.
3. The cash sale would require full payment of tax on any profit in the year of sale. The wraparound can defer tax of the profit until the years of receipt of the principal. While the wraparound provides the additional income of the interest, this will be fully taxable. The underlying interest on the old loan may well be deductible as investment interest.
4. Moving expenses are deductible only to the extent of direct expenses of the move. The former deduction for qualified real estate expenses was eliminated for 1994 and later.
5. A sale will defer tax only if the seller carries back some or all of the financing. An exchange can defer some or all of the profit into the new property acquired. The tax will then be paid upon the sale of that property.
6. Yes, they can qualify since the husband is over 55 on the date of the sale, provided this has been his principal residence for three out of the last five years.

Pauline is right that she must be able to talk intelligently about these issues.

CHAPTER 16

Important Terminology

attorney-in-fact
false promise
misrepresentation
unauthorized practice of law

Real Estate License Laws

IN THIS CHAPTER Today all states require that people in the real estate business be licensed by the state. The state's authority to require licenses falls under the state's police power to protect the health, safety, welfare, and property of its citizens. The purpose of license law legislation, then, is to protect the general public. License laws require the licensee to possess the knowledge, skill, and reputation for honesty, fair dealing, and ethical conduct necessary to participate in the real estate business. License laws also govern the licensees' conduct in their real estate business activities.

VARIATIONS IN STATE LAW

Because real estate laws vary from state to state, real estate students must become thoroughly familiar with the license law and rules and regulations in their own state or other jurisdiction where they practice. A checklist at the end of this chapter will assist in that regard.

The most important provisions of real estate law are similar, but not identical, in all states. These are based on the model recommended by the National Association of REALTORS® (NAR). Members are known as REALTORS®. Substantial uniformity among states also has resulted from efforts of the Association of Real Estate License Law Officials (ARELLO). Organized in 1930, ARELLO is made up of license law officials representing every state. ARELLO and NAR have made substantial contributions to license law legislation that have elevated the standards of the real estate industry.

Variations in license law legislation from state to state usually involve administrative matters such as requirements for license eligibility. Examples include such requirements as minimum age for licensing, amount of prelicensing education required, residence, apprenticeship, license renewal requirements, continuing education, and fees. All states require that license applicants pass a licensing examination for a broker's license and for a salesperson's license.

DEFINITION OF *BROKER* AND *SALESPERSON*

The definition of real estate broker and the definition of real estate salesperson are fairly uniform in the various state licensing laws. A real estate broker is any person, partnership, association, or corporation who, for a payment or other valuable consideration, lists or offers to list, sells or offers to sell, buys or offers to buy, auctions or offers to auction, or negotiates the purchase, sale, or exchange of real estate, or who leases or rents or offers to rent any real estate for others. Many states add to the licensee's activities the functions of property management, rental collection, and sale of business opportunities. A real estate salesperson is any person who performs any of the acts set forth in the definition of real estate broker for compensation or valuable consideration or promise of compensation or valuable consideration, but does so only while associated with and supervised by a licensed broker.

A real estate broker can own and operate a business, whereas a salesperson licensee can engage in the real estate business only when associated with and supervised by a broker. Therefore, a salesperson cannot operate independently.

Exceptions to Licensing

State laws allow certain categories of persons to perform brokerage for consideration without a license. Some examples are:

1. Owners or lessors acting in regard to property they own or lease.
2. Individuals acting as attorney-in-fact under a duly executed power of attorney authorizing the final consummation of any contract of sale, lease, or exchange of real estate. An **attorney-in-fact** is *a person or organization appointed to perform certain legal acts on behalf of another under a duly executed power of attorney.*
3. In most states, an attorney-at-law is exempt if the services are performed on behalf of clients as part of any attorney's provision of legal services to those clients.
4. Receivers, trustees in bankruptcy, guardians, administrators, or executors acting under a court order.
5. Trustees acting under trust agreements, deeds of trust or will, or trustees' salaried employees.
6. Property managers and builder–developers.

Real Estate Commission

The state assigns responsibility to a licensing board or commission to enforce real estate license law statutes. These bodies are authorized to issue licenses to qualified applicants and to revoke or suspend licenses in the event of statutory or regulatory violations by licensees. The organizations also are empowered by statute to prosecute unlicensed individuals committing acts in violation of the license law statute. These violations typically are misdemeanors or infractions, not felonies, and the license law statutes empower courts to punish the violator either by fine or by imprisonment, or both, at the court's discretion.

Prohibited Acts

Major portions of license law legislation set forth certain standards of conduct, and these are substantially uniform among the states. The standards of conduct reinforce the licensee's obligations to the principal—whether seller or buyer—and the licensee's obligations to the general public. These standards of conduct are designed to protect the general public, which is the major purpose of license law legislation. Licensees' violations of the statutory requirements subject them to license revocation or suspension.

Typical violations that subject a licensee to revocation or suspension of the license are:

1. Obtaining a license under false or fraudulent representation.
2. Having been convicted of or entering a plea of no contest upon which a finding of guilty and final judgment has been entered in a court of competent jurisdiction for

the criminal offense of embezzlement, obtaining money under false pretenses, conspiracy to defraud, forgery, or any similar offense involving moral turpitude.

3. Making any substantial and willful **misrepresentation**. For a broker or salesperson to make *an intentional false statement regarding an important matter in a real estate transaction to induce someone to contract* is a violation. If a broker or salesperson indicates knowledge of an important matter in a real estate transaction when the individual actually has no such knowledge, this is also a violation.

   As an example, the broker or a salesperson is in violation by telling a buyer that a house is well-insulated when the broker or salesperson (a) does not know whether the house is or is not insulated, or (b) knows that it is not properly insulated. If the agent should have known the facts because of his or her training and knowledge as a real estate expert, this is also a misrepresentation through a false statement.

4. Making any **false promises** of a nature likely to influence, persuade, or induce someone to contract. A false promise is simply *an untrue statement of intent to a party that something will or will not happen in a real estate transaction* when the licensee knows that just the opposite is true. A licensee who promises something when he does not know whether the promise will be kept.
5. Pursuing a course of misrepresentation or making false promises through others.
6. Acting for more than one party in a transaction without the knowledge and consent of all parties for whom the licensee acts. For a real estate broker to represent both a buyer and a seller in a real estate transaction without informing both parties of such dual representation and obtaining their agreement is a violation.
7. Accepting compensation from someone other than one's supervising broker. A salesperson licensee is required to accept compensation in a real estate transaction only from his supervising broker. Also, the salesperson may not represent (be licensed under) another broker without the knowledge and consent of the broker with whom he or she is principally associated. Both brokers must agree to such arrangements.
8. Failing to account for and remit funds belonging to others that have come into the licensee's possession. All brokers must maintain trust accounts or escrow accounts in insured banks or thrift institutions for depositing other people's monies. Brokers are prohibited from commingling the funds of others with their business or personal funds. Brokers are required to maintain adequate records regarding the deposit and disbursement of funds from this account. Salesperson licensees are required to promptly remit to their supervising broker all funds belonging to others that come into their possession.
9. Paying an unlicensed person a commission or valuable consideration for services in a real estate transaction. Paying an unlicensed person compensation for services in a real estate transaction is just as much a violation of the license law statute as the unlicensed person's receiving the compensation. Both payor and payee are in violation of the law. Real estate agents should be thoroughly knowledgeable about the policy of their state in this regard.
10. Performing or attempting to perform any legal service prohibited by the state statutes concerned with the **unauthorized practice of law**. A licensee may not prepare legal documents such as deeds or mortgages, may not give an opinion as to the legal validity of any document or the legal rights of others, and may not perform a title examination and render an opinion as to the quality of the title. In essence, a *licensee may not perform any service that must be performed by an attorney-at-law unless the licensee is an attorney-at-law*. In all legal matters affecting buyers and sellers, the licensee should recommend that the parties retain the services of a competent attorney.
11. Failing to deliver all necessary documents handled by the licensee to buyers and sellers in a real estate transaction. Licensees are required to present every written

offer to the seller. It is the seller's prerogative to accept or reject any offer. Licensees also are required to provide to the buyer and the seller copies of all documents executed by buyer, seller, or both. The buyer must receive a copy of the offer, and both buyer and seller must receive copies of the executed contract. The seller always must be given a copy of the listing contract. In addition, copies of any other documents—such as options, contract for deed, or contracts for lease—must be provided to all parties to the agreement.

12. Failing to deliver to buyers and sellers completed copies of closing statements reflecting the receipt and disbursement of funds in a real estate transaction. License law statutes may not require brokers to prepare closing statements, but they often hold brokers responsible for delivering these statements even though they are prepared by someone else.
13. Violating any rule or regulation promulgated by the licensing board or commission. The rules and regulations usually are incorporated into the statutes by statutory reference, which makes a violation of the rules and regulations a violation of law. The rules and regulations have the effect of administrative law.
14. Violating the fair housing laws.

Knowledge of the License Law

Real estate students must be thoroughly knowledgeable of the license law statute and rules and regulations currently in effect for their state or jurisdiction. Students may obtain copies of the license law statute and rules and regulations from the licensing authority in the state to which the student is applying for a real estate license. This knowledge is essential for the student to pass the state licensing examination.

Some real estate licensing examinations are divided into two parts. One part consists of questions about the license law statute and rules and regulations in effect in the state to which license application is being made. The other part consists of questions covering all other real estate subjects of which the applicant must be knowledgeable. Applicants for license must pass both parts of the examination. Other standard examinations incorporate the license law statute questions into the body of the general exam.

Real estate students also must have knowledge of their state's license law and rules and regulations to be assured that their conduct in the real estate business is in accord with the standards required by law after they are licensed. The following outline will help the student determine the license law provisions of his or her state.

Outline of License Law Provisions

Consult your state's information booklet, and here or on a separate sheet of paper, add the appropriate data to the following outline.

GENERAL PROVISIONS

Define—real estate broker

Define—real estate salesperson

Cite exemptions from license requirements

List broker office requirements

List experience requirements—broker

List experience requirements—salesperson

List educational requirements—broker

List educational requirements—salesperson

List continuing education requirements

REAL ESTATE COMMISSION

Give number of members

List qualifications and appointment

Note powers of enforcement

List all penalties for violation

Cite consent agreements and fees

GENERAL LICENSING REQUIREMENTS

Give reason for necessity for license

List qualifications for license of:

- Salesperson
- Broker
- Corporation
- Partnership
- Hybrid or limited licenses

Outline application procedures and fees for licensees

List requirements for displaying license

Specify expiration dates of and renewal procedure for license

Note effect of revocation of broker license on licenses of salespersons in his or her employ

Cite provisions for transfer of license

List branch offices

Cite provisions for discharge or termination of salesperson's employment

Give change of location requirements

Cite effect of death of broker

Note effect of contracts negotiated by licensed persons with those negotiated by unlicensed persons

Cite provisions for:

- Trust accounts
- Bonding
- Convictions
- Sponsorship
- Fee splitting with unlicensed persons
- Commingling
- Fingerprinting

Itemize other rules and regulations for:

- Rental housing
- Appraisals
- Advance fees
- Guaranty fund
- Trust accounts
- Steering/blockbusting
- Reciprocity
- Interstate land sales
- Business opportunity sales
- Time share property

Give grounds for suspension or revocation of license

List other penalties within authority of Real Estate Commission

IMPORTANT POINTS

1. License laws are an exercise of the police power of a state, and the purpose of these laws is to protect the public.
2. All states require that people be licensed to engage in the real estate brokerage business, although license laws allow certain exemptions.
3. A broker is a person or an organization who, for a consideration or promise of a consideration, performs or offers to perform acts of real estate brokerage for others.
4. A salesperson is one who performs acts that a broker is authorized to perform, but only on behalf of the broker with whom he or she is associated.
5. Real Estate Commissions are responsible for enforcing license laws in their state or jurisdiction.
6. License laws establish standards of conduct for licensees.
7. Real Estate Commissions are empowered to issue and revoke or suspend licenses and in some cases to impose fines and issue reprimands.
8. License applicants must be knowledgeable of all the provisions of the license law, commission rules, and other regulations in their state or jurisdiction.

CASE STUDY

ACTION FOR COMMISSION BY "PARTNERSHIP" FAILS

Hoffman listed his property with Real Estate Unlimited, a purported real estate brokerage partnership. Hoffman sold the real estate through his own efforts to a person he found. The buyer had no contact with Real Estate Unlimited.

Real Estate Unlimited sued Hoffman for commission. Hoffman refused to pay the commission because Real Estate Unlimited did not have a valid real estate license, nor did the person who signed the listing on behalf of the partnership.

The Court held the listing was invalid because no real estate license existed. With no listing, no commission was owed.

Hoffman v. Dunn, 1986, 496 N.E. 2d 818

REVIEW QUESTIONS

Answers to these questions are found in the *Answer Key* section at the back of the book.

1. All of the following may be specifically exempted from the licensing law requirements EXCEPT:
   a. trustees in bankruptcy
   b. attorneys-at-law
   c. receivers
   d. individuals under age 21

2. A broker must:
   a. submit all written offers to the seller
   b. give tax advice on the sale
   c. prepare the deed and abstract
   d. refuse the commission if the sale price is 10% below the listed price

3. Which of the following most correctly states the purpose of license law legislation?
   a. to provide protection for licensed brokers and salespersons from competition by unlicensed people
   b. to control the number of people entering the real estate business
   c. to protect the general public by requiring the people entering the real estate business to be adequately qualified
   d. to establish a board of arbitration to settle disputes between licensees

4. The legal authority of a state to require that real estate brokers and salespersons be licensed is derived from:
   a. enabling power
   b. executive power
   c. commission power
   d. police power

5. In an effort to induce a prospective buyer to enter into a contract to purchase a home, a real estate broker tells the buyer that the home is only four years old when it is actually eight years old. The broker knows the actual age of the home. Relying on the broker's statement, the prospect enters into a contract to purchase the property. Given this information, all of the following statements are true EXCEPT:
   a. the broker is in violation of the licensing law
   b. the broker has committed an act of willful misrepresentation
   c. the buyer can have the contract set aside
   d. the seller of the property can sue the buyer if the sale is not completed

6. A seller is so pleased with the manner in which a salesperson has handled the listing and sale of her property that she decides to pay an extra commission to go entirely to the salesperson. The salesperson may accept this special commission provided:
   a. the salesperson receives it directly from the seller
   b. the salesperson is an independent contractor
   c. the broker shares in the extra amount
   d. the seller pays the extra commission to the broker, who in turn passes it on to the salesperson

7. A broker may do all of the following without being in violation of the license law EXCEPT:
   a. market her own property through her real estate office
   b. witness a sales contract
   c. charge varying rates of commission on several different listings
   d. advise a seller as to the validity of a purchase money deed of trust taken by the seller from the buyer in a real estate transaction

8. Which of the following is typically exempt from the requirements to be licensed?
   a. a person who only lists property for sale
   b. a person who only negotiates leases for others
   c. a person engaged in the real estate brokerage business only a few months a year
   d. a person acting for another as an attorney-in-fact in a real estate transaction

9. The major distinction between a licensed salesperson and licensed broker is:
   a. the licensed salesperson must work under the supervision of a licensed broker and not independently
   b. the licensed salesperson always makes less money than a licensed broker
   c. the licensed salesperson is always younger than a licensed broker
   d. the licensed salesperson can only list property whereas a licensed broker can list and sell property

10. All of the following are violations of license laws EXCEPT:
    a. failing to remit documents of funds belonging to another that have come into the licensee's possession
    b. submitting three offers to the seller at one time
    c. signing the seller's name to an offer to purchase without a power of attorney from the seller
    d. failing to disclose to the seller that the person making the offer was really the licensee who had listed the property

CHAPTER 17

Real Estate Math

IN THIS CHAPTER Mathematics plays an important role in every real estate transaction. The mathematics normally involved in real estate transactions consists of nothing more than simple arithmetic applied to mathematical formulas. All that is required is the ability to determine what mathematical formula is involved, and then to add, subtract, multiply, or divide. These calculations are made with whole numbers, fractions, and decimal numbers.

A difficulty some people have in solving real estate mathematics problems is converting word problems into mathematical symbols illustrating the calculations to be performed. For example, the word "of" is translated into a multiplication sign meaning "to multiply." If something is one-half of something else, this means that the solution requires multiplying the fraction ½ times the other unit. "Is" or "represents" always translates into an equal sign. Saying, "Two thousand dollars represents a 10% profit" means $2,000 = a 10% profit.

This chapter sets out the different real estate formulas for finance, appraisal, closing, commissions, profit, loss, square feet, acreage, prorations, and income tax. It also provides practice problems and examples in each area.

APPLICATIONS OF REAL ESTATE MATH

Finance

Typical arithmetic calculations pertaining to real estate finance include annual interest, debt service on a loan, loan-to-value ratios in qualifying for a loan, and amortization of a loan.

Annual interest on a loan is calculated by multiplying the rate of interest as a percentage times the loan balance (also known as the principal balance). The number resulting from the multiplication is the annual interest.

The annual interest calculation also may be used in amortizing a loan on a monthly basis. The annual interest is divided by 12 (number of months in a year) to determine the monthly interest. The monthly interest then is subtracted from the monthly loan payment (principal and interest) to determine what amount of the monthly payment paid applies to reduce the loan principal.

Debt service is the annual amount to be paid to retire or regularly reduce a loan or mortgage balance. The annual debt service on a mortgage is the monthly mortgage payment times 12 (number of months in a year).

Lending institutions use loan-to-value ratios to determine the maximum loan to be issued on a given parcel of real estate. The loan-to-value ratio also can be stated as a percentage of the value of the real estate; in fact, the ratio is much more commonly expressed as a percentage. Some lending institutions lend only up to 90% of the appraised value of the property (a 9:10 ratio). If a lending institution approved a loan of 100% of the value, the loan-to-value ratio would be 1:1. If a lending institution approved a loan that was only 70% of the value, the loan-to-value ratio would be 7:10.

Appraisal

Typical arithmetic calculations involved in real estate appraisal include depreciation on improvements, comparison of properties based upon gross income, and the capitalization rate (rate of return an investor can achieve on a property based upon the present annual net income).

Depreciation on improvements is a reduction in value based upon age. The percentage of value lost each year is determined by dividing the number 1 by the number of years the improvements will last. For example, if a fence will last 15 years, the percentage lost each year is 1 divided by 15, or 6.7%. The percentage lost from passage of time multiplied by the original value shows the amount in dollars lost each year to depreciation. This is called straight-line depreciation.

Gross income on a property is the total income. Net income is the income remaining after subtracting the operating expenses of an investment from the gross income. Operating expenses are the normal day-to-day costs of the property, such as insurance, taxes, and management, but not the debt service or tax depreciation.

Capitalization rate is the percentage of the investment the owner will receive back each year from the net income from the property. This rate is based upon the dollars invested and the annual net income from the property. The capitalization formula is by far the most utilized formula for investment real estate. Investors project the rate of return of money invested based upon present value and present annual net income. Investors also can use the capitalization calculation to project the purchase price of property based upon the present annual net income and a stated desired rate of return. The capitalization formula is:

$$\text{annual net income} \div \text{rate of return} = \text{investment (value)}$$

or

$$\text{investment (value)} \times \text{rate of return} = \text{annual net income}$$

Closing

In closing a real estate transaction, the closing agent may be involved in proration of rents, interest, insurance premiums, and other shared expenses. Also at the closing, preparation of the closing statement requires an understanding of bookkeeping entries and balancing of debits and credits. See Chapter 9 for a further discussion of closing statements.

Miscellaneous Calculations

In addition to a basic understanding of finance, appraisal, and closing arithmetic principles, real estate licensees need a general understanding of commission calculations, square and cubic footage calculations, acreage calculations, profit and loss on sale of real estate, estimating net to the seller after payment of expenses of sale, basic income taxation, and ad valorem taxes.

PRACTICE IN THE MATH OF REAL ESTATE

Fractions

Many mathematical representations are made in the form of fractions. The conversion of fractions to decimal is both necessary and very easy to input into a calculator. Simply take the top numer of the fraction (the numerator) and divide by the lower number (the denominator). For example, the fraction ¼ converts by taking 1 and dividing by 4, or 1 ÷ 4 = .25.

Percentages

In the real estate brokerage business, many arithmetic calculations involve percentages. For example, a real estate broker's commission is a percentage of the sales price.

A percentage is simply a number that has been divided by 100. To use a percentage in an arithmetic calculation, the percentage must be changed to its decimal equivalent. The rule for changing a percentage to a decimal is to remove the percent sign and move the decimal point two places to the left (or divide the percentage by 100). Examples of converting a percentage to a decimal are:

98 % = .98	1½% = 1.5 % = .015
1.42 % = .0142	1¼% = 1.25% = .0125
.092% = .00092	¾% = .75% = .0075

To change a decimal or a fraction to a percentage, simply reverse the procedure. Move the decimal point two places to the right and add the percent sign (or multiply by 100). Some examples of this operation are:

1.00 = 100 %	½ = 1 ÷ 2 = .5 = 50 %
.90 = 90 %	⅜ = 3 ÷ 8 = .375 = 37.5%
.0075 = .75%	⅔ = 2 ÷ 3 = .667 = 66.7%

Formulas

Most arithmetic problems in a real estate transaction use the format of "something" × "something" = "something else." In mathematics language, "factor" × "factor" = "product." Calculating a real estate commission is a classic example:

sales price × percentage of commission = commission paid
$80,000 × 7% = $5,600

In all real estate arithmetic problems, information about two of the three numbers is provided. Calculations to find the third number are required.

If the number missing is the "product," the calculation or function is to multiply the two "factors."

If the number missing is one of the "factors," the calculation or function is to divide the product by the given "factor."

Examples for solving for product follow.

	Answers	
43,500 × 10.5% = ________	(4,567.50)	[43,500 × .105 = 4,567.50]
100,000 × 4 % = ________	(4,000.00)	[100,000 × .04 = 4,000.00]
51.5 × 125 = ________	(6,437.50)	[51.5 × 125 = 6,437.50]

Examples of solving for a missing factor follow.

			Answers
43,500 × ________		= 4,567.50	[4,567.50 ÷ 43,500 = .105 = 10.5%]
______ ×	4%	= 4,000	[4,000 ÷ .04 = 100,000]
51.5 × ________		= 6,437.50	[6,437.50 ÷ 51.5 = 125]

Commission Problems

Problems involving commissions are readily solved by the formula:

sales price × rate of commission = total commission

Sales

1. A real estate broker sells a property for $90,000. Her rate of commission is 7%. What is the amount of commission in dollars?

Solution: sales price × rate = commission
$90,000 × .07 = ________
Product missing: multiply

Answer: $6,300

2. A real estate broker earns a commission of $6,000 in the sale of a residential property. His rate of commission is 6%. What is the selling price?

Solution: sales price × rate = commission
________ × .06 = $6,000
Factor missing: divide $6,000 by .06 =

Answer: $100,000 sales price

3. A real estate broker earns a commission of $3,000 in the sale of property for $50,000. What is her rate of commission?

Solution: sales price × rate = commission
$50,000 × ________ = $3,000
Factor missing: divide $3,000 by $50,000 and convert to percentage

Answer: Rate = 6%

Rentals

4. A real estate salesperson is the property manager for the owner of a local shopping center. The center has five units, each renting for $24,000 per year. The center has an annual vacancy factor of 4.5%. The commission for rental of the units is 9% of the gross rental income. What is the commission for the year?

Solution: gross rental × rate = commission
gross rental = $ 24,000 × 5 minus the vacancy factor
vacancy factor = $120,000 × .045 = $5,400
$120,000 – $5,400 = $114,600
$114,600 × .09 = ________
Product missing: multiply

Answer: $10,314

Splits

5. A real estate salesperson sells a property for $65,000. The commission on this sale to the real estate firm with whom the salesperson is associated is 7%. The salesperson receives 60% of the total commission paid to the real estate firm. What is the firm's share of the commission in dollars?

Solution: sales price × rate = commission
$65,000 × .07 = ________
Product missing: multiply
$65,000 × .07 = $4,550
100% − 60% = 40% is the firm's share
$4,550 × .40 = $1,820

Answer: $1,820 is firm's share of the commission

6. A broker's commission is 10% of the first $50,000 of sales price of a property and 8% on the amount of sales price over $50,000. The broker receives a total commission of $7,000. What is the total selling price of the property?

Solution:

Step 1: sales price × rate = commission
$50,000 × .10 = ________
Product missing: multiply
$50,000 × .10 = $5,000 commission on first $50,000 of sales price

Step 2: Total commission − commission on first $50,000 = commission on amount over $50,000
$7,000 − $5,000 = $2,000 commission on selling price over $50,000

Step 3: Sales price × rate = commission
________ × .08 = 2,000
Factor missing: divide
$2,000 ÷ .08 = $25,000

Step 4: $50,000 + $25,000 = $75,000

Answer: $75,000 total selling price

Estimating Net to Seller

The seller the formula used to estimate the net dollars to the seller is:

sales price × percent to seller = net dollars to seller

The percent to the seller is 100% minus the rate of commission paid to the real estate agent.

7. A seller advises a broker that she expects to net $80,000 from the sale of her property after the broker's commission of 7% is deducted from proceeds of the sale. For what price must the property be sold to provide an $80,000 net return to the seller after paying the broker a 7% commission on the total sales price?

Solution: 100% = gross sales price
100% − 7% = 93%
93% = net to owner

$80,000 = .93 × sales price
Factor missing: divide
$80,000 ÷ .93 =

Answer: $86,022 (rounded)

Profit/Loss on Sale of Real Estate

Profit or loss is always based upon the amount of money invested in the property. The formula for profit is:

investment × percent of profit = dollars in profit

The formula for loss is:

investment × percent of loss = dollars lost

1. Mr. Wong buys a house for investment purposes for $48,000. He sells it six months later for $54,000 with no expenditures for fix-up or repair. What is Mr. Wong's percentage of profit?

Solution: Investment × percentage of profit = dollars in profit
$48,000 × ________ = $6,000
Factor missing: divide and convert decimal to percentage
$6,000 ÷ $48,000 =

Answer: 12.5%

2. Ms. Clary purchases some property in 1987 for $35,000. She makes improvements in 1988 costing her $15,500. In 1990 she sells the property for $46,000. What is her percentage of loss?

Solution: Investment × percentage lost = dollars in loss
$50,500 × ________ = $4,500
Factor missing: divide and convert decimal to percentage
$4,500 ÷ $50,500 = ________

Answer: 8.91%, rounded to 9%

AREA CALCULATIONS

Determining the size of an area in square feet, cubic feet, number of acres, and so forth is done quite frequently in the real estate brokerage business. In taking a listing, the broker should determine the number of square feet of heated area in the house. To establish the lot size, the number of square feet should be determined so it may be translated into acreage, if desired. Table 17.1 provides a list of measures and formulas.

Acreage

1. An acre of land has a width of 330 feet. If this acre of land is rectangular in shape, what is its length? (Each acre contains 43,560 square feet.)

Solution: L × W = A
________ × 330 = 43,560
Factor missing: divide
43,560 ÷ 330 =

Answer: The lot is 132 feet long.

Table 17.1 Measures and formulas.

Linear Measure
12 inches = 1 foot
3 feet = 1 yard
16½ feet = 1 rod, 1 perch or 1 pole
66 feet = 1 chain
5,280 feet = 1 mile

Square Measure
144 sq. inches = 1 sq. foot
9 sq. feet = 1 sq. yard
30¼ sq. yards = 1 sq. rod
160 sq. rods = 1 acre
43,560 sq. ft. = 1 acre
640 acres = 1 sq. mile
1 sq. mile = 1 section
36 sections = 1 township

Formulas
1 side × 1 side = area of a square
width × depth = area of a rectangle
1/2 base × height = area of a triangle
1/2 height × ($base_1$ + $base_2$) = area of a trapezoid
1/2 × sum of the bases = distance between the other two sides at the mid-point of the height of a trapezoid
length × width × depth = volume (cubic measure) of a cube or a rectangular solid

Cubic Measure
1,728 cubic inches = 1 cubic foot
27 cubic feet = 1 cubic yard
144 cubic inches = 1 board foot (12" × 12" × 1")

Circular Measure
360 degrees = circle
60 minutes = 1 degree
60 seconds = 1 minute

Tax Valuation
Per $100 of Assessed Value: Divide the AV by 100, then multiply by tax rate.

$$\frac{\text{Assessed Value}}{100} \times \text{Tax Rate}$$

Per Mill: Divide the AV by 1000, then multiply by tax rate.

$$\frac{\text{Assessed Value}}{1000} \times \text{Tax Rate}$$

2. If a parcel of land contains 32,670 square feet, what percent of an acre is it?

Solution: 32,670 square feet is what % of an acre?
_________ % × 43,560 = 32,670
Factor missing: divide and convert decimal to percent
32,670 ÷ 43,560 =

Answer: 75%

Square Footage

The area of a rectangle or square is determined by simply multiplying the length times the width. In a square, the length and width are the same. In terms of simple formula for a rectangle:

LENGTH times WIDTH = AREA or L × W = A

or, for a square:

SIDE times SIDE = AREA or S × S = A

The area of a triangle is calculated by multiplying one-half times the base of the triangle times the height of the triangle.

.5 × BASE × HEIGHT = AREA

3. A rectangular lot measures 185 feet by 90 feet. How many square feet does this lot contain?

Solution: L × W = A
185 × 90 =
16,650 square feet (SF) =

Answer: 16,650 SF

4. A room measures 15 feet by 21 feet. We want to install wall-to-wall carpet and need to calculate the exact amount of carpet required.

Solution: Carpet is sold by the square yard, so we need to convert square feet to square yards. Number of square feet per square yard is 3 × 3 = 9 SF per square yard. Therefore, to convert size in square feet to size in square yards, we need to divide by 9.

15 × 21 = 315 SF (AREA)
315 ÷ 9 = Square yards

Answer: 35 square yards of carpet

5. What percentage of the lot is occupied by the house shown in the diagram?

Solution:

Step 1: Divide lot into one triangle and one rectangle
.5 × base × height = Area of triangle
.5 × 250 × 150 = A
18,750 square feet = A

Area of rectangle = length × width
400 × 150 = A
60,000 square feet = A

18,750 + 60,000 = Total lot area
78,750 square feet = Lot area

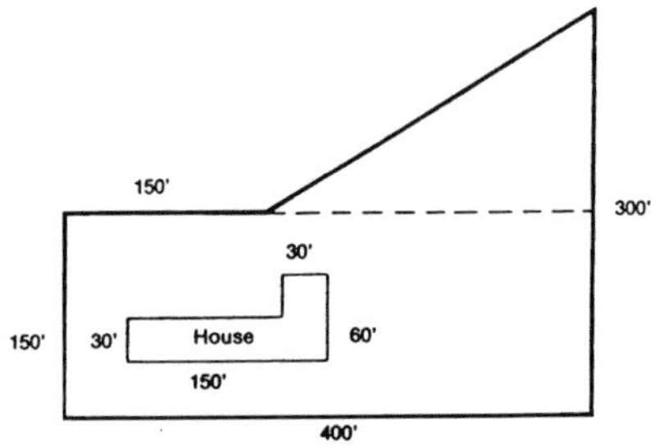

150'
300'
30'
150'
30'
House
60'
150'
400'

Step 2: Divide house into two rectangles
L × W = Area of small rectangle
30 × 30 = A
900 square feet = A

L × W = Area of large rectangle
150 × 30 = A
4,500 square feet = A

900 + 4,500 = Total area of house
5,400 square feet = A

Step 3: house footage divided by lot footage = Percentage of lot occupied by house
5,400 ÷ 78,750 = percentage

Answer: 6.85% of lot occupied by house

Cost/Size

6. A triangular lot measures 200 feet along the street and 500 feet in depth on the side perpendicular to the front lot line. If the lot sells for 10 cents per square foot (SF), what is the selling price?

Solution:
.5 × base × height = area
area × $.10 = selling price
.5 × 200 × 500 = 50,000 SF
50,000 × $.10 = ________

Answer: $5,000

7. A property owner's lot is 80 feet wide and 120 feet long. The lot is rectangular. The property owner plans to have a fence constructed along both sides and across the rear boundary of his lot. The fence is to be 5 feet high. The property owner has determined that the labor cost to construct a fence will be $2.25 per linear foot.

The material cost will be $6.00 per square yard. What is the total cost of constructing the fence?

Solution:

Step 1: First determine the linear footage to establish the labor cost
(2 × 120 ft) + 80 ft = 320 linear feet
320 feet × $2.25 per linear ft = $720 labor cost

Step 2: Establish the number of square yards in the fence to determine material cost.
5 ft × 320 ft = 1,600 sq. ft
1,600 sq ft ÷ 9 (9 square feet in 1 square yard)
= 177.78 sq. yds (rounded)
177.78 × $6.00 per sq. yd = $1,066.68 material cost

Step 3: Total cost
$1,066.68 + $720 = $1,786.68

Answer: $1,786.68 total cost

8. A new driveway will be installed, 115 feet by 20 feet. The paving cost is $.65 per square foot. What will be the minimum cost to pave the new driveway?

Solution:

Step 1: length × width = Area
115 × 20 = A
2,300 square feet = A

Step 2: 2,300 × $.65 = Cost

Answer: $1,495.00

9. A house measures 28 feet wide by 52 feet long and sells for $64,000. What is the price per square foot?

Solution:

Step 1: Calculate the area
28 × 52 = 1,456 square feet (AREA)

Step 2: Divide the sales price by the area
$64,000 ÷ 1,456 =

Answer: $43.96 per square foot

Ad Valorem Property Taxes

Certain terms must be understood to solve problems involving real property taxes. Assessed value is the value established by a tax assessor. The tax value or assessed value usually is a percentage of the estimated market value of the property and may be up to 100% of market value. The amount of tax is calculated by multiplying the assessed value by the tax rate, which is expressed either in dollars per $100 of assessed value or in mills (one mill is one-tenth of a cent) per $1,000 of assessed value. The formula for calculating property tax is:

Assessed value × tax rate = annual taxes

1. If the market value of the property is $80,000 and the assessed value is 100% of the market value, what is the annual tax if the rate is $1.50 per $100?

Solution: Assessed value × tax rate = annual taxes
$80,000 × $\frac{1.50}{100}$ = ________

Product missing: multiply
$80,000 × .0150 = $1,200

Answer: $1,200 annual taxes

2. A property sells at the market value. The annual real property tax is $588.80 at a tax rate of $1.15 per $100 of assessed value. The property is taxed at 80% of market value. What is the selling price?

Solution: Assessed value × tax rate = annual taxes
________ × $\frac{1.15}{100}$ = 588.80
Factor missing: divide
588.80 ÷ .0115 = $51,200 assessed value
Assessed value is 80% of selling price
$51,200 = .80 × ________
Factor missing: divide
$51,200 ÷ .80 = selling price

Answer: $64,000 is selling price

3. If the assessed value of property is $68,000 and the annual tax paid is $850, what is the tax rate expressed as dollars per $100 of assessed value?

Solution: Assessed value × tax rate = annual taxes
$68,000 × ________ = $850
Factor missing: divide, then convert to per $100 of value
$850 ÷ 68,000 = $1.25

Answer: Tax rate is $1.25 per $100 of assessed value

4. If the market value is $70,000, the tax rate is 120 mills, and the assessment is 80%, what is the semiannual tax bill? (To get mills, divide by 1000.)

Solution: .80 × $70,000 = Assessed value
$56,000 = Assessed value
annual taxes = Assessed value × tax rate
________ = 56,000 × 120 mills
$6,720 = Annual tax bill
$6,720 divided by 2 payments per year = Semiannual tax bill

Answer: $3,360 is semiannual tax bill

5. The real property tax revenue required by a town is $140,800. The assessed valuation of the taxable property is $12,800,000. The tax value is 100% of the assessed value. What must the tax rate be per $100 of assessed valuation to generate the necessary revenue?

Solution: Assessed value × tax rate = annual taxes
12,800,000 × ________ = $140,800
Factor missing: divide and convert to per $100 of value
$140,800 ÷ $12,800,000 = $.011 (rate per $1.00)
$.011 × 100 = $1.10 per $100

Answer: Tax rate is $1.10 per $100 of assessed value

Financial Calculations

Financial calculations include simple interest, debt service, points, loan-to-value ratios, loan yields, and qualifying for loans.

Simple Interest

Interest calculations use the formula:

loan balance × rate of interest = annual interest

1. A loan of $15,000 is repaid in full, one year after the loan is made. If the interest rate on the loan is 12.5%, what amount of interest is owed?

Solution: Loan × rate = annual interest
$15,000 × .125 = ________
Product missing: multiply

Answer: $1,875

Principal and Interest

2. On October 1, a mortgagor makes a $300 payment on her mortgage, which is at the rate of 10%. Of the $300 total payment for principal and interest, the mortgagee allocates $200 to the payment of interest. What is the principal balance due on the mortgage on the date of the payment?

Solution: $200 × 12 mo = $2,400 annual interest income
Principal × rate = annual interest
________ × 10% = $2,400
Factor missing: divide
$2,400 ÷ .10 = ________

Answer: Mortgage balance on date of payment is $24,000

3. If an outstanding mortgage balance is $16,363.64 on the monthly payment date and the amount of the payment applied to interest is $150, what is the rate of interest charged on the loan?

Solution: $150 × 12 mo = $1,800 annual interest
Principal × rate = annual interest
16,363.64 × ________ = $1,800
Factor missing: divide and convert to percentage
$1,800 ÷ $16,363.64 =

Answer: Interest rate is 11% (rounded)

Debt Service

4. The monthly amortized car payment Mr. Goldberg owes is $275. What is his annual debt service on this loan?

Solution: Debt service is monthly payment × 12
$275 × 12 =

Answer: $3,300

5. A mortgage loan of $50,000 at 11% interest requires monthly payments of principal and interest of $516.10 to fully amortize the loan for a term of 20 years. If the loan is paid over the 20-year term, how much interest does the borrower pay?

Solution: 20 years × 12 monthly payments = 240 payments
240 × $516.10 = $123,864 total amount paid
Total amount paid – principal borrowed = interest
$123,864 – $50,000 =

Answer: $73,864 interest paid

Fees and Points

The typical fees for real estate mortgages are loan origination fee, points, discount points, interest escrows, and tax escrows. The amount of the fees and escrows often depends upon the loan amount or assessed annual taxes.

The formula for calculating the dollar amount owed in points on a loan is:

loan × number of points (percentage) = dollars in points

6. A house sells for $60,000. The buyer obtains an 80% loan. If the bank charges 3 points at closing, how much in points must the buyer pay?

Solution: Loan × number of points (%) = dollars paid
($60,000 × .80) × .03 =
$48,000 × .03 =
Product missing: multiply

Answer: $1,440

7. Mr. and Mrs. Schmidt borrow $64,000. If they pay $4,480 for points at closing, how many points are charged?

Solution: loan × number of points (%) = dollars paid
$64,000 × ________ = $4,480
Factor missing: divide

Answer: 7 points

8. Mr. and Mrs. Ortega borrow $55,000 at 11% interest for 30 years. The bank requires 2 months' interest to be placed in escrow and a 1% loan origination fee to be paid at closing. What is the amount of interest to be escrowed? What is the amount charged for the loan origination fee?

Step 1: Interest escrow

Solution: $55,000 × .11 = $6,050 annual interest
$6,050 ÷ 12 = $504.17 monthly interest
$504.17 × 2 =

Answer: $1,008.34 interest escrow

Step 2: Loan origination fee

Solution: $55,000 × .01 =

Answer: $550 loan origination fee

Loan-to-Value (LTV) Ratios

9. In problem 8 above, the appraised value of the home purchased is $68,750. What is the loan-to-value ratio?

Solution: Loan ÷ value = ratio
$55,000 ÷ $68,750 = .80
.80 = 80:100

Answer: 80% loan-to-value ratio

10. The Smiths apply for a loan. The purchase price of the home is $80,000. The bank authorizes a loan-to-value ratio of 90%. What is the amount of loan authorized?

Solution: $80,000 × 90% = loan

Answer: $72,000

Yields

Loans issued by banks are repaid with interest. The interest the borrower pays is the "profit" the bank makes. The percentage of profit, however, may be greater than the interest rate charged. The percentage of profit is called the yield of the loan. Yields on loans are increased by points paid at closing. The points paid at closing reduce the amount of money the bank actually must fund. The bank can use the money paid in points to help fund the loan.

11. The First Bank lends $100,000 to the borrower and charges 3 points at closing. The interest rate on the loan is 12% for 25 years. What is the bank's effective yield on the loan?

Solution: $\frac{\text{Actual annual interest}}{\text{Amount funded}} = \text{yield}$
actual annual interest = $100,000 × .12
amount funded = $100,000 – $3,000 = $97,000
$\frac{\$12{,}000}{\$97{,}000} =$

Answer: 12.37%

Qualifying for Loan

Typically, for a borrower to qualify for a loan, the ratios of the borrower's housing and total debts to income must meet the lender's requirements. The typical housing debt-to-income ratio for conventional loans is 25–28%. The typical total debt-to-income ratio for conventional loans is 33–36%. The 25–28% means that for the borrower to qualify, PITIM (principal, interest, taxes, insurance, and mortgage insurance) must not be more than 25–28% of the borrower's monthly gross income. The 33–36% means that for the borrower to qualify, the total monthly expenses (including housing expense) must not be more than 33–36% of the borrower's monthly gross income.

12. Mr. and Mrs. Jones have a combined total monthly income of $2,500. If the lender requires a debt-to-income ratio of 25–33% for housing and total expenses, what is

the maximum house payment for which the Joneses will qualify? What is the maximum total monthly expenses besides PITIM that will be allowed?

Solution:

Step 1 Housing: \$2,500 × .25 = \$625

Step 2 Total expenses: \$2,500 × .33 = \$825
\$825 – \$625 =

Answer: \$200 other than PITIM

Prorations at Closing

Proration is involved in the real estate brokerage business in dividing between seller and buyer the annual real property taxes, rents, and homeowner's association dues to establish the buyer's cost of an insurance policy purchased from the seller. Proration is the process of dividing something into respective shares.

In prorating calculations, the best method is to first draw a timeline with beginning, ending, and date of proration, then decide which part of the timeline is asked for. In calculating prorations for closing statements, the amount is figured to the day of closing.

In prorating, every month is assumed to have 30 days. Therefore, in problems that require calculating a daily rate, the monthly rate is divided by 30, even though the month may be February.

An alternative approach to proration, as described in Chapter 9, is to reduce all costs to a daily basis. Assuming 30 days in every month and 12 months per year, we can assume 360 days per year for our purposes (and most pre-licensing exams).

One other rule to remember in prorating various costs for closing statements is that the day of closing is charged to the seller.

1. In preparing a closing statement for a closing to be held August 14, a real estate broker determines that the annual real property taxes in the amount of \$360 have not been paid. What is put in the buyer's statement as her entry for real property taxes?

   Solution:
   \$360 ÷ 12 = \$30 per month
   \$30 mo. ÷ 30 days = \$l per day
   7 mos. × \$30 = \$210
   \$210 + \$14 = \$224

   Answer: Credit to buyer in the amount of \$224. This is the seller's share of the real property taxes to cover the 7 months and 14 days of the tax year during which he owned the property.

2. A sale is closed on September 15. The buyer is assuming the seller's mortgage, which has an outstanding balance of \$32,000 as of the date of closing. The annual interest rate is 8%, and the interest is paid in arrears. What is the interest proration on the closing statements the broker prepares?

   Solution:
   \$32,000 × .08 = \$2,560 annual interest
   \$ 2,560 ÷ 360 = \$7.111 interest per day
   15 × \$7.111 = \$106.67 interest of 15 days

   Answer: Credit buyer \$106.67
   Debit seller \$106.67

   Because the interest is paid in arrears, the buyer is required to pay the interest for the full month of September when making the scheduled monthly payment on October 1. Therefore, the buyer is credited with the seller's share of 15 days' interest for September in the amount of $106.67. The entry in the seller's closing statement is a debit in this amount.

For a more complete explanation and examples of prorations and closing statements, refer to the closing examples in Chapter 9.

APPRAISAL MATH

Typical appraisal calculations deal with depreciation of improvements on property being appraised or estimation of the value of a property based upon a desired capitalization rate and the present annual net income of the property. (See Chapter 10 for a complete discussion of appraisal.)

Capitalization

As illustrated in Chapter 10, under the income approach, the estimate of value is arrived at by capitalizing the annual net income. The solution to these problems is based on the following formula:

annual net income ÷ capitalization rate = investment (value)
or
investment (or value) × capitalization rate = annual net income

1. An apartment building produces a net income of $4,320 per annum. The investor paid $36,000 for the apartment building. What is the owner's rate of return (cap rate) on the investment?

Solution: Investment × rate = annual net income
$36,000 × ________ = $4,320
Factor missing: divide and convert to percentage

Answer: 12% is annual rate of return on investment

2. An investor is considering the purchase of an office building for $125,000. The investor insists upon a 14% return on investment. What must be the amount of the annual net income from this investment to return a profit to the owner at a rate of 14%?

Solution: Investment × rate = annual net income
$125,000 × .14 = ________
Product missing: multiply

Answer: Annual net income must be $17,500

3. In appraising a shopping center, the appraiser establishes that the center produces an annual net income of $97,500. The appraiser determines the capitalization rate to be 13%. What should be the appraiser's estimate of market value for this shopping center?

Solution: Investment × rate = annual net income or value
________ × 13% = 97,500
Factor missing: divide
$97,500 ÷ .13 =

Answer: $750,000 market value

Depreciation

Depreciation is a loss in value from any cause. The two examples of depreciation that follow represent the types of depreciation problems a real estate student or practitioner may encounter. In the first problem, the present value of a building is given and the requirement is to calculate the original value. The second problem provides the original value to be used in arriving at the present depreciated value.

Depreciation problems use the formula:

original value × % of value NOT lost = present value

4. The value of a 6-year-old building is estimated to be \$45,900. What was the value when new if the building depreciated 2% per year?

Solution: 6 yrs × 2% = 12% depreciation
100% (new value) − 12% = 88% of value not lost
Original value × % not lost = present value
_________ × 88% = 45,900
Factor missing: divide
\$45,900 ÷ .88 = _________

Answer: \$52,159.09 (rounded) value when new

5. A 14-year-old building has a total economic life of 40 years. If the original value of the building was \$75,000, what is the present depreciated value?

Solution: 100% ÷ 40 yrs = 2.5% yearly depreciation rate
14 yrs × 2.5% = 35% depreciation to date
100% − 35% = 65% not lost
Original cost × % not lost = remaining dollar value
\$75,000 × .65 = _________
Product missing: multiply

Answer: Present depreciated value is \$48,750

INCOME TAX CALCULATIONS

Chapter 15 is devoted to a complete discussion of real estate taxation.

Deductions

1. Mr. Romero has owned his home for 12 years. His annual real property taxes are \$360, annual homeowner's insurance is \$270, annual principal payment on his mortgage is \$13,000, and annual interest payment on his mortgage is \$15,500. What is the total deduction allowed against his income for income tax purposes?

Solution: Only mortgage interest and property taxes are deductible when dealing with the principal residence. Total deductions are the sum of mortgage interest and taxes.

Answer: \$15,860

2. Ms. Jones and Ms. Lin are partners in a business. Total yearly expenses for the business are:

taxes	\$450
insurance	\$567
utilities	\$890

wages	$13,333
postage	$275
advertising	$875

Total income from the business is $75,880. What amount of income from the business is reportable for tax purposes?

Solution: In a business, all reasonable and necessary business expenses are deductible against income

Answer: $59,490

Basis

3. Mr. and Mrs. Swift purchased their home 15 years ago for $32,500. During their ownership, they made capital improvements totaling $19,400. They sold the home for $72,900. What amount of gain did they make on the sale?

Solution: Basis = purchase price + improvements
$32,500 + $19,400 = $51,900 basis
Sales price − basis = gain
$72,900 − $51,900 =

Answer: $21,000

4. In problem 3, above, if the Swifts were over age 55 and had never used the one-time exemption, how much gain would be taxable?

Solution: The one-time exemption for persons over age 55 allows the exemption of $125,000.

Answer: All $21,000 of gain is exempt; thus, none is taxable

5. In problem 3, above, if the Swifts purchase another home costing $90,000 and choose to defer reporting the gain, what is the basis in the new home?

Solution: Purchase price − any deferred gain = basis
$90,000 − 21,000 =

Answer: $69,000 is basis in new home

MISCELLANEOUS PROBLEMS

1. A subdivision contains 400 lots. If a broker has sold 25% of the lots and his sales staff has sold 50% of the remaining lots, how many lots are still unsold?

Solution: .25 × 400 = 100 sold by broker
400 − 100 = 300
300 × ½ = 150 sold by sales force
400 − 250 sold = 150 unsold

Answer: 150 lots still unsold

2. An owner purchases his home at 8% below market value. He then sells the property for the full market value. What is the rate of profit?

Solution: Market value = 100%
100% − 8% = 92% purchase price
8% ÷ 92% = rate of profit
.08 ÷ .92 =

Answer: 8.7% profit

Review Problems

1. A sale is closed on February 12. The buyer is assuming the seller's mortgage, which has an outstanding balance of $28,000 as of the closing date. The last mortgage payment was made February 1. The annual interest rate is 7¾%, and interest is paid in arrears. What interest proration appears in the buyer's closing statement?
   a. $72.36 credit
   b. $77.52 credit
   c. $180.83 debit
   d. $253.19 credit

2. A real estate broker earns a commission of $4,900 at a rate of 7%. What is the selling price of the property?
   a. $24,000
   b. $44,400
   c. $65,000
   d. $70,000

3. A property is sold at market value. If the assessed value is 100% of market value, the tax rate is $1.50, and the annual tax is $540, what is the selling price of the property?
   a. $24,000
   b. $27,700
   c. $36,000
   d. $81,000

4. What is the annual rent if a lease specifies the rent to be 2½% of gross sales per annum, with a minimum annual rent of $4,800, if the lessee's gross sales are $192,000?
   a. $4,800
   b. $7,680
   c. $12,000
   d. $16,000

5. A rectangular lot measures 40 yards deep and has a frontage of 80 feet. How many acres does the lot contain?
   a. .07
   b. .21
   c. .22
   d. .70

6. A real estate salesperson earns $24,000 per year. If she receives 60% of the 7% commissions paid to her firm on her sales, what is her monthly dollar volume of sales?
   a. $33,333.33
   b. $45,000.00
   c. $47,619.08
   d. $90,000.00

7. A parking lot containing 2 acres nets $12,000 per year. The owner wishes to retire and sell his parking lot for an amount that will net him $12,000 per year by investing the proceeds of the sale at 8½% per annum. What must the selling price be to accomplish the owner's objective?
   a. $96,000
   b. $102,000
   c. $120,000
   d. $141,176

8. A group of investors purchases two tracts of land. They pay $48,000 for the first tract. The first tract costs 80% of the cost of the second tract. What is the cost of the second tract?
   a. $9,600
   b. $28,800
   c. $60,000
   d. $125,000

9. An office building produces a gross income of $12,600 per year. The vacancy factor is 5%, and annual expenses are $3,600. What is the market value if the capitalization rate is 12%?
   a. $15,120
   b. $69,750
   c. $99,750
   d. $105,000

10. If the monthly interest payment due on a mortgage on December 1 is $570 and the annual interest rate is 9%, what is the outstanding mortgage balance?
    a. $61,560.00
    b. $63,333.33
    c. $76,000.00
    d. $131,158.00

11. A building has a total economic life of 50 years. The building is now 5 years old and has a depreciated value of $810,000. What was the value of the building when it was new?
    a. $891,000
    b. $900,000
    c. $972,000
    d. $1,234,568

12. If the assessed value is 100% of the market value and the market value is $63,250, what are the annual taxes if the rate is $2.10 per $100?
    a. $132.83
    b. $1,328.25
    c. $3,011.90
    d. $3,320.16

13. If Mr. Jackson buys three parcels of land for $4,000 each and sells them as four separate parcels for $4,500 each, what percent profit does he make?
    a. 33%
    b. 50%
    c. 60%
    d. 150%

14. The current value of a 12-year-old house is $56,000. If this house has an economic life of 40 years, what was its value when new?
    a. $79,550.00
    b. $80,000.00
    c. $80,500.00
    d. $82,436.86

15. The outside dimensions of a rectangular house are 35 feet by 26.5 feet. If the walls are all 9 inches thick, what is the square footage of the interior?
    a. 827.5 sq ft
    b. 837.5 sq ft
    c. 927.5 sq ft
    d. 947.7 sq ft

16. A buyer is to assume a seller's existing loan with an outstanding balance of $20,000 as of the date of closing. The interest rate is 9%, and payments are made in arrears. Closing is set for October 10. What will be the entry in the seller's closing statement?
    a. $50 credit
    b. $50 debit
    c. $150 credit
    d. $150 debit

17. A house is listed for $40,000. An offer is made and accepted for $38,500, if the seller agrees to pay 5½% discount points on a VA loan of $33,000. The broker's fee is at a rate of 6%. How much will the seller net from the sale?
    a. $34,375.00
    b. $35,875.00
    c. $36,382.50
    d. $38,500.00

18. A house and lot were assessed for 60% of market value and taxed at a rate of $3.75 per $100 of assessed value. Five years later the same tax rate and assessment rate still exist, but annual taxes have increased by $750. How much has the dollar value of the property increased?
    a. $8,752.75
    b. $20,000.00
    c. $33,333.33
    d. $38,385.82

19. What is the sales price of an apartment complex having an annual rental of $80,000 with expenses of $8,000 annually if the purchaser receives an 8% return?
    a. $66,240
    b. $800,000
    c. $864,000
    d. $900,000

20. A lease specifies a minimum monthly rental of $700 plus 3% of all business over $185,000. If the lessee does annual gross business of $220,000, how much rent is paid that year?
    a. $6,000
    b. $9,450
    c. $11,550
    d. $12,600

21. An apartment building contains 20 units. Each unit rents for $480 per month. The vacancy rate is 5%. Annual expenses are $13,500 for maintenance, $2,400 insurance, $2,500 taxes, $2,900 utilities, and 10% of the gross effective income for management fee. What is the investor's net rate of return for the first year if she paid $195,000 for the property?
    a. 7.61%
    b. 8.62%
    c. 22.05%
    d. 39.59%

22. A house has a market value of $35,000, and the lot has a market value of $7,000. The property is assessed at 80% of market value at a rate of $2.12 per $100. If the assessed valuation is to be increased by 18%, what is the amount of taxes to be paid on the property?
    a. $712.32
    b. $840.54
    c. $890.40
    d. $1,050.67

23. An owner lists a property for sale with a broker. At what price must the property be sold to net the owner $7,000 after paying a 7% commission and satisfying the existing $48,000 mortgage?
    a. $49,354
    b. $56,750
    c. $57,750
    d. $59,140

24. A tract of land is divided as follows: one-half of the total area for single-family dwellings, one-fourth of the area for shopping, and one-eighth of the area for streets and parking. The remaining seven acres are to be used for parks. What is the total acreage of the tract?
    a. 28 acres
    b. 49 acres
    c. 56 acres
    d. 70 acres

25. The value of a seven-year-old building is estimated to be $63,000. What was the value when new if the building depreciated 2½% per year?
    a. $67,725
    b. $74,025
    c. $76,363
    d. $114,975

26. An investor builds an office building at a cost of $320,000 on land costing $40,000. Other site improvements total $20,000. What must be the annual net income from the property to return a profit to the owner at an annual rate of 12%?
    a. $31,666
    b. $38,400
    c. $43,200
    d. $45,600

27. A real estate sale closes on February 20. The real property taxes have not been paid. Market value of the property is $67,500, and the assessed value is 80% of market value. Tax rate is $1.50 per $100 of assessed value. What is the proper entry on the seller's settlement statement regarding real property taxes?
    a. $112.50 credit
    b. $112.50 debit
    c. $697.50 credit
    d. $697.50 debit

28. A triangular lot measures 350 feet along the street and 425 feet deep on the side perpendicular to the street. If a broker sells the lot for $.75 (cents) per square foot and his commission rate is 9%, what is the amount of commission earned?
    a. $5,020.31
    b. $6,693.75
    c. $10,040.63
    d. $14,875.00

29. A property owner is having a concrete patio poured at the rear of the house. The patio is to be rectangular and will be 4 yards by 8 yards. The patio is to be 6 inches thick. The labor cost for the project is $3.50 per square yard, and the material cost is $1.50 per cubic foot. What will be the total cost of the patio?
    a. $112
    b. $198
    c. $328
    d. $552

30. A broker's commission is 8% of the first $75,000 of the sales price of a house and 6% of the amount over $75,000. What is the total selling price of the property if the broker receives a total commission of $9,000?
    a. $79,500
    b. $93,000
    c. $105,000
    d. $125,000

31. A buyer pays $45,000 for a home. Five years later she puts it on the market for 20% more than she originally paid. The house eventually sells for 10% less than the asking price. At what price is the house sold?
    a. $44,100
    b. $48,600
    c. $49,500
    d. $54,000

32. The owner of a rectangular unimproved parcel of land measuring 600 feet wide (front) by 145.2 feet long is offered $15 per front foot or $4,000 per acre. What is the amount of the higher offer?
    a. $2,187
    b. $7,680
    c. $8,000
    d. $9,000

33. A city with rent-control guidelines says a landlord may increase the rent on apartments by 2.25% of the cost of improvements made to the property. The landlord spends $1,200 per unit for improvements, then raises the rent from $380 to $415. By how much has the owner exceeded the guidelines?
    a. $8
    b. $15
    c. $26
    d. $35

34. $150 is 2½% of what amount?
    a. $375
    b. $600
    c. $1,666
    d. $6,000

35. After purchasing a home containing 2,300 square feet on a rectangular lot 150 feet by 210 feet, the owner adds a two-car garage with interior dimensions of 23 feet by 22 feet. The house is valued at $26 per square foot, the lot at 25 cents per square foot, and the garage at $12 per square foot. What is the percentage of increase in value of the property resulting from the addition of the garage?
    a. 8.23%
    b. 8.97%
    c. 10.15%
    d. 11.15%

36. A broker negotiates the sale of the northeast ¼ of the northeast ¼ of the northeast ¼; section 25, township 2 south; range 1 east, for $700 per acre. The listing agreement with the owner specifies a 12% commission. How much does the broker earn?
    a. $480
    b. $840
    c. $3,360
    d. $8,400

37. A tract of land containing 560 square rods is sold for 12 cents per square foot. What is the total selling price?
    a. $6,720
    b. $11,088
    c. $18,295
    d. $20,160

38. A property owner plans to fence his land, which is rectangular in shape and measures 300 feet by 150 feet. How many fence posts will be required if there is to be a post every 15 feet?
    a. 45
    b. 60
    c. 61
    d. 450

39. A triangular tract is 4,000 feet long and has 900 feet of highway frontage, which is perpendicular to the 4,000-foot boundary. How many square yards does the tract contain?
    a. 200,000
    b. 300,000
    c. 400,000
    d. 1,800,000

40. The owner of an apartment building earns a net income of $10,200 per year. The annual operating cost is $3,400. The owner is realizing a net return of 14% on investment. What price was paid for the building?
    a. $48,572
    b. $72,857
    c. $97,143
    d. $142,800

41. A percentage lease stipulates a minimum rent of $1,200 per month and 3% of the lessee's annual gross sales over $260,000. The total rent paid by the end of the year is $16,600. What is the lessee's gross business income for the year?
    a. $73,333.33
    b. $260,000.00
    c. $333,333.33
    d. $553,333.33

42. A building now 14 years old has a total economic life of 40 years. If the replacement cost of the building is $150,000, what is the present depreciated value?
    a. $52,500
    b. $60,000
    c. $97,500
    d. $202,500

43. On February 1 a mortgagor makes a $638 payment on her mortgage, at the rate of 10%. The mortgagee allocates $500 to payment of interest. What is the principal balance due on the mortgage on February 1?
    a. $38,400
    b. $60,000
    c. $79,750
    d. $95,700

44. Plans for a house under construction include a rectangular basement 30 feet wide and 90 feet long that is to be excavated to a uniform depth of 14 feet. A subcontractor receives 50 cents per cubic yard for the excavating work. How much does the subcontractor receive?
    a. $315
    b. $700
    c. $1,050
    d. $1,400

45. A house valued at $60,000 is insured for 85% of value. The annual premium is 60 cents per $100 of the face amount of the policy. The homeowner pays a three-year premium on February 28. On April 30 of the following year, she closes the sale of the home. The buyer is having this policy endorsed to him. What will be the buyer's cost?
    a. $306
    b. $357
    c. $510
    d. $561

46. The scale of a map is 1 inch equals 2½ miles. What distance is represented by 4½ inches on the map?
    a. 7 miles
    b. 11¼ miles
    c. 18 miles
    d. 180 miles

47. In planning the development of a tract of land, the developer allocates one-half of the total area to single-family dwellings, one-third to multifamily dwellings, and 20 acres for roads and recreation areas. What is the total number of acres in the tract?
    a. 36.67
    b. 56.67
    c. 120
    d. 320

48. A developer pays $900 per acre for a 125-acre tract. His costs for grading, paving, and surveying total $1,300,000. He constructs 200 houses at an average cost of $115,000 each. What is the average sales price per house if the developer realizes a net return of 14% on his total investment?
    a. $64,267.00
    b. $121,906.25
    c. $139,151.25
    d. $154,062.52

49. A lender allows a loan-to-value ratio of 85% on a home loan for a buyer. If the purchase price is $96,000 and the appraisal is $97,500, what is the buyer's required down payment?
    a. $14,400
    b. $15,000
    c. $81,600
    d. $82,875

50. A builder has 26 acres of land with 1,320 feet of depth off the road. What is the value if the local prices are $1,500 per front foot?
    a. $1,132,560
    b. $1,181,818
    c. $1,287,000
    d. $1,980,000

SOLUTIONS TO REVIEW PROBLEMS

The letter of the correct answer choice appears next to the question number.

1a. \$28,000 × .0775 = \$2,170/yr
\$2,170 ÷ 12 mos = \$180.83/mo
\$180.83 ÷ 30 days = \$6.03/day
\$6.03 × 12 days = \$72.36 used portion
As payments are made in arrears, this amount is a credit to buyer and a debit to seller

2d. Sales price × rate = total commission
× 7% = 4,900
Factor missing: divide
\$4,900 ÷ .07 = \$70,000

3c. Assessed value × tax rate = annual tax
_______ × $\frac{1.50}{100}$ = \$540
Factor missing: divide
540 ÷ .0150 = \$36,000

4a. Rent is 2½% of gross sales
2½% × gross sales = Rent
.025 × \$192,000 = ______
Product missing: multiply
.025 × \$192,000 = \$4,800

5c. 40 yds × 3 ft/yd = 120 ft
120 ft × 80 ft = 9600 sq ft
9600 sq ft ÷ 43,560 sq ft = .22 acres

6c. 24,000 is 60% of total commission
60% × total commission = 24,000
Factor missing: divide
24,000 ÷ .60 = \$40,000
Sales price × rate of comm. = total comm.
_______ × 7% = \$40,000
Factor missing: divide
40,000 ÷ .07 = 571,429 per year in sales
Divide by 12 to get monthly volume of sales
\$571,429 ÷ 12 = \$47,619.08

7d. Investment × rate of return = annual net income
_______ × 8½% = 12,000
Factor missing: divide
\$12,000 ÷ .085 = \$141,176 (rounded)

8c. 80% of second tract = first tract
.8 × ? (2nd tract) = \$48,000
2nd tract = \$48,000 ÷ .8
2nd tract = \$60,000

9b. Market value (investment) × cap rate = annual net income
12,600 − vacancy factor − expenses = Annual net income
Vacancy factor = 12,600 × .05 = \$630
\$12,600 − \$630 − \$3,600 = \$8,370 annual net income
_______ × 12% = 8,370
Factor missing: divide
\$8,370 ÷ .12 = \$69,750

10c. Loan balance × rate of interest = annual interest
_______ × 9% = (570 × 12)
Factor missing: divide
6,840 ÷ .09 = \$76,000

11b. Original value × % not lost = present value
1 ÷ 50 = 2% lost each year
_______ × (100% − 10%) = 810,000
_______ × 90% = 810,000
Factor missing: divide
810,000 ÷ .90 = \$900,000

12b. Assessed value × tax rate = annual taxes
63,250 × .0210 =________
Product missing: multiply
Annual taxes \$1,328.25

13b. 4,000 × 3 = 12,000 invested
4,500 × 4 = 18,000 sales price
18,000 − 12,000 = 6,000 profit
Investment × % of profit = dollars in profit
12,000 × ________ = \$6,000
Factor missing: divide; convert to percentage
6,000 ÷ 12,000 = 50%

14b. 40 years − 12 = 28 remaining
28 ÷ 40 = .70 = 70% not lost
Original value × % not lost = present value
_______ × 70% = 56,000
Factor missing: divide
\$56,000 ÷ .70 = \$80,000

15b. 9 inches thick on each of two ends = 1.5 ft
35 ft − 1.5 ft = 33.5 ft
26.5 ft − 1.5 ft = 25 ft
33.5 ft × 25 ft = 837.5 sq ft

16b. Loan balance × rate of interest = annual interest
$20,000 × .09 = ________
Product missing: multiply
Annual interest = $1,800
1,800 ÷ 12 months = 150 per month
150 ÷ 30 = $5 per day
10 × 5 = $50 debit to seller

17a. Expenses of sale and closing are points and commission.
Points:
Loan × number of points as percentage = dollars in points
$33,000 × .055 = ________
Product missing: multiply
Dollars in points are $1,815
Commission:
Sales price × rate of commission = total commission
38,500 × .06 = ________
Product missing: multiply
Total commission = $2,310
2,310 + 1,815 = total expenses
$38,500 – 4,125 = $34,375 net to seller

18c. $750 incr. ÷ $3.75 = 200 ($100 units)
200 ($100 units) × $100/unit = $20,000 tax value
$20,000 ÷ .60 = $33,333.33

19d. Investment of value × rate of return = annual net income
________ × 8% = 72,000
Factor missing: divide
$72,000 ÷ .08 = $900,000

20b. $700/mo × 12 mo = $8,400/year base rent
$220,000 – $185,000 = $35,000 (earnings over $185,000)
$35,000 × .03 = $1,050
$8,400 + $1,050 = $9,450

21d. 20 units × $480/mo × 12 mos = $115,200 gross rent
$115,200 – $5,760 (vacancy @ 5%) = $109,440 gross effective income
$109,440 – 32,244 (expenses) = $77,196 net income
Value × rate of return = annual net income
195,000 × ________ = $77,196
Factor missing: divide and convert to percentage
$77,196 ÷ $195,000 = 39.59% (rounded)

22b. 35,000 + 7,000 = 42,000 total assessed value
42,000 × 1.18 = 49,560 increased valuation
49,560 × .80 = 39,648 new tax basis
Assessed value × tax rate = annual taxes
39,648 × 2.12/100 = ________
Product missing: multiply
$39,648 × .0212 = $840.54 (rounded)

23d. $7,000 + $48,000 = $55,000
100% – 7% commission = 93%
$55,000 divided by .93 = $59,140 (rounded)

24c. ½ + ¼ + ⅛ = unknown area
4/8 + 2/8 + ⅛ = ⅞
8/8 – ⅞ = ⅛ remaining
Area = 7 acres = ⅛
⅛ of total = 7 acres
Total = 7 acres × 8/1 = 56 acres

25c. 7 yrs × 2.5 = 17.5% depreciation to date
100% – 17.5% = 82.5% remaining value
Original value × % not lost = present value
________ × 82.5% = 63,000
Factor missing: divide
$63,000 ÷ .825 = $76,363 (rounded)

26d. Investment × rate = annual net income
380,000 × .12 = ________
Product missing: multiply
$380,000 × .12 = $45,600

27b. Seller owes for 30 + 20 days = 50 days
67,500 × .80 = 54,000 tax value
Tax value × rate = annual taxes
54,000 × .0150 = $810
810 ÷ 12 = 67.50/month
67.50 ÷ 30 = 2.25/day
2.25 × 50 = $112.50 debit to seller

28a. Area of a triangle = ½ × base × height
½ × 350 ft × 425 ft = 74,375 sq ft
74,375 sq ft × .75/sq ft = $55,781.25 sales price
$55,781.25 × .09 = $5,020.31

29c. 4 yds × 8 yds = 32 sq yds
32 sq yds × $3.50/sq yd = $112 labor costs
½ ft × 12 ft × 24 ft = 144 cubic feet
144 cu ft × $1.50 = $216 material costs
$112 + $216 = $328

30d. \$75,000 × .08 = \$6,000 commission on first \$75,000
\$9,000 − \$6,000 = \$3,000 commission on price over \$75,000
sales price × rate = commission
________ × 6% = 3,000
Factor missing: divide
\$3,000 ÷ .06 = \$50,000 sales over \$75,000
\$75,000 + \$50,000 = \$125,000

31b. \$45,000 × 1.20 (120%) = \$54,000 asking price
\$54,000 × .90 = \$48,600 sold price

32d. 600 ft × 145.2 ft = 87,120 sq ft
87,120 sq ft ÷ 43,560 sq ft/acre = 2 acres
2 acres × \$4,000 = \$8,000 acreage basis
\$15 × 600 ft = \$9,000 front-foot basis

33a. 1,200 × .0225 = \$27 maximum allowable increase
\$415 − \$380 = \$35 increase
\$35 − \$27 = \$8

34d. 2½% × ________ = 150
Factor missing: divide
\$150 ÷ .025 = \$6,000

35b. 2,300 sq ft × \$26 = \$59,800 house value
150 ft × 210 ft = 31,500 sq ft lot area
31,500 sq ft × \$.25 = \$7,875 lot value
\$59,800 + \$7,875 = \$67,675 value of house and lot
23 ft × 22 ft = 506 sq ft interior of garage
506 sq ft × \$12 = \$6,072 garage value
Value increase ÷ original value = percentage of increase
\$6,072 ÷ \$67,675 = .0897, or 8.97%

36b. ¼ × ¼ × ¼ × 640 acres = total acres sold
.25 × .25 × .25 × 640 = 10 acres sold
10 acres × 700 = \$7,000 sales price
Sales price × rate = commission
7000 × .12 =________
Product missing: multiply
\$7000 × .12 = \$840

37c. 160 square rods = 1 acre (43,560 sq ft)
560 sq rods ÷ 160 sq rods/acre = 3.5
3.5 acres × 43,560 sq ft/acre = 152,460 sq ft
152,460 sq ft × \$.12 = \$18,295

38b. (2 × 300 ft) + (2 × 150 ft) = 900 feet
900 ft ÷ 15 ft/post = 60 posts

39a. ½ × base × height = area of a right triangle
½ × 900 ft × 4000 ft = 1,800,000 sq ft
1,800,000 sq ft ÷ 9 sq ft/sq yd = 200,000 sq yd

40b. Investment × rate = annual net income
________ × 14% = 10,200
Factor missing: divide
\$10,200 ÷ .14 = \$72,857

41c. 12 mos × 1,200 = \$14,400 minimum annual rent
\$16,600 − 14,400 = \$2,200 above minimum
\$2,200 is 3% of what amount?
3% × ________ = \$2,200
Factor missing: divide
\$2,200 ÷ .03 = \$73,333.33 over \$260,000
\$260,000 + \$73,333.33 = \$333,333.33 total sales

42c. 1 ÷ 40 years = 2½% per year depreciation
14 years × 2.5%/yr = 35% depreciation to date
100% − 35% = 65% remaining value
Replacement cost × % not lost = current value
\$150,000 × .65 = \$97,500

43b. \$500 × 12 mos = \$6,000 annual interest
Loan balance × rate = annual interest
________ × 10% = 6,000
Factor missing: divide
\$6,000 ÷ .10 = \$60,000

44b. Length × width × depth = cubic measure
90 ft × 30 ft × 14 ft = 37,800 cu ft
37,800 ÷ 27 cu ft/cu yd = 1400 cu yds
1400 cu yd × \$.50 = \$700

45d. \$60,000 × .85 = \$51,000 face amount
\$51,000 ÷ 100 = 510 units
\$.60 × 510 units = \$306 annual premium
\$306 × 3 years = \$918 premium for 3 years
\$918 ÷ 36 months = \$25.50 per month
\$25.50 × 14 months = \$357 used up
\$918 − \$357 = \$561

46b. 4½" × 2½ = ?
$\frac{9}{2} \times \frac{5}{2} = \frac{45}{4}$ = 11¼ miles

47c. ½ + ⅓ = unknown area
3/6 + 2/6 = 5/6
6/6 (entire area) − 5/6 = 1/6
Remainder = 20 acres
1/6 = 20 acres
Entire tract = 20 × 6 = 120 acres

48c. 125 acres × $900 = $112,500
200 houses × $115,000 = $23,000,000
Other costs = $1,300,000
$112,500 + $23,000,000 + $1,300,000 = $24,412,500 invested
1.14(114%) × $24,412,500 = $27,830,250 gross sales
$27,830,250 ÷ 200 houses = $139,151.25 per house

49a. The lender will lend based on the lower of appraised value or sale price
85% × $96,000 = maximum loan
.85 × $96,000 = $81,600
$96,000 price − $81,600 loan = $14,400 down payment

50c. 26 acres × 43,560 square feet per acre = 1,132,560 square feet
1,132,560 square feet ÷ 1,320 feet deep = 858 feet of frontage
858 front feet × $1,500 = $1,287,000 total value

APPENDIX A

Basic House Construction

The purpose of this chapter is to provide a basic understanding of the principles, terminology, and methods of residential construction. It is divided into 11 sections and gives an overview of the construction process from the foundation to the roof. Also included is some common terminology used in residential construction. The material in this chapter is confined to wood-frame and masonry construction.

Architectural Types and Styles

The four basic types of homes are one-story, one-and-a-half-story, two-story, and split-level. Homes of two-and-a half and three stories can be found, but these homes typically are very large and expensive and thus are not as common as the types listed above.

Although there are four basic types of homes, there are many styles of residential construction. The most common styles are **Ranch, Contemporary, Colonial, French Provincial, Tudor, Cape Cod**, and **Victorian**. This list is certainly not all-encompassing but it identifies the most common styles built in the 1900s. Drawings of the various types and styles are shown in Figure A.1.

The popularity of a particular type and style of construction varies from person to person and region to region and ultimately is a matter of functionality, affordability, and taste. The Ranch style tends to be of modest size and affordability, which contributes to its popularity. A Cape Cod one-and-a-half-story typically provides future expansion space on the upper level for a growing family. The traditional two-story is quite popular, as it can be built in a variety of styles to suit almost anyone's taste. Its extra space is perfect for a growing family or a family that needs extra room. The split-level, while not as popular as the other types of construction, takes advantage of the terrain by having the lower level partially below ground, similar to a basement. One disadvantage to this type of construction is that stairs are required to get from one level to another. In some cases, as many as two or three sets of stairs are required. This typically is a disadvantage for older homeowners who do not desire to use stairs to access all areas of the house.

Many modern styles of housing take advantage of high and open ceilings, lofts, or balconies. A variety of styles exists in this category to suit modern tastes. A renaissance of Victorian architecture has occurred, and these new homes take advantage of

FIGURE A.1
Architectural styles.

Colonial

Two-Story Contemporary

Victorian

Two-Story Tudor

French Provincial

Cape Cod

Ranch

Tri-Level

factory-built molded trim and exterior detailing in an attempt to keep costs down and make the homes more affordable.

Of course, in any type or style of construction, the floor plan must provide functional utility. Good design increases the comfort and resale potential for any home. Good design includes a modern heating and cooling system, adequate closets and storage space, a bathroom for every bedroom, living and sleeping areas of sufficient size, and the proper placement and size of windows to provide adequate light and ventilation. The grouping of bedroom and bathroom areas so as to provide privacy is also important. The kitchen should be designed to provide an efficient, attractive work area, and it should be located near a utility, rear, or side entrance, for access to the outside. The traditional living room seems to have decreased in functional significance in favor of the family room or den for the active family. Modern design may include an attached two-car garage, wood deck and/or patio, and a family room.

Location on Site

The location of the house on the building site can have a significant effect on value. Land use regulations and local covenants usually mandate a required setback from the street and side and rear property lines. A location that takes advantage of available views, privacy, terrain, and ease of access adds to the value and enjoyment of the home.

Foundations

Footings

Arguably the most important foundation building block is the footing. The footing is the concrete base below the frost line that supports the foundation of the structure. To construct the footings, the building lines are laid out with **batter boards**, temporary wood members on posts that form an L-shape outside the corners of the foundation. Strings are run from the batter boards to line up the placement of the foundation walls. Trenches are dug for the footings, which must rest on undisturbed soil. **Grade stakes** are then placed in the trenches to measure and verify proper elevation and thickness of the footing—prior to pouring the concrete. Once this is complete, the footing can be poured. Footings are composed of cast-in-place concrete. When constructing footings, it is also recommended that **reinforcement rods**, or *rebar* as it is commonly known, be placed in the concrete to aid in temperature control and make for a stronger footing. This is especially important in areas with unstable soil or a high water table and in coastal regions.

The width of the footing is twice the width of the foundation wall. The depth of the footing is usually a minimum of eight inches (one- and two-story homes), as it should be the same thickness as the foundation wall. If the wall is thicker, the footing must be thicker. Fireplace footings must be a minimum of 12 inches thick for masonry fireplaces.

The purpose of the footing is to support the foundation wall and, subsequently, the entire weight load of the structure. The footings must provide an adequate base for the structure to prevent settling of the house.

Foundation Walls

Foundation walls generally are composed of either poured concrete, masonry block, or brick. The most common type of foundation wall is one made with masonry block and brick. The masonry block forms the back half of the wall and is covered with a brick veneer on the front. Vertical masonry **piers** are built inside the foundation walls to provide additional support for the house. If only masonry block is used in the foundation wall, the exterior portions of the blocks are faced with a smooth mortar finish known as **parging**. The parged walls are painted to improve the appearance of the foundation. In some instances, foundation walls are covered with stucco to improve the appearance and hide the masonry block.

In level terrain, the foundation may be a concrete slab instead of a foundation wall. The concrete slab is poured directly on the ground and thus eliminates the crawl space or basement. The slab provides the floor of the dwelling and the support for the exterior and interior walls. The concrete slab method is less expensive than the foundation wall system or basement but is not practical in all building situations.

The foundation wall with crawl space is widely used throughout the United States. Basements, although popular, are expensive to construct and cannot be used in the eastern and coastal regions due to a high water table.

Moisture control is a serious problem that must be addressed in any foundation system. First, grading of the soil must assure that surface water is directed away from the foundation and that proper drainage is provided. Footing drain tile is used around all concrete or masonry foundations enclosing habitable or usable space, below grade. Additionally, crawl spaces under homes must be properly graded to assure positive drainage.

Equally important, **foundation vents** must be installed in foundation walls to properly ventilate the crawl space underneath the house. Some states now make the installation of an approved **vapor barrier** (usually heavy-duty plastic) mandatory in crawl spaces. The vents and vapor barrier are necessary to allow the crawl space and wood members of the floor system to remain dry and free from unnecessary moisture damage. Termite treatment is applied after the foundation is complete and prior to the vapor barrier installation. In the case of a concrete basement floor or slab, termite treatment and vapor barrier are applied prior to pouring the concrete.

FRAMING

Framing refers to the wooden skeleton of the home. Framing members are lumber with a nominal dimension of 2 inches thick. For example, a **2" × 4"** is a piece of lumber 2 inches thick by 4 inches wide. Wall **studs** are commonly 2" × 4"s; 2" × 8"s, 2" × 10"s, or 2" × 12"s are commonly used for **joists** for floor and ceiling framing. Usually 2" × 6"s or 2" × 8"s are used as **rafters** in the roof system. (See Figures A.2 and A.3.)

Flooring

The top of the foundation wall is finished off with a course of solid masonry. On top of this course of solid masonry rests the foundation **sill**. The sill is usually made up of a pressure-treated 2" × 6" or 2" × 8". In the event pressure-treated lumber is not used for the sill, then metal **flashing** must be placed between the foundation wall and wooden member. The wooden sill is fastened to the foundation wall by anchor bolts or nails. The sill is the first wooden member of the house and is used as the nailing surface for the floor system.

The box sill, or banding, rests on the sill plate and is the same size wood member as the floor joists (2" × 8", 2" × 10", or 2" × 12"). The banding runs around the top of the foundation wall, attached to the sill plate.

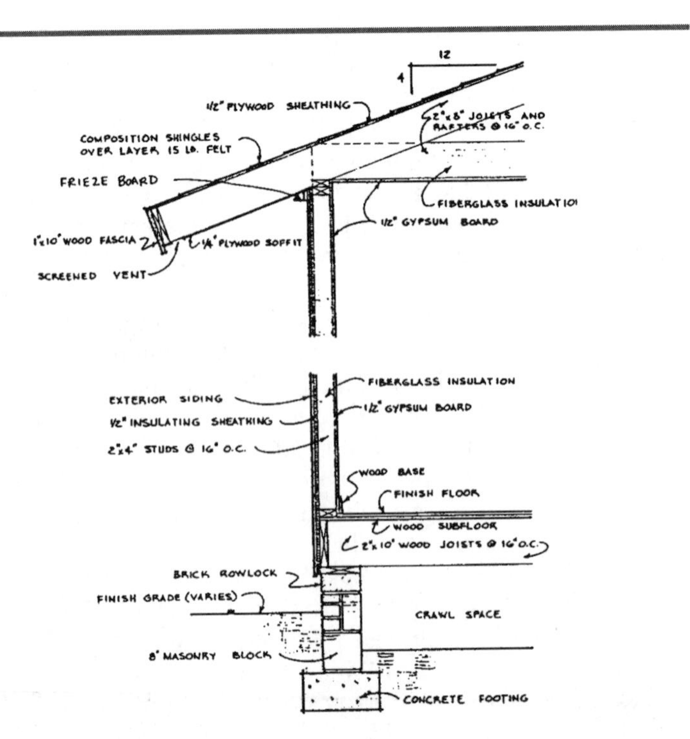

FIGURE A.2
Typical wall section.

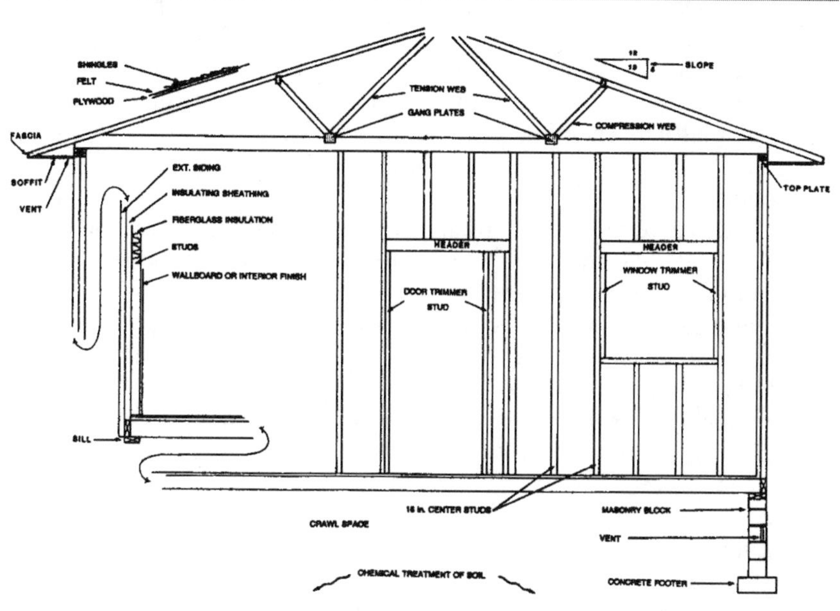

FIGURE A.3 Roof section using truss system.

The floor joists span the distance between the foundation walls and the **girder** and provide support for the subfloor. The girder is either a steel beam or several wooden members fastened together (usually 2" × 10"s, 2" × 12"s, or larger) that spans the distance from one side of the foundation to the other. The joists rest on the girder for support. Typical framing places wooden members at 16 inches **on center**. The 16" spacing of framing members depends primarily on strength considerations for lumber sizing. Additionally, covering materials such as plywood, **sheathing**, and wallboard are made in 4' widths. The 16" spacing, therefore, provides a uniform nailing pattern of four rows for each piece of covering material.

Depending upon the area to be spanned, the joists are doubled or even tripled to support the load. **Bridging** is used to provide support and "stiffening" to the joists to prevent lateral movement of the joists. Bridging is usually constructed in one of two ways. One type of bridging is solid-bridging, which utilizes the same size wooden member as the joists. This type of bridging forms a "solid" bridge between the joists. Cross-bridging uses either 1" × 4"s or 2" × 4"s in an X pattern, placed between the joists.

Some modern construction methods use wooden floor **trusses** in place of single floor joists. A truss is a support member constructed in a factory by nailing a number of smaller members (2" × 4"s or 2" × 6"s) together in a number of triangular patterns to provide maximum strength.

A plywood or particle board subflooring rests directly on top of the joists. Quality construction practice sees this subfloor glued and fastened with nails or shank screws to prevent nail-popping and squeaky floors. Finish flooring rests on top of the subflooring. Typical finish flooring includes hardwood, tile, linoleum, and carpet.

Walls

The floor system usually serves as a stage or platform for the wall system. The walls are usually built of 2" × 4" studs, 16" on center. Less common is a wall system of 2" × 6"s at 16" or 24" on center. A horizontal base plate, also called a sole plate, serves as the foundation for the wall system. A double top plate is used to tie the walls together and provide additional support for the ceiling and roof system. Both exterior and interior walls are framed in a rough carpentry skeleton. Openings in the wall for doors or windows must be reinforced to pick up the missing support for the vertical load. This is done with 2" × 8"s, 2" × 10"s, or 2" × 12"s, known as **headers**, on end, over the top of the opening. Headers should form a solid wood bridge over the opening and extend to the bottom of the top plate. The type of framing described above is known as **platform framing**, because the framing of the structure rests on a subfloor platform. Platform framing is the most common type of framing used in residential construction.

An alternative to platform framing is balloon framing. This method uses a single system of wall studs that run from the foundation through the first and second floors to the ceiling support. This method is rarely used in residential construction.

A third type of framing is **post-and-beam framing**. These members are much larger than ordinary studs and may be 4 or 6 inches square. The larger posts can be placed several feet apart instead of 16" or 24" on center. Like balloon framing, this type of framing is seldom used in residential construction.

Plumbing, electrical, and heating and cooling systems are run through the walls, floors, and ceilings before they are covered up. Inspections by the local building inspector must be made before any of these systems can be covered up with insulation and wallboard. A vapor barrier is applied to the warm (inside) wall on exterior walls. The vapor barrier is important in preventing the warm interior air from mixing with the cold exterior air and forming condensation within the wall.

Ceiling Framing and Roof

The ceiling joists rest on the top plate of the wall. These joists should be placed directly over the vertical studs for maximum bearing strength. The joists span the structure between the outer walls. In traditional framing, these joists are usually 2" × 8"s, and the inner walls are important in helping to bear the load of the roof. This is different in the contemporary use of roof truss systems, in which the truss carries the load-bearing function to the outer walls. This feature provides freedom of placement of the inner walls. Since a roof truss is made up of a number of smaller members (usually 2" × 4"s), the attic space is almost completely lost. (See Figure A.3.)

The **ridge board** is the highest part of the framing and forms the apex, or top line, of the roof. Rafters are the long wooden members that are fastened to the ends of the ceiling joists and form the gables of the roof. Rafters are usually 2" × 6"s or 2" × 8"s. The rafters are fastened to the ridge at the peak of the gable.

Contemporary residential construction sees roof styles in two varieties. These are the traditional **gable roof** and the **hip roof**. Some homes even employ both styles to create a distinctive roof line. The gable roof is the most popular roof style used in the United States. In years past, the gambrel and mansard roof styles were sometimes used, but these styles were never as popular or as functional as the gable or hip. As a result, the mansard and gambrel are rarely used. The gambrel and mansard are sometimes found on barns, stables, and other types of nonresidential structures. Figure A.4 shows the four roof styles—gable, hip, gambrel, and mansard.

The roof should extend at least 6 inches beyond the exterior of the structure. Common construction practices see a 12-inch overhang on the front and rear, with a 6-inch overhang on the side or eaves. The larger the overhang, the more protection there is from sun and rain for the exterior walls, windows, and doors.

The overhang is made up of three components: the soffit, the fascia, and the frieze board. The **soffit** is the area under the roof extension. This is either made of wood, aluminum, or vinyl (depending upon the type of siding). The area of material facing the outer edge of the soffit is called the **fascia**. The fascia is typically a 1" × 6" or a 1" × 8". If guttering is installed on the roof, it is fastened to the fascia. The third component of the overhang is the **frieze board**. This is a wooden member (usually a 2" × 4", 2" × 6", or 2" × 8") that is fastened directly under the soffit, against the top of the wall. The function of the frieze board is both decorative and functional. The frieze board

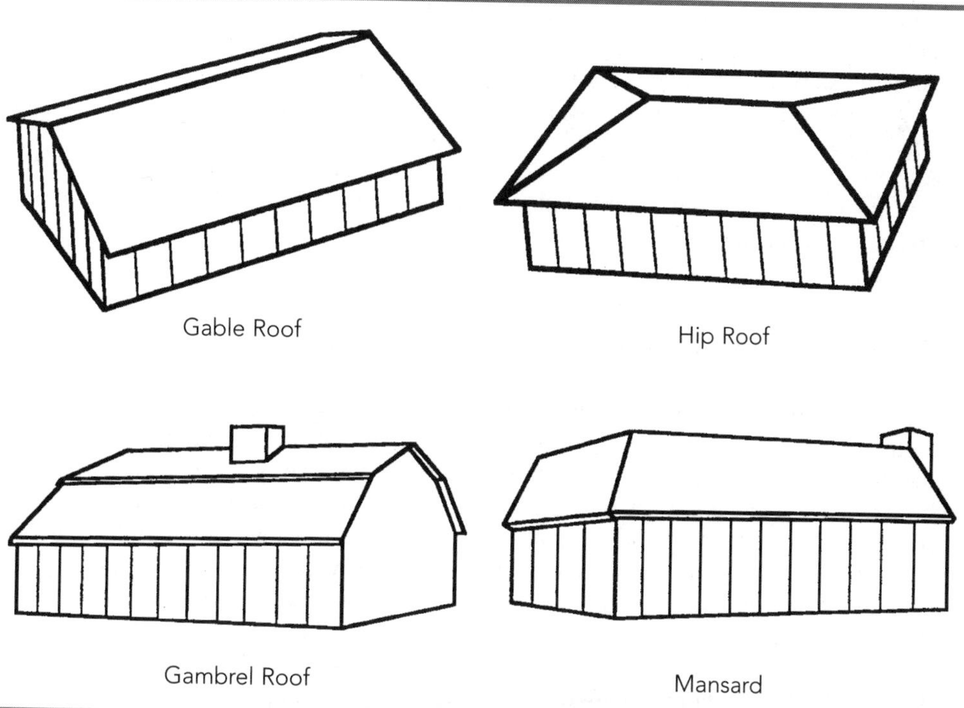

Figure A.4
Roof styles.

prevents wind and moisture from penetrating the junction of the soffit and sheathing. Depending upon the style of the home, additional trim boards are sometimes fastened on and around the frieze board to give the house the desired look.

Once the structural skeleton of the roof system is in place, it is covered with either plywood or particle board decking. On top of this, roofing paper is applied to aid in weatherproofing the structure. On top of the roofing paper, shingles are applied. Most construction utilizes the fiberglass shingle, but tile and wood shingles are also used. Just as in the crawl space below the house, proper ventilation of the attic space is important. This is accomplished through the use of vents to allow the free movement of air in the attic, which keeps moisture from forming and rotting the wood. The ventilation also aids in removing unwanted heat from the attic, allowing air conditioners to work more efficiently in cooling the home. Roof vents come in many shapes and styles. Older homes usually have gable vents at the peak on each end of the house. Newer homes often utilize a single piece ridge vent that is installed along the ridge line. Intake vents are placed in the soffit or overhang of the roof. These vents allow air to travel from the outside, through the soffit vents, through the attic, and outside through the ridge vent.

Exterior Walls

The exterior wall of the house is covered with a sheathing material. This material is usually plywood or particle board. The purpose of the sheathing is to strengthen the wall and add some insulation protection. An insulating "housewrap" is sometimes applied over this sheathing to increase the **R-factor** (resistance to heat transfer) of the walls. Upon this material, the exterior siding is applied.

There are several types of siding: aluminum, vinyl, masonite, and wood. Each type has advantages and disadvantages, and for every person who likes a particular type of siding, someone else doesn't. Regardless of the type of siding used, it should be properly installed to prevent water damage to the house and to give the house a first-rate, professional appearance.

In brick construction, builders typically install sheathing paper or housewrap, which serves to seal the home from the intrusion of moisture through the brick. A small gap exists between the brick veneer walls and the interior sheathing. This is necessary to allow any moisture that seeps through the brick mortar to run down the back of the masonry wall and out through the **weepholes**, at the bottom of the wall. Weepholes are small holes in the bottom course of brick that allow any moisture on the inside of the wall an avenue to the exterior and also allow ventilation into this area to keep the inside of the wall dry.

Windows and Exterior Doors

Windows fall into three general classes: **sliding, swinging**, and **fixed**. Although there are other classes, they are not as commonly used. Windows manufactured today are made from wood, metals such as aluminum, and even some composite materials. Whereas older windows were a single pane of glass, contemporary windows are of a thermal insulating design with a double- or even triple-glass pane. A small air space is sandwiched between the glass panes. This design provides excellent insulation and efficiency of heating and cooling, since windows make up a large portion of the wall and even roof surface area (in the case of skylights). Additionally, single-pane windows produce interior condensation in cold weather, which can damage woodwork and interior finishes. These antiquated single-pane windows require an exterior glass unit (storm window) to provide proper insulation in summer and winter.

Sliding Windows

Vertical Sliding (Double-Hung)

The most common type of windows used in residential construction are vertical sliding, known as double-hung windows (see Figure A.5). These windows are composed of two glass pane units or sashes that vertically slide by each other. In older construction, the weight of the heavy window unit was supported or balanced by a rope (sash cord) and pulley system in the wall. Lighter, modern systems are governed entirely by the friction of the unit sliding in its track.

The major parts of a window framework are labeled the same as the parts of a door opening. For example, the sill is the bottom or base part, the jamb is the side, and the header is the top of the opening.

The typical components of a window include the sash, which is the glass panel unit that slides up and down. In the past, glass manufacturers were only able to make

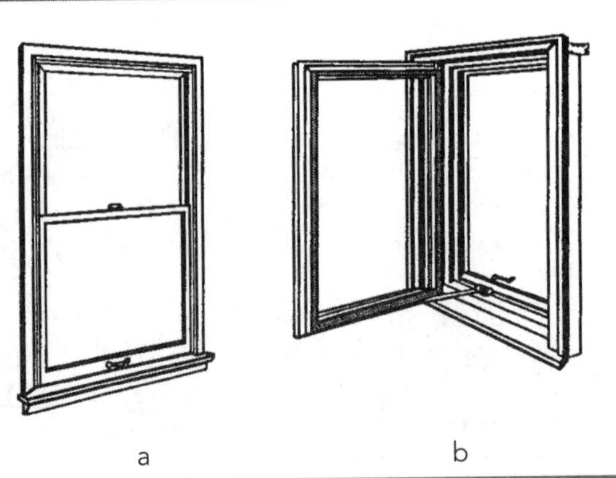

FIGURE A.5 (a) Double-hung window and (b) casement window.

small glass panes for windows. These windows were held together with wood strips known as mullions or grills. Today, many windows have nonfunctional mullions or grills added as decorative strips to simulate a multiple pane appearance. The stile is the side part of the sash, and the top and bottom portions of the sash are known as rails.

Horizontal Sliding

Horizontal sliding windows are often found in modern homes, sometimes in a bedroom. These units often have two sashes that slide by each other horizontally. In the case of a three-sash unit, the central portion is usually fixed, with only two sliding sashes. These windows are nearly identical in construction and composition to the double-hung vertical window described above, except for the manner in which they open.

Swinging Windows

The **casement window** has a sash hinged on one side, and it swings outward (see Figure A.5). The swinging mechanism is usually a geared crank system with an operating handle on the interior sill. Latches are often used to lock this type of window tight for weather-tight seal.

Older homes sometimes have jalousie, hopper, or awning windows. All these windows swing either inward or outward and as a result have limitations due to interference with living space. Typically, these windows do not insulate well, and as technology and energy efficiency have improved window construction and insulating requirements, the jalousie, hopper, and awning windows have become a thing of the past. The only swinging window that seems to have improved and kept pace with technological and architectural improvements is the casement window.

Fixed Windows

Fixed windows do not have any movable sections. As air conditioning and ventilation systems have evolved, there is less need to have windows that can be opened. The common types of fixed windows include picture, bay, bow, and palladian. In some window assemblies, a fixed window may be a center section with some form of movable and openable window on either side. These windows are designed to allow maximum lighting and are strategically placed for maximum functionality and aesthetic appeal.

Doors

Doors, like windows, come in many shapes and styles. However, there are only two classes, interior and exterior. Doors can be made of wood, steel, aluminum, composite materials, and glass. Maximum insulation is desired in exterior doors, which are usually composed of solid wood or steel with a high insulating core.

All doors and windows must be tightly sealed to prevent the movement of air around them. A high quality door coupled with proper installation is essential to maintain proper energy efficiency. External caulking around windows and doors helps complete the tight seal, as does **weather stripping** in the door frames. When you consider the large area of walls that doors and windows occupy in a typical home, you can see why it is extremely important that they be properly installed, as even tiny cracks and leaks can result in significant heating and cooling bills.

Common types of exterior doors include the flush door, which is one continuous smooth unit, and the panel door, which is composed of several recessed or raised panels that may include glass. The sliding glass door unit is very popular and is used for access to patios, decks, and porches. The glass door often has one fixed panel and one panel that slides on a track or rollers. French doors have become popular high-style decorative units that open onto patios, decks, and porches.

Interior doors are usually made of wood. These doors differ from their exterior counterparts in that they are usually not a solid core and are not designed for energy efficiency. Their main function is decoration and privacy. Interior doors can be flush, have panels, and even be glass (French door).

INSULATION

The primary purpose of insulation is resisting the flow of heat from one area to another. It provides the double benefit of preventing heat loss in the winter and protecting against heat load in the summer. The areas of the home that must be insulated are the ceiling, walls, and floor. Insulation is rated in an R-factor. The larger the R-factor, the greater the degree of insulation. Typical minimum mandated R-factors are R-31 insulation in ceilings, R-16 in walls, and R-20 in floors; some state requirements exceed these minimums, and homes built to superior energy efficient standards exceed them as well. Local utility companies usually offer discount rates to homes meeting their energy efficient standards. Additionally, they sometimes have low-cost programs to improve the insulating value of homes for homeowners.

A common form of insulation is that of fiberglass in 15½"-wide rolls, designed to fit in the space between framing members such as joists and studs. Unfaced rolls (without paper covering) and loose blown-in insulation can be added on top of existing attic insulation to improve the energy efficiency of homes. As previously discussed, exterior sheathings and housewrapping material can also provide a high degree of insulating value.

Insulation also provides a degree of sound-proofing between adjacent floors and walls of town houses, condominiums, and apartments.

INTERIOR FINISHES

In most homes, the interior walls are finished by using a wallboard material. This construction consists of **gypsum board**, or **sheetrock**, as it is commonly known. The panels essentially are a core of gypsum material covered with a treated paper. The careful placement of these sheets and the finishing of seams require a high degree of skill. Since this treatment acts as the interior finish and greatly affects the appearance of the home, usually it is done by a team of specialists. The panels are fastened with either sheetrock nails or screws or both, and the seams are bonded with a plasterlike drywall material. Once it drys, the seams are sanded and painted. Wallpaper also can be used in place of paint and is typically found in bathrooms and on accent walls.

Wood paneling, either in sheets or individual boards, makes an attractive interior finish. Often a home will contain a combination of sheetrock and paneling, although recent years have seen a decline in the amount of paneling used in residential construction. Although paneling once was used to finish entire rooms, now it is primarily used to accent other finishes such as sheetrock or wallpaper.

A durable and popular finish in bathrooms, entryways, and kitchens is ceramic tile. This tile is used on floors and walls and comes in a wide variety of styles, sizes, textures, and colors. The use of linoleum sheets or tiles often replaces ceramic tile due primarily to the cost of ceramic tile. Like ceramic tile, linoleum comes in a wide variety of styles, sizes, textures, and colors.

The use of molded fiberglass tubs and showers has gained in popularity in recent years. The relatively low cost of these fixtures often allows homeowners and builders to spend more for flooring and wall finishes. Prior to the use of these fiberglass fixtures, tubs and showers were either ceramic tile or a solid ceramic fixture. Both were more expensive than the newer fiberglass fixtures.

Such extras as hot tubs and saunas are gaining popularity among homeowners. Technology has made these once costly, hard-to-maintain systems very affordable to own and operate.

A good deal of attention should be given to the finished carpentry on the interior and exterior of the house. The quality of materials as well as the quality of work that goes into the construction of window and door frames, baseboards, crown molding, trim, cabinets, and even closets is a strong indication of the quality of the construction of the dwelling. Because a significant amount of money is spent to finish out the house, it only makes sense that it be done right and to the homeowners' quality standards.

Heating/Air Conditioning Systems

HVAC is an acronym that stands for heating, ventilation, and air conditioning. A wide variety of heating and cooling systems are available for residential construction. Older structures relied on heating systems such as fireplaces, electric baseboard heaters, or oil furnaces. Unfortunately, these systems were rather inefficient and costly to operate. In recent years there has been interest in highly efficient fireplace inserts and free-standing wood stoves. Although picturesque, a modern masonry fireplace by itself is a very inefficient heating structure. It serves largely to exhaust air (and subsequent heat) from the house.

Despite America's love affair with wood stoves and the like, the only truly efficient heating system is a central unit. Older systems relied heavily on the convection of heated and cooled air to circulate and warm the house. This system required large ducts and vents to circulate the required volume of air throughout the house.

Today's heating and cooling systems use a central blower to distribute the heated or cooled air throughout the house. Each room is required to have an air duct, and return ducts to the main unit must be centrally located to necessitate maximum efficiency. These modern systems come in a variety of sizes and capabilities to suit a particular home and can be powered by gas or electricity.

The makeup of these systems is largely one of convenience, cost, and individual preference. Efficiency and operating costs should also be top priorities for builders and homeowners. Which system (gas or electric) is the most efficient and has the lowest installation and operating costs is an ongoing debate.

Gas forced-air furnaces are popular among many homeowners due to their relatively low cost, high efficiency, and the warm, cozy environment they quickly create when the heat comes on. Electric furnaces are popular for the same reasons, but rising utility costs over the past several years have made the electric furnace less economical than in the past.

Another popular heating and cooling system is the heat pump. The heat pump extracts heat from the outside, even in moderately cold weather, and transfers the heat into the home. The cycle is reversed in the summer to extract heat from the interior and produce air conditioning. A limitation of the heat pump is that it can only operate in moderate climates. In climates that have cold winters, a separate furnace, fireplace, or wood stove is needed to provide the necessary heat when the outside temperature drops. Another drawback to the heat pump is that the heat coming out of the vent feels cooler than that generated by a furnace. For this reason, homeowners often have a backup heating system to maintain a comfortable living environment.

Air-conditioning systems usually are powered by electricity. As previously discussed, the heat pump is the only heating and cooling system that is built into the same unit. Furnaces typically are located in the utility room, basement, or garage, while the air-conditioning unit is placed outside the house. (This is necessary for proper operation and efficiency.)

Advances in technology have integrated the heating, cooling, and ventilation controls into a central thermostat, eliminating the need for separate controls. A further advance is the development of "smart houses," which utilize a central computer to automate the entire operating infrastructure of the house. With these state-of-the-art systems, you can adjust the controls of the heating and cooling system, activate the lawn sprinkler, draw your bath, or program your security system—all by telephone or computer modem link. These systems are extremely expensive but offer tremendous savings in efficiency and productivity for homeowners.

Finally, when designing, replacing, or installing a new HVAC system, builders and homeowners should ensure that the system meets the requirements of the home. Modern practice often sees duplicate systems installed in homes of two or more stories. Although individual furnaces, heat pumps, and air conditioners may be designed to heat or cool a specific size home adequately, these systems often are underpowered or overworked in order to accomplish the task. The net result is a system that does not operate at peak efficiency and ultimately breaks down sooner than expected. With the installation of dual systems (one for the upstairs and one for the downstairs), the entire system can operate more efficiently, saving the homeowner considerable money in the long run. HVAC systems are very expensive, so it makes sense that homeowners should carefully research any expenditure in this area to ensure they are getting what they want and need in a heating and cooling system.

Solar Heat

Much attention has been given to solar heat in recent years with the ever-rising cost of heating. We recognize two main types of solar heating: passive and active.

Passive solar heating simply takes advantage of exposure to the sun. Direct exposure heats a given area during the day. Indirect exposure involves heating water units or masonry surfaces to "give off" heat during the night. In order to incorporate passive solar heating into a home, the home must be situated so that the front or rear of the house faces south, and the southern exposure should incorporate sufficient windows to allow the sun's rays to penetrate the home.

Active solar heating involves a more sophisticated method of collecting, storing, and distributing heat. The system starts with a collection panel(s), a glass front, water tubing, and black flat plates. The glass is very useful in allowing the solar energy to enter while preventing its escape. The black plates absorb the heat energy for transmission to the water tubing. The heated water is pumped to a storage tank for later distribution throughout the home. A heat exchange system provides for distribution of the heat from the circulated water.

Unfortunately, solar systems cannot provide more than 50 to 60 percent of the total heating needed for a home. Thus, auxiliary systems are needed (such as a furnace or heat pump).

Electrical Systems

Like the HVAC system, the electrical system in a house serves a critical purpose. Care should be taken to ascertain the proper design, scope, and layout of electrical outlets and components and to ensure the system is adequate to handle the current and future requirements. Modern construction requires a 110/220-volt wiring system with a capacity of approximately 200 amps, fitted with circuit breakers. The electrical box/panel should be located in a utility room, basement, or garage for ease of access to reset circuit breakers and to perform maintenance.

The home should be wired with sufficient electrical wall receptacles for the use of the electricity. Utility areas such as garages and bathrooms require the installation of dedicated breakers to prevent accidental electrical shock. Additionally, the installation of smoke detectors outside sleeping areas is required to warn occupants of fire danger. These systems must be wired into the house electrical current and have a battery backup. The smoke detector must have a visible warning light, or be designed to give off a warning signal of 85 db at 10 feet. This is a new requirement for all new residential construction, as outlined in most states' residential building code.

PLUMBING SYSTEMS

The adequacy and quality of the plumbing system is another important facet in the quality of residential construction. Common construction practice uses copper, brass, cast-iron, galvanized steel, chlorinated polyvinyl chloride (CPVC), or polybutylene (PB) plastic pipe for water distribution systems. Each bathroom should be vented to the exterior by the use of a metal pipe that is run through the roof. The venting of sink traps is also required. All water fixtures should have separate cutoffs so that a repair can be made without shutting down the entire system. Like the HVAC and electrical systems, the plumbing system should be designed for maximum efficiency and functional utility. Hot water heaters should be well insulated and large enough to accommodate the demands placed upon them. Typically, single-family homes require at least a 50-gallon hot water heater. If the home has several bathrooms or is very large or if the family is large, a bigger hot water heater or multiple hot water heaters may be required.

SUMMARY

Real estate practitioners should learn to distinguish the features in a dwelling that show quality construction as well as those features that indicate construction of inferior quality. As a suggestion, those not familiar with construction techniques might well spend some time looking at homes in their area in the various stages of construction. Additionally, contact your local chapter of the National Association of Home Builders (NAHB) to get current information on building practices and trends in the industry. By doing either (or both), practitioners can gain a working knowledge of the construction process and the various qualities of workmanship and materials.

TERMINOLOGY

Batter boards temporary wood members on posts that form an L-shape outside the corners of the footing and line up the placement of the foundation walls.

Bridging wooden members (usually 1" × 4"s or solid pieces the same size as the joists) that are placed between joists to hold them in place and prevent lateral movement.

Cape Cod style a one-and-a-half-story house that is characterized by a high-pitched roof with dormers. The Cape Cod style was first constructed in New England.

casement window a window that has a sash hinged on one side and that swings outward. The swinging mechanism is usually geared by a crank, with the operating handle on the interior sill.

Certificate of Occupancy a certificate issued by the local building inspector, stating that the construction project is complete and conforms to all state and local building codes and is approved for occupancy.

Colonial style a type of residential construction (usually two-story) that incorporates architectural features found in early American homes.

Contemporary style a type of residential construction that incorporates modern designs and architectural features. A contemporary home can be in any configuration and in one, one-and-a-half, or two stories.

double-hung window a window composed of two glass panes or sashes that slide vertically past each other. The sashes are governed by the friction of the units sliding in their tracks.

fascia the wood covering attached to the end of the roof rafters at the outer end. The fascia is one of three components of the overhang.

fixed window windows that do not have any movable sections. Types of fixed windows include bay, bow, picture, and palladian.

flashing metal placed between the foundation and the first wooden member of the house. Flashing is often deleted in place of pressure-treated wood, which does not require flashing.

footing the concrete base below the frost line that supports the foundation of a structure.

foundation vents small openable vents that are placed around the foundation of a house with a crawl space. The vents are used to allow the free movement of air under the home, preventing the buildup of moisture, which can damage the wood subflooring.

framing the wooden skeleton of a home. The framing consists of the subfloor, walls, ceiling, and roof systems.

French Provincial style a type of residential construction that incorporates a hip roof and French-influenced architectural features.

frieze board a wooden member (usually a 2" × 4", 2" × 6", or 2" × 8") that is fastened directly under the soffit, against the sheathing. The frieze board is one of the three components of the roof overhang.

gable roof a roof consisting of two inclined planes joined over the center line of the house and resting on the two opposite roof plates on top of the studs. The triangular end walls are called gables.

girder a steel beam or several wooden members fastened together that span the foundation from one side to the other. The joists rest on the girder for support.

grade stakes small wooden stakes placed in the bottom of the footing trenches that are used to measure and verify the proper elevation and thickness of the footing.

gypsum board (sheetrock) large panels of gypsum material, covered in treated paper, that are used as finish for interior walls. The gypsum board is fastened directly to the studs and ceiling joists.

header wooden members used to support the free ends of joists, studs, or rafters over openings in the frame.

hip roof a roof consisting of four inclined planes joined together to form a rectangle.

HVAC an acronym that stands for heating, ventilation, and air conditioning.

insulation material used in construction to prevent heat loss in the winter and to protect against heat load in the summer. Insulation is usually fiberglass material either in rolls or loose. The material is placed in the floor, exterior walls, and ceiling of homes.

joist a large wooden member (usually a 2" × 8", 2" × 10", 2" × 12", or larger) that is placed on edge horizontally to support a floor or ceiling.

on center refers to the placement of wooden members in the construction process. Usually joists, studs, and rafters are placed at 16" or 24" on center to maximize strength and fastening of wallboard, plywood, and sheathing.

parging a smooth, mortar-based finish that is used to cover exposed masonry blocks to hide mortar joints and seams.

piers vertical masonry structures (usually poured concrete, cement block, or brick) that are placed inside the foundation walls to support the subflooring. Piers are not used with concrete slabs or basements.

platform framing the most common type of framing used in residential construction. Platform framing is the construction of a floor system that serves as a stage or platform for the walls and the rest of the structure.

post-and-beam framing a type of framing in which large wooden members are placed several feet apart, instead of at 16" or 24" on center. Post-and-beam framing is rarely used in residential construction.

rafter the large, long wooden members that are fastened to the ends of the ceiling joists and ridge board. The rafters form the pitch of the roof. Plywood is fastened to the rafters to form the underlay of the roof covering.

Ranch style a one-story home that is usually of modest size and affordability and that can be finished in siding, brick, or other types of exterior coverings.

reinforcement rods (rebar) metal rods that can be placed in footings and poured concrete to aid in temperature control and strengthening of the concrete. Highly recommended in areas with poor soil or a high water table.

R-factor stands for resistance to heat transfer. Insulation is rated in R-factors. The greater the R-factor, the greater the degree of insulation.

ridge board the highest part of the framing, forming the apex, or top line, of the roof.

sheathing wooden or composite material used to cover the exterior walls and roof of a house. Sheathing comes in various thicknesses and R-factors. The exterior siding and roof covering are fastened to the sheathing.

sill wooden member of the frame that is attached to the foundation. Sills must either be flashed or be pressure treated to aid in termite control.

sliding window one of the most common types of windows used in residential construction. Sliding windows come in various sizes that slide either vertically or horizontally to open.

soffit one of the three components of the overhang. The soffit is the area under the overhang extension that is composed of wood, aluminum, or vinyl. Usually intake vents are installed in the soffit to aid in ventilation of the attic.

stud a vertical wooden member (2" × 4" or 2" × 6") that is used in the framing of a house. Studs are fastened between the sole and top plates and form the walls of a house.

swinging window a type of window that swings either in or out to open. The most common type of swinging window used in residential construction is the casement window.

truss a triangular framework of wooden members (usually 2" × 4"s), nailed in W-shaped patterns to provide support over a long span. The truss is used in subfloor and roof construction.

Tudor style a type of architecture that incorporates English designs and features. Tudor-style homes can be one-story, two-story, or split-level.

2" × 4" a piece of lumber 2 inches thick by 4 inches wide.

vapor barrier heavy duty plastic installed under concrete floor slabs, under homes with crawl spaces, and in exterior walls to prevent the intrusion of moisture into a structure.

Victorian style a type of architecture designed and built during the Victorian era. Victorian-style homes are characterized by large turrets, intricate detailing and trimwork, and large porches. This type of architecture is once again popular in certain regions of the state and country.

weather stripping foam or metal insulating material that is placed around door and window frames to aid in preventing the intrusion of air into a home. Weather stripping comes in various thicknesses and sizes to meet many applications.

weepholes small holes in the bottom course of brick that allow any moisture on the inside of the wall an avenue to the exterior. The weepholes also allow ventilation of the interior wall to keep it dry.

APPENDIX B

A Guide to Common Real Estate Environmental Hazards*

INTRODUCTION

Does this home fit my needs and those of my family? Is this a safe, secure home, free from potential hazards? Is this home a good investment and will it retain and increase its value in the years ahead?

These are among the hundreds of questions that home buyers ask themselves as part of the home-buying thought process. It is a good policy, this questioning, a means of gathering hard facts that can be used to balance the emotional feelings that are so much a part of buying a home.

In ever-increasing numbers, home buyers today find it necessary to add new kinds of questions to their quest for information. Environmental concerns are becoming an element of the home-buying thought process.

Although it is unrealistic to expect that any home will be free of all forms of environmental influences, most homes (and the areas surrounding most homes) in the United States generally do not contain materials and substances that pose a health threat. However, in recent years, new concerns have been raised as our understanding of the natural environment has increased. Substances, such as radon gas and asbestos, have provoked new questions about how and where we build homes and manage their upkeep.

HOME-BUYING CONSIDERATIONS

For the majority of Americans, the purchase of a home is the single greatest investment of a lifetime. Will the presence of an undetected environmental hazard have a long-term negative impact on that investment? Does the presence of a hazard have the potential to affect the health of the occupants? If hazards can be safely removed or mitigated, will the process alter the homeowner's lifestyle? These questions—and others like them—are, and should be, part of the home buyer's thought process today.

As our knowledge of the natural environment evolves, the body of law governing potentially harmful environmental hazards and their effect on real estate transactions also is evolving. The rights and responsibilities of buyers and sellers are determined by state and local laws or terms negotiated into the sales contract between the buyer and seller.

Thus, before buying a home, prudent home buyers may want to obtain information about the potential impact of environmental hazards. Local, county, or state health or environmental departments are sources of such information. And while builders, real estate appraisers, real estate sales licensees, and lenders are not experts about the environment, these individuals may be of assistance in locating additional sources of information regarding environmental matters. Private home inspectors also may be useful in detecting the existence of potentially hazardous conditions if the sales contract provides for such an inspection.

The pages that follow provide general information about some of the environmental hazards that have the potential to affect the home environment. While this information is believed to be accurate, it is not meant to be comprehensive or authoritative. This publication provides introductory information to help home buyers understand the possible risk of exposure to potentially harmful environmental hazards in and around the home.

The agencies and individuals contributing to or assisting in the preparation of this booklet—or any individual acting on behalf of any of these parties—do not make any

---

*Compiled by: National Council of Savings Institutions; Office of Thrift Supervision; Society of Real Estate Appraisers; The Appraisal Foundation; U. S. Environmental Protection Agency; U. S. League of Savings Institutions. This document is in the public domain.

warranty, guarantee, or representation (express or implied) with respect to the usefulness or effectiveness of any information, method, or process disclosed in this material or assume any liability for the use of (or for damages arising from the use of) any information, method, or process disclosed in this material.

RADON

What is radon and where is it found?

Radon is a colorless, odorless, tasteless gas that occurs worldwide in the environment as a byproduct of the natural decay of uranium present in the earth. Radon is present in varying quantities in the atmosphere and in soils around the world.

How does radon enter a home?

Radon that is present in surrounding soil or in well water can be a source of radon in a home. Radon from surrounding soil enters a home through small spaces and openings, such as cracks in concrete, floor drains, sump pump openings, wall/floor joints in basements, and the pores in hollow block walls. It also can seep into ground water and remain entrapped there. Therefore, if a home is supplied with water taken from a ground water source (such as a well), there is greater potential for a radon problem. The likelihood of radon in the water supply is greatly reduced for homes supplied with water from a municipal water supply.

Is radon found throughout a home, or just in certain rooms or areas?

Radon generally concentrates most efficiently in the areas of a home closest to the ground. Radon levels generally decrease as one moves higher up in the structure.

How can I tell if a home has a radon problem?

The only way to know whether or not a home has a radon problem is to test it. Radon levels vary from house to house depending on the construction of the house and the soil surrounding it. There are several ways to make a preliminary screening test for radon. Preliminary screening test kits can be bought over-the-counter in many hardware, grocery, and convenience stores. Tests that measure the amount of radon in water normally require you to send a sample of tap water to a laboratory for analysis. State agencies should be consulted if the home water supply is suspected as a source of radon.

When purchasing a radon detection kit, you should examine the package for indications that the kit has been approved by federal or state health, environmental protection, or consumer protection agencies. Directions should be followed carefully when using a radon detection kit to assure that proper measurements are obtained. Short-term testing (ranging from a few days to several months) is one way to determine if a potential problem exists. Long-term testing (lasting for up to one year) is a more accurate way to determine if radon is present. Both short- and long-term testing devices are easy to use and relatively inexpensive.

Why is radon harmful?

Radon gas breaks down into radioactive particles (called decay products) that remain in the air. As you breathe these particles, they can become trapped in your lungs. As these particles continue to break down, they release bursts of energy (radiation) that can damage lung tissue. This damage can cause lung cancer. When radon gas and its decay products enter your home, they remain in circulation in the enclosed air. Out of doors, radon is not a problem for human beings because the surrounding air allows the gas to diffuse in the atmosphere.

What health risks are associated with radon?

The health risk associated with prolonged inhalation of radon decay products is an increased risk of developing lung cancer. There are indications that risk increases as the level of radon concentration and duration of exposure increase. The U.S. Environmental Protection Agency (EPA) has determined that short-term exposure to a high concentration of radon is not as severe a risk as long-term exposure to a lower level of the gas.

What is an acceptable level of indoor radon?

The concentration of radon in air is measured in units of picocuries per liter of air (pCi/L). Estimates suggest that most homes will contain from one to two picocuries of radon per liter of air. If preliminary tests indicate radon levels greater than four picocuries per liter of air in livable areas of the home, the EPA recommends that a follow-up test be conducted. No level of radon is considered safe; there are risks even at very low levels. To put this into perspective, the EPA estimates that the risk of dying from lung cancer as the result of an annual radon level of four picocuries is equivalent to the risk from smoking 10 cigarettes a day or having 200 chest x-rays a year. A picocurie level of 40 equates to smoking two packs of cigarettes a day, while a level of 100 equates to 2000 chest x-rays a year.

How are radon risk levels calculated?

The EPA's risk assessments assume an individual is exposed to a given concentration of radon over a lifetime of roughly 70 years, and spends 75 percent of his or her time in the home.

Can the level of radon in a home be reduced?

Yes, there are many effective and relatively inexpensive methods of reducing radon levels in a home. The method used will vary from house to house and from region to region. The techniques used will depend on the source of the gas, the ways in which it enters the home, and the kind of construction used in the home. If radon is present in water supplies, it can be removed altogether or reduced by the installation of special filter systems.

What will it cost to reduce the level of radon in a home?

The costs for radon reduction will depend on the number of sources, the amount of radon in the surrounding land or in the water supply, and the kind of construction used in the home. Normally, the costs of installing radon reduction equipment range from several hundred dollars to several thousand dollars. If the system chosen involves fans, pumps, or other appliances, operating costs for these devices may cause increases in monthly utility bills.

Is radon removal a "do-it-yourself project"?

Not usually. In some cases, homeowners should be able to treat the problem themselves; however, it is not always possible for homeowners to diagnose the source of radon or to install systems that will reduce the level. Radon source diagnosis and mitigation normally require skills, experience, and tools not available to the average homeowner; therefore, it is always prudent to consider the use of trained personnel. When seeking a contractor to assist with a radon problem, you should first consult local, county, or state government agencies for recommendations of qualified radon-reduction contractors.

What is the government doing about radon?

The federal government has undertaken an extensive public outreach effort to encourage individuals to test their homes. This effort includes a national hotline, 1-800-SOS-RADON, for obtaining further information on radon testing. EPA also is working closely with state and local governments and the private sector to research and demonstrate cost-effective methods for reducing indoor radon levels and with builders to develop radon-resistant new construction techniques.

You also may contact your state's radon office at the telephone number listed below.

State Radon Offices

Alabama (205) 261-5315
Alaska (907) 465-3019
Arizona (602) 255-4845
Arkansas (501) 661-2301
California (415) 540-2134
Colorado (303) 331-4812
Connecticut (203) 566-3122
Delaware (800) 554-4636
Florida (800) 543-8279
Georgia (404) 894-6644
Hawaii (808) 548-4383
Idaho (208) 334-5933
Illinois (217) 786-6384
Indiana (800) 272-9723
Iowa (515) 281-7781
Kansas (913) 296-1560
Kentucky (502) 564-3700
Louisiana (504) 925-4518
Maine (207) 289-3826
Maryland (800) 872-3666
Massachusetts (413) 586-7525
or in Boston (617) 727-6214
Michigan (517) 335-8190
Minnesota (612) 623-5341
Mississippi (601) 354-6657
Missouri (800) 669-7236
Montana (406) 444-3671
Nebraska (402) 471-2168
Nevada (702) 885-5394
New Hampshire (603) 271-4674
New Jersey (800) 648-0394
New Mexico (505) 827-2940
New York (800) 458-1158
North Carolina (919) 733-4283
North Dakota (701) 224-2348
Ohio (800) 523-4439
Oklahoma (405) 271-5221
Oregon (503) 229-5797
Pennsylvania (800) 23-RADON
Puerto Rico (809) 767-3563
Rhode Island (401) 277-2438
South Carolina (803) 734-4631
South Dakota (605) 773-3153
Tennessee (615) 741-4634
Texas (512) 835-7000
Utah (801) 538-6734
Vermont (802) 828-2886
Virginia (800) 468-0138
Virgin Islands (809) 774-3320
Washington (800) 323-9727
Washington, DC (202) 727-7728
West Virginia (304) 348-3526
Wisconsin (608) 273-5180
Wyoming (307) 777-7956

The following resources and publications can provide additional information about radon.

Brochures

- *A Citizen's Guide to Radon*
- *Radon Reduction Methods (A Homeowner's Guide)*
- *Removal of Radon from Household Water*
- *The Inside Story—A Guide to Indoor Air Quality*

The above are available from:

U. S. Environmental Protection Agency
Public Information Center
401 M Street, SW
Washington, DC 20460
(202) 475-7751

ASBESTOS

What is asbestos and where is it found?

Asbestos is a fibrous mineral found in rocks and soil throughout the world. Asbestos has been used in architectural and construction applications because it is strong, durable, fire retardant, and an efficient insulator. Alone or in combination with other materials, asbestos can be fashioned into a variety of products that have numerous applications within the building industry—such as flooring, walls, ceiling tiles, exterior housing shingles, insulation or fire retardant for heating and electrical systems, etc.

Is asbestos dangerous?

Asbestos has been identified as a carcinogen. Once ingested, asbestos fibers lodge in the lungs. Because the material is durable, it persists in tissue and concentrates as repeated exposures occur over time. It can cause cancer of the lungs and stomach among workers and others who have experienced prolonged work-related exposure to it. The health effects of lower exposures in the home are less certain; however, experts are unable to provide assurance that any level of exposure to asbestos fibers is completely safe.

Under what circumstances do asbestos-containing products in the home become a health risk?

Home health risks arise when age, accidental damage, or normal cleaning, construction, or remodeling activities cause the asbestos-containing materials to crumble, flake, or deteriorate. When this happens, minute asbestos fibers are released into the air and can be inhaled through the nose and mouth. The fibers can cling to clothing, tools, and exposed flesh; cleanup operations can then dislodge the fibers and free them to circulate in the air.

Can I expect to find asbestos in newer homes, and where in the home should I look for asbestos?

According to the EPA, many homes constructed in the United States during the past 20 years probably do not contain asbestos products. Places where asbestos sometimes can be found in the home include: around pipes and furnaces in older homes as insulating jackets and sheathing; in some vinyl flooring materials; in ceiling tiles; in exterior roofing, shingles, and siding; in some wallboards; mixed with other materials and troweled or sprayed around pipes, ducts, and beams; in patching compounds or textured paints; and in door gaskets on stoves, furnaces, and ovens.

How can I identify asbestos in the home?

You may hire a qualified professional who is trained and experienced in working with asbestos to survey the home. A professional knows where to look for asbestos, how to take samples properly, and what corrective actions will be the most effective. EPA regional asbestos coordinators can provide information on qualified asbestos contractors and laboratories. In addition, the manufacturer of a product may be able to tell you, based on the model number and age of the product, whether or not the product contains asbestos.

What should I do if I think there is asbestos in a home I have purchased?

Generally, if the material is in good condition and is in an area where it is not likely to be disturbed, leave the asbestos-containing material in place. Extreme care should be exercised in handling, cleaning, or working with material suspected of containing asbestos. If the material is likely to be banged, rubbed, handled, or taken apart—especially during remodeling—you should hire a trained contractor and reduce your exposure as much as possible. Common construction and remodeling operations can release varying amounts of asbestos fibers if the material being worked on contains asbestos. These operations include hammering, drilling, sawing, sanding, cutting, and otherwise shaping or molding the material. Routine cleaning operations (such as brushing, dusting, vacuum cleaning, scraping, and scrubbing) can also release hazardous fibers from asbestos-containing materials. Vinyl flooring products that contain asbestos can be cleaned in a conventional manner, but these products can release some asbestos fibers if they are vigorously sanded, ground, drilled, filed, or scraped.

The repair or removal of asbestos-containing products from a home is generally a complicated process. It depends on the amount of these products present, the percentage of asbestos they contain, and the manner in which asbestos is incorporated into the product. Total removal of even small amounts of asbestos-containing material is usually the last alternative. You should contact local, state, or federal health or consumer product agencies before deciding on a course of action. To assure safety and elimination of health hazards, asbestos repair or removal should be performed only by properly trained contractors.

Many home repair or remodeling contractors do not yet have the requisite tools, training, experience, or equipment to work safely with asbestos or to remove it from a home. Furthermore, asbestos removal workers are protected under federal regulations that specify special training, protective clothing, and special respirators for these workers.

Are exterior asbestos shingles a health risk?

When properly installed on the exterior of a home, asbestos-containing products present little risk to human health. However, if siding is worn or damaged, spray painting it will help seal in the fibers.

What is being done about the potential problem of exposure to asbestos in the home?

Over the years, the U.S. Environmental Protection Agency (EPA) and the Consumer Product Safety Commission (CPSC) have taken several steps to reduce the consumer's exposure to asbestos. Most recently these steps include requiring labeling of products containing asbestos and announcing a phased-in ban of most asbestos products by 1996.

The following sources and publications can provide additional information about asbestos in the home.

BROCHURES

- *Asbestos (Environmental Backgrounder)*
- *The Inside Story—A Guide to Indoor Air Quality*

The above are available from:

U.S. Environmental Protection Agency

Public Information Center
401 M Street, SW
Washington, DC 20460
(202) 475-7751

- *Asbestos in the Home*

Available from:

U. S. Environmental Protection Agency
TSCA Assistance Information Service
401 M Street, SW
Washington, DC 20460

Hotline

- *The Toxic Substances Control Act (TSCA) Assistance Information Service Hotline*

  This Hotline provides both general and technical information and publications about toxic substances (including asbestos) and offers services to help businesses comply with TSCA laws (including regulatory advice and aid, publications, and audiovisual materials). The Hotline operates Monday through Friday from 8:30 A.M. to 5:00 P.M., Eastern Time. (202) 554-1404

LEAD

What is lead, and why is it hazardous to our health?

Lead is a metallic element found worldwide in rocks and soils. The toxic effects of lead have been known since ancient times. Recent research has shown that lead represents a greater hazard at lower levels of concentration than had been thought. Airborne lead enters the body when an individual breathes lead particles or swallows lead dust. Until recently, the most important source of airborne dust was automobile exhaust.

When ingested, lead accumulates in the blood, bones, and soft tissue of the body. High concentrations of lead in the body can cause death or permanent damage to the central nervous system, the brain, the kidneys, and red blood cells. Even low levels of lead may increase high blood pressure in adults.

Infants, children, pregnant women, and fetuses are more vulnerable to lead exposure than others because the lead is more easily absorbed into growing bodies and their tissues are more sensitive to the damaging effects of the lead. Because of a child's smaller body weight, an equal concentration of lead is more damaging to a child than it would be to an adult.

What are the sources of lead in and around the home?

Lead can be present in drinking water, in paint used to decorate the interior or exterior of a home, in the dust within a home, and in soil around the home.

Lead in Drinking Water

Are there acceptable levels of lead in drinking water?

The EPA Office of Drinking Water has proposed regulations under the Safe Drinking Water Act (SDWA) that establish a maximum contaminant level for lead in drinking water of five micrograms per liter and a maximum contaminant level goal of zero. [Note: One microgram per liter is equal to one part per billion (ppb).] These levels or goals are set by EPA to control contamination that may have an adverse effect on human health. Nonenforceable health-based goals are intended to protect against known or anticipated adverse health effects with an adequate margin of safety. Both the current maximum contamination level and goal are 50 micrograms per liter. Although the Public Health Service first set these levels in the 1960s before much of the current knowledge about the harmful effects of lead at low levels was gained, the EPA included them unchanged in the Safe Drinking Water Act of 1985. EPA, however, is now revising these standards to reflect its increased concern.

I have heard that materials containing lead have been banned from use in public water supplies. If this is true, how does lead enter drinking water in the home?

In 1986, amendments to the Safe Drinking Water Act banned any further use of materials containing lead in public water supplies and in residences connected to public water supplies. In 1988, the U. S. Congress banned the use of lead-based solder in plumbing applications within homes and buildings. However, many homes built prior to 1988 contain plumbing systems that use lead-based solder in pipe connections. In such systems, lead can enter drinking water as a corrosion byproduct when plumbing fixtures, pipes, and solder are corroded by drinking water. In these instances, lead levels in water at the kitchen tap can be far higher than those found in water at treatment plants.

The combination of copper pipes connected with lead-based solder is found in many homes and can result in high levels of lead in water. In these circumstances, galvanic corrosion between the two metals releases relatively large amounts of lead into the water. The amount of lead in this kind of home water system will be higher when water has been at rest in the pipes for a period of time.

The EPA has determined that newly installed solder is most easily dissolved. As the home ages, mineral deposits build up on the inner walls of water pipes and act as an insulating barrier between the water and the solder. Data compiled by the EPA indicates that during the first five years following home construction, water in the home may have high levels of lead, with the highest levels recorded during the first 24 months.

Can I tell by looking at pipes and plumbing fixtures whether or not water in the home will contain harmful levels of lead?

No. Visual inspection of pipe joints and solder lines is not an accurate means of determining whether or not decaying solder is a source of lead.

A simple chemical test can determine whether the solder used in a home is lead-containing or not. Many jurisdictions make use of this test as a regular procedure in plumbing inspections. And while many newer homes rely on non-metallic plumbing lines, the majority of faucets and plumbing fixtures used today can contribute some lead to home water supplies. However, these contributions can be eliminated effectively by running the faucet for 15 seconds before drawing drinking water.

How can I tell if a home has a problem with lead in the water?

The only way to determine lead levels in water is to test a sample of the water. Should you suspect that lead is present in drinking water, or if you wish to have water tested, contact local, county, or state health or environmental departments for information about qualified testing laboratories.

Is lead in water a concern in newly renovated older homes?

If the renovation included replacement of aging water pipes with copper or other metal piping, you should check with the renovating contractor to ensure that lead solder was not used in pipe joints. Further, some old homes contain water systems made of pipes that can contain high levels of lead. If the original water lines remain in the house, you should question the renovating contractor regarding his or her knowledge of pipe composition.

Lead-Based Paint

How prevalent is lead-based paint?

According to the EPA, it is estimated that lead-based paint was applied to approximately two-thirds of the houses built in the United States before 1940; one-third of the houses built from 1940 to 1960; and an indeterminate (but smaller) portion of U. S. houses since 1960.

How can I tell whether the paint in a home contains lead?

The only accurate way to determine if paint in a home contains lead is to remove a sample of the paint and have it tested in a qualified laboratory. Should you suspect that lead is present in paint, or if you wish to have paint tested, contact local, county, or state health or environmental departments for information about qualified testing laboratories.

I have heard about problems when children eat chips of lead-based paint, but are there any other ways that lead-based paint can be harmful?

While the health hazards to children from eating lead-based paint chips have been known for some time, other sources of exposure to lead in household air and dust have been documented only recently.

Lead can enter the air within a home when surfaces covered with lead-based paint are scraped, sanded, or heated with an open flame in paint-stripping procedures. Once released into the home atmosphere, lead particles circulate in the air and can be inhaled or ingested through the mouth and nose. Lead particles freed in fine dust or vapors settle into carpet fibers and fabric and can be recirculated in the air by normal household cleaning (such as sweeping and dusting) and through the normal hand-to-mouth behavior of young children, which results in the ingestion of potentially harmful amounts of any lead present in household dust. Fine lead particles penetrate the filter systems of home vacuum cleaners and are recirculated in the exhaust air streams of such appliances. Lead also can enter household air from outdoor sources (such as contaminated soil) and from recreational activities that require the use of solder or materials containing lead.

How can I get rid of lead-based paint safely?

It is best to leave lead-based paint undisturbed if it is in good condition and there is little possibility that it will be eaten by children. Other procedures include covering the paint with wallpaper or some other building material, or completely replacing the painted surface. Pregnant women and women who plan to become pregnant should not do this work. Professional paint removal is costly, time-consuming, and requires everyone not involved in the procedure to leave the premises during removal and subsequent clean-up operations. In addition, if the house was built prior to 1950, there is a good chance that lead from exterior surface paint has accumulated in surrounding soils. Keep the yard well vegetated to minimize the likelihood of children being exposed to contaminated dust. Clean the floors, window-sills, and other surfaces regularly, preferably with wet rags and mops. Practice good hygiene with your children, especially frequent hand washing.

The following publications provide additional information about lead in the home.

Brochures

- *Is Your Drinking Water Safe?*
- *Lead and Your Drinking Water*
- *The Inside Story—A Guide to Indoor Air Quality*

The above are available from:

U. S. Environmental Protection Agency
Public Information Center
401 M Street, SW
Washington, DC 20460
(202) 475-7751

Hotline

For additional information about lead in drinking water, contact EPA's Safe Drinking Water Hotline: (800) 426-4791; (202) 382-5533 (in the Washington, DC, area)

HAZARDOUS WASTES

What are hazardous wastes?

Hazardous wastes are those waste products that could pose short- or long-term danger to personal health or the environment if they are not properly disposed of or managed. These wastes can be produced by large business and industries (such as chemical and manufacturing plants), by some small businesses (such as drycleaners and printing plants), and by individuals who improperly apply, store, or dispose of compounds that contain potentially toxic ingredients (which can be found in chemical fertilizers, pesticides, and household products).

Concentrations of hazardous wastes occur in the environment when these wastes are handled, managed, or disposed of in a careless or unregulated manner. For many decades, hazardous industrial wastes were improperly disposed of on land, and their toxic components remained in the earth or seeped into ground water and drinking water supplies. The widespread use of pesticides and other agricultural chemicals also has resulted in the seepage and run-off of toxic compounds into land and water supplies. In addition, EPA estimates that as many as two million of the more than five million underground storage tanks in the United States may be leaking—discharging gasoline, petroleum products, and other hazardous liquids into the soil and, potentially, into ground water sources.

What is being done to locate and clean up hazardous waste sites?

During the past 20 years, the U. S. Congress has enacted a body of interlocking laws and regulatory procedures aimed at the abatement of environmental hazards. The Superfund Act was enacted in 1980 (and amended in 1986) to provide more than $10 billion for the detection and cleanup of sites where hazardous waste is a problem.

The revenue for Superfund is raised through taxes on petrochemical companies and other manufacturers. Under the law, the EPA, other federal agencies, and individual states may draw the necessary funds to allow them to react in hazardous waste emergency situations and to conduct long-term, permanent cleanups of hazardous waste sites.

How can I determine if a home is affected by a hazardous waste site?

Generally, testing for hazardous waste involves skills and technology not available to the average homeowner or home remodeling contractor.

The EPA has identified more than 30,000 potentially contaminated waste sites nationwide and has completed a preliminary assessment of more than 27,000 of these sites. The Agency publishes a National Priorities List of sites that will require action through the Superfund. Sites suspected of containing hazardous wastes are mapped at the time of the EPA preliminary assessment and communities likely to be affected by the site are notified. Thus, the nearest regional office of the EPA should have information on the location and status of local hazardous waste sites. The addresses and telephone numbers of these regional offices are listed in the back of this publication.

Furthermore, local and state governments maintain offices and agencies for locating and managing hazardous waste sites. These offices often are good sources for current information about the location and possible effects of these sites.

What are the primary health hazards associated with hazardous wastes?

The specific health hazards in homes contaminated by hazardous wastes are determined by the kinds and amounts of toxic substances present. Some hazardous wastes can cause death even when ingested in small amounts. Other hazardous wastes have been linked to elevated risks of cancer, permanent damage to internal body organs, respiratory difficulties, skin rashes, birth defects, and diseases that attack the central nervous system.

Can hazardous waste concentrations be removed from my property or reduced to non-hazardous levels?

The ability to remove or mitigate hazardous wastes will depend on the kinds, amounts, and sources of the wastes that are present. Generally, the removal of hazardous wastes from a property is beyond the capability of an individual homeowner.

The following sources and publications provide additional information about hazardous wastes.

Brochures

- *A Consumer's Guide to Safer Pesticide Use*
- *Citizen's Guide to Pesticides*
- *Hazardous Wastes (Environmental Backgrounder)*

The above are available from:

U. S. Environmental Protection Agency
Public Information Center
401 M Street, SW
Washington, DC 20460
(202) 475-7751

Hotlines

- *National Poison Control Center Hotline*

  This Hotline provides information on accidental ingestion of chemicals, poisons, or drugs. The Hotline is operated by Georgetown University Hospital in Washington, DC. (202) 625-3333

- *RCRA (Superfund) Hotline*

  This Hotline responds to questions from the public and regulated community on the Resource Conservation and Recovery Act and the Comprehensive Environmental Response, Compensation and Liability Act (Superfund). The Hotline operates Monday through Friday from 8:30 A.M. to 7:30 P.M., Eastern Time. (800) 424-9346; (202) 382-3000 (in the Washington, DC, area)

- *Emergency Planning and Community Right-to-Know Information Hotline*

  This Hotline complements the RCRA (Superfund) Hotline and provides communities and individuals with help in preparing for accidental releases of toxic chemicals. The Hotline operates Monday through Friday from 8:30 A.M. to 7:30 P.M., Eastern Time. (800) 535-0202; (202) 479-2449 (in the Washington, DC, area)

GROUND WATER CONTAMINATION

What causes ground water contamination?

Ground water contamination occurs when hazardous chemical wastes, pesticides, or other agricultural chemicals (such as fertilizer) seep down through the soil into underground water supplies. Faulty private septic systems, improperly managed municipal sewer systems, and leaking industrial injection wells can also contribute to ground water contamination. In recent years, leaking underground storage tanks also have posed a threat to ground water. Half of all Americans and 95 percent of rural Americans use ground water for drinking water.

Is ground water contamination harmful?

The U. S. Center for Disease Control reports an average of approximately 7,500 cases of illness linked to drinking water in the United States each year. This estimate generally is thought to be considerably lower than the actual figures because drinking water contaminants are not always considered in the diagnoses of illnesses.

How can I tell if the water in a home is contaminated?

The only way to know whether or not the water in a home is contaminated is to test it. Since 1977, federal law has required water suppliers to periodically sample and test the water supplied to homes. If tests reveal that a national drinking water standard has been violated, the supplier must move to correct the situation and must also notify the appropriate state agency of the violation. Customers must be notified also, usually by a notice in a newspaper, an announcement on radio or television, or a letter from the health department that supervises the water supplier. If the home is supplied with water from its own private well, laboratory testing of a water sample is the only way to determine if the water supply is contaminated. Should you suspect that water is contaminated, or if you wish to have water tested, contact local, county, or state health or environmental departments for information about qualified testing laboratories.

What can be done to decontaminate a home water supply?

If the home is supplied by an outside water supply source, federal law requires the provider to correct any contamination problems. When homes are supplied by private wells, analysis and treatment of the contaminated water may solve the problem.

What will it cost to decontaminate a home water supply?

Normally, consumers bear no direct financial responsibility for eliminating contamination from water supplied by an outside source (if the water was contaminated when it was delivered); the supplier bears the primary responsibility for correcting contamination problems. In the case of contaminated water supplied from a private well (or water from an outside source that becomes contaminated after it is received from the supplier), the cost of decontamination will depend on the kinds and amounts of contaminants present.

In the majority of cases, decontamination of a private water source involves technology and knowledge beyond the scope of the average homeowner. State and local environmental and water quality officials may be able to provide additional information and assistance for decontamination of private water sources.

What is being done about ground water contamination?

The U. S. Environmental Protection Agency has the lead responsibility for assuring the quality and safety of the nation's ground water supply. The EPA's approach is focused in two areas: minimizing the contamination of ground water and surface waters needed for human consumption and monitoring and treating drinking water before it is consumed.

In 1986, the U. S. Congress passed a set of amendments that expanded the protection provided by the Safe Drinking Water Act of 1974. These amendments streamlined the EPA's regulation of contaminants, banned all future use of lead pipe and lead solder in public drinking water systems, mandated greater protection of ground water sources, and authorized EPA to file civil suits or issue administrative orders against public water systems that are in violation of the Act.

Working with the states, EPA has set national standards for minimum levels of a number of contaminants and is mandated to set such standards for additional contaminants by 1991. In addition, EPA and the states are working to devise a national strategy for the monitoring and management of ground water supplies.

The following sources and publications provide additional information on ground water contamination.

Brochure

- *Is Your Drinking Water Safe?*

Available from:
U. S. Environmental Protection Agency
Public Information Center
401 M Street, SW
Washington, DC 20460
(202) 475-7751

Hotline

- *Safe Drinking Water Hotline*

  This Hotline provides information and publications to help the public and the regulated community understand EPA's drinking water regulations and programs. The Hotline operates Monday through Friday, 8:30 A.M. to 4:30 P.M., Eastern Time. (800) 426-4791; (202) 382-5533 (in the Washington, DC, area)

FORMALDEHYDE

What is formaldehyde?

Formaldehyde is a colorless, gaseous chemical compound that is generally present at low, variable concentrations in both indoor and outdoor air. It is emitted by many construction materials and consumer products that contain formaldehyde-based glues, resins, preservatives, and bonding agents. Formaldehyde also is an ingredient in foam that was used for home insulating until the early 1980s.

Where is formaldehyde found in the home?

Sources of formaldehyde in the home include smoke, household products, and unvented fuel-burning appliances (like gas stoves or kerosene space heaters). Formaldehyde, by itself or in combination with other chemicals, serves a number of purposes in manufactured products. For example, it is used to add permanent press qualities to clothing and draperies, as a component of glues and adhesives, and as a preservative in some paints and coating products.

In homes, the most significant sources of formaldehyde are likely to be in the adhesives used to bond pressed wood building materials and in plywood used for interior or exterior construction. Urea-formaldehyde (UF) resins are found in wood products that are intended for indoor use. Phenol-formaldehyde (PF) resins are used in products intended for exterior uses. UF resins emit significantly more formaldehyde gas than PF resins.

Certain foam insulating materials once widely used in housing construction (urea-formaldehyde foam or UFFI) also contain large amounts of formaldehyde. While contractors have voluntarily stopped using UFFI foam insulation, the material is present in many homes that were originally insulated with UFFI.

What health risks are associated with formaldehyde?

Formaldehyde has been shown to cause cancer in animals, but there is no definitive evidence linking the chemical to cancer in humans. Higher-than-normal levels of formaldehyde in the home atmosphere can trigger asthma attacks in individuals who have this condition. Other health hazards attributed to formaldehyde include skin rashes; watery eyes, burning sensations in the eyes, throat, and nasal passages; and breathing difficulties. Most persons will first react to formaldehyde when the levels are in the range of 0.1 to 1.1 parts per million. Some individuals acquire a reduced tolerance to formaldehyde following their initial exposure to the gas. In these instances, subsequent exposures to even small amounts of formaldehyde will cause reactions.

Do some kinds of homes carry a greater formaldehyde health risk than others?

Yes, materials containing formaldehyde were used extensively in the construction of certain prefabricated and manufactured homes. Since 1985, the federal government, through the U. S. Department of Housing and Urban Development, has enforced regulations that sharply curtail the use of materials containing formaldehyde in these types of housing to the lower-emitting products. However, use of formaldehyde compounds is still widespread in the manufacture of furniture, cabinets, and other building materials.

What can be done to reduce formaldehyde levels in a home?

Reducing formaldehyde levels in the home can be a simple or complex task depending on the source of the gas. Initial procedures often include steps to increase ventilation and improve circulation of outside air through the home. If new furniture, drapery, or other sources are contributing to higher-than-normal levels of formaldehyde, removal of these items (or limiting the number of new items introduced into the home) may be all that is needed.

In some instances, home subflooring or walls may be the source of formaldehyde, or foam insulation between inner and outer walls may be emitting the gas. If increased ventilation does not produce acceptable results in these instances, homeowners may be required to remove the formaldehyde-bearing material. Such procedures will be costly, time-consuming, and temporarily disruptive of life in the home.

How can I tell if the home I wish to buy contains formaldehyde-bearing materials?

In the case of a new home, you should consult with the builder before you purchase the house if you suspect the presence of materials that emit high levels of formaldehyde. Most builders will be able to tell you if construction materials contain urea-formaldehyde or they may direct you to manufacturers who can provide information about specific products. In the case of an older home, formaldehyde-emitting materials may not be visually evident and the current owners may not have specific product information. Because formaldehyde emissions from building materials decrease as the materials age (particularly over the first two or three years), older urea-formaldehyde building materials most probably will not be a significant source of formaldehyde emissions.

If you suspect the presence of formaldehyde, you may wish to hire a qualified building inspector to examine the home for the presence of formaldehyde-emitting materials. In addition, home monitoring kits are currently available for testing formaldehyde levels in the home. Be sure that the testing device will monitor for a minimum of 24 hours to assure that the sampling period is truly representative.

The following sources and publications provide additional information about formaldehyde in the home.

Brochures

- *The Inside Story—A Guide to Indoor Air Quality*

Available from:

U. S. Environmental Protection Agency
Public Information Center
401 M Street, SW
Washington, DC 20460
(202) 475-7751

- *Air Pollution in Your Home*
- *Home Indoor Air Quality Checklist*

Available from:

Local chapters of the American Lung Association.

- *Formaldehyde: Everything You Wanted to Know But Were Afraid to Ask*

Send a self-addressed, stamped envelope to:

Consumer Federation of America
1424 Sixteenth Street, NW
Washington, DC 20036

SOURCES OF ADDITIONAL INFORMATION

The EPA operates a variety of telephone hotlines to provide the public with easy access to EPA's programs, capabilities, and services. In addition to the hotlines, EPA has a variety of clearinghouses, libraries, and dockets that may provide information about a broad range of environmental issues. Information related to all of these sources is published in the *Guide to EPA Hotlines, Clearinghouses, Libraries, and Dockets*, which is available from EPA's Public Information Center (401 M Street, SW, Washington, DC 20460).

The regional offices of the U. S. Environmental Protection Agency are perhaps the best sources of additional information about environmental hazards in specific states and local areas. Each EPA regional office has information on states and areas within a single geographic area.

EPA Region 1
John F. Kennedy Federal Building
Room 2203
Boston, MA 02203
(617) 565-3715
Areas served: Connecticut, Maine, Massachusetts, New Hampshire, Rhode Island, and Vermont

EPA Region 2
26 Federal Plaza
New York, NY 10278
(212) 264-2515
Areas served: New Jersey, New York, Puerto Rico, and Virgin Islands

EPA Region 3
841 Chestnut Street
Philadelphia, PA 19107
(800) 438-2474
Areas served: Delaware, Maryland, Pennsylvania, Virginia, Washington, DC, and West Virginia

EPA Region 4
345 Courtland Street, NE
Atlanta, GA 30365
(800) 282-0239 in Georgia
(800) 241-1754 in other Region 4 states
Areas served: Alabama, Florida, Georgia, Kentucky, Mississippi, North Carolina, South Carolina, and Tennessee

EPA Region 5
230 South Dearborn Street
Chicago, IL 60604
(800) 572-2515 in Illinois
(800) 621-8431 in other Region 5 states
Areas served: Illinois, Indiana, Michigan, Minnesota, Ohio, and Wisconsin

EPA Region 6
1445 Ross Avenue, Suite 1200
Dallas, TX 75202
(214) 655-2200
Areas served: Arkansas, Louisiana, New Mexico, Oklahoma, and Texas

EPA Region 7
726 Minnesota Avenue
Kansas City, KS 66101
(913) 236-2803
Areas served: Iowa, Kansas, Missouri, and Nebraska

EPA Region 8
999 18th Street, Suite 500
Denver, CO 80202
(800) 759-4372
Areas served: Colorado, Montana, North Dakota, South Dakota, Utah, and Wyoming

EPA Region 9
215 Fremont Street
San Francisco, CA 94105
(415) 974-8076
Areas served: Arizona, California, Hawaii, and Nevada

EPA Region 10
1200 Sixth Avenue
Seattle, WA 98101
(206) 442-5810
Areas served: Alaska, Idaho, Oregon, and Washington

APPENDIX C

Preparing for Your Real Estate Exam

General Preparation for Your State's Real Estate Exam

Although the strategy you develop to study for your exam should reflect your own test-taking experiences and strengths, the following guidelines should prove helpful:

1. Set aside regular periods of time to study, review, and *practice* test taking.
2. Don't study for too long a period. Although everyone's attention span is different, studies show that several short sessions with a break are much more effective than one long session.
3. You will find studying more enjoyable and efficient if you set up a specific study corner where you can read, take notes, file your materials, etc.
4. Study when you are most alert. Some of us are morning people, and some of us are not.
5. In reviewing your text prior to the test, use a three-step approach to your study sessions. First, prepare yourself for the information by *scanning* (reading heads and bolded or italicized material), noting key terms, and examining summary information at the end of the chapter. If necessary, reread all or portions of the material—underlining, highlighting, or taking notes as you go. Finally, *review* the chapter briefly and *do the review questions.* Since the review questions are very important, do not skip or shortchange this part of your preparation. Check your answers immediately and note any particular areas that require additional review.
6. Take the two practice exams at the back of the book, reviewing any missed questions and referring back to the text when necessary. Remember that these practice tests are intended to prepare you for the *uniform* (or national) portion of your exam.

Before the Test Date

You will find the real estate examination less stressful if you learn as much as you can about the test ahead of time. Test preparation booklets will be provided by your school or the state. Go through them thoroughly. Find out as soon as you can who the testing agency is, what the percentage of state versus general questions is, and what percentage of the questions on the exam are math-specific. Unless you are told otherwise, you should assume that all of the questions on the examination will be multiple choice. That means your test-taking strategy should reflect this format. (See the section on taking multiple-choice tests under Taking the Test.)

Visit the testing site ahead of time to see approximately how much time it will take to get there. Find the building and room you will be taking the test in, and locate parking if you will need a place to park. After you have made your test reservation, it is a good idea to check with the testing agency a day or two later to confirm that you are registered (and to verify the date, time, and location of your examination).

Finally, make sure that any equipment or supplies that you plan to bring with you are acceptable. Calculators, especially, should be given some thought. Find out what restrictions the testing agencies place on their use and type. Solar-powered calculators, for example, may not be allowed. Test your calculator's batteries the day before you take the exam. And this isn't the time to get a new, complicated calculator that you are unfamiliar with.

Taking the Test

Plan to be there early. If there is time, take a short walk to relax a bit. Above all, don't stress yourself with last-minute cramming. As you enter the room and begin pre-examination activities, resist the temptation to rush into the examination. The allotted time should be enough to complete the test. So, take a few deep breaths and pay close attention to the instructions. Be certain that you understand them, and ask questions if you do not. Before beginning the exam, establish a rough timetable. First, divide your test-taking time into two parts—general and state—if your exam is structured that way. Remember, the two portions of the test probably will not be equal in length so adjust your overall timetable to reflect this fact. Then, divide each section of the exam into two parts (allow about two-thirds of the time for taking the examination and one-third for reviewing it).

Although only a specified number of questions will count (usually 80–100), you may find more questions than that on the exam. That is because they may be testing some questions for later use in their testing program. Don't worry about it. Just answer all questions asked.

General Guidelines for Taking Multiple-Choice Examinations

1. If you find yourself rushing through the questions, try reading each question twice. This will slow you down and help you avoid misreading the question.
2. Work by a process of elimination if you aren't certain about the correct answer. As you eliminate answers that you believe are incorrect, you automatically increase your chance of answering the question correctly.
3. If you feel certain that two answers are correct, you may be misreading the question. Rephrase the question in your own words.
4. If two answers mean the same thing (like nonfreehold estate and leasehold estate), eliminate them as possibilities. There will never be two correct answers to one question.
5. Never leave an answer blank. Since you are not penalized for wrong answers, you have a 25 percent chance of being right if you guess without having eliminated any possibilities.

6. During the test, pay particular attention to negatives (EXCEPT, NOT, FALSE, LEAST). These words are warning signs to help you interpret the question correctly.
7. Don't assume that all the information embedded in the question is needed. Math questions, especially, are designed to test your ability to eliminate irrelevant information.

Handling Math Questions on the Exam

Math questions, more than any other category, are likely to frighten students. If you have reviewed your study materials carefully, however, there is no reason to panic. Real estate math is not complex; nor does it comprise a very large segment of the exam. If you are concerned about these questions, keep the following suggestions in mind:

1. Do these questions last. Just mark them for future attention and move on. This allows you to work through the test in a timely way.
2. An alternative to this is to read through each math question quickly as you encounter it. If you are confident that you know how to answer the question, go ahead and do it. Working some of the math problems as you go through the examination will give you confidence for later ones you are less sure of.
3. When in doubt, make your best guess. Even a 25 percent chance is better than no chance!
4. Look the problem over and "guesstimate" what the answer should be. You will then have some sort of ballpark figure to compare your computations to. If your answer is wildly different, you may have made a basic mathematical error, used an incorrect process (for example, dividing when you should have multiplied), or used information that was not relevant. Testers derive some "wrong" answers by selecting common mistakes made by students.
5. If you find yourself taking too long or getting confused, take your best guess, mark the question for later review, and move on. Often, students find that a break from the question helps them see it more clearly.

Review

One final note: do leave adequate time for review, but use that time wisely. First, go back to all the unanswered questions you marked and go over them. At times, the correct answer will suddenly be clear. Unless you know why you are changing an answer, however, it is usually best to leave the answer you initially chose. When you have finished the marked questions, begin a review of each question by reading each question and the answer you chose. In a few cases, you may find that information embedded in later questions gives you a different perspective on earlier ones. You may also be more relaxed now—and less error-prone. Finally, don't feel that you have to use all the time available to you. If you have completed the exam, reviewed all marked items with special care, and reviewed the test as a whole, you should consider your job done. Studies show that over-reviewing results in lower test scores. Your first, intuitive choice is most often the correct one.

Testing Agencies

The standard examinations for a state's real estate license fall into four primary categories:

1. Assessment Systems, Inc. (ASI) Program

2. Psychological Services, Inc. (PSI)
3. Applied Measurement Professionals, Inc. (AMP)
4. In-house programs prepared by the state's own licensing and regulatory agency

Because these standard exams have many common features, we can discuss their format in general as a guide to preparing you for your own state exam. However, you must learn which examination program your state uses and obtain a specific content outline for the exam from the testing service or from your state's real estate licensing agency (your instructor probably will give you information regarding this). Plan to obtain all this information as early as possible so you can prepare for your exam.

All categories of real estate licensing examinations follow a common format. The examinations are approximately 80–100 questions in length and consist entirely of objective test items with four answer options (multiple-choice). The questions, and to some extent the subject areas, are different on the exams for salespersons and for brokers.

The uniform test covers a variety of subjects that are standard, or uniform, in all jurisdictions. To be successful in taking some examinations, the applicant must pass both the state test and the uniform test. In case of failure, some jurisdictions require the applicant to retake only that test, state or uniform, that the applicant did not pass, rather than retake the entire examinations. The regulation in this regard is completely determined by each state licensing agency.

The state portion of the test is based on the license law and rules and regulations of the jurisdiction where the student has applied for a real estate license. The state tests typically consist of 30–50 questions.

The examinations must be completed within the time allotted by each jurisdiction. If the applicant is adequately prepared and does not waste time, the amount of time allowed is sufficient to complete the examination successfully.

Scores

The passing score required for the examinations is established by each jurisdiction. Passing scores typically are 70 percent to 75 percent. A jurisdiction may specify different percentages for the state and the uniform tests. The testing agency, or its appointed agents, grades the exam.

If testing is by electronic pad, score reports usually are provided immediately at the test site. If testing is by paper-and-pencil mode, the testing agency sends score reports to applicants. If an applicant is successful, the score report reads PASS (the score may also be given). If the applicant is not successful, the report states FAIL, gives the percentage correct, and also gives the results by subject area. This method of reporting the results enables the applicant to determine the subject area(s) on which to concentrate in preparing to retake the examination. Neither the testing agency nor licensing agencies provide for a review of test results with applicants on a question-by-question basis.

Bulletins of Information

Each testing service provides a bulletin about its exam. The Assessment Systems, Inc., Psychological Services, Inc., and Applied Measurement Professionals, Inc. publish Candidate Guides for Applicants that provide detailed information about the examinations, including sample questions illustrating the types of questions on each of the two examinations. The bulletins are available at no charge from licensing agencies using the testing services, from prelicensing real estate schools, or directly from the services themselves. Correspondence should be addressed to:

REAL Program
ASI Processing Center
718 Arch Street
Philadelphia, PA 19106

Psychological Services, Inc. (PSI)
100 West Broadway, Suite 1100
Glendale, CA 91210

Applied Measurement Professionals, Inc.
8310 Nieman Road
Lenexa, KS 66214

APPENDIX D

Practice Exam 1

1. A salesperson associated with Lighthouse Realty effects a sale of property listed in the MLS with a universal offer of subagency by Point Hazard Realty. In this transaction the salesperson is a subagent of which of the following?
   a. seller
   b. Lighthouse Realty
   c. buyer
   d. seller and buyer

2. All of the following statements about agency are correct EXCEPT:
   a. the principal is responsible for acts of his agent while engaged in activities concerning the agency
   b. the agent is in a fiduciary relationship to her principal
   c. the agent in a real estate listing is usually the seller
   d. the principal has a duty to cooperate with the agent

3. If a salesperson lists and sells a property for $90,000 and receives 60% of the 7% commission paid to her employing broker, how much does the salesperson receive?
   a. $2,520
   b. $3,780
   c. $5,400
   d. $6,300

4. Sara Seller is satisfied with all of the terms of an offer to purchase her property from Bill Buyer except the date of possession, which she changes from April 9 to April 10. Which of the following is correct?
   a. Sara's acceptance creates a valid contract
   b. Sara cannot make a counteroffer
   c. Sara can always accept Bill Buyer's original offer if the April 10th date is not accepted
   d. Sara has rejected Bill Buyer's offer

5. A salesperson sold one-quarter of the southeast quarter of section 12 for $1,800 per acre. If the salesperson's commission was 60% of the 10% commission her broker received, how much did the salesperson earn?
   a. $2,880
   b. $4,320
   c. $11,520
   d. $17,280

6. At the time of listing a property, the owner specifies that he wishes to net $65,000 after satisfying a mortgage of $25,000 and paying a 7% brokerage fee. For what price should the property be listed?
   a. $90,000
   b. $94,550
   c. $96,300
   d. $96,774

7. When an option is exercised, it becomes which of the following?
   a. lease
   b. offer
   c. multiple listing
   d. contract of sale

8. An agreement that is a financing instrument and a contract of sale is called a(n):
   a. option
   b. lease
   c. contract for deed
   d. exclusive agency

9. A real estate broker sells a tract of land (described in the figure below) for $1,600 per acre and earns a 9% commission. How much does the broker receive? (answers rounded)
   a. $661
   b. $952
   c. $992
   d. $1,983

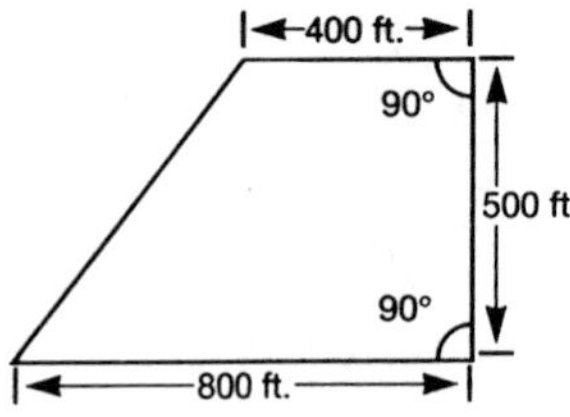

10. A lease agreement in which the landlord accepts another tenant and relieves the vacating tenant of any liability is:
    a. novation
    b. assignment
    c. accord and satisfaction
    d. carryover contract

11. Which of the following is a key word used to determine whether a real estate broker is or is not legally entitled to a commission?
    a. acceptance
    b. accountability
    c. assignment
    d. assumption

12. Buyer Berta makes an offer to purchase seller Steve's land if she also decides to buy another tract that adjoins his land. Which of the following describes Berta's offer?
    a. indefinite
    b. illusory
    c. unilateral
    d. fraudulent

13. Failure to comply with the terms of an offer as to the manner of communicating acceptance will result in which of the following?
    a. termination of the offer
    b. extension of the offer
    c. acceptance of the offer
    d. duress

14. The party who assigns a contract interest to another is the:
    a. grantor
    b. assignee
    c. assignor
    d. grantee

15. From the standpoint of both the agent and the seller, the best type of listing contract is:
    a. open
    b. exclusive agency
    c. net
    d. exclusive right to sell

16. In making an FHA-insured loan of $45,000, a lending institution charges sufficient discount points to increase the yield on the loan from 9% to 9¾%. The cost of the points is:
    a. $1,350
    b. $1,800
    c. $2,700
    d. $5,400

17. If the monthly payment on a $60,000 fully amortizing mortgage loan at 12% APR for a 20-year term is $660.65, how much is the principal reduced by the first monthly payment?
    a. $60.65
    b. $72.00
    c. $600.00
    d. $612.20

18. Hypothecate most nearly means:
    a. selling real estate
    b. pledging real estate as collateral for a loan
    c. leasing real estate
    d. giving an easement

19. The monthly payment of principal and interest on a 30-year mortgage at 10% for $40,000 is $351.03. How much interest will the borrower pay over the 30-year term?
    a. $40,000
    b. $86,371
    c. $126,371
    d. $160,000

20. Which of the following most accurately describes the major purpose of a mortgage or a deed of trust?
    a. to secure the payment of a note
    b. to convey a title to the trustee
    c. to provide for equity of redemption
    d. to prevent assumption

21. The acceleration clause provides for which of the following?
    a. equity of redemption
    b. prepayment penalty
    c. right of lender to require immediate payment of principal balance when borrower is in default
    d. alienation by borrower

22. Which of the following liens takes priority over mortgage foreclosure sale proceeds?
    a. mortgage lien
    b. income tax lien
    c. real property tax lien
    d. mechanic's lien

23. An alienation clause makes a mortgage:
    a. defeasible
    b. unassumable
    c. incontestable
    d. adjustable

24. A lending institution's sharing in the appreciation in value of property and sharing in the equity of property is called:
    a. shared appreciation mortgage
    b. amortization
    c. liquidation
    d. hypothecation

25. All of the following may be required prepaid items by the mortgagee EXCEPT:
    a. real property taxes
    b. hazard insurance
    c. property owner's assessment
    d. broker's commission

26. FHA requires which of the following documents to be signed by borrowers purchasing a home built before 1978?
    a. commission disclosure form
    b. lead-based paint test results disclosure
    c. lead-based paint information disclosure
    d. Fair Housing Disclosure form

27. Which of the following is a way in which a veteran borrower can have eligibility fully restored?
    a. sell the property on contract
    b. sell the property to a nonveteran who assumes the VA-guaranteed loan
    c. dispose of the property and pay off the VA-guaranteed loan
    d. lease the property with an option to buy

28. The financing arrangement in which the borrower and lender hold equitable title to the real estate and a disinterested third party holds legal title is:
    a. deed of trust
    b. note
    c. junior mortgage
    d. contract for deed

29. Nonjudicial foreclosure occurs in:
    a. friendly foreclosure
    b. foreclosure by action
    c. strict foreclosure
    d. foreclosure under power of sale

30. Minor changes to a signed accepted offer to purchase require each amendment or change to be initialed by:
    a. all parties
    b. buyer only
    c. broker and seller
    d. seller only

31. A blanket mortgage usually contains which of the following?
    a. closed-end clause
    b. release clauses
    c. good faith estimate
    d. due-on-sale clause

32. Which is the true statement regarding FHA loan assumptions?
   a. buyers must always qualify
   b. the need for buyer qualification depends on date of original loan origination
   c. FHA loans are not assumable
   d. buyers need not qualify

33. Which of the following regulates the advertisement of credit terms available for a house offered for sale?
   a. RESPA
   b. Fannie Mae
   c. Equal Credit Opportunity Act
   d. Regulation Z

34. Which of the following is limited to purchasing FHA-insured and VA-guaranteed mortgages?
   a. Fannie Mae
   b. Freddie Mac
   c. Maggie Mae
   d. Ginnie Mae

35. If a lease specifies the rent to be 2% of the gross sales per annum, with a minimum annual rent of $8,000, what is the annual rent if gross sales are $1,200,000?
   a. $8,000
   b. $12,000
   c. $24,000
   d. $28,000

36. Which of the following provides the grantee with the greatest assurance of title?
   a. special warranty deed
   b. deed of gift
   c. general warranty deed
   d. grant deed

37. Which of the following is a benefit of recording a deed?
   a. it prevents any liens from being filed against the property
   b. it protects the grantee against the grantee's creditors
   c. it protects the grantee against future conveyances by the grantor
   d. it makes a mortgage lien subordinate

38. Which of the following requires the grantor to execute a deed of confirmation if needed?
   a. covenant of seisin
   b. covenant for further assurances
   c. covenant against encumbrances
   d. covenant of right to convey

39. Which of the following statements about the rollover rule is correct?
   a. it is mandatory if the transaction qualifies
   b. it may be used only once in a lifetime
   c. it allows exemption of the gain from tax
   d. it applies only if the real estate was a principal residence five of the last eight years

40. All of the following are rights of a life tenant EXCEPT:
   a. encumber
   b. use
   c. alienate
   d. waste

41. Which of the following statements is correct?
   a. an easement provides right of possession
   b. an easement in gross has no servient tenement
   c. an easement is a fixture to real estate
   d. an appurtenant easement can be obtained by necessity

42. If the market value of a property is $90,000, the tax rate is 90 mills, and the assessment is 70%, what is the amount of the annual tax bill?
   a. $567
   b. $5,670
   c. $7,000
   d. $8,100

43. The owner(s) of real property may hold title in all of the following ways EXCEPT:
   a. tenants in common
   b. lessees
   c. severalty
   d. joint tenants

44. A claim, lien, charge, or liability attached to and binding upon real property is a(n):
   a. encumbrance
   b. community property
   c. license
   d. syndication

45. An owner of a condominium office:
    a. has a proprietary lease
    b. is assessed by the property owners association for maintenance to his office unit
    c. may pledge his property as security for a mortgage loan
    d. owns a share of stock in the corporation that owns the real estate

46. Timesharing is commonly associated with which of the following?
    a. cooperatives
    b. profits
    c. joint ventures
    d. condominiums

47. Which of the following clauses in an accepted offer to purchase protects the buyer from losing her earnest money in the event financing is not obtained?
    a. habendum
    b. contingency
    c. defeasance
    d. subordination

48. The Fair Housing Act of 1968 prohibits discrimination in the rental of all of the following EXCEPT:
    a. offices
    b. apartments
    c. houses
    d. residential lots

49. The Fair Housing Act of 1968 prohibits all of the following EXCEPT:
    a. discriminatory advertising
    b. use of brokerage services
    c. steering
    d. redlining

50. Inducing an owner to list property by telling the owner that people of a certain national origin are moving into the neighborhood is called:
    a. steering
    b. redlining
    c. blockbusting
    d. profiteering

51. Exemptions to the Fair Housing Act of 1988 are lost by all of the following EXCEPT:
    a. use of discriminatory advertising
    b. use of a broker
    c. use of a sign that states "Room for Rent"
    d. use of a REALTOR®

52. A property manager's fee usually consists of a base fee plus:
    a. a percentage of the rental income received
    b. a percentage of the gross potential income
    c. a percentage of the net income
    d. a percentage of the stabilized budget

53. When a lessee installs trade fixtures, these are:
    a. a permanent part of the real estate
    b. owned by the lessor
    c. the personal property of the lessee
    d. real property

54. A person living on the managed premises as a salaried employee engaged to manage and lease apartments is called a(n):
    a. property manager
    b. rental agent
    c. employee manager
    d. resident manager

55. The monthly accounting by the property manager is called a:
    a. stabilized budget
    b. property management report
    c. management budget
    d. financial report

56. All of the following are required of property managers EXCEPT:
    a. showing and leasing property
    b. deciding owner's objectives
    c. collecting rent
    d. providing for the protection of tenants

57. A buyer assumes a seller's existing 11%, $80,000 first deed of trust on the settlement date of June 12. The seller makes the monthly payment on June 1 with interest in advance. Which of the following is a correct settlement statement entry for the interest?
    a. $293.28 buyer's credit
    b. $439.92 seller's credit
    c. $293.28 seller's debit
    d. $439.92 seller's debit

58. Which of the following types of listing contracts gives the broker commission entitlement if anyone sells the listed property during the listing term?
    a. net
    b. open
    c. exclusive agency
    d. exclusive right to sell

59. A real estate salesperson advises a prospective buyer that the property the buyer is considering is scheduled for annexation into the city limits. This disclosure constitutes which of the following?
    a. disloyalty to principal
    b. misrepresentation
    c. required disclosure to buyer
    d. violation of disclosure of information by salesperson

60. After inspecting a property, the prospective buyer tells the salesperson that she likes the property but will not pay the listed price of $75,000. Knowing that the owner is anxious to sell, the salesperson suggests that the prospective buyer make an offer of $70,000. Which of the following statements about this situation is correct?
    a. the salesperson is violating his obligation as a special agent
    b. because the salesperson knows the owner is anxious to sell, he is acting correctly
    c. the salesperson is violating his obligations as a universal agent
    d. the prospective buyer can be found guilty of conversion

61. A salesperson receives two offers for a listed property within a 10-minute period. One offer is 2% less than the listed price, and the other is 6% less than the listed price. The salesperson should present to the seller:
    a. neither offer
    b. both offers
    c. the highest offer
    d. the first offer

62. Closing on a commercial property is April 18. The seller had paid real property taxes in the amount of $5,760 for the tax year that began June 1 of the previous year. Which of the following is the correct closing statement entry for taxes?
    a. $672 buyer's credit
    b. $5,088 buyer's credit
    c. $672 seller's credit
    d. $5,088 seller's credit

63. The amount of a purchase money mortgage appears in the closing statement as:
    a. seller's credit only
    b. buyer's debit only
    c. seller's debit; buyer's credit
    d. seller's credit; buyer's debit

64. A seller paid an annual hazard insurance premium of $540 for a policy effective February 12. At settlement on April 16 of the same year, the buyer purchased the policy from the seller. This transaction is correctly entered on the settlement statements as:
    a. $96 buyer's credit
    b. $444 buyer's credit
    c. $96 seller's credit
    d. $444 seller's credit

65. The amount of earnest money appears on closing statements as a:
    a. credit to buyer
    b. debit to seller
    c. credit to seller
    d. debit to buyer

66. When listing real property for sale, a real estate broker:
    a. does a competitive market analysis
    b. makes an appraisal to estimate market value
    c. estimates residual income
    d. correlates reproduction cost

67. An apartment building produces an annual net income of $10,800 after deducting $72 per month for expenses. What price for the property would provide a buyer with a net return of 12%?
    a. $90,000
    b. $97,200
    c. $116,641
    d. $129,600

68. An apartment building contains 30 units. Each unit rents for $200 per month. The vacancy rate is 4%. Annual expenses are $3,000 for maintenance, $1,100 insurance, $1,600 taxes, $1,200 utilities, and 15% of the gross effective income for management fee. What is the investor's net rate of return for the first year if he paid $260,000 for the property?

a. 6.69%
b. 11.64%
c. 14.94%
d. 19.94%

69. If a rental property provides the owner with an 11% return on her investment of $780,000, what is the net annual income from the property?

a. $70,512
b. $70,909
c. $85,800
d. $141,025

70. Which of the following methods is used to estimate the value of the land only, on which an apartment building is to be located the next year?

a. cost approach
b. income approach
c. market data approach
d. replacement cost

71. Gross rent multipliers are used in connection with which of the following?

a. condominiums
b. schools
c. vacant land
d. income property

72. Adherence to which of the following has the effect of maximizing land value?

a. principle of contribution
b. principle of change
c. principle of anticipation
d. principle of highest and best use

73. Which of the following statements about zoning is correct?

a. in exclusive-use zoning, property may be used only for the uses specified for that specific zoned area
b. if a nonconforming structure is destroyed, it may be replaced by another nonconforming structure
c. all nonconforming uses are illegal
d. a preexisting nonconforming use requires a variance

74. Restrictive covenants are:

a. conditions
b. encumbrances
c. public land use controls
d. zoning classifications

75. When land is torn away by the violent action of a river it is called:

a. erosion
b. avulsion
c. reliction
d. alluvion

76. The characteristic of land that has the greatest effect on land value is:

a. nonhomogeneity
b. location
c. indestructibility
d. immobility

77. All of the following are examples of public land use controls EXCEPT:

a. deed restrictions
b. building codes
c. zoning
d. environmental control laws

78. An estate created for the life of a person other than the life tenant is called a life estate:

a. in remainder
b. pur autre vie
c. by dower
d. in reversion

79. Freehold estates that are not inheritable are called:

a. defeasible estates
b. leasehold estates
c. life estates
d. fee simple estates

80. Which of the following is a right in the land of another by the owner of adjoining land?

a. profit
b. easement appurtenant
c. license
d. easement in gross

81. A trespass on the land of another as a result of an intrusion by some structure or other object is an:
a. encroachment
b. easement
c. estate
d. emblement

82. Easements may be created in all of the following ways EXCEPT:
a. prescription
b. condemnation
c. lis pendens
d. dedication

83. An owner lists her property with three brokerage firms. In each case she retains the right to sell the property herself without being obligated to pay a commission to any of the brokers. The type of listing contract given to each broker is called:
a. exclusive right to sell
b. open
c. multiple
d. net

84. As a result of a salesperson's negligence in filling in the provisions in a contract of sale, the seller incurs a financial loss. Liability for this loss may be imposed on:
a. both the salesperson and the employing broker
b. the salesperson's employing broker only
c. the salesperson only
d. neither party

85. A contract for deed or installment land contract is a(n):
a. contingent proposition
b. offer to purchase
c. form of financing instrument and contract for sale
d. option to purchase

86. All of the following are remedies available to a party to a contract upon breach of the contract EXCEPT:
a. specific performance
b. liquidated damages
c. estoppel
d. compensatory damages

87. A gift of real property at death is a(n):
a. devise
b. bequest
c. escheat
d. demise

88. Of the following types of deeds, which provides the grantee with the LEAST assurance of title?
a. bargain and sale
b. quitclaim
c. grant
d. special warranty

89. Recording protects which of the following parties?
a. grantor
b. seller
c. vendor
d. grantee

90. All of the following are rights of a mortgagor EXCEPT:
a. defeasance
b. foreclosure
c. equity of redemption
d. possession

91. Which of the following gives the mortgagee the right to declare the entire principal balance immediately due and payable if the mortgagor is in default?
a. acceleration clause
b. alienation clause
c. statutory foreclosure clause
d. assignment clause

92. Using the amortization schedule on page 161, determine which of the following is the monthly payment of principal and interest required to fully amortize a $50,000, twenty-year mortgage loan at 9.5% interest:
a. $357.14
b. $466.07
c. $512.18
d. $592.50

93. Which of the following provides the highest loan-to-value ratio?
a. conventional
b. FHA 245
c. 95% insured conventional
d. FHA 203B

94. On June 16, a seller closes on the sale of her home. Annual taxes of $861 for the current year were paid in full by the seller prior to the sale. If these payments are prorated, which amount will be returned to the seller?

a. $357
b. $397
c. $430
d. $464

95. If the GIM is 7.5 and the annual gross income is $250,000, what is the estimated property value?

a. $1,875,000
b. $2,500,000
c. $3,000,000
d. $3,333,000

96. Restrictive covenants are:

a. private land use controls
b. public land use controls
c. variances
d. statements of record

97. A right granted to a lessee to purchase a property if the owner decides to sell, where no price is established and no specific sum is paid for the right, is a(n):

a. option
b. right to the obligor
c. defeasance clause
d. right of first refusal

98. All of the following statements about the age-55-and-over exclusion are correct EXCEPT:

a. it may be taken only once in a lifetime
b. it is available to co-owners
c. it is up to $125,000
d. it is available on commercial property

99. In a tax-deferred exchange, which of the following is taxable in the year of sale?

a. like-kind property
b. boot
c. exchange property
d. salvage value

100. A salesperson licensee may receive commissions from which of the following?

a. cooperating broker
b. buyer
c. seller
d. employing broker

APPENDIX E

Practice Exam 2

1. Mary Seaver, a salesperson associated with Leisure Homes Realty, advised a seller that his property would sell for at least $150,000. Relying on this price quotation, the seller listed the property at a price of $150,000. Comparable sales and listings of competitive properties at the time were in the range of $105,000 to $110,000. The seller refused several offers between $106,000 and $112,000 during the 120-day term of the listing contract. The seller eventually sold his property for $98,000 because of depressed economic conditions since expiration of the listing with Leisure Homes. Which of the following statements about these events is true?
   a. Mary has done nothing wrong and thus is not liable for any damage
   b. because Mary is an agent of Leisure Homes Realty, Leisure Homes is the only party that may be held liable for the seller's damages
   c. Mary committed an act of misrepresentation and may be liable for the resulting financial loss the seller incurred
   d. because the seller did not sell the property during the listing period, Mary is entitled to a commission

2. While a broker was inspecting a property for listing, the property owner told the broker that the house contains 2,400 square feet of heated living area. Without verifying this information, the broker listed the property and represented it to prospective buyers as containing 2,400 square feet. After purchasing the property, the buyer accurately determined that the house has only 1,850 square feet and sued for damages for the difference in value between 2,400 square feet and 1,850 square feet. Which of the following is correct?
   a. the broker is not liable because he relied on the seller's positive statement as to the square footage
   b. the seller is not liable because the broker, not the seller, represented the property to the buyer as containing 2,400 square feet
   c. the theory of caveat emptor applies; thus, neither the seller nor the broker is liable to the buyer
   d. both the broker and the seller are liable to the buyer

3. The sales associates of Executive Realty, Ltd., obtained several excellent listings in Exclusive Estates by advising homeowners that a number of Chinese families were moving into Exclusive Estates and therefore their property values would be substantially depressed. This activity is most accurately described as:
   a. steering
   b. blockbusting
   c. soliciting
   d. redlining

4. A real estate salesperson earned $48,000 in commissions in one year. If she received 60% of the 6% her broker received, what was her average monthly sales volume?
   a. $66,666
   b. $80,000
   c. $111,111
   d. $133,333

5. The type of listing contract that is most beneficial to the broker and the seller is:
   a. exclusive right to sell
   b. net
   c. open
   d. exclusive agency

6. A real estate broker is responsible for all of the following EXCEPT:
   a. acts of sales associates while engaged in brokerage activities
   b. appropriate handling of funds in trust, or escrow, accounts
   c. adhering to commission schedule recommended by the local board of REALTORS®
   d. representing property honestly, fairly, and accurately to prospective buyers

7. A triangular tract of land is 8,000 feet long and has highway frontage of 4,000 yards. If Ajax Realty Company lists this property at 9% commission and sells it for $1,600 per acre, what amount of commission does Ajax receive?
   a. $105,785
   b. $158,678
   c. $218,160
   d. $317,355

8. When listing a home for sale, the broker advises the seller that because he owns only one house, the listing is exempt from prohibitions of the Fair Housing Act of 1968. Which of the following statements about the broker's advice is true?
   a. the broker is acting correctly in advising the seller about the exemption
   b. the broker always should give good legal advice to sellers and buyers
   c. the broker is in error because the exemption is from the Civil Rights Act of 1866
   d. the broker is acting incorrectly in that the property is not exempt because the seller is using a broker

9. A broker deposited a buyer's check for earnest money in the amount of $6,000 in her escrow account. Prior to the closing and at the seller's request, the broker took $1,200 from the escrow account to pay for the cost of damage repairs caused by termites in the house. This expense was necessary so the seller could provide the required termite certificate to the buyer at the closing. Which of the following statements about this transaction is correct?
   a. because the $1,200 disbursement from the broker's escrow account was made at the seller's request and benefitted both buyer and seller, the broker acted properly
   b. the broker's action constituted an act of commingling and, as such, was improper
   c. the broker's action was not proper and constituted collusion
   d. the broker's action was not proper without the buyer's agreement

10. A salesperson associated with Metro Realty, Inc., obtained an offer for a property listed by Preferred Real Estate Company, which she gave to Sam Slicker, the listing agent with Preferred, for presentation to the property owner. Realizing that the amount of the offer was such that it probably would not be accepted, Sam increased the amount by $3,000 prior to presentation. Which of the following statements correctly characterizes Sam's action?
    a. to make the change a proper and appropriate act, Sam should have obtained the approval of Metro Realty before changing the offer
    b. Sam's action was in violation of his fiduciary obligations and was completely improper
    c. Sam's action would have been appropriate with the seller's consent
    d. Metro Realty, Inc., will be entitled to the entire commission because of Sam's actions

11. In the process of preparing an offer for commercial property, a broker was asked by two potential purchasers to recommend the most beneficial way for them to take title to the property. Which of the following should the broker recommend?
    a. tenants in common
    b. in severalty
    c. ask an attorney
    d. ask the listing broker

12. Upon the broker's recommendation, a seller accepted an offer that was 8% below the listed price. The broker did not disclose to the listing seller that the buyer was the broker's brother-in-law. Which of the following is correct?
    a. the broker violated his obligations as agent of the seller
    b. the fact that the buyer is related to the broker is not required to be divulged to the seller
    c. the broker has done nothing wrong as long as he doesn't take any commission
    d. the broker has done nothing wrong if the appraised value of the home matches the offered price

13. Due to the curvature of the earth, under the rectangular survey method, adjustments must be made to the north and south baseline of every fourth township. These adjustments are called:
    a. curvature lines
    b. correction lines
    c. rectangular line adjustments
    d. base line adjustments

14. All of the following usually appear only in the seller's closing statement EXCEPT:
    a. broker's fee
    b. deed preparation
    c. prepayment penalty
    d. earnest money

15. If the closing date is November 10 and the seller had paid the real property taxes of $2,880 for the current tax year of January 1 through December 31, which of the following is the correct closing statement entry for taxes?
    a. seller's credit of $400
    b. seller's debit of $2,480
    c. buyer's credit of $400
    d. buyer's debit of $2,480

16. RESPA requires lending institutions to provide borrowers with which of the following at the time of or within three days after application for a mortgage loan for housing?
    a. good faith estimate
    b. HUD Form No. 1
    c. disclosure statement
    d. nonrecourse note

17. The buyer assumes a 9% loan with a balance of $74,000 mortgage at closing on July 12. The seller has already made the July 1 payment; the next payment of $638.69, including principal and interest for July, will be due on August 1. Which of the following is the correct closing statement entry for interest?
    a. buyer's debit of $222.00
    b. buyer's credit of $638.69
    c. seller's debit of $222.00
    d. seller's credit of $638.69

18. A sales contract provided that the buyer was to pay $65,000 for a seller's property by giving a purchase money mortgage for $30,000 and the balance in cash at closing. The buyer made a good faith deposit of $6,500 when he made the offer. The seller's share of the real property taxes credited to the buyer was $850. The buyer's other closing costs totaled $900. What amount must the buyer pay at closing?
    a. $27,650
    b. $27,700
    c. $28,550
    d. $35,050

19. Which of the following individuals usually brings the earnest money to the final settlement?
    a. broker
    b. buyer
    c. lender
    d. seller

20. Which of the following is most likely to have been prepared by a broker?
    a. deed
    b. closing statement
    c. certificate of occupancy
    d. lien waivers

21. A property manager's responsibilities include all of the following EXCEPT:
    a. maintenance
    b. collecting rents
    c. commingling
    d. negotiating leases

22. Which of the following is one of the basic responsibilities of a property manager?
    a. appraising the property annually
    b. evicting all minority tenants to provide for a more stable complex
    c. producing the best possible net operating income for the owner
    d. preparing the annual tax returns and attending audits with the IRS

23. What net annual operating income must a property manager produce from a property to provide an 8% return to the owner, who paid $763,000 for the property?
    a. $9,538
    b. $61,040
    c. $95,375
    d. $104,849

24. Which of the following most accurately describes a property manager?
    a. fiduciary
    b. trustee
    c. escrow agent
    d. resident manager

25. When all parties agree to the terms and conditions of a real estate contract, there is said to be:
    a. mutual satisfaction
    b. *sui juris*
    c. meeting of the minds
    d. equitable consent

26. A roofline extending without permission onto an adjoining property is an example of:
    a. easement appurtenant
    b. encroachment
    c. license
    d. easement in gross

27. John owns an apartment building in a large city. After discussing the matter with his legal advisers, he decides to alter the type of occupancy in the building from rental to condominium status. This procedure is known as:
    a. conversion
    b. partition
    c. deportment
    d. amendment

28. In the preceding question, after checking the applicable laws, John discovers that he must offer to sell each unit to the current tenant. If the tenant does not accept the offer, he then may offer the unit for sale to the general public. This requirement to offer the property to the present tenant is known as:
    a. contingent restriction
    b. conditional sales option
    c. covenant of present possession
    d. right of first refusal

29. An owner's office building is producing a net annual operating income of $140,000. If the owner paid $1,166,666 for the property, what rate of return is she receiving on her investment?
    a. 8.3%
    b. 12%
    c. 14%
    d. 16.3%

30. All of the following statements about options are correct EXCEPT:
    a. they must be in writing to be enforceable
    b. they are binding upon optionor and optionee
    c. when exercised, they become contracts of sale
    d. optionor and optionee must be competent

31. Which of the following is both a contract of sale and a financing instrument?
    a. installment land contract
    b. sale and leaseback
    c. lease with option to purchase
    d. executed contract

32. A lease providing for rental changes based on changes in the Consumer Price Index is which of the following?
    a. escalated
    b. graduated
    c. percentage
    d. index

33. Deed restrictions enforced by a suit for damages or by an injunction are:
    a. conditions
    b. conveyances
    c. covenants
    d. considerations

34. Public land use controls in the form of subdivision ordinances are an exercise of:
    a. power of eminent domain
    b. general plan for development
    c. police power of the government
    d. Interstate Land Sales Full Disclosure Act

35. A property owner in a recently zoned area is permitted to continue to use his property in a manner that does not comply with the zoning requirements. This use is described as:
    a. exclusive-use zoning
    b. deviation
    c. nonconforming use
    d. private control of land use

36. The covenant for further assurances may require the grantor to execute a(n):
    a. deed of confirmation
    b. executor's deed
    c. certificate of title opinion
    d. deed of devise

37. A life tenant may convey her life estate by executing which of the following?
    a. quitclaim deed
    b. deed of confirmation
    c. judicial deed
    d. certificate of title registration

38. A deed is made eligible for recording on the public record by which of the following?
    a. abstract
    b. avoidance
    c. alienation
    d. acknowledgment

39. A real estate broker may do all of the following EXCEPT:
    a. have a buyer's deed recorded
    b. make a title examination
    c. act as agent of the grantee to accept deed delivery
    d. execute a certificate of title opinion

40. Which of the following provides the exclusive right of possession and control of real property?
    a. easement
    b. leasehold
    c. license
    d. encumbrance

41. A co-owner of real property automatically received a deceased co-owner's share of ownership. This is called:
    a. intestate succession
    b. inheritance by devise
    c. right of survivorship
    d. inheritance by descent

42. Four brothers received title to a large tract of land from their grandfather, who gave each brother a one-fourth undivided interest with equal rights to possession of the land. All four received their title on their grandfather's seventieth birthday. The brothers most likely hold title in which of the following ways?
    a. in severalty
    b. as tenants in common
    c. as tenants by the entirety
    d. as remaindermen

43. John and his wife, Mary, live in a community property state. Mary inherits a large shopping mall in the city where they live. Which of the following statements about Mary's ownership of the mall is correct?
    a. Mary and John hold the property as tenants by the entirety
    b. Mary may encumber or convey the title only with John's participation in a mortgage or deed
    c. Mary holds title as separate property
    d. the property is considered community property because of the marriage status at the time of inheritance

44. Which of the following statements about the creation of a condominium is FALSE?
    a. a Declaration, Articles of Association, and Association Bylaws must be recorded in the public record in the county where the property is located
    b. a parking garage with rental spaces can be converted to condominium ownership
    c. an apartment complex can be converted to condominiums only with a majority vote of the tenants
    d. a shopping center can be converted to condominium ownership

45. All of the following are correct EXCEPT:
   a. owners of condominium apartments are assessed for their share of the cost of operating and maintaining the common areas
   b. stockholders occupying apartments under a lease pay fees as specified in the lease for maintenance and operation of the common areas of a cooperative
   c. owners of condominium apartments are assessed a prorated share of the real estate taxes on the entire complex
   d. stockholders in a cooperative do not receive an abstract, title insurance, or deed on the leased unit

46. The state took a part of an owner's property for construction of a building. Which of the following statements about this event is correct?
   a. the property owner must be compensated for the difference in market value of the property before and after the partial condemnation
   b. the building to be constructed may be used for the sole use and benefit of a private corporation
   c. the property owner has no recourse to challenge taking his property
   d. the value established is the average of the owner's desired value, the state's desired purchase price, and an independent appraisal

47. An easement that exists across adjoining land is a(n):
   a. easement in gross
   b. dedicated easement
   c. prescriptive easement
   d. appurtenant easement

48. A property with a market value of $80,000 is assessed at 75%. What is the tax rate per $100 if the tax bill is $900?
   a. $1.125
   b. $1.50
   c. $11.25
   d. $15.00

49. An encroachment is which of the following?
   a. lien
   b. party wall
   c. trespass
   d. fixture

50. In estimating the value of an office building containing 22,400 square feet, an appraiser established the annual rental income to be $400,000. The appraiser also learned that monthly expenses averaged $16,700. If the average investor in this type of property was realizing a net return of 13.5%, what would be the appraiser's estimate of the value of the property?
   a. $1,478,518
   b. $1,484,444
   c. $2,962,962
   d. $2,964,600

51. A competitive market analysis is performed when:
   a. assessing property
   b. pricing property
   c. appraising property
   d. condemning property

52. For which of the following types of property would the market data approach be the most relevant appraisal method?
   a. vacant industrial land
   b. library
   c. condominium office
   d. farm land with a large hog operation

53. The principle providing that the highest value of a property has a tendency to be established by the cost of purchasing or constructing a building of equal utility and desirability is the principle of:
   a. highest and best use
   b. competition
   c. supply and demand
   d. substitution

54. Dick and Jane's property has no road frontage. A property adjoining theirs that has road frontage was offered for sale. The value of the available property to Dick and Jane is most accurately described as:
   a. market value
   b. objective value
   c. appraised value
   d. subjective value

55. All of the following are included in a competitive or comparative market analysis EXCEPT:
   a. properties that have sold recently
   b. properties currently on the market
   c. properties sold at foreclosure
   d. properties sold by the owner without a REALTOR®

56. An appraiser who is estimating the value of a four-story government building determines that each floor measures 90 feet by 80 feet with a replacement cost of $60 per square foot. She also observes that the building has depreciated 25% as the result of physical and functional obsolescence. Other site improvements are estimated to have depreciated 20% from a new value of $160,000. The appraiser also estimates the land associated with the building to be worth $362,000. What is the correct estimate of the property value by the cost approach?

a. $814,000
b. $846,000
c. $1,786,000
d. $1,818,000

57. A building now 21 years old has a total economic life of 40 years. If the replacement cost of the building is $1,200,000, what is the value?

a. $228,571
b. $252,631
c. $570,000
d. $630,000

58. Which of the following is the most likely result of the homogeneous development of a residential subdivision?

a. overinflated values
b. maximized values
c. stabilized values
d. depressed values

59. Which of the following approaches to value is the most appropriate for estimating the value of a condominium apartment?

a. cost approach
b. income approach
c. comparable approach
d. gross rent multiplier

60. In the sale of a capital asset held for 12 months, the seller realizes a gain of $242,000. The amount of taxable gain is:

a. $96,800
b. $145,200
c. $193,600
d. $242,000

61. If a property producing an annual gross income of $290,000 sells for $2,465,000, what is the GRM?

a. 7.2
b. 8.0
c. 8.5
d. 11.8

62. The monthly payment necessary to fully amortize a 15-year mortgage loan of $100,000 at 8.5% APR is $984.74. How much interest will the mortgagor pay over the 15-year term?

a. $77,253.20
b. $127,500.00
c. $176,892.41
d. $276,892.41

63. In the preceding question, how much of the borrower's first monthly payment is applied to reducing principal?

a. $57.32
b. $276.41
c. $458.33
d. $568.50

64. A lender charges a 2% loan origination fee and three discount points to make a 95% conventional insured mortgage loan in the amount of $47,500. What is the cost of these charges to the borrower?

a. $922
b. $1,188
c. $1,425
d. $2,375

65. All of the following statements about promissory notes are correct EXCEPT:

a. they are executed only by the borrower
b. they provide evidence that a valid debt exists
c. they provide security for a valid debt
d. they are considered a negotiable instrument

66. Which of the following enables the mortgagor to avoid a record of foreclosure after default and prior to a foreclosure sale?

a. statutory redemption
b. deed in lieu of foreclosure
c. deed of trust
d. foreclosure by action

67. All of the following are ways in which a seller may finance the sale of her property for a buyer EXCEPT:
    a. wraparound purchase money mortgage
    b. contract for deed
    c. FHA-insured mortgage
    d. purchase money first mortgage

68. Bill and Betty Brown execute and deliver a $50,000 mortgage to Ajax Financial Associates at 10:30 A.M. on April 1. At 11:30 A.M. on the same day, they give a $10,000 mortgage pledging the same property to Fidelity Finance, Inc. Fidelity's mortgage is recorded at 1:10 P.M. that day, and the mortgage to Ajax is recorded at 1:42 P.M. on April 1. Which of the following statements about these mortgages is correct?
    a. because the mortgage to Ajax was executed and delivered first, Ajax holds the first mortgage
    b. Fidelity has the second mortgage because it was executed and delivered after the mortgage given to Ajax
    c. Ajax and Fidelity will be co-first mortgage holders because both mortgages were signed on the same day
    d. because the mortgage to Fidelity was recorded first, Fidelity holds the first mortgage

69. When a buyer signs a purchase contract and the seller accepts, the buyer acquires an immediate interest in the property known as:
    a. legal title
    b. statutory title
    c. equitable title
    d. defeasible title

70. Regulation Z specifies that the only specific credit term that may appear in an advertisement of a house for sale without the requirement of a full disclosure is which of the following?
    a. SAM
    b. APR
    c. ECOA
    d. RESPA

71. In the sale of their home, Van and Vera Vendor were required to satisfy their existing first mortgage of $40,000 so the buyers could obtain a first mortgage to finance their purchase. The Vendors' closing statement contained a debit in the amount of $800 because the Vendors paid off their loan prior to the full term. From this information, it can be determined that the Vendors' mortgage contained a(n):
    a. acceleration clause
    b. alienation clause
    c. prepayment clause
    d. defeasance clause

72. A developer gave the seller a $385,000 purchase money first mortgage to secure payment of part of the purchase price for a tract of land. The developer was able to convey unencumbered titles to the first six lot purchasers by paying only $8,000 on the purchase money mortgage because the mortgage contained:
    a. release clauses
    b. due-on-sale clauses
    c. prepayment clauses
    d. mortgaging clauses

73. In the purchase of an office building, the buyer gave the seller a mortgage for $200,000 more than the seller's first mortgage and took title to the property subject to the first mortgage. The purchase money mortgage required payments of interest only for the first five years, at which time the principal has to be paid and a new purchase money mortgage created. All of the following statements about these financial arrangements are correct EXCEPT:
    a. the purchase money mortgage is a wraparound term mortgage
    b. for this arrangement to work satisfactorily, the seller's first mortgage must not contain an alienation clause
    c. this arrangement must be approved by Fannie Mae
    d. the purchase money mortgage has a balloon payment

74. When Mr. Black bought real estate for investment purposes, he realized there would be certain expenditures for repair or replacement, maintenance, and management; however, the appraiser advised him to be aware of the point beyond which capital outlays would not result in increased returns. The appraiser was referring to which appraisal principle?
    a. supply and demand
    b. diminishing returns
    c. capitalization
    d. economic depletion

75. The definition of personal property is:
    a. any building permanently attached to real estate
    b. any tree or bush growing on real estate
    c. anything that is not real property
    d. the right to use the air above real estate

76. The real estate market is:
    a. quick to react to changes in supply and demand
    b. not subject to economic cycles
    c. subject to economic cycles
    d. not affected by supply and demand

77. The private ownership of land is known as:
    a. feudal ownership
    b. government ownership
    c. allodial ownership
    d. eminent domain

78. All of the following are powers of government EXCEPT:
    a. police power
    b. escheat
    c. taxation
    d. estovers

79. All of the following are specific liens EXCEPT:
    a. mortgage lien
    b. mechanic's lien
    c. judgment lien
    d. real property tax lien

80. A listing contract creates an agency relationship in which:
    a. the broker is a general agent
    b. the seller is the principal
    c. the seller is a general agent
    d. the broker is the principal

81. When a real estate broker or seller conceals a known defect, this is an example of:
    a. mutual mistake
    b. unintentional misrepresentation
    c. fraud
    d. mistake of law

82. An action or inaction by the lessor resulting in the property being unusable is:
    a. actual eviction
    b. assignment
    c. sandwich lease
    d. constructive eviction

83. A lease is all of the following EXCEPT:
    a. contract
    b. nonfreehold estate
    c. freehold estate
    d. binding obligation on the parties

84. All of the following are required to effect voluntary alienation of title during life EXCEPT:
    a. recordation of the deed
    b. acceptance of delivery by grantee
    c. delivery of a valid deed to grantee
    d. legal capacity of grantor

85. The statement made by a grantor to a qualified public official that the signing of a deed was done by her and was a voluntary act is called a(n):
    a. abstract
    b. acknowledgment
    c. covenant
    d. conveyance

86. A property description reading "¼ of the northeast ¼ of section 22" describes how many acres?
    a. 20
    b. 40
    c. 160
    d. 240

87. Which of the following enables the mortgagee to sell the mortgage in the secondary mortgage market?
    a. assignment clause
    b. due-on-sale clause
    c. mortgaging clause
    d. power-of-sale clause

88. Friendly foreclosure is also called:
    a. beneficial foreclosure
    b. statutory foreclosure
    c. strict foreclosure
    d. deed in lieu of foreclosure

89. Brantley Buyer obtained an FHA-insured loan to purchase a home. The difference between the purchase price and the loan amount was $3,100. Which of the following statements about the $3,100 is correct?
    a. Brantley must pay this amount from his existing assets, borrow on the security of another asset such as his stocks, or acquire it as a bona fide gift from a close relative or friend
    b. Brantley may satisfy this amount by giving the seller a purchase money second mortgage
    c. Brantley may borrow the $3,100 from a relative at 6% interest
    d. Brantley may obtain the money by giving a lending institution a second mortgage

90. When a buyer purchases a home using a VA-guaranteed loan, he is allowed to:
    a. pay a loan origination fee
    b. pay discount points
    c. purchase the property to be used as a rental
    d. both a and b

91. On April 1, Chuck and Sara Vollaro make the mortgage payment of principal and interest for March on their home, in the amount of $402.50. On April 20, the Vollaros close on the sale of their home to the Hudsons. The Hudsons assume the Vollaro's mortgage with a principal balance of $42,000 and an interest rate of 9%. Which of the following is the correct closing statement entry for interest?
    a. buyer's debit of $105
    b. buyer's credit of $105
    c. seller's debit of $210
    d. seller's credit of $210

92. The type of demand that affects market value is called:
    a. urgent
    b. unlimited
    c. effective
    d. restrictive

93. An owner whose property is condemned is entitled to be compensated for:
    a. book value
    b. assessed value
    c. market value
    d. mortgage value

94. Deed restrictions that provide for a reversion of title are called:
    a. certificates
    b. covenants
    c. clusters
    d. conditions

95. The Interstate Land Sales Full Disclosure Act requires which of the following?
    a. property report
    b. enabling act
    c. zoning
    d. cumulative use

96. Redlining applies to which of the following?
    a. brokers
    b. developers
    c. lenders
    d. landlords

97. A lease is a contract that is:
    a. bilateral
    b. unilateral
    c. collateral
    d. trilateral

98. Which of the following is a deductible expense for homeowners?
    a. real property taxes
    b. maintenance
    c. mortgage principal payments
    d. energy usage

99. Which of the following reduces the basis of a new residence?
    a. depreciation
    b. energy credits
    c. gain on which tax is postponed
    d. installment sale

100. All of the following may lead to the revocation or suspension of a license EXCEPT:
   a. failing to submit all written offers to the listing seller
   b. advising a prospective buyer that the seller will take a certain price for a property that is less than the listed price
   c. failing to obtain an accepted offer during the term of the listing
   d. failing to account for all funds belonging to other persons that come into the licensee's hands

ANSWER KEY

ANSWER KEY TO CHAPTER-END REVIEW QUESTIONS

CHAPTER 1 BASIC REAL ESTATE CONCEPTS

1. c
2. b
3. a
4. d
5. d
6. c
7. b
8. d
9. b
10. c
11. b
12. c
13. c
14. d
15. a

CHAPTER 2 PROPERTY OWNERSHIP AND INTERESTS

1. c
2. a
3. b
4. d
5. c
6. b
7. b
8. a
9. c
10. c
11. b
12. c
13. a
14. c
15. b
16. d
17. b
18. c
19. d
20. c

CHAPTER 3 ENCUMBRANCES, GOVERNMENT RESTRICTIONS, AND APPURTENANCES

1. a
2. d
3. d
4. d
5. b
6. a
7. b
8. d
9. c
10. a
11. d
12. c
13. c
14. b
15. d
16. b
17. d
18. a
19. b
20. b
21. c
22. b
23. c
24. a
25. d

CHAPTER 4 BROKERAGE AND AGENCY

1. d
2. a
3. b
4. a
5. c
6. c
7. d
8. d
9. c
10. c
11. c
12. b
13. a
14. c
15. a
16. a
17. b
18. b
19. b
20. c

CHAPTER 5 REAL ESTATE CONTRACTS

1. c
2. c
3. d
4. d
5. a
6. d
7. b
8. b
9. d
10. c
11. b
12. a
13. c
14. b
15. c
16. d
17. c
18. b
19. d
20. c

CHAPTER 6 TRANSFER OF TITLE TO REAL PROPERTY

1. b
2. a
3. a
4. c
5. d
6. d
7. b
8. a
9. d
10. c
11. c
12. a
13. a
14. b
15. b
16. c
17. d
18. b
19. a
20. a

CHAPTER 7 REAL ESTATE FINANCE PRINCIPLES

1. d
2. d
3. d
4. b
5. a
6. b
7. a
8. d
9. a
10. c
11. b
12. d
13. b
14. b
15. c

CHAPTER 8 REAL ESTATE FINANCE PRACTICES

1. d
2. d
3. a
4. c
5. b
6. b
7. d
8. a
9. d
10. b
11. c
12. b
13. b
14. d
15. a
16. a
17. a
18. a
19. c
20. a

CHAPTER 9 CLOSING REAL ESTATE TRANSACTIONS

1. a
2. d
3. c
4. a
5. a
6. a
7. a
8. b
9. d
10. b

CHAPTER 10 PROPERTY VALUATION

1. d
2. b
3. c
4. b
5. d
6. c
7. a
8. a
9. c
10. a
11. b
12. b
13. b
14. d
15. c
16. d
17. b
18. b
19. b
20. d

CHAPTER 11 LAND USE CONTROLS

1. d
2. d
3. b
4. d
5. b
6. b
7. d
8. b
9. a
10. c
11. a
12. b
13. c
14. c
15. d
16. b
17. a
18. b
19. c
20. c

CHAPTER 12 FAIR HOUSING

1. b
2. c
3. a
4. d
5. b
6. d
7. c
8. b
9. d
10. a
11. d
12. b
13. b
14. b
15. a

CHAPTER 13 LEASEHOLD ESTATES (LANDLORD AND TENANT)

1. a
2. b
3. c
4. c
5. b
6. a
7. b
8. a
9. d
10. d
11. c
12. c
13. a
14. b
15. c
16. a
17. a
18. a
19. c
20. c

CHAPTER 14 PROPERTY MANAGEMENT AND INSURANCE

1. c
2. a
3. b
4. c
5. a
6. b
7. b
8. a

CHAPTER 15 FEDERAL INCOME TAXATION AND BASIC REAL ESTATE INVESTMENT

1. c
2. b
3. b
4. a
5. a
6. b
7. c
8. b
9. c
10. b
11. c
12. c
13. c
14. c
15. c

CHAPTER 16 REAL ESTATE LICENSE LAWS

1. d
2. a
3. c
4. d
5. d
6. d
7. d
8. d
9. a
10. b

Answers to the Review Problems found at the end of Chapter 17, Real Estate Math, appear in the solutions at the end of that chapter.

ANSWER KEY TO PRACTICE EXAM 1 (APPENDIX D)

1. a
2. c
3. b
4. d
5. b
6. d
7. d
8. c
9. c
10. a
11. a
12. b
13. a
14. c
15. d
16. c
17. a
18. b
19. b
20. a
21. c
22. c
23. b
24. a
25. d
26. c
27. c
28. a
29. d
30. a
31. b
32. b
33. d
34. d
35. c
36. c
37. c
38. b
39. a
40. d
41. d
42. b
43. b
44. a
45. c
46. d
47. b
48. a
49. b
50. c
51. c
52. a
53. c
54. d
55. b
56. b
57. b
58. d
59. c
60. a
61. b
62. c
63. c
64. d
65. a
66. a
67. a
68. d
69. c
70. c
71. d
72. d
73. a
74. b
75. b
76. b
77. a
78. b
79. c
80. b
81. a
82. c
83. b
84. a
85. c
86. c
87. a
88. b
89. d
90. b
91. a
92. b
93. d
94. d
95. a
96. a
97. d
98. d
99. b
100. d

ANSWER KEY TO PRACTICE EXAM 2 (APPENDIX E)

1. c
2. d
3. b
4. c
5. a
6. c
7. b
8. d
9. d
10. b
11. c
12. a
13. b
14. d
15. a
16. a
17. c
18. c
19. a
20. b
21. c
22. c
23. b
24. a
25. c
26. b
27. a
28. d
29. b
30. b
31. a
32. d
33. c
34. c
35. c
36. a
37. a
38. d
39. d
40. b
41. c
42. b
43. c
44. c
45. c
46. a
47. d
48. b
49. c
50. a
51. b
52. a
53. d
54. d
55. c
56. c
57. c
58. b
59. c
60. d
61. c
62. a
63. b
64. d
65. c
66. b
67. c
68. d
69. c
70. b
71. c
72. a
73. c
74. b
75. c
76. c
77. c
78. d
79. c
80. b
81. c
82. d
83. c
84. a
85. b
86. b
87. a
88. d
89. a
90. d
91. c
92. c
93. c
94. d
95. a
96. c
97. a
98. a
99. c
100. c

GLOSSARY

Abandonment The surrender or release of a right, claim, or interest in real property.

Abstract continuation An update of an abstract of title by a memorandum of a new transfer of title.

Abstract of title A history of a title and the current status of a title based on a title examination.

Accelerated depreciation Regarding federal income tax, being able to take more depreciation in early years than in later years.

Acceleration clause A provision in a mortgage or deed of trust that permits the lender to declare the entire principal balance of the debt immediately due and payable if the borrower is in default.

Acceptance Voluntary expression by the person receiving the offer to be bound by the exact terms of the offer; must be unequivocal and unconditional.

Access The right to go onto and leave a property.

Accidental agency An individual's being led to believe by a broker/salesperson's actions and representations that the broker/salesperson is representing (is an agent for) the individual.

Accord and satisfaction A new agreement by contracting parties that is satisfied by full performance, thereby terminating the prior contract as well.

Accretion The gradual building up of land in a watercourse over time by deposits of silt, sand, and gravel.

Accrued depreciation (a) The loss in value in a structure measured by the cost of a new replacement. (b) The amount of depreciation taken, as of a given date, for tax purposes.

Accrued expenses Expenses seller owes on the day of closing but for which the buyer will take responsibility (such as property taxes).

Acknowledgment A formal statement before an authorized official (e.g., notary public) by a person who executed a deed, contract, or other document that it was (is) his or her free act.

Acquisition The act of acquiring a property.

Acquisition cost The basis used by the FHA to calculate the loan amount.

Acre A land area containing 43,560 square feet.

Action to quiet title A lawsuit to clear a title to real property.

Actual age Chronological age.

Actual eviction The removal of a tenant by the landlord because the tenant breached a condition of a lease or other rental contract.

Actual notice The knowledge a person has of a fact.

Adjoining lands Lands sharing a common boundary line.

Adjustable rate mortgage (ARM) One in which the interest rate changes according to changes in a predetermined index.

Adjusted basis Value of property used to determine the amount of gain or loss realized by owner upon sale of the property; equals acquisition cost plus capital improvements minus depreciation taken.

Adjusted sales price The amount realized minus selling expenses.

Adjustments Additions or subtractions of dollar amounts to equalize comparables to subject property in the market data approach to estimating value.

Administrative law judge (ALJ) A judge who hears complaints regarding violations of 1988 Fair Housing Act Amendments.

Administrator A man appointed by a court to administer the estate of a person who has died intestate.

Administrator's deed One executed by an administrator to convey title to estate property.

Administratrix A woman appointed by a court to administer the estate of a person who has died intestate.

Ad valorem Latin meaning "according to value"; real property is taxed on an ad valorem basis.

Adverse possession A method of acquiring title to real property by conforming to statutory requirement; a form of involuntary alienation of title.

Affirmative easement A legal requirement that a servient owner permit a right of use in the servient land by the dominant owner.

Age-55-and-over exclusion A tax exemption available to sellers of a principal residence who are age 55 or older.

Agency The fiduciary relationship between a principal and an agent.

Agent A person authorized by another to act on his or her behalf in communications with third parties.

Agreement A contract requiring mutual assent between two or more parties.

Air rights Rights in the air space above the surface of land.

Alienation Transfer of title to real property.

Alienation clause A statement in a mortgage or deed of trust entitling the lender to declare the entire principal balance of the debt immediately due and payable if the borrower sells the property during the mortgage term. Also known as due-on-sale clause.

Allodial system The type of land ownership existing in the United States whereby individuals may hold title to real property absolutely.

Alluvion Increased soil, gravel, or sand on a stream bank resulting from flow or current of the water.

Amenities Benefits resulting from the ownership of a specific property.

Americans with Disabilities Act A federal law protecting the rights of individuals with physical or mental impairments.

Amortization schedule Designation of periodic payments of principal and interest over a specific term to retire a loan.

Amortizing Applying periodic payments first toward the interest and then toward the principal to eventually pay off a debt.

Amortizing loan One in which uniform installment payments include payment of both principal and interest.

Anchor store A well-known commercial retail business, such as a national chain store or regional department store, placed in a shopping center to generate the most customers for all stores in the shopping center.

Annexation Addition of an area into a city.

Annual Yearly.

Annual percentage rate (APR) The actual effective rate of interest charged on a loan expressed on a yearly basis; not the same as simple interest rate.

Anticipation The principle that property value is based on expectations or hopes of the future benefits of ownership.

Appraisal An estimate of value of a particular property at a particular time for a specified purpose.

Appraisal by capitalization Income approach to appraise income-producing real estate.

Appraisal process An organized and systematic process for estimating real property value.

Appraisal report Documentation containing an estimate of property value and the data on which the estimate is based.

Appreciation An increase in property value.

Approaches to valuation Methods of estimating real property value: market data, income, and cost.

Appurtenances All rights or privileges that result from ownership of a specific property and move with the title.

Appurtenant easement A right of use in the adjoining land of another that moves with the title to the property benefiting from the easement.

Arrears Delinquency in meeting an obligation; or, paid at the end of a period (e.g., at the end of the month) for the previous period; payments in arrears include interest for using the money during the previous period.

Artificial person A corporation or other legally recognized entity that is not a human being.

Asking price The price of a property specified in a listing contract.

Assessed value The dollar amount of worth to which a local tax rate is applied to calculate the amount of real property tax.

Assessment A levy against property.

Assessor An official of local government who has the responsibility for establishing the value of property for tax purposes.

Assignee One to whom contractual rights are transferred.

Assignment Transfer of legal rights and obligations by one party to another.

Assignment of lease Transfer by a lessee of the entire remaining term of a lease without any reversion of interest to the lessee.

Assignor The person transferring contractual rights to another.

Association of Real Estate License Law Officials (ARELLO) Founded in 1929, a group of real estate license law officials that regulates more than two million real estate licensees.

Assumable mortgage One that does not contain an alienation clause.

Attestation Witnessing of a document.

Attorney-at-law A person licensed by a state to practice law.

Attorney-in-fact A person appointed to perform legal acts for another under a power of attorney.

Auction A form of property sale in which people bid against each other.

Availability An economic characteristic of land denoting that land is a commodity with a fixed supply base.

Avulsion Sudden loss or gain of land as a result of water or shift in a bed of a river that has been used as a boundary.

Bail bond A bond given by a defendant under criminal charges to obtain release from custody.

Balloon loan One in which the scheduled payment will not fully amortize the loan over the loan term; therefore, to fully satisfy the debt, it requires a final payment called a balloon payment, larger than the uniform payments.

Bargain-and-sale deed A form of deed usually without covenants of title.

Baselines East-west lines in the rectangular method of property description.

Base rent The fixed or minimum rent portion in a percentage lease.

Basis The value of property for income tax purposes; consists of original cost plus capital improvements less accrued depreciation.

Beneficial title Equitable title to real property retained by a trustor conveying legal title to secure a deed of trust debt.

Beneficiary (a) Recipient of a gift of personal property by will. (b) Lender in a deed of trust.

Bequest A gift of personal property by will.

Bilateral contract An agreement based on mutual promises that provide the consideration.

Bill of sale An instrument transferring ownership of personal property.

Blanket mortgage One in which two or more parcels of real property are pledged to secure payment of the note.

Blockbusting For profit, to induce or attempt to induce any person to sell or rent any dwelling by representations regarding the entry or prospective entry into the neighborhood of a person or persons of a particular race, color, religion, sex, national origin, handicap, or children.

Bona fide In good faith.

Book value Dollar value as it appears on the owner's books, usually for tax purposes; also known as historic value.

Boot Cash or unlike property received in a tax-free exchange.

Breach of contract Failure, without legal excuse, to perform any promise that forms the whole or part of a contract.

Broker A person or an organization acting as agent for others in negotiating the purchase and sale of real property or other commodities for a fee.

Brokerage The business of bringing buyers and sellers together and assisting in negotiations for the terms of sale of real estate.

Budget A plan for systematic spending and receiving of income.

Budget loan *See* Impound account.

Building codes Public controls regulating construction.

Bundle of rights The rights of an owner of a freehold estate to possession, enjoyment, control, and disposition of real property.

Buyer brokerage An agency relationship between a buyer and a broker.

Capital gain Tax laws allowing sellers a lower tax rate on their profit on real estate investments.

Capital improvement An item that adds value to the property, adapts the property to new uses, or prolongs the life of property; maintenance is not a capital improvement.

Capitalization The process of converting future income into an indication of the present value of a property by applying a capitalization rate to net annual income.

Capitalization formula Investment or value of real estate equals the annual net income of the real estate divided by the capitalization rate.

Capitalization rate The rate of interest appropriate to the investment risk as a return on the investment.

Capital reserve budget Projected budget over the economic life of improvements on the property for repairs, decorating, remodeling, and capital improvements.

Cap rate Another name for capitalization rate.

Carryover clause A statement in a listing contract protecting the broker's commission entitlement for a specified period of time after the contract expires; also called extender clause or protection clause.

Cash flow Income produced by an investment property after deducting operating expenses and debt service.

Caveat emptor Latin meaning "let the buyer beware"; applies to "sales talk" and not to statements of material facts.

Certificate of eligibility A statement provided to veterans of military service setting forth the amount of loan guarantee to which they are entitled at that time.

Certificate of occupancy A document issued by a local government agency, after a satisfactory inspection of a structure, authorizing that the structure can be occupied.

Certificate of reasonable value A document setting forth the value of a property as the basis for the loan guarantee by the Veterans Administration to the lender.

Certificate of title opinion A report, based on a title examination, setting forth the examiner's opinion of the quality of a title to real property.

Chain In land measurement, a distance of 66 feet.

Chain of title Successive conveyances of title to a specific parcel of land.

Change The principle stating that change is continually affecting land use and therefore continually altering value.

Chattel Personal property.

Chattel loan One in which personal property is pledged to secure payment of a debt.

Chattel real Nonfreehold interests in real property; also includes fixtures.

Chronological age Actual age of an item.

Civil action A lawsuit between private parties.

Civil Rights Act of 1866 A federal law that prohibits all discrimination on the basis of race.

Civil Rights Act of 1968. *See* Fair Housing Act of 1968.

Client The person who selects the agent to act on his or her behalf; principal.

Closed-end loan One that cannot be refinanced.

Closed loan One that imposes a prepayment penalty.

Closing The consummation of a real estate contract; also called settlement.

Closing costs Expenses incurred in the purchase and sale of real property paid at the time of settlement or closing.

Closing (or settlement) statement An accounting of the funds received and disbursed in a real estate transaction.

Cloud on a title A claim against a title to real property.

Cluster zoning A form of zoning providing for several different types of land use within a zoned area.

Code of ethics A standard of conduct required by license laws and by the National Association of REALTORS®.

Coinsurance clause A requirement of hazard insurance policies that property be insured for a certain percent of value to obtain the full amount of losses claimed.

Collateral Property pledged as security for payment of a debt.

Color of title A defective claim to a title.

Commercial property Property used in business.

Commingling An agent's mixing money or property of others with the agent's personal or business funds or other property.

Commission A fee paid for the performance of services, such as a broker's commission.

Commissioner's deed A form of judicial deed executed by a commissioner.

Commitment A promise, such as a promise by a lending institution to make a certain loan.

Common areas Property to which co-owners hold title as a result of ownership of a condominium or townhome unit.

Common law Law by judicial precedent or tradition as contrasted with a written statute.

Community-based planning A form of land use control originating in the grassroots of a community.

Community planning A plan for the orderly growth of a city or county to result in the greatest social and economic benefits to the people.

Community property A form of co-ownership in several states limited to husband and wife; does not include the right of survivorship.

Comparable A property that is similar to a property being appraised by the market data approach.

Comparison approach *See* Market data approach.

Compensatory damages The amount of money actually lost, which will be awarded by a court in case of a breached contract.

Competent parties Persons and organizations legally qualified to manage their own affairs, including entering into contracts.

Competition The principle stating that when the net profit a property generates is excessive, very strong competition will result.

Complete performance Execution of a contract by virtue of all parties having fully performed all terms.

Condemnation Exercise of the power of eminent domain; taking private property for public use.

Condemnation value Market value of condemned property.

Condition Any fact or event which, if it occurs or fails to occur, automatically creates or extinguishes a legal obligation.

Conditional sales contract *See* Contract for deed.

Conditional use permit Special permission, with conditions, to use property not in compliance with zoning ordinances.

Condominium A form of ownership of real property, recognized in all states, consisting of individual ownership of some aspects of the property and co-ownership in other aspects of the property.

Condominium declaration The document that, when recorded, creates a condominium; also called a master deed.

Conforming loans Those processed on uniform loan forms and complying with FNMA/FHLMC guidelines.

Conformity Homogeneous uses of land within a given area, which results in maximizing land value.

Consideration Anything of value, as recognized by law, offered as a benefit of a contract.

Construction loan A short-term loan, secured by a mortgage or deed of trust, to obtain funds to construct an improvement on land.

Construction mortgage Interim, short-term financing for creating improvements on land.

Constructive eviction Results from some action or inaction by the landlord that renders the premises unsuitable for the use agreed to in a lease or other rental contract.

Constructive notice One in which all affected parties are bound by presumed knowledge of a fact even though they have not been actually notified of such fact.

Consumer Price Index (CPI) An index of the change in prices of various commodities and services, providing a measure of the rate of inflation.

Contingency A condition in a contract relieving a party of liability if a specified event occurs or fails to occur.

Contract An agreement between competent parties upon legal consideration to do, or abstain from doing, some legal act.

Contract buyer's policy Title insurance that protects contract buyer against defects in contract seller's title.

Contract for deed A contract of sale and a financing instrument wherein the seller agrees to convey title when the buyer completes the purchase price installment payments; also called installment land contract, land contract, and conditional sales contract.

Contract rent The amount of rent agreed to in a lease.

Contribution The principle that, for any given part of a property, its value is the result of the contribution that part makes to the total value by being present, or the amount that it subtracts from total value as a result of its absence; used in comparative market analysis (CMA) and market data appraisal.

Conventional life estate One created by intentional act of the parties.

Conventional loan One in which the federal government does not insure or guarantee payment to the lender.

Conversion Change in a form of ownership, such as changing rental apartments to condominium ownership.

Convey To pass to another (as in title).

Conveyance Transfer of title to real property.

Cooling-off period A three-day right of rescission for certain loan transactions.

Cooperating broker One who participates in the sale of a property through the listing broker.

Cooperative A form of ownership in which stockholders in a corporation occupy property owned by the corporation under a proprietary lease.

Co-ownership Title to real property held by two or more persons at the same time; also called concurrent ownership.

Corporation A form of organization existing as a legal entity under state law.

Corporeal Tangible.

Corrective maintenance Repairs of a nonfunctioning item.

Cost approach An appraisal method whereby the cost of constructing a substitute structure is calculated, depreciation is deducted, and land value is added.

Counteroffer A new offer made by an offeror rejecting the previous offer.

Covenant A promise in writing.

Covenant against encumbrances A promise in a deed that the title causes no encumbrances except those set forth in the deed.

Covenant for further assurances A promise in a deed that the grantor will execute further assurances that may be reasonable or necessary to perfect the title in the grantee.

Covenant of quiet enjoyment A promise in a deed (or lease) that the grantee (or lessee) will not be disturbed in his or her use of the property because of a defect in the grantor's (or lessor's) title.

Covenant of right to convey A promise in a deed that the grantor has the legal capacity to convey the title.

Covenant of seisin A promise in a deed assuring the grantee that the grantor has the title being conveyed.

Covenant of warranty A promise in a deed that the grantor will guarantee and defend the title against lawful claimants.

Credit In a closing statement, money to be received or credit given for money or an obligation given.

Creditor One to whom a debt is owed.

Cubic-foot method A means of estimating reproduction or replacement cost, using the volume of the structure.

Cul-de-sac A dead-end street with a circular turnaround at the dead end.

Cumulative zoning A type of zoning permitting a higher-priority use even though it is different from the type of use designated for the area.

Curable depreciation A condition of property that exists when correction is physically possible and the cost of correction is less than the value increase.

Curtesy A husband's interest in the real property of his deceased wife.

Customer A consumer who is not a client, but must be treated fairly; third party.

Damages The amount of financial loss incurred as a result of another's action.

Debit In a closing statement, an expense or money received against a credit.

Debt service Principal and interest payments on a debt.

Decedent A dead person.

Declaration Master deed containing legal description of the condominium facility, a plat of the property, plans and specifications for the building and units, a description of the common areas, and the degree of ownership in the common areas available to each owner.

Declaration of restrictions The instrument used to record restrictive covenants on the public record.

Decree A court order.

Dedication An appropriation of land or an easement therein by the owner to the public.

Deductible expenses Costs of operating property held for use in business or as an investment. These expenses are subtracted from gross income to arrive at net income.

Deed A written instrument transferring an interest in real property when delivered to the grantee.

Deed in lieu of foreclosure Conveyance of title to the mortgagee by a mortgagor in default to avoid a record of foreclosure. Also called friendly foreclosure.

Deed in trust A deed transferring title to a trustee in a land trust.

Deed of bargain and sale A deed with an implied covenant that the grantor has title and possession.

Deed of confirmation A deed executed to correct an error in a prior deed; also called a deed of correction.

Deed of gift A warranty or quitclaim deed conveying title as a gift to the grantee.

Deed of release A deed executed by a mortgage lender to release a title from the lien of a mortgage when the debt has been satisfied; also used to release a spousal right.

Deed of surrender A deed executed by a life tenant to convey his or her estate to the remainder or reversionary interest.

Deed of trust A form of lien wherein there is a third party who is called a trustee and who holds legal title pending satisfaction of the debt.

Deed restriction Limitation on land use appearing in deeds.

Default Failure to perform an obligation.

Defeasance clause A statement in a mortgage or deed of trust giving the borrower the right to redeem the title and have the mortgage lien released at any time prior to default by paying the debt in full.

Defeasible Subject to being defeated by the occurrence of a certain event.

Defeasible fee A title subject to being lost if certain conditions occur.

Deficiency judgment A court judgment obtained by a lender for the amount of money a foreclosure sale proceeds were deficient in fully satisfying the debt.

Delivery and acceptance A transfer of a title by deed requires the grantor to deliver and the grantee to accept a given deed.

Demise To convey an estate for years; synonymous with lease or let.

Density Number of persons or structures per acre.

Department of Housing and Urban Development (HUD) A federal agency involved with housing.

Depreciable asset Property, other than land, held as an investment or for use in a business.

Depreciated value The original basis of a property less the amount of depreciation taken at any point in time.

Depreciation (a) Loss in value from any cause. (b) Deductible allowance from net income of property when arriving at taxable income.

Descent The distribution of property to legally qualified heirs of one who has died intestate.

Description by reference Refers to a plat (map) and lot number that has been recorded.

Devise A gift of real property by will.

Devisee The recipient of a gift of real property by will.

Disability Defined in USC 42, Sec. 12101, as a physical or mental impairment that substantially limits one or more of the major life activities of a person.

Disclosure of information The prompt and total communication to the principal by the agent of any information that is material to the transaction for which the agency is created.

Disclosure statement An accounting of all financial aspects of a mortgage loan required of lenders to borrowers in residential mortgage loans by Regulation Z of the Federal Reserve Board.

Discount points A percentage of the loan amount the lender requires for making a mortgage loan.

Discriminatory advertising Any advertising that states or indicates a preference, limitation, or discrimination on the basis of race, color, religion, sex, national origin, handicap, or familial status in offering housing for sale or rent.

Disintermediation The loss of funds available to lending institutions for making mortgage loans, caused by depositors' withdrawal of funds for making investments that provide greater yields.

Dominant tenement Land benefiting from an easement appurtenant.

Dower A wife's interest in her deceased husband's real property.

Down payment The portion of the price of property that is paid in cash.

Dual agency A broker/salesperson's representing both buyer and seller in the same transaction.

Due-on-sale clause *See* Alienation clause.

Duress The inability of a party to exercise his or her free will because of fear of another party.

Duty of disclosure A responsibility for revealing all information that affects the agency agreement.

Earnest money A deposit a buyer makes at the time of submitting an offer, to demonstrate the true intent to purchase; also called binder, good faith deposit, escrow deposit.

Easement A nonpossessory right of use in the land of another.

Easement appurtenant *See* Appurtenant easement.

Easement by condemnation Created by the exercise of the government's right of eminent domain.

Easement by grant Created by the express written agreement of the land owners, usually in a deed.

Easement by implication Arising by implication from the conduct of the parties.

Easement by necessity Exists when a land owner has no access to roads and is landlocked.

Easement by prescription Obtained by use of the land of another for the legally prescribed length of time.

Easement in gross A personal right of use in the land of another without the requirement that the holder of the right own adjoining land.

Economic depreciation Loss in value due to surrounding conditions and influences.

Economic life The period of time during which a property is financially beneficial to the owner.

Economic obsolescence Loss in value caused by things such as changes in surrounding land use patterns and failure to adhere to the principle of highest and best use; usually incurable.

Economic rent The amount of rent established by the market value of a property.

Effective age The age of a property based on remaining economic life.

Effective demand A desire for property accompanied by financial ability to satisfy the desire by purchasing the property.

Effective interest rate Actual rate of interest being paid.

Egress The right to leave a parcel of land entered (ingress) by law.

Ejectment A legal action to evict a tenant from property.

Emblements Personal property growing in the soil, requiring planting and cultivation; annual crops.

Eminent domain The power of government to take private property for public use.

Enabling acts Laws passed by state legislatures authorizing cities and counties to regulate land use within their jurisdictions.

Encroachment Trespass on the land of another as a result of intrusion by some structure or other object.

Encumbrance A claim, lien, charge, or liability legally affecting real property.

Endorsement Additional coverage on an insurance policy to include a specific risk.

Enforceable A contract in which the parties may legally be required to perform.

Environmental impact statement A requirement of the National Environmental Policy Act prior to initiating or changing a land use that may have an adverse effect on the environment.

Environment Policy Act A federal law that requires filing an environmental impact statement with the EPA prior to changing or initiating a land use or development.

Environmental Protection Agency (EPA) A federal agency that oversees land use.

Equal Credit Opportunity Act (ECOA) A federal law prohibiting discrimination in consumer loans.

Equitable title An interest in real estate such that a court will take notice and protect the owner's rights.

Equity of redemption The borrower's right to redeem the title pledged or conveyed in a mortgage or deed of trust after default and prior to a foreclosure sale by paying the debt in full, accrued interest, and lender's costs.

Escalated lease One in which the rental amount changes in proportion to the lessor's costs of ownership and operation of the property.

Escalation clause A statement in a lease or loan permitting the lessor or lender to increase the rent.

Escheat The power of government to take title to property left by a person who has died without leaving a valid will (intestate) or qualified heirs.

Escrow The deposit of funds or documents with a neutral third party, who is instructed to carry out the provisions of an agreement.

Escrow account (a) An account maintained by a real estate broker in an insured bank for the deposit of other people's money; also called trust account. (b) An account maintained by the borrower with the lender in certain mortgage loans to accumulate the funds to pay an annual insurance premium, a real property tax, or a homeowner's association assessment.

Escrow agent A neutral third party named to carry out the provisions of an escrow agreement.

Escrow instructions Written directions to the escrow agent setting forth terms for the escrow closing.

Estate at sufferance Continuing to occupy property after lawful authorization has expired; a form of leasehold estate.

Estate at will A leasehold estate that may be terminated at the desire of either party.

Estate for years A leasehold estate of definite duration.

Estate from year-to-year A leasehold estate that automatically renews itself for consecutive periods until terminated by notice by either party; also called estate from period-to-period or periodic tenancy.

Estate in fee An estate in fee simple.

Estate in real property An interest sufficient to provide the right to use, possession, and control of land; establishes the degree and duration of ownership.

Estoppel Preventing a person from making a statement contrary to a previous statement or conduct.

Estoppel certificate A document executed by a mortgagor or mortgagee setting forth the principal amount; executing parties are bound by the amount specified. Also used in leasing.

Estovers The right of a life tenant or lessee to cut timber on the property for fuel or to use in making repairs.

et al. Latin for "and others."

et ux. Latin for "and wife."

Evaluation A study of the usefulness or utility of a property without reference to the specific estimate of value.

Eviction A landlord's action that interferes with the tenant's use or possession of the property.

Exclusive agency listing A listing given to one broker only (exclusive), who is entitled to the commission if the broker or any agent of the listing broker effects a sale, but imposes no commission obligation on the owner who sells the property to a person who was not interested in the property by efforts of the listing broker or an agent of the listing broker.

Exclusive-right-to-sell listing A listing given to one broker only, who is entitled to the commission if anyone sells the property during the term of the listing contract.

Exclusive-use zoning A type of zoning in which only the specified use may be made of property within the zoned district.

Executed contract An agreement that has been fully performed.

Execution Signing a contract or other legal document.

Execution of judgment Judicial proceeding in which property of a debtor is seized (attached) and sold to satisfy a judgment lien. Also called writ of execution.

Executor A man appointed in a will to see that the terms of the will are carried out.

Executory contract An agreement that has not been fully performed.

Executrix A woman appointed in a will to see that the terms of the will are carried out.

Exercise of option Purchase of optioned property by the optionee.

Express agency An agency relationship created by oral or written agreement between principal and agent.

Express contract One created orally or in writing by the parties.

Extended coverage An insurance term referring to the extension of a standard fire insurance policy to cover damages resulting from wind, rain, and other perils.

Extender clause *See* Carryover clause.

Face amount Amount of insurance coverage shown on the declaration page.

Face-to-face closing Closing in which the buyer, seller, and closing agent meet for execution of documents and disbursement of funds.

Fair Housing Act of 1968 A federal prohibition on discrimination in the sale, rental, or financing of housing on the basis of race, color, religion, sex, or national origin.

Fair Housing Amendments Act of 1988 A law adding to the Fair Housing Act of 1968 provisions to prevent discrimination based on mental or physical handicap or familial status.

Fair market value A price for property agreed upon between buyer and seller in a competitive market with neither party being under undue pressure.

False promise An untrue statement of intent to a party that something will or will not happen.

Familial status Status granted to an adult with children under 18, a person who is pregnant, one who has legal custody of a child, or who is in the process of obtaining such custody.

Fannie Mae The shortened name for the Federal National Mortgage Association (FNMA), a privately owned corporation that purchases FHA and VA as well as conventional loans.

Federal Home Loan Bank System The U. S. agency that regulates federally chartered savings and loan associations.

Federal Housing Administration (FHA) The U. S. agency that insures mortgage loans to protect lending institutions.

Federal Reserve System The U. S. agency that regulates monetary policy and, thereby, the money supply and interest rates.

Fee simple An inheritable estate in land providing the greatest interest of any form of title.

Fee simple determinable A defeasible fee (title), recognizable by words "as long as."

Fee simple subject to a condition subsequent A defeasible fee (title), recognizable by words "but if."

Feudal system A type of land ownership previously existing in England, whereby only the king could hold absolute title to real property.

FHA-insured loan A loan in which payments are insured by the Federal Housing Administration.

Fiduciary A person, such as an agent, placed in a position of trust in relation to the person for whose benefit the relationship is created.

Final settlement Consummation of a contract to buy and sell real property.

Finance charge An amount imposed on the borrower in a loan, consisting of origination fee, service charges, discount points, interest, credit report fees, and finders' fees.

Fire insurance policy *See* Homeowner's policy.

First mortgage One that is superior to other mortgages encumbering the same property.

Fixed expenses Expenditures such as property taxes, license fees, and property insurance; subtracted from effective gross income to determine net operating income.

Fixed lease One in which the rental amount remains the same for the entire lease term; also called flat, straight, or gross lease.

Fixed-rate mortgage One in which the interest does not change.

Fixture Personal property that has become real property by having been permanently attached to real property.

Fix-up expenses Costs incurred by the seller of a principal residence in preparing it for sale.

Flat lease One in which the rental amount does not change during the lease term.

FNMA Pass-Through Certificate A negotiable security secured by a pool of FNMA mortgages with income and principal "passing through" to the investor.

Foreclosure The legal procedure of enforcing payment of a debt secured by a mortgage or other lien.

Forfeiture clause A statement in a contract for deed providing for giving up all payments by a buyer in default.

Fraud An intentional false statement of a material fact.

Freddie Mac A nickname for Federal Home Loan Mortgage Corporation (FHLMC), a corporation wholly owned by the Federal Home Loan Bank System that purchases conventional loans as well as FHA and VA loans.

Freehold estate A right of title to land.

Free market An economic condition in which buyer and seller have ample time to negotiate a beneficial purchase and sale without undue pressure or urgency.

Friendly foreclosure An absolute conveyance of title to the lender by the mortgagor in default to avoid a record of foreclosure. Also called deed in lieu of foreclosure.

Front foot A linear foot of property frontage on a street or highway.

Front-loaded depreciation *See* Accelerated depreciation.

Fruits of industry Items on real estate that are not part of real estate but instead are personal property, such as crops.

Fruits of nature Items on real estate that are part of real estate, such as trees and shrubs.

Fully amortizing loan One in which the scheduled uniform payments will pay off the loan completely over the term.

Functional obsolescence Loss in value resulting from things such as faulty design, inadequacies, overadequacies, and equipment being out-of-date.

Future interest The rights of an owner of an estate who will vest at some upcoming time.

Gain realized The excess of the amount realized over the adjusted basis.

General agent One with full authority over one area of a principal's interest, such as a property manager.

General lien One that attaches to all of the property of a person within the court's jurisdiction.

General plan A plan setting forth development of a subdivision.

General warranty deed A deed denoting an unlimited guarantee of title.

GIM *See* Gross income multiplier.

Ginnie Mae A nickname for Government National Mortgage Association (GNMA), a U.S. government agency that purchases FHA and VA loans.

Good faith estimate Lender's estimate of borrower's settlement costs, required by RESPA to be furnished to borrower at time of loan application.

Government survey system *See* Rectangular survey system.

Graduated lease One in which the rental amount changes in specified amounts over the lease term.

Graduated payment adjustable loan A combination of the graduated payment loan and the variable rate loan.

Graduated payment mortgage (GPM) One in which the payments are lower in the early years but increase on a scheduled basis until they reach an amortizing level.

Grant A transfer of title to real property by deed.

Grant deed A statutory form of deed in which the warranties are implied from the statute rather than being spelled out in the deed.

Grantee One who receives title to real property by deed.

Granting clause The statement in a deed containing words of conveyance.

Grantor One who conveys title to real property by deed.

Gross effective income Total potential income less deductions for vacancy and credit losses plus other income.

Gross income multiplier (GIM) A factor used in calculating estimated value of income property.

Gross lease One in which the lessor pays all costs of operating and maintaining the property and real property taxes.

Gross operating income *See* Gross effective income.

Gross potential income The amount of rental income that would be received if all units were rented 100 percent of the time and there were no credit losses. Also called gross scheduled income.

Gross rent multiplier (GRM) Also called gross scheduled income. A method of estimating the value of income property.

Ground lease A lease of unimproved land.

Ground rent Lessee's payment under a ground lease.

Growing equity mortgage (GEM) Loan for which the monthly payments increase annually, with the increased amount applied directly to the loan's principal, thus shortening the term of the loan.

Habendum clause The statement in a deed beginning with the words "to have and to hold" and describing the estate granted.

Habitable Suitable for the type of occupancy intended.

Handicap A mental or physical disability that impairs any life functions.

Heirs Persons legally eligible to receive property of a decedent.

Hereditament Any property or property right capable of being inherited, whether real, personal, corporeal, or incorporeal.

Heterogeneous A variety of dissimilar uses of property; nonhomogeneous.

Highest and best use The use of land that will preserve its utility and yield a net income flow in the form of rent that, when capitalized at the proper rate of interest, represents the highest present value of the land.

Holding period The length of time a property is owned.

Holdover clause A lease clause predicting and addressing the possibility of a tenant's failure to vacate upon the expiration of an estate for years. It usually results in the extended tenancy being treated as a periodic estate.

Holdover tenant A tenant who remains in possession of property after a lease terminates.

Holographic will One handwritten by the testator.

Home Buyer's Guide A booklet explaining aspects of loan settlement required by RESPA.

Homeowners' association An organization of owners having the responsibility to provide for operation and maintenance of common areas of a condominium or residential subdivision; also called property owners association.

Homeowner's policy An insurance policy protecting against a variety of hazards.

Homeowner's warranty policy An insurance policy protecting against loss caused by structural and other defects in a dwelling.

Homestead The land and dwelling of a homeowner.

Homestead exemption An exemption of a specified amount of value of a homestead from the claims of creditors or taxation; provided by state statute.

Homogeneous Similar and compatible, as in land uses.

Horizontal Property Act The title of condominium statutes in some states.

Housing and Urban Development (HUD) An agency of the federal government concerned with housing programs and laws.

HUD Form No. 1 A standard settlement form required by RESPA.

Hypothecate To pledge property as security for the payment of a debt without giving up possession.

Illusory offer One that does not obligate the offeror.

Immobility Incapable of being moved, fixed in location; an important physical characteristic of land.

Implied agency Agency that exists as a result of the conduct of the parties.

Implied contract One created by deduction from the conduct of the parties rather than from the direct words of the parties; opposite of an express contract.

Implied warranty One presumed by law to exist in a deed, though not expressly stated.

Impound account Another term for escrow account.

Improved land Land on which structures or roads exist.

Improvements Changes or additions made to a property, such as walls or roads, and so on. These typically increase the value of a property, except in cases of overimprovement.

Inchoate In suspension or pending, possibly occurring at some future time.

Income approach The primary method for estimating the value of properties that produce rental income; also called capitalization.

Income property One that produces rental income.

Income shelter Deductible allowances from net income of property to arrive at taxable income and tax losses allowed to offset passive and active income.

Incompetent Describes a person who is not capable of managing his or her own affairs, under law.

Incorporeal Intangible things such as rights.

Incurable depreciation That which is not physically correctable or not economically practical to correct.

Indemnification Reimbursement or compensation paid to someone for a loss already suffered.

Indestructibility A physical characteristic of land describing that land as a permanent commodity that cannot be destroyed.

Index lease One in which the rental amount changes in proportion to changes in the Consumer Price Index.

Ingress The right to enter a parcel of land; usually used as "ingress and egress" (both entering and leaving).

Inheritance basis The market value of property at date of decedent's death, for tax purposes.

Injunction A court instruction to discontinue a specified activity.

Installment land contract *See* Contract for deed.

Installment sale A transaction in which the seller receives the sale price in more than one tax year.

Instrument A written legal document such as a contract, note, mortgage.

Insurable interest The extent of interest qualifying for insurance.

Insurance value The cost of replacing a structure completely destroyed by an insured hazard.

Insured conventional loan One in which the loan payment is insured by private mortgage insurance to protect the lender.

Interest (a) Money paid for the use of money. (b) An ownership or right.

Interim financing A short-term or temporary loan such as a construction loan.

Intermediate theory A modified plan of either the title or lien theory, functioning much like a mortgage or lien theory, but the lender does not have to wait until the foreclosure to obtain possession of the property.

Interstate Land Sales Full Disclosure Act A federal law regulating the sale across state lines of subdivided land under certain conditions.

Interval ownership *See* Timesharing.

Intestate The condition of death without leaving a valid will.

Intestate succession Distribution of property by descent as provided by statute.

Invalid Not legally enforceable.

Investment The outlay of money for income or profit.

Investment syndicate A joint venture, typically controlled by one or two persons, hoping for return to all investors.

Involuntary alienation Transfer of title to real property as a result of a lien foreclosure sale, adverse possession, filing a petition in bankruptcy, condemnation under power of eminent domain, or, upon the death of the title holder, to the state if no heirs.

Irrevocable That which cannot be changed or canceled.

Joint tenancy A form of co-ownership that includes the right of survivorship.

Joint venture Participation by two or more parties in a single undertaking.

Judgment A court determination of the rights and obligations of parties to a lawsuit.

Judgment lien A general lien resulting from a court decree.

Judicial deed One executed by an official with court authorization.

Judicial foreclosure A court proceeding to require that property be sold to satisfy a mortgage lien.

Junior mortgage One that is subordinate to a prior mortgage.

Jurisdiction The extent of authority of a court.

Laches Loss of legal rights because of failure to assert them on a timely basis.

Land The surface of the earth, the area above and below the surface, and everything permanently attached thereto.

Land capacity The degree to which land can sustain improvements created to make the land productive.

Land contract *See* Contract for deed.

Land grant Conveyance of land as a gift for the benefit of the public.

Landlocked Describes property with no access to a public road.

Land trust Type of trust in which title to land is held by a trustee for the benefit of others.

Land use controls Governmental restrictions on land use (e.g., zoning laws and building codes).

Lawful Legal, not prohibited by law.

Lease A contract wherein a landlord gives a tenant the right of use and possession of property for a limited period of time in return for rent.

Leased fee Lessor's interest in leased property.

Leasehold estate Nonfreehold estate; of limited duration, providing the right of possession and control but not title.

Leasehold mortgage One in which a leasehold (nonfreehold) estate is pledged to secure payment of the note.

Leasehold title insurance policy One insuring a lessee against defects in the lessor's title.

Legacy A gift of personal property by will at the death of a person.

Legal capacity The ability to contract.

Legal description A description of land recognized by law.

Legal entity A person or organization with legal capacity.

Legality of object Legal purpose.

Legal life estate One created by exercise of the right of dower, curtesy, or a statutory substitute.

Legal rate of interest The maximum rate permitted by law. *See* Usury.

Lessee A tenant under a lease.

Lessor A landlord under a lease.

Less than freehold estate *See* Nonfreehold estate.

Leverage The use of borrowed funds; the larger the percentage of borrowed money, the greater the leverage.

Levy Imposition of a tax, executing a lien.

License A personal privilege to do a particular act or series of acts on the land of another.

Lien A claim that one person has against the property of another for some debt or charge, entitling the lienholder to have the claim satisfied from the property of the debtor.

Lienee One whose property is subject to a lien.

Lien foreclosure sale Selling property without consent of owner who incurred the debt resulting in a lien, as ordered by a court or authorized by state law, and title conveyed to purchaser by judicial deed.

Lienor The one holding a lien against another.

Lien theory The legal tenet holding that a mortgage creates a lien against the real property pledged in the mortgage to secure payment of a debt.

Life estate A freehold estate created for the duration of the life or lives of certain named persons; a noninheritable estate.

Life estate in remainder A form of life estate in which certain persons, called remaindermen, are designated to receive the title upon termination of the life tenancy.

Life estate in reversion A form of life estate that goes back to the creator of the estate in fee simple upon termination.

Life estate pur autre vie An estate in which the duration is measured by the life of someone other than the life tenant. *See also* Pur autre vie.

Life tenant One holding a life estate.

Like-kind property Real or personal property that qualifies for tax treatment as a tax-free exchange.

Limited partnership An organization consisting of one or more general partners and one or more partners with lesser roles.

Liquidated damages Money to be paid and received as compensation for a breach of contract.

Liquidity The attribute of an asset's being readily convertible to cash.

Lis pendens Latin meaning "a lawsuit pending."

Listing contract A contract whereby a property owner employs a real estate broker to market the property described in the contract.

Litigation A lawsuit.

Littoral rights Rights belonging to owner of land that borders a lake, ocean, or sea.

Loan commitment Obligation of a lending institution to make a certain loan.

Loan-to-value ratio The relationship between the amount of a loan and the lender's opinion of the value of the property pledged to secure payment of the loan.

Location (Situs) An economic characteristic of land having the greatest effect on value in comparison to any other characteristic.

L.S. Signifies locus sigilli, a Latin term meaning "place of the seal."

Management agreement A contract wherein an owner employs a property manager.

Management plan A long-range program prepared by a property manager indicating to the owner how he or she will manage a property.

Management proposal A program for operating a property submitted to the owner by a property manager.

Margin Measure of profit.

Marketable title One that is free from reasonable doubt and that a court would require a purchaser to accept.

Market data method The primary approach in estimating the value of vacant land and single-family, owner-occupied dwellings. Also called comparison approach.

Market value A property's worth in terms of price agreed upon by a willing buyer and seller when neither is under any undue pressure and each is knowledgeable of market conditions at the time.

Master deed The instrument that legally establishes a condominium; also called condominium declaration.

Material fact Important information that may affect a person's judgment.

Materialman's lien *See* Mechanic's lien.

Mechanic's lien A statutory lien available to persons supplying labor (mechanics) or material (materialmen) to the construction of an improvement on land if they are not paid.

Meeting of the minds A condition that must exist for creation of a contract.

Merger The absorption of one thing into another.

Metes and bounds A system of land description by distances and directions.

Mill One tenth of a cent.

Millage One tenth of a cent in tax per dollar of value.

Mineral lease A nonfreehold (leasehold) estate in the area below the surface of land.

Mineral rights A landowner's ability to take minerals from the earth or to sell or lease this right to others.

Minor A person who has not attained the statutory age of majority.

Misrepresentation (a) A false statement or omission of a material fact. (b) In real estate, making an intentionally false statement to induce someone to contract.

Modification by improvement An economic characteristic of land providing that the economic supply of land is increased by improvements made to the land and on the land.

Mortgage A written instrument used to pledge a title to real property to secure payment of a promissory note.

Mortgage assumption The transfer of mortgage obligations to purchaser of the mortgaged property.

Mortgage banker A form of organization that makes and services mortgage loans.

Mortgage broker One who arranges a mortgage loan between a lender and a borrower for a fee.

Mortgagee The lender in a mortgage loan, who receives a mortgage from the borrower (mortgagor).

Mortgagee's title lender insurance policy A policy that insures a lender against defects in a title pledged by a borrower to secure payment of a mortgage loan.

Mortgage insurance premium (MIP) A payment for insurance to protect the lender and/or insurer against loss if default occurs.

Mortgage loan value The value sufficient to secure payment of a loan.

Mortgage principal The amount of money (usually the loan amount) on which interest is either paid or received.

Mortgage satisfaction Full payment of a mortgage loan.

Mortgaging clause The statement in a mortgage that demonstrates the mortgagor's intention to mortgage the property to the mortgagee.

Mortgagor The borrower in a mortgage loan who executes and delivers a mortgage to the lender.

Multiple exchange A transaction in which more than two like-kind properties are exchanged.

Multiple listing service (MLS) An organized method of sharing or pooling listings by member brokers.

Mutual assent The voluntary agreement of all parties to a contract as evidenced by an offer and acceptance.

Mutual mistake An error of material fact by both parties.

Mutual rescission The agreement of all parties to an executory contract to release each other.

Mutual savings banks Similar to the savings and loan associations; an institution that provides a substantial source of financing for housing.

Narrative appraisal report A statement of an opinion of value containing the element of judgment as well as the data used in arriving at the value estimate.

National Association of REALTORS® (NAR) The largest and most prominent trade organization of real estate licensees.

Negative amortization When loan payment amount is not sufficient to cover interest due, the shortfall added back into principal, causing principal to grow larger after payment is made.

Negative covenant *See* Restrictive covenant.

Negative easement A right in the land of another prohibiting the servient owner from doing something on the servient land because it will affect the dominant land.

Negligence Legal term describing failure to use the care that a reasonable person would use in like circumstances.

Net income Gross income less operating expenses; also called net operating income.

Net lease One in which the lessee pays a fixed amount of rent plus the costs of operation of the property.

Net listing Not a type of listing but a method of establishing the listing broker's commission as all money above a specified net amount to the seller.

Net operating income Gross operating income minus operating expenses.

Net salvage value *See* Salvage value.

Nonconforming use Utilization of land that does not conform to the use permitted by a zoning ordinance but that is in use before the ordinance.

Nonfreehold estate Leaseholds; estates with a length determined by agreement or statute; establishes possession of land as opposed to ownership in fee.

Nonhomogeneity A physical characteristic of land describing that land as a unique commodity.

Nonjudicial foreclosure A form of foreclosure that does not require court action to conduct a foreclosure sale; also called foreclosure under power of sale.

Nonrecourse note A note in which the borrower has no personal liability for payment.

Notary public A person authorized by a state to take oaths and acknowledgments.

Notice of lis pendens A statement on the public record warning all persons that a title to real property is the subject of a lawsuit and any lien resulting from the suit will attach to the title held by a purchaser from the defendant.

Novation Substitution of a new contract for a prior contract.

Null and void Invalid; without legal force or effect.

Obligee One to whom an obligation is owed.

Obligor One who owes an obligation to another.

Obsolescence Loss in property value caused by economic or functional factors.

Occupancy Physical possession of property.

Offer A promise made to another conditional upon acceptance by a promise or act made in return.

Offer and acceptance Necessary element for the creation of a contract.

Offeree One to whom an offer is made.

Offeror One making an offer.

Open-ended listing contract One without a termination date.

Open-end mortgage One that may be refinanced without rewriting the mortgage.

Open listing A listing given to one or more brokers wherein the broker procuring a sale is entitled to the commission but imposes no commission obligation on the owner in the event the owner sells the property to someone who was not introduced to the property by one of the listing brokers.

Open mortgage One that does not impose a prepayment penalty.

Operating budget A yearly budget of income and expense for a specific property, prepared by a property manager.

Operating expenses Costs of operating a property held as an investment.

Operating statement A report of receipts and disbursements resulting in net income of rental property.

Operation of law The manner in which rights and liabilities of parties may be changed by application of law without the act or cooperation of the parties.

Opinion of title *See* Certificate of title opinion.

Opportunity cost Lost potential profits or receipts in transactions that are not undertaken.

Optionee One who receives an option.

Optionor One who gives an option.

Option to purchase A unilateral contract whereby a property owner (optionor) sells a right to purchase his or her property at an established price to a prospective buyer (optionee).

Option to renew A provision setting forth the method and terms for renewing the lease.

Ordinance A law enacted by a local government.

Origination fee A service charge by a lending institution for making a loan.

Overimprovement An improvement to land that results in the land not being able to obtain its highest and best use.

Ownership The right to use, control, possess, and dispose of property.

Ownership in severalty Title to real property held in the name of one person only.

Owner's title insurance policy A policy insuring an owner of real property against financial loss resulting from a title defect.

Package loan One in which personal property as well as real property is pledged to secure payment of the note.

Package policy Insurance coverage for property damage and liability loss all within one premium.

Paired sales analysis The comparison of two closely comparable sales with only one significant difference.

Parol evidence rule A concept allowing that oral explanations can support the written words of a contract but cannot contradict them.

Partially amortizing loan One in which the schedule of uniform payments will not completely satisfy the debt over the mortgage term and therefore will require a final payment larger than the uniform payments to completely satisfy the debt; the final payment is called a balloon payment.

Participation loan (a) One in which two or more lenders share in making the loan. (b) One in which a lender shares in the profit produced by an income property pledged to secure the loan payment in addition to receiving interest and principal payments.

Partition A legal proceeding dividing property of co-owners so each will hold title in severalty.

Partnership A form of business organization in which the business is owned by two or more persons, called partners.

Party wall A common wall used by two adjoining structures.

Percentage lease One in which the rental amount is a combination of a fixed amount plus a percentage of the lessee's gross sales.

Perch A surveyor's measure 16½ feet in length.

Percolation (perc) test A test of soil to determine if it is sufficiently porous for installation of a septic tank.

Periodic lease *See* Periodic tenancy.

Periodic tenancy A lease that automatically renews for successive periods unless terminated by either party; also called an estate from year-to-year or periodic estate.

Personal property All property that is not land and is not permanently attached to land; everything that is movable; chattel.

Physical deterioration Loss in value caused by unrepaired damage or inadequate maintenance.

PITI Acronym denoting that a mortgage payment includes principal, interest, taxes, and insurance.

Placed in service The date when an asset is ready and available for a particular use.

Planned unit development (PUD) A form of cluster zoning providing for both residential and commercial land uses within a zoned area.

Planning A program for the development of a city or county designed to provide for orderly growth.

Plat A property map, recorded on the public record in plat books.

Pledge To provide property as security for payment of a debt or for performance of a promise.

Plottage Combining two or more parcels of land into one tract that has more value than the total value of the individual parcels.

Points *See* Discount points.

Police power The power of government to regulate the use of real property for the benefit of the public.

Population density The number of people within a given land area.

Positive misrepresentation A person's actual statement that is false and known to be false; fraud.

Potential income *See* Gross potential income.

Power of attorney An instrument appointing an attorney-in-fact; creates a general or universal agency.

Prepaid expenses Costs the seller pays in advance but were not fully used up (such as property taxes due) shown as a credit to the seller and debit to the buyer.

Prepaid items Funds paid at closing to start an escrow account, as required in certain loans; also called prepaids.

Prepayment penalty A financial charge imposed on a borrower for paying a loan prior to expiration of the full loan term.

Prescription A method of acquiring an easement by continuous and uninterrupted use without permission.

Prescriptive easement One obtained by prescription.

Preventive maintenance Program of regularly scheduled checks on equipment to assure proper functioning.

Prima facie Latin meaning "on the face of it"; a fact presumed to be true unless disproved by contrary evidence.

Prima facie case A suit that is sufficiently strong that it can be defeated only by contrary evidence.

Primary financing The loan with the highest priority.

Primary mortgage market The activity of lenders' making real estate loans to individual borrowers.

Prime rate The interest rate a lender charges to the most creditworthy customers.

Principal (a) In the law of agency, one who appoints an agent to represent him or her. (b) Amount of money on which interest is paid or received.

Principal meridians North-south lines in the rectangular method of property description.

Principal residence The home the owner or renter occupies most of the time.

Priority liens Special liens that receive preferential treatment (such as property tax liens).

Private land use control Regulations for land use by individuals or nongovernment organizations in the form of deed restrictions and restrictive covenants.

Private mortgage insurance (PMI) A form of insurance coverage required in high loan-to-value ratio conventional loans to protect the lender in case the borrower defaults in loan payment.

Private property That which is not owned by government.

Privity of contract An agreement that exists only between contracting parties for the right to demand and receive the specific benefit.

Probate The procedure for proving and carrying out the provisions of a will.

Procuring cause The basis for a direct action that results in successfully completing an objective.

Profit or Profit á prendre The right to participate in profits of another's land.

Promissory note A written promise to pay a debt as set forth in the writing.

Promulgate To put in effect by public announcement.

Property description An accurate legal description of land.

Property Disclosure Form A comprehensive checklist pertaining to the condition of the property including its structure and any environmental hazards in and around the property.

Property management Comprehensive, orderly, continuing program analyzing all investment aspects of a property to ensure a financially successful project.

Property management report A periodic financial report prepared for the owner by a property manager.

Property manager One who manages properties for an owner as the owner's agent.

Property report Disclosure required under Interstate Land Sales Full Disclosure Act.

Proprietary lease A lease in a cooperative apartment.

Proration Division of certain settlement costs between buyer and seller.

Public land use control Regulation of land use by government organizations in the form of zoning laws, building codes, subdivision ordinances, and environmental protection laws.

Public property That which is owned by government.

Public record Constructive notice, for all to see, of real property conveyances and other matters.

Punitive damages Court-ordered awards for extremely bad behavior by a party; intended to punish and indicate that the behavior will not be tolerated.

Pur autre vie Latin meaning "for the life of another"; a life estate measured by the life of someone other than the life tenant.

Purchase money mortgage A lien given by a buyer to a seller to secure payment of all or part of the purchase price.

Quantity survey A method for estimating replacement or reproduction cost.

Quarter section One-fourth of a section, containing 160 acres.

Quiet enjoyment Use or possession of property that is undisturbed by an enforceable claim of superior title.

Quiet title action A lawsuit to remove a cloud on a title.

Quitclaim To relinquish or release a claim to real property.

Quitclaim deed A deed that contains no warranty of title; often used to remove a cloud on a title.

Radius Distance from the center of a circle to the perimeter; part of a metes and bounds description.

Range An area of land defined by the rectangular survey system of land description.

Rate of return Percentage of net income produced by a property or other investment.

Ratify To reaffirm a previous action.

Ready, willing, and able Describes a buyer who is ready to buy, willing to buy, and financially able to pay the negotiated price.

Real estate Land and everything permanently attached to land; sometimes used interchangeably with the terms real property and realty.

Real estate broker A person or organization who negotiates real estate sales, exchanges, or rentals for others for compensation or a promise of compensation.

Real Estate Commission A state agency charged with enforcing real estate license laws.

Real Estate Investment Trust (REIT) A form of business trust owned by shareholders making real estate loans or other real estate investments.

Real estate market A local activity in which real property is sold, exchanged, leased, and rented at prices set by competing forces.

Real estate salesperson A person performing any of the acts included in the definition of real estate broker but while associated with and supervised by a broker.

Real Estate Settlement Procedures Act (RESPA) A federal law regulating activities of lending institutions in making loans for housing.

Reality of consent Mutual agreement between the parties to a contract; meeting of the minds; to exist and be free of duress, fraud, undue influence, and misrepresentation.

Realized gain Actual profit resulting from a sale.

Real property The aggregate of rights, powers, and privileges conveyed with ownership of real estate.

REALTOR® A registered trademark of the National Association of REALTORS®; its use is limited to members only.

Realty Land and everything permanently attached to land.

Reappraisal lease One in which changes in rental amount are based on changes in property value, as demonstrated by periodic reappraisals of the property.

Reciprocity Mutual agreement by states to extend licensing privileges to licensees in each state.

Recognized gain The amount of profit that is taxable.

Reconciliation (a) The process of checking accounting of settlement statement. (b) The adjustment process in appraising, whereby comparables are adjusted to the subject property or the results of different approaches are weighted to reach a rational estimate of property value.

Recordation Written registration of an owner's title in public records to protect against subsequent claimants.

Recording Registering a document on the public record.

Rectangular survey system A type of land description utilizing townships and sections.

Redemption *See* Equity of redemption.

Redlining The refusal of lending institutions to make loans for the purchase, construction, or repair of a dwelling because the area in which the dwelling is located is integrated or populated by minorities.

Reentry The owner's right to regain possession of real property.

Referral fee A percentage of a broker's commission paid to another broker for sending a buyer or seller to him or her.

Refinancing Obtaining a new mortgage loan to pay and replace an existing mortgage.

Regulation Z Requirements issued by the Federal Reserve Board in implementing the Truth-in-Lending Law, which is a part of the Federal Consumer Credit Protection Act.

Reject To refuse to accept an offer.

Release clause A provision in a mortgage to release certain properties from the lien when the principal is reduced by a specified amount.

Release of liability An agreement by the non-assigning party to a contract to relieve the assignor of all obligations.

Remainder A future interest in a life estate.

Remainderman One having a future interest in a life estate.

Remise To release or give up.

Replacement cost The amount of money required to replace a structure with another structure of comparable utility.

Replacement reserve A fund to replace assets when they wear out.

Repossession Regaining possession of property as a result of a breach of contract by another.

Reproduction cost The amount of money required to build an exact duplicate of a structure.

Rescission Cancellation of a contract when another party is in default.

Resident manager A person employed to manage a building; may live on the premises.

Residual income Income allocated to the land under the principle of highest and best use.

Restrictive covenant Restriction placed on a private owner's use of land by a nongovernmental entity or individual.

Reverse annuity mortgage (RAM) Mortgage allowing elderly homeowners to borrow against the equity in their homes to help meet living expenses.

Reversion Return of title to the holder of a future interest, such as the grantor in a life estate not in remainder.

Reversionary interest A provision stating the owner's interest: that possession of property will go back to owner at end of lease.

Revocation Withdrawal of an offer.

Right of assignment Allows lender to sell mortgage at any time and obtain money invested rather than wait for completion of loan term.

Right of first refusal An agreement giving a person an opportunity to purchase the property on a potential buyer's terms before the offer is accepted.

Right of inheritance The right for property to descend to the heirs of the owner as set out by will or by intestate succession.

Right of survivorship The right of an owner to receive the title to a co-owner's share upon death of the co-owner, as in the case of joint tenancy and tenancy by the entirety.

Right to emblements The right of former owners or former tenants to reenter property to cultivate and harvest annual crops planted by them.

Riparian rights The rights of an owner of property adjoining a watercourse such as a river, including access to, and use of, the water.

Risk factor The potential for loss.

Risk management Controlling and limiting risk in property ownership.

Rollover rule A mandatory provision in the tax law providing that tax on any gain realized in the sale of a principal residence must be postponed if the sale and repurchase qualify.

Running-with-the-land Rights moving from grantor to grantee along with a title.

Sale and leaseback A transaction whereby an owner sells his or her property to an investor who immediately leases the property to the seller as agreed in the sales contract.

Sales contract An agreement between buyer and seller on the price and other terms and conditions of the sale of property.

Salvage value The amount estimated by an owner that will be realized from the sale of an asset at the end of the useful life of the asset.

Savings and loan associations (S&Ls) A major source of funds for financing residential real estate.

Scarcity (a) An economic characteristic of real property. (b) In appraisal, supply of property in relation to effective demand.

"S" corporation Corporate formation whereby corporate income and expenses flow through to shareholders as if a partnership.

Secondary mortgage market The market in which lenders sell real estate loans.

Second mortgage One that is first in priority after a first real estate loans.

Section A 1-mile-square area of land described by the rectangular survey system, consisting of 640 acres.

Security deposit A sum of money that the landlord requires of the tenant prior to lease, to be refunded at end of lease based upon condition of the premises.

Seisin (or Seizin) Possession of a freehold estate in land.

Separate ownership Ownership in severalty by one's spouse.

Separate property Any property acquired by one spouse during marriage by gift or inheritance or purchased with the separate funds of a husband or wife or brought into the marriage by one spouse.

Servient tenement Land encumbered by an easement.

Setback The distance from a front or interior property line to the point where a structure can be located.

Settlement Consummation of a real estate contract; also called closing.

Settlement costs Expenses paid by buyers and sellers at the time they consummate a real estate sales contract; also called closing costs.

Severalty Ownership by only one person.

Shared appreciation mortgage (SAM) One in which the lender shares in the appreciation in property value in return for making the loan at a fixed rate lower than the rate in effect at the time the loan is made.

Situs Location of land.

Sole proprietorship A business owned by one individual.

Special agent Agent with limited authority to act on behalf of the principal, such as created by a listing.

Special assessment A levy by a local government against real property for part of the cost of making an improvement to the property, such as street paving, installing water lines, or putting in sidewalks.

Special warranty deed A deed containing a limited warranty of title.

Specific lien One that attaches to one particular property only.

Specific performance A court instruction requiring a defaulting party to a contract to buy and sell real property to specifically perform his or her obligations under the contract.

Spot zoning Rezoning of a certain property in a zoned area to permit a different type of use than that authorized for the rest of the area; may be valid or invalid.

Square-foot method A technique used to estimate the total cost of construction, in which the total number of square feet to be constructed is multiplied by a cost per square foot figure to derive total cost.

Stabilized budget A forecast of income and expense as may be reasonably projected over several years, prepared by a property manager.

Standard fire policy The most common fire insurance policy indemnifying the insured against loss by fire.

Standards of practice Established practices set out in the Code of Ethics established by NAR.

Starker exchange Exchange of like-kind property in which the exchange property is not identified at the time of exchange (Internal Revenue Code 1031).

Starker trust Trust account where money from a Starker exchange is placed until exchange property can be identified.

Statute of Frauds A law in effect in all states requiring certain contracts to be in writing to be valid.

Statute of limitations State laws establishing the time period within which certain lawsuits may be brought.

Statutory redemption A foreclosure proceeding that allows a statutory time period after a foreclosure sale during which the borrower may still redeem the title.

Steering The practice of directing prospective purchasers toward or away from certain neighborhoods to avoid altering the racial/ethnic makeup of these areas.

Straight-line depreciation A depreciation method whereby the property is depreciated in equal annual installments over the years of useful life.

Strict foreclosure A proceeding in which a court gives a borrower in default a specified time period in which to satisfy the debt and thereby prevent transfer to the lender of the title to the property.

Strip center More than four stores located conveniently and with easy access to a main roadway.

Subagent A person appointed by an agent to assist in performing some or all of the tasks of the agency.

Subdivision regulation (Ordinance) Public control of the development of residential subdivisions.

Sublease The transfer of only part of a leasehold right term with reversion to the lessee. Also called sandwich lease.

Subordinate Lower in priority.

Subrogation of rights The substitution of the title insurance company in the place of the insured for filing a legal action.

Substitution The principle providing that the highest value of a property has a tendency to be established by the cost of purchasing or constructing another property of equal utility and desirability provided that the substitution can be made without unusual delay.

Substitution of entitlement In a VA loan, the stipulation that simply paying the loan in full is not sufficient to restore the entitlement; the veteran must no longer own the property.

Subsurface rights Rights to the area below the earth's surface.

Supply and demand The principle stating that the greater the supply of any commodity in comparison to demand, the lower the value; conversely, the smaller the supply and the greater the demand, the higher the value.

Survivorship The right of the surviving co-owner to automatically receive the title of a deceased co-owner immediately without probate.

Take-out loan Permanent financing arranged to replace a short-term construction loan.

Taking title subject to a mortgage Accepting a title pledged to secure a mortgage and with no personal liability for payment of the note.

Taxable gain The amount of profit subject to tax (recognized gain).

Taxation One of the four powers of government, to tax, among other things, real property.

Tax basis *See* Basis.

Tax credit An amount of money that may be deducted from a tax bill to arrive at the net amount of tax due.

Tax-deductible expense An amount of money that may be deducted from gross income in arriving at net taxable income.

Tax depreciation A provision of tax law permitting a property to take an ordinary business deduction for a portion of an asset's cost.

Tax-deferred exchange Trading of like-kind properties held as an investment or for use in business.

Tax shelter A method of tax avoidance such as protecting income from taxation by allowable depreciation.

Tenancy by the entirety A form of co-ownership limited to husband and wife, with the right of survivorship.

Tenancy in common A form of co-ownership that does not include the right of survivorship.

Tenements Inherent rights of ownership of real estate that arise from owning land.

Term loan One that requires the borrower to pay interest only during the loan term, with the principal due in full at the end of the term.

Testate To have died leaving a valid will.

Testator A man who has died and left a valid will.

Testatrix A woman who has died and left a valid will.

Third party Another name for *customer*.

Time value of money Discounting future receipt of money to reflect the equivalent value in the present.

Timesharing A form of ownership in which the purchaser owns the property for a certain specified time interval.

Title Ownership.

Title examination A search of the public record to determine the quality of a title to real property.

Title insurance An insurance policy protecting the insured from a financial loss caused by a defect in a title (superior claim) to real property.

Title theory The legal theory followed in some states, holding that a mortgage conveys a title to real property to secure payment of a debt.

Title transfer tax A tax imposed on the conveyance of title to real property by deed.

Torrens system A system of title recordation.

Township An area of land 6 miles by 6 miles, as defined by rectangular survey system.

Tract An area of land.

Trade fixtures Items that are installed by a commercial tenant and are removable upon termination of the tenancy.

Transferability The ability to transfer property ownership from seller to buyer.

Trapezoid An area with two parallel sides and two nonparallel sides.

Trespass Unlawful entry on the land of another.

Trust A legal relationship under which title to property is transferred to a person known as trustee.

Trust deed *See* Deed of trust.

Trustee One who holds title to property for the benefit of another called a beneficiary.

Trustor One who conveys title to a trustee.

Truth-in-Lending Simplification and Reform Act (TILSRA) *See* Regulation Z.

Unauthorized practice of law Performing any service that must be performed by an attorney-at-law.

Underimprovement Use of land that is not its highest and best use and thus does not generate the maximum income.

Underwriting The act of reviewing loan documentation and evaluating borrower's ability and willingness to repay the loan and sufficiency of collateral value of the property.

Undisclosed principal A principal whose identity is not disclosed by an agent.

Undivided interest Ownership of fractional parts not physically divided.

Undue influence Any improper or wrongful influence by one party over another whereby the will of a person is overpowered so that he or she is induced to act or prevented from acting according to free will.

Unencumbered property Property that is free of any lien.

Unenforceable contract One that appears to meet the requirements for validity but would not be enforceable in court.

Uniform Commercial Code (UCC) A standardized and comprehensive set of commercial laws regulating security interests in personal property.

Unilateral contract An agreement wherein there is a promise in return for a specific action, which together supply the consideration.

Uninsured conventional loan One in which the loan payment is not insured to protect the lender.

Unintentional misrepresentation An innocent false statement of a material fact.

Unities of title Time, title, interest, and possession.

Unity-in-place method Technique used in appraising real estate under the cost approach, in which the cost of replacement or reproduction is grouped by stages of construction.

Universal agent Agent that has complete authority over any activity of principal; for example, power of attorney.

Unlike-kind property Property that is not similar in nature and character to the property exchanged.

Useful life The period of time that a property is expected to be economically useful.

Usury Charging a rate of interest higher than the maximum rate allowed by law.

Utility Capable of serving a useful purpose.

Vacancy rate A projected rate of the percentage of rental units that will be vacant in a given year.

VA-guaranteed loan A mortgage loan in which the loan payment is guaranteed to the lender by the Department of Veteran Affairs.

Valid contract An agreement that is legally binding and enforceable.

Valuable consideration Anything of value agreed upon by parties to a contract.

Valuation Establishes an opinion of value utilizing an objective approach based on facts related to the property, such as age, square footage, location, cost to replace, and so on.

Value in exchange The amount of money a property may command for its exchange; market value.

Value in use The present worth of the future benefits of ownership; a subjective value that is not market value.

Variance A permitted deviation from specific requirements of a zoning ordinance because of the special hardship to a property owner.

Vendee Purchaser.

Vendor Seller.

Vendor's affidavit Document signed under oath by vendor stating that vendor has not encumbered title to real estate without full disclosure to vendee.

Voidable contract An agreement that may be voided by a party without legal consequences.

Void contract An agreement that has no legal force or effect.

Voluntary alienation The transfer of title freely by the owner.

Waste Allowing devaluation of a property which harms the interest of another party in interest.

Weighted average In the market data method of appraisal, reconciliation by giving more weight to comparables with high degree of similarity or the most appropriate approach.

With reserve Concerning auction sales, seller may specify this, meaning the seller does not have to accept any bids.

Words of conveyance Wording in a deed demonstrating the definite intention to convey a specific title to real property to a named grantee.

Wraparound loan A junior loan in an amount exceeding a first loan against the property.

Writ of attachment Court order preventing any transfer of attached property during litigation.

Yield The return on an investment.

Zoning A public law regulating land use.

Zoning map A map that divides the community into various designated districts.

Zoning ordinance A statement setting forth the type of use permitted under each zoning classification and specific requirements for compliance.

INDEX